BEETLES
of Eastern North America

BEETLES
of Eastern North America

Arthur V. Evans

Princeton University Press
Princeton and Oxford

DEDICATION

This book is dedicated to CHARLES "CHUCK" LAWRENCE BELLAMY (1951–2013) and RICHARD LAWRENCE HOFFMAN (1928–2012) in recognition of their years of friendship, good cheer, support, and shared passion for all things beetle. I miss them both very much.

Copyright © 2014 by Princeton University Press
Published by Princeton University Press, 41 William Street, Princeton, New Jersey 08540
In the United Kingdom: Princeton University Press, 6 Oxford Street, Woodstock, Oxfordshire OX20 1TW

nathist.princeton.edu

Front cover photograph: *Phanaeus vindex* male, by David Almquist
Spine photographs, top to bottom: *Dynastes tityus*, by Christopher C. Wirth; *Ellipsoptera gratiosa*, by Arthur V. Evans
Back cover photographs, left to right: *Typocerus velutinus* (1) and *Strangalia luteicornis* (3); *Chrysochus auratus*; *Alaus oculatus*; all by Arthur V. Evans
Title-page photograph: Flat-headed Redbud Borer *Ptosima gibbicollis*, by Arthur V. Evans

Library of Congress Cataloging-in-Publication Data

Evans, Arthur V.
    Beetles of eastern North America / Arthur V. Evans.
        p. cm.
    Includes bibliographical references and index.
    ISBN 978-0-691-13304-1 (pbk. : alk. paper)
        1. Beetles—North America—Identification. I. Title.

    QL581.E93 2014
    595.76—dc23
                    2013028570

British Library Cataloging-in-Publication Data is available

This book has been composed in Arial MT (main text) and Avant Garde Gothic PS (headings and captions).

Printed on acid-free paper. ∞

Typeset and designed by D & N Publishing, Baydon, Wiltshire, UK

Printed in the United States of America

10 9 8 7 6 5 4 3 2 1

CONTENTS

CONTENTS

6

PREFACE

When I moved from California to Virginia some 14 years ago, I found myself surrounded by a beetle fauna that was at once familiar, yet exotic. Familiar because, as a scarab beetle specialist, I had more than a working familiarity with the scarab fauna of eastern North America and its literature. Exotic because most of the beetles in other families were entirely new to me. I took the opportunity to extend my focus beyond scarabs to include all families of beetles that occurred in my newly adopted state. Through fieldwork, macro photography, literature searches, and the examination of museum collections, I soon discovered that Virginia's coastal, sandhill, piedmont, and montane plant communities served as habitats for a tremendous diversity of beetles that included those with decidedly boreal or austral distributions. In other words, studying the beetles of Virginia was like taking a crash course in the fauna of all of eastern North America.

Several books became my primary entrée to the beetles of the region, including *An Illustrated Descriptive Catalogue of the Coleoptera or Beetles (exclusive of the Rhynchophora) Known to Occur in Indiana* (Blatchley 1910) and *Rhynchophora or Weevils of North Eastern America* (Blatchley and Leng 1916). *A Manual of Common Beetles of Eastern North America* (Dillon and Dillon 1972) was also very helpful. *The Beetles of Northeastern North America* (Downie and Arnett 1996) provided numerous keys for identifying species. The two-volume *American Beetles* (Arnett and Thomas 2000, Arnett et al. 2002) provided a badly needed taxonomic update for the North American beetle fauna supported with well-illustrated keys and extremely useful bibliographies. Much of the published taxonomic, biological, ecological, and distributional information for the species that inhabit eastern North America is tucked away, however, among thousands of notes, articles, and monographs published in hundreds of departmental circulars, newsletters, peer-reviewed journals, regional guides, and various online resources.

Beetles likely make up nearly one-fifth of all plant and animal species found in eastern North America. Although beetles are frequently eye-catching because of their color, form, or habit, no one photographic guide covering species in all 115 families known in the region has been attempted until now. Most of the 1,409 species that appear in this work are quite conspicuous and found throughout the region, while a few are decidedly boreal or Floridian in distribution; however, it must be remembered that the species presented within these pages represent fewer than 10% of the entire eastern beetle fauna. As such, readers should not expect to find every species they encounter described among these pages; for example, typically rare forms excluded from this book may become locally common under extraordinary conditions. Still, readers using this book are likely to identify the majority of conspicuous beetles that cross their paths to the species level and should be able to reliably assign others to their appropriate genus or family.

The primary goal of this book is to present the beetles of eastern North America in an engaging format that is accessible to the amateur naturalist interested in beetles, yet authoritatively written to serve the needs of the professional biologist. I hope this richly illustrated book will increase the enjoyment of all interested in the natural world, serve as an introduction for students desiring to know more about beetles, and stimulate those who have already embraced the world's largest and most diverse group of animals as their life's work.

ACKNOWLEDGMENTS

First and foremost, I thank Robert Kirk, executive editor at Princeton University Press, for the opportunity to write this book. His support, guidance, and, most importantly, patience, were instrumental in the creation of this work. I also appreciate the dedication and expertise of Mark Bellis and Lorraine Doneker at Princeton University Press, copyeditor Lucinda Treadwell, and typesetter David Price-Goodfellow for their encouragement, advice, creativity, and expert copyediting.

A book of this size, depth, and quality would have been impossible to achieve were it not for the excellent images supplied by a talented and dedicated cadre of photographers. Their persistence in seeking out and capturing images of all kinds of beetles served as an inspiration to me as I compiled this work. I am particularly grateful for the efforts of Chris Wirth and Tom Murray, whose stunning work represents a significant portion of the images that appear on these pages. The contributions of the following photographers provided this book with the taxonomic breadth and depth required to establish its utility, and enhance its aesthetic appeal: Ken Allen, Dave Almquist, Jerry Armstrong, Lyn Atherton, Troy Bartlett, Christy Beal, Paul Bedell, Christoph Benisch, Thomas Bentley, Ashley Bradford, Donna Brunet, Val Bugh, Bob Carlson, Chris Carlton, Carmen Champagne, Jan Ciegler, Patrick Coin, Alan Cressler, Stephen Cresswell, Rob Curtis, Denis Doucet, Josef Dvořák, Charley Eiseman, Mardon Erbland, John Frisch, David Funk, Nicolas Gompel, Henri Goulet, Bob Gress, Joyce Gross, Guy Hanley, Randy Hardy, Phil Harpootlian, Jeff Hollenbeck, Scott Justis, James Kalisch, WonGun Kim, Thor Kristiansen, Jessica Lawrence, René Limoge, Ilona Loser, Stephen Luk, Ted MacRae, Crystal Maier, Daniel Marlos, Steve Marshall, Ole Martin, Charles Matson, John Maxwell, Sean McCann, Richard Migneault, Graham Montgomery, Roy Morris, Tim Moyer, Steve Nanz, Scott Nelson, Mark O'Brien, Jenn Orth, Johnny Ott, Nikola Rahme, Jon Rapp, Jennifer Read, David Reed, Lary Reeves, Charles Robertson, Matt Roth, Kurt Schaefer, Lynnette Schimming, Kyle Schnepp, Jimmy Sherwood, Tom Schultz, Roy Sewall, Ken Schneider, Marvin Smith, Gayle (deceased) and Jeanell Strickland, Tracy Sunvold, Mike Thomas, Alexey Tishechkin, Ed Trammel, Donna Watkins, Alex Wild, Jane Wyche, Dan Young, and Robert Lord Zimlich. I am forever grateful to all these superb photographers for their generosity and enthusiasm for this project.

Jennifer Read expertly prepared all 1,500+ images used in this work. She converted jpegs into tifs when needed and, when absolutely necessary, cropped, sharpened, adjusted exposures, repaired or replaced the occasional missing or damaged appendage, and removed dust and stray hairs so that each and every image in this book would look its absolute best. Jen also rendered the illustrations accompanying the key to families. Many thanks to Graham Wilson and Megan Rollins for their assistance in the initial phase of developing these illustrations.

I thank the following friends and colleagues for their assistance with specimen identifications, sorting out taxonomic issues, providing pertinent literature, collecting live specimens to photograph, supplying unpublished biological and geographic data, and reviewing portions of the manuscript: Albert Allen, Bob Anderson, Bob Androw, Chuck Bellamy (deceased), Vassili Belov, Larry Bezark, Yves Bousquet, Michael Brattain, Carlyle Brewster, Adam Brunke, Chris Carlton, Mike Caterino, Don Chandler, Anne Chazal, Jan Ciegler, Andy Cline, Maureen Dougherty, Hume Douglas, Terry Erwin, David Funk, François Genier, James Gibbs, Bruce Gill, Phil Harpootlian, Chris Hobson, Richard Hoffman (deceased), W.M. Hood, Mike Ivie, Paul Johnson, Kerry Katovich, Sergey Kazantsev, John Kingsolver, Nadine Kriska, John Lawrence, John Leavengood, Rich Leschen, Stephané Le Tirant, Steve Lingafelter, Darren Loomis, Chris Ludwig, Ted MacRae, Chris Majka, Blaine Matheson, Adriean Mayor, Chuck McClung, Will Merrit, Alfred Newton, Rolf Obeprieler, Charlie O'Brien, M.J. Paulsen, Stewart Peck, Keith Philips, Keith Pike, John Pinto, Darren Pollock, Jens Prena, Jennifer Read, Steve Roble, Bill Shepard, Floyd Shockley, Derek Sikes, Paul Skelley, Charlie Staines, Warren Steiner Jr., Margaret Thayer, Mike Thomas, Alexey Tishechkin, Natalia Vandenberg, Robert Vigneault, Graham Wilson, Rebecca Wilson, Norm Woodley, and Dan Young.

Finally, I thank my wife, Paula, whose love and support have made all my entomological pursuits in this century possible. Without her I would never have been able to undertake or complete this book.

I share the success of *Beetles of Eastern North America* with all the aforementioned individuals, but the responsibility for any and all of its shortcomings, misrepresentations, inaccuracies, and omissions is entirely my own.

HOW TO USE THIS BOOK

To get the most out of this book, read its introductory sections before venturing out into the field. Once you have become familiar with the bodies and lives of beetles, when to find them, where they live, and how to collect them, move on to the family diagnoses that punctuate the species accounts. Begin learning the physical features that characterize each family and distinguish them from similar families. Then peruse the individual accounts to get an idea of where and when to look for specific species. With this information at your disposal, you will be much better prepared to find and observe beetles and recognize the specific characteristics that will aid in their identification.

CLASSIFICATION

Numerous and substantial changes have been made in the classification of the Coleoptera since the appearance of the *American Beetles* volumes, and this process is ongoing. The families and species covered in this book mostly follow the order presented in *Family Group Names in Coleoptera (Insecta)* (Bouchard et al. 2011). In this book, the Cybocephalidae, treated elsewhere as a subfamily of the Nitidulidae, is treated as a family. The Ischaliidae, also recognized in this book, has been considered either its own family or a subfamily of the Anthicidae by previous authors. See the appendix, Classification of the Beetles of Eastern North America (p.501), for further details.

KEY TO FAMILIES

To assist with the correct placement of the most commonly encountered beetles in their proper family, a dichotomous key is presented (pp.53–7). This key consists of a series of "either–or" choices based on the quality of physical features possessed by a specimen. As with a road map, the reader is directed to a series of junctions called *couplets* that, through a process of elimination, will lead to a smaller and more manageable subset of the most commonly encountered families with which the beetle in question can be compared, checked against similar families, and, it is hoped, matched to a species photo and account.

FAMILY DIAGNOSES

Each family diagnosis provides information on the accepted common family name, pronunciation of the scientific family name, a brief overview of the natural history of the species in the family, and family diagnosis based on morphological features, including length in millimeters, shape, color, and features of the head, thorax, abdomen, and appendages. This information is augmented by descriptions of select features of other families of beetles containing species superficially similar in appearance or habit. Finally, the numbers of species and genera of each family (if known) found in the Nearctic and eastern North America are presented to give readers an idea of the beetle diversity in the region and how it compares with the combined fauna of Canada and the United States. Some of these numbers are only estimates since many taxa are inadequately known.

SPECIES ACCOUNTS

The species accounts provide the accepted common name (if any), scientific name, length in millimeters, overall form, and color of living beetles. The bright colors (pink, red, orange, yellow, green) of some living beetles frequently fade after death, while metallic colors and iridescence are usually permanent, except in some tortoise beetles (Chrysomelidae). Read the species accounts carefully to discern species-specific features that may not be evident in the photo. As good as the photographs are in this book, they sometimes do not adequately highlight the subtle characters necessary for accurate species identification. Snap judgments based solely on overall appearance and color often result in misidentifications. Information on distinguishing males and females is presented for many species in which the sexes markedly differ from one another externally. Brief notes on seasonality, habitat, food preferences (for adults and occasionally larvae), and distribution are also provided. The origin of species not native to North America, either purposely or accidentally introduced, is indicated when appropriate. Every effort has been made to ferret out published distributional records and augment them with unpublished data gleaned from local lists, records provided by avocational coleopterists, and specimens in select museums. Still, the actual distributions

A representative page showing the main elements of the family diagnoses and species accounts (see p.9).

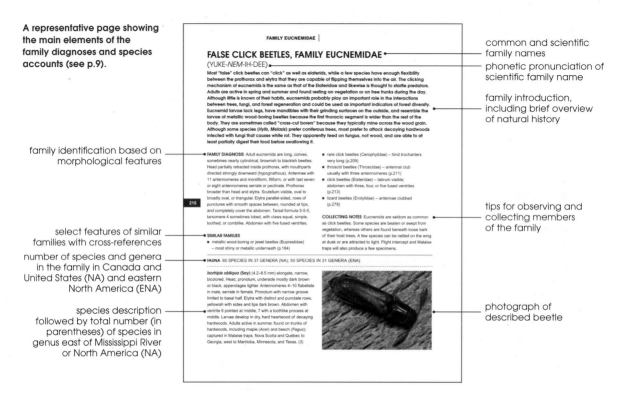

common and scientific family names

phonetic pronunciation of scientific family name

family introduction, including brief overview of natural history

family identification based on morphological features

select features of similar families with cross-references

number of species and genera in the family in Canada and United States (NA) and eastern North America (ENA)

species description followed by total number (in parentheses) of species in genus east of Mississippi River or North America (NA)

tips for observing and collecting members of the family

photograph of described beetle

of many species described in this guide are very likely broader than indicated in this book. At the end of most accounts is the total number of species in the genus known east of the Mississippi river.

SPECIES IDENTIFICATION

The identification of beetles can be challenging. Many conspicuous species are easily identified by direct comparison with a photograph, but most beetles are small and the characters necessary for species identification simply are not going to be available for examination without the specimen in hand. This is why it is best to capture and properly prepare a short series of specimens and have them available for detailed microscopic examination. Although 10× or 20× hand lenses are very useful for this purpose, a stereoscopic dissecting microscope with good lighting is ideal. Using a hand lens or microscope to examine specimens takes a bit of practice at first, but once you have mastered these indispensible tools, you will never again waste time by straining your unaided eyes to count tarsomeres and antennomeres or examine genitalia.

Many beetles can be positively identified to species only through examination of the male reproductive organs and comparison with detailed illustrations, photos, or previously identified specimens that were determined by experts.

Although providing detailed drawings of thousands of beetle genitalia is well beyond the scope of this book, it is useful to get into the habit of extracting the male genitalia while the specimen is still fresh and pliable so they can be easily examined by a specialist or compared to literature that depicts the genital structures of closely related species. You can extract the genitalia from the posterior opening of the abdomen by gently pulling them out with fine-tipped forceps or with the aid of a fish-hooked insect pin. Extracting genitalia from dried specimens requires that the specimens first be softened in a relaxing chamber, or placed in boiling water with a few drops of dish soap added as a wetting agent. Once the genitalia are extracted, you can leave them attached to the tip of the abdomen by their own tissue, where they will dry in place, or remove them entirely and glue to an insect mounting point, and pin the point just below the pinned specimen for later examination. Some beetles, especially very small species, require specialized techniques for extracting and preserving their genitalia. Consult the pertinent literature or a specialist before undertaking the dissection of these specimens.

Readers requiring accurate species identification, especially for control of horticultural, agricultural, and forest pests, are encouraged to consult coleopterists affiliated with cooperative extension offices or the entomology department of a museum or university for verification.

INTRODUCTION TO BEETLES

BEETLE ANATOMY

Although colors and patterns are sometimes useful, beetles are classified and more reliably identified on the basis of their anatomical features. Therefore, a basic understanding of beetle anatomy (Fig. 1) is essential for better understanding of not only their evolutionary relationships, but also the terminology used in the family diagnoses and species accounts that appear in this book.

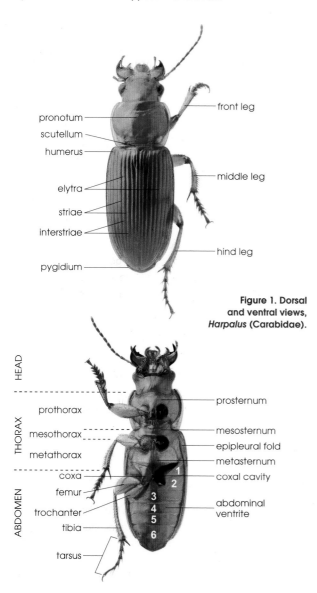

Figure 1. Dorsal and ventral views, *Harpalus* (Carabidae).

Labels (top): pronotum, scutellum, humerus, elytra, striae, interstriae, pygidium, front leg, middle leg, hind leg

Labels (bottom): HEAD, THORAX, prothorax, mesothorax, metathorax, coxa, femur, trochanter, tibia, tarsus, ABDOMEN, prosternum, mesosternum, epipleural fold, metasternum, coxal cavity, abdominal ventrite

EXOSKELETON

Adult beetles are covered and protected by a highly modified *exoskeleton* that functions as both skeleton and skin. Internally, the exoskeleton serves as a foundation for powerful muscles and organ systems, while externally providing a platform for important sensory structures connecting them to their surrounding environment. The exoskeleton is light yet durable and composed of a multilayered structure comprising the polysaccharide *chitin* and the protein *sclerotin*.

The exoskeleton is subdivided into *segments*, some of which are composed of smaller plates, or *sclerites*. The segments are joined into functional units that form appendages (mouthparts, antennae, legs) and three body regions (head, thorax, abdomen). Segments are joined together by membranes of pure chitin or separated by narrow furrows called *sutures*. The division of the exoskeleton into body regions and sclerites affords flexibility to beetle bodies, much the way the joints and plates of armor allowed knights to maneuver in battle.

BODY SHAPE

The basic body shape (Figs. 2a–n) of a beetle when viewed from above is sometimes variously described as elongate, oval, triangular, or antlike, among others. Parallel-sided refers to the straight and parallel sides of the elytra, the wing covers of a beetle. Terms like *convex*, *hemispherical*, flat, and flattened are useful too for describing the upper or *dorsal* surface, a description best determined when viewed from the side. Lady beetles (Coccinellidae) and some leaf beetles (Chrysomelidae) are sometimes referred to as "hemispherical" because their dorsal surface is very convex while the *ventral* surface or underside is relatively flat. *Cylindrical* is usually applied to elongate, parallel-sided species with convex dorsal and ventral surfaces and suggests that they would appear almost circular in cross section.

SURFACE SCULPTURING

The nature of the body surface on beetles, or surface sculpturing, is very useful in species identification. Surfaces can be shiny like patent leather or dulled (*alutaceous*)

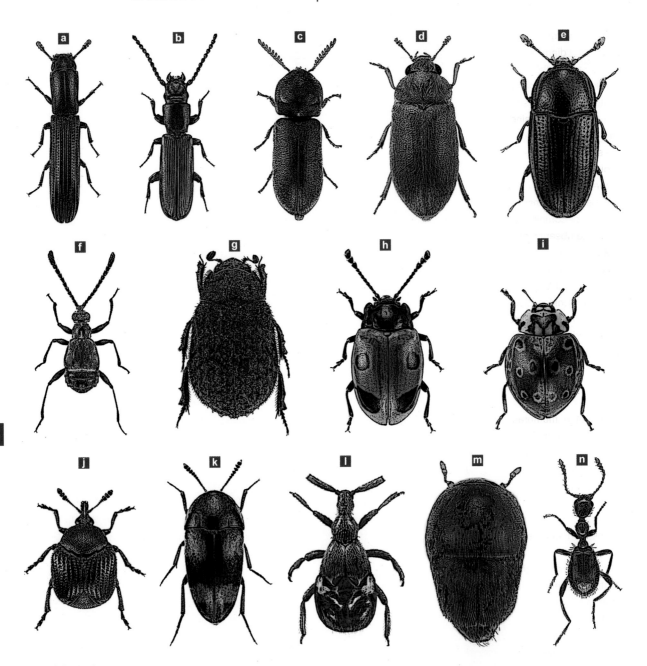

Figure 2. Body shapes.
a. elongate, *Colydium* (Zopheridae); b. elongate, *Catogenus* (Passandridae); c. elliptical, *Ptilinus* (Ptinidae); d. elongate-oval, *Byturus* (Byturidae); e. elongate-oval, *Philothermus* (Cerylonidae); f. elongate-oval, *Ctenisodes* (Staphylinidae); g. oval, *Trox* (Trogidae); h. oval, *Endomychus* (Endomychidae); i. broadly oval, *Anatis* (Coccinellidae); j. broadly oval, *Pterocolus* (Attelabidae); k. obovate, *Holostrophus* (Tetratomidae); l. triangular, *Adranes* (Staphylinidae); m. limuloid, *Sepedophilus* (Staphylinidae); n. antlike, *Acanthinus* (Anthicidae).

by a minute network of fine cracks resembling those of human skin. The surfaces of the head and legs, especially in burrowing species, are sometimes dulled by normal abrasion as the beetle burrows through soil or wood. Sometimes the surface is *glaucous*, or coated with a grayish or bluish coating of waterproof wax secreted by epidermal glands underlying the exoskeleton. This coating is easily rubbed off or dissolved in chemical preservatives and is usually evident only in freshly emerged individuals.

Shiny or not, many beetle bodies are typically covered to varying degrees with small pits called *punctures*. Punctures range from very small (*finely punctate*) to large (*coarsely punctate*) and may be shallow or deep. The density or distance of punctures from one another is often reported in terms of the degree of separation in relation to the puncture's diameter. Contiguous or nearly contiguous punctures are those with rims that touch one another, or nearly so. In *rugopunctate* surfaces, the punctures are so tightly spaced, the surface appears rough. Punctures sometimes bear a single hairlike *seta* (pl. *setae*). Setae are fine or bristly, stand straight up (*erect*), or lie nearly flat on the surface (*recumbent*). Flattened setae, or *scales*, range in outline from nearly round, to *oval* (egg-shaped), *obovate* (pear-shaped), *lanceolate* (spear-shaped) to linear (long and slender). Densely setose or scaled surfaces may be partially or completely obscured from view, while the complete absence of setae or scales altogether is referred to as *glabrous*.

An *impunctate* surface lacks punctures altogether, while *rugose* (rough) surfaces have raised areas that are formed by small wrinkles, distinct ridges, bumps, or fingerprint-like whorls. *Granulate* surfaces consist of many small, distinct, and rounded bumps, like the pebbled surface of a basketball.

HEAD AND ITS APPENDAGES

The capsule-shaped *head* (Fig. 3) is attached to the thorax by a flexible, membranous neck that is sometimes visible from above (e.g., Meloidae) but usually hidden, along with part of the head, within the first thoracic segment, or *prothorax*. In the fireflies (Lampyridae), some hooded beetles (Corylophidae), and other beetle families, the head is completely hidden from above by a hoodlike extension of the dorsal sclerite of the prothorax, or *pronotum*.

The compound eyes are usually conspicuous and composed of dozens or hundreds of individual facets or lenses. Awash in light, the lenses of day-active (*diurnal*) beetles are relatively small and flat, while nocturnal species have more convex lenses that gather all available light. Flightless, cave-dwelling, and subterranean species often have small compound eyes with only a few lenses or may lack eyes altogether. Compound eyes are typically round, or oval to kidney-shaped in outline. The front margins of kidney-shaped eyes are weakly to strongly notched, or

emarginate; the antennae of some species may originate within or near the emargination. The eyes are sometimes partially divided in front by a narrow ridge of cuticle called the *canthus*. In whirligigs (Gyrinidae) and some throscids (Throscidae) and longhorns (Cerambycidae), the canthus completely divides the eye. Some skin beetles (Dermestidae) and omaline rove beetles (Staphylinidae) also possess a simple eye, or *ocellus*, comprising a single lens located on the front of the head between the compound eyes.

The males of several eastern species (e.g., Geotrupidae, Scarabaeidae, and Tenebrionidae) have horns on their heads modified into spikes, scooped blades, or paired knobs that are used in mostly "bloodless" battles with other males of the same species over resources that will attract females. The variation of horn size in males of the same species is of particular interest to scientists who study mate selection. Environmental factors, especially larval nutrition, often play a more important role in horn development than genetic factors. Although outgunned in battle, lesser endowed males are still fully capable of mating with females and fertilizing their eggs when the opportunity arises.

The mouthparts of all beetles follow the same basic plan: an upper lip (*labrum*), two pairs of jaws (*mandibles*, *maxillae*), and a lower lip (*labium*). Although the mandibles of beetles are variously modified to cut and tear flesh (e.g., Carabidae), grind leaves (e.g., Chrysomelidae), or strain fluids (some Scarabaeidae), they also serve other purposes. The outsized mandibles of some male stag beetles (Lucanidae) are not used for feeding at all, but rather for battling other males over females. The tile-horned prionus, *Prionus imbricornis* (Cerambycidae) uses its imposing mandibles to tunnel out of wood as well as for weapons of defense. Male tiger beetles (Carabidae) use their mandibles to firmly grasp the female during copulation. Attached to the maxilla and labium are delicate, flexible, fingerlike structures, or *palps*, that assist beetles in the manipulation of food. The long and conspicuous maxillary palps of water scavengers (Hydrophilidae) are easily mistaken for antennae. Each palp is divided into articles or

13

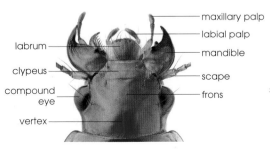

maxillary palp
labial palp
mandible
scape
frons

labrum
clypeus
compound eye
vertex

labial palp
glossa
mandible
submentum
gula

maxillary palp
galea
lacinia
maxilla
mentum
gena

Figure 3. Dorsal and ventral views of head, *Harpalus* (Carabidae).

sections called *palpomeres*. Protecting the mouthparts from above in most beetles is a broad plate of cuticle formed by the leading edge of the head, or *clypeus*. Below the head at the base of the labium in most beetles are two sclerites: *mentum* and *gula*.

The mouthparts of predatory and some wood-boring beetles are typically *prognathous* (Fig. 4), directed forward and parallel to the long axis of the body. *Hypognathous* mouthparts (Fig. 5) are directed downward and typical of most plant-feeding beetles, including chafers

Figure 4. Prognathous mouthparts, *Hesperandra* (Cerambycidae).

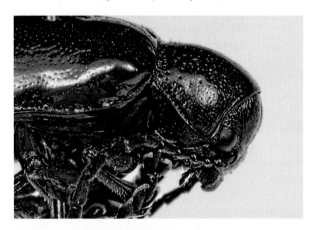

Figure 5. Hypognathous mouthparts, *Chrysochus* (Chrysomelidae).

Figure 6. Rostrum, *Curculio* (Curculionidae).

(Scarabaeidae), some longhorn beetles (Cerambycidae), leaf beetles (Chrysomelidae), and weevils (Curculionidae). The hypognathous mouthparts of some net-winged beetles (Lycidae) and narrow-waisted beetles (Salpingidae), and many weevils and their relatives (Curculionidae, Nemonychidae, Brentidae, Anthribidae) are drawn out into a short, broad beak, or an elongate *rostrum* (Fig. 6).

The *antennae* are beetles' primary organs of smell and touch and usually attached to the sides of the head, often between the eyes and the bases of the mandibles. Although the antennae exhibit an incredible diversity of sizes and shapes, they all consist of three basic parts: *scape*, *pedicel*, and *flagellum* (Fig. 7). The usual number of antennal articles is 11, but 10 or fewer are common in some groups, while 12 or more occur only rarely. Insect morphologists note that only the scape and pedicel have their own internal musculature and are the only true antennal segments, while the remaining articles of the flagellum lack intrinsic musculature and are called *flagellomeres*. Distinguishing segments and flagellomeres to communicate information about the number of antennal articles and the like is unwieldy at best. For the sake of morphological correctness and clarity, all visible antennal articles are referred to as *antennomeres*. The scape is antennomere 1 and the pedicel is antennomere 2. Antennomeres 3–11 refer to the articles of the flagellum.

The antennae are generally shorter than the body and somewhat similar in both sexes; however, male pine sawyers in the genus *Monochamus* (Cerambycidae) have long, threadlike antennae up to three times the length of the body, while those of the female are only slightly longer than the body. In other species, the ornate antennal modifications possessed by male *Polyphylla* (Scarabaeidae), *Phengodes* (Phengodidae), *Sandalus* (Rhipiceridae), and wedge-shaped beetles (Ripiphoridae) are packed with sensory pits capable of tracking pheromones released by distant or secretive females.

The principal forms of beetle antennae (Figs. 8a–l) include the following:

- *filiform*, or threadlike, with antennomeres uniformly cylindrical, or nearly so
- *moniliform*, or beadlike, with round antennomeres of uniform size
- *serrate*, or saw-toothed, with flattened, triangular antennomeres
- *pectinate*, or comblike, with short antennomeres each bearing a prolonged extension
- *bipectinate*, or comblike, with short antennomeres each bearing two prolonged extensions

- *flabellate*, or fanlike, with antennomeres bearing long extensions that fit together like a fan
- *plumose*, or featherlike, with antennomeres bearing long, slender, flexible extensions
- *clavate*, with outermost antennomeres gradually enlarged to form a distinct symmetrical club
- *capitate*, with outermost antennomeres abruptly enlarged to form a round or oval symmetrical club
- *lamellate*, with outermost antennomeres flat, forming a distinct, lopsided club
- *geniculate*, or elbowed, with a long, slender scape with pedicel and flagellomeres attached at a distinct angle; pedicel and capitate or lamellate flagellomeres are collectively referred to as the funicle

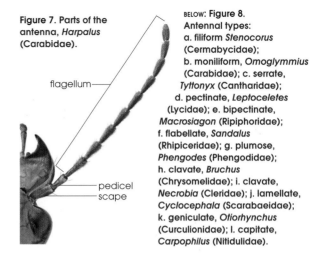

Figure 7. Parts of the antenna, *Harpalus* (Carabidae).

flagellum

pedicel
scape

BELOW: **Figure 8.** Antennal types: a. filiform *Stenocorus* (Cermabycidae); b. moniliform, *Omoglymmius* (Carabidae); c. serrate, *Tyttonyx* (Cantharidae); d. pectinate, *Leptoceletes* (Lycidae); e. bipectinate, *Macrosiagon* (Ripiphoridae); f. flabellate, *Sandalus* (Rhipiceridae); g. plumose, *Phengodes* (Phengodidae); h. clavate, *Bruchus* (Chrysomelidae); i. clavate, *Necrobia* (Cleridae); j. lamellate, *Cyclocephala* (Scarabaeidae); k. geniculate, *Otiorhynchus* (Curculionidae); l. capitate, *Carpophilus* (Nitidulidae).

THORAX AND ITS APPENDAGES

Like that of all insects, the beetle thorax is divided into three segments, the *prothorax*, *mesothorax*, and *metathorax*, each bearing a pair of legs. The underside of the thorax is sometimes modified with impressions or distinct grooves that accommodate the antennae or legs.

The prothorax is always exposed and forms the distinctive "midsection" of the beetle body, while the remaining wing-bearing mesothorax and metathorax, or *pterothorax*, are hidden beneath the wing covers, or *elytra*. The prothorax is either firmly or loosely attached to the pterothorax. The dorsal sclerite of the prothorax, or *pronotum*, is sometimes hoodlike and extends forward to partially (e.g., Corylophidae) or completely (e.g., Lampyridae) cover the head when viewed from above. In some males, the pronotal surface is modified with horns, pits, bumps, or ridges that are useful in species identification. The sides, or lateral margins of the prothorax may be partly or completely sharply ridged or keeled (e.g., Carabidae, Gyrinidae, Dytiscidae), or distinctly rounded (e.g., Meloidae, some Cerambycidae). Underneath, the central portion of the prothorax is called the *prosternum* and is sometimes attenuated into a spinelike structure directed toward the head or backward. The prosternum is flanked on either side by the *propleuron*. Sometimes the propleuron is divided into two sclerites by the *pleural suture*; the sclerite in front is called the *proepisternum*, while the sclerite behind is the *proepimeron*. A distinct line delimits the outer portion of propleuron or suture that separates it from the pronotum called the *notopleural suture* in the Carabidae, Gyrinidae, Haliplidae, Noteridae, and Dytiscidae. The front legs are inserted into prothoracic cavities called *procoxal cavities*. Although sometimes very difficult to see, the nature of these cavities is important in the identification of families, subfamilies, and tribes of beetles. If the cavities are enclosed behind by the *proepimeron*, or a junction of the proepimeron and the prosternum, they are said to be "closed behind" (Fig. 9a). If these cavities open directly to the mesothorax, they are said to be "open behind" (Fig. 9b).

The segments of the pterothorax are broadly united with one another. The mesothorax bears the middle legs below and is largely covered by the elytra above. In many beetles, the mesothorax is evident dorsally by the presence of a small triangular or shield-shaped sclerite called the *scutellum*. The scutellum, if visible, is always located directly behind the pronotum, at the base and between the elytra. The hind thoracic segment, or metathorax, bears the hind legs and, if present, flight wings folded beneath the elytra. The hind coxae are usually wide, or *transverse*. In the Carabidae, Gyrinidae, Haliplidae, Noteridae, and Dytiscidae, the hind

16

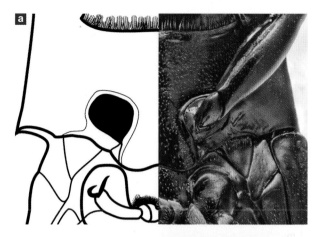

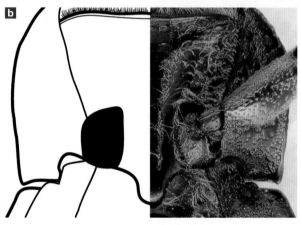

Figure 9. Procoxal cavities.
a. closed; b. open.

coxae are immovably fused to the *metasternum* and extend backward past or "completely divide" the first abdominal segment. In the crawling water beetles (Haliplidae), the hind coxae form broad plates that conceal nearly the entire abdomen. In all other families, the hind coxae are "free," or not fused to the metasternum and do not extend past or "divide" the first abdominal segment. The segments of the pterothorax are usually shortened in wingless (*apterous*) or reduced-wing (*brachypterous*) species.

The most conspicuous and unique feature of nearly all adult beetles are the modified mesothoracic wings, or elytra (sing. *elytron*) that partially or completely cover the abdomen. The elytra are opaque, soft, and leathery (e.g. Lycidae, Phengodidae, Lampyridae, Cantharidae), or rigid. At rest, the elytra usually meet over the middle of the back along a distinct and straight line called the *elytral suture*. The tips, or apices, of the elytra usually meet at the elytral suture, too, although they are often slightly separated; distinctly diverging elytral tips, such as those seen in *Lichnanthe* (Glaphyridae) are referred to as *dehiscent*. The outer basal angle of each elytron, or "shoulder," is called the *humerus* (pl. *humeri*). Punctures irregularly scattered over the elytral surface are referred to as *confused*. Elytra with punctures arranged in rows that may or may not be connected by impressed lines or that occur within narrow grooves (*striae*) running lengthwise are called *punctostriate*. The spaces between striae are called *intervals*. The portion of side margins of each elytron that is folded down is called the *epipleural fold*. Bordering the epipleural fold is a narrow inner edge, or *epipleuron* (pl. *epipleura*) that is of variable width and may or may not extend to the tip of the elytron.

The elytra are typically short in the rove (Staphylinidae), clown (Histeridae), and sap beetles (Nitidulidae). The elytra of male glowworms (Phengodidae) are oarlike, while those of some ripiphorids (Ripiphoridae) resemble flaplike scales. In most species, the elytra are lifted and separated when airborne, but in the fruit chafer genera *Cremastocheilus*, *Cotinis*, and *Euphoria* (Scarabaeidae), and in the metallic wood-boring beetles *Acmaeodera* (Buprestidae), the elytra are partially or totally fused along the elytral suture. When taking to the air, these fast-flying beetles lift their elytra slightly as the membranous flight wings unfold and expand through broad notches along the lateral margins near the bases.

The membranous flight wings are supported by a network of hemolyph-filled veins that help them to expand or fold. Some of these veins are hinged so that the wings can be carefully tucked and folded under the elytra. Flight wings are seldom used to identify genera or species, but their venation patterns do offer important clues to the relationships of families. The flight wings of some species (e.g., some female Scarabaeidae, Tenebrionidae, some female Cerambycidae, Curculionidae) are reduced in size or absent altogether. Adult females of all phengodids

(Phengodidae) and some glowworms (Lampyridae) are *larviform* and lack both flight wings and elytra altogether.

Beetle legs are subdivided into six segments (Fig. 10). The *coxa* (pl. *coxae*) is generally short and stout, and it firmly anchors the leg into the coxal cavity of the thorax while allowing for the horizontal to-and-fro movement of the legs. The *trochanter* is usually small, freely movable in relation to the coxa, but fixed to the femur. The *femur* (pl. *femora*) is the largest and most powerful leg segment and greatly enlarged in species that jump (e.g., Scirtidae, Chrysomelidae). The *tibia* (pl. *tibiae*) is usually long and slender but often modified into a rakelike structure on the forelegs of burrowing species. The *tarsus* (pl. *tarsi*), if present, is typically divided into multiple articles called *tarsomeres* that lack their own internal musculature, and the *pretarsus* that bears the claws.

The tarsi are of particular value in beetle identification. Each tarsus consists of up to five tarsomeres. The three-digit tarsal formulas used in this guide, such as 5-5-5, 5-5-4, or 4-4-4, indicate the number of articles (tarsomeres) on the front, middle, and hind legs, respectively. Some articles, especially the last tarsomere, are difficult to see without careful examination under high magnification and are typically denoted as "appears 4-4-4, but actually 5-5-5." The front tarsi of some male predaceous diving beetles (e.g., *Cybister*, *Dytiscus*) are highly modified into adhesive pads that enable them to grasp the female's smooth and slippery elytra while mating, or absent altogether in some dung beetles (Scarabaeidae). The feet of some longhorn (Cerambycidae) and leaf beetles (Chrysomelidae) are equipped with broad, brushy pads that are tightly packed with setae that help them to walk on smooth vertical surfaces or cling to uncooperative mates, while those of some click beetles and other species have tarsomeres with membranous flaps that project outward.

The claws of beetles are frequently modified (Figs. 11a–f). *Cleft* or *incised* claws are finely notched near the tip. *Toothed* claws have one or more distinct teeth underneath. *Appendiculate* claws have a broad flange at the base. *Serrate* claws have finely notched undersides resembling the teeth of a saw. *Pectinate* claws have comblike teeth underneath. *Simple* claws, which are typical of many beetles, lack any such modifications.

ABDOMEN

Beetles typically have nine abdominal segments, but only five or six segments are usually visible. These segments are ringlike and consist of two sclerites: a dorsal *tergum* (pl. *terga*) or *tergite*, and the ventral *sternum* (pl. *sterna*);

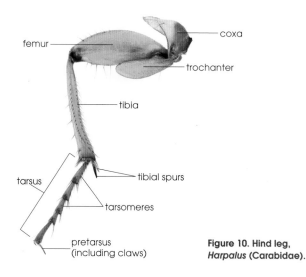

femur
coxa
trochanter
tibia
tibial spurs
tarsus
tarsomeres
pretarsus (including claws)

Figure 10. Hind leg, *Harpalus* (Carabidae).

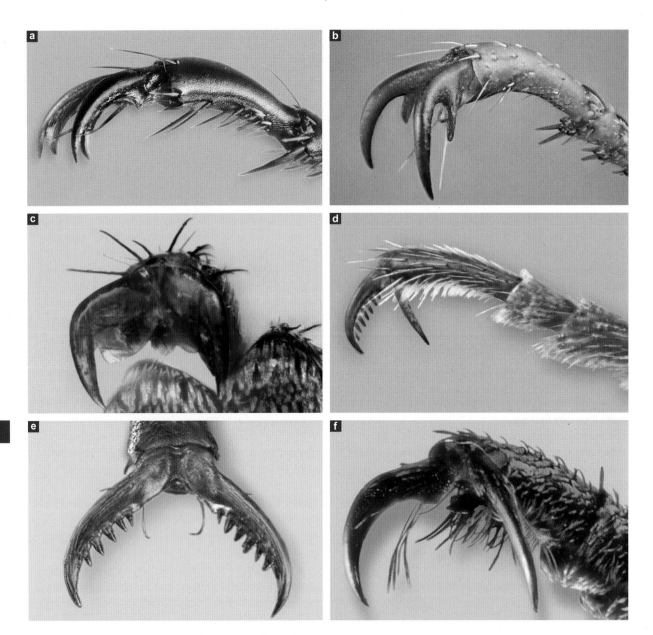

Figure 11. Claws. a. cleft, *Macrodactylus* (Scarabaeidae); b. toothed, *Polyphylla* (Scarabaeidae); c. appendiculate, *Oberea* (Cerambycidae); d. pectinate, *Melanotus* (Elateridae); e. serrate, *Synuchus* (Carabidae); f. simple, *Alaus* (Elateridae).

some segments may be only partially ringlike. The terga are thin and flexible in beetles with abdomens completely covered by the elytra, but are thicker and more rigid in species with short elytra. The penultimate and ultimate terga are called the *propygidium* and *pygidium*, respectively. The abdominal spiracles are in the pleural membrane between the dorsal and ventral sclerites or on the edges of the terga.

The visible abdominal sternites are called *ventrites*, and each is numbered beginning from the base of the abdomen regardless of the true morphological segment it represents.

For example, ventrite 1 is usually abdominal sternite 2. The ventrites are of varying lengths in relation to one another and are either distinctly or barely separated by deep to shallow sutures or narrow membranes, especially, down the middle. Ventrites that are fused together, as evidenced by shallow or obsolete sutures, are said to be fused or *connate*, while "free" ventrites are those that are separated by distinct membranes. In some families, some or all of the ventrites are connate.

The remaining segments are internal and variously modified for reproductive activities: egg laying in females and copulation in males. Long *ovipositors* are characteristic of beetles that deposit their eggs deep in sand or plant tissues, while short and stout ovipositors are indicative of species that deposit their eggs directly on the surface of various substrates. The often elaborate male reproductive organs are of considerable value in species identification and sometimes the only method of separating closely related species.

BEHAVIOR AND NATURAL HISTORY

The mating behaviors, developmental strategies, and life cycles of most of the beetles in eastern North America assure their reproductive success by maximizing their efforts to locate mates, eliminating competition for food and space between larvae and adults, and adapting them to cope with dramatic seasonal shifts in temperatures that are typical of a temperate climate. With their compact and armored bodies, chewing mouthparts, and specialized limbs, beetles are equipped to occupy and thrive in a staggering array of habitats. They chew, dig, mine, and swim their way through a myriad of habitats in sandy coastal beaches and dunes, arid sandhills, backyards, urban parks, agricultural fields, lush woodlands, wetlands, and rocky mountain outcrops. Their ability to fly increases their chances of finding food and mates, and affords them opportunities to seek out and colonize new habitats.

MATING BEHAVIOR

With relatively short lives that last only weeks or months, most beetles have little time to waste in finding mates. They have developed various channels of communication that enhance their efforts at finding a mate, including scent, sight, or sound. These strategies are often remarkably effective, luring in numerous eager mates from considerable distances. Sex-attractant *pheromones* are used by many species to attract and locate mates over long distances. Males of these species often have longer or more elaborate antennal structures (e.g., Scarabaeidae, Ptilodactylidae, Rhipiceridae, Phengodidae, some Elateridae, Ripiphoridae, Cerambycidae) that provide more surface area for incredibly sensitive sensory pits capable of detecting just a few molecules of the female's pheromone wafting about in the air. These males typically track and locate females by flying in a zigzag pattern until they cross through the female's "odor plume" of pheromone. Once the plume is located, the male follows the increasing concentration of pheromone molecules directly to its source. Compounds other than pheromones are used for intersexual communication. For example, male *Neopyrochroa flabellata* (Pyrochroidae, p.375) secrete cantharidin into a large cranial pit located between their eyes not only to attract females, but also to inform them of their fitness as a mate.

The best-known example of visual communication in beetles is that of *bioluminescence*. Bioluminescence is a characteristic of many eastern fireflies (Lampyridae) and larval and adult female glowworms (Phengodidae) (Figs. 12a–b), as well as some click beetles (Elateridae). The whitish, greenish-yellow, or reddish light emanating from these insects is produced by special abdominal (e.g., Lampyridae, Phengodidae) or pronotal (e.g., Elateridae) organs with tissues that are supplied oxygen by numerous tracheae. The brightness and duration of these lights are controlled by the nervous system, which regulates the amount of oxygen reaching these tissues and reacting with the pigment luciferin, a chemical reaction sped up by the presence of the enzyme luciferase; color of the

Figure 12. *Phenogodes* (Phengodidae) larva.

light may vary depending on temperature and humidity. Bioluminescence in fireflies is virtually 100% efficient, with almost all the energy that goes into the system given off as light. In fact, the light produced by just one firefly produces 1/80,000th of the heat produced by a candle flame of the same brightness. By comparison, notoriously inefficient incandescent lightbulbs lose up to 90% of their electrical energy as heat.

Some male death-watch beetles (Ptinidae) bang their heads against the walls of their wooden galleries to lure females into their tunnels, but most beetles produce sound by rubbing two ridged or roughened surfaces together in a process known as *stridulation*. Stridulation generally occurs during courtship, confrontations with other beetles, or in response to other stressful situations, such as attack by a predator. Longhorn (Cerambycidae), June (Scarabaeidae), and bark beetles (Curculionidae) stridulate by rubbing their elytra with their legs or abdomen to create a chirping or squeaking sound when handled or attacked, possibly to startle predators; some aquatic species stridulate by rubbing their elytra and abdomen together.

Adult bess beetles (Passalidae) stridulate to communicate with their larvae. Using a pair of rasplike, oval patches located on the fifth abdominal segment, bess beetles raise their abdomen slightly to rub these patches against hardened folds on their membranous flight wings to produce a clearly audible squeaking noise. At least 14 different signals have been documented in this species that are associated with various behaviors, including aggression, courtship, or responses to threats and other disturbances. The larvae respond to stridulating adults by rapidly vibrating their stumpy, pawlike hind legs over a ribbed area at the base of the second pair of legs. Their incessant squeaking is feeble in comparison to that of the adults but still perceptible to the human ear. Communication between the larvae and adults is thought to help keep them in close proximity to one another, a theory partly supported by the dependence of the larvae on the adults for a steady food supply in the form of chewed wood and feces. Hungry *Nicrophorus* (Silphidae) larvae are also summoned to feed by stridulating parents rubbing a pair of abdominal files against the underside of their elytra.

In beetles, elaborate courtship behaviors are rare; however, some species may engage in nibbling (Cantharidae), licking (Cerambycidae), or antenna pulling (Meloidae) just prior to copulation, with the male typically mounting the female from above and behind. Females usually have enormous reserves of eggs awaiting fertilization, but need to mate only once, in spite of being courted by numerous enthusiastic males responding to

Figure 13. Mate guarding or postinsemination association, *Habroscelimorpha* (Carabidae).

their pheromones. Sperm is usually stored internally in a socklike reservoir called the *spermatheca*. Fertilization does not occur until her eggs travel past the spermatheca, just as they are about to be laid. In these females, it is the sperm of the last male that fertilizes the eggs. To assure their paternity, male tiger beetles (Carabidae) continue to tightly grasp their partners with their mandibles (Fig. 13) after copulation is completed until the eggs are laid, a behavior called *postinsemination association*.

Not all species of beetles must mate to reproduce. *Parthenogenesis*—development from an unfertilized egg— occurs among several families of beetles including leaf beetles (Chrysomelidae) and weevils (Curculionidae). Males of parthenogenetic species are rare or unknown altogether. The females of these species are solely responsible for maintaining the population and do so by producing cloned offspring. Telephone-pole beetles (Micromalthidae) exhibit an extreme form of this type of reproduction. They develop in rotting wood and must multiply quickly to take advantage of the patchy and ephemeral food source. They have evolved the singular ability to reproduce not only sexually as adults, but also asexually as larvae, a phenomenon known as parthenogenetic *paedogenesis*.

PARENTAL CARE

For most species of beetles, care of offspring is limited to selection of the egg-laying site; however, in a select few groups, relatively elaborate provisions are made to ensure the survival of the eggs and larvae. Some ground beetles (Carabidae) deposit their eggs in carefully constructed cells of mud, twigs, and leaves. Some water scavenger (Hydrophilidae) and minute moss beetles (Hydraenidae) enclose their eggs singly or in batches within cocoons made of silk secreted by special glands in the female's reproductive system. Depending on the species, leaf beetles (Chrysomelidae) apply a protective coating of their own feces to the eggs that are laced with distasteful chemicals sequestered from the tissues of the host plant. Leaf-mining metallic wood-boring beetles (Buprestidae) and weevils (Curculionidae) provide their offspring with both food and shelter by sandwiching their eggs between the upper and lower surfaces of leaves. Some longhorn beetles provide their larvae with dead wood by girdling, or chewing, a ring around a living tree branch and laying their eggs on the soon-to-be-dead outer tip. Dying branch tips quickly turn brown, a phenomenon called *flagging*, and stand in stark contrast to healthy green foliage. The girdle eventually weakens the branch, causing it to break and fall to the ground where the larvae can feed and develop inside, undisturbed. Female leaf-rolling weevils (Attelabidae) cut the leaf's midrib before laying their eggs in the rolled-up portion of the leaf.

Dung scarabs (Scarabaeidae) and *Nicrophorus* burying beetles (Silphidae) exhibit varying degrees of parental care well beyond the egg stage. Both males and females may cooperate in digging nests for their eggs and provision them with dung or carrion, respectively, for their brood. Dung and carrion are rich in nutrients, and competition for these resources can be fierce. Many dung- and carrion-feeding beetles have evolved tunneling or burying behaviors to quickly hide excrement or dead animals from the view of other scavenger species. Burial not only secures food for their young, it also helps to maintain optimum moisture levels for successful brood development. *Nicrophorus* beetles exhibit *the most advanced form of parental care known in beetles.* They meticulously prepare corpses as food for their young by removing feathers and fur, reshape them by removing or manipulating legs and wings, all while coating the carcass in saliva laced with antimicrobials that slow decomposition. Females lay their eggs in the burial chamber and remain with the young larvae as they feed and develop. The brood's first meal consists of droplets of chewed carrion regurgitated by the mother in a broad depression on the carcass.

Ambrosia and bark beetles (Curculionidae) also provide food and shelter for their young, carving elaborate galleries beneath the bark of trees or in galleries that penetrate the sapwood. Adult females cultivate and store ambrosia fungus in their *mycangia*, specialized pits on their bodies. As they colonize and tunnel into new trees, they introduce the "starter" ambrosia fungus into the brood chambers, where it will be used as food for both themselves and their developing larvae.

METAMORPHOSIS AND DEVELOPMENT

Beetles develop by a process called *holometaboly*, or complete metamorphosis that usually involves four distinct stages: egg, larva, pupa, and adult. The egg stage is sometimes absent in telephone-pole beetles (Micromalthidae), while the pupal stage may be greatly modified in female glowworms (Phengodidae) and some female fireflies (Lampyridae). Each developmental stage is adapted to a particular season and set of environmental factors that ultimately enhances the individual beetle's ability to survive extreme conditions. Adults and larvae are seldom found together in the same place at the same time, thereby functioning in the environment as two distinct species. The spatial and temporal separation of the larvae and adults within the same species effectively eliminates competition for the basic resources of food and space.

Females lay eggs singly or in batches (Fig. 14) through a membranous and sometimes very long tube, or *ovipositor*, usually on or near suitable larval foods. Aquatic species lay their eggs singly or in small batches on submerged rocks, plants, or chunks of wood and other objects. Ground-dwelling beetles that scavenge plant and animal materials often deposit their eggs in soil, leaf litter, compost heaps, dung, carrion, and other sites rich in decomposing organic materials and animal waste. Plant-feeding species drop their eggs at the base of the larval food plant or glue them to various vegetative structures; some species carefully apply a protective coating of their own feces on the eggs. Wood borers, such as longhorn beetles (Cerambycidae), deposit their eggs in cracks, crevices, and wounds of bark.

The larvae of most beetles bear no resemblance whatsoever to the adults and function as though they were entirely different species in terms of food and habitat preferences. Growth is typically rapid, and the outgrown exoskeleton is replaced with a new and roomier one

21

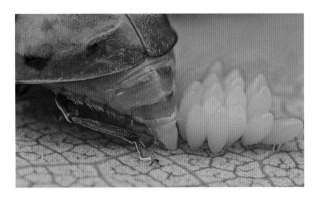

Figure 14. Egg laying or oviposition,
Harmonia (Coccinellidae).

22

Figure 15. Larval body types. a. eruciform, *Harmonia* (Coccinellidae); b. scarabaeiform, *Valgus* (Scarabaeidae); c. elateriform, *Alaus* (Elateridae); d. vermiform, *Aethina* (Nitidulidae); e. campodeiform, *Galerita* (Carabidae); f. fusiform, *Pyractomena* (Lampyridae); g. onisciform, *Aphorista* (Endomychidae); h. cheloniform, *Psephenus* (Psephenidae).

secreted from underneath by a layer of epidermal cells, a process called *molting*. The stage between each larval molt is called an *instar*. Most species pass through three to five instars, although some may have as few as two (Histeridae) or as many as seven (Dermestidae) or more.

The five basic larval types (Figs. 15a–h) recognized in beetles are based on body form. The slow and caterpillar-like larvae of lady beetles (Coccinellidae) and some leaf beetles (Chrysomelidae) are called *eruciform*; they typically have well-developed heads, legs, and fleshy abdominal protuberances. Sluggish, C-shaped *scarabaeiform* grubs have distinct heads and well-developed legs suited for burrowing through the soil or rotten wood and are characteristic of scarab beetles and their kin (Scarabaeidae, Lucanidae, Trogidae, etc.). The *elateriform* larvae of click beetles (Elateridae) and many darkling beetles (Tenebrionidae) have long, slender bodies with short legs and tough exoskeletons. Thick, legless, maggot-like weevil grubs are called *vermiform*, while the flattened, elongate, and leggy predatory larvae of ground (Carabidae), whirligig (Gyrinidae), predaceous diving (Dytiscidae), water scavenger (Hydrophilidae), and rove beetles (Staphylinidae) are *campodeiform*. The broadly oval and distinctly segmented water penny larvae (Psephenidae) are *cheloniform*, or turtle-shaped, while those of some Silphidae resemble pillbugs, or are *onisciform*. *Fusiform* larvae are broad in the middle and narrowed at the ends.

Each successive instar is generally similar to the last in form, but larger in size; however, the larvae of telephone-pole beetles (Micromalthidae), cicada parasite beetles (Rhipiceridae), blister beetles (Meloidae), and wedge-shaped beetles (Ripiphoridae) develop by a special type of holometaboly called *hypermetamorphosis*. Hypermetamorphosis is characterized by two or more distinct larval forms. The first active, leggy instar is called a *triungulin*, adapted for seeking out the appropriate host. Once the triungulin has located a host, it molts into a decidedly less active larva with short, thick legs and begins to feed. This form is followed by a fat, legless grub that eventually develops into a more active short-legged grub that spends most of its time preparing a pupal chamber.

Although beetle larvae lack compound eyes, most possess from one to six simple eyes on each side of the head called *stemmata*, while others lack any visual organs and are blind. Their mouthparts are adapted for crushing, grinding, or tearing foodstuffs. Predatory larvae are liquid feeders that pierce and drain victims of their bodily fluids. Some species have sickle-like and grooved mouthparts that channel digestive fluids into insect prey to liquefy their tissues and organs. The antennae of larvae consist of only two or four simple segments. Giant water scavenger larvae (*Hydrophilus*), known as water tigers, use their sharp, pointed antennae in concert with their mandibles to tear open insect prey.

The thorax consists of three very similar segments, the first of which may have a thickened plate across its back. Legs, if present, typically have six or fewer segments. Larvae with legs greatly reduced or absent generally feed inside plant tissues or parasitize other insects.

Beetle larvae have 9- or 10-segmented abdomens that are usually soft and pliable, allowing their food-filled bodies to rapidly expand without having to molt. Although legless, the abdomen in some species possesses segments equipped with fleshy wartlike protuberances that afford the larva a bit of traction as it moves about. The terminal abdominal segment may end in a pair of fixed or segmented projections called *urogomphi* (Fig. 16).

Beetle larvae live in all kinds of terrestrial and aquatic habitats, especially in leaf litter, rotten wood, and various kinds of fungi. They feed on a wide variety of organic

23

Figure 16. Larval urogomphi, *Dendroides* (Pyrochroidae).
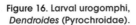

Figure 17. Tiger beetle larva,
Cicindela (Carabidae).

Figure 18. Glowworm larva, *Phengodes*
(Phengodidae), attacking a millipede.

materials, including plant and fungal structures, as well as on living and dead animals. *Phytophagous*, or plant-feeding, larvae attack living and decomposing flowers, fruits, seeds, cones, leaves, needles, twigs, branches, trunks, and roots. Leaf-mining species tunnel between the upper and lower surfaces of living leaves, leaving discolored blotches, blisters, or meandering tunnels trailing in their wake. Wood-boring larvae tunnel between the bark and wood and, depending on species, either pupate there or tunnel their way into the sapwood. Others attack only the heartwood and leave the outer, living sapwood intact. Some larval carrion beetles (Silphidae) feed on accumulations of plant material, while dung-feeding larvae (Geotrupidae, Scarabaeidae, etc.) eat plant materials that have been partially decomposed within the digestive tracts of vertebrates.

The fleet-footed larvae of several families actively hunt for prey in leaf litter or under bark, while decidedly stationary tiger beetle larvae (Carabidae) (Fig. 17) ambush prey that stray too close to the entrance of their vertical burrows. Some larval ground beetles and rove beetles (Staphylinidae) actively seek out and consume the pupae of leaf and whirligig beetles, and flies. A glowworm larva (Phengodidae) overpowers its prey by coiling itself around the front of a millipede's body (Fig. 18). It bites the millipede just behind and underneath the head with sharp and channeled sickle-shaped mandibles that deliver gut fluids laced with paralyzing toxins and digestive enzymes. Immobilized almost instantly, the millipede is unable to release its noxious defensive chemicals and quickly dies as its internal organs and tissues are liquefied. The phengodid larva consumes all but the millipede's exoskeleton and defensive glands. The larvae of blister beetles (Meloidae)

attack underground grasshopper egg masses or invade subterranean nests of solitary bees to raid their stores of pollen and nectar. Rhipicerid and ripiphorid larvae are ectoparasitoids that attack cicada nymphs and various mud-nesting wasps, respectively.

Beetle larvae employ a variety of morphological and chemical strategies to defend themselves. Dermestid larvae (Fig. 19) have clusters of bristly hairlike setae that are irritating deterrents to predatory mammals, reptiles, and birds. Located on the upper surface of the abdomen, these setae are arrayed like a defensive fan to ward off potential enemies and entangle the mouthparts of ants and other small arthropod predators. These very same structures are common components of house dust; they trigger allergic reactions and are linked to asthma attacks. Tortoise beetle larvae (Chrysomelidae) carry racks of fecal material and cast larval skins over their backs (Fig. 20) under which they can hide, while other leaf beetles construct protective cases from their waste that cover their entire bodies (Fig. 21).

Figure 19. Dermestid larva,
Anthrenus (Dermestidae).

Figure 20. Tortoise beetle larva, *Gratiana*
(Chrysomelidae), with defensive rack of fecal material.

Figure 21. Case-bearing leaf beetle larva
(Chrysomelidae, Cryptocephalinae).

The last larval instar, sometimes called the *prepupa*, develops into the pupa. Dramatic physiological and morphological transformations take place during the pupal stage (Fig. 22), marking the end of a larva adapted primarily for feeding and the beginning of an adult whose life is dominated by reproduction. During this stage, the first physical details of the adult are apparent. Most beetle pupae are of the *adecticous exarate* type and lack functional mandibles (*adecticous*) and have legs not tightly appressed (*exarate*) to the body. Some species (Ptiliidae, some Staphylinidae, Clambidae, Coccinellidae, some Chrysomelidae) have adecticous pupae with legs that are tightly appressed (*obtect*) along the entire length of the body. Many pupae have functional abdominal muscles that allow for some movement. Some of these species have specialized teeth, or sharp edges along the opposing

abdominal segments known as *gin-traps* that snap shut on the appendages of ants, mites, and other small predators and parasites.

In eastern North America, many beetles overwinter as pupae within chambers located deep in soil, humus, or the tissues of plants where they are less likely to be subjected to freezing temperatures. Some scarab beetle larvae (e.g., *Cotinis*, *Cremastocheilus*, *Dynastes*, *Euphoria*) and other species construct protective pupal chambers from their own fecal material. Leaf beetles (Chrysomelidae) generally pupate in the soil, sometimes inside a "cocoon" within a specially dug chamber, although the larvae of *Ophraella* typically anchor their meshlike cocoons up on their host plant. In glowworms (Phengodidae) and some fireflies (Lampyridae), the females undergo a modified pupal stage that closely resembles the last larval instar. Adult *larviform* females emerge without wings and are best distinguished from the larvae by the presence of compound eyes externally and reproductive organs internally.

25

ADULT EMERGENCE

The requisite combination of time, temperature, and moisture triggers adult emergence, or *eclosion*, from the pupa. Freshly eclosed adults are typically soft and pale, or *teneral* (Fig. 23). Their exoskeleton hardens as it undergoes chemical changes akin to the tanning process and gradually takes on its normal color. Adult beetles are at their full size and never molt again; however, the abdomens of some soft-bodied leaf and blister beetles are capable of limited expansion as they stuff themselves with food or become filled with eggs. Once fully developed, adult beetles may or may not feed, but they are ready to mate and reproduce.

Figure 22. Pupa,
Harmonia (Coccinellidae).

Figure 23. Teneral multicolored Asian lady beetle, *Harmonia* (Coccinellidae).

FEEDING

Equipped with powerful mandibles, beetles are capable of cutting, grinding, or boring their way through all kinds of plant and animal materials, living or dead. Most beetles are herbivores and obtain their nutrition by consuming living plant tissues. Scarabs (Scarabaeidae), blister beetles (Meloidae), leaf beetles (Chrysomelidae), and weevils (Curculionidae) are among the species that are particularly fond of leafy foliage and will strip leaves of their tissues or completely defoliate plants. Pestiferous beetles in these families hungrily consume turf, garden vegetables, ornamental shrubs, and shade trees as well as agricultural or horticultural crops, while their subterranean larvae frequently attack roots.

Pollen- and nectar-producing flowers are particularly attractive to some species (e.g., Scarabaeidae, Cantharidae, Lycidae, Mordellidae, Cerambycidae), but

the role of beetles as pollinators (Fig. 24) requires further study. Many wood-boring beetles (e.g., Buprestidae, Cerambycidae, Curculionidae) feed on dead or dying wood. Their tunneling and feeding activities in twigs, limbs, trunks, and roots hasten decay and attract a succession of additional beetles and other insects that prefer increasingly rotten wood. Scavengers prefer their plant foods "cured" by the action of fungi and bacteria. Dung-feeding beetles (some Hydrophilidae, Geotrupidae, Scarabaeidae) consume plant materials already partially broken down by the digestive tracts of horses, cattle, dogs, and other vertebrates. These beetles consume and bury feces as food for their young and are among the most beneficial, yet least appreciated insects.

Several families of beetles are directly or indirectly dependent on fungi as food for themselves and their larvae. Bark beetles (Curculionidae) infect trees with fungal spores that kill twigs and branches or eventually the entire tree. Some of these species have special cavities associated with their head or thorax called *mycangia* that are specifically adapted for storing fungal spores. Ambrosia beetles chew tunnels in wood and introduce into them a specific type of fungus that lines the chambers and serves as food for both larvae and adults. These and other fungi are often dependent on beetles for their distribution. The larvae of some species are unable to complete their development in wood unless the tree has been previously weakened or killed. Featherwing beetles (Ptiliidae), round fungus beetles (Leiodidae), minute brown scavenger beetles (Latridiidae), and others are frequently found with mold and other fungi, and slime mold. Some flat bark beetles (Trogossitidae), pleasing fungus beetles (Erotylidae), handsome fungus beetles (Endomychidae), some darkling beetles (Tenebrionidae) (Fig. 25), tetratomid beetles (Tetratomidae), fungus weevils (Anthribidae),

LEFT: **Figure 24.** Jewel beetles on a flower, *Acmaeodera* (Buprestidae).

ABOVE: **Figure 25.** *Neomida* (Tenebrionidae) on fungus.

and other families are also associated with sac fungi (Ascomycota) and mushrooms, puffballs, bracket fungi, and kin (Basidiomycota).

Ground and tiger beetles (Carabidae) are formidable hunters that rely on speed and powerful mandibles (Fig. 26) to overpower and tear apart a broad range of insect and other invertebrate prey. Rove (Staphylinidae) and clown beetles (Histeridae) hunt for maggots, mites, and other small arthropods living among leaf litter, dung, carrion, under bark, in decaying plant and fungal tissues, and sap flows; some are specialists living in bird and mammal nests. Burrowing water beetles (Noteridae), predaceous diving beetles (Dytiscidae), and whirligigs (Gyrinidae) all attack aquatic invertebrates or terrestrial insects trapped on the water's surface. Many water scavenger beetles (Hydrophilidae) feed on both animal and plant tissues. Predatory scarab beetles (Scarabaeidae) are rare, but adult *Phileurus* have been observed eating various insects, while ant-loving scarabs (*Cremastocheilus*) prey on ant brood. Checkered beetles (Cleridae) and some soldier beetles (Cantharidae) prey on wood-boring and sap-feeding insects, respectively. Lady beetles (Coccinellidae) consume a variety of foodstuffs, especially pollen and molds, but are also predators of aphids, mealybugs, and other plant pests.

Carrion and burying beetles (Silphidae) scavenge freshly dead carcasses, occasionally preying on fly maggots that compete for the same juicy resource. Hide beetles (Trogidae) derive most of their diet from keratin-rich feathers, fur, claws, and hooves. Ham beetles (Cleridae) gnaw on dried tissues and will attack dried meats, while skin beetles (Dermestidae) infest study skins and insect specimens. Natural history museums around the world enlist the services of select dermestid beetles to clean animal skeletons used in research collections and exhibits, while others are strictly monitored and controlled as museum pests.

DEFENSE

Beetles are continually beset by various insectivorous predators, parasites, and pathogens. Birds, bats, rodents, small to medium-sized mammalian predators, reptiles, amphibians, and fishes are among the vertebrates that regularly prey on them, while spiders, ants, and other beetles rank high among invertebrate predators. They often rely on morphological and behavioral adaptations to avoid becoming a meal for a hungry predator. Daytime predation by birds is likely to have played a dominant role in the evolution of cryptic and aposematic coloration in beetles, while the stridulatory, chemical, and non-aposematic

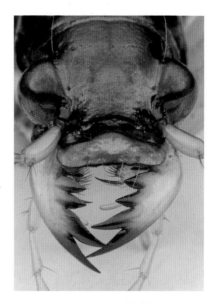

Figure 26. Mandibles of a tiger beetle, *Tetracha* (Carabidae).

BELOW: **Figure 27.** Padded and adhesive feet of a leaf beetle, *Hemisphaerota* (Chrysomelidae).

defenses of nocturnal species are especially effective deterrents against mammals, amphibians, and invertebrate predators.

Ground and tiger beetles (Carabidae) back up their bursts of speed to evade predators with sprays of noxious chemical compounds. Others, such as *Hemisphaerota cyanea* (Chrysomelidae) (Fig. 27), simply stay put. When attacked, they hunker down by using their oily and bristly feet to cling mightily to the surface of a palmetto leaf. Their tortoise-like carapace is broadly flanged around the edges and completely covers the beetles' appendages, robbing marauding ants of any opportunity to gain purchase.

Adult flea (Chrysomelidae) and some marsh beetles (Scirtidae) have muscular hind jumping legs that quickly propel them out of harm's way in an instant. Click beetles (Elateridae), false click beetles (Eucnemidae), and throscids (Throscidae) all, more or less, have the ability to jump by "clicking" themselves away from danger.

Figure 28. Clicking mechanism of
a click beetle, *Alaus* (Elateridae).

They accomplish this feat by contracting ventral muscles
that bring a prosternal spine up against a corresponding
groove on the mesoternum (Fig. 28). As tension builds, the
spine suddenly snaps into the groove with a clearly audible
and startling click, propelling the beetle into the air. For
some large longhorn beetles (Cerambycidae) and scarabs
(Scarabaeidae), size alone—backed up by powerful
mandibles, horns, and claws—may be enough to deter all
but the most determined predators.

Death feigning, or *thanatosis*, is a behavioral strategy
employed by hide beetles (Trogidae), certain fungus-feeding
darkling beetles (Tenebrionidae), zopherids (Zopheridae),
weevils (Curculionidae), and many others. When disturbed,
they "play possum" by pulling their legs and antennae up
tightly against their bodies; some of these species have
special grooves to receive and protect these appendages.
Faced with impenetrable bodies that lack any movement,
most small predators quickly lose interest and simply give up.

Other species employ varying degrees of camouflage
to blend in with their background and avoid detection by
predators. Somber-colored brown or gray wood-boring
beetles and weevils blend in perfectly with the rough bark
and gnarled branches of their food plants. Pale tiger beetles
(Carabidae) almost disappear among the sandy shores
of beaches, rivers, and streams. Even a few members of
the usually brightly colored lady beetles (Coccinellidae)
are tan or striped, enabling them to remain undetected
among pine needles. Some seemingly conspicuous bright
metallic green beetles (e.g., Scarabaeidae, Buprestidae,
Chrysomelidae) disappear among the needles and leaves
of their food plants. Longhorn beetles (Cerambycidae)
and fungus weevils (Anthribidae) may have markings that
resemble lichen-covered bark. Other cryptic beetles, such
as the avocado weevil, *Heilipus apiatus* (Curculionidae)

(Fig. 29), which looks very much like a bird dropping, are of
no interest to predators. The small, dark, and chunky warty
leaf beetles *Chlamisus*, *Exema*, and *Neochlamisus* (p.453)
(Chrysomelidae) hide right out in the open and are often
overlooked by predator and collector alike because of their
strong resemblance to caterpillar feces (Fig. 30).

Although incapable of inflicting harm themselves, some
beetles mimic the appearance or behavior of stinging or
distasteful insects, a phenomenon known as *Batesian
mimicry*. Flower-visiting *Acmaeodera* (Buprestidae),
scarabs (Scarabaeidae), and longhorns (Cerambycidae) all
sport fuzzy bodies, bold colors and patterns, and behaviors
that make them striking mimics of stinging bees and
wasps. In flight, the American carrion beetle, *Necrophila
americana* (Silphidae) looks very much like a bumble bee.
Several species of checkered beetles (Cleridae) are boldly
colored to resemble pugnacious ants or wingless wasps
known as velvet ants. Their quick, jerky movements further

Figure 29. Bird dropping mimic,
Heilipus (Curculionidae).

Figure 30. Caterpillar feces mimic,
Neochlamisus (Chrysomelidae).

Figure 31. Eyespots on pronotum of the eyed click beetle, *Alaus* (Elateridae).

Figure 32. Eyespots on pygidium of flower chafer, *Trichiotinus* (Scarabaeidae).

reinforce the charade. But stinging insects are not the only models for beetles seeking protection. Several species of click (Elateridae) and longhorn beetles (Cerambycidae) strongly resemble distasteful fireflies (Lampyridae), soldier (Cantharidae), and net-winged beetles (Lycidae).

Eyespots or sudden flashes of bright colors are thought to startle or confuse would-be predators. The outsized eyespots of the eyed click beetle, *Alaus oculatus* (Elateridae) (Fig. 31), may momentarily confuse a predator trying to direct a sneak attack, allowing the beetle an extra moment or two to escape. *Trichiotinus* beetles (Scarabaeidae) have bold eyespots on their pygidium (Fig. 32) that may suggest the face of a stinging wasp to potential attackers. Some carrion beetles (Silphidae), many dullcolored metallic wood-boring beetles (Buprestidae), and tiger beetles (Carabidae) may also startle predators by revealing flashes of bright iridescent blue, green, or red under their elytra or on their abdomens as they take flight.

Some beetles possess arsenals of noxious chemicals produced by specific glands in the body or extracted from their food and sequestered in special chambers or within the blood (*hemolymph*) that are used as repellents, insecticides, or fungicides. The abdominal defensive glands of ground beetles (Carabidae) produce hydrocarbons, aldehydes, phenols, quinones, esters, and acids and release them as noxious streams through the anus. For example, aposematically colored *Galerita* beetles spray mostly formic acid. Smaller, yet similarly colored bombardier beetles (*Brachinus*) release small, yet potent boiling clouds of hydrogen peroxide gas laced with hydroquinones and various enzymes, among other components, with considerable accuracy through their anal turret with an audible pop. When attacked, carrion and burying beetles (Silphidae) emit oily, smelly anal secretions with a strong

ammonia odor. Most rove beetles (Staphylinidae) and darkling beetles (Tenebrionidae) have eversible abdominal or anal glands that produce a wide range of defensive substances.

Many net-winged (Lycidae), soldier (Cantharidae), lady (Coccinellidae), blister (Meloidae), and milkweed beetles (Cerambycidae) are sluggish insects that boldly display their *aposematic*, or warning colors for all to see. Their conspicuously bright and bold patterns serve to warn predators up front of their bad taste. Bright red and black-spotted milkweed borers in the genus *Tetraopes* (Cerambycidae) (Fig. 33) sequester toxic cardenolides from the milky sap of milkweeds. Like the monarch caterpillar, they co-opt the milkweed's defense system by shunting these harmful compounds out of their digestive tract and into their body wall. Lady and blister beetles engage in a behavior known as *reflex bleeding* and will purposely exude bright orange or yellow hemolymph laced with noxious chemicals from their leg joints (Fig. 34) to repel predators.

29

Figure 33. Milkweed borer, *Tetraopes* (Cerambycidae).

Figure 34. Reflex bleeding from femero-tibial joints, *Meloe* (Meloidae).

Cantharidin is an incredibly caustic chemical compound found in the tissues of blister (Meloidae) and false blister beetles (Oedemeridae). It functions as a powerful feeding deterrent to predators and, even in low doses, will blister and burn mucous membranes and other sensitive tissues. Male antlike beetles (Anthicidae) gather cantharidin from dead or dying blister beetles for their own protection and to attract mates. Males pass along large amounts of cantharidin to the females through copulation that—in turn—is passed along to the eggs and larvae as a defensive chemical compound. Other anthicids have thoracic glands that produce chemicals that are particularly distasteful to ants, the primary predator of ground-dwelling insects. *Neopyrochroa* and *Pedilus* (Pyrochroidae) also sequester cantharidin, possibly from blister beetles (Fig. 35) or other natural, yet unknown cantharidin sources.

30

SYMBIOTIC RELATIONSHIPS

Some beetles have intimate and specialized, or *symbiotic*, relationships with other organisms. Symbiotic relationships that benefit both the beetle and its partner organism are examples of *mutualism*. *Commensalism* is a form of symbiosis where one symbiotic organism clearly benefits while the other is not adversely affected by the relationship. *Parasites*, on the other hand, live at the expense of their hosts.

All plant-feeding beetles, especially wood-boring species, rely on mutualistic *endosymbiotic microorganisms*, such as bacteria, fungi, and yeasts that live within special pockets called *mycetomes* in their digestive tracts and assist in digesting the primary component of all plant-based foods, cellulose. The larvae of these species do not begin their lives with these vital organisms in place and must either obtain them by consuming their eggshells, which were coated by their mothers in residues laden with endosymbionts, or by consuming adult waste (*feces*, *frass*) that is teeming with them.

Larger beetles in the families Scarabaeidae, Elateridae, and Cerambycidae often harbor pseudoscorpions (Fig. 36). These tiny arachnids are occasionally found in a killing jar used to dispatch these large beetles. Pseudoscorpions depend on their insect hosts for transportation, a type of commensalism known as *phoresy*. They hunt under tree bark for small insect larvae and mites among the chewed galleries and frass left in the wake of wood-boring insects. As their prey populations are depleted, pseudoscorpions seek out and attach themselves to a beetle to hitch a ride to another fallen tree where food is more abundant. Burying beetles (Silphidae) possess phoretic mites that prey on the eggs of carrion-feeding flies, thus reducing the competition for their host beetles. The mites found on bess beetles (Passalidae) and longhorn beetles (Cerambycidae) are not phoretic, but feed on the beetle's bodily fluids (Fig. 37).

LEFT:
Figure 35. *Pedilus* (Pyrochroidae) on an oil beetle, *Meloe* (Meloidae).

RIGHT: **Figure 36.** A pseudoscorpion.

Figure 37. Mites on a bess beetle, *Odontotaenius* (Passalidae).

Ant-loving beetles, or *myrmecophiles*, in the families Staphylinidae, Histeridae, and Scarabaeidae are more or less adapted for living in the nests of ants. Some myrmecophilous beetles are simply opportunists and live on the fringes of colonies where they scavenge bits of food left behind by the ants. However, other species are much better adapted to living with ants and have evolved various degrees of behavioral, chemical, or tactile mimicry to integrate themselves into the host ants' social system. Host ants tolerate their beetle guests with varying degrees of hospitality, but the benefits derived from the relationship nearly always favor the beetle. Species in these and other families similarly adapted to living with termites are referred to as *termitophiles*.

A few beetle larvae are ectoparasitoids of other animals. For example, the larvae of *Brachinus* and *Lebia* (Carabidae) attack the larvae and pupae of aquatic beetles and leaf beetles, respectively. The larvae of cicada parasite beetles (Rhipiceridae) attack cicadas, while those of wedge-shaped beetles (Ripiphoridae) parasitize solitary wasps. Larval passandrids (Passandridae) and bothriderids (Bothrideridae) attack the larvae and pupae of wood-boring longhorn (Cerambycidae) and jewel beetles (Buprestidae); however, the most specialized ectoparasitic beetle known in eastern North America is a mammal specialist. Both the flattened, louselike adults of the beaver parasite beetle, *Platypsyllus castoris* (Leiodidae) (p.120) and its larvae live on beavers where they feed on their host's skin and bodily fluids.

AQUATIC BEETLES

Aquatic beetles are variously adapted behaviorally and morphologically for living on the surface of, within, or on the bottom of standing and flowing bodies of water. Winged species are generally good to strong fliers and sometimes attracted to lights at night in large numbers. Based on adult modes of locomotion, water beetles are divided into two basic groups: swimmers and crawlers.

The flattened middle and hind legs of swimmers (Haliplidae, Gyrinidae, Noteridae, Dytiscidae, some Hydrophilidae) are fringed with setae and used like oars to propel their mostly smooth, rigid, streamlined bodies through standing or slow-moving waters. All but the gyrinids spend most of their adult lives submerged underwater and must regularly bring fresh supplies of air into contact with spiracles through which they breathe. Water scavengers (Hydrophilidae) accomplish this by breaking through the surface tension headfirst with their antennae to draw a layer of air over the underside of their abdomen. Crawling water (Haliplidae), burrowing water (Haliplidae), and predaceous diving beetles (Dytiscidae) all trap air under their elytra in the *subelytral cavity* by breaching the water surface with the tips of their abdomens.

Whirligigs (Gyrinidae) are adapted for life on the surface of standing and slow-moving waters, although they can dive and remain submerged for short periods of time when threatened. They propel themselves with highly modified and paddlelike middle and hind legs, and steer with the rudderlike tip of the abdomen that bends down almost at a right angle. Their compound eyes are completely divided into two different sets of lenses, allowing them to see in both air and water. With special organs in their antennae, whirligigs can detect surface vibrations emanating from other whirligigs, predators, and struggling insect prey. Dead and dying insects are grasped with *raptorial*, or grabbing front legs.

Contrastingly, beetles that crawl in the water (Hydraenidae, some Hydrophilidae, Elmidae, Dryopidae, some Curculionidae) have legs adapted not for swimming, but for clinging, as evidenced by their long pretarsi tipped with well-developed claws. They are partly or wholly clothed in a dense, velvety, and water-repellent pubescence called a *hydrofuge* that continuously envelops their bodies in a silvery layer of air that draws a steady supply of oxygen from the surrounding water and allows carbon dioxide to diffuse out— a system called *plastron breathing*. Plastron breathing is not very efficient and is largely restricted to sedentary grazers in the families Dryopidae and Elmidae living in shallow, well-oxygenated waters. Once submerged, plastron-breathing beetles seldom, if ever, need to surface or leave the water.

BEETLES AS PESTS

As a group, beetles are among the most beneficial animals, but it shouldn't be a surprise that species that have evolved to scavenge animal nests, carrion, dead insects, seeds, and decaying plant materials in nature are also adapted to exploit these very same materials improperly stored in our pantries, warehouses, and museum collections. Beetles in several families infest and damage stores of grains and other cereal products, dried meats and fruits, legumes, nuts, and spices. Others are serious museum pests that destroy often-irreplaceable study skins, and insect and herbarium specimens.

Wood borers are essential for breaking down and recycling nutrients bound up in dead wood, while other phytophagous species help to keep plant populations in check via consumption of reproductive and vegetative structures; however, when some beetles direct these activities to ornamental and horticultural plants, agricultural crops, forests managed for timber, or wood products, the results are catastrophic in terms of significant monetary losses as a direct result of lost production, trees killed, damaged goods, and pest control efforts. Ptinids and bostrichids that tunnel into dry wood have become pests of wood carvings,

Figure 38. Asian longhorn beetle,
Anoplophora glabripennis (Cerambycidae).

Figure 39. Emerald ash borer,
Agrilus planipennis (Buprestidae).

furniture, flooring, and paneling. Both native and adventive bark and ambrosia beetles (Curculionidae) regularly attack and kill trees in forests and along city streets, usually focusing their efforts on recently dead, injured, or felled trees, or on trees stressed by drought or overwatering. Others attack the roots and branches of fruit and nut trees in orchards, severely impacting crop yields. The tunneling activity of these and other wood-boring beetles disrupts a tree's ability to transport water and nutrients, and also introduces debilitating and lethal fungal infections.

Two of the most notorious wood-boring beetles in eastern North America were accidentally introduced from Asia. A native of China and Korea, the Asian longhorn beetle, *Anoplophora glabripennis* (Motschulsky) (Fig. 38) (12.0–39.0 mm) is a large, shiny black longhorn beetle (Cerambycidae) with irregular white spots on elytra and bluish or white legs. It has long antennae that are ringed in pale blue or white and extend past the elytra by five antennomeres in the male, but by just one or two in the female. The elytra are smooth, shiny or dull and only rarely densely spotted or spotless. The tunneling activities of the larvae weaken and kill otherwise healthy trees and threaten millions of street trees and the maple syrup industry. Infestations of this beetle were first reported in New York in 1996, but it was probably introduced about 10 years earlier in untreated wood used to crate heavy equipment. Infestations of this destructive beetle have since been reported from New Jersey, southern Ontario, northeastern Illinois, and Ohio, with additional individuals intercepted elsewhere in the Northeast and upper Midwest. Efforts to eradicate this destructive species involve cutting down, chipping, and burning thousands of trees.

The emerald ash borer, *Agrilus planipennis* Fairmaire (Fig. 39) (8.0–14.0 mm), is a slender, bright metallic green, rarely blue-green or violet jewel beetle (Buprestidae), much larger than native species of *Agrilus*. It also has a distinct ridge down the middle of the pygidium that extends beyond the tip. Emerald ash borers were first discovered in Detroit, Michigan, and Windsor, Ontario, during the summer of 2002, but they likely arrived in wood packing materials from eastern Asia in the early 1990s. Since then, this species has become established throughout much of the Northeast and upper Midwest. It has destroyed millions of ash trees in Michigan, southern Ontario, and Québec and threatens to destroy ash trees across North America. Ash species are important street trees and a vital source of wood for making furniture, tool handles, and baseball bats. Efforts are under way to control the spread of the emerald ash borer with the introduction of biological control agents imported from China.

WHEN AND WHERE TO FIND BEETLES

One of the most appealing aspects of studying beetles is that opportunities to discover and observe unfamiliar species and behaviors are everywhere. You can ramble about backyards, vacant lots, and parks, or explore more distant coastal habitats, woodlands, wetlands, or montane regions year-round, especially in the southeast along Atlantic and Gulf coasts where temperatures are relatively mild in winter. Visiting familiar areas and habitats in all seasons year after year will likely produce a breathtaking diversity of species. Even in more northern regions, overwintering beetles are found tucked away under snow-covered bark, buried deep in rotten wood or leaf litter, or hiding under boards and other debris to avoid lethal frosts. Many water beetles remain active throughout winter and are sometimes seen swimming under the ice of frozen ponds and lakes; however, some species are adapted to reach peak activity levels in fall and late winter, at least at lower elevations.

Spring through midsummer is the best time to find the greatest diversity of beetles in eastern North America. The beginning of beetle activity varies depending on weather conditions and location, the latter of which is largely influenced by latitude and elevation. Spring conditions arrive later in the north and at higher elevations. As early as February, the first sustained period of warm weather in northern Florida will drive many small ground beetles (Carabidae), scarabs (Scarabaeidae), weevils (Curculionidae), and other beetles into the air to search for food and mates, while much of the region to the north is still firmly in the grip of winter. The front of spring progresses northward through the Coastal Plain and penetrates the interior uplands via the lower reaches of riverine valleys before reaching southeastern Canada by mid-May. By the middle of June all of eastern North America, save for its northernmost reaches and highest mountains, is or is about to be warmed by a blanket of heat and humidity that drives most beetle populations into high gear for the rest of the summer. The first hints of fall, as evidenced by shorter days, cooler nights, and the turning of autumn leaves, occur in September in southeastern Canada and montane habitats elsewhere in the east, and progresses steadily southward over the next several weeks. By November most of the remaining conspicuous beetle activity in the region is evident only along the coastal states of the southeastern United States.

Time and experience will teach you the best times and places to look for beetles. The following are some of the more productive habitats to search for beetles in eastern North America. Exploring these and other habitats throughout the day and year will likely reveal a surprisingly diverse fauna that will enhance your enjoyment and appreciation of beetles. Be sure not to damage host plants and always return rocks, logs, and bark to their original positions. Such actions not only keep these sites productive for future visits, but also help to preserve the aesthetics of the habitat for the enjoyment of all.

FLOWERS AND VEGETATION

Spring and summer blooms rich in sweet nectar and high-protein pollen are especially attractive to flower-visiting beetles, such as Queen Anne's lace (*Daucus carota*), goldenrod (*Solidago* species), buttonbush (*Cephalanthus occidentalis*), joe pye weed (*Eutrochium*), milkweed (*Asclepias* species), and lizard's tail (*Saururus cernuus*). Several native and introduced blooming shrubs and trees are popular with beetles, including dogwood (*Cornus*), redbud (*Cercis canadensis*), New Jersey tea (*Ceanothus americanus*), autumn olive (*Elaeagnus umbellata*), serviceberry (*Amelanchier*), spicebush (*Lindera*), viburnum (*Viburnum*), hydrangea (*Hydrangea*), cherry (*Prunus*), tulip tree (*Liriodendron tulipifera*), and elderberry (*Sambucus*).

Beetles also exploit many other vegetative structures as food, places to mate and reproduce, or habitats in which to hunt for prey. Carefully examine fruits, seedpods, cones, needles, leaves, and roots of grasses, forbs, vines, shrubs, and trees. The young spring foliage of deciduous shrubs and trees is especially attractive to many plant-feeding species. Some herbivorous beetles are specialists and are seldom found on anything other than the adult or larval host plant. For example, some *Rhyssomatus* (Curculionidae) and all *Tetraopes* species (Cerambycidae) feed on milkweeds in the genus *Asclepias* and seldom occur on other plants.

Slime flux is a bacterial disease of some hardwoods that forces sap attractive to many species of beetles out of tree limbs and trunks through freeze cracks, insect emergence holes, and other wounds (Fig. 40). Check not only the nooks and crannies of sap-soaked bark for beetles, but also the sap-drenched soil and litter beneath for smaller species and their larvae.

FRESHLY CUT AND BURNED WOOD

The smell of freshly cut or recently burned wood is especially attractive to beetles, particularly those looking for mates and egg-laying sites. Slash piles (stacks of freshly cut branches) in wooded areas are particularly productive, especially in spring and early summer. You can also attract

33

Figure 40.
Green June
beetles, *Cotinis*
(Scarabaeidae),
attracted to slime
flux.

34

beetles with bundles of fresh-cut branches placed in forest openings, along woodland edges, or in canopy-covered habitats that are only partially exposed to sunlight. Inspect the bundles at weekly intervals, day and night, and note which beetles are attracted to the branches of which species of tree. Another technique is to lay branches, bark, or a slab of trunk 4 to 6 inches thick across the top of a fresh-cut stump in spring and check the top of the stump regularly for beetles that have taken shelter there. Wood smoke, especially that generated by burning pine trees, also attracts wood-boring and bark beetles.

FUNGI, MUSHROOMS, MOSSES, LICHENS

Species in several families are found commonly on fungi, slime molds, mosses, and lichens. Carefully inspect fungi with a hand lens and leave them in good condition so they continue to lure new beetles. Fleshy and relatively ephemeral puff balls and mushrooms are also attractive, while more durable woody shelf fungi provide food and breeding sites for other species. Still other species seek out fungal tissues growing on or under bark, or in the soil. In addition to *mycophagous*, or fungal-feeding beetles, predatory rove (Staphylinidae) and clown beetles (Histeridae) frequent fungi infested with insects and mites as hunting grounds. Adults and larval pill or moss beetles (Byrrhidae) are obligate moss feeders that graze on vegetative surfaces or burrow in the soils beneath. Tread very lightly in these habitats so that future visits are

equally productive. Only when fungal, moss, and lichen examples are in abundance should samples be collected for microscopic examination or extraction of specimens with a Berlese funnel (see p.41).

SNAGS, LOGS, AND STUMPS

Standing snags dry from the top down, and most of their beetles are concentrated at or near the base. Moist rather than dry wood harbors more species. Some species prefer primarily shady habitats, while others prefer more open, sun-drenched wood, although this latter niche dries out more quickly. As the wood decomposes, its quality changes in terms of its suitability as beetle food and egg-laying sites, attracting a progression of beetle species over time. Checking these microhabitats every few weeks over a period of years may reveal an amazing diversity of beetle species.

Recently dead trees with tight-fitting bark are more likely to harbor the adults of smaller or flatter species than those with bark that is easier to remove. As the wood dries and its bark loosens, larger and more robust species are able to take shelter. Peeling back dead bark, or "barking," is best accomplished during the cooler winter and spring months. Use a broad-blade knife, screwdriver, or dandelion weeding tool to peel back bark and examine all the freshly exposed areas carefully. Whenever possible, replace the bark by nailing or tying it back in place so the site will continue to be colonized by additional individuals and species. Many small species are best found by placing crumbling and rotten wood onto a light-colored surface for immediate inspection or into a Berlese funnel or some other insect extraction system.

Night collecting on dead wood with a headlamp or flashlight, particularly on warm evenings in the spring and summer when beetles are emerging from their tunnels or wandering about limbs and trunks in search of mates, is an especially fruitful activity.

STREAM BANKS, LAKESHORES, AND COASTLINES

Plant debris on the surfaces of streams and rivers contains flying and crawling beetles trapped by floodwaters. Some species typically spend their daylight hours hidden under debris washed up on lakeshores and ocean beaches. Flying beetles of all sorts fly or are windblown out over lakes and oceans only to drown and be washed back up on shore, sometimes by the thousands. The high waterlines along these shores are often littered with thousands of beetles from various families. Burrowing species that are adapted to living in flat sandy, gravelly, or muddy shorelines are flushed from their burrows by splashing water across the substrate. Ground and tiger beetles (Carabidae) are commonly found hunting, flying, or mating on sandy or muddy substrates along the edges of various wetlands.

FRESHWATER POOLS, STREAMS, AND LAKES

While some beetles prefer cold, fast streams, others favor ponds or slow-moving streams. Look for rafts of whirligig beetles (Gyrinidae) on the surface of ponds or protected, slow-moving pools in streams and along the edges of rivers. Predaceous diving beetles (Dytiscidae) are often found on gravelly bottoms or beneath submerged objects, while water scavengers (Hydrophilidae), crawling water beetles (Haliplidae), and long-toed water beetles (Dryopidae) are found swimming near aquatic plants, crawling among mats of algae, or clinging under logs and rocks. Carefully pick up and examine rocks lifted out of flowing waters for larval water pennies (Psephenidae) and riffle beetles (Elmidae) clinging to their surfaces.

COASTAL DUNES, SAND SCRUB, AND SANDHILLS

Various small, sand-loving, or *psammophilic* beetles hide among flowing sand and plant debris at the bases of dune grasses and other plants. They are typically found down in the moisture layers, or in or under accumulations of detritus closer to the surface. They typically move up and down through the sand as they follow the seasonal moisture and temperature gradients to maintain ideal living conditions. Sandhill, sand scrub, and pine barren beetles are variously adapted for living in hot, dry, sandy habitats. Most are burrowers that are active on the surface only for very brief periods of time. These habitats, which stretch from the pine barrens of New Jersey to the isolated pockets of sand scrub in Florida, are habitat for many rare, endangered, poorly known, or undescribed beetle species.

CARRION

Dead animals provide food and shelter for adult and larval beetles. Look for them on, in, and under the carcass, as well as buried in the soil directly beneath the body. Carrion and burying beetles (Silphidae) feed primarily on fresh, juicy flesh, while most skin beetles (Dermestidae) scavenge dried tissues. Hide beetles (Trogidae) are among the last

contingent of insects to visit a carcass and gnaw on the keratin-rich hair, feathers, hooves, and horns. Predatory species seek out and devour the eggs of other carrion-feeding insects and mites. Other beetles are attracted to carrion simply because of the available moisture and shelter.

DUNG

The most conspicuous dung beetles in the region belong to the families Geotrupidae and Scarabaeidae. Several genera of smaller dung scarabs feed on the small dung pellets produced by flying squirrels or deer. Deer dung specialists are typically active during the cooler months in fall and spring. Many of our larger species are drawn to the big, juicy feces produced by cattle, pigs, horses, and humans. Dog and cat feces attract only a few, mainly introduced species of dung scarabs. Clown (Histeridae) and rove beetles (Staphylinidae) are commonly associated with dung as predators of fly eggs and larvae.

BENEATH STONES AND OTHER OBJECTS

Many beetles occasionally or habitually take shelter under rocks, logs, boards, and other debris on the ground, especially in grassy areas and habitats along the edges of ponds, lakes, streams, rivers, and other wetlands. For the benefit of the people following your footsteps and the organisms living underneath, always return these objects to their original places and positions. Also look for antlike flower (Anthicidae) and false blister beetles (Oedemeridae) under driftwood that has washed up along coastal beaches and rivers, especially along the lower reaches that are regularly influenced by the tides.

35

LEAF LITTER, COMPOST, AND OTHER ACCUMULATIONS OF PLANT MATERIALS

Layers of leaves and needles that gather beneath trees, accumulate along streams and rivers as flood debris, or wash up on beaches and lakeshores after storms frequently harbor all kinds of beetles. Beetles overwintering in these habitats are collected by placing debris in plastic bags and bringing the samples inside to check for individuals that have become active. Backyard compost heaps, decaying piles of mulch, and other natural or artificial accumulations of decomposing grass, leaves, branches, and other vegetative structure are particularly productive. Some coastal rove beetles (Staphylinidae) live under decomposing piles of seaweed washed up along the beach.

LIGHTS

Incandescent, fluorescent, and neon lights on porches and storefronts, especially in undeveloped wooded areas, are very attractive to many kinds of beetles. The bright bluish glow of a mercury vapor streetlight is much more attractive to beetles and other insects than the dull yellowish light emitted by their sodium vapor counterparts. Although many beetles will settle on the ground or wall directly beneath or behind the light, others, especially the largest species, may prefer to remain on plants and other surfaces just beyond the light's glow.

INDOORS

Look for living and dead beetles on windowsills and light fixtures inside houses, garages, sheds, and warehouses. Household and structural pests, as well as other beetles trapped indoors are usually attracted to well-lit windows and other light sources. High numbers of skin beetles (Dermestidae) or pantry pest species are indicative of infested stored foods, skins, plant materials, wood products, and insect collections.

OBSERVING AND PHOTOGRAPHING BEETLES

Making a beetle collection (see p.45) is the best way to learn about beetles. Only by having them in hand will you have the opportunity to critically examine the physical features necessary to facilitate accurate species identification and develop an understanding of their evolutionary relationships and classification; however, some readers may prefer instead to simply observe or photograph them alive in the wild.

BEETLES THROUGH BINOCULARS

Close-focusing binoculars allow you to observe beetles on flowers or shorelines less than 6 feet away with amazing color and clarity. The larger the diameter of the eyepiece, or objective, the more light that is gathered to form the image. The best binoculars for handheld use are 8 × 42 or 10 × 42. An objective magnification of 8 produces an image as if the viewer were 8 times closer to the subject. A 10-power binocular will make the image larger, but the smaller field of view can make tracking of moving beetles a bit more of a challenge. Lower power binoculars with smaller oculars (e.g., 7 × 36) are also useful. They are smaller and less expensive, but your subjects will not be as magnified or

brilliant. When buying a pair of close-focusing binoculars, compare several brands at the same time to determine which model and magnification works best for you and fits your budget. Close-focusing monoculars are also useful, less expensive, and easily stowed in your field kit.

A pair of compact binoculars with the front lenses closer together than the eyepiece lenses (reverse Porro prism design) can be modified for close-up beetle watching. Screw a two-element Nikon 5T or 6T close-up lens into a soft lens hood, place the hood with lens in front of the binoculars, and affix them using heavy rubber bands to achieve a close-focusing capability.

BEETLE MACRO PHOTOGRAPHY

Macro, or close-up photography was once the domain of highly proficient photographers using expensive and complex equipment. Good quality macro photographs are easier to take, review, and share now than ever. Today, even the most casual photographer can capture good images with relatively inexpensive point-and-shoot digital cameras with macro-like capabilities. However, the very best images, including most of the photos that grace these pages, were taken with a digital single-lens reflex camera with dedicated macro lenses with focal lengths of 50 mm, 90 mm, or 100 mm that allow focusing on beetles just a few millimeters from the lens. The distance between the lens and the beetle is called the *working distance*. When fully extended, macro lenses allow you to fill the frame of your photograph with an up to life-size (1:1) image of a beetle. Some beetles are a bit skittish at these close working distances, while others seem not to notice the camera at all. Macro lenses with longer focal lengths (150 mm, 200 mm) have greater working distances and still offer 1:1 capability, but they are bulky, difficult to hold steady, and very expensive. To obtain magnifications greater than life size, 1:2 or more, doublers, teleconverters, and extension tubes of 25 mm or more are placed between the lens and the camera body. High-quality close-up lenses of varying magnifications screwed on the front of the macro lens can be useful, but will reduce already close working distances and sometimes degrade image quality.

In macro photography, focus is best achieved not by using the camera's autofocus feature, but by selecting the desired magnification in advance based on the beetle's size and the kind of picture you want to take. Once the lens is extended, aim the camera at your subject and look through the viewfinder to compose the shot. Then slowly rock back and forth until the subject is in focus and take the picture. Most beetle images look best when the subject, especially the eyes, and background are both in sharp focus. The depth of focus in a photo, usually referred to as the depth of field, is the distance between the nearest and farthest objects in the photo that are in focus. Think of text on a page photographed at an angle—the sentences in the image that are in focus are indicative of the depth of field. Depth of field is determined by the opening at the back of the lens, or aperture. The aperture is expressed as an *f*-stop; the bigger the *f*-stop number, the smaller the aperture. Decreasing the aperture, or stopping down to $f/16$ or $f/22$, increases the depth of field; however, decreasing the *f*-stop also requires using flash to compensate for the reduced amount of natural light reaching the sensor.

Because of the long barrel of the macro lens, the built-in flash on your camera's body will cast a shadow across your beetle and ruin the image; therefore, additional and adjustable external flashes attached to the end of the lens are your best bet. Two adjustable flashes are better than one and always better than the flat lighting provided by a ring flash. Placing these flashes at a 30-degree angle to the long axis of the lens barrel will create the effect of natural morning or afternoon sunlight; however, you may want to adjust one or both flashes to properly expose your subject and its background. Macro photographers often use one flash on the subject while a second flash provides a weaker "fill light" on a nearby background. Distant backgrounds that are underexposed appear dark or black and the overall impression of the photograph is often not pleasing, even if the subject is in perfect focus and properly exposed. The easiest way to compensate for this is by making sure that the background is close enough to the subject to be properly exposed by the flash. Always try to photograph a beetle resting on a leaf or flower rather than one perched on an isolated branch tip. Whenever possible, make sure the background is not so cluttered or busy that it distracts from your subject. Always use the highest shutter speed (1/125 sec., 1/250 sec., etc.) possible that synchronizes your camera with the flash system to freeze the action of your subject and mitigate camera movement in order to capture a razor-sharp image.

Take lots and lots of pictures. Experiment with different combinations of apertures, shutter speeds, and flash settings under a variety of conditions, and carefully record these in a small notebook. Compare your notes with the resultant images to establish the settings and conditions that work best for your camera. Carefully review all your images either in camera or on your computer, then select

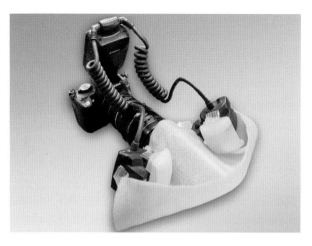

Figure 41. Camera equipment used by the author.

and keep only the very best for each species. There is no point in tying up valuable space on your hard drive with inferior images. Store your images using one of many software applications, and be sure to label each image with locality data and any other pertinent information as if it were a specimen in a collection. This way, your images can be easily retrieved and become part of a permanent record of your travels and observations. Your best photos will be those that are well exposed and in focus and tell a story of beetles feeding, mating, laying eggs, or otherwise going about their business undisturbed in their own habitat.

There is no one way to photograph a beetle. Every photographer has his or her own favorite setup and method of working based on a combination of aesthetics, experience, taxonomic interests, available camera equipment, and degree of patience to experiment with said equipment. Most of my images reproduced in this guide were photographed with a Canon EOS Digital Rebel XTi set at ISO 100 with a 100 mm macro lens, up to 50 mm of extension tubes, and a Macro Twin Lite MT-24EX (Fig. 41). Each strobe was placed about 90 degrees apart, aimed at about 30 degrees from the axis of the macro lens, and fitted with Stoffen and Puffin diffusers. Both flashes were further diffused with a sheet of 3/32-inch (2 mm) sheet of polyethylene foam taped to the camera to help reveal subtle surface sculpturing in all but the most shiny of black beetles. I generally used $f/16$–22 and a shutter speed of 1/125 to 1/200 of a second. Instead of lugging a tripod around to steady my camera, I strap on knee and elbow pads to absorb the shock to my joints produced by hunkering down on the ground or bracing myself against trees and boulders.

37

BEETLE CONSERVATION AND THE ETHICS OF COLLECTING

Commercial and residential development, conversion to agricultural lands, agricultural runoff, grazing, logging, inundation by water impoundments, wetland draining, indiscriminate use by off-road vehicles, and overuse and abuse of pesticides and herbicides in urban and agricultural areas are just a few of the many human activities that adversely affect, alter, or destroy beetle habitats. The ever-growing list of exotic insect introductions, including those purposely introduced as biological control agents, can inflict unintended and possibly catastrophic consequences on indigenous beetle populations by choking out native food plants or outcompeting native beetles for food, shelter, and egg-laying sites. Climate change, too, will certainly affect many beetle populations for better or worse.

Beetles restricted to ever-shrinking habitats are particularly susceptible to habitat destruction and invasive species. Populations of *saproxylic*, or rotten wood-feeding beetles (e.g., Tetratomidae, Melandryidae, Synchroidae, Stenotrachelidae, Scraptiidae) in old growth forests are significantly related to forest structure. The impacts of current forest management practices that fragment these mature growth forests and reduce coarse woody debris could severely impact the availability of food for both the larvae and adults. The sandhill habitats of the southeastern United States also support unique beetle species, yet these habitats are under constant threat of invasive plant species, agricultural conversion, logging, mining, fire and fire suppression, ditching, and recreational use.

Although beetles are among the most conspicuous and charismatic of all insects, our overall lack of knowledge of their biology, ecology, and distribution hampers efforts to identify species in need of conservation. With the exception of some tiger beetles and cave-dwelling ground beetles (Carabidae), relatively few species in eastern North America are recognized as threatened or endangered and afforded legal protection. To find out more about rare, threatened, and endangered beetles in eastern North America, visit the NatureServe Explorer website at www.natureserve.org/explorer/.

ETHICS OF BEETLE COLLECTING

Unlike most birds, butterflies (and some moths), dragonflies, and damselflies that are easily identified on sight, many beetles must be in hand to facilitate close examination or dissection before accurate species identifications are possible. Their capture and preservation not only assures identification, but also represents the first important step toward their conservation. The data associated with these specimens contributes to our understanding of their habitat preferences, activity period, and distribution. Beetle collecting, collections, and collectors all provide critical information that land managers and other decision makers need to develop and implement the best land-use practices that will protect beetles and other natural resources.

Whether you are a professional biologist investigating a particular avenue of research, or a student or amateur naturalist desiring to learn more about insects and the natural world, you need not worry that your collecting activities will adversely affect most beetle populations. Such efforts at beetle collecting pale in comparison to the proficiency demonstrated by hungry insectivorous animals, or to the deleterious effects of pesticide use, mowing, vehicular traffic, artificial lights, and bug zappers. Habitat degradation and destruction, combined with invasive species—not collecting or collectors—pose the greatest threats to beetles and their habitats in eastern North America.

Beetles with small populations living in sensitive, specialized, or patchy and ephemeral habitats, such as those living in sand dunes, wetlands, and vernal pools or dependent on populations of rare plants, are potentially sensitive to adverse changes in their environments, and should be collected only in small numbers; however, the reproductive capacity of most beetles is much greater and differs dramatically from that of vertebrates. Birds, fish, reptiles, amphibians, and mammals all produce relatively few young and must invest enormous amounts of time and effort in nest building and caring for their young to ensure the survival of enough individuals to maintain stable populations. Removal of even a small number of these animals—parents or offspring—can have a major impact on local populations; however, a single female beetle may produce hundreds of young that require little if any parental care at all. Of these, only a few need to survive and reproduce to sustain a thriving population.

Adopt a collecting ethic that embraces the need to conserve beetle populations and their habitats, and recognizes the rights of landowners. Collecting large numbers of the same species at the same time and place adds little to our knowledge of beetles and does not enhance the diversity that is the mark of a good reference collection. Such a collection, supported by accurate specimen label data and field notes, can only be built over time. The collection of beetles listed as endangered or threatened is strictly regulated, and it is the responsibility of the collector to know which species are afforded protection and to adhere to those regulations. When moving beetles, living or dead, be sure to comply with county, state, and federal agricultural and wildlife regulations. Generally speaking, transporting any living beetles or other insects across county, state, or international borders requires written permission from state or federal agricultural authorities, or both.

Always obtain permission to collect on private lands. Collecting on public lands, such as county, state, and national parks, state and national forests, monuments, and recreational areas generally requires written permission, but these requirements may vary depending on locality and the purpose for collecting specimens. Managers of public lands are usually happy to issue permits to individuals conducting beetle surveys or other ecological studies, especially if they are affiliated with museums, universities, and other research institutions. Your efforts will provide data needed to effectively manage and preserve habitats for all wildlife. Always conduct your fieldwork within the conditions set forth in your permit and be respectful of other visitors. Once your project is completed, promptly share your data with the permitting agency and other researchers, and deposit voucher specimens in a permanent museum or university entomology collection.

COLLECTING AND PRESERVING BEETLES

The scientific data generated by professionals and dedicated amateurs collecting beetles are important not only to document the fauna of a given jurisdiction or region, but also to track species diversity and faunal composition over time. The collections of amateur coleopterists working in concert with museum scientists are particularly useful for filling gaps in permanent collections of museums and universities and often provide the basis for both scientific and popular publications. On a more basic level, collecting beetles is a great way to get outside, sharpen your skills of observation, and learn firsthand the biology and ecology of the most diverse group of animals in eastern North America. Beetle collecting is also an excellent way of getting youngsters outdoors and introducing them to the diversity of nature. Many scientists and educators, including the author of this book, cite the activity of collecting beetles and other insects as the spark that launched their lifelong careers of research and public service.

The initial cost of collecting beetles is minimal, since the basic "tools" required are a sharp pair of eyes, patience, persistence, a few containers, and a bit of luck. Nets,

beating sheets, and other collecting equipment listed below are also useful. As your knowledge of the seasonal and habitat proclivities of beetles increases, so will your desire to explore new habitats and try out different collecting equipment and techniques. With time and experience, your collecting activities will become more targeted, and these efforts will contribute to the overall diversity of your collection. For detailed information on techniques and equipment for collecting and preserving beetles and other insects, consult *Collecting and Preserving Insects and Mites. Techniques and Tools* (Schauff 1986) or *Collecting, Preparing, and Preserving Insects, Mites, and Spiders* (Martin 1977).

BASIC TOOLS FOR HANDLING AND EXAMINING BEETLES

Forceps made of spring aluminum are known as "featherweights." They are extremely useful for picking up small beetles without damaging them, while camel-hair brushes are used to probe for and dislodge beetles from their resting and hiding places. Aspirators of various designs are useful tools for sucking small beetles from beating sheets, nets, and other substrates into a glass or plastic vial. Protective gauze over the intake tube prevents the accidental inhalation of beetles and other bits, while an inline fuel filter will extract smaller particles, but neither of these protections will completely prevent the inhalation of molds, spores, insect feces, or the noxious defensive odors produced by many beetles. Blowing aspirators or those using a suction bulb do not involve sucking air through a mouthpiece and alleviate these potential hazards, but they are not widely used. No one who spends any time in the field should be without a good quality hand lens. Available from biological supply companies, hand lenses are small and compact devices for revealing beetle anatomy and other details that might otherwise escape notice by the naked eye. Magnifications of 8× or 10× are ideal, with some units employing several lenses in concert to increase magnification. The trick is to hold the hand lens close to your eye and then move in on your subject until it comes into sharp focus.

KILLING JARS AND KILLING AGENTS

Beetles retained as specimens for a collection must be dispatched quickly and humanely. Freezing is an easy and nontoxic method, but the specimens must be kept cool and calm in a small ice chest until they can be placed in a freezer overnight. Using a killing jar with a bit of loosely crumpled paper that is freshly charged with several drops of ethyl acetate or some other killing agent is often a more practical solution. Ethyl acetate is available from biological and scientific supply houses. Although it is relatively safe to use, avoid getting it on your skin, breathing the fumes, or using it near an open flame. The wadded paper toweling not only holds the killing agent, but also absorbs excess fluids produced by your catch and protects your delicate specimens from jostling. Continually opening and closing the killing jar will result in the loss of its potency, so you will have to recharge the killing jar from time to time. A small, 2-ounce squeeze bottle filled with ethyl acetate makes this task easy. Note that ethyl acetate dissolves anything made of styrene, including clear hard plastic bottles and polystyrene foam. Any jar will serve as a killing jar as long as it has a broad mouth and tight-fitting screw-top lid to retain volatile killing agents. Long cylindrical jars, such as those used for olives, pickled onions, or spices, that are no more than 6 inches tall slip easily into a pocket or collecting bag.

Dark, colorfast beetles with few setae are sometimes killed and temporarily stored by placing them directly in fluid preservative such as 70–95% ethyl alcohol (ethanol) or 70% rubbing alcohol (isopropyl). For long-term storage of larger specimens, pour off the old alcohol and replace it with fresh after a week or two. Although there is no one method for killing beetles for morphological examination, beetles intended for use in tissue studies or molecular analysis must be placed directly in 95% ethanol. Ethanol is generally unavailable to private individuals, with the exception of prohibitively expensive neutral grain spirits, or pure grain alcohol that can be purchased in liquor stores. Isopropyl in concentrations of 70% and 91% is readily available in drug and grocery stores, but over time, 91% isopropyl dries out specimens and makes them quite brittle.

NETS

Nets are essential for capturing beetles on the wing, resting on vegetation, or living in aquatic habitats. Flying beetles are best caught with aerial nets with a rim diameter of 12 or 15 inches and a handle 3 feet long. The rim is usually reinforced with canvas or some other heavy material to prevent the net bag from tearing. The net bag is made of cotton bobbinet or some other soft and translucent material that will hold its shape and is long enough to easily fold over the rim to trap beetles inside. The tip of the bag is typically rounded, not pointed, so that beetles and other insects are easily removed after capture. These lightweight and durable nets are easily maneuvered when swung through the air. Aerial nets are also used to capture tiger beetles by clapping them over the beetle and then holding the tip of the net bag so that the beetle will climb up into the net. Heavy-duty aerial nets are available commercially and have a net bag that is half canvas and half mesh; these are used for light-duty sweeping through herbaceous vegetation.

Sweep nets are used to dislodge beetles from the tops of grasses, shrubs, and tree branches. They have shorter, thicker handles, sturdy net rings, and net bags constructed completely of canvas to endure repeated brushing through dense vegetation. Beetles are more likely captured in a sweep net if the rim is kept vertical to the ground. After completing a series of sweeps, swing the net back and forth several times and fold it over the rim to trap the insects inside toward the tip of the net bag. Slowly open the net to release stinging bees and wasps before removing beetles inside by hand, with forceps, or with an aspirator and transferring them to a killing jar.

Aquarium nets are useful for capturing aquatic beetles swimming along the edges of ponds and slow-moving streams. Long-handled dip nets are helpful for scooping beetles swimming in open water further out. D-frame nets have rims that are flat on one side and are dragged along the bottom of standing and moving waters to dislodge specimens resting on rocks and plants. Each of these nets placed vertically on the substrate in moving waters will capture beetles dislodged by lifting stones or disturbing vegetation upstream.

BEATING SHEET

Beating the branches and foliage of trees and shrubs is an incredibly productive method for collecting beetles. Beating

Figure 42. Author beating vegetation at night with headlamp and aspirator.

sheets (Fig. 42) are typically square sheets of light-colored canvas or ripstop nylon stretched out with two hardwood dowels or plastic tubes as crosspieces, with their ends slipped into reinforced pockets sewn into each corner of the sheet. To collect beetles, place the sheet beneath the foliage and then strike a large branch directly above with another dowel or net handle. Beetles and other insects and arthropods jarred loose from their perches fall onto the sheet where they are collected using forceps or an aspirator. Beating is most productive in the cooler morning or evening hours in spring and summer. During the heat of the day, beetles will usually take flight the moment they hit the sheet.

SIEVING

Beetles are extracted from ground litter, fungi, lichens, mosses, soil, and decaying wood samples using various containers fitted with a screened bottom. The size of the mesh is determined by the size of beetles sought. Place the substrate in the container, shake it gently over a white or light-colored pan, sheet, or shower curtain, and collect the beetles with forceps, aspirator, or camel-hair brush. Kitchen strainers work well for sifting beach sand and other fine, dry soils. Beetles and larger pieces of debris retained in the screen are dumped onto a light-colored surface for further sorting, or placed in a Berlese or Tulgren funnel, or other separator.

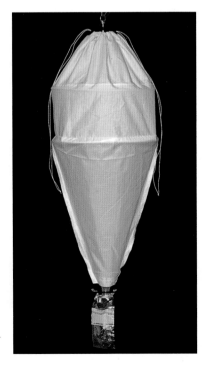

Figure 43. Collapsible Berlese funnel for extracting small beetles and other arthropods from litter.

BERLESE FUNNELS AND SEPARATORS

The *Berlese* or *Tulgren funnel* (Fig. 43) uses the combination of light and heat from a low-wattage incandescent lightbulb to extract beetles from debris samples. Place a piece of coarse screen above the opening of the funnel to prevent debris from falling into the jar. Then fill the funnel with beach wrack, fungi, leaf litter, rotten wood, and other plant debris and place the light bulb above to drive beetles and other arthropod inhabitants downward into a glass jar half-filled with a 50-50 mixture of water and 70% isopropyl. The time required to extract all the beetles from a sample varies from hours to days and depends on the size and moisture content of the sample.

Separators known as *photoeclectors* or Winkler/Moczarski eclectors also extract beetles from organic samples but require no electricity to generate light or heat. Using a cloth sleeve open on both ends, attach a strong drawstring to each end. Affix a coarse screen sieve over the mouth of a one-quart canning jar half-filled with a 50-50 mixture of water and 70% ethanol or isopropyl. Attach the sleeve to the jar using the drawstring at one end of the bag. Fill the bag about halfway with a lightweight litter sample and tie off the top of the bag. Hang the photoeclector in a well-ventilated place where the material inside will air dry and drive the beetles down into the jar.

FLOATING

Another useful method for separating beetles from plant materials—particularly clumps of grass, but also fungi, bark, and dung—is to drop the materials into a bucket of water. Beetles and other insects will float to the surface, where they can be scooped up with a small kitchen strainer or collected by hand.

COLLECTING AT LIGHTS

The most productive method of collecting beetles at night involves attracting them with a light suspended in front of or over a white sheet or cloth shower curtain. Almost any light will attract night-flying beetles, but ultraviolet light, or black light (Fig. 44) is the most effective. Commercially available black lights operate on house current or 12-volt batteries. Mercury vapor lights using 175-watt bulbs are also very attractive to beetles and other night-flying insects and require house current or a generator to operate. Note that these bulbs will become extremely hot and break should they come into contact with rain or other sources of moisture. Suspend a freshly laundered sheet between two trees or poles over a ground sheet. Suspend the light

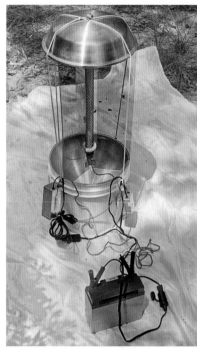

FAR LEFT: **Figure 44.** Blacklight sheet for attracting nocturnal beetles and other insects.

LEFT: **Figure 45.** 12-volt blacklight bucket trap.

BELOW: **Figure 46.** Pitfall array.

about a foot away and parallel to the upright sheet at about eye level to achieve maximum illumination. Be sure to regularly patrol the ground and nearby shrubs just beyond the illuminated area with a headlamp to free both your hands for collecting beetles crawling on the ground or wandering about plants, trees, stumps, and logs. Spring and summer nights that are warm (65 °F or higher), especially with little or no moon, are the most productive. The bulk of species will come in within 2 hours of sunset, but other beetles, especially large species, fly later in the evening. Light traps (Fig. 45) use a black light suspended over a funnel placed on a 3- or 5-gallon bucket. Acrylic or metal vanes help to direct beetles and other insects down the funnel and into the bucket. By supplying the bucket with plenty of wadded-up paper towels, you can reduce the wear and tear on beetles and other insects caught in the trap.

TRAPPING BEETLES

Methods for trapping beetles, with or without the use of baits, lures, lights, and other attractants, are just as diverse as the beetles themselves. The performance of these traps is dependent on season, local conditions, and trap site. Pitfall traps are designed to capture beetles crawling on the ground. Using a trowel or small shovel, dig a small hole just large enough to accommodate a 16-ounce plastic deli or drink cup. Place the cup in the hole so the rim is flush with

the surface of the ground. Then place an identical cup within the first cup. Nesting the cups in this fashion allows easy inspection of the trap without having to redig the hole at every visit. Cover the trap with a flat stone or slab of wood raised on small stones, leaving a space large enough for beetles but small enough to keep out larger animals. Place unbaited pitfall traps along natural barriers, such as rock ledges and logs. Wood, metal, or plastic drift fences, will also increase the effective surface area for each trap (Fig. 46). Pitfalls baited with small amounts of fresh dung, carrion, rotting fruit, or chopped mushrooms will attract and capture beetles over a large surface area without the aid of physical obstacles. Solid and liquid baits are wrapped in cheesecloth or placed in small plastic sauce cups, respectively, and suspended over the trap opening with sticks, wires, or string (Fig. 47). Liquid baits consisting of equal parts molasses and water, or malt with a pinch of yeast, will attract species naturally drawn to sap flows. For traps that are checked daily, place crumpled paper towels or leaves at the bottom of each trap to provide beetles with a bit of cover. Pitfalls left out for a week or more should be supplied with a preservative to prevent struggling beetles from damaging each other and decomposing shortly after they die. Add an inch or two of a 50-50 mix of propylene glycol and water to kill and preserve beetles. Unlike ethylene glycol (antifreeze), propylene glycol is not toxic to wildlife.

Fruit traps (Fig. 48) made from plastic drink bottles or cups and hung at various heights in trees and shrubs are very attractive to beetles. Be sure to check these traps regularly and provide a rain guard of some sort to prevent specimens from being washed out of the trap. Pan traps (Fig. 49) consisting of shallow plastic bowls, especially bright yellow ones, filled with an inch or two of water, are especially attractive to some jewel beetles (Buprestidae),

tumbling flower beetles (Mordellidae), and other flower-visiting insect species. A drop or two of dish soap added to the water will break the surface tension, making it harder for the beetles to escape.

Flight intercept traps (Fig. 50) are extremely useful for sampling small, crepuscular beetles that are seldom attracted to light. They comprise a dark mesh nylon screen suspended between two poles or trees and are placed across a trail, next to a log, or in a field. A shallow trough or a series of roasting pans containing soapy water or propylene glycol are laid end to end directly below the screen. Beetles flying into the screen will fall down into the fluid, where they are killed and temporarily preserved. A plastic roof placed over the top of the screen will prevent rainwater from diluting the fluid. A Malaise trap (Fig. 51) is

LEFT: **Figure 47.** Pitfall trap of soapy water baited with feces on a stick.

RIGHT: **Figure 48.** Fruit trap made from plastic soft drink bottle.

BELOW LEFT: **Figure 49.** Yellow pan trap filled with soapy water to attract flower-visiting and other beetles.

BELOW RIGHT: **Figure 50.** Flight intercept trap.

essentially a tent with a wall or partition on the inside. Flying beetles strike the interior walls and fly up into a collecting jar filled with 70% ethanol or isopropyl alcohol. Shallow troughs or roasting pans filled with fluid are sometimes placed under the wall of the trap to capture specimens that drop to the ground rather than fly up into the collecting jar. This trap produces large numbers of diurnal and nocturnal species that are not readily collected via other methods. Several styles are available commercially and all are somewhat expensive.

Lindgren funnel traps (Fig. 52) consist of a series of four or more black funnels suspended over one another and hung from a branch, rope between two trees, or some other hanger. At the bottom of the funnels is a collecting container that is either dry or partially filled with propylene glycol or some other preservative. The stack of funnels resembles a tree trunk and is attractive to wood-boring beetles and other species that crawl or land on tree trunks. They are sometimes baited with chemicals that mimic those released by dead and dying conifers and hardwoods, such as turpentine and alcohol. Specimens in dry containers are best removed every few days.

ABOVE: **Figure 51.** Malaise trap.

LEFT: **Figure 52.** Lindgren funnel trap.

TEMPORARY STORAGE OF SPECIMENS

Beetles should be prepared immediately after they are collected, but this is not always possible. Specimens left in killing jars charged with adequate amounts of ethyl acetate will remain relaxed for several days or weeks and can be handled without damage. They can also be transferred to a tightly sealed container and stored in the freezer. For longer periods of storage, carefully place specimens between layers of paper towels moistened with a few drops of ethyl acetate or preserved by adding chlorocresol crystals and store in soft plastic storage boxes with airtight lids. Specimens stored in this manner will keep indefinitely, but delicate colors will fade and setae become matted. Large numbers of beetles collected from Berlese funnels, pitfalls, and blacklight traps can be placed in 70% ethanol or isopropyl alcohol. After about a week, replace the fluid with fresh alcohol. Always include basic collecting information (locality, date, collector) inside each container, using pencil or permanent ink on good quality acid-free paper. Samples without this information are of little value and should be discarded.

RECORDS AND FIELD NOTES

Always record the date, place, and collector's name for your specimens. Be sure to include the country, province or state, and county or parish, as well as the name of the nearest city or town, mileage and direction from the nearest road junction, latitude and longitude, and any other locality data that will help fix your collecting locality on a map. These data will become the basis for the locality labels for your specimens and serve as directions to others who may want to retrace your steps to find a specific locality to search for a particular beetle.

Dead beetles in collections reveal little of their lives, so it is important to spend some time observing their behaviors whenever possible and record them in your field notes. Your observations should always include time of day, temperature and humidity, plant or animal associations, and reproductive and feeding behaviors; such details are all worthy of note and could easily be new to science.

Whenever possible, record your observations in the field, as they are happening. Never trust your memory for long because it is all too easy to confuse bits of information in time and place. With practice, you will settle on a routine for noting and recording pertinent observations.

Maintaining a detailed and accurate field notebook is an important component of a carefully curated beetle collection, and the value of the notes is enhanced if they are clearly associated with specific specimens, especially those identified to species. Select a well-bound notebook with acid-free paper that is small enough to pack in your field kit, but large enough not to be easily lost or misplaced, and will withstand the rigors of field use. Fine-tip marking pens with permanent ink, such as the Pigma Micron available in art supply stores, or pencils are the most reliable for writing in all sorts of weather.

MAKING A BEETLE COLLECTION

There is still much to learn about the beetles living in eastern North America. Carefully prepared collections supported by accurate label data, field notes, and photographs will add enormously to our understanding of their seasonality, distribution, and food and habitat preferences, as well as provide a historical record that will offer insights into the possible impacts of climate change. If properly cared for, beetle collections will last hundreds of years to inspire and inform future generations of coleopterists and naturalists. Coleopterists—professionals and amateurs alike—are but temporary caretakers of collections that ultimately belong to the greater scientific community. Should you lose interest, lack adequate storage space, or simply want to preserve the legacy of your hard work long after you are gone, consider donating your collection and its associated records to an appropriate research institution dedicated to housing permanent insect collections and making them available to researchers and students. Below are some tips and tools for building and maintaining a scientifically valuable and aesthetically pleasing insect collection.

PINNING AND POINTING SPECIMENS

Dead, dried beetles are very brittle, and touching them will result in broken and lost appendages that will make their identification difficult, if not outright impossible. In order for specimens to be manipulated without damage, they must be mounted on pins that are safely used as handles. Always use black-enameled or stainless steel insect pins because sewing pins are too short and thick and will corrode. Insect pins are available through entomological supply houses in packets of 100 in several sizes (diameters). Sizes 0–3 are suitable for most of the species found in eastern North America. Sizes 00 and 000 bend easily and are not recommended for mounting beetles.

Pin beetle specimens when their appendages are still pliable enough to manipulate without damage. Working only with beetles collected at the same place and time, temporarily place your specimens on a folded tissue or paper towel for several minutes to absorb excess moisture. After selecting the appropriate-size pin, grasp your specimen firmly between the thumb and forefinger or brace it on the table with its topside up. With your other hand, push the pin through the base of the right elytron so that it will exit underneath between the middle and hind legs. Before driving the pin all the way through, check relative alignment of the specimen carefully to make sure that the

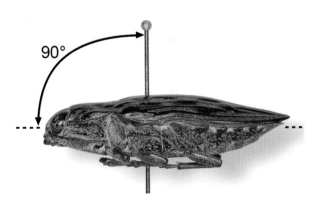

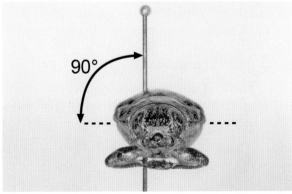

Figure 53. Proper longitudinal and transverse orientation of a beetle specimen on pin.

Figure 54. Pinning block.

shaft of the pin is perpendicular to the long and transverse axes of the body (Figs. 53a–b). Once the pin is all the way through, use the highest or shortest step of your pinning block to adjust the height of the beetle on the pin so about a quarter-inch space is left between the top of the specimen and the head of the pin. A pinning block (Fig. 54) is a small block of hardwood with three or four fine holes drilled successively deeper in quarter-inch increments, beginning with one-quarter inch. Using this simple tool will enable you to consistently space the head of the pin above the specimen and the intervals between the specimen and its labels underneath.

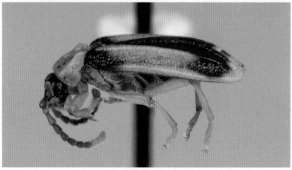

Figure 55. Proper longitudinal and transverse orientation of a beetle specimen on a point.

Specimens that are 5 mm or less or very narrow and likely to be damaged by direct pinning are best preserved on points (Fig. 55). Points are isosceles triangles of acid-free cardstock that are about 7 mm long and 2 mm wide at the base. The occasional point can be cut with sharp scissors, but a point punch, available from entomological supply houses, is desirable for making large numbers of uniform points. Push an insect pin (no. 2 or 3) through the broad end of the point and adjust its height on the shaft using the highest step on your pinning block. Using fine-tipped forceps, slightly bend down the tip of the point before attaching it to the specimen. For the sake of convenience, prepare several dozen points in advance to have them ready. Affixing a beetle to a point is best done under well-illuminated magnification provided by an optical visor or binocular dissecting microscope. Place the specimen to be pointed on its back (dorsum) or underside (ventrum) on a smooth, light-colored surface so the head is to the right and you have unfettered access to the beetle's right-hand side. Then dip the tip of the point into adhesive that is soluble in water (e.g., Elmer's blue gel) or alcohol (shellac, polyvinyl acetate) and affix it to the area of the thorax between the middle and hind legs. Be sure that there is enough glue to securely attach the specimen to the point, but not so much that it spreads and obscures important features needed for identification. Alcohol-soluble adhesives normally thicken with use and can be thinned by adding a bit more alcohol. If too thin, leave the container open for a brief period to allow excess alcohol to volatilize. Once the beetle is glued to the point, minor adjustments can be made so that its body axes are perpendicular to the shaft of the pin.

SPREADING SPECIMENS

Accurate species identification in beetles often requires careful examination of a specimen's appendages, mouthparts, body segments, and genitalia. Familiarity with these features will help to guide and improve your efforts to properly prepare and spread specimens. A spreading board (Fig. 56) is the best way to position and set a beetle's antennae and legs in place. Purchase a small sheet (no more than 12 × 18 inches) of polystyrene foam 1 inch thick (30 × 46 × 2.5 cm) from a craft store and wrap it in newsprint to prevent claws and mouthparts of dried specimens from catching on the board's rough surface and breaking off. Start by pinning a temporary locality label in the upper left corner of the spreading board. To the right of the label, push the first pinned beetle into the spreading board so the underside of the body rests directly on the board's surface. Carefully position the legs and antennae

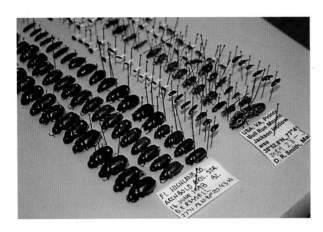

Figure 56. Spreading board with beetle specimens.

with brace pins so that these structures are symmetrical and observable from all angles. Tuck in legs and antennae, since specimens with outstretched appendages take up valuable space and are likely to be broken. Be sure to keep spread specimens from each locality separate so they can be accurately labeled when they are dry. It may take a week or so for specimens to dry, depending on the size of the specimen and relative humidity. You may want to keep your spreading boards in a protected yet airy space, such as in a covered box, in a cupboard, or on shelves with doors so that your specimens don't get dusty. Once the specimen is dried, carefully remove the brace pins to avoid damaging the now brittle appendages.

LABELING

To be of any scientific value, each and every specimen must have a permanent, carefully composed, and neatly produced locality label. Laser printers set to print at 1200 dpi or 600 dpi professional using a bold sans serif font (Arial, Geneva, Helvetica) of 4 or 5 point size on acid-free 65 lb. (176 g/m^2) card stock give good results. Each finished label should be no more than 0.8 inches across and five lines long, although some adjustments may be required depending on the length and the nature of the data. Cut the labels into strips and then individually with sharp scissors so that all four sides are neatly trimmed right up to the text.

Locality labels should include the following information on the first line: country (abbreviated as USA or CAN), state or province (e.g., VA for Virginia, ON for Ontario), and county or parish. The remaining four or five lines of the label includes the general locality, specific locality (if applicable), elevation (in feet ['], or meters [m]), latitude and longitude (in degrees, minutes, and seconds or decimal degrees), date (with month spelled out, or as a Roman numeral

[ex., vii for July] and full year), collector(s) name, and collecting method. A sample locality label is shown below:

USA: VA, Charles City Co.
VCU Rice Center, elev. 45′
N37.32605° W077.20593°
4 July 2014
A.V. Evans, under pine bark

An additional label may be added to more fully flesh out the method of collection, host plant data, other ecological data, and a cross-reference number that connects the specimen to photographs and field notes. Once the beetle is identified to species, a determination label containing the species name, name of determiner, and year of determination (as shown below) can be added as the very last label:

Dynastes
tityus
(Linnaeus, 1767)
det. A.V. Evans, 2014

Align the pinned specimen and its label so the beetle's head is directed toward the label's left margin. Center the specimen over the label and push the pin part way through. Select the appropriate step on the pinning block to adjust the height of the label on the pin. When labeling pointed specimens, both the beetle and the point are centered over the label with the point directed toward the label's left margin and the beetle's head off to the right of the point.

RELAXING SPECIMENS

To prepare dried specimens, or to reposition appendages or dissect those already mounted, specimens must first be "relaxed." Beetles that are not delicately patterned or colored, or those lacking any kind of setose or waxy vestiture that could become matted, discolored, or dissolved are placed directly in hot water. Simply bring filtered or distilled water to a boil and then add a drop of dish soap as a wetting agent. After several minutes, specimens submerged in this solution should become pliable enough to manipulate safely; larger and bulkier specimens may take longer. Another method is to use a relaxing chamber. Place a layer of clean sand, cardboard, blotter paper, or some other relatively sterile and porous substrate in a soft (polyethylene) plastic shoe box or food storage container. Saturate the substrate with warm water and pour off the excess. Place dry specimens in a plastic jar lid so they will not come into direct contact with wet surfaces. Add a couple of mothballs to the chamber to

47

discourage mold. Smaller beetles with more delicate bodies will become sufficiently relaxed overnight, but larger, heavier-bodied specimens may take several days to soften. Inspect the chamber every few days for mold that will damage or destroy specimens. Insect pins that corrode in a relaxing chamber should be replaced.

PRESERVING LARVAE AND PUPAE

Larvae and pupae, especially those with ecological data and positively associated with adult voucher specimens, are extremely valuable and should be permanently preserved. Place them in boiling water to fix their tissues and kill the microorganisms that will hasten tissue decay. Then place them directly in 70% ethanol or isopropyl alcohol. After a day or so, place these specimens (one species per collection) in glass vials with screw caps or neoprene stoppers supplied with a fresh supply of alcohol for permanent storage. Each vial must have its own label inside to be of any scientific value. Long shelf life for wet labels can be problematic because of the effects of preservatives on various papers, ink, and laser-printed text and is still undergoing study. For now, the simplest solution is to use acid-free 100% rag paper with pencil or to print laser labels at 1200 dpi or 600 dpi professional. Before cutting the sheet into individual labels, coat it with clear acrylic spray sealer to increase its durability. Those interested in building and maintaining extensive collections of beetle larvae and pupae would do well to keep up with published literature and LISTSERV discussions on the latest materials and techniques.

COLLECTION STORAGE

Sturdy, airtight specimen boxes with tight-fitting lids are a must for the permanent storage of beetle specimens. Dermestids, both larvae and adults, and booklice (Psocodea) can slip through the narrowest of spaces and, in a relatively short period of time, reduce pinned beetle collections to dust. Fluctuating temperatures, humidity, and sunlight will also destroy collections over time, so it is important to store them in dark and temperature-controlled spaces.

Storing specimens in tightly sealed glass-topped drawers that are kept in sealed cabinets is the best hedge against light and pest damage, but these systems are expensive. Wooden specimen boxes with tight-fitting lids, known as Schmitt or Schmitt-type boxes, also provide adequate protection for specimens, but are also expensive. Entomology departments at museums or universities occasionally offer surplus drawers and boxes at reasonable prices. A relatively inexpensive system consists of

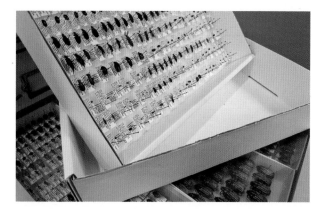

Figure 57. Beetle collections are stored in cardboard specimen boxes or glass-topped drawers supplied with unit trays.

commercially available cardboard specimen boxes with separate lids and foam bottoms that are slipped into 2-gallon resealable plastic bags to keep out pests (Fig. 57).

None of these systems is completely effective, especially if beetles are left out on spreading boards or open trays and become infested with the eggs or larvae of pests and are then introduced into otherwise pest-proof containers. Constant vigilance for fine powder accumulating beneath specimens is essential for identifying those infested with booklice or dermestid larvae. Remove these specimens immediately, take their labels off the pin, and immerse them in alcohol for at least one day. If several specimens within the same box are affected, place the entire box in a very cold freezer for at least a week. This process may need to be repeated, as freezing will usually kill all the dermestid larvae present but may leave eggs unaffected.

CURATING YOUR COLLECTION

Align your specimens in neat columns and rows using either the label or specimen itself as a guide to create neat, straight rows. Orient each specimen so that the head of the pinned beetle or the tip of the point is directed toward the top of the box. Avoid entangling legs and antennae by not overcrowding specimens. Organize your collection first by family and subfamily, then by tribe, genus, and species. A good reference collection not only contains well-prepared specimens accompanied by accurate label data, but also is organized to facilitate the easy retrieval of specimens and data. As your collection grows in size and diversity, you might consider adopting a glass-topped drawer system housed in cabinets. These drawers are supplied with interchangeable cardboard unit trays of various sizes lined with polyethylene foam bottoms called unit trays. Unit tray systems simplify curation and are easily expanded to accommodate the addition of new taxa and specimens. Glass-topped drawers with pinned beetles intended primarily for display must be kept dry and away from extreme temperatures to avoid the growth of mold, and out of direct sunlight to prevent fading. Display cases fitted with UV-filtered Plexiglas will slow, but not prevent, the fading of specimens exposed to sunlight.

KEEPING AND REARING BEETLES IN CAPTIVITY

Live beetles kept at home, in a classroom, or in a laboratory provide numerous opportunities to observe and photograph beetles as they undergo basic life processes. They require little space and are easy to display and maintain. In young students, caring for beetles instills a basic sense of awareness of the natural world by bringing into sharp focus the basic environmental and nutritional needs of organisms. For older students, captive beetles provide opportunities to engage in directed and open inquiry investigations into their behavior. Although few species of live beetles are sold commercially in North America, an amazing diversity of native species is available in nearby vacant lots, parks, and natural areas. Transporting live beetles may be regulated within counties, states, and provinces, and is strictly regulated across state, provincial, and international borders (see Beetle Conservation and the Ethics of Collecting).

TRANSPORT FROM THE FIELD

When transporting live beetles from the field, it is important to remember that even the briefest exposure to direct sunlight or the temperatures inside a closed car at the

Figure 58. Plastic food containers are perfect for transporting live beetles.

height of summer will quickly kill them, especially those species adapted to cool or moist habitats. Half- or 1-pint deli cups or similar resealable plastic food containers (Fig. 58) are perfect for transporting beetles so they arrive alive and unharmed. They are inexpensive, lightweight, unbreakable, and easily nested for packing. Before placing beetles in the container, supply it with a piece of paper towel, some leaf litter, or a piece of moss and slightly moisten this substrate with water to provide your animals with a bit of comfort and protect them from the rigors of travel. Always use moistened paper towels or moss when transporting aquatic beetles. Placing them in even small amounts of water for short periods may lead to their death by drowning. Then put the containers in an ice chest supplied with one or more frozen water bottles to keep them cool in transit. As long as the beetles are kept cool and not crowded in their containers, it is not necessary to punch air holes in the lids of their containers, especially for day trips.

HOUSING FOR ADULT TERRESTRIAL BEETLES

Keeping beetles in captivity requires some knowledge of their food and moisture requirements so that these conditions can be duplicated in captivity. Supply at least 1 inch (25 mm) of a 50-50 mixture of sterile sand and potting or forest soil on the bottom of an appropriately sized terrarium or deep plastic food container. Based on your observations of the beetles in the field, add rocks, bark, chunks of moss, or dried leaves for shelter, and branches and twigs for climbing. Beetles don't require a lot of air, but they do require good ventilation to release heat and control humidity. A secure screened lid attached with binder clips will not only prevent the escape of your animals but also provide plenty of ventilation to minimize the growth of harmful mold and fungi. Regularly mist the enclosure with distilled or filtered water and install a vial of water plugged with cotton and placed on its side. The cotton enables beetles to drink from the vial and also acts as a wick that allows moisture to evaporate from the vial into the enclosure to help maintain humidity.

Offer predatory species appropriately sized adult and immature insects as food. Remember that the feeder insects must spend most of their time where they will be found by your beetles. Climbing and flying species are likely to be missed by mostly ground-dwelling predators. Provide plant feeders with fresh cuttings of their host plants placed in small jars or vials of water to maintain freshness as long as possible. Stuffing cotton into the top of the jar to hold the plants in place will prevent beetles from crawling or falling inside and drowning. Some phytophagous species will accept romaine lettuce or other leafy greens, oatmeal, potato slices, and various kinds of fruit. Always remove uneaten plant and animal foods after a day or two to prevent the buildup of mold, mites, and other pests.

Bess beetles (*Odontotaenius disjunctus*), green June beetles (*Cotinis nitida*), eastern Hercules beetles (*Dynastes tityus*), caterpillar hunters (*Calosoma* species), and tiger beetles (*Cicindela*, etc.) are all relatively large and hardy species that do well in captivity. Bess beetles are kept in well-ventilated containers (Fig. 59) supplied with moist but not wet chunks of decaying wood to provide them with both food and shelter. Green June beetles thrive in a terrarium supplied with several inches of sandy loam, branches to climb, and a variety of soft fruits (peaches, grapes, strawberries, bananas, etc.) to eat. They will mate and lay eggs readily in their enclosure. The C-shaped grubs will develop in a deep, organic substrate supplied with a mixture of leaf litter, grass clippings, and crushed dry dog food. Eastern Hercules beetles (*Dynastes tityus*) are kept in similar enclosures with thicker branches for climbing and will also eat soft fruits, especially peaches and bananas. They will accept cotton balls or sponges soaked in a 50-50 solution of water and real maple syrup as food. Several caterpillar hunters can be kept together in an open terrarium supplied with branches to climb and plenty of prey. They prefer to eat caterpillars, but will accept commercially available crickets and mealworms. Tiger beetles will do well in a terrarium filled with several inches of clean sand. Keep one corner of the terrarium moist and cover the entire enclosure with a lid fitted with a 40-watt aquarium bulb to supply heat and light. A rock or piece of wood will give them something to burrow under, if they so choose. They will accept a variety of live insects every other day, as long as the prey items are no larger than the beetles themselves.

Figure 59. Keep bess beetles in well-ventilated containers supplied with moist chunks of wood.

SETTING UP AN AQUARIUM

Aquatic beetles are relatively easy to keep in an aquarium and will provide hours of great beetle watching and photography. A light hood on the aquarium is essential for illuminating your beetles and preventing their escape. Although several filtration systems are available, under-gravel filter systems are particularly easy to maintain for beginners. After assembling and installing the under-gravel filter plate and snapping the clear filter stack pipes in place, place 1 or 2 inches of sealed aquarium gravel on the filter plate. Then half-fill the tank with distilled or filtered water, or tap water that has been allowed to stand in a clean bucket for 24 hours. Add artificial or real plants and some larger rocks, and then top off the water level of the tank. Branches and aquatic vegetation added to the tank may be attractive, but they are likely to introduce unwanted algae to your aquarium.

Whirligigs (Gyrinidae) and predaceous diving beetles (Dytiscidae) will eat living or frozen crickets placed on the surface of the water. Mosquito and mayfly larvae are excellent sources of wild insect food, if they are sufficiently available on a regular basis. Hungry predators and scavengers alike readily accept bits of raw meat, fish, and shellfish, but these items will quickly foul the water, requiring frequent water and filter cartridge changes. Water scavenger beetles (Hydrophilidae) will also devour bits of romaine lettuce or aquatic plants. Living aquarium plants or submerged rocks covered with algae will provide food for most herbivorous beetles (Elmidae, Dryopidae), but the presence of algae will require greater vigilance to keep the aquarium clean.

KEEPING BEETLE LARVAE

Unlike butterfly and moth collectors who dedicate much of their time to searching for and rearing caterpillars, coleopterists seldom collect and keep beetle larvae in captivity, partly because of their varied and often specialized feeding requirements, secretive habits, and extended periods of time needed to reach adulthood; however, taking the trouble to rear beetle larvae leads to a better understanding of their biology and is a way of securing adults of species that are otherwise difficult to obtain. The challenge of rearing beetle larvae is in recognizing and duplicating natural conditions in captivity, and maintaining optimal conditions and food quality for the duration of larval and pupal development. Too little moisture results in dehydration that hampers hatching, molting, and pupation, while excess moisture often leads to fatal fungal infections or drowning. Eggs, larvae, pupae, and teneral adults should be handled as little as possible and with great care by using featherweight forceps to avoid inflicting injury.

REARING GROUND-DWELLING BEETLES

Place mating pairs or gravid females of predatory ground beetles (Carabidae) and rove beetles (Staphylinidae) in small transparent plastic containers with airtight lids supplied with about a quarter inch (1 cm) of moist soil consisting of sand, loam, forest soil rich in organics, or peat moss. The substrate should be moist enough to remain compacted when squeezed, but without dripping water. To prevent these carnivorous beetles from eating their own eggs, keep their appetites sated with chopped mealworms. Females usually begin laying eggs right away and are removed immediately, or left in the container until the eggs hatch. Place the eggs and young larvae in their own containers to avoid cannibalism. The containers should be kept cool, about 68 °F (20 °C). Check for and remove dead eggs and larvae immediately, especially those attacked by fungi, to avoid spreading infections. Uneaten food should also be removed every other day to limit fungal growth and the proliferation of mites. Species that undergo winter diapause may require an extended cold period to complete their development.

REARING AQUATIC LARVAE

Predaceous diving beetles (Dytiscidae), whirligigs (Gyrinidae), and water scavenger beetles (Hydrophilidae) generally lay their eggs on the water's surface or on submerged rocks or vegetation. Their larvae are predatory and require a steady supply of live insect food to complete their development. You can collect feeder insects from natural habitats, or can purchase mealworms and flightless fruit flies from dealers or pet shops. Be sure to remove uneaten food to avoid fouling the water. The mature larvae leave the water to pupate in relatively dry subterranean chambers or other protected places just beyond the shoreline. Successful rearing of these beetles requires removing mature larvae and placing them in a container with moist soil, or providing them with the means for crawling out of the tank and into a moist but not wet substrate covered with chunks of wood or moss.

REARING LARVAE FROM STEMS

Some species of tumbling flower beetles (Mordellidae) are reared from larvae developing in pithy stems. Identify plants

Figure 60. Mordellids are reared from pithy galls and stems.

in late summer while they still have leaves and flowers, then return to the site in late winter and early spring to select large, upright stems and cut them off at ground level. Cut the stems into sections (Fig. 60) and place them in 2-gallon resealable bags. To maintain the stems under reasonably natural conditions, place the bags outdoors in a protected area that is exposed to ambient temperatures, but not direct sunlight. Add a few drops of water to avoid dehydration, or open the bags to dry out samples showing signs of condensation or mold.

REARING LARVAE FOUND UNDER BARK

The larvae and pupae of several beetle families (Lycidae, Elateridae, Pythidae, Tenebrionidae, Stenotrachelidae) found under loose bark on snags, stumps, and logs are often more commonly encountered than the adults. One method of rearing these larvae is to place them in a covered petri dish containing a small amount of the substrate in which they were collected. Another method involves using glass vials, each filled with approximately a quarter inch (1 cm) of compact, moist paper towel covered with a quarter inch of loose substrate found under the bark from which the larvae were collected. The size of the vials and type of tree material can be altered depending on species. The tops of the vials are either left open or loosely plugged with crumpled paper towel and kept upright in a lidded box at room temperature. Both the paper toweling and natural substrate not only serve as food, but also help to regulate the moisture content of each vial. Many species require cold before completing their development. These vials are stored in a box and placed in a plastic bag punched with holes and set outside in the fall for exposure to cold winter temperatures. In spring, the larvae are brought back indoors to complete their life cycle. Because

51

the larvae are kept individually, accurate notes can be kept regarding their behavior and length of life cycle with minimal disturbance during examination.

REARING LARVAE FROM WOODY FUNGI AND DECAYING WOOD

Late winter and early spring are good times to gather woody fungi, dead limbs, and rotten logs and stumps containing pupae or mature larvae preparing to pupate. Plastic food containers with resealable lids are practical and inexpensive rearing chambers. Cheesecloth or window screen stretched over the tops of these containers and secured with heavy rubber bands allows excess moisture to escape, but requires a bit more vigilance to avoid dehydration, especially in air-conditioned and heated environments. Keep containers away from outside doors, windows, and heating and cooling ducts to avoid exposing your animals to extreme temperatures. Depending on species, consistently warm indoor temperatures may accelerate or hinder their development.

For larger rearing operations, place dead limbs in large, sturdy black or blue plastic storage or filing bins with snap-on lids; clear plastic boxes can be wrapped with black garbage bags to keep out light. Make sure these containers have tight-fitting lids or wrap them in plastic to prevent emerging beetles from escaping. Cut a hole in the end of each container and screw in the neck of a small jar or vial so the bulk of the jar is on the outside. Beetles emerging from the rearing materials inside are drawn to the light and find their way into the jar where they are easily seen and collected. Adding a bit of water to the rearing material from time to time will prevent it from completely drying out. Keeping rearing chambers indoors is likely to speed up the emergence of some beetles, but it may delay those that require a period of cold temperatures to complete their development. Accurate records of host plants and parasitoids are important contributions to beetle study, especially for species with poorly understood or unknown biologies.

TAKING AN ACTIVE ROLE IN BEETLE RESEARCH

The natural history notes that appear in peer-reviewed journals, newsletters, and coleopterological LISTSERVs are not only written by professional biologists, but also contributed by observant students and naturalists who keep meticulous notes. Although the beetles making up the fauna of eastern North America are relatively well known taxonomically, there is still much to be learned about various aspects of their lives, including reproduction and development, food preferences and foraging behavior, adult and larval habitat selection, seasonality, number of generations produced annually, and distribution. The bold and distinctive color patterns of some adults have been noted for decades, but little experimental work has been carried out to determine how potential predators of beetles perceive these colors. Geographic variation within beetle populations is poorly documented in most families. Behavioral, ecological, and distributional data gleaned from carefully executed beetle surveys and mark-recapture studies, especially those conducted over a period of several successive years on school grounds, parks, vacant lots, or nearby woods can be of considerable value. Coordinating such efforts through citizen science organizations or with researchers at universities and natural history museums will facilitate the inclusion of these data into ongoing scientific research.

Traditionally, the study of larvae and of adults have been treated as separate endeavors, but more and more coleopterists today have come to embrace the value of studying both the adult and immature stages simultaneously, especially when studying their evolutionary relationships. Students and naturalists with a knack for rearing beetle larvae associated with reliably identified adults can make enormously important contributions to our understanding of the development of beetles and their evolutionary relationships.

A bioblitz is a very popular and expedient way of gathering beetle and other invertebrate data for national and state forests, parks, and other natural areas that lack this information. Because of their short duration, the findings of these intensive one-day surveys are unduly influenced by season, lunar cycle, local weather conditions, and personnel available to gather samples. As such, these events provide only a snapshot of beetle diversity and thus are not substitutes for well-managed, long-term monitoring efforts. Still, bioblitzes do generate useful species lists that support effective natural resource management and suggest avenues for sustained research programs and conservation measures in the future. These events also provide opportunities for students and naturalists to meet professional biologists and work with them in the field.

It is hoped that books such as this and other regional identification manuals will increase general interest in beetles and inspire citizen scientists, students, and naturalists to take up the cause of their study and conservation.

This key is intended to serve only as a "quick guide" to the most commonly encountered families (**bold** type), while less common families are suggested within square brackets in plain type. As such, the key includes only 68 of the 115 families known to occur in eastern North America. It should be used in combination with the "Similar families" sections included in each family diagnosis for proper family placement. For detailed keys, see *American Beetles* (Arnett and Thomas 2001; Arnett et al. 2002).

1. Metacoxae may or may not be enlarged, basal half of hind femora and ventrites clearly visible .... **GO TO 2**

1'. Metacoxae greatly enlarged to conceal basal half of legs and most of first three ventrites:

Haliplidae (p.96)

2. Head without rostrum .... **GO TO 3**

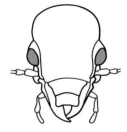 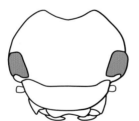

2'. Head with distinctly long or broad rostrum:

Curculionidae (p.469); Anthribidae (p.458); Brentidae (p.466)
[see also Nemonychidae (p.457); Belidae (p.462); Attelabidae (p.462)]

 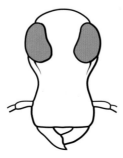

ILLUSTRATED KEY TO THE COMMON BEETLE FAMILIES OF EASTERN NORTH AMERICA (*CONTINUED*)

3. Hind coxae not immovably fused to metathorax and not dividing the first ventrite .... **GO TO 4**

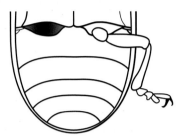

3'. Hind coxae fused to metathorax and dividing the first ventrite:

Carabidae (p.63); Dytiscidae (p.99); Gyrinidae (p.94) [see also Noteridae (p.97)]

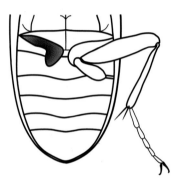

4. Elytra long, covering all or nearly all of the abdomen .... **GO TO 5**
4'. Elytra short, exposing two or more terga:

Staphylinidae (p.124); Silphidae (p.120); Histeridae (p.110); Nitidulidae (p.295); Mordellidae (p.333)
[see also Buprestidae (p.184); Phengodidae (p.233); Cantharidae (p.238); Ripiphoridae (p.338);
Cerambycidae (p.388)]

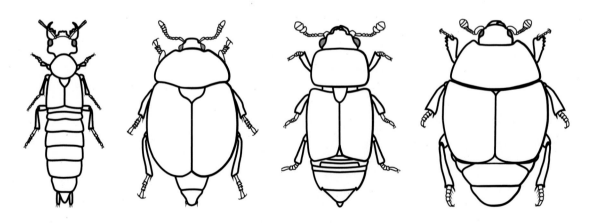

5. Antennae not lamellate .... **GO TO 6**

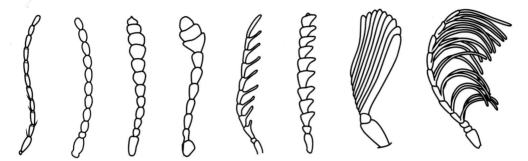

5'. Antennae lamellate with apical three to seven antennomeres forming distinctly asymmetrical or one-sided club:

Scarabaeidae (p.156)

[see also Lucanidae (p.142); Passalidae (p.145); Glaresidae (p.146); Trogidae (p.147); Geotrupidae (p.149); Ochodaeidae (p.152); Hybosoridae (p.153); Glaphyridae (p.155)]

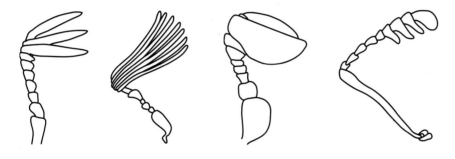

6. Tarsal formula not 5-5-4 .... **GO TO 7**

6'. Tarsal formula 5-5-4:

Tenebrionidae (p.344); Melandryidae (p.329); Synchroidae (p.359); Meloidae (p.365)

[see also Mycetophagidae (p.323); Tetratomidae (p.327); Mordellidae (p.333); Ripiphoridae (p.338); Zopheridae (p.340); Stenotrachelidae (p.360); Oedemeridae (p.362); Pyrochroidae (p.373); Anthicidae (p.377); Aderidae (p.382); Scraptiidae (p.384)]

7. Tarsal formula variable; maxillary palps long, usually conspicuous; antennae variable, not more than half the length of the body .... **GO TO 8**

7'. Tarsal formula often appears 4-4-4, actually 5-5-5 with small fourth tarsomere surrounded by bilobed third tarsomere, or distinctly 5-5-5; maxillary palps short, often not conspicuous; antennae never clubbed and more than or less than half the length of body:

Cerambycidae (p.388); Chrysomelidae (p.429)

[see also Megalopodidae (p.428); Orsodacnidae (p.429)]

8. Body with scattered setae or scales, if present at all; head without ocelli .... **GO TO 9**

8'. Body densely covered with setae or scales; head often with one ocellus

Dermestidae (p.246)

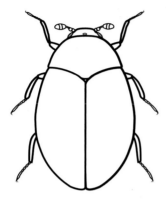

9. Antennae not clubbed or club not velvety; maxillary palps much shorter than antennae;
legs not modified for swimming .... **GO TO 10**

9'. Antennae with antennomeres 7–9 forming loose, velvety club; maxillary palps long, always half the
length of antennae, usually as long or longer; legs often fringed with setae, modified for swimming:

Hydrophilidae (p.105)

10. Elytra hard and shell-like .... **GO TO 11**

10'. Elytra soft and leathery:

Cantharidae (p.238); Lampyridae (p.234); Lycidae (p.229)
[see also Omethidae (p.237); Melyridae (p.271)]

11. Ventrites variable, never iridescent or metallic .... **GO TO 12**

11'. Ventrites 1 and 2 fused with no trace of suture between, all iridescent or metallic:

Buprestidae (p.184)

12. Body variable .... **GO TO 13**

12'. Body strikingly flat:

Cucujidae (p.288)
[see also Laemophloeidae (p.291)]

13. Body usually elongate, somewhat flattened or nearly cylindrical, tarsal formula variable .... **GO TO 14**

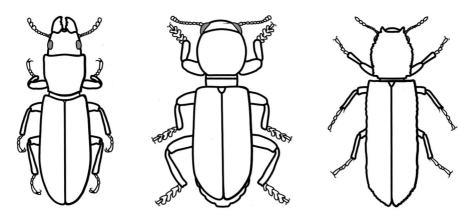

13'. Body typically compact, round, convex dorsally and flattened ventrally; tarsal formula usually appearing 3-3-3, actually 4-4-4:

Coccinellidae (p.311)

[see also Erotylidae (p.277); Endomychidae (p.308)]

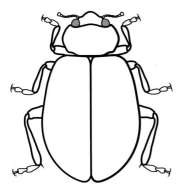

14. Body, legs, and antennae variable .... **GO TO 15**

14'. Prothorax long, loosely articulated with rest of body; antennae usually serrate; legs long, slender:

Elateridae (p.213)

[see also Eucnemidae (p.210); Throscidae (p.211)]

15. Head distinctly visible from above:

Trogossitidae (p.259); Cleridae (p.263); Melyridae (p.271)

[see also Bostrichidae (p.250)]

15'. Head hidden from above by hoodlike prothorax:

Bostrichidae (p.250); Ptinidae (p.252)

[see also Curculionidae (p.469)]

BEETLES
OF
EASTERN
NORTH
AMERICA

RETICULATED BEETLES, FAMILY CUPEDIDAE
(CUE-*PEH*-DIH-DEE)

Cupedids are a small and unusual family of primitive beetles with more than 30 species worldwide, two of which are found in eastern North America. Adults and larvae bore into fungus-infested wood beneath the bark of limbs and logs.

FAMILY DIAGNOSIS Adult cupedids are slender, parallel-sided, strongly flattened, roughly sculpted, and clothed in broad, scalelike setae. Head and pronotum narrower than elytra. Antennae thick, filiform with 11 antennomeres. Prothorax distinctly margined or keeled on sides, underside with grooves to receive legs. Elytra broader than prothorax, strongly ridged with square punctures between. Tarsal formula 5-5-5; claws simple. Abdomen with five overlapping ventrites.

SIMILAR FAMILIES
- net-winged beetles (Lycidae) – head not visible from above (p.229)
- hispine leaf beetles (Chrysomelidae: Cassidinae) – antennae short, clavate; head narrower than pronotum (p.429)

COLLECTING NOTES Adult cupedids are found in late spring and summer by chopping into old decaying logs and stumps, netted in flight near infested wood, and beaten from dead branches. They are sometimes common at light.

FAUNA FOUR SPECIES IN FOUR GENERA (NA); TWO SPECIES IN TWO GENERA (ENA)

- -

Cupes capitatus **Fabricius** (7.0–11.0 mm) is elongate, narrow, bicolored with reddish or golden head and remainder of body grayish black. Adults active late spring and summer, found under bark and on bare trunks of standing dead oaks (*Quercus*); attracted to light. Nothing has been published on immature stages. New England to Georgia, west to Ontario, Michigan, Kansas, and Missouri. (1)

Tenomerga cinereus **(Say)** (8.0–13.0 mm) is elongate, narrow, pale brownish or ashy gray with darker oblong patches or blotches on the elytra. Larvae tunnel into solid, decaying poles, rotting oak (*Quercus*) trestle timbers, and pine (*Pinus*). Adults active late spring and summer, found beneath bark, sometimes associated with old wood frame houses; attracted to light. Ontario and New Hampshire south to Florida, west to Michigan and Texas. (1)

TELEPHONE-POLE BEETLES, FAMILY MICROMALTHIDAE
(MY-KRO-*MAL*-THIH-DEE)

Micromalthids are utterly bizarre animals in terms of their unusual reproductive biology that involves different types of parthenogenesis (reproduction without sex) and paedogeneisis (larval reproduction). Under stressful environmental conditions, the highly mobile caraboid larva (so named because it resembles larvae of carabid ground beetles) metamorphoses into a cerambycoid larva (so named because it resembles the larva of a longhorn beetle) that either develops into an adult female or a paedogenetic female- or male-producing larva that gives birth to caraboid larvae. Or the cerambycoid larva can develop directly into a male-producer by laying eggs that hatch into curculionoid larvae that eventually develop into adult haploid males. The ability to reproduce as both larvae and adults affords micromalthids the opportunity to multiply quickly and fully exploit patchy and ephemeral resources. Micromalthid larvae feed and develop in moist, decaying logs and stumps in the red-rotten or yellowish-brown rotten stages of decomposition. Although they will occasionally attack rotting telephone poles, hence their common name, micromalthids are neither structural pests nor of any economic importance.

FAMILY DIAGNOSIS Adult micromalthids are elongate, somewhat flattened, with large head and bulging compound eyes broader than pronotum, mouthparts directed forward (prognathous), antennae moniliform, with 11 short, bead-shaped antennomeres. Pronotum narrower than head, widest in front. Elytra straight-sided, short, leaving five abdominal ventrites exposed. Legs slender, with tarsal formula 5-5-5, and claws simple. Abdomen with six ventrites, ventrites 3–5 of male each with large central cavity filled with setae.

SIMILAR FAMILIES
- rove beetles (Staphylinidae) – elytra usually shorter; antennae not moniliform (p.124)
- small soldier beetles (Cantharidae) – antennae filiform (p.238)
- checkered beetles (Cleridae) – antennae never moniliform (p.263)
- soft-winged flower beetles (Melyridae) – pronotum with well-defined side margins (p.271)

COLLECTING NOTES Although sometimes locally abundant, telephone-pole beetles are seldom seen and rarely collected. Adults emerge briefly in large numbers to mate and locate new breeding sites. They are sometimes captured in Malaise or flight intercept traps. Specimens are best obtained by rearing the small whitish larvae that are sometimes abundant in moist, but not wet, oak or pine logs and stumps in the advanced stages of red-rotten decay. Larvae collected in late winter or early spring and kept indoors will emerge as adults in a few months.

FAUNA ONE SPECIES, *MICROMALTHUS DEBILIS* LECONTE (NA)

Micromalthus debilis LeConte (1.5–2.5 mm) is small, flat, shiny brown to black with yellowish antennae and legs. Head wider than pronotum. Pronotum widest in front, without keeled margins or grooves. Elytra short, exposing part of abdomen. Rarely seen adults briefly emerge in large numbers, captured in Malaise or flight intercept traps. Larvae sometimes abundant in moist, but not wet, oak or pine logs and stumps that are in the advanced stages of red-rotten decay. Likely from Massachusetts to Florida, west to Michigan, Illinois, and probably Texas. (1)

MINUTE BOG BEETLES, FAMILY SPHAERIUSIDAE
(SFER-EE-OO-SIH-DEE)

Minute bog beetles, known formerly in the family Microsporidae, are found along the edges of streams and rivers in mud, under stones, on algae, among roots associated with riparian plants, in moss associated with wetland edges, or in moist leaf litter. Adults breathe water by storing oxygen under their elytra. These very small, shiny black or brown beetles are convex with large heads and have distinctly clubbed antennae, large thoracic and posterior coxal plates underneath, and three visible abdominal ventrites that are uneven in length. The sole genus *Sphaerius* includes 19 species on all continents, except Antarctica, and is in need of revision.

FAMILY DIAGNOSIS Adult sphaeriusids are broadly oval, and shiny; underside mostly flat. Head large with mouthparts directed forward, partly visible from underneath pronotum, eyes prominent, antennae with 11 antennomeres and a cone-shaped club, last antennomere with long bristles. Prothorax short, with pronotum narrowed in front and widest at elytra, underside with mesosternum small and fused with metasternum to form a large plate. Elytra very convex and cover abdomen. Abdomen with three ventrites, first and last wide and long, middle narrow. Middle legs widely separated at base, hind legs nearly touching at base with coxal plates large and covering femora and first abdominal ventrite, tarsal formula 3-3-3, first tarsomere much longer than second, with claws simple and unequal.

SIMILAR FAMILIES

- featherwing beetles (Ptiliidae) – pronotum less narrowed in front (p.115)
- minute beetles (Clambidae) – can partially roll up their bodies (p.179)
- lady beetles (Coccinellidae) – antennae club gradual, not distinct (p.311)
- minute fungus beetles (Corylophidae) – head covered; antennae club gradual, not distinct (p.320)

COLLECTING NOTES Sphaeriusids are rarely collected and usually associated with wet environments. Look for them by carefully searching along the edges of bodies of water in wet mud, sand, or gravel, and among roots, on algae, and under rocks; also extracted from plant debris using a Berlese funnel.

FAUNA THREE SPECIES IN ONE GENUS (NA); ONE SPECIES IN ONE GENUS (ENA)

Sphaerius **species** (0.5–1.2 mm) is shiny black. Head large. Pronotum widest at base near elytra. Thorax underneath forming a large plate with coxae of hind legs. Elytra are strongly convex, long, and completely cover all of abdominal ventrites. Adults and larvae are extremely small and live among spaces between wet sand grains and gravel and eat algae. Adults are found in damp environments along the shores of wetlands, sometimes in association with hydraenids, small hydrophilids, limnichids, and elmids. Alabama, possibly distributed throughout Gulf Coast states. (1)

GROUND, TIGER, AND WRINKLED BARK BEETLES, FAMILY CARABIDAE
(KUH-*RAB*-IH-DEE)

Carabids range in habit from blind and flightless cave dwellers to fully winged species with decided preference for living on the ground or up on trees and shrubs. Most species are shiny, dark, and sometimes metallic or patterned. The bright, shiny colors and distinct markings of tiger beetles help them blend into their background, making it difficult for potential predators to track them. Most carabids are fleet of foot and, equipped with long legs and powerful jaws, perfectly adapted for hunting, capturing, and killing insect prey. Both adults and larvae attack all sorts of insects, as well as their eggs, larvae, and pupae, and are considered largely beneficial when they prey on pest species. Although most adults are opportunistic predators and eat whatever they can catch, some appear to specialize on caterpillars (*Calosoma*) or snails (*Scaphinotus, Sphaeroderus*). A few species (*Amara, Harpalus*) prefer eating mainly plant materials, especially fruits and seeds. Most tiger beetles hunt during the warmest part of the day, while many ground beetles search for prey at dusk or at night. The genera *Clinidium* and *Omoglymmius* (formerly Rhysodidae) are aberrant carabids that spend most of their lives deep inside rotten, fungal-ridden wood, consuming the amoeboid stage of slime molds and possibly the mycelia of other fungi. Adult mandibles are not for chewing, but instead protect special needlelike appendages associated with the maxillae. With these specialized mouthparts, wrinkled bark beetles pin down amoebae, rip open their cell membranes, and lap up leaking cellular fluids. Many species of carabids ably defend themselves when threatened or disturbed by releasing noxious fluids from a pair of abdominal glands near their anus, sometimes with amazing force and accuracy. These smelly and sometimes caustic fluids are produced by pygidial glands located at the tip of the abdomen and contain a potent chemical cocktail of various hydrocarbons, aldehydes, phenols, quinones, esters, and acids.

63

FAMILY DIAGNOSIS Carabids are elongate, flattened or almost cylindrical, generally hairless and somewhat tapered at both ends. Usually uniformly shiny and dark, sometimes brownish or pale, metallic, or bi- or tricolored, often with brightly marked patterns of yellow or orange on the elytra; tiger beetles often with bold white or yellow, enamel-like markings on otherwise metallic elytra. Mouthparts directed forward (prognathous). Antennae threadlike (filiform) or beadlike (moniliform) with 11 antennomeres. Pronotum usually narrower than elytra, with sides sharply margined (less so in tiger beetles). Scutellum visible except in round sand beetles (*Omophron*). Elytra always completely covering the abdomen and fused in flightless species; surface smooth, punctured, and/or grooved (striate). Flight wings fully developed, reduced in size, or absent. Hind trochanter large and offset from femur; tarsal formula 5-5-5, with claws equal, simple, saw-toothed (serrate) or comblike (pectinate). Abdomen usually with six ventrites (*Brachinus* has seven or eight); first ventrite divided by hind coxae.

SIMILAR FAMILIES

- *Ceruchus, Platycerus* (Lucanidae) – antennae geniculate with lamellate clubs (pp.143, 144)
- lined flat bark beetles (Laemophloeidae) – distinct lines along sides of head, pronotum (p.291)
- bothriderid beetles (Bothrideridae) – antennae clubbed; tarsal formula 4-4-4 (p.305)
- colydiine beetles (Zopheridae) – antennae clubbed; tarsal formula 5-5-4 (p.340)
- darkling beetles (Tenebrionidae) – tarsi 5-5-4; antennae sometimes clavate (p.344)
- comb-clawed beetles (Tenebrionidae) – tarsi 5-5-4; claws serrate (pp.351–3)
- *Ditylus* (Oedemeridae) – tarsi 5-5-4 (p.363)
- dead log beetles (Pythidae) – tarsi 5-5-4 (p.372)
- narrow-waisted bark beetles (Salpingidae) – tarsi 5-5-4 (p.376)
- *Hesperandra, Neandra* (Cerambycidae) – tarsi appear 4-4-4 (p.389)
- straight-snouted weevils (Brentidae) – head with distinct beak (p.466)

COLLECTING NOTES Look for ground beetles under bark, rocks, boards, logs, especially along the banks of ponds, streams, and rivers. Flush beetles from their hiding places in mud and sand along shorelines by pouring or splashing water over the substrate. Raking leaves and sifting litter in these habitats are productive. Inspect bases of plant rosettes, or within the axils of reeds and grasses growing in wetlands. Beat and sweep vegetation, or check tree trunks at night. Pitfall traps, especially those baited with meat, are useful for monitoring some ground beetle populations. Many nocturnal species are attracted to lights. *Clinidium* and *Omoglymmius* are found under loose bark of moist, firm, fungus-ridden logs and stumps, as well in rotten centers of large, living trees. Tiger beetles are mostly diurnal, extremely alert, and quickly take flight when threatened, fly for a short distance, and land facing the collector. Most are active on hot, bright days in spring and summer, especially in sunny, open places along roads and trails, ocean beaches, lakeshores, riverbanks, and mudflats; they hide in burrows under stones, or beneath loose bark at night or during bad weather.

FAUNA 2,439 SPECIES IN 208 GENERA (NA)

Lacustrine Gazelle Beetle *Nebria lacustris* **Casey**
(9.5–11.7 mm) is shiny black with yellowish to pale reddish legs. Top of head without reddish spots. Pronotal margin with seta at middle. Elytra with tips distinctly and obliquely truncate at suture. Nocturnal and fast-running adults active mostly in spring and summer; hide during day under stones and other debris on open gravelly or rocky shores of rivers and larger streams. New Brunswick to North Carolina, west to Manitoba, Minnesota, Iowa, and Indiana. (3)

Brassy Big-eyed Beetle *Notiophilus aeneus* **(Herbst)**
(5.0–6.0 mm) is shiny black with a brassy tinge, antennae and femora reddish yellowish. Head broad with deep grooves between large, prominent eyes. Pronotum distinctly constricted at base. Elytra with grooves equally spaced and coarsely punctate at base, much less distinct at tips, each elytron with a pair of seta-bearing punctures just before tip. Mostly diurnal adults active in spring and early summer; found in forest moss and leaf litter and probably prey on small insects. Maritime Provinces to Georgia, west to Ontario, Minnesota, Nebraska, Missouri, and Tennessee. (9)

Notiophilus novemstriatus **LeConte** (4.0–4.7 mm) is shiny black, brassy. Head wide with deep grooves between large, prominent eyes. Antennomeres 1–4 pale. Elytra each with two punctures bearing setae just before tip and broad area next to suture without grooves. Legs with femora dark, tibiae pale. Diurnal and fleet-footed adults active late winter through early summer, late summer and fall, found in leaf litter and bare ground in open woodlands, especially near streams; occasional at light. Winged and wingless, mostly the latter. New England to Florida, west to South Dakota, Oklahoma, and Arizona. (9)

Calosoma calidum (Fabricius) (19.0–27.0 mm) is black, sometimes with bronze luster, and elytra margined with metallic green. Elytra with rows of deep punctures, each elytron with three rows of large metallic red, gold, or green pits; flight wings developed. Underside metallic. Legs dark. Adults and larvae prey on moth caterpillars, especially cutworms, armyworms, tent caterpillars. Adults active mostly spring and summer, found in meadows, open fields, and disturbed habitats; fly to light. Across Canada and northern United States; in east, south to northern Georgia and Missouri. (9)

Cold-country Caterpillar Hunter *Calosoma frigidum* **Kirby** (16.0–27.0 mm) is black with or without bronze luster, sides of pronotum and elytra metallic green; appendages dark. Elytra each with three rows of widely spaced metallic green or sometimes gold or purplish pits, spaces between with four deep, punctate grooves; flight wings developed. Underside black, sides with green or purplish luster. Adults active mostly spring and summer, found in wooded habitats under debris; fly to light. Across southern Canada and northern United States; in east, south to Georgia and Texas. (9)

Say's Caterpillar Hunter *Calosoma sayi* **Dejean** (25.0–28.0 mm) is large, black with green or bronze luster, and with elytral margins blue or green. Elytra deeply grooved with coarse punctures, each elytron with three rows of metallic red or green pits. Adults and larvae prey on caterpillars, beetle larvae, and pupae. Adults active mostly at dawn and dusk, often found under stones and other debris in disturbed habitats and agricultural fields during day; attracted to light. New York to Florida, west to Iowa, Oklahoma, and California. (9)

Fiery Searcher *Calosoma scrutator* (Fabricius) (23.0–36.0 mm) is large, black with violet luster. Pronotum dark blue or violet with broad purple, coppery, or golden green margins. Elytra bright green with metallic reddish or gold margins. Legs with femora black with blue luster, middle tibiae of male strongly curved with reddish setal brushes at tip. Adults found in various open habitats and woodland edges on caterpillar-infested shrubs in spring; sometimes common at light. Like other species of *Calosoma*, adults release a foul-smelling defensive fluid when disturbed. In east from southeastern Canada to Florida, west to Dakotas and Texas. (9)

Forest Caterpillar Hunter *Calosoma sycophanta*
(Linnaeus) (22.0–25.0 mm) is large with bright golden green
elytra. Maxillary palps with last two palpomeres of similar
length and width. Pronotum black with metallic blue
margins. Elytra distinctly grooved with reddish luster on
sides. Underside black and distinctly broadly metallic blue
or violet along sides. Femora dark brown or black, without
metallic luster. Adults active in late June and July, found in
trees and on ground mostly in deciduous forests. Introduced
as biological control agent for caterpillars of gypsy moth
(*Lymantria dispar*) and browntail moths (*Euproctis
chrysorrhea*). Europe, established from New England to
northern Virginia, west to Pennsylvania and West Virginia. (9)

Wilcox's Caterpillar Hunter *Calosoma wilcoxi* LeConte
(15.0–24.0 mm) is metallic dark or bronze green with purple
or golden margins. Head, pronotum, and underside dark
green or black with purplish luster. Antennomere 2 about
one-third length of 3. Flight wings fully developed. Legs
of male with tibiae straight and without setal brush. Adults
most active in spring and prey on caterpillars, found in
various habitats climbing trees or under bark and logs; fly
to light. Québec and Ontario to Georgia, west to Minnesota,
Kansas, and Texas. (9)

Golden Worm and Slug Hunter *Carabus auratus*
Linnaeus (20.0–27.0 mm) is brilliant metallic green with
elytra that each have three distinct ridges. Antennomeres
1–4, femora, and tibiae red. Legs with front tarsomeres 1–4
expanded with spongy setose pads beneath and apical half
of middle tibiae with setal brushes on inside margin in male.
Flightless, diurnal, and long-lived adults active spring and
summer, found in gardens, parks, and open fields, where
they prey mostly on earthworms, caterpillars, and other
invertebrates; first introduced to control gypsy
moth caterpillars in 1908. Europe, established
from Maine to Connecticut. (10)

Woodland Worm and Slug Hunter *Carabus nemoralis*
Müller (21.0–26.0 mm) is black with upper surface more or
less metallic, bronze or coppery green, and sides of pronotum
and elytra usually broadly bluish or violet. Head finely wrinkled,
with fine ridge in front of each eye. Pronotum with broad
basal angles protruding backward. Elytra with rows of widely
spaced punctures, spaces between irregularly sculptured, side
margins smooth; flight wings reduced. Flightless and nocturnal
adults active mostly spring and summer, found in various
disturbed habitats under debris. Europe, established in east
from Maritime Provinces and New England to Virginia, west to
Ontario, Minnesota, and Illinois. (10)

Serrate-shoulder Worm and Slug Hunter *Carabus serratus* Say (15.0–24.0 mm) is elongate-oval, somewhat slender, and black with metallic blue or violet pronotal and elytral margins, and elytra without ridges. Elytra with two or three small notches on sides near base, each with three rows of widely separated punctures, spaces between with three irregular rows of punctures; flight wings fully developed or reduced. Adults active primarily spring and summer, found in various habitats under debris during day; attracted to light. Across southern Canada and northern United States; in east, south to Georgia, Illinois, and Iowa. (10)

Sylvan Worm and Slug Hunter *Carabus sylvosus* Say (21.0–30.0 mm) is dull black with purplish margins. Head with ridge along inside margin of eye, antennomere 3 without ridge and twice as long as 2, and tip of maxillary palp broad. Elytra sometimes faintly purplish overall, each elytron with three rows of shallow pits, spaces between with multiple and uninterrupted rows of close-set punctures. Flightless adults found year-round, active late spring and summer, found under rocks, logs, and other debris; overwinter beneath objects on ground and in soil. Maine and Québec to Florida, west to Ontario, Wisconsin, Kansas, and Texas. (10)

Round Worm and Slug Hunter *Carabus vinctus* (Weber) (20.0–28.0 mm) is black with a brassy sheen, especially on elytra. Antennomere 3 without ridge and twice as long as 2. Elytra each with three distinct ridges higher and wider than rest and interrupted by large pits, spaces between finely ridged. Front tarsomeres 1–4 broad in male. Adults active spring through fall, found in wet deciduous woodlands, often near water under leaf litter, bark, logs; also attracted to light and banana bait. Ontario to Florida, west to Illinois and Mississippi. (10)

Andrew's Snail-eating Beetle *Scaphinotus andrewsii* (Harris) (18.0–29.9 mm) is elongate-oval and black with bluish or violet luster. Head and mandibles slender, longer than pronotum. Pronotum mostly smooth, punctate on sides, margins narrowly flat and slight elevated, longer than wide, somewhat heart-shaped, with hind angles obtuse. Elytra ovate (egg-shaped) with deep grooves irregularly punctured, spaces between convex. Nocturnal and flightless adults eat snails and berries; active in spring and summer, found under logs, bark, and debris in moist hardwood forests, especially along streams; in pitfall traps. Eleven subspecies inhabit mostly mountain habitats from Pennsylvania to Georgia, west to Ohio and Kentucky. (20)

LeConte's False Snail-eating Beetle *Sphaeroderus stenostomus lecontei* **Dejean** (11.5–15.0 mm) is elongate-oval, somewhat flattened, black, with pronotal depressions, elytra or just elytral margins bluish. Head tapered with four setae across deeply forked labrum, two at base of notch, and black palpi. Pronotum with oblique hind angles. Elytra with 14-16 more or less irregular punctostriate, striae closely punctate, with intervals interrupted at apical half. Tarsi black. Flightless adults found among rocks, and under bark and debris in moist habitats and wetlands. Newfoundland and Maritime Provinces to Georgia, west to Manitoba, Minnesota, and Iowa. (5)

Pan American Big-headed Tiger Beetle *Tetracha carolina* **(Linnaeus)** (12.0–20.0 mm) is metallic purple and green with appendages pale yellowish brown. Head broad with prominent eyes and distinct mandibles. Pronotum with front angles forming lobes extending forward. Elytra bright reddish purple, shiny green on sides, with large pale curved markings on tips. Front tarsi of male widened with setose brushes underneath. Nocturnal adults active mostly in summer, found along sandy and muddy edges of lakes and rivers, and in moist, grassy upland areas; attracted to light. Maryland to Florida panhandle, west to southeastern California. (3)

Virginia Big-headed Tiger Beetle *Tetracha virginica* **(Linnaeus)** (16.0–25.0 mm) is dark green with pale reddish-brown appendages. Head broad, metallic green with prominent eyes and distinct mandibles. Pronotum with front angles forming lobes extending forward. Elytra bluish black, dark green on sides, with small pale mark on tips. Front tarsi of males widened with setose brushes underneath. Nocturnal adults active mostly in summer on wet silt flats, stream cuts, or edges of woods, found during day under debris; fly to light. Opportunistic hunters that prey on various insects. New York and Connecticut to Florida, west to Nebraska and Texas. (3)

Twelve-spotted Tiger Beetle *Cicindela duodecimguttata* **Dejean** (12.0–15.0 mm) is dark brown to blackish above and metallic blue-green underneath. Pronotum widest in front, with front constriction across top not as deep as one in back. Elytral markings are thin and complete, or broken into a series of dots, sometimes 12, never with comma-shaped markings at humerus or with complete lines along sides. Larvae prefer steep banks for burrowing and take two years to reach adulthood. Adults active in spring and early summer, and late summer found along moist edges of ponds and slow-moving streams in upland habitats. Atlantic Canada to Georgia, west to Alberta and Texas. (21)

Hairy-necked Tiger Beetle *Cicindela hirticollis hirticollis* **Say** (10.5–15.0 mm) is brown or reddish brown with thick white markings. Prothorax with tufts of white setae on sides. Elytra with G-shaped mark on humerus. Adult activity peaks spring and early summer, then late summer, found on sandy edges of large rivers and ocean. In east, Atlantic and Gulf coasts, from New Jersey to Louisiana. *Cicindela h. rhodensis* Calder is larger, darker with broken or thin lines, Atlantic Canada, New England, Great Lakes states; *C. h. shelfordi* Graves larger, reddish brown, marking heavy and connected along sides; Mississippi River Valley. (21)

Common Claybank Tiger Beetle *Cicindela limbalis* **Klug** (11.0–16.0 mm) is bright reddish to reddish green with distinct elytral markings. Elytra with middle markings usually straight cross, kinked at middle, and reaching side margin, sometimes short and not reaching side. Underside metallic copper and green. Adults active spring and early summer, again in late summer, found on bare and red clay soils on road banks, forest openings, and sparsely vegetated patches. Across Canada, south to New Jersey, West Virginia, Ohio, Missouri, Kansas, New Mexico, and Utah. DNA analysis suggests this species might be synonymous with *C. splendida* Hentz. (21)

Northern Barrens Tiger Beetle *Cicindela patruela* **Dejean** (12.0–14.0 mm) is iridescent green or greenish brown with distinct white markings on elytra. Elytra with humeral spots and almost complete sinuous band across middle. Larva has a two-year life cycle. Adults are active in spring and later in fall in habitats with dry sandy soils within mixed pine-oak forest, including dirt roads, open and eroded slopes, and in sand quarries; also in sparsely vegetated clearings with sandstone substrate. Québec and Ontario to Georgia, west to Minnesota, Indiana, Kentucky, and Tennessee. (21)

Bronzed Tiger Beetle *Cicindela repanda repanda* **Dejean** (11.0–13.0 mm) is bronze-brown, usually with three distinct whitish markings on each elytron. Prothorax with setae on somewhat parallel sides inconspicuous or absent. Elytron with C-shaped mark at base, sometimes connected to other markings along sides; markings thinner in some populations. Adults active spring and early summer, late summer, found on open sandy beaches, strands, and broad flat rocks along rivers, lakes, and ocean, often in good numbers. Widely distributed in eastern North America. *Cicindela r. novascotiae* Vaurie is redder with smaller markings; Cape Breton Island to Nova Scotia. (21)

69

Wrinkle-fronted Tiger Beetle *Cicindela scutellaris rugifrons* **Dejean** (11.0–14.0 mm) has a relatively chunky body and short legs; males with labrum white, females black. Elytra black (New Jersey pine barrens) or dull green (coastal and southern populations) with white triangles on sides and C-shaped mark on tips. Adults inhabit sparsely vegetated deep sand habitats in spring and fall. East of Appalachia from Massachusetts to North Carolina. Five additional subspecies occur in eastern North America with numerous intergrade populations. (21)

Six-spotted Tiger Beetle *Cicindela sexguttata* **Fabricius** (10.0–14.0 mm) is brilliant metallic green with six white spots on elytra; some individuals or populations with four, two, or no spots. Populations in Nova Scotia black, purplish in Nebraska. Larvae burrow in sandy, clay, or loamy soils along roads and dry creek beds. Adults active in spring and early summer, rarely in fall. Inhabits deciduous woodlands and forests, often seen on sunlit roads, trails, gaps, and edges; hides under bark in winter and during inclement weather. Maritime Provinces to northern Florida, west to South Dakota and Texas. (21)

Splendid Tiger Beetle *Cicindela splendida* **Hentz** (12.0–15.0 mm) has a bright, shiny, green or blue body contrasting with coppery to brick-red elytra (sometimes green in Arkansas, Louisiana). Pronotum about one-third wider than long with wrinkles across surface. Elytra with one or two spots or crescent-shaped spot on outer bases of elytra, short middle band, apical bar, sometimes a dot just before apex. Larva burrows in patchy, open, red clay soils in road cuts, banks, roads, and sparsely vegetated habitats; life cycle two to three years. Adults active late winter through spring, again in late summer and early fall, found in larval habitats. Pennsylvania to South Carolina, west to South Dakota, Wyoming, and Texas. DNA analysis suggests this species might be synonymous with *C. limbalis* Klug. (21)

Oblique-lined Tiger Beetle *Cicindela tranquebarica* **Herbst** (11.0–15.0 mm) is dark brown, gray, or blackish above with thin to broad markings on elytra. Elytra marked with narrow crescent at shoulder, broader bent line at middle with expanded tips and not reaching suture, and wider crescent at tip; no white mark along sides. Underside metallic green and copper to purple. Adults found in many habitats from beach to mountains. Newfoundland to northern Florida, west to Nebraska and northern Texas. A detailed examination of color and pattern variation in this species will likely eliminate many subspecies outside the East. (21)

Eastern Pine Barrens Tiger Beetle *Cicindelidia abdominalis* **(Fabricius)** (8.0–11.0 mm) is shiny black above with hints of greenish blue. Prothorax metallic blue with row of white hairlike setae. Elytra with shallow, sinuate line of greenish pits, markings consist of white marks at middle and tip of each elytron, latter sometimes extending slightly forward along side. Abdomen below brownish and red with scattered white setae; brownish-red upper surface exposed in flight. Adults most common in summer, found along roads, paths, and other open, sandy habitats in pine barren, sand hill, and scrubland habitats. Atlantic and Gulf Coast states, from New York to Florida, west Louisiana. (21)

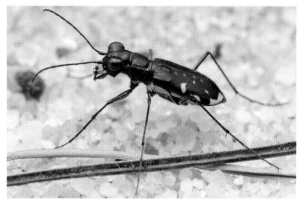

Punctured Tiger Beetle *Cicindelidia punctulata* **(Olivier)** (10.0–13.0 mm) is black to dark olive above with a row of large green or coppery punctures down each side of elytral suture. Head has a labrum with single tooth. Elytra with small spots and short, straight line on outer margin of each elytron near tip. Abdomen protruding from tip of elytra dark. Adults occur in a wide variety of open, sparsely vegetated, and disturbed habitats such as paths, dirt roads, field edges, and eroded gullies during the summer; good fliers and attracted to light. Québec and Maine to Florida, west to Alberta, Montana, Kansas, and Texas. (21)

Eastern Red-bellied Tiger Beetle *Cicindelidia rufiventris rufiventris* **(Dejean)** (9.0–12.0 mm) is dull dark brown to black with thin markings broken up into small spots; underside metallic blue with orangish abdomen. Upper surface of abdomen also orange and clearly visible in flight. Mostly solitary adults active in summer, found in dry, open, upland habitats on rocky outcrops and other sparsely vegetated openings. Massachusetts to Florida panhandle, southwest to Illinois and Missouri. Intergrades with *C. r. cumatilis* (LeConte) (dark blue, markings small or absent) from southern Missouri to Louisiana west to Oklahoma and Texas; dark brown *C. r. hentzi* (Dejean) restricted to moss-covered rocky substrates near Boston. (21)

One-spotted Tiger Beetle *Cylindera unipunctata* **(Fabricius)** (14.0–18.0 mm) is large, dull brown with single white spot on each elytron. Elytra somewhat flat, with many shallow green pits. Underside metallic violet-blue green. Solitary adults active primarily in summer, found in and under leaf litter in shaded woodland habitats, sometimes found in open patches and road tracks on overcast days; weak flier, runs or remains motionless when approached and is easily overlooked. New York to Georgia, west to Missouri, northern Arkansas, and northern Mississippi. (2)

Moustached Tiger Beetle *Ellipsoptera hirtilabris* **(LeConte)** (9.0–11.0 mm) is slender, parallel-sided, pale, leggy, with brown-bronze pattern down elytral suture. Labrum covered with white setae, or "moustache." Head and pronotum densely clothed in white setae. Pronotum longer than wide and narrower than head. Elytral markings with rough edges. Underside and legs mostly covered with white setae. Adults active in summer, sometimes abundant but local on dry, level white sand along trails and roads and in sparsely vegetated patches of white sand in pine scrub flatwoods. Southeastern Georgia and northern Florida. (10)

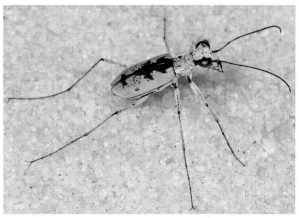

Ghost Tiger Beetle *Ellisoptera lepida* **(Dejean)** (9.0–11.0 mm) is mostly whitish above with white legs. Solitary adult active mostly in midsummer in sandy habitats, including coastal and inland dunes and open, sparsely vegetated sand ridges in wooded areas; populations shrinking due to sand mining and development. Often stands still, difficult to see. Widespread; in east from southern Québec and Ontario to coastal Maryland, southwest along St. Lawrence River to Michigan, Minnesota, Arkansas, and Mississippi River Delta. Federally listed as threatened in United States. (10)

Margined Tiger Beetle *Ellisoptera marginata* **(Fabricius)** (11.0–14.0 mm) is greenish or brownish bronze. Elytra with complete marginal line. Adults prefer coastal and bay habitats with sand-mud substrates, such as salt marshes, saline flats, back beaches, tidal mudflats; also sandy beaches. Active day and night and attracted to lights from February through September; most common in mid-summer. Very wary and will fly out over shallow water and swim back to shore. Atlantic and Gulf coasts, from Maine to Florida. (10)

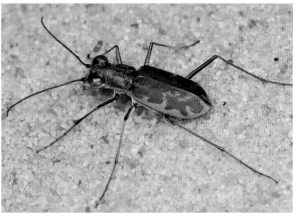

Northeastern Beach Tiger Beetle *Habroscelimorpha dorsalis dorsalis* **(Say)** (13.0–15.0 mm) is mostly white with variable bronze markings; becomes smaller, darker in south. Elytral tips rounded (male) or broadly notched (female). Underside dark bronze to blackish green with dense white setae on thorax. Legs with hind femora long, with one-third extending beyond body, claws nearly as long as last tarsomere. Adults active in summer on open beaches where they feed on amphipods and insects. Massachusetts and shores of Chesapeake Bay in Maryland and Virginia. Federally listed as endangered in the United States. Three additional subspecies further south. (2)

California Marsh and Bog Beetle *Elaphrus californicus* **Mannerheim** (6.3–8.0 mm) is dull greenish to brassy above, metallic green below. Elytra with large purple impressions. Tibia and part of femora reddish, hind femur with long whitish setae on broad dorsal surface near apex. Males with front tarsi 1–3 dilated. Adults somewhat gregarious and found running over sparsely vegetated wet ground, muddy edges of ponds and lakes, and silted shores of streams and rivers year-round, especially in late spring and summer; overwinter in higher, drier habitats. Widely distributed throughout North America. (11)

American Round Sand Beetle *Omophron americanum* **Dejean** (5.0–7.0 mm) is broadly oval, convex, with metallic luster on dark areas. Head with V-shaped pale area. Pronotum with dark spot broad across base and interior margins of pale sides uneven. Scutellum not visible. Elytra mostly dark, sides not forming continuous arc with sides of pronotum. Adults found mostly in spring and summer along open beaches or rivers, lakes, ponds, and other bodies of water; occasionally fly to light. When alarmed, adults run, make a squeaking noise, or quickly burrow into sand. Newfoundland to Florida panhandle, west to Idaho and northeastern Arizona; Mexico. (6)

73

Large-lipped Round Sand Beetle *Omophron labiatum* **(Fabricius)** (4.8–6.3 mm) is broadly oval, convex, with dark areas lacking metallic luster. Pronotum mostly dark with wide pale margins even, sides forming continuous arc with sides of elytra. Scutellum not visible. Elytra mostly dark, with grooves somewhat indistinct along sides and at tips. Front tarsi of males expanded and covered underneath with setose pads. Mostly nocturnal adults are fast runners and strong burrowers, found on wet sand near streams mostly in spring and summer; attracted to light. Coastal provinces and states, Nova Scotia to Florida, west to southeastern Texas. (6)

Mosaic Round Sand Beetle *Omophron tessellatum* **Say** (5.4–7.0 mm) is broadly oval, convex, with metallic green markings. Head with pale M-shaped area. Pronotum with central dark area not reaching front or basal margins. Scutellum not visible. Sides of pronotum and elytra not forming a continuous arc. Elytra with light and dark areas about even. Mostly nocturnal adults found year-round on wet sand near bodies of water in varied habitats, fast runners and strong burrowers; collected by splashing water on shore, also attracted to light. In east from Maritime Provinces and New England to Virginia, west to Minnesota and Texas. (6)

Digger Slope-rumped Beetle *Clivina fossor* **(Linnaeus)**
(5.5–6.5 mm) is mostly brown or black, with head and
prothorax loosely attached to rest of body; appendages
reddish. Pronotum same color or paler than elytra, sides
each with one very small tooth toward base. Elytra
sometime reddish along sides, surface, including suture,
without markings, each with four seta-bearing punctures;
flight wings fully developed or reduced. Abdominal ventrite
2 without lines, 3–6 with microscopic meshlike sculpturing.
Middle tibiae with long, sharp protuberance tipped with
single seta. Adults active in spring and summer; attracted to
light. Europe; in east from Maritime Provinces to New York,
west to Ontario, Wisconsin, and Illinois. (16)

Pale Slope-rumped Beetle *Clivina pallida* **Say**
(4.0–5.2 mm) is slender, elongate, and uniformly reddish
brown. Head with frons smooth. Lateral bead of pronotum
attains basal margin. Middle tibia with prominent, spine-like
peg on outer edge near apex. Elytra each typically with
four setigerous punctures, striae wide with wavy edges.
Nocturnal adults found in mixed woodlands nearly year
round under bark of loblolly pine (*Pinus taeda*) logs, stones,
wood, and in tree hollows. Maine to Florida, west to Indiana
and Texas. (16)

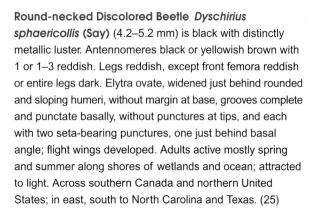

Round-necked Discolored Beetle *Dyschirius*
sphaericollis **(Say)** (4.2–5.2 mm) is black with distinctly
metallic luster. Antennomeres black or yellowish brown with
1 or 1–3 reddish. Legs reddish, except front femora reddish
or entire legs dark. Elytra ovate, widened just behind rounded
and sloping humeri, without margin at base, grooves complete
and punctate basally, without punctures at tips, and each
with two seta-bearing punctures, one just behind basal
angle; flight wings developed. Adults active mostly spring
and summer along shores of wetlands and ocean; attracted
to light. Across southern Canada and northern United
States; in east, south to North Carolina and Texas. (25)

Two-spot Slope-rumped Beetle *Paraclivina bipustulata*
(Fabricius) (6.0–7.5 mm) is elongate, cylindrical, mostly
brown or black, with head and prothorax loosely attached to
rest of body. Pronotum nearly smooth, without punctures.
Elytra with deeply punctate grooves (punctostriate) with basal
and preapical red spots that nearly reach suture. Antennae,
middle and hind legs reddish; middle tibiae preapical peg
absent. Adults are burrowers and found year-round, active
especially in spring and summer in various lowland habitats,
usually in layers of leaf litter, roots of shore grasses, or
decaying plant debris along shorelines; often attracted to
lights. Ontario to Florida, west Wisconsin and Texas. (16)

74

Green Semipoint-mouth Beetle *Semiardistomis viridis* **(Say)** (5.0 mm) is elongate-oval, convex, and shiny greenish black; appendages reddish brown. Head with long, slender mandibles. Pronotum convex, smooth, with impressed line down middle. Elytra not grooved, but with rows of fine, shallow punctures, each bearing a seta distinctly visible from side. Underside with long, sparse setae. Legs with front tibiae each with long tooth at tip, tarsomeres broad in both sexes, wider and notched in male. Adults are found spring and summer along stream and river banks; attracted to light. New York to Florida, west to Wisconsin, and Texas. (2)

Margined Warrior Beetle *Pasimachus marginatus* **(Fabricius)** (26.0–32.0 mm) is black, with or without violet margins. Antennomeres 2–4 more or less sharply ridged and abdominal ventrites 3–5 without setae-bearing punctures. Base of pronotum margined next to scutellum, margins extend to sides or not. Elytra distinctly ridged with widely expanded margins. Flightless adults active in summer in open, dry or sandy habitats on open ground at night in summer or hiding under loose bark on logs or in burrows beneath logs during day. Maryland to Florida, west to Texas, and north up Mississippi River. (6)

Moderately Sulcate Warrior Beetle *Pasimachus subsulcatus* Say (19.0–22.0 mm) is black. Head flattened between eyes, antennomeres each ridged on top and bulging on tip, labrum deeply lobed with middle lobe rounded. Elytra smooth, without raised intervals, ridge at humeri short and not sharp, with sides rounded or nearly parallel at middle. Middle tibiae with fixed spine slender and pointed at tip. Flightless adults active spring through fall, found on ground or under debris in sparsely vegetated sandhill habitats. Coastal Plain, from South Carolina to Florida, west to Louisiana. (6)

Tunneling Large Pedunculate Beetle *Scarites subterraneus* Fabricius (15.0–30.0 mm) is elongate, robust, parallel-sided, with forebody loosely attached to rest of body. Head with large mandibles, antennomeres 8–10 moniliform. Pronotum somewhat square, widest near middle, with hind angles rounded. Elytra without ridges at humeri, each with six complete and widely separated shallow grooves, outermost groove next to side margin incomplete. Front tibiae with one small tooth followed by three large ones. Adults most active spring and summer; attracted to light. Throughout eastern North America. (6)

Carved Sloped Beetle *Clinidium sculptile* **(Newman)** (6.5–7.6 mm) is elongate, narrow, and shiny reddish brown. Pronotum with deep groove down middle flanked by two short, deep impressions; underside of male with central patch of setae. Elytra deeply grooved, spaces between without punctures. Female third and fourth abdominal sternites depressed at sides. Flightless adults are typically found in spring and early summer, and again in summer and fall under bark or in partially decayed wood of logs, dead roots, and lower stumps of pitch pine (*Pinus rigida*) and tulip tree (*Liriodendron tulipifera*). New York to Florida, west to Indiana and Louisiana. (5)

American Crudely Carved Wrinkle Beetle *Omoglymmius americanus* **(Laporte)** (6.0–8.0 mm) is elongate, narrow, and shiny reddish brown to dark brown. Back of head broad with upper surface divided by a distinct groove down middle. Pronotum with three deep grooves. Elytra have distinct rows of punctures. Adults and larvae live in various fungus-infested deciduous trees, especially elm (*Ulmus*), maple (*Acer*), and oak (*Quercus*); adults are seldom found outside this habitat. Ontario and New York to Florida, west to Minnesota and Texas. (1)

76

Trechus apicalis **Motschulsky** (4.0–4.7 mm) is light brown to black, appendages and elytra paler, and elytra without setae. Head without distinct neck, and mouthparts with last two palpomeres about equal in size. Eyes present, each surrounded by distinct groove and two setae above. Pronotum with hind angles each without small tooth. Adults found under leaves and stones in damp habitats. Elytra combined with fewer than 11 grooves, each with a groove along suture curving back up and a broad groove along side at tip. Alaska, across Canada, south through Rockies to Colorado, also Ohio and Appalachia to West Virginia. (65)

Bembidion castor **Lindroth** (3.4–4.3 mm) is black with a brassy head and pronotum; appendages reddish yellow-brown. Antennomeres 2–3 at least partly pale on top. Legs with femora and tibiae reddish yellow to brownish red. Elytra black or blackish with irregular pale and broken bands at base, middle, and just before tips not reaching suture. Adults active mostly spring and summer along borders of running water, wetlands, and ocean beaches; attracted to light. Across Canada; in east, south to Virginia, Ohio, and Iowa. *Bembidion* is a large genus; species sometimes challenging to identify. (253 NA)

Bembidion rapidum (**LeConte**) (3.8–4.4 mm) is black with brassy, greenish, or bluish reflections, and reddish antennal bases and legs. Head with eyes large, mouthparts with slender tip of maxillary palp short. Pronotum not strongly constricted at base, with obtuse hind angles. Elytra not iridescent, each with only one spot near tips, surface punctures not in contact with grooves; elytral grooves fine, distinct from bases to tips, densely punctate along basal half. Abdominal ventrites each with one pair of seta-bearing punctures. Adults active spring and summer in open, wet habitats; flies to light. *Bembidion* is a large genus; species sometimes challenging to identify. (253 NA)

Mioptachys flavicauda (**Say**) (1.5–1.8 mm) is very small, blackish brown, with apical third of elytra and all appendages pale. Head without grooves. Pronotum wider than long, margins broad and pale. Elytra each usually with 1–4 punctured grooves. Adults found year-round under loose bark of dead or dying trees and logs, especially hardwoods (*Acer*, *Juglans*, *Populus*); occasionally attracted to light in spring and summer. Widespread in North America; in east from Nova Scotia to Florida, west to Dakotas and Texas. (1)

Paratachys rhodeanus (**Casey**) (2.8–3.0 mm) is brown or reddish brown with pale appendages and elytral markings. Head small with pair of deep pits on underside behind mouthparts on mentum, flattened eyes, and long, slender antennae. Pronotum as wide in front as at base, distinctly sinuate before posterior angles. Elytra with anterior discal seta-bearing puncture near stria 4, large, dark central cloud and dark spots at base. Fast-running adults are strong burrowers and found at base of plants and under stones and litter along margins of marshes, lakes, and slow-moving rivers spring through summer; crepuscular and nocturnal, attracted to light. Maritime Provinces to South Carolina, west to Ontario, Ohio, and Alabama. (11)

Tachyta kirbyi **Casey** (2.6–3.0 mm) is small and dull black with grooves flanking suture curved upward at tips along side margins. Head with area between furrows somewhat convex at middle, antennomere 2 longer than 3, underneath with plate behind mouthparts without pits. Pronotum with side margins shallow, sinuation short in basal half, angle slightly obtuse. Elytra each with three seta-bearing punctures, one at base next to scutellum. Males with front tarsomeres 1–2 expanded with setose pads underneath. Adults found nearly year-round under bark of fallen trees; attracted to light. In east from Maritime Provinces and New England to Ontario. (4)

77

Patrobus longicornis **(Say)** (9.0–15.0 mm) is shiny black with reddish-brown antennae and paler legs. Head and pronotum narrower than elytra. Eyes each with two setae above. Antennae half as long as body. Pronotum with sides sinuate behind middle, with deep furrow across front and down middle, and basal impression deep and coarsely punctate. Elytra lack margin across base; flight wings developed or reduced. Adults active spring and summer, usually found near water; attracted to light. Throughout eastern North America to northern Florida and Oklahoma. (3)

Narrow-necked Little Bombardier Beetle *Brachinus tenuicollis* **LeConte** (11.9–14.5 mm) is mostly reddish above with blue-black elytra. Head with mentum glabrous. Sides of pterothorax dark. Elytra distinctly ribbed, ribs glabrous at base, with intervals clothed in short, pale setae. Abdomen reddish, becoming darker at sides, more toward thorax. Legs uniformly reddish. Nocturnal adults are gregarious and often found hiding under rocks and debris in spring through fall in various habitats, especially around water; fly to light. Larvae are ectoparasitoids of pupae of giant water scavenger (*Hydrophilus*, Hydrophilidae). Québec and Ontario to Florida, west to Wyoming and New Mexico. (28)

Cyclotrachelus sigillatus **(Say)** (15.2–19.8 mm) is shiny black, narrow with a "waist," and sides of elytra moderately rounded. Penultimate palpomere with 4-5 setae along front edge. Pronotum square, widest before middle, deeply impressed across front at middle, sides mostly straight, with or without shallow sinuation in front of posterior angle. Elytra somewhat dull. Front tarsi of males with setose pads on tarsomeres 1–3. Nocturnal and flightless adults active mostly during spring and summer in various open and wooded habitats and attracted to light; days spent sheltered under rocks, logs, and other debris. Massachusetts to Florida panhandle, west to West Virginia and Alabama. (40)

Myas cyanescens **Dejean** (13.5–15.5 mm) is robust, shiny black, usually with strong metallic purplish or violet luster on elytra and pale red appendages. Mouthparts with tips of palpomeres widened. Pronotum convex, broad as elytra, with marginal beads along sides not particularly widened at basal half. Elytra with deep grooves lacking punctures and underturned rim pale reddish; flight wings reduced. Legs with front tarsomeres 1–3 expanded in male. Abdomen underneath tipped with two (male) or usually four (female) setae. Flightless adults found in leaf litter and under debris in spring and summer; attracted to light. Maritime Provinces to Georgia, west to Minnesota and Alabama. (3)

Poecilus chalcites (Say) (10.0–13.0 mm) is green, bronze to almost black above, black underneath. Antennomeres 1–3 reddish, 2–3 finely ridged and somewhat flattened. Pronotum slightly wider than long, widest just before middle, with sides and outer basal margins distinctly defined by fine groove or bead. Elytra with epipleura interrupted or crossed by ridge near tip; flight wings fully developed. Front tarsomeres 1–3 widened with setose pads underneath. Nocturnal adults active year-round, found under debris during day in disturbed habitats and wetland edges; attracted to light. New Brunswick to Florida, west to Colorado, Kansas, and New Mexico. (2)

Poecilus lucublandus (Say) (9.0–14.0 mm) is greenish or coppery, bluish, or black above. Antennomeres 2–3 somewhat flattened and finely ridged. Pronotum without distinct marginal bead along sides, outermost impression at base indefinitely delimited. Elytra with deep and sometimes fine punctures; flight wings slightly reduced, occasional flier. Abdomen with two (male) or four (female) setae near tip. Underside black. Adults active mostly spring and summer in many disturbed areas and other; attracted to light. Across southern Canada and northern United States; in east, south to Georgia, Tennessee, Missouri, and Kansas. (2)

Pterostichus adoxus (Say) (12.9–15.2 mm) is shiny black with iridescent elytra and dark reddish-brown antennae and mouthparts. Pronotum with posterior angles obtuse, blunt. Tip of abdomen underneath with two setae in male, four in female. Male with front tarsomeres 1–3 dilated, thick pads of setae underneath; apical tarsomeres in both sexes without setae underneath. Flightless and nocturnal adults active in spring and summer in deciduous and mixed forests in wet habitats, often under loose bark of fallen trees, or inside or under decaying logs. Cape Breton Island to Minnesota, south along the Appalachian Mountains to Tennessee and South Carolina. (~180 NA)

Amara pallipes Kirby (6.2–8.0 mm) is oval and shiny black with brassy reflection, with reddish-brown appendages. Head with a pair of seta-bearing punctures above each eye. Pronotum with a single seta-bearing puncture at each hind angle. Elytra with side margins crossed over themselves behind middle. Legs with apical tibial spur on front legs with three teeth. Adults feed on seeds and are found in meadows and cultivated fields, along roads, and in other open, often grassy habitats, especially near water. Southern Canada and northern United States; in east, south to Virginia, Iowa, and Minnesota. (105 NA)

Acupalpus testaceus Dejean (2.5–3.0 mm) is small, slender, uniformly reddish brown above, elytra with or without diffuse patch. Head pale with eyes dark; underneath without small tooth immediately behind mouthparts. Pronotum sometimes darker, wide as long, sides broadly curved, hind angles distinctly rounded, with hind margin shallowly impressed with a few large punctures at middle. Elytra with short groove on either side of suture faint or absent. Male with front tarsi unmodified. Adults active spring and summer in leaf litter; attracted to light. New England and Québec to Florida, west to Ontario, South Dakota, and Texas. (13)

Amphasia interstitialis (Say) (8.5–10.2 mm) is oval and bicolored with head, pronotum, and appendages reddish yellow or reddish brown, elytra blackish. Pronotum wider than long, coarsely and roughly punctate at base, sparse elsewhere. Elytral surface mostly dark with suture and side margins paler, grooves finely punctate, spaces between grooves somewhat convex, conspicuously punctate, and covered with short golden setae. Front tarsomeres 2–4 wide and densely setose underneath in male. Adults found under stones, logs, and leaf litter; overwinter under stones and in litter and debris. Québec and Ontario to South Carolina, west to South Dakota, and Texas. (2)

80

Anisodactylus rusticus (Say) (7.2–12.6 mm) is dull black. Head with one seta on each side of clypeus, antennomeres 1–2 pale. Pronotum widest at base, with sides expanded, translucent, and becoming wider at base. Elytra with basal margin not ending in a small tooth at basal angle when viewed from above, grooves somewhat deep, and spaces between flat, and tips moderately sinuate; flight wings fully developed. Legs blackish with femora darker, front tibia with spur three-pronged. Adults active spring and summer in open and disturbed habitats; attracted to light. Prince Edward Island to Florida, west to Manitoba, Wyoming, Colorado, and eastern Texas. (20)

Anisodactylus sanctaecrucis (Fabricius) (8.0–10.5 mm) is bicolored with head, pronotum, underside black, pronotal margins and elytra brownish or yellowish. Underside of head with plate (mentum) behind mouth lacking a tooth. Pronotum widest before middle, sides sinuate to distinct hind angles. Elytra almost flat between grooves, with or without a darkened cloud not extended to base. Males with foot pads on front and middle legs. Adults active spring and summer, found in various habitats on open ground, under bark and debris; attracted to light. North America; in east from Maritime Provinces and New England to Georgia, west to Ontario and Louisiana. (20)

Cratacanthus dubius (Palisot de Beauvois) (7.5–11.5 mm) is blackish to black, somewhat shiny, without setae, ventral surface paler, and appendages pale to dark reddish brown. Head broad, larger in male, both sexes with triangular process in front of each eye and projecting over bases of antennae and angulate ridge on mandible. Pronotum with sides broadly rounded and distinctly sinuate at base. Elytra shorter in male, both sexes with grooves not punctate and spaces between slightly convex; wings developed for flight or not. Tarsi not or only slightly expanded. Adults found in open, sandy, or disturbed habitats in summer; flies to light. In east from New York to Florida, west to southern Alberta, and southern Arizona; Mexico. (1)

Euryderus grossus (Say) (10.5–16.5 mm) is robust and somewhat shiny black with mouthparts, appendages, and side margins lighter brown. Eyes each with one seta above. Pronotum with two setae on sides, at middle and rear angles. Elytra each with two rows of several deep punctures, each with a single long seta. Front tibiae with long, thick, fingerlike projection on side at tip. Adults active late spring and summer in mostly open habitats; attracted to light. Across southern Canada and northern United States, in east, south to Georgia and Texas. (1)

81

Geopinus incrassatus (Dejean) (13.0–17.0 mm) is robust, convex, and mostly pale reddish yellow-brown. Head short, not narrowed behind eyes. Pronotum mostly smooth, wider than long, widest in front of middle; front and base of equal width, sides sinuate just before hind angles. Elytra distinctly grooved, areas between slightly convex. Front tarsomeres 2–4 of male with spongy setose pads underneath. Nocturnal adults active year-round, feed on seeds and caterpillars, found walking on or burrowing in sandy soils, wet sand, and dunes, especially along rivers and streams; attracted to light. New England and Québec to southern Georgia, west to Idaho, Nevada, and northern Arizona. (1)

Harpalus caliginosus (Fabricius) (14.0–35.0 mm) is mostly black with male shinier than female; antennomeres 1–2 and tarsi reddish brown. Head with punctures coarser and denser near eyes. Pronotum distinctly wider than long, as wide as base of elytra, and with hind angles squared. Elytral striae deep, punctate, with intervals convex, third interval without setae-bearing punctures. Adults found nearly year-round in open habitats on ground, under debris; sometimes attracted to light in large numbers. They feed on insects, pollen, and seeds. Stridulate and release pungent odor in smokelike cloud when threatened. Widespread across southern Canada and United States. (46)

Harpalus erythropus **Dejean** (10.6–13.2 mm) is black, faintly shiny with reddish-brown appendages. Pronotum nearly square, with sides slightly curved and a broad depression near each posterior angle. Elytra with bases mostly impunctate, deeply grooved, grooves without punctures. Front and middle tarsi of males dilated; hind legs of both sexes with tarsomeres 1–4 grooved on outer sides; all apical tarsomeres with or without dorsal setae. Nocturnal adults active mostly in spring and summer and fly to light in various open habitats, edges, and open woods, also near human dwellings; found under stones and other debris during day. Widely distributed in eastern North America. (46)

Harpalus faunus **Say** (8.4-13.0 mm) is uniformly dark reddish brown. Pronotum almost square, with sides broadly translucent, front half smooth, and impressions at base broad, shallow, and punctate, punctures extending across base. Elytra grooved, spaces between without setae, smooth (male) or punctate toward sides at base only (female). Middle and hind tarsi with sparse setae on top. Adults found year-round. New England and Québec to Florida panhandle, west to Manitoba, Dakotas, Colorado, and Arizona. (46)

Notiobia terminata **(Say)** (7.5–9.1 mm) is oblong-oval, black; front of head, sometimes between eyes, pronotal and elytral margins reddish yellow-brown. Head with labial palpomere 2 with several setae, underneath with plate behind mouthparts with distinct tooth in front. Pronotum with rear angles rounded. Elytra with greenish or bluish luster, without tooth on basal angle, epipleura reddish yellow-brown. Abdomen with two (male) or four (female) setae near tip. Male with front and middle tarsomeres expanded with spongy setose pads below, middle tarsomeres usually with a few setae on top, hind tarsomere 1 about as long as 2–3 combined. Adults found in various habitats; attracted to light. Widespread in eastern North America. (5)

Selenophorus opalinus **(LeConte)** (9.2–10.7 mm) is black with distinctly iridescent elytra; underside sometimes paler. Pronotum and elytra with pale margins. Elytra each with three rows of small setae, with tips sinuate and pointed. Tip of abdomen underneath with two setae in male, four in female. Male with front and middle tarsomeres 1–3 dilated, with thick pads of setae underneath. Nocturnal adults found year-round in open habitats, along forest edges, and in disturbed areas, especially those with sandy, sparsely vegetated soils; flies to light. New Brunswick to Florida, west to southeastern Manitoba, South Dakota, and eastern Texas. (19)

Stenolophus comma (Fabricius) (5.3–7.7 mm) is yellowish brown with spot on elytra; appendages pale except antennomeres 3 or 4-11 darker. Head blackish. Pronotum reddish brown, with or without dark spot at center, sides in front of middle not sinuate, and hind angles broadly rounded. Scutellum flanked by short grooves on elytra. Elytra each with dark spot extended forward only on second interval out from suture that is about same color as sides. First hind tarsomere not ridged, not distinctly longer than 2. Across North America, south to South Carolina, northern Alabama, and southeastern California. (16)

Stenolophus lecontei (Chaudoir) (5.3–7.2 mm) is mostly yellowish brown with dark stripes flanking elytral suture. Head black or blackish with two reddish spots on top. Pronotum pale or with central dark spot, with basal margin or bead absent. Elytra with dark stripes often extended forward on the inside (*S. lineola* similar, stripes extended on outside and suture lighter), or not, meshlike microsculpture, and darker along suture than rest of surface. Tarsomeres 5 without setae underneath. Adults found in spring and summer in various habitats; attracted to light. Maine to Florida, west to South Dakota and eastern Texas. (16)

Stenolophus lineola (Fabricius) (7.0–9.1 mm) is pale reddish yellow with with a dark mark between the eyes and two distinct spots on pronotum. Elytra with outer and inner margins of dark areas closest to base. Adults are active from spring through early fall and found in various habitats. They eat insects and corn seeds; occasionally a pest in cornfields. Commonly collected at light and in pitfall traps. Across southern Canada and United States. (16)

Stenolophus ochropezus (Say) (4.8–6.7 mm) is blackish with all margins on pronotum and elytra pale. Pronotum with broad, shallow, distinctly punctate impressions at base. Elytra distinctly iridescent. Legs and first two or three antennomeres pale yellowish brown. Adults are active from spring through fall in various habitats and commonly attracted to light, sometimes in large numbers. Nova Scotia to Florida, west to Saskatchewan, Texas, and California. (16)

Trichotichnus dichrous (Dejean) (9.0–11.0 mm) is bicolored with head and pronotum reddish yellow or blackish and usually with reddish-brown pronotal margins, and elytra distinctly iridescent; appendages pale. Pronotum with sides not sinuate in basal half, side depressions becoming wider behind marginal seta. Elytral grooves without punctures, surface microscopically wrinkled. Adults active in summer; attracted to light. New Hampshire and Québec to Georgia, west to Alberta and Arizona. (3)

Badister neopulchellus Lindroth (5.0–6.2 mm) is bicolored with distinctly iridescent head and pronotum. Head black and right mandible crossed with deep notch, left mandible normal. Pronotum and elytra orange or yellowish brown. Pronotum narrowest at base, broadly notched in front, with front angles rounded and not protruding, and base distinctly margined within hind angles. Elytra shallowly grooved, spaces between flat; flight wings developed. Front tarsomeres expanded, tarsomere 5 on all tarsi setose underneath. Adults found year-round along edges of standing waters; attracted to light. Widespread in North America; in east, south to Georgia and Kansas. (13)

84

Dicaelus elongatus Bonelli (14.0–19.0 mm) is somewhat shiny, black. Head with outer margins of mandibles nearly symmetrical, labial palpomere 2 with two setae, and antennae mostly pale, dark at base. Pronotum somewhat squarish and sides with three or more seta-bearing punctures along slightly raised margins. Elytra with grooves deep and without punctures, spaces between convex and granular, with a ridge along side extending from basal angle to apical third. Adults active spring and summer, found on ground, tree trunks. Maine and Ontario to Florida, west to South Dakota and Texas. (11)

Dicaelus purpuratus Bonelli (20.0–25.0 mm) is large and typically purplish, sometime black or greenish. Head with mandibles asymmetrical, labial palpomere 2 with four setae, and antennae mostly pale, dark at base. Pronotum squarish, margins distinctly raised with hind angles narrowly rounded, and almost wide as elytra. Elytra with grooves deep and without punctures, spaces between convex, with a ridge along sides from basal angle to apical third. Adults active spring through fall, found under logs, bark, and other debris. Massachusetts and Ontario to Georgia, west to Wisconsin, and eastern Texas. (11)

Dicaelus sculptilis Say (14.0–26.0 mm) is broad, somewhat convex and shining. Head broad. Pronotum rectangular, broadest at base. Elytra with broad ridges interrupted by ringlike punctures, ridge at basal angle sharply raised, spaces between ridges wider with more ringlike punctures. Nocturnal and flightless adults active spring and summer, found under logs and stones, on tree trunks in various habitats; collected in pitfall traps. Three subspecies based on pronotal and elytral sculpturing. Ontario to Virginia, west to Iowa, Kansas, and Oklahoma. (11)

Diplocheila striatopunctata **(LeConte)** (12.5–17.9 mm) is black, sometimes with even intervals on elytra brown or reddish. Left mandible with small bump usually visible from side. Pronotum with side margins straight or slightly sinuate behind middle, angles broad. Elytra with deep grooves punctate, spaces between slightly convex, with one or no seta-bearing punctures; flight wings developed. Adults active mostly spring and summer on shorelines next to permanent standing water, including ditches and canals; attracted to light. Good burrowers and swimmers. Widespread, in east from southern New England and Québec to New Jersey, west to Ontario, Minnesota, and Kansas. (8)

Panagaeus fasciatus Say (8.2–9.0 mm) is brown or blackish, bristling with erect setae, with reddish-brown or orange elytra marked with black band behind middle and black tips. Elytra with rows of widely spaced, deep punctures. Front tarsi of males wide with setose pads underneath. Adults active primarily spring and summer, found under loose bark and debris on ground; attracted to light. Massachusetts to Florida, west to Ontario, Illinois, Kansas, and Texas. *Panagaeus crucigerus* Say (11.0–11.5 mm) is similar in form, black with two large reddish-orange spots on each elytron; Delaware to Florida, west to Indiana and Texas. (2)

Chlaenius aestivus Say (14.5–17.0 mm) has a metallic green or bronze head and pronotum and dull, blue-black elytra. Head with mandibles short and curved, antennomere 3 longer than 1 + 2 and 4. Pronotum nearly long as wide, densely punctured, distinctly sinuate at sides near base, with a seta-bearing puncture near each hind angle. Elytra grooved with fine punctures, spaces between with fine, indistinct punctures, humeri distinct, with hind wings fully developed or not. Legs reddish yellow-brown, middle tibiae near tips with setal brushes on outer surface in male. Adults active spring through summer, found under rocks and logs; occasionally attracted to light. Massachusetts and Ontario to Florida, west to Wisconsin, Missouri, and Arkansas. (34)

Chlaenius niger **Randall** (11.3–15.0 mm) is entirely black, pronotum and elytra setose, with flattened margins of pronotum sometimes brown. Head with a pair of seta-bearing punctures above, mandibles short, curved. Pronotum with coarse punctures becoming dense in depression across base, widest just behind middle, sides broadly rounded, and with seta-bearing punctures at hind angles. Front tarsi of male broad, with thick and setose pads underneath. Elytra conspicuously pubescent. Nocturnal adults active year-round, found along moist edges of wetlands; attracted to light. Can stay underwater for several minutes. Throughout eastern North America. (34)

Chlaenius sericeus **(Forster)** (11.4–16.1 mm) is setose, bright metallic green, occasionally with a bronze or bluish luster; appendages reddish brown. Head shiny, with mandibles short and curved, with two seta-bearing punctures above each eye. Antennomere 3 longer than 1 and 2, longer than 4. Pronotum less shiny, slightly wider than long, sides slightly sinuate behind middle, hind angles obtuse with a single puncture bearing a long seta. Elytra dull with shallow grooves with fine punctures; hind wings fully developed. Underside black. Legs of male with front tarsomeres broad and setose underneath. Widely distributed in North America. (34)

Chlaenius tomentosus **(Say)** (12.5–18.0 mm) is broadly oval, bronze or green with head shiny, pronotum less so, elytra dull; appendages mostly black; antennomere 1 pale. Pronotum coarsely punctured throughout, with four or more seta-bearing punctures along each side, widest and densely punctate at base. Elytra with bases sharp, rectangular. Usually nocturnal adults active mostly late spring and summer, found in many habitats, especially disturbed areas; attracted to light. Maine to Florida, west to southern Alberta and southeastern Arizona. (34)

Oodes fluvialis **(LeConte)** (11.6–14.8 mm) is large, dull black, oval, somewhat flattened, with base of pronotum as wide as base of elytra. Labrum with six seta-bearing punctures, clypeus with two. Pronotum with a seta-bearing puncture on each side at middle, but not at hind angles. Elytra with uniformly impressed grooves, punctures distinct but of variable depth and distance to one another, each with two seta-bearing punctures. Front tarsi of males somewhat expanded, middle and hind tarsi not densely setose underneath. Wetland edges; attracted to light. New England and Québec to Florida, west to Ontario, Minnesota, and Louisiana. Distinguished from *O. americanus* Dejean (Coastal Plain, Maryland to Louisiana) only by male genitalia. (4)

86

Leptotrachelus dorsalis (Fabricius) (7.0–8.5 mm) is elongate, with narrow head and slender prothorax, and long elytra completely covering abdomen; appendages and elytra yellowish brown. Head blackish, shiny, longer than prothorax. Prothorax cylindrical, usually dark or blackish. Elytra about twice width of prothorax, with rows of deep, close-set punctures, spaces between slightly convex. Tarsi broad with tarsomere 4 deeply notched and bilobed. Larvae prey on caterpillars. Adults active late spring and early summer, found in leaf litter and on foliage, including corn (*Zea*), and sugar cane (*Saccharum*). Rhode Island and Connecticut to Florida, west to Ontario, South Dakota, and Texas. (3)

Agonum extensicolle (Say) (6.8–10.4 mm) is elongate, shiny black, and distinctly metallic, with head and pronotum greenish or bronze, elytra dark bronze, bright green, or purplish; mouthparts, legs, antennomeres 1–3 or 4 reddish yellow-brown. Neck without broad depression across top when viewed from side. Pronotum with sides straight or sinuate at base, narrower than elytra, and base roughly punctate, impression with/without small bump. Elytra with shallow grooves without punctures, intervals with row of 4–5 seta-bearing punctures; flight wings developed or reduced. Maritime Provinces and Québec to Florida, west to Alberta, Montana, Utah, and Arizona. (130 NA)

87

Agonum octopunctatum (Fabricius) (7.5–8.5 mm) is elongate, bright metallic green. Head with broad groove across neck when viewed from side, antennal bases brown, antennomere 3 with setae only around tip. Pronotum wider than long with sides rounded to very finely margined base, depressions ill-defined. Elytra with grooves without punctures or finely punctate, spaces between flat, each with distinct humeri and row of four distinct seta-bearing pits, area next to suture brassy, sides contrasting greenish; flight wings developled. Tarsomere 5 with long setae underneath. Adults active mostly spring and summer, found in moist habitats and fields; attracted to light. Maritime Provinces and New England to Florida, west to Manitoba and Texas. (54)

Calathus opaculus LeConte (7.5–11.0 mm) is elongate-oval, dark reddish black or blackish with pale pronotal and eltyral margins; appendages yellowish brown. Head and pronotum shiny, elytra dull. Pronotum wider than long, with sides slightly curved and nearly parallel and becoming wider toward rounded hind angles. Elytra dull with grooves shallow and not punctate; flight wings developed. Nocturnal adults active year-round, under rocks and leaves during the day; occasionally at light. New England and Québec to Florida, west to Ontario, Michigan, Colorado, Utah, and Arizona. (5)

Platynus cincticollis **(Say)** (10.5–11.5 mm) is shiny blackish or black, with margins of pronotum and elytra paler. Head with neck broadly impressed when viewed from side. Pronotum small, short, widest just before middle, side margins flattened and narrowed toward base, and hind angles indicated by small, blunt tooth. Elytra with fine grooves lacking punctures, spaces between flat, and each elytron with three seta-bearing punctures. Hind femora with setae on front edge, hind tarsomere 5 without distinct setae underneath. Nocturnal adults active mostly spring and summer, found on tree trunks, under bark and debris; attracted to light. Widespread in eastern North America to Georgia and Texas. (10)

Platynus tenuicollis **(LeConte)** (9.5–13.0 mm) is slender, shiny black except for pale pronotal margins and elytral margins and suture. Pronotum with hind angles distinct to rounded, with basal impression lacking punctures. Elytra with or without impression across apical fourth. All legs with tarsomere 5 lacking setae underneath, middle and hind tarsomeres 1–3 each with a ridge on top. Nocturnal adults active spring and summer in deciduous and mixed forests, found under debris during day, on tree trunks at night; attracted to light. Cape Breton Island to Georgia, west Colorado and Texas. (10)

Synuchus impunctatus **(Say)** (8.7–11.2 mm) is mostly black with paler pronotal and elytral margins, space between suture and first groove reddish, ventral surface paler, and appendages reddish. Pronotum wider than long, sides broadly rounded, as are front and hind angles. Elytra each with two or three seta-bearing punctures, humeri rounded, and spaces between grooves smooth, almost without punctures; flight wings developed or reduced. Legs with claws toothed, hind tarsomeres 1–4 without ridge on top, and front tarsi widened in male. Adults active spring and summer in woodlands, usually found in leaf litter and under debris; occasionally attracted to light. In east from Maritime Provinces and New England to northern Georgia, west to Ontario, Minnesota, and Missouri. (1)

Ega **(formerly** *Calybe***)** *sallei* **(Chevrolat)** (4.0 mm) is antlike, with reddish head and pronotum and brown elytra with white spots. Antennae with last four antennomeres dark. Elytra with grooves along their entire length and pale erect setae. Legs with light and dark brown femora, pale tibiae, and light brown tarsi. Diurnal adults active spring and summer, found on bare shores of ponds, pools, and slow-moving streams under mats of algae and debris. South Carolina to Florida, west to Illinois and Arizona. (1)

Cosnania (formerly *Colliuris*) *pensylvanica* (Linnaeus) (5.8–7.2 mm) has a distinctly rhomboidal head and long, cylindrical "necklike" prothorax. Head and pronotum black. Elytra somewhat oval with distinctly punctate grooves near bases, dull red with black spots and tip and appear somewhat cut off and lack any setae. Legs black or pale, "knees" dusky. Adults found in open grassy habitats and wetland edges on plants during day or under debris year-round, especially in late spring and summer; attracted to light. Eastern United States, also Ontario and Québec. (2) *Colliuris ludoviciana* (Sallé) similar, with base of head, front and base of pronotum reddish; Connecticut and New York to Florida, west to Louisiana.

Tetragonoderus latipennis (LeConte) (4.5–5.0 mm) is somewhat oval, flattened, appendages pale yellow, underside dark. Head and pronotum blackish with bronze reflections. Pronotum wider than long. Elytra pale with dark markings, posterior margins notched before somewhat straight and oblique elytral tips. Hind tibial spurs finely notched, longest spur almost as long as first tarsomere. Diurnal adults are quick to run and fly; found mostly in lowland habitats, especially on sandy, sparsely vegetated soils along rivers and lakes; occasionally attracted to light. Alabama and Arkansas to Arizona. (4)

Apenes sinuata (Say) (6.5–7.5 mm) has a blackish head and prothorax, brassy dark brown elytra with pale humeri, with spots before tips distinct or nearly absent, and pale reddish-brown appendages. Head sparsely punctured. Prothorax about one-third wider than long, sparsely punctured, wider at base than behind head, sides with margins curved, narrowly flattened, and hind angles distinct. Elytra oblong-oval with finely punctured grooves (punctostriate). Adults found in variety of woodland habitats at bases of trees and stumps year-round; also attracted to light in spring and summer. Ontario to Florida, west to Illinois and Texas. (6)

Calleida punctata LeConte (7.0–8.5 mm) is reddish and bright metallic green. Head black with short pubescence, antennae blackish except for basal antennomeres, eyes small and flat. Pronotum reddish, longer than wide, slightly wider than head, with side margins narrow with sparse setae. Elytra oblong, gradually becoming wider toward rear, black with bright green luster, and intervals flat with few punctures. Legs yellowish with tips of femora and tarsi blackish, tops of tarsi convex, not furrowed; front, middle tarsi broad with rows of thick setae underneath in male. Québec to South Carolina, west to Manitoba and Kansas. *Calleida decora* (Fabricius) similar, eyes prominent, tarsi flat and furrowed. (5)

Coptodera aerata **Dejean** (5.5–7.0 mm) is black or blackish with dark brown legs and strongly metallic blue-green elytra. Antennae dark brown, basal articles paler, antennomeres 1–3 and part of 4 glabrous. Pronotum twice as wide as long, side margins and rear angles broadly rounded, with rear margin not lobed. Males with front tarsi slight dilated and middle tibiae notched inside near tip; tarsal claws of both sexes serrate. Found in spring and summer under bark and at light. Connecticut and New York to Florida, west to Nebraska and Texas. (1)

Cymindis limbata **Dejean** (8.5–10.5 mm) is dark brown to blackish with sides of pronotum and elytra paler. Antennomeres 1–3 with few setae compared to 4-11. Pronotum about a third wider than long, sides narrow toward rear with margins wide and upturned at hind angles. Elytral surfaces between grooves somewhat convex with fine mesh and a single row of very small punctures; tips appear obliquely cut off. Appendages mostly yellowish brown. Males with front tarsi wide, expanded tarsomeres each with two rows of thick setae underneath. Nocturnal adults found year-round on tree trunks, under loose bark, stones, and debris; fly to light. Québec and Ontario to Florida, west to North Dakota, Iowa, Missouri, Oklahoma, and Texas. (9)

Lebia analis **Dejean** (4.3–6.0 mm) has a mostly black head finely grooved between eyes, with palps and tips of mandibles darkened, and antennomeres 1–3 pale, 4–11 mostly darker with each lighter at tips, and slightly narrower than pronotum. Prothorax pale, finely grooved, wider than long, narrower at base than elytra. Elytra entirely dark to extensively pale with epipleura pale, grooves distinct with spaces between moderately convex, with tips appearing obliquely cut off. Abdomen underneath mostly pale, darker at tip. Legs entirely pale, claws comblike. Adults active spring and summer; attracted to light. Eastern United States and southern Ontario; also in Southwest. (20)

Lebia fuscata **Dejean** (4.3–7.7 mm) is small, bicolored, with head almost as wide as pronotum that is narrower than elytra. Head black, finely wrinkled or punctate next to eyes. Pronotum black, twice as wide as long, with side and sinuate basal margins pale. Elytra distinctly grooved, spaces between somewhat convex, with pale brownish-yellow side margins before tips crossed over, apices obliquely cut off, sinuate. Appendages pale, antennae with outer antennomeres darker. Claws comblike, front tarsomeres 1–3 broad with adhesive pads below in male. Québec to Florida, west to Ontario, Minnesota, Kansas, and eastern Texas; also on West Coast. (20)

Lebia grandis **Hentz** (8.5–10.5 mm) has a reddish-orange head, thorax, and legs. Elytra usually metallic blue, abdomen black. Adults found in open fields and woods on vegetation of plants and trees during day and at light year-round, especially in spring and summer. They prey on all immature stages of Colorado potato beetles (*Leptinotarsa decemlineata*); larvae are ectoparasitoids of *Leptinotarsa* pupae. Widespread in North America, seldom found in Midwest. (20)

Lebia ornata **Say** (4.0–5.5 mm) is dark, without metallic reflections, clear pale markings on elytra, appendages entirely yellowish; underside pale or dark. Head blackish, smooth, without pubescence. Pronotum smooth, uniformly pale or dark with pale margins, and with incomplete bead along margin before elytra. Elytra with ridge at base short, distinctly grooved with variable yellowish spots along margins connected or not, and small spots at tips hooked. Front tibia simple and tipped with spur and all femora pale. Adults found on vegetation and flowers and beneath debris in spring through fall; also attracted to light and baited pitfall traps. Widespread in eastern North America. (20)

91

Lebia pectita **Horn** (6.5–7.2 mm) is reddish yellow-brown with broad black and white stripes on elytra. Head nearly as broad as pronotum, with mouthparts dark, antennomere 1 pale, 2–3 dark. Pronotum narrower than elytra. Elytra with stripe along entire suture, side stripes not reaching base, and central stripe whitish; side margins crossed over just before sinuate and obliquely cut-off tips. Legs black, except for basal two-thirds of femora, claws comblike. Adults active spring and summer, found on flowers and vegetation; also attracted to light. New Hampshire to Georgia, west to Michigan, Kansas, and New Mexico. (20)

Lebia solea **Hentz** (4.5–6.2 mm) is reddish yellow-brown, except for two black stripes on each elytron; antennomeres 4-11 also darker. Head almost as wide as pronotum. Pronotum narrower than elytra with side margins flattened and wider toward rounded angles at base. Elytra with distinct grooves, spaces between moderately convex, with margins underneath crossed over near obliquely cut-off tips. Front tarsomeres broad with adhesive pads underneath in male, claws comblike. Larvae ectoparasitoids on leaf beetle pupae. Diurnal adults active late spring through summer, on flowers, trees, and shrubs. Nova Scotia to Florida, west to Manitoba, Oklahoma, and Texas. (20)

Lebia tricolor **Say** (6.5–9.0 mm) is tricolored with a black head, reddish pronotum, and black elytra with shiny metallic green reflections. Head finely wrinkled along sides. Pronotum narrower than elytra, side margins flattened and broadest at rear. Elytra distinctly grooved, sides black or blackish, with margins underneath crossed over near sinuate and obliquely cut-off tips. Appendages reddish yellow-brown with claws comblike. Mostly diurnal adults active late spring and summer, on flowers and vegetation; attracted to lights. New Brunswick and Nova Scotia to Florida, west to Ontario, Minnesota, Arkansas, and Texas. (20)

Lebia viridis **Say** (4.6–6.6 mm) is uniformly shiny green or dark purplish blue. Antennae mostly blackish, antennomeres 1–3 greenish. Underside and legs blackish. Head with fine grooves along sides. Pronotum narrower than elytra, side margins flattened and narrow, except at distinct hind angle. Elytral grooves very fine, spaces between somewhat flat to slightly convex, with margins underneath crossed over near sinuate and obliquely cut-off tips. Claws comblike, male with front tarsomeres 1–3 expanded, adhesive pads underneath. Mostly diurnal adults active late spring and summer, on flowers and vegetation; attracted to light. Widespread in North America. (20)

Lebia vittata **(Fabricius)** (5.5–8.0 mm) is reddish orange, with elytra each with a pale stripe flanked by thick black stripes, inner black stripes in contact with suture at about apical two-thirds; appendages mostly dark. Head with eyes black and basal antennomeres pale. Elytra with marginal bead from humeri to scutellum. Adults primarily active spring and summer in moist situations in various habitats, found on foliage and flowers; attracted to light. Throughout eastern North America. (20)

Phloeoxena signata **(Dejean)** (5.5–6.0 mm) is bicolored yellowish brown and black; appendages pale. Pronotum uniformly pale or with black spot on middle, sides with two pairs of setae. Elytra pale with irregular black bands and base and just behind middle connected along suture, each with three setae down middle. Adults active mostly in spring and summer in oak-pine forests under bark of oak (*Quercus*) or pine (*Pinus*), on flowers. Maryland to Florida, west to Louisiana; Mexico. (1)

Plochionus timidus **Haldeman** (6.5–7.5 mm) is mostly dark without metallic luster, brown to blackish with pale pronotal and elytral margins. Pronotum wider than long, widest at base, with sides round, with fine wrinkles across surface and fine line down middle. Elytra with grooves deep, not punctured, spaces between without setae and convex, and tips appear cut off. Male with tarsomeres 1–3 of forelegs broad, each with two rows of dense setae underneath; tarsomere 4 of both sexes deeply notched. Adults and larvae prey on caterpillars. Adults found under tree bark year-round in lowland deciduous forests; attracted to light. New Hampshire and New York to Florida, west to Wisconsin, Iowa, Kansas, and Texas to southern California. (6)

Pseudaptinus pygmaeus **(Dejean)** (6.0–6.5 mm) is flat, neck broader (see *Zuphium*), brownish yellow with dense yellow setae; head and centers of elytra darker, appendages lighter. Antennomeres 2–4 each about equal in length, almost wide as long. Pronotum longer than wide, widest in front, distinct hind angles in front of basal margin, and distinct line down middle. Elytra finely and densely punctate. Adults active spring and summer, found in lowland habitats along shores of lakes and canals; occasional at light. Virginia to Florida, west to Arkansas and Louisiana. (3)

Zuphium americanum **Dejean** (5.2–6.0 mm) is flat, very narrow-necked, mostly pale brownish, with upper surface setose; head and center of elytra darker, appendages lighter. Head with single seta on each side of clypeus. Pronotum wide as long, sides rounded from neck, straight before middle, then converging to base. Elytra with faint grooves, spaces between moderately punctate. Adults active year-round near wetlands under stones and debris; flies to light. New Jersey and southern Ontario to Florida, west to South Dakota, Kansas, and Texas. (3)

Galerita bicolor **(Drury)** (17.0–22.0 mm) is large, elongate, densely setose, bicolored, with a distinct neck. Head narrow, longer than wide, and black with small reddish spot on top, area behind eyes longer than eyes when viewed from above. Eyes somewhat flat. Antennae pale at bases. Pronotum red, longer than wide, with angles obtuse; clothed in short yellowish erect setae. Elytra black with dense, short, bristlelike setae over basal third. Legs reddish brown. Adults found year-round under bark; sometimes attracted to light. New York to Florida, west to South Dakota, Kansas, and Texas. (3)

93

Helluomorphoides praestus bicolor (Harris) (13.0–18.0 mm) is somewhat flattened, and bicolored, usually with head, pronotum, and sometimes base of elytra reddish brown, rest or all of elytra black. Head with distinct neck. Antennae becoming progressively wider toward tips, antennomeres 5–10 wider than long, hirsute, each with shiny triangles not coarsely punctured. Front tarsi of males not widely expanded, but with very fine adhesive setae underneath. Flight wings developed. Adults active in summer in upland woodlands; attracted to light. Can detect chemical trails and will steal and eat brood from migrating columns of army ants (*Neivamyrmex*). New Hampshire to Georgia, west to Wyoming, Colorado, and Kansas. *Helluomorphoides p. floridanus* Ball similar, uniformly reddish brown; Florida. (6)

WHIRLIGIG BEETLES, FAMILY GYRINIDAE
(JYE-*RIN*-IH-DEE)

Whirligigs are so named because of their wild gyrations on the surface of the water when disturbed. They are the only beetles that use the surface tension of water for support. Moving about singly or in large groups, these streamlined beetles search for mates and insect prey on ponds or along the edges of slow-moving streams, as well as in cattle tanks, canals, swimming pools, even rain puddles. They produce defensive secretions from the tips of their abdomens that not only are feeding deterrents to fish, amphibians, birds, and other predators, but also may serve as an alarm pheromone that alerts whirligigs nearby of possible danger. The pungent odor of these secretions smells like apples and has inspired the nicknames "apple bugs," "apple smellers," and "mellow bugs." This passively released secretion is also a water repellent that lowers the surface tension and enables whirligigs to "ride" on a wave of recoiling water molecules. Recently emerged adults sometimes congregate by the dozens or hundreds in shady or sheltered spots in late summer and fall. Some smaller species (*Gyretes*, *Gyrinus*) often climb out of the water onto emergent leaves, twigs, and roots to rest. *Gyretes* and the seldom encountered *Spanglerogyrus* prefer shaded undercuts and hollowed-out pockets along the banks of small streams. The predatory larvae crawl about the bottom debris of ponds and streams in search of immature insects and other small invertebrates. Mature larvae pupate within a case constructed of sand and debris and are located on shore (*Dineutus*) or attached to plants above the water surface (*Gyrinus*).

FAMILY DIAGNOSIS Adult gyrinids are oval, flattened, and uniformly shiny or dull black, or white underneath (*Spanglerogyrus*). Combined margins of the head, thorax, and abdomen form a continuous outline. Mouthparts directed forward (prognathous). Antennae short, clubbed, with 8–11 antennomeres. Compound eyes distinctly divided. Scutellum visible (*Gyrinus*, *Spanglerogyrus*) or not (*Dineutus*, *Gyretes*). Elytra smooth (margins lined with pubescence in *Gyretes*) and do not completely cover the abdomen. Front legs raptorial, adapted for grasping prey. Tarsal formula 5-5-5, middle and hind legs flattened and paddlelike. Abdomen has six ventrites.

SIMILAR FAMILIES The completely divided eyes, paddlelike legs, and habits of whirligigs are distinctive.

COLLECTING NOTES Rapidly sweeping an aquatic net through groups of beetles swimming on the surface of ponds and streams is the best way to collect specimens. Individuals may dive beneath the water to avoid capture but will soon resurface. Also investigate shaded undercuts and hollowed-out pockets with trailing roots from terrestrial vegetation along stream banks. Some whirligigs are readily attracted to lights at night.

FAUNA 56 SPECIES IN FOUR GENERA (NA); 32 SPECIES IN FOUR GENERA (ENA)

Dineutus emarginatus **(Say)** (8.5–11.0 mm) is broadly oval and bronzy black with underside shinier than dorsal surface. Front legs mostly dark brown, middle and hind legs lighter. Males with padded front tarsi and distinctly angulate tooth near tip of front tibiae. Elytral apices of both sexes rounded or slightly irregular, not finely notched. Adults active from spring through late fall on ponds, lakes, rivers, and swamps; also attracted to light. New Hampshire to Florida, west to Michigan and Texas. (9)

Gyrinus **species** (3.3–7.0 mm) are small and shiny, live on surface of still or slow-moving waters, and have long forelegs. Dorsal and ventral eyes completely divided, inset from lateral margin of head by at least half width of eye. Pronotum and elytra without setae. Elytra with 11 distinct and punctured grooves. Underside of front tarsi of male with dense brush of setae. Tarsomeres 2–4 on middle and hind legs much broader than long. Identification to species difficult. Adults active spring through early fall. Throughout eastern North America. (20)

Gyretes iricolor **Young** (4.5–5.0 mm) has pubescence on both sides of pronotum. Elytra with pubescence along sides, very narrow, less than half width on pronotum, extending to tips (female) or not (male), surface smooth and without rows of punctures, and tips flat (male) or sharp (female). Abdomen with last ventrite long, without tooth on penultimate ventrite. Front tarsi broad and flat (males), or not (females). Adults active spring and summer, found in streams under overhanging banks and root tangles. Florida panhandle and Alabama, possibly Mississippi. *Gyretes sinuatus* LeConte with pubescence on sides of elytra half or more that of pronotum; western Virginia to Alabama, west to Indiana and California. (2)

CRAWLING WATER BEETLES, FAMILY HALIPLIDAE
(HA-*LIP*-LIH-DEE)

Crawling water beetles resemble small, loosely built predaceous diving beetles (Dytiscidae) and move their legs alternately, like water scavenger beetles (Hydrophilidae). They are easily distinguished from all other aquatic beetles by their enlarged coxal plates that obscure most of the abdomen, and by the broadly tapered head and posterior. Haliplids typically live along the edges of standing or slow-moving freshwater habitats with good water quality, where they crawl over mats of algae and submerged vegetation and prey on small invertebrates. In spite of their common name they are fair swimmers thanks to long hairlike setae on their legs that increase the effectiveness of these limbs as oars. Eggs are laid on the surfaces of aquatic plants (*Peltodytes*) or in cavities chewed in algae or other aquatic vegetation (*Haliplus*) from spring through summer and possibly in fall. The larvae feed on algae and pupate in a chamber on shore, usually beneath stones and logs.

FAMILY DIAGNOSIS Adult haliplids are yellowish or brownish yellow with black spots and oval bodies broadly tapered at each end. Mouthparts directed forward (prognathous). Antennae with 11 antennomeres, 1–2 short and broad, 3–11 longer and filiform. Prothorax widest at base and keeled below, with margins rounded (*Haliplus, Peltodytes*), or parallel-sided (*Brychius*); pronotum unmarked or with two distinct black spots at base (*Peltodytes*). Scutellum not visible. Elytra cover abdomen completely; each elytron with 10 or more rows of large, dark punctures. Tarsal formula 5-5-5. Abdomen mostly concealed by large, flattened coxal plates of hind legs, one or more ventrites exposed.

SIMILAR FAMILIES
- burrowing water beetles (Noteridae) – abdominal ventrites visible, not covered by expanded coxal plates (p.97)
- predaceous diving beetles (Dytiscidae) – abdominal ventrites visible, not covered by expanded coxal plates (p.99)

COLLECTING NOTES Look for adult haliplids crawling over and feeding on mats of stringy green algae and other submerged vegetation growing in weedy ditches or along the edges of ponds, lakes, or small and slow-moving streams (*Haliplus, Peltodytes*); *Brychius* prefers coarser substrates along rivers and lakes. Lightly sweep a dip net or small aquarium net through algae and aquatic vegetation in these habitats. Also drag aquatic vegetation on shore and hand-collect beetles as they attempt to crawl back to the water. Haliplids also fly to lights at night.

FAUNA 65 SPECIES IN FOUR GENERA (NA); 41 SPECIES IN THREE GENERA (ENA)

Hungerford's Crawling Water Beetle *Brychius hungerfordi* Spangler (3.7–4.4 mm) is relatively long, narrow, shining yellow-brown. Pronotum with sides straight, parallel. Elytra slightly broader than pronotum at base, becoming wider at middle before narrowing at tips, side margins behind humeri with small teeth, each with 10 rows of punctures. Adults found among algae-laden gravel and cobble at edges of pools and along streams with high oxygen content. Federally listed as endangered in the United States and is illegal to collect. Southern Ontario and Michigan. (1)

Haliplus pantherinus Aubé (3.5–4.0 mm) is brownish yellow or brownish. Pronotum with dark spot rounded to strongly tapered, front margin lacking fine bead or groove at sides. Underside with ridges along sides between coxal plates covering abdomen and middle legs darker than rest of surface. Middle trochanter without coarse deep punctures. Adults active spring and summer, found along margins of permanent standing water with rooted vegetation and debris on bottom. Québec to Georgia, west to South Dakota and Tennessee. (25)

Peltodytes muticus (**LeConte**) (3.5–3.8 mm) is oblong, ovate, and usually pale yellow. Pronotum with two spots at base. Elytron without distinctly dark patch below humerus, and blotch just behind middle usually coalesces with dark suture that is narrowed at base and not in contact with rows of punctures; punctures in front large, small and scattered on apical half, not in regular rows. Hind femur uniformly dark. Adults found year-round along edges of slow streams and rivers, lakes, Carolina bays, also in ditches and pools; attracted to light. Massachusetts to Florida, west to Illinois and Louisiana. (15)

BURROWING WATER BEETLES, FAMILY NOTERIDAE
(NO-*TAIR*-IH-DEE)

Burrowing water beetles live along the edges of weedy ponds and lakes. The adults are strong swimmers, move their legs in unison like predaceous diving beetles (Dytiscidae) and prey on larvae of midges (Chironomidae), insect eggs, and other small aquatic species; some are also known to eat plant debris. Life cycles of North American species are unknown but probably similar to that of predaceous diving beetles, except that they pupate underwater. Eggs are presumably laid in aquatic vegetation or soft mud during late spring and early summer; larvae are present from June through August. They are mostly carnivorous, but also scavenge dead insects and plant detritus. Their powerful legs are adapted to burrowing in the mud. Pupation underwater takes place in a specially prepared cell.

FAMILY DIAGNOSIS Adult noterids are small, smooth, shiny, streamlined, broadly to elongate oval, flat underneath and convex to strongly convex above, reddish brown to black. Serrate antennae with 11 antennomeres. Pronotum widest at base. Scutellum not visible. Front tibiae usually with a strong hook or curved spine. Tarsal formula 5-5-5. Hind tarsi usually with 2 equally curved claws. Abdomen with five ventrites.

SIMILAR FAMILIES
- crawling water beetles (Haliplidae) – head small and hind coxae expanded, covering most of abdomen (p.96)
- predaceous diving beetles (Dytiscidae) – larger, scutellum usually visible (p.99)
- water scavenger beetles (Hydrophilidae) – antennae clubbed; mouthparts (maxillary palps) long; underside flat, sometimes with a spinelike keel (p.105)

COLLECTING NOTES Adults of *Hydrocanthus* and *Suphisellus* are collected by vigorously sweeping an aquarium or dip net through emergent weedy or decaying vegetation, and mats of floating vegetation and algae associated with pond and lake edges; they are also attracted to lights in spring and summer. Smaller species, such as *Notomicrus*, are most abundant in debris, mats of plant roots, or floating aquatic vegetation. They are best collected by placing suitable substrate on a screen over a light-colored pan or directly into a Berlese funnel. *Suphis* prefers permanent and acidic sinkholes, ponds, lakes, and marshes. *Pronoterus* lives in ponds filled with aquatic plants. *Mesonoterus addendus* (Blatchley) is known only from southern Florida and found among water hyacinth and other emergent aquatic plants in ponds and canals.

FAUNA 14 SPECIES IN SIX GENERA (NA); 13 SPECIES IN SIX GENERA (ENA)

Hydrocanthus iricolor **Say** (4.3–5.5 mm) is relatively large, obovate, convex, distinctly narrowed behind, and reddish-yellow with darker elytra. Elytra with three distinct rows of punctures. Front tibiae with curved spur at tip, hind femora with thick brush of setae, and tarsi 5-5-5. Adults active spring and summer, found in temporary pools and permanent ponds with various kinds of submerged and emergent vegetation, in root mats, and in rice fields; attracted to light. Québec and Ontario to South Carolina, west to Wisconsin, Missouri, Arkansas. (4)

Suphis inflatus **(LeConte)** (3.0–3.5 mm) is globose, nearly hemispherical, dull black with irregular reddish markings, and gradually tapered toward elytral apices. Antennae yellowish. Pronotum about a third of overall length. Elytra and rest of upper surface appearing wrinkled with coarse and moderately dense punctures. Legs reddish with tarsi lighter. Adults active spring through fall, found among emergent vegetation surrounding permanent ponds, marshes, lakes, rivers, and Carolina bays. North Carolina to Florida, west to Arkansas and Texas. (1)

PREDACEOUS DIVING BEETLES, FAMILY DYTISCIDAE
(DYE-*TISS*-IH-DEE)

Adult and larval diving beetles are predators and scavengers, consuming both invertebrate and vertebrate tissues. They are strong swimmers and occur in a variety of aquatic habitats, particularly along the edges of pools, ponds, and slow streams where emergent vegetation grows. A few species are specialists, preferring cold-water streams, seeps, and springs, or other specialized bodies of water. Their oval and flattened bodies are streamlined to reduce drag as they swim. The short, fringed hind legs move in unison, propelling the beetle through the water. The hind legs are placed well back on the body to increase speed and maneuverability. Most diving beetles are capable of flight and sometimes migrate in large numbers to new bodies of water. They are quite awkward on land because their legs are attached to plates that are tightly fused to the body and incapable of moving up and down like those of terrestrial beetles. Predaceous diving beetles are chemically defended and possess a pair of thoracic glands located just behind the head that secrete steroids that are particularly distasteful to fish. Larvae are strong swimmers and voracious predators; larger species are sometimes called water tigers. They consume the larvae of mosquitoes, biting midges, and other biting insects. Mature larvae leave the water to construct pupal chambers beneath streamside objects. Overwintering typically occurs during the adult stage; they are sometimes active in the winter and are visible under the ice.

FAMILY DIAGNOSIS Adult dytiscids are oval, streamlined, and usually reddish brown to black or pale, with or without distinct markings. Mouthparts directed forward (prognathous). Antennae with 11 moniliform antennomeres. Pronotum widest at base. Scutellum visible or not. Elytra usually smooth and polished, sometimes pitted, sparsely hairy, or grooved, and always completely covering abdomen. Tarsal formula is 5-5-5, sometimes appearing 4-4-4. Claws equal or unequal in size, never toothed. Abdomen with six ventrites.

SIMILAR FAMILIES
- whirligig beetles (Gyrinidae) – eyes divided; antennae clubbed (p.94)
- crawling water beetles (Haliplidae) – head small and hind coxae expanded, covering most of abdomen (p.96)
- burrowing water beetles (Noteridae) – scutellum not visible and hind tarsus with two similar claws (p.97)
- water scavenger beetles (Hydrophilidae) – antennae clubbed; mouthparts (maxillary palps) long; underside flat, sometimes with a spinelike keel (p.105)

COLLECTING NOTES Adults are sometimes common at lights in spring and summer. Sweeping an aquatic net through exposed and shaded vegetated shallows of ponds, lakes, and other standing bodies of water with and without aquatic vegetation on various substrates will produce the greatest diversity of species; some species prefer streams. Underwater light traps placed in these habitats will also attract specimens.

FAUNA 513 SPECIES IN 51 GENERA (NA); ~ 200 SPECIES IN 41 GENERA (ENA)

Copelatus glyphicus (Say) (4.2–4.6 mm) is elongate, oval, flat, usually uniformly dark or light reddish brown, underside dark brown or blackish, with conspicuously grooved elytra; base of pronotum and elytra without lengthwise grooves. Head with eye margins notched. Pronotum smooth, sides with (female) or without (male) a few fine wrinkles. Scutellum visible. Elytra with 10 grooves, alternate grooves shorter, intervals with inconspicuous punctures. Adults found in summer in shallow permanent and temporary pools, especially over mats of leaves. Maritime Provinces and New England to Florida, west to Minnesota, Nebraska, and Texas; also California, Oregon. (6)

Agabetes acuductus (Harris) (6.5–7.5 mm) is oval, somewhat flattened, dull, brown to dark brown with head, pronotal and elytral margins lighter. Pronotum short with sides broadly rounded. Surfaces of pronotum and basal two-thirds of elytra densely sculptured with many short, lengthwise scratches and not round punctures, more so on elytra. Males with very long front claws and pair of lengthwise grooves on last abdominal ventrite. Adults active late spring and summer, found in woodland pools and temporary ponds among dense leaf litter. New England and Québec to Florida, west to Wisconsin, Indiana, Tennessee, and Texas. (1)

Laccophilus maculosus Say (4.6–6.4 mm) is oval, broadest just before middle, and yellowish to pale brown with prominent pale spots on elytral margins. Scutellum hidden. Elytra speckled, without distinct irregular bands. Underside yellow to brown. Legs with 5 tarsomeres, each about equal in length, and hind tibiae with spurs notched at tips, male with file at base of middle legs. Adults active spring and late summer, found among rooted vegetation in shallow waters in permanent pools and ponds in forested habitats; attracted to light. Widespread in eastern North America. (7)

Laccophilus undatus Aubé (3.2–4.3 mm) is oval, broadest at base of elytra with margins of pronotum and elytra continuous; underside yellow to darker reddish brown. Head, basal antennomeres, and mouthparts pale, latter darkened at tips or not. Pronotum pale yellow to reddish brown. Scutellum hidden. Elytra yellow with darker blotchy and undulating bands. Legs with 5 tarsomeres, each about equal in length, and hind tibiae with spurs notched at tips. Adults active in late spring and summer in permanent and temporary shady ponds, also in intermittent pools along streams. Massachusetts to Washington, DC, west to Wisconsin and Illinois; likely in southern Ontario. (7)

Celina hubbelli Young (3.6–4.3 mm) has front and middle tarsi with five tarsomeres; fourth tarsomere mostly concealed by lobes of third. Pronotum with micropunctures and some larger punctures. Elytra elongate, parallel-sided and abruptly tapered behind middle to apex, mostly brown with distinct and broad yellowish band at base. Scutellum is large. Adults are found in ponds and seepages among plant debris year-round; also attracted to lights. Ontario to Florida, west to Colorado and Texas. (8)

Hydroporus tristis **(Paykull)** (2.8–3.2 mm) is small, narrowly oval, reddish brown to black, dorsal surface with minute wrinkles; ventral surface dark. Head reddish with pair of blackish spots between and behind eyes; spots behind sometimes coalesce. Pronotum and elytra without lengthwise grooves. Pronotum with narrow upturned margin. Scutellum visible. Front and middle tarsi apparently with four tarsomeres; process between bases of hind legs straight. Adults found among dense emergent vegetation at margins of shaded pools in forested habitats. Canada and across most of northern United States; also Eurasia. (44)

Hygrotus sayi **Balfour-Browne** (2.8–3.2 mm) is small, oval, body outline continuous. Tips of labial palps pointed or shallowly emarginate. Head and pronotum reddish. Scutellum visible. Elytra with epipleuron near base crossed by diagonal ridge, surface color variable with diffuse light and dark patterns or reddish to dark brown. Legs pale reddish, fore- and middle tarsi apparently with four tarsomeres, front tarsi of male not expanded, process between hind legs expanded toward sides, partly covering trochanter. Ventral surface reddish to reddish blackish. Adults prefer sun-warmed, vegetated margins of ponds and slow-flowing streams. Throughout North America, except Southeast. (18)

Neoporus undulatus **(Say)** (3.9–4.5 mm) is broadly oval or somewhat oval, shiny (male), or dull (female) reddish yellow, finely and uniformly wrinkled, with variable reddish-brown markings. Outer antennomeres darker. Pronotum with front and rear margins dark and side margins appearing expanded, flattened. Elytra blackish with three light irregular bands interrupted at suture. Front tarsi of male expanded. Adults found almost year-round among emergent vegetation along edges of permanent water with little movement, such as pools, ponds, small lakes, and margins of slow marshy streams; attracted to light. Across Canada, south to Georgia, Arkansas, and Dakotas; also Pacific Northwest. (17)

Coptotomus longulus lenticus **Hilsenhoff** (6.8–8.2 mm) is narrowly oval pale, with yellowish-brown and dark markings. Head pale with dark posterior margin, eye with front margin notched. Tips of labial and maxillary palps notched. Base of pronotum and elytra without a pair of fine longitudinal grooves. Pronotum pale with anterior and posterior margins dark at middle. Scutellum visible. Elytral markings variable with sutural stripe, surface finely wrinkled at base in female. Hind femur without line of setae near apex, claws nearly equal in length. Adults prefer open ponds, barrow pits, and stock ponds lined with cattail (*Typha*). Eastern North America. (4)

***Matus bicarinatus* (Say)** (7.7–9.3 mm) is elongate, oval, tapered toward rear, and uniformly brownish red; head, mouthparts, appendages, and side margins of elytra paler. Elytral surface with microscopic meshlike sculpturing, punctation finer and sparser than on pronotum. Underside with coxal plates at bases of hind legs polished, shining. Adults active in late spring through early summer, again in late summer, mainly in marshes and permanent ponds with dense vegetation and debris on bottom. Southern Ontario to Florida, west to Wisconsin and Texas. (3)

***Agabus* species** (5.0–12.5 mm) ovate, convex above, flattened underneath, mostly brown to black or with paler margins; a few pale with dark stripes. Head with pale spots between eyes, front margin of eyes notched. Males with front tarsomeres 1–3 slightly to broadly widened and adhesive setal pads underneath, hind legs of both sexes with angles at femoral tips with small group of short, stiff setae, claws about equal in length. Found around vegetated margins of shallow standing and flowing water. Eastern North America. (38)

***Colymbetes paykulli* Erichson** (15.7–18.6 mm) is very dark. Pronotum largely black, with side margins and small reddish patch near sides reddish. Elytra dark brown, crossed with numerous nearly parallel ridges. Appendages and underside completely dark. Front tarsi distinctly broad in male; hind tarsi in both sexes without fringe of setae on posterior angle. Adults prefer cold, small sphagnum ponds with emergent sedges (*Carex*). Atlantic Canada and New England, west to Minnesota; also western Canada and Rocky Mountains. (4)

***Ilybius biguttulus* (Germar)** (8.4–11.4 mm) is oval, appearing totally black, usually with one or two triangular light markings near elytral margins. Eye notched in front. Underside with surface between middle and hind legs appearing finely and distinctly scratched; last abdominal ventrite with distinct ridge. Front and middle tarsi of male with long patches of yellow setae, hind femur in both sexes with row of setae on apical angle and hind claws unequal in length. Adults active late spring and summer in sun-warmed ponds with densely vegetated margins; also at lights. Atlantic Canada and New England to Georgia, west to Ontario, Dakotas, Colorado, Utah, and New Mexico. (10)

Rhantus wallisi **Hatch** (9.4–11.6 mm) is broadly oval and flat with bicolored pronotum. Head black, except for front, clypeus, and spots or bar between eyes, with front margin of eyes notched. Pronotum reddish with dark narrow anterior and posterior margins. Elytra yellowish brown, darkly speckled, speckles larger and merging at tip. Underside mostly black. Hind femur lacks fringe of setae on posterior angle, hind claws unequal in length. Adults inhabit vegetation-rich, sun-warmed margins of ponds in woods or near wooded areas. Boreal North America; in east from Atlantic Canada to Massachusetts, west to Manitoba, Minnesota, Iowa, and Illinois. (6)

Dytiscus carolinus **Aubé** (22.0–26.4 mm) is broadly oval and greenish black with pale margins. Clypeus and side margins of pronotum and elytra brownish yellow. Elytra smooth (male) or grooved (female). First abdominal ventrite and adjacent metasternum dark, rest range from mostly dark reddish with black bands to black. Legs with expanded front tarsi circular and middle tarsi without smooth area dividing setal pad in male, hind tibial spurs of both sexes about equal in diameter. Adults found in open, deeper water among debris; attracted to light. Massachusetts to Georgia, west to Wisconsin and Arkansas. (8)

Hydaticus piceus **LeConte** (11.6–14.0 mm) is dark reddish brown to almost blackish. Head yellow to brown, darker behind, brown underneath. Pronotum yellow to dark brown, central part with irregular blotches darker, sides paler. Scutellum brown. Elytra yellowish to dark reddish brown, areas near base and sides speckled with coalescent spots, sides paler, but not distinctly so. Legs mostly dark, light brown to blackish, with front and middle femora yellowish. Active spring through fall, found in shaded pools in deciduous woodlands with organic substrate and diverse divergent vegetation; also attracted to light in summer. Nova Scotia to Pennsylvania, west to Alberta and Illinois. (5)

Acilius mediatus **(Say)** (10.2–12.5 mm) is shiny, brownish black with wavy band behind middle of elytra. Head reddish yellow with inverted blackish W or V and bar at base. Pronotum pale with two black bars. Elytra dark with side margins and band yellow, pale areas with black coalescing speckles. Adults prefer small forest pools with bare bottoms, often next to slow-flowing brown water streams. Maritime Provinces and New England to Florida, west to Ontario, Minnesota, Missouri, and Mississippi. (4)

Acilius semisulcatus **Aubé** (12.5–15.6 mm) is broadly oval, yellowish brown and speckled with dark spots; underside black. Head yellowish brown to reddish except for dark M-shaped mark and posterior margin. Pronotum pale with two black bars. Elytra grooved at base (female) or not (male), with punctures crescent-shaped, especially at base, and narrow, wavy band behind middle. Hind femur usually yellowish brown or reddish. Adults found in broad range of ponds, barrow pits, ditches, and small lakes without fish. Alaska and Canada; New England to South Carolina, west to Dakotas, Colorado, and Illinois. (4)

Graphoderus liberus **(Say)** (10.4–12.4 mm) is broadly oval, widest just behind middle. Head and pronotum uniformly yellowish-to-reddish brown. Elytra yellowish, appearing dark with dense speckles. Underside and appendages yellowish brown to reddish. Adults active in spring and summer in rivers, often localized boggy ponds and lakes, beaver ponds, and open woodland pools, beaver ponds, and Carolina bays. Across Canada; New England to Florida, west to Minnesota, Missouri, and Alabama. (4)

Thermonectus basillaris **(Harris)** (9.0–11.5 mm) is ovate and flattened, usually with narrowly pale elytral bases. Head with yellow across front and middle. Pronotum with yellow line down each side and across middle. Elytra black, sometimes dark brown with scattered irregular yellow markings along margin, female with deep scratches along basal half. Legs with smaller hind tibial spur notched; male lacks adhesive pads on middle tarsi. Underside dark, smooth, almost without punctures. Adults found in ponds, ditches, swamps, and other standing waters; attracted to light. New York to Florida, west to Wisconsin and Texas. (2)

Cybister fimbriolatus **(Say)** (26.0–33.0 mm) is large, ovate and broadest behind middle, blackish with greenish sheen, with narrow yellow band along sides of pronotum and elytra. Male front tarsi each with tarsomeres forming an oval, not circular, adhesive pad. Female with rough sculpturing on pronotum sometimes extending to elytra. Prothorax distinctly greenish underneath. Elytra broadly rounded at tips. Adults found year-round in more open, deeper water in permanent ponds, ditches, and other standing water; attracted to light. Nova Scotia to Florida, west to North Dakota, Kansas, and southern California. (1)

WATER SCAVENGER BEETLES, FAMILY HYDROPHILIDAE
(HI-DRO-*FIL*-IH-DEE)

Hydrophilidae is one of the largest families of aquatic beetles, second only to the Dytiscidae. Most hydrophilids live in ponds, streams, and lakes with an abundance of plants or organic debris; they are often among the first to arrive at rain pools and other new aquatic habitats. Adults are sometimes common along the vegetated edges of ponds and lakes, as well as in slow-moving streams and springs; few are found in brackish water. They are sometimes attracted to shiny car surfaces and blue tarps. Adults are usually good swimmers, but some are slow and awkward. They propel themselves through the water by moving their legs in an alternate fashion, unlike predaceous diving beetles (Dytiscidae) that move their legs in unison. At night, aquatic beetles often take to the air in search of new habitats and are sometimes attracted to lights. Hydrophilid larvae are mostly predatory, but the adults are vegetarians or omnivores, occasionally predators or scavengers. Predaceous species feed on a variety of animal foods, including snails and other small invertebrates; omnivorous species supplement their diets with spores, algae, and decaying vegetation. Mature larvae construct their pupal chambers of mud near the shore either buried in the soil or tucked beneath a rock or other object and are suspended within by strategically placed setae. The common name "water scavenger beetle" is somewhat misleading since some hydrophilids prefer to live on land in wet sand, rich organic soil, moist leaf litter, fresh mammal dung, or extremely decayed animal carcasses.

FAMILY DIAGNOSIS Adult hydrophilids are mostly broadly oval, distinctly convex on top and flattened underneath. Dorsal surface black, black with brownish markings, or rarely greenish or with cream markings. Mouthparts are directed downward (hypognathous). Antennae with 6–10 antennomeres, last three forming a variable club usually nested within a cup-shaped antennomere. Maxillary palps of aquatic species often exceed length of antennae, but usually equal in length or shorter in terrestrial species. Pronotum broader than head and usually wider than long. Scutellum visible. Elytra widest at middle and broader at base than pronotum, surface smooth or rough and sometime covered with rows of small pits, and completely conceal abdomen. Tarsal formula 5-5-5, 5-4-4 (*Cymbiodyta*), rarely 4-5-5 (male *Berosus*); claws generally simple; foretarsi sometimes modified in males (*Berosus*). Abdomen usually with five, rarely six ventrites.

SIMILAR FAMILIES

- burrowing water beetles (Noteridae) – antennae filiform; mouthparts inconspicuous; body not flattened underneath (p.97)
- predaceous diving beetles (Dytiscidae) – antennae filiform; mouthparts inconspicuous; body not flattened underneath (p.99)
- minute moss beetles (Hydraenidae) – abdomen with six or seven ventrites (p.114)
- dung beetles (Scarabaeidae) – antennal club with lamellae (p.156)
- riffle beetles (Elmidae) – small; legs long with large claws (p.196)
- minute flower beetles (Phalacridae) – small (1.0– 3.0 mm); maxillary palps short; tarsal formula 5-5-4 (p.290)

COLLECTING NOTES Sweeping an aquatic net along the shallow, vegetated margins of ponds, lakes, and slow moving streams is usually productive; searching among submerged organic debris and algae along the margins is particularly rewarding, especially with a flashlight at night. Another technique is to disturb aquatic substrates and vegetation to dislodge small, nonswimming species that become trapped on the surface film. Organic debris raked up on shore in an open sandy area or on a white shower curtain will reveal numerous beetles as they attempt to escape back into the water. Small amounts of debris are placed in a white pan for sorting. Look for terrestrial species by picking through wet leaf litter, moist cow dung, decaying vegetation on shores, or under very rotten carcasses. A Berlese funnel is useful for removing individuals from leaf litter. Well-lit storefronts, street lights, and UV traps near bodies of water will attract aquatic hydrophilids, sometimes in large numbers.

FAUNA 258 SPECIES IN 35 GENERA (NA)

Helophorus grandis Illiger (4.5–7.7 mm) is robust, with head and pronotum distinctively metallic greenish copper. Head with stem of Y-shaped groove slightly widened in front, antennae with nine antennomeres. Elytra barely metallic, if at all, with alternating flat and barely raised ridges; fine groove running alongside scutellum and suture. Tip of abdominal ventrite 5 with flat teeth on posterior margin. Found in temporary ponds and weedy margins of ponds and lakes. Europe; established from Nova Scotia and New Brunswick to New England, west to Ontario and New York. (3)

Hydrochus squamifer LeConte (3.3–4.2 mm) is elongate, moderately convex, surface of head and pronotum densely granulose, dark reddish black to blackish above with more or less metallic reflections; appendages mostly reddish yellow-brown, tip of maxillary palps dark. Head with Y-shaped groove on top and distinct neck behind protruding eyes. Pronotum about as long as wide. Elytra inconspicuously granulose, with grooves coarsely and distinctly punctured, and long, metallic stripes. Adults found along edges of lakes, ponds, swamps, marshes, and roadside ditches; also sphagnum bogs. Transcontinental, south to New Jersey and Missouri in east. (15+)

Sperchopsis tessellata (Ziegler) (6.5–7.6 mm) is broadly oval, almost hemispherical, reddish yellow-brown to reddish brown; appendages reddish yellow-brown. Pronotum coarsely and irregularly punctate, with vague spot on middle. Elytra grooved with confused darker pattern, except at base, side margins serrate. Tarsal claws simple in both sexes. Adults found in undercut sandy or gravelly banks with overhanging roots along clear, cold, and rapidly flowing streams. Atlantic Canada to Florida, west to Wisconsin and Arkansas. (1)

Berosus ordinatus LeConte (4.5–6.5 mm) is oval, convex, and shiny greenish yellow-brown with deep grooves on elytra. Elytra with grooves distinct at base, punctures in and some between grooves about same size, sides rough, and tips obtuse and divergent from suture; most specimens with indistinct spot on side. Abdomen with posterior margin of last ventrite notched with two small teeth in center. Adults active spring and summer, found in ponds and pools along river; attracted to light. Massachusetts to Florida, west to Minnesota and Alabama. (14+)

106

Enochrus cinctus (**Say**) (4.9–7.5 mm) is oval, very convex, black with sides of pronotum, elytra variably and narrowly pale; antennae and palps mostly pale. Head with clypeus yellow in front of eyes, maxillary palps longer than antennae, with second maxillary palpomere curved forward. Prothorax without ridge between front legs. Elytra with faint rows of punctures. Abdomen with last ventrite deeply notched. Legs dark with paler tarsi 5-5-5, tarsomere 5 short; front claws of both sexes similar. Adults poor swimmers in standing waters associated with streams, swamps, ponds, and ditches; attracted to light. New Brunswick to Florida, west to Saskatchewan, Wisconsin, Kansas, and eastern Texas. (12)

Enochrus ochraceus (**Melsheimer**) (2.5–4.0 mm) is somewhat elongate-oval and convex, yellowish to dark brown. Head black with clypeus entirely pale to variably darkened in middle, last maxillary palpomere shorter than penultimate. Pronotum and elytra yellowish to dark brown, underneath with process between legs not ridged. Elytra with turned-under edges dark. Underside reddish brown to blackish, with process between middle legs low and smoothly rounded. Abdomen with tip notched somewhat deep and wide. Front claws of male distinctly enlarged at base. Adults found year-round in many types of moving and standing waters; attracted to light. Widespread in eastern North America. (12)

107

Helobata larvalis (**Horn**) (5.0–6.0 mm) is elongate-oval, somewhat flattened, and dull yellowish brown with broad and flat pronotal and elytral margins. Head with broad clypeus covering labrum. Elytra each with 10 grooves, two outermost very faint. Adults found tightly affixed to submerged rocks and plants, e.g., pickerel weed (*Pontederia*) along margins of ponds, lakes, rivers; also in beach drift, brackish water, and attracted to light. Females carry eggs sacs under abdomen. Atlantic and Gulf Coast states, from Virginia to Florida, west to Texas. (1)

Helocombus bifidus (**LeConte**) (5.8–7.6 mm) is oval, convex, dark brown to black with pronotal and elytral margins lighter. Head with mouthparts and antennae reddish brown. Pronotum moderately punctate, punctures becoming coarser toward sides. Elytra each with 10 grooves, three or four nearest suture extending only to half or basal third from tips. Legs brown to blackish with tarsi paler, tarsi 5-4-4, claws each with basal tooth, tooth less prominent in female. Adults active year-round, found among emergent vegetation of ponds, streams, ditches; attracted to light. New Brunswick and Québec to Florida, west to British Columbia and Colorado. (1)

***Hydrobius fuscipes* (Linnaeus)** (5.4-8.0 mm) is oblong-oval, somewhat convex, finely and densely punctate, and dark brown to blackish with faint metallic luster. Maxillary palps and antennae yellowish brown, tip of last maxillary palpomere usually dark. Elytra sometimes becoming gradually paler on sides, each with 10 distinct punctate grooves extending nearly to base. Legs reddish yellow-brown with femora darker, and tarsal formula 5-5-5. Adults active spring and summer, found in shallow pools, swamps, and sphagnum bogs; attracted to light. Widespread in Northern Hemisphere. (3)

***Hydrochara soror* Smetana** (14.0–19.0 mm) is broadly oval, convex, shiny black. Head punctate, labrum hard and dark like clypeus, clypeus straight across front; maxillary palps long, pale, palpomere 3 is 1.3× length of 4, 4 at least slightly darkened at tip. Eytral margins and surface smooth. Underside with keel on pterothorax not more than slightly dilated nor spinelike, extending past first of five abdominal ventrites. Adults active primarily in late spring and summer, found in ponds, streams, ditches, shallow lake margins; also attracted to light. Connecticut to Florida, west to Minnesota, Kansas, and Texas. (6)

***Hydrophilus ovatus* Gemminger & Harold** (31.0–33.0 mm) is large, oblong-ovate, convex, dark greenish black with appendages pale reddish brown. More broadly rounded in front and rear than *H. triangularis*. Prothorax underneath with channel in front of legs open and lobed on each side behind head. Elytra smooth, each with three rows of indistinct punctures, and tips without a tooth. Adults found year-round in deep, vegetated ponds and lakes; attracted to light. Québec and Ontario to Florida, west to Michigan and Texas. (3)

***Hydrophilus triangularis* Say** (28.0–38.0 mm) is large, elongate-oval, shiny black with greenish blue or purplish luster. Narrow and more pointed on ends than *H. ovatus*. Antennae yellowish brown to black becoming paler toward tips. Prothorax underneath with channel in front of legs closed and hoodlike behind head. Elytra smooth, each with five rows of punctures, third row out from suture abbreviated at both ends, and tip without a tooth. Underside of abdomen brownish black to black, ventrites each with white spots on sides. Legs dark with tarsi usually paler. Adults found year-round in deep, vegetated ponds and lakes; attracted to light. Québec and throughout United States. (3)

Tropisternus blatchleyi d'Orchymont (7.0–10.5 mm) is oval, body completely black with hint of brassy sheen. Legs with tip of femora and middle of tibiae yellowish brown to reddish yellowish brown, basal third of hind femur covered with somewhat triangular pubescent patch extending past trochanter. Adults prefer shallow pools, ponds, ditches, and lake margins, especially when thickly vegetated. New Jersey and New York to Florida, west to Iowa and Texas. (8)

Tropisternus collaris (Fabricius) (7.0–11.0 mm) is shiny dark olive to blackish with alternating light and dark stripes on elytra; stripes sometimes restricted to mostly near margins. Elytral stripes yellowish. Last abdominal ventrite without spine. Adults found year-round in shallow permanent and temporary fresh water ponds of various sizes, usually with organic debris and algae; tolerant of pine needles in water; attracted to light. New York to Florida, west to Kansas and Texas. (8)

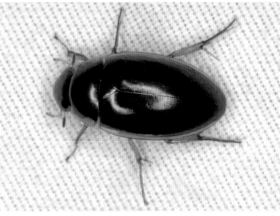

Tropisternus lateralis nimbatus (Say) (7.5–10.5 mm) is narrowly oval, moderately convex, and shiny black with metallic luster and pale yellowish-brown side margins only on pronotum and elytra. Prothorax underneath with channel in front of coxae closed in front by prominent ridge. Underside with thoracic plates between middle and hind legs forming keel down middle projecting over first visible abdominal sternite as a sharp spine. Fifth visible abdominal tergite with spine on tip. Adults found year-round in all kinds of wetlands, including brackish water; attracted to light. Widespread in eastern North America. (8)

Cercyon praetextatus (Say) (2.4–3.5 mm) is shiny, blackish to black, with two pale and sometimes obscure yellowish- to reddish-brown spots on head. Elytra with large, distinct yellowish to reddish-yellow spots on elytral apices that often extend along lateral margins. Adults found in wet habitats along the edges of wetlands, as well as in debris, decaying vegetation, and animal droppings (cattle, horse); also commonly attracted to light. Prince Edward Island and Nova Scotia to Manitoba, widespread throughout United States to South America. (35)

Sphaeridium scarabaeoides (Linnaeus) (4.0–7.1 mm) is oval, convex, and mostly black with reddish and yellow markings. Pronotum with front angles or sides yellowish, hind angles broadly angled, basal margin sinuate. Elytra often with reddish spot at humeri with yellowish area at tips extending halfway up side, but not reaching suture. Legs mostly yellowish red with dark, variably marked femora. Adults active nearly year-round, found in cow, horse, and other mammal dung. Southern Canada and most of United States, except Florida and Gulf Coast. (3)

CLOWN BEETLES, FAMILY HISTERIDAE
(HISS-*TAIR*-IH-DEE)

The Histeridae are a fascinating family of beetles. The adults and larvae are primarily carnivorous and prey on insects; some species feed on fungal spores as adults. Species in the genera *Atholus*, *Hister*, and *Margarinotus* typically prey on fly and beetle larvae in dung, carrion, and decaying plants. Xylophilic (wood-loving) species of *Hololepta*, *Platysoma*, and *Platylomalus* are small and/or flat, adaptations for moving easily under the bark of dying or decaying dead trees. Cylindrical species of *Teretrius* are found in the galleries of wood-boring beetles, especially those of bark beetles (Curculionidae). Sand-dwelling species (*Hypocaccus*) live among the roots of plants. Species of *Haeterius* and *Psiloscelis* are found only in ant nests, where they scavenge or prey on the immature stages of their hosts. When threatened, adults pull their head inside their prothorax and tuck their legs tightly beneath their shiny, round, compact bodies. The larvae are unusual among beetles, molting only twice (instead of three or more times), including the molt to the pupal stage. The thoracic legs are small and not useful for walking; the larvae move by contracting and relaxing the muscles of the abdomen. They feed on liquids and must digest their food outside the body using digestive fluids.

FAMILY DIAGNOSIS Most adult histerids are small, oval, convex or flat, shiny black, sometimes with distinct red markings, or reddish, metallic blue, or green. Head with prominent and relatively large mandibles. Geniculate (elbowed) antennae with 11 antennomeres, elbowed, 9–11 fused to form a compact club often clothed in patches of sensory hairs. Scutellum usually visible. Elytra usually distinctly grooved and/or punctured, short, appearing cut off to expose last two abdominal tergites. Coxae widely separated, tarsal formula 5-5-5 or 5-5-4, with claws usually equal in size and simple. Abdomen with five ventrites.

SIMILAR FAMILIES

- some water scavenger beetles (Hydrophilidae) – elytra completely covering abdomen; antennal club not as compact; maxillary palps long (p.105)

- some round fungus beetle (Leiodidae) – antennal club long; antennomere 8 usually smaller than 7 and 9 (p.118)
- shining fungus beetles (Staphylinidae) – antennae weakly clubbed, long, and not tucked under body; abdomen pointed (p.132)
- some dung beetles (Scarabaeidae) – antennae lamellate (pp.159, 160)
- short-winged flower beetles (Kateretidae) – antennae not geniculate (p.293)
- sap beetles (Nitidulidae) – antennae not geniculate; tarsi usually expanded and hairy beneath; fourth tarsomere reduced (p.295)

110

COLLECTING NOTES Adult histerids are found under dead animals, in dung or rotting vegetation, on tree wounds, or under the bark of recently dead or dying hardwoods and conifers. Some species are located by sifting sand from beneath coastal plants. They are occasionally found flying during the day over sandy shores or grassy areas. Baiting pitfall traps with carrion is the most productive method for collecting some species.

FAUNA 435 SPECIES IN 57 GENERA (NA)

Plegaderus transversus **(Say)** (1.2–1.6 mm) is dark reddish brown. Pronotum with long grooves on each side, distinctly divided by a transverse groove, lobes at front third with punctures as fine or finer than those across middle; plate between front legs with large cavity edged by dense setae, flanked on each side by broad, deep, curved groove. Elytra with fine, scratchlike grooves between coarse, teardrop-like punctures. Abdomen with pygidium covered in coarse punctures separated by half their diameters or less. Adults found in spring and summer under bark of dead pine (*Pinus*); prey on brood of *Ips* bark beetles. Southern Ontario and southwestern Québec to Florida, west to Arizona. (5)

Aeletes politus **(LeConte)** (0.8–1.0 mm) is very small, oval, convex, smooth, and yellowish or reddish brown. Pronotum without grooves or band of elongate punctures at middle of base, underneath with process between legs not lobed, with mouthparts exposed. Scutellum not visible. Adults active early spring and summer, found under bark and in accumulations of plant debris, including forest litter, rotten logs, bracket fungi, tree holes, and compost. Maritime Provinces and Québec to Florida, west to Ontario, Iowa, and Kansas. (3)

Euspilotus assimilis **(Paykull)** (3.5–5.5 mm) is oval, convex, and shiny black with coarse punctures on elytra becoming finer at sides. Pronotum with shallow impressions behind front angles. Elytra each with four coarsely punctured grooves, outer pair extending past and inner pair almost reaching middle, and coarse punctures reaching middle at suture. Abdomen with pygidium coarsely punctate and bearing a marginal groove just before tip interrupted in middle (male) or not (female). Adults active in spring and summer, found on carrion. Maritime Provinces and New England to Florida, west to Manitoba and Texas. (10)

Hypocaccus dimidiatipennis **(LeConte)** (3.2–4.5 mm) is broadly oval, shiny black, and elytra sometimes with wide reddish triangular area on sides at middle. Head smooth. Pronotum smooth except for narrow band of punctures across base, with marginal grooves along sides not or only slightly extended onto basal margin. Elytra with punctate area from midsuture to sutural and humeri. Metatibiae with three rows of spines. Adults active spring and early summer along sandy Atlantic coastline and associated bays, found flying low, under seaweed and sometimes carrion. Atlantic Canada to Georgia. (10)

Hypocaccus fraternus **(Say)** (2.5–4.2 mm) is broadly oval, shiny, with areas of coarse punctation. Front of head with transverse ridge. Pronotum coarsely punctate except for triangular area on top. Elytra with groove along suture distinct at basal half, spaces between three grooves on sides densely punctate and with short, fine grooves. Hind tibiae each with two rows of spines along side. Adults found year-round in sandy habitats, especially along shores of water bodies, sometimes on carrion, where they prey on maggots. Newfoundland to Florida panhandle, west to British Columbia and California. (10)

Saprinus pensylvanicus **(Paykull)** (4.5–5.0 mm) is bright metallic green, sometimes with bronze sheen. Groove along elytral suture strongly curved at base. Prosternum lacks apical pits, grooves along edges diverge toward head and meet at lateral grooves. Margins of pygidium not grooved. Adults found in spring and early summer under carcasses in coastal habitats. This species is found along Atlantic coast from Massachusetts to Florida. (6)

Paromalus bistriatus **Erichson** (1.8–2.2 mm) is moderately convex, oval, and shiny dark reddish brown to black above. Head with distinct marginal groove across middle. Pronotum finely punctate, punctures mostly uniform, occasionally slightly coarser at base. Elytra with fine punctures along base of suture coarser than on pronotum, striae weak, sutural stria absent. Abdomen with male pygidium smooth, grooved in female; first tergite of male with small bump at middle of posterior edge. Adults found under bark of decaying deciduous trees, including oak (*Quercus*), ash (*Fraxinus*), sycamore (*Platanus*), cottonwood (*Populus*), elm (*Ulmus*), and beech (*Fagus*). Southeastern Ontario to Florida and Lousiana. (5)

Platylomalus aequalis **(Say)** (3.0–3.5 mm) is flat, shiny, and dark reddish brown to black. Pronotum sparsely punctured. Elytra sparsely punctured down middle, punctures slightly more coarse along sides, all but one partial groove at base indistinct or absent, and no groove present along suture. Process between forelegs with more or less parallel grooves. Adults found under bark of deciduous trees, especially oak (*Quercus*), ash (*Fraxinus*), sycamore (*Platanus*), maple (*Acer*), and aspen and cottonwood (*Populus*). Widely distributed in North America; in east from southern Québec to Florida, west to Manitoba and Kansas. (1)

Platysoma coarctatum **LeConte** (2.7–3.5 mm) is elongate, narrow, slightly convex, parallel-sided, shiny dark reddish brown to black. Pronotum uniformly punctured, punctures becoming coarse toward sides. Elytra with outer grooves running almost entire length, two closest to suture shorter and not distinct at basal third. Adults found underneath bark of conifers, especially pine (*Pinus*) and spruce (*Picea*), often in association with bark beetle galleries. Maritime Provinces to Florida, west to Alberta and Northwest Territories, and Oklahoma. (10)

113

Platysoma leconti **Marseul** (2.5–3.5 mm) is elongate, wide, oval, flat, shiny, and black. Pronotum with marginal groove complete behind head, not interrupted at middle, and punctures becoming coarse at sides. Elytron with three entire grooves and two shorter grooves that nearly reach tip. Adults are found under bark of dead trees, typically in bark beetle galleries. Widely distributed in North America; in east from Nova Scotia and Ontario to Florida westward. (10)

Hololepta aequalis **Say** (8.0–11.5 mm) is flat, shiny black, somewhat rectangular, and with long, prominent mandibles. Elytral grooves short, restricted to basal third. Adults are found under tight bark of recently dead poplars (*Populus*), willows (*Salix*), elms (*Ulmus*), tulip tree (*Liriodendron tulipifera*), and pines (*Pinus*); often with mesostigmatid mites attached. Ontario to Florida, west to British Columbia and Texas. (5)

Hister furtivus **LeConte** (5.0–8.0 mm) is shiny black. Prothorax underneath with plate behind mouth somewhat straight (male) or broadly notched (female). Elytra with three complete grooves, fourth restricted to apical half, fifth restricted to apical fourth, area outside and below humeri with a series of punctures near middle present or absent. Tip of abdomen (pygidium) coarsely and deeply punctured, surface between punctures finely wrinkled. Adults found on carrion, dung, rotting mushrooms, and compost. Across southern Canada, south to Georgia and Arizona. (~20)

MINUTE MOSS BEETLES, FAMILY HYDRAENIDAE
(HI-*DREEN*-IH-DEE)

Adult minute moss beetles are extremely small, mostly aquatic but do not swim, and they typically live along the margins of various bodies of freshwater among wet vegetation or sand where they feed on plant tissues. Some species burrow in damp sand or soil on shore, while others cling to rocks or chunks of waterlogged wood in streams. They are often very abundant in these microhabitats in western North America and probably play an important role in recycling plant detritus. The dense setae on the underside of their body traps a bubble of air and allows them to breathe underwater. Adults of *Hydraena*, *Limnebius*, and *Ochthebius* use patches of setae on their legs to distribute a special chemical on their bodies when they are out of water that increases the respiratory effectiveness of their respiratory bubble of air when submerged. The larvae are semiaquatic and usually found in the damp margins of aquatic habitats that harbor adults. Eggs are generally laid singly in damp places out of water on leaves, rocks, and algae along the edges of water bodies. The eggs are secured to these substrates with silklike strands. The feeding habits of the adults and larvae are largely unknown, other than some graze microorganisms from wet stones, sand grains, and plant matter.

FAMILY DIAGNOSIS Adult hydraenids are black to yellowish brown, sometimes with metallic reflections. Head with mouthparts directed downward (hypognathous), maxillary palps long, and eyes prominent. Antennae with nine antennomeres, last five forming club clothed in velvety pubescence. Thorax broader than head. Scutellum small and visible. Elytra completely conceal abdomen, surface with rows of punctures. Legs short and stout, or long and slender; tarsal formula 5-5-5 with first three tarsomeres short, last tarsomere long, sometimes appearing 4-4-4 or 3-3-3. Abdomen with seven ventrites, sometimes withdrawn into six.

SIMILAR FAMILIES
- water scavenger beetles (Hydrophilidae) – usually larger; abdomen with five ventrites (p.105)
- riffle beetles (Elmidae) – maxillary palps not elongate (p.196)

COLLECTING NOTES Hydraenids are neither abundant nor commonly collected in eastern North America. Look carefully for adults along the margins of streams and ponds, cascades, rills, and waterfalls in splash zones among leaf packs, matted roots, moss-covered rocks, and other wet plant materials. Stir the sand and gravel at the waterline and wait for the beetles to float to the surface. Others are found in the wet, sandy margins of streams, potholes, submerged rocks, and other debris.

FAUNA 67 SPECIES IN SIX GENERA (NA); 19 SPECIES IN FIVE GENERA (ENA)

Hydraena pensylvanica Kiesenwetter (1.8–2.2 mm) is elongate, oval, and brown with lighter elytral margins. Head and pronotum darker than elytra. Pronotum rectangular, surface coarsely, densely punctate, sides sinuate and narrower at base. Elytra with yellowish-brown basal and apical margins and 10 or more grooves with coarse, squarish punctures, spaces between narrow and convex. *Hydraena* species are best identified by examination of male genitalia. Adults found in association with moss and litter, especially near bogs and swamps; also at light. New England and Québec to South Carolina, west to Minnesota. (12)

Enicocerus benefossus (LeConte) (1.5–1.6 mm) is somewhat ovate, convex, and brown. Antennae with nine antennomeres. Eyes with row of setae behind. Pronotum distinctly sculptured, widest in front of middle, with only sides behind bulge translucent. Elytra each with six rows of punctures, spaces between flat with row of seta-bearing punctures, and sides expanded along entire length. Québec to Virginia, west to Indiana. (1)

FEATHERWING BEETLES, FAMILY PTILIIDAE
(TIH-*LEE*-IH-DEE)

Ptiliids are the smallest of all beetles. Both the adults and larvae are usually found in moist, decaying organic matter that supports the growth of fungi, where they feed on spores. In addition to their small size, featherwing beetles are notable in that some species reproduce by parthenogenesis, while others have strikingly different body forms. The typical form in these species has normally developed compound eyes, wings, and body pigmentation, while vestigial forms have eyes, wings, and other structures greatly reduced or absent. The featherlike flight wings may extend more than twice the length of the body. Each wing consists of a central thin and curved shaft bearing long setae on each side that greatly increase its surface area. The males of some species are unknown, and females reproduce by parthenogenesis. Eggs are typically laid one at a time. Adults and larvae both eat fungal hyphae and spores and are usually found in same place at the same time.

FAMILY DIAGNOSIS Adult ptiliids are minute, moderately to strongly convex, yellow, brown, reddish brown, or blackish, and somewhat pubescent. Clubbed antennae with 8–11 antennomeres, 1–2 enlarged, last two or three form loose club, each with a whorl of setae. Elytra long, completely covering abdomen, or short and exposing three to five abdominal tergites. Abdomen with six ventrites. Tarsal formula 3-3-3, tarsomere 1 short, second very small, 3 long and slender; claws equal or nearly equal in length and simple.

SIMILAR FAMILIES

- limulodine rove beetles (Staphylinidae) – abdomen tapered at tip (p.129)
- minute beetles (Clambidae) – capable of partly rolling up (p.179)
- minute fungus beetles (Corylophidae) – pronotum usually conceals head (p.320)

COLLECTING NOTES The best method for finding these small but seldom collected nocturnal beetles is to extract them from organic material using a Berlese or Tullgren funnel. Productive sources of organic materials include tree holes, bark-covered rotten logs, clumps of moss, and piles of plant debris (leaf mold, grass compost, sawdust). Look for *Nanosella* and its relatives in the spore tubes on the underside of shelf fungi (Polyporaceae) and pick them off with the wetted tips of forceps as they attempt to escape across the fungal surface. *Actidium* and its relatives found on bare sand and gravel bars along watercourses are collected by flotation.

FAUNA 117 SPECIES IN 29 GENERA (NA); 23 GENERA (ENA)

Ptenidium pusillum **(Gyllenhal)** (1.0–1.5 mm) is ovate, borad, convex, and mostly shiny blackish with long, sparse, silvery pubescence and yellowish appendages. Pronotum short, widest behind middle, sides rounded, with surface distinctly punctate and deep, transverse groove on each side at base. Elytra tips broadly reddish yellow-brown. Inhabits tree holes, forest leaf litter, mammal nests; found on decaying green cracking russula mushroom, *Russula virescens*. North America and Europe, widely distributed in east. (12+ NA)

Nanosella atrocephala **Dury** (0.42–0.50 mm) is elongate-oval, yellowish brown. Head darker between coarsely faceted eyes. Antennae with 11 antennomeres, last three forming loose club. Pronotum widest before base. Adults and larve found on surface or inside spore tubes of bracket or woody fungi (Polyporaceae, Hydnaceae). *Nanosella fungi* (LeConte) (0.25 mm) is more slender and pale. Among world's smallest known beetle species. Widespread in eastern United States. (2)

PRIMITIVE CARRION BEETLES, FAMILY AGYRTIDAE
(UH-*JER*-TIH-DEE)

Agyrtids were once placed as a subfamily of the carrion beetles (Silphidae), but are now recognized as a distinct family more closely related to the round fungus beetles (Leiodidae). Of the six species found in North America, only one is found east of the Mississippi River. The secretive and wingless adults of *Necrophilus pettiti* Horn live in moist or wet habitats under rocks or in loose soil and leaf litter, sometimes along the margins of mountain streams and springs, and at cave entrances. They are attracted to carrion and fungi in these habitats. In captivity, they have been reared on mouse feces and decayed squirrel flesh. Reproduction takes place during the winter.

FAMILY DIAGNOSIS Adult agyrtids are somewhat oval and flattened, yellowish to dark reddish brown, and the dorsum without any setae. Mouthparts with prominent mandibles directed forward (prognathous). Antennae with 11 antennomeres, clavate, club with fine antennomeres clothed in velvety setae, 8 never smaller than 7 or 9. Surface of pronotum smooth, without pits and margins broadly flattened. Each elytron with nine rows of large, distinct, and deep punctures, and apex broadly rounded with short, sharp tooth at suture; abdomen completely covered. Tarsal formula 5-5-5. Abdomen with five ventrites.

SIMILAR FAMILIES
- carrion beetles (Silphidae) – elytra with punctures and/or ribs, never with distinct grooves (p.120)

COLLECTING NOTES Primitive carrion beetles are difficult to find and seldom collected. Adults are attracted to pitfall traps baited with carrion or feces and placed in moist woods and other habitats near springs, creeks, and streams.

FAUNA 11 SPECIES IN SIX GENERA (NA); ONE SPECIES, *NECROPHILUS PETTITI* HORN (ENA)

Necrophilus pettiti Horn (9.0–12.0 mm) is broadly oval and shining reddish brown. Antennae weakly clubbed. Pronotum wider than long, almost as wide as elytra just before base, with side margins broadly flattened and densely punctured, sparsely punctate on middle. Elytra each with nine punctate grooves, punctures large and deep, even intervals raised, apical fourth sharply sloped down, with angle at tip of suture sharp; flight wings absent. Adults active mostly in fall through early spring at lower elevations, and summer in mountains, found on carrion, feces, and fungi in forested habitats. Southern Ontario to northern Florida, west to Illinois and Louisiana. (1)

ROUND FUNGUS BEETLES, FAMILY LEIODIDAE
(LIE-*OH*-DIH-DEE)

Eastern leiodids, commonly known as round fungus, small carrion, and mammal nest beetles, are a diverse family of small and secretive insects that feed and develop in accumulations of moist plant and animal tissues. *Catops, Prionochaeta, Dissochaetus,* and *Sciodrepoides* are scavengers of decaying organic matter, especially carrion, while *Nemadus* and *Ptomaphagus* are associated with accumulations of decaying plant material, dung, and carrion, or are associated with animal burrows, harvester ant nests, and caves. Blind and flightless, *Catopocerus* scavenge subterranean fungi growing in moist forest litter and soil, rotten logs, and occasionally caves. *Leiodes* and probably *Colon* also feed on subterranean fungi in forest litter habitats. *Agathidium* and *Anisotoma* eat mostly the fruiting bodies and plasmodia of slime molds. The mouse nest beetle, *Leptinus testaceus* Müller, is found in rodent nests. *Leptinillus validus* Horn is a scavenger in beaver lodges,while the highly modified and flealike beaver parasite beetle, *Platypsyllus castoris* Ritsema, is an ectoparasite on beavers.

FAMILY DIAGNOSIS Most adult leiodids are best distinguished from other small, oval beetles by the noticeably smaller eighth antennomere. Broadly oval to somewhat elongate, slightly flattened to very convex. Head partly visible from above, with distinctly clubbed antennae, club usually with five antennomeres and interrupted (not in *Colon*) by reduced antennomere 8. Prothorax with sides strongly keeled. Prothorax and elytra often granular or finely wrinkled across surface. Elytra long, covering abdomen (except *Platypsyllus*). Legs with usually front tarsi expanded (male) or narrow (female), tarsal formula usually 5-5-5, sometimes 3-3-3; also 5-5-4 (male *Agathidium, Anisotoma, Stetholiodes*), 5-4-4 (*Cainosternum*), or 4-4-4 (female *Agathidium, Anisotoma, Stetholiodes*). Abdomen with six ventrites.

SIMILAR FAMILIES The combination of body shape and clavate antennae with reduced antennomere 8 are distinctive.

COLLECTING NOTES Look for leiodids primarily in wooded habitats. Winged species (*Catops, Dissochaetus, Nemadus, Ptomaphagus, Sciodrepoides, Prionochaeta*) are captured in pitfall traps baited with dung and carrion, or in flight intercept traps. Flightless species are extracted from leaf litter by using Tulgren or Berlese funnels with presifted samples, or found under large rocks and logs in montane forests.

FAUNA 381 SPECIES IN 38 GENERA (NA); ~106 SPECIES IN 26 GENERA (ENA)

Leiodes species (1.5–6.4 mm) are small, oval or hemispherical beetles, and shiny yellowish-to-reddish brownish or blackish. Head with grooves underneath for antennae with 11 antennomeres, 7–11 forming a long, loose club. Tarsi 5-5-4 in both sexes. Larvae and adults feed mostly on subterranean fungi. Adults active in summer in forested habitats, found by sweeping grasses and herbaceous plants along roads and paths along forest edges, and in meadows and clearings at dusk; also found in refuse floating on rising floodwaters, unbaited pitfall trips, flight intercept traps, and at light. Mostly Northeast, further south in Appalachia, some in Coastal Plain. (29)

Agathidium species (4.0–6.0 mm) are convex, hemispherical, surfaces polished, reddish brown to black, and capable of rolling up into a ball concealing appendages. Head with grooves underneath for antennae with 11 antennomeres, 8 smaller than 7 or 9, last three (sometimes five) forming loose club; in some species, males with left mandible with a tusklike projection. Pronotum with broadly expanded sides, as broad as elytra. Elytra with few, if any, scattered punctures. Male with expanded front and middle tarsi. Adults generally found in moist, forested habitats in decaying logs, or under loose bark feeding on slime molds. Northeast and mid-Atlantic states. (3).

Catops basilaris Say (3.0–4.1 mm) is oblong, brown, surface granular and pubescent, with head and pronotum darker. Back of head sharply margined, antennomere 8 reduced, asymmetrical and pointed on one side. Base of pronotum evenly arched. Last tergite (propygidium) of female abdomen notched and grooved. Legs with tibial spurs long, not finely notched, tarsi 5-5-5. Active year-round in woodlands and forests, mostly early fall to late spring in northern part of range. Found under carrion and owl pellets, or in decaying fungus, leaf litter, and sometimes in the nests of moles, shrews, and rodents. Widespread; in east from Atlantic Canada to Georgia, west to Ontario, Wisconsin, and Iowa. (12)

Small Carrion Beetle *Prionochaeta opaca* (Say) (4.0–5.5 mm) is oblong-oval, blackish, and narrowed behind middle with pronotal and elytral margins nearly continuous. Antennae with nine antennomeres, as long as pronotum, 8 smaller than 7 or 9, club with five. Pronotum and elytra smooth with numerous setae borne on prominent sockets. Elytra with blue-grey coating, distinctly grooved along suture, faintly so at tips. Male front tarsi expanded, first tarsomere of middle leg not enlarged; hind tibiae with spur longer than first tarsomere, sides serrate. Active mostly spring and summer in broadleaf forests and cave entrances on carrion, dung, fungi, and other decomposing matter, sometimes rotting fruit; also in mammal and bird nests, tree holes. Eastern North America. (1)

Ptomaphagus brevior Jeannel (2.4–3.1 mm) is brownish black. Head with large eyes and short antennae not reaching base of pronotum. Pronotum with very fine ridges across surface. Hind tibia with two long spurs and fringed with smaller ones. Adults active late spring and late summer. Adults found in leaf litter, pitfall traps baited with human feces, carrion, and skunk cabbage leaves. Southern Ontario and Québec to Appalachian states, west to Iowa; replaced by the similar *P. consobrinus* LeConte in Coastal Plain states to central Texas. (52 NA)

Leptinus orientamericanus **Peck** (2.0–2.5 mm) is oblong-oval, flat, uniformly pale yellowish. Head with eyes reduced with crest across back of head overlapping front margin of pronotum. Prothorax underneath with prosternum short and sharp in front, not extending between bases of front legs, which are open behind, not surrounded by thoracic plates. Adults, most active in fall and winter, are ectoparasites and found mostly on fur or in nests of short-tail shrews, eastern moles, and mice. Older references to *L. testaceus* Müller (a European species) east of the Mississippi River are of this species. New York to Florida, west to Mississippi River. Similar *Leptinus americanus* LeConte is west of Mississippi River. (1)

Beaver Parasite Beetle *Platypsyllus castoris* **Ritsema** (1.9–2.2 mm) strongly resembles a flattened flea with flaplike elytra about as long as pronotum. Yellowish brown with darker markings. Adults and larvae are true ectoparasites of beavers. Adults collected by combing fur of captured or recently dead beavers; more than 60% of beavers in some populations may harbor up to nearly 200 beetles. Like its host, this beetle occurs across southern Canada and most of United States. (1)

BURYING AND CARRION BEETLES, FAMILY SILPHIDAE
(*SIL*-FIH-DEE)

Silphids, also known as burying, or carrion beetles (sexton beetles in England), are often large, conspicuous insects. Burying beetles (*Nicrophorus*) have long attracted attention because they exhibit some of the most advanced parental care behaviors known in beetles. Most adult silphids eat decaying flesh and are typically found in large numbers on or under carcasses. They may supplement their diets with maggots and rotting fungi, while a few feed exclusively on living plants or scavenge decomposing plant materials. Larval silphids feed almost exclusively on dead flesh. Adults often harbor predatory mites that help them to compete with other insect scavengers. The adults and larvae of species other than *Nicrophorus* opportunistically feed on carcasses or in accumulations of plant material as they find them and prepare nothing for their young. Adults defend themselves by oozing or spraying a dark, foul-smelling fluid from their anus that smells like rotting flesh to deter predators and collectors alike, while some day-flying species (*Nicrophorus, Oiceoptoma*) mimic bumble bees in flight.

FAMILY DIAGNOSIS Adult silphids are somewhat to strongly flattened and mostly black, sometimes with yellow, orange, or reddish markings on the pronotum and elytra. Head and mouthparts are directed forward (prognathous). Antennae with 11 antennomeres and gradually (clavate) or abruptly clubbed (capitate), clubs covered with velvety setae. Pronotum broader than head with edges sharply margined. Scutellum visible. Elytral surface never grooved, either smooth (*Nicrophorus*), or rough, sometimes with three longitudinal ridges or branched ribs (Silphinae). Apices of elytra either rounded, drawn out into sharp points, or appear as though they have been squarely cut off (truncate) and exposing one or more abdominal tergites. Tarsal formula 5-5-5, with simple claws equal in size. Abdomen with six (females), or seven (males) ventrites.

SIMILAR FAMILIES

■ primitive carrion beetles (Agyrtidae) – elytra with distinct grooves (p.117)

COLLECTING NOTES Search on or beneath vertebrate carcasses for adults. Dead pigs, rabbits, chickens, or juvenile turkeys are relatively cheap and readily obtained from farms and butchers for use as bait to attract these and other carrion-visiting beetles. Secure carcasses with chicken wire and tent stakes, or cover them with plywood weighed down with rocks or logs to discourage raccoons, skunks, coyotes, and other scavengers from stealing the bait. Pitfall traps baited with shrimp, fish, or chicken wings or other parts, and sunk in the ground or attached to trees placed in more or less open situations will also attract silphids. *Necrodes* and some species of *Nicrophorus* are attracted to lights in spring and summer. *Necrophila* and *Oiceoptoma* fly during the day and are sometimes found in large numbers on fungus; *Necrophila* rarely at sap flows.

FAUNA 30 SPECIES IN EIGHT GENERA (NA): 19 SPECIES IN SIX GENERA (ENA)

Red-lined Carrion Beetle *Necrodes surinamensis* **(Fabricius)** (12.0–24.0 mm) is mostly black with red markings on tips of ridged elytra and large eyes. Pronotum circular in outline, widest at middle, shiny. Elytra each with three long ridges, surface between distinctly rough, with variable row of reddish spots across tips sometimes extending up sides. Hind legs of male with curved tibiae and expanded femora. Nocturnal adults, active spring and summer, feed on maggots and carrion; attracted to light. Exude a vile-smelling chemical from special rectal glands. Newfoundland south to Florida, west to British Columbia, Oregon, Colorado, and New Mexico. (1)

American Carrion Beetle *Necrophila americana* **(Linnaeus)** (13.0–20.0 mm) is mostly dull black, pronotum with broad yellow margins and central black spot. Elytron with three ridges, surfaces wrinkled between ridges. Elytral tips of male normal, prolonged in female; both sexes tipped with yellow in northern populations, uniformly black in south. Diurnal adults in flight resemble bumble bees; found on carrion, fungus, and sapping tree wounds in moist woods from spring through summer. Nova Scotia south to Florida, west to Manitoba and eastern Texas. (1)

Ridged Carrion Beetle *Oiceoptoma inequale* **(Fabricius)** (13.0–15.0 mm) is black, covered with fine black pubescence, and with three distinct ridges on each elytron. Head with short row of erect setae behind eyes. Elytra with humeri each with tooth, surfaces between ridges flat, and width of upper oblique portion of epipleura twice that of lower vertical portion. Diurnal adults active late winter and spring, found on carrion and fungus. New Hampshire and Québec to northern Georgia, west to Ontario, Dakotas, and northeastern Texas. Replaced by *O. rugulosum* Portevin, with narrow elytra epipleura, upper and lower portions about equal; southeastern Coastal Plain, North Carolina to Florida, west to Texas. (3)

Oiceoptoma noveboracense **(Forster)** (13.0–15.0 mm) is dark brownish or black with distinct orangeish- or pinkish-red pronotal margins. Head black and eyes small with short row of long erect hairs behind. Each elytron with three ridges, smooth spaces between, and toothed elytral shoulders. Diurnal adults active spring and early summer, found on carrion and fungus, and at sapping tree wounds in forested habitats. Maritime Provinces and New England to Georgia, west to Alberta, Montana, Wyoming, Colorado, Oklahoma, and Mississippi. (3)

Thanatophilus lapponicus **(Herbst)** (9.4–14.0 mm) is dull black, clothed in dark setae, and elytra each with three ridges separated by rows of bumps. Head and pronotum covered in dense gray pubescence. Elytra each with tips broadly rounded (male) or extended at suture (female). Adults active in spring through early fall, found in open habitats on carcasses where they are scavengers and predators. Atlantic Canada to Rhode Island, west to Minnesota; also in western North America. (3)

122

American Burying Beetle *Nicrophorus americanus* **Olivier** (20.0–35.0 mm) is distinguished from all other *Nicrophorus* by large size and mostly orange pronotum with black border. Once widespread in eastern North America, now patchily distributed along western fringes of former range in South Dakota, Nebraska, Kansas, Oklahoma, Arkansas, and northeastern Texas; also on Block Island, Rhode Island. Decline attributed to loss of appropriately sized carrion and increase in vertebrate scavengers. Adults attracted to carrion and light. Federally listed as endangered in the United States and illegal to collect. Submit photos of beetles found elsewhere east of Mississippi River to U.S. Fish and Wildlife Service. (9)

Nicrophorus defodiens **Mannerheim** (12.0–18.0 mm) has black antennal clubs. Pronotum shiny black, somewhat squarish in outline, with broad margins along sides and base. Elytra with distinct pattern, epipleura black on ends, red in middle; red markings sometimes reduced. Underside with plate around hind legs clothed in dense yellow pubescence. Legs with hind tibiae straight. Adults active late spring and summer; attracted to light. Carrion buried under leaves and not soil. Alaska and across Canada, New England west to Minnesota, south through Appalachian Mountains to North Carolina and Tennessee; also in northwestern United States. (9)

Nicrophorus orbicollis Say (15.0–22.0 mm) has a shiny black, almost circular pronotum with wide side and basal margins. Antennal club orange, basal antennomeres black. Elytra with distinct pattern, surface covered with long erect setae, folded-under rim along sides entirely black; red markings sometimes reduced. Underside with brown pubescence. Legs with hind tibiae straight, not curved. Adults active late spring and summer, found in various habitats, especially wooded areas; attracted to light. Nova Scotia west to Saskatchewan, Dakotas, and eastern Texas. (9)

Nicrophorus pustulatus Herschel (15.0–20.0 mm) has antennal club with three orange antennomeres beyond one black one at base. Pronotum completely black and somewhat square, wider than long. Elytra black with red markings sometimes difficult to see; epipleuron entirely black. Underside of thorax sparsely clothed in yellowish brown pubescence; epimeron lacks setae. Hind tibiae straight. Nocturnal adults attracted to light, especially in forested habitats. Scant evidence suggests that they prefer to forage high in the canopy, possibly in tree holes, and rear their young on black rat snake eggs rather than carrion. Nova Scotia to Florida, west to Alberta, North Dakota, and eastern Texas. (9)

Nicrophorus sayi Laporte (15.0–23.0 mm) is shiny black with side margins of elytra reddish orange. Antennal club with three orange antennomeres. Pronotum round, black, without setae. Metasternal pubescence yellowish, brown and sparse, metepimeron with few black setae. Elytra each with two broad reddish-orange spots. Hind tibiae strongly curved. Nocturnal adults active in spring and summer; mostly montane in southern part of range. Newfoundland and Nova Scotia to Georgia, west to Alberta, Arkansas, and Oklahoma. (9)

Nicrophorus tomentosus Weber (11.0–19.0 mm) is the only species of *Nicrophorus* that has a pronotum densely clothed in long yellow setae. It also has completely black antennal clubs and straight hind tibiae. In flight, this diurnal beetle strongly resembles a bumble bee. Adults active in summer and found in various habitats, including woodlands and open grasslands. They do not bury carcasses, instead placing them in shallow pits and covering them with leaf litter. Found throughout eastern North America north to Nova Scotia, west to Saskatchewan, Montana, Colorado, and New Mexico. (9)

ROVE BEETLES, FAMILY STAPHYLINIDAE
(STAFF-EH-*LIN*-IH-DEE)

Rove beetles are the largest family of beetles in North America. They are found in nearly every type of terrestrial habitat and typically eat almost everything except living tissues of higher plants. Most species prey on insects and other invertebrates, but there are several subfamilies with species that feed entirely on fungi or decaying organic matter. Although a few large and conspicuous species are found on carrion and dung, most are decidedly more secretive and inhabit leaf litter, mosses, and rotting plant matter. They live under rocks and plant debris, especially in woodlands or along the shores of ponds, lakes, streams, and other wetlands; a few species are restricted to ocean beaches. Still others are found under bark, on living plants and fungi, and in the nests of animals. Most rove beetles are quick to take to the air. Many run on the ground with their abdomen waving menacingly in the air as if they could sting, but they cannot. Depending on the species, staphylinid larvae are predaceous, mycophagous, or scavengers and live in habitats similar to those of the adults. Staphylinid species are challenging to identify. Their identification often requires the examination of carefully prepared specimens with the aid of detailed monographs.

FAMILY DIAGNOSIS Adult staphylinids are incredibly diverse in form and habit. The majority of species are distinguished from other families of beetles by their long, slender, nearly parallel-sided, and flexible abdomens, threadlike (filiform) or gradually clubbed (clavate) antennae, and short elytra exposing five to six abdominal tergites. *Baeocera* and *Scaphidium* are small, broadly oval, compact, and leggy with elytra exposing one or two abdominal tergites. Other very small species are elongate-oval with distinctly clubbed antennae, more compact and rigid bodies, with short elytra generally exposing three to five abdominal tergites (Pselaphinae), or covering the abdomen entirely (Scydmaeninae). Tarsal formula usually 5-5-5, 3-3-3 (e.g., Pselaphinae), sometimes 4-4-4, 2-2-2, 4-5-5, or 4-4-5. Abdomen with six, sometimes seven ventrites.

SIMILAR FAMILIES Several other families (Micromalthidae, Cleridae, Cantharidae, Phengodidae, Nitidulidae, Meloidae, Cerambycidae) have species with short elytra exposing just a few abdominal tergites, but their overall appearance and form of antennae will usually distinguish them from most staphylinids.

COLLECTING NOTES Look for rove beetles on dung, carrion, under bark, in fungi, beneath objects and debris on the ground, especially in riparian habitats and along the shores of permanent bodies of standing and running water. Sweeping flowers and other herbaceous vegetation, or beating foliage of trees and shrubs are also productive. Some species are best located by sifting leaf litter and detritus, or extracted from these and other substrates gathered in suitable habitats by using Berlese-Tulgren funnels or Winkler/Moczarski eclectors. Many species are attracted to lights at night.

FAUNA 4,360 SPECIES IN 539 GENERA (NA)

Arpedium schwarzi **Fauvel** (2.4–3.3 mm) is flat, slightly convex, without pubescence, reddish brown to blackish. Head narrower than pronotum, with vague depression and small pits in front of simple eyes, antennae dark brown to blackish. Pronotum densely punctate, widest just before middle, with margins sometimes irregularly yellowish. Elytra densely punctate, punctures evenly distributed or arranged in vague rows, without impressions, with tips yellow. Abdomen finely punctate. Legs yellow. Adults active spring and summer, found in litter in forest floor, and under debris along waterways or damp soil. Massachusetts to North Carolina and Alabama, west to Michigan, Illinois, Missouri, Arkansas, and Louisiana. (5)

Olophrum obtectum Erichson (3.6–5.5 mm) is dark reddish brown to blackish with margins of pronotum and tips of elytra narrowly yellowish-to-reddish brown. Elytra diverging from base to broadly rounded tips, surface coarsely and evenly punctate, punctures not in rows; flight wings fully developed. Appendages light brown to reddish brown. Adults are found in spring and summer on vegetation along creeks and streams; also attracted to lights. Québec and Ontario to North Carolina, west to Wisconsin, Kansas, and Tennessee. (3)

Trigonodemus striatus LeConte (4.5–5.0 mm) is robust, flattened, and orange-red with dark markings. Elytra long; legs and antennal bases pale brown. Head long but not extended into a beak. deeply impressed beside each bulging eye. Antennomere 1 long, 2 shorter than 3, 4 smallest, 5–11 abruptly thickened and densely pubescent. Pronotum widest across base, somewhat parallel-sided toward rear, becoming broadly arched across front. Elytra together oval, at base with angles rounded and broader than prothorax, covering all but last two abdominal tergites. Tarsi 5-5-5, first hind tarsomere shorter than last. Adults found on fungi and in rotten logs. Nova Scotia and New England to Pennsylvania, west to Ontario. (1)

Batrisodes lineaticollis (Aubé) (formerly *B. globosus* LeConte) (1.8–2.2 mm) is robust, cylindrical, sparsely and finely pubescent, shining, and uniformly reddish brown. Head with ridge down middle, small pits between eyes deep and round, more or less connected by deep, curved groove. Antennomere 1 large, 2 conical, equal in width to 3 and 8. Pronotum slightly wider than long, widest before middle. Elytra very finely punctate, one-half longer than pronotum, each with raised basal angles, three small punctures at base, and short, shallow grooves. Adults found in ant nests, under stones, and in caves. Widespread in eastern North America. (84 NA)

Brachygluta abdominalis (Aubé) (1.9–2.0 mm) is slender, smooth, and uniformly reddish brown, with head and pronotum each with three pits; pronotal pits about equal in size, pubescent. Head squarish, wide as prothorax, with antennae half as long as body. Pronotum not very convex, widest at middle, with two pits on sides at base clearly visible from above. Elytra together slightly wider than long, each with prominent humeri. Abdomen of male with tergites 1–3 distinctly lobed on hind margins, those on 1 swollen, broadly rounded. Adults found under leaf litter and stones, or in mosses along ponds, marshes, and streams. Atlantic coast, from Maritime Provinces and New England to Georgia, Pennsylvania. (22 NA)

125

Decarthron velutinum **(LeConte)** (1.2 mm) is elongate, slender, clothed in short and sparse pubescence, reddish brown. Head squarish, flattened, with two large pits on top. Antennae with 10 antennomeres in both sexes. Pronotum nearly circular with deep pits. Elytra shorter than head and pronotum combined, distance across base equal to length, not twice as wide as pronotum. Abdomen short, with first tergite three times wide as long, ridges entire over one-third of surface. Middle femora enlarged in male, scooped out from middle almost to tip, with large sharp spine above. In leaf litter and moss. Eastern United States. (23)

Reichenbachia facilis **(Casey)** (1.3 mm) is sparsely clothed in short reclining setae, and blackish with reddish elytra and pale reddish-yellow legs. Head longer than wide, without punctures between prominent eyes, and with three deep pits of similar size arranged in equilateral triangle, narrower than head. Antennae longer than head and prothorax combined. Pronotum slightly wider than long, widest before middle. Elytra at base slightly wider than pronotum, each with groove along suture and down middle. Abdominal tergites convex, polished, first tergite with small punctures and divergent fine ridges. In leaf litter and moss. Ontario to Georgia, west to Illinois and Mississippi. (33)

Adranes coecus **LeConte** (1.8 mm) is orange-yellow with elytra each bearing a row of stiff setae. Head cylindrical, eyes absent, palps with one palpomere, antennae short with three antennomeres, 1 extremely small. Prothorax cone-shaped. Elytra with rows of short, recumbent, reclining setae. Abdomen above smooth, with tergites fused. Legs with tarsomeres 1 and 2 very short, 3 very long, each with single claw. Adults found in ant (*Aphaenogaster*, *Lasius*) nests. New York to Georgia, west to Illinois, Missouri, and Alabama. (2)

Cedius spinosus **LeConte** (1.9–2.0 mm) is stout, somewhat convex, reddish brown with sparse pubescence. Head wider than long; maxillary palps short, palpomere 3 with inward projection and about half as long as 4; last three antennomeres gradually enlarged; 8 obliquely produced, pointed at tip and partly enclosing 9 in male. Pronotum finely, sparsely punctate; front half without pits, pair of basal pits connected by fine transverse groove. Elytra short, finely and sparsely punctate, with pits at base. Abdomen margined on sides with six (female) or seven (male) ventrites. Front femora each with cone-shaped spine at base and small tooth at basal third, bases of middle legs separated. Found with ants in rotten logs or under bark. New York to Florida, west to Illinois and Texas. (3)

Ceophyllus monilis LeConte (3.3 mm) is elongate-ovate, smooth, reddish brown. Head convex, as long and nearly as wide as pronotum. Maxillary palpomere 3 leaflike. Antennae robust, without club, antennomeres 5, 6, 8 enlarged (male) or beadlike (female). Pronotum bell-shaped with fine impression down middle flanked by two pits at base. Elytra flat, wider at base than pronotum, widest at apical third, with groove along suture long or short. Legs slender, front femora each with three spines at base, tarsi long and slender, half as long as tibiae, and claws equal in length, inner one thicker. Adults found in ant (*Lasius*) nests. Ontario to North Carolina, west to Manitoba, Wisconsin, and Alabama. (1)

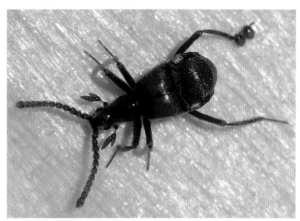

Tyrus semiruber Casey (1.6–1.7 mm) is somewhat stout, convex, very shiny with sparse tiny punctures, dark reddish brown with elytra reddish and abdomen black; appendages pale yellowish brown. Head long, broadly rounded in front, with maxillary palpomeres 3 and 4 elongate. Antennae short, very slender, gradually clubbed, barely half as long as body. Pronotum barely wider than long, widest and somewhat rounded in front of middle. Elytra half again wider than long, sides diverging to broadly rounded tips, with abdomen wider and longer than prothorax. Adults found under bark of conifer and deciduous trees, also in decayed wood. Maritime Provinces and New England to Georgia, west to Manitoba, Wisconsin, and Missouri. (2)

127

Charhyphus picipennis (LeConte) (2.7–3.9 mm) is reddish to blackish brown; legs yellowish brown to pale reddish brown. Head strongly flattened, with mouthparts and antennae paler, and large, coarse, deep punctures. Pronotum with large, deep, coarse, and dense punctures. Elytra yellowish-to-reddish brown with infusions of black, and distinct ridge along sides. Abdomen with only one pair of plates on sides of each tergite. Adults active spring and summer, found beneath bark of oak (*Quercus*) and other logs. New Hampshire to Georgia, west to Ontario, Wisconsin, and Illinois. (1)

Olisthaerus substriatus Paykull (5.0–5.5 mm) is elongate, parallel-sided, and reddish brown with head and elytra darker. Antennae attached on sides of clypeus. Pronotum wider than elytra, margins not expanded or flattened, sparsely punctate, with a pair of circular impressions at base; underneath with small triangular plate behind front leg without spiracle. Abdomen ridged on sides. Front tarsi not expanded. Adults found under bark of dead conifers. Holarctic; in North America from Alaska, across Canada, New England, and New York. (2)

Lordithon cinctus (Gravenhorst) (4.4-6.2 mm) is bicolored with an elongate head. Last two antennomeres distinctly contrasting, with last pale and penultimate dark. Pronotum uniformly reddish yellow to reddish orange. Elytra with fewer punctures along suture and across middle, each with distinctly pale base and darker markings restricted to apical two-thirds. Abdomen with tergites more densely punctate along rear margins. Adults active mostly late summer, found on fungus, e.g., sulphur polypore (*Laetiporus sulphureus*) and *Suillus*. New Brunswick and New England to Georgia, west to Wisconsin, Kansas, and Texas. (16)

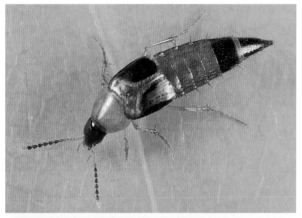

Lordithon facilis (Casey) (2.6–4.9 mm) is light reddish yellow to dark reddish brown with distinct bicolored pattern on elytra. Head short, blackish to black, antennae dark with basal three or four antennomeres paler. Pronotum yellowish. Elytra yellowish with dark sides and suture, dark triangular markings on tips, and punctate rows each consisting of 7–14 seta-bearing punctures. Adults active almost year-round, especially in summer, found on mature gill mushrooms and polypore fungi. Atlantic Canada to Georgia, west to Ontario, Michigan, Iowa, and Arkansas. (16)

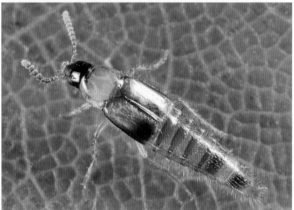

128

Lordithon fungicola Campbell (4.6–6.9 mm) is elongate, narrow, sides strongly tapering to rear, smooth and shiny. Head long, black, antennae dark with basal three or four antennomeres paler. Pronotum uniformly pale to vaguely dark with pale margins. Elytra pale with large, elongate brown to blackish spot from just before middle almost to tip. Abdomen above usually with basal tergites uniformly brown to blackish, penultimate tergite (propygidium) dark brown to black at base and pale across rear, tip dark except at extreme base, sometimes uniformly dark reddish brown, or basal half of each tergite dark reddish brown to black and rear half pale to light reddish brown. Adults on mature gill mushrooms and polypore fungi. Transcontinental, in east from Atlantic Canada to New Jersey, west to Wisconsin. (16)

Lordithon kelleyi (Malkin) (formerly *L. bimaculatus* Couper) (4.4–5.9 mm) is elongate, narrow, sides strongly tapering to rear, smooth and shiny. Head and scutellum black. Basal three or four antennomeres pale. Pronotum uniformly pale, often broadly blackish across middle, or black with pale margins. Elytra yellowish, each with large triangular dark spot starting at basal two-fifths and ending near tip, spot deeply notched on side at base and tip. Abdomen variable, usually dark with tip and base of 7–8 respectively, pale. Adults active spring and summer, found on fruiting fungal bodies. Transcontinental, in east from Maritime Provinces and New England to North Carolina, west to Minnesota and Illinois. (16)

***Coproporus ventriculus* (Say)** (1.5–1.7 mm from front of head to elytral tip) is broadly oval with triangular abdomen, black or blackish with lighter margins. Head with mouthparts pointed down, narrower than pronotum and partly inserted inside prothorax. Pronotum wider than long, widest at base, and evenly convex, with surface punctate and no microsculpture. Elytra with tips lighter. Abdomen with sides evenly tapered from base to tip, underside of tip with four setose lobes (female) or simple (male). Adults active mostly spring through summer, found under loose bark of conifers and hardwoods. Widespread in eastern North America. (6)

***Sepedophilus* species** (1.2–3.2 mm) are broadly elongate-oval, usually uniformly brownish to reddish brown to blackish, broadest across pronotum or base of elytra, and clothed in dense pubescence. Elytra along suture longer or shorter than pronotum. Abdomen without ridges along sides, tip notched (male) or not (female). Front tibiae with distinct row of spines along outer margins. Adults, and probably larvae, eat fungus found in moldy forest litter and other decaying debris, also under loose bark or on fleshy and polypore fungi. Some species run rapidly when disturbed, others remain immobile. Eastern North America. (21)

***Tachinus fimbriatus* Gravenhorst** (7.0–10.5 mm) is oblong, robust, flattened, and bicolored with head, pronotum, abdomen shiny black, and elytra reddish brown with tips narrowly dark. Antennae mostly dark, basal four pale, tip sometime pale. Elytra combined as wide as long. Abdomen with first two ventrites ridged between bases of hind legs in both sexes, dorsal surface of tergite 6 without spongy spot at middle, tip notched in female. Front tarsi of male expanded. Adults active spring and summer, found on fleshy fungi and decaying fruit. Maritime Provinces and New England to Georgia, west to Ontario, Wisconsin, and Arkansas. (22)

***Tachyporus elegans* Horn** (1.6–1.8 mm) is teardrop-shaped, moderately convex, and mostly yellowish brown to reddish orange with bicolored abdomen. Head blackish. Pronotum with sides broadly rounded. Scutellum and surrounding elytral surfaces blackish. Elytra with sides straight, slightly narrowed from base to tips, and a distinct ridge. Abdomen with six ventrites, first ventrite pale, last two blackish. Adults active year-round, often found in spring and fall under bark, from wet clumps of grass and moss, in decayed logs, and in nesting material of rodents. New Brunswick and New England to montane North Carolina, west southern Ontario and eastern Nebraska. (19)

Aleochara littoralis **(Mäklin)** (3.5–7.0 mm) is elongate, somewhat parallel-sided, and uniformly black with surface of head, pronotum, and elytra with distinct hexagonal microsculpture. Mouthparts rusty brown. Antennomere 4 spherical, 6–10 each twice as wide as long. Pronotum with pubescence directed toward sides. Elytra sometimes rusty brown. Abdomen somewhat shiny, sparsely pubescent, ventrites 1–3 deeply and 4 shallowly impressed. Adults found late winter to midsummer, restricted to coastlines, under decaying seaweed teeming with maggots, also under carrion on beaches. Atlantic and Pacific coasts, in east from Newfoundland to Florida. (29)

Meronera venustula **(Erichson)** (1.6–1.8 mm) is very small, stout, and brown with yellowish-brown legs and antennal bases. Head with distinct and narrow neck. Antennomeres become progressively wider toward tip. Pronotum wider than long, slightly wider than head, very convex, sides rounded at apical third and weakly convergent to base, and without depression at base. Elytra often partly or wholly blackish, wider than pronotum, at middle only slightly longer than pronotum, less coarsely punctured than head or pronotum. Underside with bases of middle legs widely separated. Adults and larvae feed on fungal structures in leaf litter in various habitats. Widespread in eastern North America. (1)

Falagria dissecta **Erichson** (1.9–2.6 mm) is small, elongate, slender, sparsely pubescent and finely punctate, and blackish or black, with elytra and base of abdomen dark brown. Head with narrow neck, antennae attached between eyes. Pronotum barely wider than long, sides strongly rounded in front, widest before middle, with a fine deep groove down middle sometimes interrupted by small pocket. Scutellum with two distinct ridges. Elytra distinctly wider than pronotum. Abdomen at base narrower than elytra, without long setae along sides and underneath tip. Legs brownish yellow. Adults found year-round, under decaying vegetation, dung, carrion, rotting fungi, and in rodent nests; attracted to light. Widespread in North America. (2)

Gymnusa atra **Casey** (5.0–6.5 mm) is elongate, slender, narrowed at both ends, head directed downward, and black with black pubescence. Top of head smooth, shiny. Antennae attached between eyes, antennomere 1, sometimes 2 reddish brown to brown, and almost equal in length. Abdomen with ventrites 3–6 fringed with setal combs. Legs with tarsi 5-5-5, tarsomere 5 without long setae, claws simple. Adults found in vegetation along margins of bogs, marshes, ponds, and streams. Maritime Provinces and New England to Manitoba, Iowa, and Illinois. (5)

Gyrophaena species (1.2–3.5 mm) are elongate-oval, flattened, coarsely and distinctly punctured, yellowish, brown, blackish, or black, often bicolored. Antennae with antennomeres each becoming wider toward tips. Eyes prominent and finely faceted. Mandibles well-developed, right mandible with single tooth on inner margin. Pronotum wider than long, constricted behind middle. Elytra usually wider and always longer than pronotum. Tarsi 5-5-4. Abdomen tapering to tip. Adults prefer fresh mushrooms, where they feed, mate, and lay eggs on fruiting bodies; also found in moist forest litter and under logs. Eastern Canada south to North Carolina and Missouri. (47)

Hoplandria lateralis (Melsheimer) (2.8–4.0 mm) is narrowly oval and mostly shiny yellowish brown to reddish with bicolored elytra. Head dark brown, mouthparts pale, eyes large, and antennomeres 6–10 each twice as wide as long. Abdomen with sides broadly arched, male with U-shaped process on second ventrite. Legs with coxae and femora pale. Elytra each usually with dark oblique stripe from inner front angle to outer angle at tip. Adults active mainly spring and summer, found on feces and carrion in hardwood forests, by sweeping herbaceous vegetation; attracted to light. Québec and Ontario to Florida, west to South Dakota and Arizona. (10)

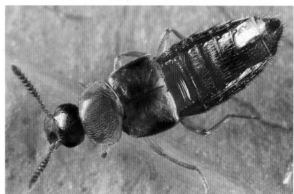

131

Drusilla canaliculata (Fabricius) (4.0–4.8 mm) is reddish brown with head and abdominal tergites 4–5 darker; legs and antennal bases yellowish brown. Head with narrow neck. Pronotum longer than wide, widest in front, with sides narrowed behind middle, broad oval impression, and narrow groove down middle ending in pit at base. Elytra wider and shorter than pronotum. Abdomen of male with broad notch at tip lined with small teeth. Tarsi 4-4-5. Adults active spring and summer, prey on ants, found under stones and in leaf litter associated with river margins, flood debris, and other disturbed habitats. Europe; in east from Maritime Provinces to Connecticut and Pennsylvania, west to Ontario and Kentucky. (2)

Philotermes cubitopilus Seevers (2.1–2.5 mm) is small, broad, clothed in pale and reclining pubescence, and light brown. Head large, sloping only slightly down, with some erect setae on top, antennomeres stout, 2–11 are 1.7–1.8 times longer than pronotum. Pronotum wider than long, with base and side margins continuously arched. Abdomen moderately broad, flat, with sides parallel. Legs short, tarsi 4-4-5. Adults found in logs with eastern subterranean termites (*Reticulitermes flavipes*). District of Columbia to Florida, west to Arkansas and Alabama. (7)

Scaphidium quadriguttatum Say (3.8–4.5 mm) is oval, convex, and mostly or completely shiny black. Head with eyes notched. Base of pronotum and elytra each with distinct row of deep punctures. Each elytron with two to four short rows of punctures and with or without two red spots. Last abdominal tergite (pygidium) exposed and strongly pointed. Males with underside of metasternum depressed, punctate, and hairy. Adults found year-round beneath bark of decaying, fungus-covered hardwood logs; also attracted to lights in late spring and summer. Ontario and Québec, south to Georgia, west to Iowa and Texas. (~5)

132

Baeocera species (1.3–2.6 mm) are very small, ovate or oblong-ovate, convex, and shiny blackish. Eye shallowly, narrowly notched. Antennae slender and not distinctly clubbed, antennomere 3 long, slender, cylindrical, not much shorter than 4. Pronotum with hind angles sharp, but not produced. Scutellum absent. Elytra without rows of punctures, widest near base and weakly tapering to broadly square tips. Adults active year-round, found in forest leaf litter, around decaying logs, and on fungi, especially slime molds (Myxogastria). Species identification often requires examination of male genitalia. Widespread in eastern North America. (22)

Scaphisoma rubens Casey (1.7–1.9 mm) is very small, narrowly oval, strongly convex, uniformly pale reddish yellow-brown. Head with eyes not notched. Antennae slender and not clubbed, antennomere 3 short, triangular and flattened, not much shorter than 4. Head and pronotum vaguely punctured. Scutellum very small, triangular. Elytra with fine scattered punctures, widest at basal third, sides rounded and narrowed to tips. Adults feed on spores, found on logs and polypore fungi. Maritime Provinces and New England to New York, west to Ontario. (20)

Siagonium americanum (Melsheimer) (5.0–6.5 mm) is elongate, flattened, and uniformly yellowish-to-reddish brown. Head and pronotum finely punctate. Head of male with depression flanked by a pair of horns. Pronotum narrowed behind middle, with trace of fine groove down middle. Elytra each with single punctate groove along suture, rest of surface irregularly wrinkled and punctured. Adults active in summer, usually found under bark of decaying trees, especially conifers; attracted to light. Maritime Provinces and New England to Georgia, west to Nebraska, Kansas, and Arkansas. *S. punctatum* LeConte has smooth or finely wrinkled pronotum and 4-5 punctate grooves on elytra; widespread in East. (3)

Thoracophorus costalis (Erichson) (2.0–2.5 mm) is elongate, slender, somewhat cylindrical, dull reddish brown, and very roughly sculptured. Head with one pair of longer and two pairs of shorter ridges, eyes small and not visible from above, antennae attached on margin in front of eyes, with 11 antennomeres. Pronotum somewhat squarish with six ridges, pronotum, and narrower than base of elytra. Elytra each with four ridges and microscopic polygons. Abdomen not distinctly ridged along sides. Tarsal formula 3-3-3. Adults found under bark of dead oak (*Quercus*) and other deciduous trees; some Neotropical species associated with termites. New England and Québec to Florida, west to Manitoba. (3)

Bledius mandibularis Erichson (6.0–11.0 mm) is somewhat cylindrical and mostly pale to dark reddish brown, legs and elytra paler; inland populations darker than coastal. Head with large mandibles and geniculate antennae, surface more deeply impressed in male. Pronotum and abdomen with black infusions. Elytra yellowish brown with broad infusions of brown on surface. Tibiae spiny, tarsal formula 4-4-4. Active spring and summer, year-round in South. Adults live in coastal and salt lake habitats, excavating galleries marked by casts of lighter substrates into open mudflats; attracted to light in large numbers. Massachusetts to Florida, west to southern Manitoba, Utah, and New Mexico. (90 NA)

133

Anotylus rugosus (Fabricius) (4.0–5.0 mm) is elongate, black, with reddish-brown appendages, pronotum and elytra sometimes brownish; appendages reddish brown. Head with opaque square area in front. Pronotum with four ridges, pair in middle divergent in front. Elytra combined wider than long, longer than pronotum. Abdomen ridged along sides. Tarsomeres 1 and 2 nearly equal in length. Adults found on dung, carrion, and decaying vegetable matter. Europe, now established in east from Québec and Ontario to Florida, west to Indiana and Texas; also Pacific Northwest and California. (14)

Oxyporus quinquemaculatus LeConte (5.3–8.0 mm) is robust, shiny yellow to reddish yellow with bold dark markings. Head and mandibles large, antennomeres 6–10 narrow, no more than 1.5 times wider than long, pale at base and tip. Pronotum with hind angle distinct and with a distinctly convex ridge. Abdomen with middle of first two and all of last three tergites black. Legs pale. Adults and larvae feed on fungus. Adults often gregarious, active in late spring and early summer, found on mushrooms including *Laccaria*, *Psilocybe*, *Hypholoma*, *Tricholomopsis*, and *Pluteus*; also in Malaise traps. Nova Scotia and Québec to Georgia, west to Ontario, Illinois, and Tennessee. (12)

Oxyporus rufipennis LeConte (8.5–13.0 mm) is robust, black with orange-red elytra and reddish-yellow mouthparts and tarsi. Head and mandibles large, antennomeres 6–10 more than twice as wide as long. Pronotum with hind angle distinct and with a distinctly convex ridge. Elytral tips with outer angles black. Abdomen with middle of first two and all of last three tergites black. Legs pale. Adults and larvae feed on fungus. Adults active in late spring and summer, found on mushrooms including *Pholiota* and *Pluteus*. Maritime Provinces and New England to Maryland, west to Ontario, Michigan, Iowa, and Kansas. (12)

Oxyporus vittatus Gravenhorst (5.5–7.3 mm) is robust and shiny yellow and black or mostly black, with large conspicuous mandibles directed forward; color pattern variable. Head with mandibles larger in male, large, crescent-shaped labial palpi, and antennomeres 6–11 more than twice as wide as long. Adults active spring and summer, found on bolete (*Suillus*) and gilled (*Naucoria, Hypholoma, Pleurotus,* and *Laccaria*) mushrooms. Maritime Provinces to northern Florida, west to Manitoba, Iowa, and Kansas. (12)

Colour variation in
Oxyporus vittatus.

Euconnus salinator (LeConte) (1.5 mm) is oval, robust, narrowed at ends, and shiny blackish with dark reddish tinge on elytra with no pubescence on head or elytra. Head with eyes in front of middle, narrow neck, nearly as long as wide with a puncture bearing thick seta on each side. Clubbed antennae black, reddish brown at base with antennomeres 3–7 equal in length, club formed by 8–10, each progressively longer. Prothorax as long as wide, slightly wider than head, pronotum with black setae and four pits across base. Scutellum not visible. Elytra longer than wide, wider than pronotum, each with deep pit at middle of base. Adults found in moist litter, rotting logs, tree hollows; attracted to light. New England to Florida, west to Wisconsin, Iowa, and Tennessee. (~100)

Stenus colon Say (3.6–4.0 mm) is slender, shining black elytra, with pale reddish-yellowish spot just behind middle. Head slightly more than twice as wide as long, eyes bulging, deeply impressed and coarsely punctate between eyes, antennae not reaching middle of pronotum, with antennomere 3 one-half longer than 4. Prothorax widest at middle, pronotum with deep narrow groove just behind middle. Elytra at base narrower than head, wider than pronotum, coarsely and densely punctate. Diurnal adults prey on springtails and other arthropods with extendable mouthparts, swim on water surface with aid of glandular secretion, found under rocks and debris along streams and rivers. Widespread in eastern United States; also Ontario. (192 NA)

Pseudopsis subulata Herman (3.0–4.0 mm) is somewhat flattened and reddish brown with distinct and sharp longitudinal ridges on head, pronotum, and elytra. Head, pronotum, and each elytron with three, four, and five ridges, respectively. Antennae stout. Middle lobe of male genitalia tapered to a sharp tip. Adults collected in leaf litter in mixed deciduous woodlands. Atlantic Canada and Québec to North Carolina, west to Ontario and Illinois. *Pseudopsis sagitta* Herman (2.6–5.0 mm), middle lobe of male genitalia arrowhead-shaped; Québec. (2)

Astenus brevipennis (Austin) (3.0–3.7 mm) is very elongate, slender, and yellowish brown with head and last two or three abdominal tergites dark or black. Head rectangular, coarsely punctured, wider than pronotum. Pronotum longer than wide with sides broadly rounded at apical third or fourth before converging to basal angles. Elytra about same length and width as pronotum. Legs with tarsomere 4 lobed, hind tarsomere 1 long. Adults found in moist habitats; attracted to light. Québec and Ontario to Virginia, west to Manitoba, Michigan, Iowa, and Missouri. (16)

135

Homaeotarsus bicolor (Gravenhorst) (7.5–10.0 mm) is large and bicolored black and brown with prominent mandibles each with three teeth on inside margins. Head black with a distinct neck, coarsely punctate, mouthparts and antennae brown. Basal antennomere elongate. Pronotum longer than wide, brown, and smooth at middle, more coarsely punctate on sides. Elytra brown, one-third wider and longer than pronotum, with ridge from basal to outer apical angle. Abdomen ridged on sides, slightly narrower than elytra, black with last two tergites brown. Legs pale, with front tarsi not expanded, hind tarsomere 4 not lobed underneath. Adults found under stones and debris in wet or damp habitats, especially along streambeds. New Brunswick to Florida, west to Ontario and Iowa. (25)

Lathrobium convolutum Watrous (7.8–8.9 mm) is narrowed at both ends and mostly black. Head oval, labrum deeply notched and without teeth, distinct narrow neck; underneath with pair of fine grooves behind mouth widely separated and parallel. Pronotum longer than wide. Elytra about as long as combined width, long as pronotum, mostly red with triangular blackened area at base. Abdomen of male above with tergites 4-7 with bare, shallow longitudinal impressions along middle, tip underneath notched (male) or not (female). Legs yellowish brown, with front tarsi not expanded. Adults found among leaf litter in riparian habitats. Québec to New Jersey, west to Manitoba and Ohio. (67 NA)

Lobrathium collare (Erichson) (4.5–6.0 mm) is small, somewhat flattened, narrowed at both ends, and bicolored black and reddish brown. Head black with distinct neck, tip of maxillary palp cone-shaped and pointed. Pronotum slightly longer than wide, wider than head, with smooth line down middle. Elytra barely wider than pronotum and coarsely punctate, each without ridge along sides, with punctate grooves. Abdomen slightly narrower than elytra, densely and finely punctate, tip lighter. Adults found under litter and debris in riparian habitats. Maritime Provinces to Florida, west to Manitoba and Iowa. (69 NA)

Paederus littorarius Gravenhorst (4.0–5.5 mm) is elongate, slender, sparsely clothed in erect setae, and bicolored reddish yellow and black. Head dark with distinct pale neck. Antennae blackish in middle, pale at base and very tip. Pronotum elongate, convex, slightly narrower than head, finely punctate, and sides slightly arched. Elytra with dark blue sheen, punctures coarse, deep, and dense. Abdomen narrower than elytra, parallel-sided, with last two tergites black. Legs with tarsomere 4 bilobed underneath. Adults active in spring under rocks in damp habitats; produce defensive skin irritant, paederin. Widespread in Canada and northern United States. (10)

Sunius confluentus (Say) (3.0–4.0 mm) is dark reddish brown or darker, appendages and tips of elytra paler. Head finely wrinkled, wider than long, as wide as elytra, straight behind eyes, hind angles rounded. Pronotum narrower than head, "necklike" behind head, finely wrinkled, with posterior angles rounded and distant from humeral angles of elytra. Elytra finely, closely punctate. Legs with front femora distinctly toothed. Predatory adults found under loose bark of recently dead trees and in association with fungi; sometimes brought indoors with firewood. Prince Edward Island and Québec to Florida, west to Manitoba, Minnesota, Indiana, and Alabama. (7)

Palaminus testaceus Erichson (3.0–4.0 mm) is slender, somewhat cylindrical, and shiny pale yellowish brown with bristling yellowish setae. Head wider than long, abruptly stops behind eyes; antennae longer than head and prothorax. Head and pronotum coarsely, sparsely punctured. Pronotum only slightly narrowed from front to back. Elytra slightly wider, twice as long as pronotum. Abdomen narrower and darker than elytra, cylindrical, with sides not ridged, with tip double-notched (male) or with deep single notch (female). Adults found in spring and early summer on foliage of trees and shrubs. (12)

Pinophilus latipes Gravenhorst (14.0–19.5 mm) is elongate, slender, and black with appendages yellowish brown. Head with mandibles nearly symmetrical, each with long two-tipped tooth at middle, many medium and small punctures, as well as larger ringed seta-bearing punctures. Pronotum dull with larger ringed seta-bearing punctures and many smaller punctures between. Elytra longer and wider than pronotum. Protarsi widely expanded in both sexes. Adults active spring and summer; attracted to light. New Jersey to Florida, west to Iowa and eastern Texas. (6)

Diochus schaumii Kraatz (3.4–4.2 mm) is elongate, slender, narrowed at both ends, and variable in color. Individuals are uniformly yellowish brown, reddish yellow-brown, or reddish yellow-brown with head, elytra (except apical margin) and abdomen (except apical margins of tergites and tip) variably dark. Head with narrow neck, antennae not elbowed, with basal antennomere somewhat long and robust, and maxillary palpomeres 2–3 pubescent. Pronotum longer than wide, widest behind middle, wider than head. Elytra wide as pronotum, not overlapping. Abdomen elongate-oval. Adults found in forest litter, especially near swamps, marshes, and edges of lakes and ponds. Québec and southern Ontario, eastern United States. (1)

Atrecus americanus (Casey) (4.5–5.7 mm) is dark brownish black to blackish. Head as wide as pronotum, with fine, dense grooves across top, antennae short, antennomere 3 slightly longer than 2, 4 and 5 about as long as wide, 4 sometimes longer, 6–11 wider than long. Pronotum longer than wide, at base narrower than elytra, with many fine wrinkles across surface becoming meshlike on sides in front. Elytra slightly and indistinctly paler along base and suture. Adults found under bark of dead trees. Maritime Provinces to Appalachian Mountains of North Carolina, west to Ontario and Michigan. (2)

Acylophorus species (4.8–8.0 mm) are elongate, narrowed at both ends, pronotum usually dark (*A. flavicollis* Sachse bright red), with head and pronotum shiny, and elytra and abdomen punctured and setose. Mandibles long, slender, pointed. Antennae geniculate, antennomere 1 very long, about as long or longer than 2–5 combined. Pronotum widest at base, underneath with front angles projecting forward. Adults found in wet moss and debris near water. Tarsi 5-5-5, front claws longest, front tarsomeres 1–4 expanded, bristly on sides and setose on top, middle and hind tarsi smooth on top. Examination of male genitalia essential for species determination. Widespread in eastern North America. (15)

Belonuchus rufipennis (Fabricius) (4.6–8.5 mm) is black, with elytra and first four abdominal tergites reddish yellow or reddish brown. Labial palpomeres long, narrow, 4 longer and narrower than 2. Pronotum longer than wide, with rows of 4–5 punctures on top, sides 5–6. Front and hind femora more spinose in male than female. Front tarsi simple, tarsomeres with upper surface bare, except for scattered, long setae along margins, below without setose pads. Adults attracted to decaying organic matter, including carrion, dung, rotting plant and fungal tissues, fermenting fruit and sap; also in forest litter and tree holes. New England to Florida, west to Ontario, Colorado, and New Mexico. (4)

Bisnius blandus (Gravenhorst) (4.9–6.7 mm) is bicolored. Head, elytra, and abdomen from fourth tergite on dark; legs uniformly yellowish brown. Pronotum and first three visible abdominal tergites reddish yellow-brown. Pronotum as long as wide to slightly longer, punctate rows with 4-5 punctures. Elytra at suture as long as pronotum, at sides longer. Front tarsi simple, tarsomeres with upper surface bare, except for scattered, long setae along margins, below without setose pads. Adults found on or near deciduous trees, either under bark or in rotten wood, on sap drip, among polypores, or on carrion. Maritime Provinces to Georgia, west to Ontario, Minnesota, Nebraska, and Oklahoma. (7)

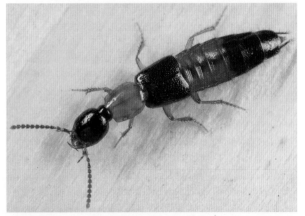

Hairy Rove Beetle *Creophilus maxillosus villosus* (Gravenhorst) (11.0–23.0 mm) is large and shiny black with vestiture on back of head, anterior pronotal angles, pterothorax, and abdominal tergites 4–5 mostly whitish grey. Produce an irritating defensive chemical at tip of abdomen. Adults appear in late spring, again in late summer; feed on maggots at carcasses in open, wooded, and coastal habitats; not uncommon in urban and suburban habitats. Widely distributed in North America to northern Central America. European *C. m. maxillosus* (Linnaeus) forebody vestiture mostly black, abdomen whitish grey; Québec and Ontario. (1)

Erichsonius patella (Horn) (4.7–5.5 mm) is elongate, blackish chestnut, bases of antennae and abdomen lighter. Head squarish, sparsely punctate, widest at eyes; antennomeres 1–2 wider than 3. Pronotum oval, barely wider than head, with irregular rows of eight or more punctures on each side. Elytra longer than wide, finely punctate, barely wider than pronotum. Abdomen slightly broadened, tapering toward tip. Front tarsomeres of male expanded. Ontario to North Carolina, west to Michigan, Illinois, and Louisiana. (15)

Hesperus baltimorensis (Gravenhorst) (9.5–13.8 mm) is blackish to black, with elytra and abdomen, except front of eighth tergite, reddish. Mouthparts brownish, antennae stout and blackish, gradually becoming paler toward tips. Pronotum long, narrowed behind, with surface sparsely, irregularly punctured and a smooth narrow strip down middle. Elytra at base wider and at suture as long as pronotum. Abdomen slightly iridescent. Legs reddish brown to blackish, tarsi paler; tarsi of male expanded and bilobed with setal pads underneath. Adults under bark and in decaying wood of old hardwoods and conifers. New Hampshire to Georgia, west to Iowa, Nebraska, and Louisiana. (6)

Heterothops fumigatus LeConte (previously known as *H. fusculus* LeConte) (3.2–5.2 mm) is usually reddish or yellowish brown, head and front of abdomen often darker. Surfaces of head and pronotum with microsculpture of fine transverse lines. Head with four large seta-bearing punctures along each side and a pair at base, narrower than pronotum, with three basal antennomeres pale, last maxillary palpomere very small, thin, straight, and sharp at tip. Pronotum with rear margin broadly arched, underneath with front angles projecting forward. Elytra at suture about as long as pronotum. Tarsi 5-5-5, above with setae. Adults found under debris and leaf litter, near old trees, in tree holes, under decaying organic matter; also mammal nests. Transcontinental; in east south to North Carolina and Iowa. (4)

Laetulonthus laetulus (Say) (5.8–8.2 mm) is elongate, parallel-sided, and bicolored. Black with pronotum and first three visible abdominal tergites red or reddish. Head with distinct neck. Antennae blackish. Elytra at suture as long as pronotum, at sides longer, punctate and pubescent, surface between punctures without microsculpture. Abdomen above punctate and pubescent, surface very finely wrinkled across tergites. Legs pale with femoral tips, tibiae and tarsi dark, front tarsi of both sexes expanded, less so in female. Adults found under bark of rotting logs, in leaf litter at bases and in tree holes of live trees; attracted to light. New England and Québec to Florida, west to Ontario, Wisconsin, and Texas. (1)

Ocypus nitens **(Schrank)** (11.0–20.0 mm) is large, elongate, narrowed in back, and black with very short elytra. Prothorax underneath without distinct translucent process behind base of leg. Elytra shorter than pronotum at midline; flight wings reduced, scarcely longer than elytra. Flightless adults active year-round, especially in spring, found in open and forested habitats, often around human dwellings; attracted to carrion. Europe and Middle East, established along Atlantic states from Maine to New York. (2)

Ontholestes cingulatus **(Gravenhorst)** (13.0–21.0 mm) is elongate, robust, dark brown or blackish with heavy pubescence forming irregular black spots. Head densely punctate as wide pronotum, with large eyes and slender antennae. Pronotum wide as long, widest in front, densely and finely punctate. Elytra not much wider than pronotum, surface finely granulate. Tip of abdomen and underside of last thoracic segment with bright gold setae. Adults active from spring through fall, found on carrion and dung. Eastern North America. (2)

Philonthus caeruleipennis **(Mannerheim)** (12.0–15.0 mm) is elongate, robust, black with shiny blue or green elytra; antennae and tarsi dark brown. Head shiny with few punctures, round, with distinct neck, and wide or wider than pronotum. Pronotum shiny, slightly longer than wide, side and posterior margins rounded, narrowing toward head. Elytra equal or slightly wider than pronotum, not overlapping, widest at tips. Abdomen iridescent, finely and densely setose. Legs dark brown. Adults active in summer, associated with fungi, compost, and decaying vegetation in or near wooded habitats; attracted to carrion pitfall traps. Widely distributed in North America and Europe. (114 NA)

Philonthus flumineus **Casey** (5.1–6.7 mm) is elongate, somewhat parallel-sided, with shiny head and pronotum, and setose elytra and abdomen. Antennae short, antennomere 1 pale, 2–3 short and almost equal in length, each longer than 7. Pronotum wider than head, on top with rows of six punctures each, those on sides with two. Elytra at suture as long as midline and wider at tips than pronotum. Legs uniformly yellowish brown, with front tarsomeres 1–3 somewhat bilobed underneath in both sexes, less so in female. Adults found in various habitats associated with standing and moving water. Atlantic Canada to Georgia, west to Manitoba, Minnesota, Kansas, and Texas; Montana. A genus with many species requiring examination of male genitalia for species identification. (114 NA)

Red-spotted Rove Beetle *Platydracus fossator*
(Gravenhorst) (13.0–17.0 mm) is robust and dimorphic,
uniformly dull black, or black with a large patch of golden or
orange-red pubescence on outer tip of each elytron. Head
and pronotum coarsely, densely punctate. Pronotum with
smooth line down middle at basal half. Elytra with slight
bluish or purplish reflections, densely and roughly punctate,
clothed in dark setae, and wide as pronotum. Both sexes
with padded front tarsi. Adults active late summer through
fall, found on decaying fleshy fungi, e.g., oyster mushroom
(*Pleurotus ostreatus*). In east from New Brunswick to
Florida, west to Manitoba and Texas. (21)

Platydracus maculosus **(Gravenhorst)** (18.0–25.0 mm) is
the largest rove beetle in North America. Body is elongate,
robust, and dark reddish brown, with antennal bases, tibiae,
and tarsi pale. Head and pronotum with brassy luster,
coarsely and densely punctate, with at least a trace of shiny
line down middle. Elytra and abdomen with variegated
reddish spots. Tip of abdomen pale reddish brown, femora
dark with ventral edges pale, both sexes with padded front
tarsi. Adults active spring and summer, attracted to carrion,
decaying fungi, and dung. Widely distributed in eastern
United States to Ontario and Québec. (21)

Quedius capucinus **(Gravenhorst)** (6.0–9.0 mm) is
elongate, slender, narrowed in front and back, and shiny
black with iridescent pronotum and abdomen. Antennae
reaching middle of pronotum, antennomere 2 half as long
as 3. Pronotum about as wide as long, broadly rounded
behind and narrowed in front. Elytra slightly narrower than
pronotum, together longer than wide, sometimes dark
reddish brown, sparsely punctate, as long as pronotum
at midline. Legs brownish red to dark brown, tarsi paler,
tarsomeres with setae on top. Adults found on decaying
fungi, carrion, and feces. Québec to Georgia, west to
Ontario, Wisconsin, Kansas, and Texas. (98 NA)

Quedius peregrinus **(Gravenhorst)** (6.0–9.5 mm) is
elongate, slender, narrowed in front and back, and blackish
with pronotum, elytra, or both sometimes reddish brown;
appendages reddish yellow-brown, antennae may be darker.
Head longer than wide, behind only slightly constricted.
Pronotum convex, about as long as wide, base broadly
rounded and narrowed toward front. Scutellum without
punctures. Elytra at suture slightly shorter than pronotum.
Abdomen with front margins of ventrites and abdominal
tips paler. Tarsomeres with setae on top. Adults found on
fungus and under bark. Maritime Provinces to Florida, west to
Michigan, Iowa, Missouri, and Tennessee. (98 NA)

Gyrohypnus fracticornis (Müller) (6.4–8.2 mm) is elongate, parallel-sided, blackish or black, sometimes with blackish-brown elytra and abdomen. Head barely longer than wide before eyes, slightly wider at rear, with large punctures mostly on sides. Pronotum longer than wide, slightly narrowed toward rear, with curved rows of coarse punctures, middle rows with three to seven and outer rows with 7–9 punctures; sides with double margins at rear united at middle. Abdomen with fine, sparse punctures. Elytra at midline equal to length of pronotum, with ridge along each side, coarse and sparse punctures forming two irregular rows along sides. Adults found in compost, grass piles, and dung. Europe and North America; in east from Atlantic Canada to North Carolina, west to Ontario, Wisconsin, Iowa, and Arkansas. (3)

STAG BEETLES, FAMILY LUCANIDAE
(LOO-*KAN*-IH-DEE)

The common name "stag beetle" is in reference to the large antlerlike mandibles found in some males, such as the giant stag beetle *Lucanus elaphus*. Mandible size within a species is directly proportionate to the size of the body and regulated by genetic and environmental factors. Males use their oversized mouthparts to engage in grappling contests with rival males in order to mate with a nearby female. Stag beetles are more or less restricted to moist habitats where dead, decomposing wood is plentiful. Eggs are laid in crevices of logs and stumps, and among roots of both deciduous and coniferous trees. The C-shaped grubs eat decaying wood, but do not damage homes or other buildings. Adults sometimes drink sap from wounds on tree trunks or flower nectar.

FAMILY DIAGNOSIS Adults lucanids are robust, oval (*Nicagus*) or elongate, somewhat flattened to nearly cylindrical (*Ceruchus*), usually dull, shiny black or reddish brown, sometimes with a hint of a greenish sheen (*Platycerus*). Head and mouthparts directed forward (prognathous). Mandibles of both males and females prominent and visible from above (except *Nicagus*), usually more developed in males. Lamellate antennae with 10 antennomeres, straight with last three antennomeres forming club (*Ceruchus, Nicagus*), or elbowed (geniculate) at first antennomere and with club of three or four antennomeres (*Lucanus, Dorcus, Platycerus*); club antennomeres thick, velvety (except in *Ceruchus*) and do not form a compact club (loose club in *Nicagus*). Pronotum narrower at base than elytra and lacks ridges, grooves, horns, or other projections. Elytra are smooth or grooved with lines of punctures. Legs adapted for digging, tarsal formula 5-5-5, with tarsal claws equal in size and simple; outer margin of front tibiae distinctly toothed (dentate) or sawlike (serrate) with large and smaller teeth. Abdomen has five ventrites; a portion of sixth is visible in *Platycerus*.

SIMILAR FAMILIES
- ground beetles (Carabidae) – antennae filiform, not clubbed (p.63)
- hide beetles (Trogidae) – club lamellae fold tightly together; side margins of pronotum not crenulate; setae short, thick (p.147)
- sand-loving scarab beetles (Ochodaeidae) – meso- and metatibial spurs finely notched (p.152)
- scarab beetles (Scarabaeidae) – club lamellae fold tightly together (p.156)
- powder-post beetles (Bostrichidae) – antennal club not elongated; mouthparts directed downward (hypognathous); pronotum usually with bumps or small horns (p.250)
- bark-gnawing beetles (Trogossitidae) – antennal club symmetrical (p.259)
- some genera of darkling beetles (Tenebrionidae) – antennae moniliform; tarsal formula 5-5-4 (p.344)

COLLECTING NOTES Eastern stag beetles are active in late spring through midsummer in moist, wooded habitats,

142

as well as in open sandy spaces, especially near bodies of water. Most species fly at dusk and early evening, or are found walking on downed logs, climbing up tree trunks, or crawling over the ground. Adults and larvae are found throughout the year in decaying wood, especially beneath loose bark of rotten logs and stumps. Adults are usually collected by hand, by netting on the wing, or by beating and sweeping vegetation. Some species are attracted to lights at night. *Platycerus* and *Nicagus* are active during the day. *Platycerus* rests on vegetation and flowers, while *Nicagus* flies along sandy shorelines of creeks, streams, rivers, and lakes, or clings to or hides beneath chunks of driftwood and other debris scattered along the shore.

FAUNA 25 SPECIES IN EIGHT GENERA (NA); NINE SPECIES IN FIVE GENERA (ENA)

Nicagus obscurus **(LeConte)** (5.5–10.0 mm) is oval, dark brown to black, elytra sometimes lighter, with setae pale, erect. Both sexes lack enlarged mandibles; antennae not elbowed, antennomeres 1 and 2 short, nearly equal, club with three antennomeres. Sides of pronotum finely notched. Elytral surfaces not grooved, coarsely and densely punctured. Larvae developing in decomposing branches washed up along rivers and lakes reach maturity in late summer. Adults overwinter, emerge in spring, fly during day over shores and sandbars, difficult to see against sand and debris. Ontario and Québec to Georgia, west to Minnesota, Illinois, and Iowa. (1)

Ceruchus piceus **(Weber)** (10.0–18.0 mm) is shiny, reddish brown to black, almost cylindrical and nearly devoid of setae. Antennae with 10 articles, not elbowed (geniculate), and club with three antennomeres. Mandibles of male long or longer than head, each mandible with two teeth directed upward; those of female shorter than head. Elytra distinctly grooved. Adults and larvae found in logs and stumps of pine (*Pinus*), beech (*Fagus*), birch (*Betula*), oak (*Quercus*), and other hardwoods in advanced stages of red-rot decay; also attracted to light in summer. Nova Scotia south to Georgia, and west to Manitoba, Nebraska, Kansas, and Tennessee. (1)

Antelope Beetle *Dorcus parallelus* **(Say)** (15.0–26.0 mm) is dull black. Head shorter and narrower than pronotum, which is slightly wider than elytra. Hind pronotal angles distant from elytral bases. Elytra deeply grooved and punctured, more so in females than males. Middle tibiae of male with dense setae. Adults on roots and stumps in spring and summer, at light in deciduous woodlands and pine barrens. Larvae in decaying roots and stumps of hardwoods. Ontario and Québec to Georgia, west to Wisconsin, Nebraska, and northeastern Texas. *Dorcus brevis* (Say) male more robust, forebody distinctly broader than faintly grooved elytra, middle tibia lacks dense setae near tip. (2)

Yellow-thighed Stag Beetle *Lucanus capreolus*
(Linnaeus) (20.0–36.0 mm, excluding mandibles) is
faintly shining, light to dark reddish brown with distinctly
yellow-brown femora. Mandibles of major males as long
as pronotum, those of minor males and females are
shorter. Head of male slightly broader than pronotum.
Inner margins of mandibles of both sexes have only one
tooth. Live in deciduous hardwood forests, parks, and older
neighborhoods with mature trees. They fly with a loud
buzzing noise at dusk and early evening and are attracted
to lights. Ontario and Québec and northeastern United
States south to Florida, west to Wisconsin, Nebraska,
Kansas, and eastern Texas. (3)

Giant Stag Beetle *Lucanus elaphus* Fabricius
(28.0–40.0 mm, excluding mandibles) is chestnut brown
with uniformly dark legs. Head of major male wider than
prothorax, fork-tipped mandibles sometimes long as elytra,
always longer than head and pronotum combined; female
with shorter mandibles; labrum of both sexes somewhat
triangular, rounded in front. Larvae develop in moist,
decayed wood. Adults active at dusk, found in summer on
stumps, sapping wounds, or at light; hide under logs during
day. Pennsylvania to northern Florida, west to southeastern
Nebraska and eastern Texas. *Lucanus placidus* Say with
labrum flat in front, mandibles shorter than forebody;
Midwest and Northeast, not mid-Atlantic or Southeast. (3)

Platycerus virescens **(Fabricius)** (7.0–12.0 mm) is
usually black, sometimes reddish black to reddish, always
with bluish, greenish, or bronzy luster. Inside margins of
mandibles lack teeth, and club antennomeres are stout
and blunt, with basal antennomere reduced. Females
have mandibles less developed than males, legs and
abdominal ventrites sometimes reddish brown. Elytra finely
impressed with rows of punctures. Adults active in spring
and early summer and found perching on vegetation or
on the flowers of trees and shrubs; also under bark and in
wood of decaying logs and stumps of pine and deciduous
hardwoods. Nova Scotia to Georgia, west to Ontario,
Nebraska, and northeastern Texas. (2)

144

BESS BEETLES, FAMILY PASSALIDAE
(PAH-*SAL*-IH-DEE)

Passalids are unusual among beetles in that adults and larvae live together in overlapping generations in loose colonies in galleries chewed in rotten logs and stumps. The tunneling and feeding activities of the adults help to break down and recycle decomposing wood, but they do not damage buildings and other structures made from sound or treated wood. The larvae are completely dependent on the adults for food and shelter and eat wood chewed by the adults. Both larvae and adults supplement their diets with adult feces to beef up the supply of gut microorganisms that aid in the digestion of wood. In spite of their conspicuous mandibles, the adults do not bite. Several species of armored mites live on bess beetle bodies, sometimes encrusting the head, coxae, edges of the elytra, or underside of the abdomen. Highly specialized, these mites seldom leave their beetle hosts and are harmless to humans and other animals.

FAMILY DIAGNOSIS Adult passalids are large, shiny black, with horned heads in both sexes, and deeply grooved elytra are distinctive in the region. Head with conspicuous mandibles directed forward (prognathous). Lamellate antennae with 10 thick antennomeres curved, 8–10 not forming a compact club. Pronotum shallowly grooved down middle, loosely attached to rest of body. Straight-sided elytra deeply grooved and completely cover abdomen. Legs stout with tarsal formula 5-5-5, and claws simple and equal. Abdomen with five ventrites.

SIMILAR FAMILIES

- stag beetles (Lucanidae) – large species with geniculate antennae; head without horn (p.142)

COLLECTING NOTES Bess beetles are found year-round but reach their peak of activity in late spring and summer. Both adults and larvae are commonly found under bark in large rotten hardwood and pine logs and snags. Look for telltale accumulations of coarse sawdust around logs inhabited by these insects. Adults occasionally come to lights and are sometimes seen flying at dusk.

145

FAUNA FOUR SPECIES IN TWO GENERA (NA); TWO SPECIES IN ONE GENUS (ENA)

Horned Passalus *Odontotaenius disjunctus* **(Illiger)** (28.0–37.0 mm), also known as bess, patent leather, or peg beetle, is elongate, robust, slightly flattened, shiny black with a thick curved horn on head and deeply grooved elytra. Freshly emerged individuals are soft, reddish brown. Mandibles large, but never bite when handled. Widespread throughout deciduous woodlands and mixed forests of eastern Canada and United States, from Ontario to Florida, west to Manitoba, Minnesota, southeastern Nebraska, and eastern Texas. *Odontotaenius floridanus* Schuster is similar, but has wider foretibia and a shorter, much less curved horn; restricted to the sandhills of central Florida. (2)

ENIGMATIC SCARAB BEETLES, FAMILY GLARESIDAE
(GLAH-*REES*-IH-DEE)

The family Glaresidae includes about 55 very similar species in the genus *Glaresis* that are distributed on all continents except Australia. They are enigmatic because only adults are known, and very little is known of their habits, other than they are usually found in dry, sandy habitats and are attracted to light. When handled, they can produce a faint squeaking sound. It has been suggested that, based on an examination of their mouthparts, the adults eat subterranean fungi. Once part of the family Trogidae, the Glaresidae is believed to be one of the most primitive families of scarab beetles and their relatives. In North America, glaresids are usually encountered in appropriate habitats in the Southwest and Midwest. The sole species found east of the Mississippi River, *G. inducta* Horn, is also the most widespread species of the Nearctic glaresid fauna.

FAMILY DIAGNOSIS Adult glaresids are small, oblong-oval, and light brown, with moderately dense short setae. Head without horns or bumps, mandibles barely projecting beyond clypeus; clubbed antennae with 10 antennomeres, 8–10 forming a compact, velvety club; eyes divided by narrow strip of cuticle (canthus). Scutellum visible. Elytra convex, long and fully concealing abdomen, each with 10 distinct ridges. Wings developed. Abdomen with five ventrites. Legs with meso- and metatibiae with two apical spurs, metafemora and metatibia enlarged, obscuring abdomen, tarsal formula 5-5-5, claws equal and simple.

SIMILAR FAMILIES

- hide beetles (Trogidae) – larger; eyes not divided by canthus (p.147)
- earth-boring scarab beetles (Geotrupidae) – larger; 11 antennomeres (p.149)
- sand-loving scarab beetles (Ochodaeidae) – eyes not divided by canthus; meso- and metatibial spurs finely notched (p.152)
- scarab beetles (Scarabaeidae) – club antennomeres fold tightly together (p.156)

COLLECTING NOTES Look for *Glaresis* at lights along sandy lakeshores and sandhills along the western fringes of the eastern hardwood forest during the summer months.

FAUNA 20 SPECIES IN ONE GENUS (NA); ONE SPECIES, *GLARESIS INDUCTA* HORN (ENA)

Glaresis inducta Horn (2.7–3.3 mm) is oblong-oval and dark yellowish brown; dorsal surface with short, stout, setae. Eyes divided in half by canthus. Abdomen underneath mostly covered by enlarged hind femora and tibiae; two teeth on hind femora near rear margin variably developed and sometimes difficult to see. Nothing is known of the biology of this species, other than adults are attracted to lights in summer on sandy lakeshores of Lake Michigan and sandhill habitats. Wisconsin and Indiana to California, Arizona, and Texas. (1)

146

HIDE BEETLES, FAMILY TROGIDAE
(*TRO*-GIH-DEE)

Trogids are dull grayish, reddish, or blackish, rough, and are frequently covered in mud and mites. Adults and larvae of *Omorgus* and *Trox* are keratin feeders and scavenge hair, hooves, and feathers from dried animal carcasses left behind by other carrion visitors and are typically found during the final stage of decomposition. Some species prefer accumulations of feathers or hair in bird nests or rodent burrows, while others are attracted to the hair-laden feces of carnivores. When alarmed, adults feign death by pulling in their legs and remaining motionless for long periods of time to avoid detection. Encrusted with debris, they look very much like a pebble, clump of earth, or some other inanimate object. Both *Omorgus* and *Trox* stridulate, or make a chirping sound by rubbing a patch of ridges on the penultimate abdominal tergite (propygidium) against the inner margin of the elytra. The larvae of *Omorgus* and *Trox* generally develop in burrows in the soil under or next to caracass or other keratin source.

FAMILY DIAGNOSIS Adult trogids are oval or somewhat parallel-sided, convex, rough, reddish brown, brown-gray, or black, often encrusted with dirt, or a gray or brown crust that forms a subtle pattern; underside flat. Head with mandibles inconspicuous and directed downward (hypognathous), eyes not divided by strip of cuticle (canthus). Lamellate antennae with 10 antennomeres, 8–10 forming a compact, velvety club. Pronotum squarish or rectangular with sharp side margins. Scutellum visible, arrowhead-shaped (*Omorgus*) or oval (*Trox*). Elytra strongly ridged or covered with rows of small raised bumps; completely conceal abdomen. Legs with tarsal formula 5-5-5, with all claws equal and simple, not toothed. Abdomen with five ventrites.

SIMILAR FAMILIES
- *Nicagus* (Lucanidae) – body long; lamellate antennomeres do not form club (p.143)
- scarab beetles (Scarabaeidae) – abdomen with six ventrites (p.156)
- *Endecatomus* (Endecatomidae) – clubbed antennae capitate, not lamellate (p.249)
- horned fungus beetles (Tenebrionidae) – tarsi 5-5-4; antennae not abruptly clubbed; male pronotum horned (p.348)

COLLECTING METHODS *Omorgus* and *Trox* are most commonly collected at lights; also look for them on aged carcasses and in animal nests and burrows. Check the soil carefully beneath old carcasses and hair-packed scats for larval burrows and soil-encrusted adults.

147

FAUNA 57 SPECIES IN TWO GENERA (NA); 24 SPECIES IN TWO GENERA (ENA)

- -

Omorgus monachus (**Herbst**) (12.0–15.0 mm) has a head with two tubercles, ridged pronotum, hatchet-shaped scutellum, and elytra with distinct tubercles and covered entirely with short velvety coating. Adults usually found at light, also on carcasses. Maryland to Florida, west to Kansas and eastern Texas. (7)

Omorgus suberosus (Fabricius) (11.1–14.1 mm) has a head with two tubercles, pronotum relatively smooth and convex with long fine setae on margins notched just before base, hatchet-shaped scutellum. Elytra appearing almost smooth with weakly developed ridges and tubercles. Adults found in spring and summer at carrion and at lights. Widespread in eastern United States, except in New England. (7)

Trox capillaris Say (8.0–10.3 mm) is unique among North American *Trox* species by having widely separated clumps of shiny dark or black scales not associated with tubercles on the elytra and smooth elytral intervals. Head with four setose tubercles across front. Pronotum tomentose with sparse pale setae. Scutellum more or less oval, not constricted at base. Elytra with odd intervals usually not elevated, extreme base of interval 3 sometimes ridged. Adults are found on carcasses and owl pellets, or with fur associated with fox dens. Ontario to South Carolina, west to Nebraska and Texas. (16)

148

Trox scaber (Linnaeus) (5.0–7.0 mm) is oblong and blackish. Antennal club reddish brown. Pronotum coarsely punctate with broad furrow running down entire middle and deeper round impressions on each side, and side margins not notched at bases. Scutellum oval, not constricted at base. Elytra with alternating rows of long and short patches of reddish-brown setae. Legs with hind tarsomeres smooth. Adults active spring and summer, found under carrion, owl pellets, and feathers and in bird and mammal nests. Widely distributed in Northern Hemisphere; in east from Nova Scotia and New Brunswick and Québec to Florida, west to Minnesota and Texas. (16)

Trox tuberculatus (De Geer) (7.5–11.0 mm) has four tufts of black setae across head, no tubercles. Pronotum with broad depression down middle, surface obscured by thick woolly setae, base sinuate before angles. Elytra with alternating ridges higher, margins at middle with setae sparse and separated by their own lengths or clumped. Adults active spring and early summer, found on carrion; attracted to light. Massachusetts to Florida, west to Colorado and New Mexico. (16)

Trox unistriatus Palisot de Beauvois (9.0–12.0 mm) is dull black with distinct ridges and punctures on elytra. Pronotum covered with dense woolly pubescence, with broad groove down middle, base straight before angles. Scutellum more or less oval, sides not constricted. Elytra with distinct ridges topped with double row of short setae and separated by paired rows of large squarish punctures, side margins not notched, and upturned rims along sides of elytra without row of bumps extending entire length. Adults at carrion; attracted to light. Southern Canada and Northern United States; in east to South Carolina and Tennessee. (16)

EARTH-BORING SCARAB BEETLES, FAMILY GEOTRUPIDAE
(JEE-OH-*TROOP*-IH-DEE)

Adults geotrupids are mostly nocturnal, feed on fungi, leaf litter, and dung, and spend much of their lives burrowing deep into the soil. The burrows of *Peltotrupes profundus* Howden average nearly 6 feet in depth and may reach 10 feet in loose sand. Some geotrupids prefer more mesic habitats, while others are more commonly encountered in xeric situations, such as sandhill habitats with deep, well-drained soils. Their vertical burrows are often marked by conspicuous "push-ups," piles of soil or sand dug up from the burrow below. Some species, especially those living in restricted habitats such as sandhills, often dig their burrows in groups. The burrows end in one or more chambers and are provisioned with a wide array of organic materials, including leaf litter, fungi, or dung; one species occasionally uses carrion; *Mycotrupes* sometimes uses acorns and dog food. These materials are pushed down into the burrow and formed into a plug on which the grubs feed. The adults do not stay in the burrow to care for the young. Dung-feeding species often harbor phoretic mites. Most adult and larval geotrupids are capable of producing sound by stridulation, but there are few published records of this behavior. Geotrupids are of no economic importance, although they are sometimes considered a nuisance when their push-ups appear in lawns, especially in Florida.

149

FAMILY DIAGNOSIS Adult geotrupids are oval or round, strongly convex or hemispherical, yellowish or reddish brown, brown, black, shiny black with metallic reflections, or metallic blue, green, or purple. Head with conspicuous mandibles prognathous, often with distinct horn, tubercle, or ridge. Antennae with 11 antennomeres, 9–11 forming a compact club, 9 large, cup-shaped, with club equal in length to all previous articles combined (*Bolbocerosoma*, *Bradycinetulus*, *Eucanthus*, *Odonteus*), or small, about half as long (*Geotrupes*, *Mycotrupes*, *Peltotrupes*). Pronotum broad, convex, wider or subequal to elytra, with or without tubercles, ridges, horns, grooves, and excavations. Scutellum visible. Elytra convex, smooth, or distinctly striate, and completely concealing abdomen. Legs adapted for digging, tarsal formula 5-5-5, tarsi with claws equal in size and simple. Abdomen with six ventrites.

SIMILAR FAMILIES Geotrupids are easily distinguished from other scarabaeoids in eastern North America by having antennae with 11 antennomeres.

- sand-loving scarab beetles (Ochodaeidae) – small (4.2–7.5 mm); antennae with 10 antennomeres; eyes bulging; spurs on ends of middle tibiae finely notched (p.152)

COLLECTING NOTES Adults of many geotrupids (*Bolbocerosoma*, *Bradycinetulus*, *Eucanthus*, *Geotrupes*, *Odonteus*) are nocturnal and attracted to lights. Both *Geotrupes* and *Mycotrupes* are attracted to herbivore and human feces and captured in pitfall traps baited with these materials. Some species (*Geotrupes*, *Mycotrupes*, *Peltotrupes*) are attracted to fermenting malt and molasses baits. *Mycotrupes*, *Odonteus*, and some *Geotrupes* eat fungus. Look for push-ups along paths and track roads in sandy habitats, marking the burrows of *Bolbocerosoma*, *Bradycinetulus*, *Eucanthus*, and *Odonteus*.

FAUNA 56 SPECIES IN 11 GENERA (NA); 36 SPECIES IN 7 GENERA (ENA)

Bolbocerosoma farctum (Fabricius) (9.0–13.0 mm) is hemispherical and bicolored black and yellowish brown to reddish brown. Pronotum without black spot or stripe on middle. Each elytron with five deep grooves strongly punctate between suture and humerus; female with apical black spots variable, joining both black suture and marginal stripe. Adults found beneath logs and in burrows marked by push-ups along sandy tracts in Piedmont and Coastal Plain from spring through early fall; attracted to light and collected in Malaise traps. New York to Georgia, west to Ohio and Mississippi. (7)

Bradycinetulus ferrugineus (Palisot de Beauvois) (17.0–21.0 mm) is uniformly brown, weakly shining, with eyes only partly divided by canthus. Head with short horn and evenly rounded clypeus in female, hornless and shovel-like clypeus in male. Antennal club large and almost as long as remaining articles. Pronotum with protuberances, male with distinct horns. Elytra each with seven striae between suture and humerus, humerus rounded. Adults are active from spring through early fall. Push-ups found in sandy turkey oak habitats with burrows averaging 2–3 feet in depth; occasional at light. Virginia to Florida, west to Mississippi. (1)

Eucanthus lazarus (Fabricius) (6.4–14.0 mm) is smooth and shining between punctures, orange-brown to dark red-brown. Eyes partly divided by canthus with front edge straight, outer angles not produced. Antennal club larger than underside of eye, yellow-brown to brownish red. Front margin of pronotum sinuate, front angles sharp, area in front of medial pronotal swelling without dense punctures down middle, basal margin complete. Each elytron with five deeply punctate grooves between suture and humerus. Adults active mostly late spring and summer, generally found in clay soils in sparsely treed habitats; attracted to light. Ontario to northern Georgia, west to South Dakota and Arizona. (4)

Odonteus darlingtoni Wallis (5.0–10.0 mm) is oblong-oval, convex, and uniformly shiny reddish brown; major male with long slender horn set in shallow pit curving back over head. Head with eyes almost completely surrounded by narrow and evenly curved canthus, clypeus without a small thin ridge down middle. Pronotum of major male with deep pits and sharp ridges (not horns) on sides, basal margin sinuate just before angles. Adults active nearly year-round, found in sandy habitats and dug from burrows; attracted to light. Coastal Plain, from Massachusetts to Florida, west to Mississippi. (4)

Blackburn's Earth-boring Beetle *Geotrupes blackburnii blackburnii* **(Fabricius)** (6.5–11.0 mm) is shiny coppery black to black. Front tibiae of male expanded and produced inwardly, underside with largest teeth at tip, both sexes with row of setae along their lengths not interrupted by parrallel ridge. Elytra with moderately punctured grooves. Adults active in spring, fall, and warm winter days and nights. Found in dung, carrion, decaying fungi, and at lights. Vermont and New Hampshire south to Florida, west to Ohio and Tennessee. Males of subspecies *G. b. excrementi* Say have largest teeth under foretibiae at middle and vaguely punctured elytra. Mostly west of the Appalachian Mountains, from Iowa and Indiana to Texas. (9)

Geotrupes splendidus **(Fabricius)** (13.0–18.0 mm) is usually bright, shining green (more yellow west of Appalachian Mountains), although some individuals are light blue or purplish black overall. Antennae dark reddish brown with clubs lighter. Elytra with deep, punctured groove along scutellum not reaching base, punctures similar in color to surrounding surface. Adults are active in spring and summer, then again in later summer and fall. Adults provision brood burrows with dead leaves. Prefer fungi as food, as well as feces, carrion, feathers, and fermenting malt; also drawn to isoamylamine and butyric and proprionic acids. New Brunswick and Ontario to Florida, west to Wisconsin, Nebraska, and Oklahoma. (9)

151

Cartwright's Mycotrupes *Mycotrupes cartwrighti* **Olson & Hubbell** (15.0–15.2 mm) is oval, very convex, with surface distinctly granular, and wingless with fused elytra. Pronotum with distinct conical horn (male) or low rounded nodule or callus (female) on front margin. Elytral grooves seldom apparent. Adults active year-round, especially October through March, found in sandy habitats in mixed woodlands; found under dung (deer, horse), in pitfall traps baited with malt, molasses, and dung. Southern Georgia and northern Florida. (5)

Mycotrupes retusus **(LeConte)** (10.0–16.0 mm) is oval, very convex, and wingless with fused elytra. Pronotum with distinct bump in front, if present, and without punctures. Elytral surface evenly and densely covered with distinct granules, with little or no trace of grooves. Front tibiae of male with front tooth extending forward, bending downward. Adults active mostly in fall and winter, found in deep burrows marked by push-ups in sandy, ancient coastline habits; attracted to traps with fungus, fermenting malt; occasionally associated with mammal dung. Inland Coastal Plain of central and southern South Carolina. (5)

Florida Deep-digger Scarab *Peltotrupes profundus*
Howden (15.0–23.0 mm) is oval, somewhat flat on top,
and black with shiny bright iridescent blue or purple,
especially male. Head with mandibles visible. Scutellum
flanked by elytral suture. Elytra not fused together, smooth,
with faint rows of fine, shallow punctures, and side margins
widely flared, especially in front. Outer surface of middle
and hind tibiae with only a trace of a ridge at tip. Adults fly
at dusk from January through April, in scrub and sandhill
habitats with deep sand; attracted to traps baited with malt,
molasses, and honey, and occasionally at lights. Northern
and central Florida. Ocala deep-digger scarab, *Peltotrupes
youngi* Howden, usually black with iridesecent green; suture
next to scutellum obscure. (2)

SAND-LOVING SCARAB BEETLES, FAMILY OCHODAEIDAE
(O-KO-*DEE*-IH-DEE)

Sand-loving scarabs resemble small bolboceratine earth-boring scarab beetles (Geotrupidae), but are
easily distinguished by their antennae and meso- and metatibial spurs. About 80 species and 12 genera of
ochodaeids are found in all biogeographic regions except Australasia. Nearly all of the 21 species of North
American ochodaeids occur in the Southwest. Very little is known of the natural history of ochodaeids,
other than they are nocturnal and seem to prefer sandy soils in prairies, or open grassy habitats within
deciduous hardwood forests. Some species stridulate, but it is not known if any of the eastern species
produce sound. The larvae of all but the California genus *Pseudochodaeus* remain unknown.

FAMILY DIAGNOSIS Adult ochodaeids are round,
somewhat convex, reddish brown, and covered with
short erect hairs. Head with eyes bulging and distinct
mandibles directed forward (prognathous); clypeus
with (*Neochodaeus*) or without (*Xenochodaeus*) central
tubercle. Lamellate antennae with 10 antennomeres,
8–10 forming compact, velvety club, 8 somewhat cup-
shaped and surrounding 9 and 10. Scutellum visible and
rounded. Elytra with rows of punctures along entire length;
spaces between rows with smaller punctures, each with
a small bump in front armed with a stiff hair. Meso- and
metatibial spurs finely notched or pectinate. Tarsal formula
5-5-5, claws simple, equal. Abdomen with six ventrites,
penultimate tergite above (propygidium) long with straight-
edged groove (*Xenochodaeus*), or short with edges of
groove converging (*Neochodaeus*).

SIMILAR FAMILIES
- stag beetles (*Nicagus*, Lucanidae) – tibial spurs
  not notched (p.143)
- earth-boring scarab beetles (Geotrupidae) –
  antennae with 11 antennomeres; tibial spurs
  not notched (p.149)
- scarab beetles (Scarabaeidae) – tibial spurs
  not notched (p.156)

COLLECTING NOTES Adults are nocturnal and attracted
to lights in summer. Individuals are occasionally dug from
burrows marked by push-ups of soil on bare ground along
forested trails and road tracks. *Neochodaeus frontalis*
(LeConte) (Georgia and Florida, west to New Mexico)
was taken in a trap baited with amyl acetate in Florida.

Xenochodaeus musculus (Say) (5.5–6.0 mm) is oval, convex, light yellowish or reddish brown, sparsely clothed in short, stiff setae. Pronotum with surface between punctures smooth. Hind leg of male with distinct tooth on tip of femora and inside margin of tibia. Adults inhabit eastern hardwood forests from Ontario to northern Florida, west to southwestern Wisconsin, southeastern Nebraska, and eastern Texas. *Xenochodaeus americanus* (Westwood) (4.2–7.5 mm) has minute tubercles between pronotal punctures, male hind legs not toothed; plains habitats in Wisconsin and Iowa to Montana and Colorado. (2)

SCAVENGER AND PILL SCARAB BEETLES, FAMILY HYBOSORIDAE
(HI-BO-*SOR*-IH-DEE)

Very little is known of the natural history of hybosorids. The larvae of *Hybosorus roei* develop in the soil and are collected among the roots of plants, including fennel (*Foeniculum*) and Bermuda grass (*Cynodon dactylon*). Adults have been observed emerging from golf courses. Although the turf is not harmed, the small mounds of soil they leave behind are sometimes considered a nuisance by golfers and greens keepers alike. They are thought to prey on insects at carrion and dung. *Ceratocanthus* and *Germarostes* are associated with decomposing hardwoods and all stages of both genera are associated with fungal-ridden tree cavities in the boles of living trees and snags. Adults and larvae are found in tree holes high above the ground (*Ceratocanthus*) or in tunnels and among the frass of bess beetles (Passalidae) and under bark of dead trunks worked by wood-boring insects (*Germarostes*).

FAMILY DIAGNOSIS Adult hybosorids are shiny light brown, black, greenish black, or purplish, sometimes with a metallic luster, oval and convex (*Hybosorus*); *Ceratocanthus* and *Germarostes* have retractile appendages and can roll up into a compact ball. Head with distinct mandibles directed forward (prognathous). Lamellate antennae with 9–10 antennomeres, last three forming compact, velvety club, last two surrounded by somewhat cup-shaped antennomere. Scutellum visible. Elytra smooth or with rows of linear punctures, completely covering abdomen. Legs with meso- and metatibial spurs simple; tarsal formula 5-5-5, claws simple, equal. Abdomen with six ventrites.

SIMILAR FAMILIES
- Earth-boring scarab beetles (Geotrupidae) – antennae with 11 antennomeres (p.149)

- Scarab beetles (Scarabaeidae) – first club antennomere not cup-shaped (p.156)

COLLECTING NOTES Adults are nocturnal and attracted to lights in summer. *Hybosorus* is also collected in carrion and dung; *Germarostes* is occasionally found at carrion. *Germarostes* is found under the loose bark of hardwood snags, especially oak (*Quercus*) and has been found on the trunks of standing dead or dying trees as night; they are occasionally taken in Malaise traps. *Ceratocanthus* are collected in flight intercept traps suspended in hardwood tree canopies, while *Germarostes* have been taken in Lindgren funnels baited with sawdust. Both *Ceratocanthus* and *Germarostes* are beaten from dead branches and vines.

153

FAUNA FIVE SPECIES IN FOUR GENERA (NA); FOUR SPECIES IN THREE GENERA (ENA)

Hybosorus roei **Westwood** (7.0–9.0 mm) is oval and shiny dark reddish brown. Little is known of the natural history of this species and the larvae are undescribed. Adults are collected at lights and in carrion and dung, where they sometimes prey on or scavenge the remains of other beetles. Old World species probably introduced into southeastern United States during mid-nineteenth century; established from Virginia to Florida, west to Kansas, Arizona, and southern California; also Mexico to northern South America and the Caribbean. (1)

Ceratocanthus aeneus **(MacLeay)** (7.0 mm, not rolled up) is shiny and metallic. Pronotum with anterior margin incomplete and angles lacking depressions; posterior angles broadly rounded, not angulate. Elytra with rows of punctures not extending to base. Middle and hind tibiae completely flattened. Adults beaten from vines, found under loose bark of rotten logs, and collected from tree holes, flight intercept traps suspended in tree canopy, and Lindgren funnel traps baited with sawdust. Virginia to Florida, west to Tennessee and Alabama. (1)

Germarostes aphoidioides **(Illiger)** (3.8–6.0 mm) is dark purplish black or purplish brown with a metallic sheen. Clypeus densely punctate, most punctures round. Elytral margins behind humeri smooth, not serrate. Adults capable of stridulation and are found singly or in clusters under bark or beaten from dead branches from late spring through summer. Maryland to Florida, west to Illinois to Texas. *Germarostes globosus* (Say) (4.2–5.2 mm) is similar in form, black, occasionally with bluish reflections; clypeus mostly with fingerprint-like whorls; elytral margins behind humeri distinctly serrate; Pennsylvania to Florida, west to Illinois to Texas. (2)

BUMBLE BEE SCARABS, FAMILY GLAPHYRIDAE
(GLA-*FEER*-IH-DEE)

Bumble bee scarabs are so named because the adults are often hairy, brightly colored, and fast and agile fliers. This small family comprises seven genera distributed in Europe, Asia, and North America. Of these, only *Lichnanthe* occurs in North America, two species of which occur in eastern North America. One of these, the cranberry grub, *Lichnanthe vulpina* (Hentz), is a pest of cranberry bogs in northeastern United States, where the larvae attack the roots. *Lichnanthe lupina* LeConte, a possibly extinct species from coastal New Jersey and New York, is the most aberrant of the North American glaphyrid fauna because its elytra meet along the entire length of the elytral suture, but gradually or sharply diverge in all other species. Adult *Lichnanthe* are active from midmorning to midafternoon and are often observed hovering near flowers and foliage or flying over sandy areas. They are sometimes found on flowers, but it is not clear whether they actually feed on pollen. At the end of the daily flight period, both males and females burrow into the soil. The larvae feed on layers of decaying leaf litter and other plant debris buried in sandy areas along streams and rivers.

FAMILY DIAGNOSIS Adult glaphyrids are elongate with long yellowish-orange or pale yellowish setae. Head with mouthparts directed downward. Lamellate antennae with 10 antennomeres, 8–10 forming compact, velvety club. Pronotum convex, somewhat rectangular. Scutellum visible and triangular. Elytra short, smooth, somewhat transparent, and diverging along suture (*L. vulpina*) or not (*L. lupina*); last abdominal tergite (pygidium) is completely exposed. Tarsi 5-5-5, claws equal, toothed. Abdomen with six ventrites.

SIMILAR FAMILIES
- scarab beetles (Scarabaeidae) – elytra long and never divergent, pygidium not completely exposed above (p.156)

COLLECTING METHODS Bumble bee scarabs are collected on the wing or while resting on the ground or on vegetation in riparian or coastal dune habitats. Males are sometimes found on flowers. They are usually active during the late morning and early afternoon hours on sunny or slightly overcast days during the summer.

FAUNA EIGHT SPECIES IN ONE GENUS (NA); TWO SPECIES IN ONE GENUS (ENA)

Cranberry Root Grub *Lichnanthe vulpina* (Hentz) (12.0–18.0 mm) is beelike in flight and clothed almost entirely in long yellow-orange setae. Head, pronotum, scutellum, and underside reddish brown. Antennal club with three velvety and asymmetrical antennomeres. Elytra light reddish brown, clothed in short dark setae, do not meet along entire length of suture, tips divergent. Abdomen exposed beyond elytra. Larvae eat roots of shrubs and are pests in cranberry bogs. Diurnal adults active in late spring and early summer, fly along riparian corridors and in cranberry bogs, hovering over flowers and vegetation; also at light. New England to Maryland, through Appalachia to northern Georgia. (2)

SCARAB BEETLES, FAMILY SCARABAEIDAE
(SCARE-EH-*BEE*-IH-DEE)

Scarab beetles form one of the largest and most diverse families of beetles in the region. They have long attracted attention because of their large and colorful bodies, conspicuous and interesting behaviors, or abundance. Their roles as bioindicators, recyclers, and pollinators are often underappreciated. The adults of many species are diurnal or crepuscular, but most are nocturnal. Several genera (e.g., *Maladera, Nipponoserica, Serica, Phyllophaga, Pelidnota, Cyclocephala, Eutheola, Dyscinetus*) are already familiar to homeowners in residential areas because they are attracted to porch lights at night, sometimes in large numbers. Some species are considered garden and agricultural pests. The larvae of some *Ataenius* damage lawns, especially in parks and golf courses. Japanese beetle (*Popillia japonica*) and masked chafer (*Cyclocephala*) grubs are also turf pests. Adults of several genera (*Maladera, Nipponoserica, Serica, Dichelonyx, Macrodactylus, Diplotaxis, Polyphylla, Hoplia, Anomala,* and *Exomala*) may defoliate potted plants, deciduous garden shrubs, vegetable crops, and orchard trees as well as some conifers in managed forests. Their larvae feed on the tender roots of seedling trees and shrubs and are sometimes particularly destructive in nurseries. Several genera of dung beetles are attracted to all kinds of mammal dung, but a few prefer deer dung. Some species live with ants (*Euparia, Martineziella, Cremastocheilus*) or termites (*Valgus*). One rarely collected species, *Saprosites ventralis* (Horn) is found in the tunnels of horned passalus (Passalidae)

FAMILY DIAGNOSIS Adult scarabs are oval-oblong, somewhat flattened or cylindrical, and mostly black, brown, yellowish brown, occasionally green, metallic, or scaled with blotched or striped patterns. Head with mouthparts inconspicuous, mandibles visible or not, and weakly directed downward (hypognathous), sometimes with a small tubercle or distinctive horn. Lamellate antennae with 8–10 antennomeres, last 3–7 flat antennomeres (lamellae) can spread out fanlike or form a compact, usually bare or sometimes velvety (dung scarabs) club. Pronotum variable, with or without horns, tubercles, and excavations; sides always distinctly margined. Scutellum hidden (*Canthon, Deltochilum, Melanocanthon, Pseudocanthon, Copris, Ateuchus, Dichotomius, Euoniticellus, Digitonthophagus, Onthophagus, Phanaeus*) or visible. Elytra slightly rounded or parallel-sided, with surface smooth, distinctly pitted, grooved, or covered with scales, and completely covering abdomen (dung scarabs) or with one tergite (pygidium) partially exposed. Legs strong, adapted for burrowing; tarsal formula usually 5-5-5 (front tarsi absent in *Deltochilum*, male *Phanaeus*), claws equal in size or not, simple, toothed, or narrowly split at tips. Abdomen with six ventrites.

SIMILAR FAMILIES

- stag beetles (Lucanidae) – antennae usually geniculate, club not compact (p.142)
- enigmatic scarab beetles (Glaresidae, *Glaresis*) – abdomen with five ventrites (p.146)
- hide beetles (Trogidae) – abdomen with five ventrites (p.147)
- earth-boring scarab beetles (Geotrupidae) – antennae with 11 antennomeres (p.149)
- sand-loving scarab beetles (Ochodaeidae) – mandibles exposed; spurs on middle and hind tibiae finely notched (p.152)
- scavenger and pill scarab beetles (Hybosoridae) – mandibles exposed; first club antennomere cup-shaped (p.153)
- bumble bee scarabs (Glaphyridae) – elytra short, tips usually separated exposing tergites (p.155)

COLLECTING METHODS Most nocturnal scarabs are strongly attracted to ultraviolet or mercury vapor lights. Others are found by sweeping, beating, and searching vegetation at night. Diurnal species are found on or under fresh dung, sapping tree wounds, or on flowers. Female *Cotinis* and *Euphoria* are often found flying over turf, compost, and dung heaps in search of egg-laying sites. Scarab burrows in sandy soils in road tracks and along trails are often marked by conspicuous mounds of sand called push-ups. Very small species (*Aegialia, Rhysothorax, Odontopsammodius, Neopsammodius, Geopsammodius, Leiopsammodius*) are sifted from sand at the base of plants or accumulations of vegetation along rivers and in coastal dunes. Hanging traps baited with rotting fruit or malt and molasses are attractive to some species, especially sap feeders. Dung beetles are attracted to pitfall traps baited with human, pig, sheep, horse, or cow feces, while some species prefer carrion. Deer dung, especially during the cooler parts of the year, attracts specialist species (*Aphotaenius, Dialytes*) that usually ignore other kinds of feces.

FAUNA ~1,700 SPECIES IN 125 GENERA (NA)

Aphodius fimetarius **(Linnaeus)** (6.5–9.5 mm) is oblong, robust, black with red elytra. Head black with three sharp bumps across front, clypeus without sharp teeth or broad angles. Pronotum mostly black with front angles reddish yellow, with frontal depression at middle in male. Adults found nearly year-round in open and lightly shaded habitats in cattle dung, occasionally in other accumulations of plant debris. Genetic data suggest this species may be two very similar species. Europe; widely established in North America from southwestern and southeastern Canada south. (1)

Blackburneus stercorosus **(Melsheimer)** (3.0–4.6 mm) is oblong, convex, mostly reddish brown with ill-defined lighter margins. Pronotum finely punctured, punctures becoming coarser toward sides. Scutellum triangular. Elytra broadly rounded at rear. Front tibiae with distinct, scattered punctures on upper surface, hind tibiae fringed with small, unequal spines, and hind tarsi with tarsomere 1 as long as 2–4 combined. Adults feed on decaying plant materials, small mammal feces, and cow dung; attracted to light. New England and Québec to northern Florida, west to eastern Kansas and eastern Texas. (7)

Calamosternus granarius **(Linnaeus)** (3.4–6.0 mm) is usually black, sometimes with obscure reddish margins on sides of pronotum; occasionally head and pronotum black with dark brown elytra. Head with three small bumps across front. Pronotum with line across basal margin. Scutelum small, one-sixth length of elytra, and pentagonal. Elytral surface shiny, without setae, and humeri without sharp tooth. Legs with front tibiae with upper surface smooth, without punctures, and middle and hind tibiae fringed with small spines about equal length. Adults found in dung carrion, and decaying plant materials; at light. Europe; established throughout North America. (1)

Dialytes striatulus **(Say)** (3.5–4.7 mm) is dark grayish black with sharply ridged elytra. Front tibiae each with four teeth on outer margin, last two teeth strong and parallel to spur on tip. Front margin of head with two broad angles, coarsely punctate, punctures more than twice in diameter of those on head, with distinct impression down middle. Scutellum small, less than one-sixth length of elytra. Elytra with sharp tooth at basal angle and spaces between ridges rough and vaguely punctate. Adults typically found on deer dung in forested habitats in spring and summer. Maritime Provinces to Georgia, west to Manitoba, Nebraska, and Mississippi. (4)

Flaviellus phalerioides **(Horn)** (4.0–6.6 mm) is mostly yellow with yellowish-brown head and faint or distinct markings elsewhere. Pronotum flattened with brownish-yellow spot on middle or either side of middle. Elytra lacking setae on sides and tips, with dark suture, often with faint markings, and fringed with setae mostly shorter than scutellum except at base. Tips of hind tibiae fringed with short, unequal spines, and first hind tarsomere shorter than spur above; male front tibiae with inner margin somewhat wavy. Adults found in coastal dunes at light in summer. *Flaviellus phalerius* Gordon & Skelley has long, unequal spines on hind tibiae; inner margin of male front tibiae straight. Coastal, from New York to South Carolina. (2)

Labarrus **(formerly *Aphodius*)** *pseudolividus* **(Balthasar)** (3.5–5.8 mm) has distinctively yellowish-brown and brown markings. Head brown to blackish with variable amounts of yellowish brown on side of clypeus, with three small tubercles, center tubercle higher. Pronotum brown with yellowish-brown sides and pale membrane across front. Elytra yellowish brown with brown stripe down middle, punctostriate, intervals flat. Longest spur of hind tibia slender, gradually tapering to tip and subequal in length to first tarsomere. Adults very common in herbivore dung and at lights. Maryland to Florida, west to Iowa, Kansas, and California. (2)

Pseudagolius bicolor **(Say)** (5.0–7.0 mm) is mostly shiny black above and yellowish or reddish yellow below, including legs. Head without bump across surface, clypeus with pair of feeble angulations and setae along margin. Coarsely punctured with front margin reddish brown. Pronotum uniformly and densely punctured, punctures separated by own diameters or less, with basal margin weakly sinuate and a narrow channel. Scutellum short. Elytra not ridged, with uniform rows of punctures. Adults usually associated with deer dung in forested habitats and cow dung. Michigan and southern Ontario to Florida, west to Wisconsin, Kansas, and eastern Texas. (1)

Ataenius imbricatus **(Melsheimer)** (3.3–4.3 mm) is dull grayish brown to grayish black with distinct grooves on elytra and dark brown legs, and covered with very short, stubby setae. Head convex, clypeus broadly notched. Elytra twice as long as wide, sides almost parallel, spaces between rows of punctures flat with row of short coarse setae, and humeri sharply toothed and directed forward. Adults active mostly spring through summer, found under leaves and cattle dung; attracted to light. Widespread in eastern United States to Ontario. (34)

Black Turfgrass Ataenius *Ataenius spretulus*
(Haldeman) (3.6–5.5 mm) is shiny black with legs and
clypeal margins reddish, and grooved elytra. Head with
clypeus wrinkled in front. Pronotum with coarse, sparse
punctures becoming slightly more dense at sides, with
base distinctly margined. Elytra one-half longer than wide,
with humeri sharp, toothlike. Hind face of front femora
mostly smooth, with few, if any coarse punctures; hind
legs with femora with line halfway from knee to trochanter,
tibia usually with fringe of five setae at tip, first tarsomere
longer than tibial spur. Adults active almost year-round, turf
pests, occasionally at dung; attracted to lights. Ontario,
widespread in United States. (34)

Canthon pilularius **(Linnaeus)** (12.0–17.0 mm) is matte
black (northern), often with bronze, bluish, or coppery
reflections, or greenish (southern). Upper surface more
or less uniformly sculptured with mixed granules. Head
with clypeus bearing two broadly rounded teeth at middle
and, when viewed from above, narrow crescent-shaped
eyes. Elytra each with eight fine shallow grooves. Adults
active spring through early fall, found in association with
mammal dung, occasionally carrion; not attracted to light.
Massachusetts and Florida, west to Montana and eastern
Texas. (6)

Canthon viridis **(Palisot de Beauvois)** (2.0–4.7 mm) is
small, round, convex, and metallic. Upper surface purplish
with bronze reflections (northern) or shiny bright green
(southern); some populations with both color forms.
Clypeus of head with two small teeth at middle. Hind
tibiae each with a single spur on tip. Diurnal adults most
active spring and early summer, found in wooded habitats
perching on vegetation or in pitfalls baited with fungi,
carrion, or vertebrate feces. New York to Florida, west to
Wisconsin, Nebraska, and Texas. (6)

Deltochilum gibbosum **(Fabricius)** (20.0–25.0 mm) is
oval, dull black, sometimes with hint of purplish luster. Head
with four teeth on clypeal margin, inner pair sharp. Elytra
with (male) or without (female) prominent bumps at basal
third, tips of both sexes with five short, distinct ridges. Front
legs lack tarsi and hind tibiae long, slender, and curved
abruptly inward. Adults active late spring and summer in
wooded habitats, attracted to carrion, feathers, dung, and
rotten fruit. Virginia to Florida, west to Illinois and Texas;
Mexico. (1)

Melanocanthon bispinatus **(Robinson)** (6.0–10.0 mm) is broadly oval and dull gray-black. Resembles *Canthon*, but with two apical spurs on posterior tibiae. Clypeus with four distinct and sharp angles, or teeth. Adults active spring through fall, usually found in sandhill habitats and pine barrens where they fly low over roads and sparsely vegetated areas, and bury dead insects, dried fungi, and deer dung. Atlantic and Gulf states from New York to Mississippi. (4)

Copris fricator **(Fabricius)** (13.0–18.0 mm) is broadly oval, robust, slightly shiny black. Head with sharp horn (male) or bump (female) on top. Pronotum densely, coarsely punctate, crest with three bumps, middle bump notched or divided, most prominent in male. Adults found under or burrowing below cow dung mostly in piedmont and montane habitats; attracted to light. Elytra grooved, spaces between convex, finely and densely punctate. New England and Québec to Florida, west to Ontario, South Dakota, and Texas. *Copris howdeni* Matthews & Halffter similar, head unarmed in both sexes, elytra with spaces between grooves flatter, coarsely and densely punctate; coastal southeastern Virginia to Florida. (3)

Copris minutus **(Drury)** (8.0–13.0 mm) is shiny black with head horn developed in both sexes. Horn ranges from a short ridge across front (minor male, female) to long and narrow (major male). Pronotum with prominence across middle straight (male) or more curved and well developed (female). Clypeus of male with deep V-shaped notch at middle. Elytra distinctly grooved with deep punctures, spaces between smooth and convex. Adults active year-round; attracted to light. New England and Québec to Florida, west to Ontario, Iowa, Nebraska, and Texas. (3)

Ateuchus histeroides **Weber** (6.0–7.0 mm) is small, oval, convex, robust, and black with bronze sheen, with head and pronotum unarmed. Head coarsely punctate, punctures in front separated by less than their own diameters, antennae with nine antennomeres. Pronotum hind angles evident and below level of sides of elytra, and basal margin without fine groove or bead. Scutellum not visible. Elytra each with eight grooves, spaces between convex. Adults attracted to dung, carrion, fungi, especially in wooded areas; occasionally attracted to light. Bases of front legs broad, not conical or prominent. New Jersey to Florida, west to Mississippi. (2)

Dichotomius carolinus **(Linnaeus)** (19.8–30.0 mm) is the largest and heaviest dung beetle in the east. Very robust. Head with horn or tubercle in front of eyes (male), or nearly between (female); elytra noticeably grooved, grooves densely packed with setae near posterior. Adults prefer open habitats; attracted to lights in summer. Entrances to burrows dug adjacent to dung pads marked with large mounds of excavated soil. New York to Florida, west to Nebraska and Texas. (1)

Phanaeus vindex **MacLeay** (11.0–22.0 mm) is robust and bright metallic green with gold reflections and coppery red. Head metallic green, major male with prominent curved horn. Pronotum rough with well-defined ridges with distinct margins, coppery red on top, green on sides, surface shieldlike in male. Scutellum hidden. Elytra bright green with smooth base near scutellum with two or three distinct ridges separated by shallow grooves flanked by rough wrinkles and elongate punctures. Legs with front and middle tarsi lacking claws, and hind leg with first tarsomere shorter than the next three. Larvae develop in dung. Adults active in spring and summer, found under dung, in burrows. Massachusetts to Florida, west to South Dakota and Arizona. (3)

Euoniticellus intermedius **(Reiche)** (7.0–9.0 mm) is elongate, somewhat flat, and yellow-brown with dark markings. Male with short, curved, blunt horn on head. Adults dig branched tunnels under cattle feces and supply blind ends with pear-shaped brood balls; in dry conditions brood balls placed immediately beneath dung to take advantage of moisture. Intentionally introduced into California, Georgia, and Texas in the late 1970s, early 1980s to reduce accumulations of cattle dung serving as breeding sites for pestiferous flies. Active year-round, prefers open, relatively dry habitats. Africa and Middle East; established from Florida to California, south to Costa Rica. (1)

Digitonthophagus gazella **(Fabricius)** (6.0–13.0 mm) is greenish brown to coppery black with yellowish-brown markings. Head, most of pronotum, portions of underside and tibiae, and large oval spots on middle and hind femora mostly greenish or coppery black. Male with pair of slender, curving horns on head; female with distinct transverse ridge. Pronotum with pale margins at side and base. Elytra light brown, with or without dark markings. Larva develops primarily in cow dung, sometimes dog feces. Nocturnal adults active late spring through fall, found under dung; attracted to light. African-Asian species now established across southern third of United States; Central and South America, Australia, Japan. (1)

Onthophagus depressus **Harold** (6.0–7.7 mm) is oval, dull gray to brownish black, without horns or protuberances on head or pronotum in either sex. Clypeus with two teeth on front margin. Pronotum covered with small seta-bearing bumps, each surrounded by round puncture. Elytral surface sculpted similarly to pronotum with seta-bearing bumps surrounded by nearly round punctures, not as dense as pronotum. Adults active spring and summer, found in scrub habitats on cattle dung; attracted to light. African; established from southern South Carolina to Florida. (7)

Onthophagus hecate **(Panzer)** (5.2–9.5 mm) is uniformly dull black, sometimes dull brassy, with dorsal surface covered in small, rounded bumps. Male with broadly triangular clypeus upturned. Pronotum of major male with flat, notched horn with two middle teeth projecting forward over head. Specimens from Carolinas to Florida with horn shorter, broader, and middle teeth reduced to blunt process with two points. Elytra shiny with punctured grooves. Adults active late spring and summer, attracted to cow dung and other animal feces, as well as rotting fungi, fruit, and carrion; also attracted to light. Maritime Provinces and Québec to Florida, west to Alberta, Montana, Utah, and Arizona. (7)

Onthophagus nuchicornis **(Linnaeus)** (6.3–8.1 mm) is oval, dull black with tan or brown elytra mottled with black. Male with horn on top of head between eyes. Female with small hump on pronotum just behind head. Pronotum coarsely punctate, spaces between very finely wrinkled. Scutellum not visible. Elytra with grooves not deeply impressed, spaces between not distinctly convex. Front legs with tarsi, middle and hind tibiae widened at tips. Adults found on cow and horse dung in summer. Europe, established across southern Canada and northern United States, in east from Maritime Provinces and New England to New Jersey and Maryland, west to Wisconsin and Missouri. (7)

Onthophagus taurus **(Schreber)** (8.0–10.0 mm) is dark brown to black, sometimes with elytra slightly paler. Major male distinctive with pair of long curved horns sweeping back over pronotum. Pronotum with impressions on sides to receive horns (male), or evenly convex (female). Adults active in summer, usually found in vertebrate feces, especially dog, cow, and horse. Old World, established across southern half of United States, in east from New York to Florida, west to Ohio, Missouri, and Texas. (7)

Asiatic Garden Beetle *Maladera castanea* (Arrow) (8.0–9.0 mm) is oval, broad, robust, chestnut-brown, with dull, slightly iridescent surface. Head in front of eyes shiny. Antennae with 10 antennomeres. Legs with hind tibiae broad and flat, hind tibiae with two spurs on tip located above and below tarsal attachment. Larvae feed on roots, sometimes pest of turf, vegetable gardens, and flower beds. Nocturnal adults active late spring and early summer, found feeding on leaves of shrubs and trees; attracted to light. Japan; established from Nova Scotia to Florida, west to Illinois, Kansas, and Alabama. (1)

Nipponoserica peregrina (Chapin) (8.0–8.9 mm) is pale yellowish brown with a dark frons and eyes. Antennae with nine antennomeres. Elytra with narrow membranous borders at tips. Leg spurs on tips of hind tibiae located above and below tarsal attachment. Adults commonly attracted to lights at night in summer. First reported in United States from Long Island, New York in 1938. Nocturnal adults found on vegetation and at light in summer. Asia; established from Massachusetts to Virginia, west to New York and West Virginia. (1)

Serica atracapilla (Kirby) (8.0–11.0 mm) is elongate-oval, smooth, shiny chestnut brown, without traces of iridescence. Head with clypeus smooth, slightly sunken with raised central area, front of clypeus distinctly raised and notched on sides. Antennae with nine antennomeres. Pronotum wider than long, convex. Elytra without membranous border. Genital organs of male without setae and resemble two ping-pong paddles. Nocturnal adults active spring and early summer, found on vegetation; attracted to light. Maritime Provinces and New England to Florida, west to Ontario, Michigan and Alabama. Species of *Serica* are best determined by examination of male genitalia. (34)

European Chafer *Amphimallon majale* (Razoumowsky) (13.0–15.0 mm) is uniformly light reddish brown. Head with notch in labrum distinctly separated from clypeus and antennae with nine antennomeres, 7–9 forming lamellate club. Pronotal surface appears silky. Elytra with weakly raised ridges. Larvae eat roots of wild grasses, turf, clover, small grains, soybeans, and containerized nursery stock. Adults active in summer; attracted to light. Europe; established from New England and Québec to Connecticut, west to Ontario, Indiana, and West Virginia. (1)

Florida Hypotrichia *Hypotrichia spissipes* LeConte (12.4–16.0 mm) is oblong, brown or dark brown; males are dull. Head, except clypeus, pronotum, and scutellum covered in dense, long setae. Antennal club with three antennomeres. Elytra without grooves, long and covering abdomen, clothed in short pubescence; flight wings developed in both sexes, females not known to fly. Front claws of all legs in both sexes with distinctive lobelike tooth. Underside covered with long, silky setae, abdomen with sutures between ventrites distinct across middle. Diurnal males found after rains from spring through fall just beneath surface of soil under small push-ups or flying over grassy areas in urban and other areas located in upland sand ridge habitats and sand pine scrub, also in Malaise traps; shiny, flightless females located by following males. Peninsular Florida. (5)

TOP RIGHT: *Hypotrichia spissipes* male.
BOTTOM RIGHT: *Hypotrichia spissipes* female.

164

Phyllophaga crenulata (Froelich) (14.8–22.2 mm) is robust, oblong-oval, tan to brown, feebly shining, and clothed in intermixed long and short setae. Head with margin of clypeus turned up, antennae with 10 antennomeres, male club shorter than remaining antennomeres combined. Legs with tarsal claws strongly toothed at middle in both sexes. Larvae sometimes pests of sod, field crops, and coniferous nurseries. Adults active mostly in spring and early summer and eat leaves of various native and introduced deciduous trees and shrubs. New England to Florida, west to South Dakota and eastern Texas. (86)

Phyllophaga micans (Knoch) (15.0–17.0 mm) is dull reddish black to blackish with permanent dustlike whitish coating, especially on elytra. Antennae with 10 antennomeres. Pronotum with coarse punctures larger than those on head and deeper than punctures on elytra. Claws with tooth at middle. Nocturnal adults active spring and early summer, feed on various hardwoods; attracted to light. Connecticut and New York to Georgia, west to Wisconsin, Iowa, Kansas, and Texas. (86)

Polyphylla comes Casey (23.0–26.0 mm) is large, robust, and mostly brown with scattered pale patches and stripe along suture. Head black, antennal club large with seven (male) or smaller with five (female) antennomeres. Pronotum wider than long with three indistinct stripes. Elytra with lines interrupted into scattered patches, except for thick stripe along suture. Larvae sometimes pests in pastures. Adults active in summer, mostly in montane habitats; attracted to light. Southwestern Virginia to Georgia, west to Mississippi. (10)

Polyphylla occidentalis (Linnaeus) (20.2–25.0 mm) is easily distinguished by its clearly striped elytra. Males have large antennal clubs, while those of females are much less conspicuous. Adults feed on pine (*Pinus*) and are attracted to lights. Larvae feed on roots of sedges. This primarily coastal plain species ranges from Virginia south to Florida, west to Mississippi. (10)

Polyphylla variolosa (Hentz) (20.2–23.0 mm) is broad, robust, mostly light to dark reddish brown, sometimes with black head. Antennal club long (male) or short (female), with seven antennomeres. Pronotum wider than long with punctures dense to widely separated. Elytra with blotches scattered randomly, occasionally in very poorly defined stripes, often without stripe down suture. Adults primarily active in summer, found in association with sedgelike grasses in sandy soils and dune habitats; attracted to light. Primarily coastal and along Great Lakes, New England and Québec to northern Virginia, west to Ontario and Pennsylvania. (10)

Diplotaxis liberta (Germar) (10.5–13.0 mm) is large, robust, not clothed in setae, shiny black, occasionally dark reddish. Head without swollen area behind clypeus, labrum at narrowest point about same thickness as upturned front of clypeus. Pronotum with clear, membranous border in front, sparsely and irregularly punctured with scattered smooth patches on middle, front angles sharp, narrow, and extending forward. Scutellum distinctly and densely punctured. Hind tarsi longer (male) or shorter (female) than tibiae. Elytra with paired rows of fine punctures with scattered coarse punctures between. Adults active in spring in association with pine (*Pinus*); attracted to light. New England and Ontario to northern Florida, west to Iowa, and Louisiana. (12)

Diplotaxis sordida **(Say)** (10.0–12.0 mm) is dull black, roughly punctured, and distinctly clothed in short, fine, reddish-yellow erect setae. Elytra sometimes with impressions between basal (humeral) angles. Adults are attracted to lights in spring and summer and are especially common in sandhill habitats. Québec and Ontario to Georgia, west to Indiana and Mississippi. (12)

Hoplia trivialis **Harold** (6.0–8.0 mm) is black with long grayish scales in both sexes. Head without ridge across front of eyes. Pronotum with side margins nearly straight or slightly bowed just in front of hind angles. Middle legs each with two claws, single hind claw entire, not cleft or notched. Underside with scales oval to elongate, usually separated by their own width. Adults active in spring, found on vegetation, flying over open ground and leaves, and swarming on branches or prominent light-colored surfaces. Maritime Provinces and New England to Georgia, west to Ontario, North Dakota, Iowa, and Texas. (8)

166

Dichelonyx albicollis **(Burmeister)** (11.0–12.0 mm) is elongate, parallel-sided, with metallic green elytra faintly striped with pale setae. Head and pronotum reddish yellow. Pronotum with distinct groove down middle. Elytra with narrow, slightly raised ridges less punctate and setose than spaces between. Male hind tibia with larger spur twisted, tip blunt, appearing cut off, and four times wider than smaller spur. Adults active in late spring and early summer, found on pine (*Pinus*) and other conifers; attracted to light. Maritime Provinces and New England to South Carolina, west to Ontario, Minnesota, and Indiana. (9)

Dichelonyx linearis **(Gyllenhal)** (8.0–11.1 mm) has a blackish or reddish head with clypeus uniformly colored except for narrowly reflexed rim. Pronotum convex with punctures somewhat confluent down middle. Elytra light to dark reddish brown with weak to strong metallic green reflection, always with paler lateral and apical borders. Legs mostly pale, hind tibial apices and tarsi dark. Adults active in spring and early summer, and feed on conifers and hardwoods, occasionally damaging ornamental trees and shrubs; also attracted to light. Québec and Ontario to Georgia, west to North Dakota, Nebraska, and Oklahoma. (9)

Macrodactylus angustatus **(Palisot de Beauvois)** (7.0–10.0 mm) is elongate, densely clothed in yellow scales, with long, mostly reddish legs. Female pronotum covered with erect pubescence on disc; underneath with spine between legs of male half as long as coxae when viewed from side. Middle and hind tarsi much longer than tibiae, hind tibial apices with spurs. Abdominal midline with many large punctures bearing long setae. Adults found on shrubs; maybe at light. Massachusetts and New York to Florida, west to Indiana and Texas. Rose Chafer, *M. subspinosus* (Fabricius) similar, pronotum with recumbent setae in both sexes, male prosternal spine as long as coxae, female abdomen with short setae along midline; eastern North America. (2)

Plectris aliena **Chapin** (10.0–14.0 mm) is robust, clothed in short, erect and dense setae, and reddish-to-yellowish brown, underside and legs paler. Head with clypeus deeply concave with margin raised and slightly notched in front. Pronotum strongly convex, wider than long, with side margins nearly parallel behind middle. Elytra each with four indistinct ridges, between with seta-bearing punctures. Claws divergent, those in front not equal in size, finely notched at tips, with outer claw longer and stouter than inner. Larvae feed on roots of turf, sweet potatoes (*Ipomoea batatas*). Adults active spring and summer, males found flying over turf at dusk; attracted to light. Argentina; established from South Carolina to Florida, west to Alabama; also Australia. (1)

Anomala lucicola **(Fabricius)** (8.0–10.0 mm) is usually dull brown, sometimes completely black. Pronotum with or without central black spot or pair of spots. Head with clypeus moderately concave. Elytra weakly grooved. Front and middle legs with largest claws distinctly cleft, bases of middle legs separated by distinct process. Adults found on wild grape (*Vitis*). Maine to Florida, west to Ontario, Michigan, and Kansas. (12)

Anomala undulata **Melsheimer** (7.0–11.0 mm) is variably marked. Head not distinctly bicolored. Pronotum with broadly rectangular mark with sides not constricted toward front and front not pointed, or mark reaching base. Scutellum usually black, sometimes light in middle. Elytra spotless to spotted, banded, but never entirely black, with humeri seldom dark. Adults active mostly in spring, found on various plants; attracted to light. Southern New England to Florida, west to Minnesota and Texas. *Anomala innuba* (Fabricius) (6.0–9.0 mm) similar, sometimes entirely black, pale forms with humeri almost always dark, scutellum black in black form only and pale or dark margined in paler forms, active in summer. (12)

Callistethus marginatus (Fabricius) (11.0–16.0 mm) is light or dark reddish brown with a distinct metallic green sheen, sides of pronotum usually with pale borders. Base of pronotum is broadly rounded, nearly as wide as the base of elytra, and metasternum produced into a distinct spine. Adults are commonly attracted to lights during the summer and sometimes found resting on low vegetation during the day. Maryland south to Florida, west to Indiana and Texas. May belong in genus *Anomala*. (1)

Oriental Beetle *Exomala orientalis* (Waterhouse) (7.0–13.0 mm) is incredibly variable in color, all with slight metallic sheen. Pronotum ranges from unmarked to black, with or without a pair of spots. Elytra pale, with or without darks spots or bands. Each elytron with six distinct grooves between the suture and shoulders. Nocturnal adults feed on the leaves of ornamentals, such as rose, phlox, and petunia. Larvae feed on roots and are sometimes turf pests. This immigrant species from Asia is now established from Maine south to Georgia, west to Wisconsin. (1)

Japanese Beetle *Popillia japonica* Newman (8.9–11.8 mm) is only North American beetle with five white tufts along each side of abdomen. Head, pronotum, and legs are coppery green, while elytra are reddish brown. Larvae eat roots and are serious pests of turf in lawns, parks, and golf courses; they also attack the roots of ornamental plants and vegetables. Adults eat more than 300 species of plants, consuming leaves, flowers, and fruits. Asian; now established in Southern Ontario and Maine south to Georgia, west to Minnesota, Nebraska, Kansas, Arkansas, and Mississippi. (1)

Strigoderma arbicola (Fabricius) (7.6–13.0 mm) has yellowish-brown elytra, each elytron with eight grooves. Head shiny black or light brown, and pronotum black with metallic green, coppery, or brassy reflections. Adults feed on many plant species and occasionally attack crops, including peanuts. They are active in summer and are found on plants, flying during the day, or in Japanese beetle traps. Ontario and Québec south to Georgia, west to Colorado and Texas. (2)

Strigoderma pygmaea (Fabricius) (4.5–6.2 mm) is small, shiny, and variable in color and markings. Head and pronotum brown or black with slight greenish-violet iridescence. Pronotum densely clothed in yellow setae. Elytra each with five grooves between suture and basal angle, and ranges from uniformly brown or black to pale yellow, or with dark with light patches. Abdomen and legs reddish brown to black. Underside with long, dense setae. Diurnal adults active in summer, found on various shrubs, low herbaceous growth, and grasses, or flying over open ground, especially in sandy areas; attracted to light. New Jersey to Florida, west to Missouri and Alabama. (2)

Goldsmith Beetle *Cotalpa lanigera* (Linnaeus) (19.2–26.0 mm) with head and pronotum metallic golden yellowish brown with faint pale greenish reflection. Pronotal punctures separated by one to three of their own diameters, base sinuate. Elytra creamy yellow, yellowish, or yellowish white. Underside with dense white setae. Nocturnal adults active late spring and early summer, found flying at dusk or feeding on leaves of poplar and cottonwood (*Populus*), oak (*Quercus*), hickory (*Carya*), pear (*Pyrus*), silver maple (*Acer saccharinum*), sweetgum (*Liquidambar styraciflua*), and willow (*Salix*); at light. Maine to Florida, west to Wisconsin and Louisiana. (1)

Grapevine Beetle *Pelidnota punctata* (Linnaeus) (18.0–27.0 mm) is shiny yellowish to reddish brown above, with one small spot on each side of the pronotum and three small spots along sides of each elytron; underside ranges from yellowish brown to black. Northern populations often have larger, more distinct spots, while those in south sometimes lack spots altogether, especially in Florida. Larvae develop on or near large roots of various kinds of hardwood stumps; complete life cycle requires two years. Adults attracted to lights during the summer, or found clinging to vegetation during the day, especially grapes. Ontario and Maine to Florida, west to South Dakota and Texas. (1)

Northern Masked Chafer *Cyclocephala borealis* **Arrow** (11.0–14.0 mm) is oblong-oval, mostly shiny light reddish brown. Head smooth and dark between eyes, front margin of semicircular clypeus not thickened, sharply and narrowly upturned when viewed from side. Pronotum without tubercles, setae, or marginal bead at base. Males with thickened foreclaws and setae on elytra. Metasternum of male and female densely punctured with long, dense pubescence. Larvae eat grass roots. Nocturnal adults fly over turf in summer; also attracted to light. New York to Florida, west to Iowa, Kansas, and Texas. (7)

Dyscinetus morator (Fabricius) (15.0–20.0 mm) is oblong-oval, robust, shiny brownish black to black with clypeus somewhat flat to slightly concave in front. Adults are attracted to lights, sometimes in large numbers, from late spring through summer. Larvae develop in moist accumulations of plant materials, including sod and compost heaps. In North America from New York and Connecticut to Florida, west to Iowa, eastern Nebraska, and Texas. (1)

Aphonus castaneus (Melsheimer) (8.6–12.2 mm) is oval, slightly pear-shaped, convex, shining reddish brown. Head small, weakly punctate and wrinkled, with a ridge across front and mandibles rounded externally and usually hidden from above. Pronotum uniformly punctate, evenly convex, with front angles sharp, sides round, and hind angles obtuse. Front tibiae tridentate, apical tooth small. Pygidium finely wrinkled (male) or punctate (female). Larvae develop in sandy soil, sometimes abundant in turf. Adults active primarily in summer; attracted to light. New England and Québec to Florida, west to Tennessee and Alabama. (4)

Sugarcane Beetle *Eutheola humilis* (Burmeister) (10.8–14.5 mm) is dull, chunky black with a smooth pronotum. Adults are commonly found at lights or on sidewalks in parks and suburban neighborhoods from spring through early fall. They feed on young shoots and ground-level leaves of grasses, sedges, and rushes and are sometimes minor pests of cotton, sweet potatoes, corn, rice, and sugarcane. Possession of an earlike structure may help them to avoid predation by bats. Larvae feed on roots of grasses and are sometimes abundant in well-drained grassy habitats. Maryland south to Florida, west to Nebraska and Texas, southward to Argentina. (1)

Parastasia brevipes (LeConte) (14.0–17.0 mm) is dark, shiny reddish brown to black with long club antennomeres; club twice as long as previous antennomeres in male. Elytra with rows of large pits. Adults active during summer in woodlands, usually found at light. Larvae feed and develop in rotten wood, including oak (*Quercus*) and sycamore (*Platanus*). New York to Florida, west to Nebraska and Kansas. *Parastasia* consists of mostly Asian species. (1)

Carrot Beetle *Tomarus gibbosus* **(De Geer)** (10.0–17.0 mm) is robust and reddish brown to black. Clypeus narrowed, with two small upturned teeth; mandibles with three outer teeth. Front pronotal margin with tubercle at middle. Surface of front tibia outside long row of coarse setae-bearing punctures with fine to coarse punctures. Adults commonly attracted to lights in spring and summer. Larvae develop in soils rich in organic matter or in sandy soils feeding on the roots of many plants. Widespread across southern Canada and the United States. (4)

Strategus aloeus **(Linnaeus)** (31.0–60.9 mm) is dark mahogany to black. Head with pair of tubercles, mandibles visible from above. Pronotum of male with three blunt to sharply pointed horns; female unarmed. Elytra mostly smooth, with deep groove along entire suture in both sexes. Front tibiae with five teeth. Females lay eggs in rotten wood where larvae feed and develop. Adults found mostly in later spring and summer; are attracted to light, especially females. Georgia to Florida, west to Arizona, south to South America. (3)

Ox Beetle *Strategus antaeus* **(Drury)** (18.2–40.7 mm) is smaller and reddish in north, becoming larger and darker south. Head without tubercles, mandibles visible from above. Pronotum of male varies from three bumps to slender horns; female unarmed. Elytra mostly smooth, grooves lacking along entire suture, sometimes faintly indicated at tips. Females dig vertical burrows 6–8 inches deep terminating in up to five or more horizontal chambers, and provision each chamber with decayed oak leaves for their larvae. Adults found in summer at tree roots and on trunks, or walking across roads in sandhill habitats in the late afteroon and early evening; also attracted to light. Atlantic Coast, from Massachusetts to Florida, west to Oklahoma and eastern Texas. (3)

Strategus splendens **(Palisot de Beauvois)** (25.0–36.0 mm) is broadly oval, shiny chestnut-brown to black. Pronotum of male with conspicuous short horn and erect transverse bump in front only, no major or minor development; female unarmed. Elytra each with complete punctate groove along suture. Adults active mostly spring and summer, sometimes associated with palms and palm nursery stock; attracted to light. Coastal plain of southeastern United States, from North Carolina to Florida, west to Mississippi. (3)

Rhinoceros Beetle *Xyloryctes jamaicensis* **(Drury)** (21.0–33.7 mm) is dark reddish brown with long, dense reddish setae underneath. Head with mandibles not visible from above, males with single horn on head, and females have conical tubercle between eyes. Elytra of both sexes deeply grooved. Adults feed and lay their eggs at base of white ash (*Fraxinus americana*). Larvae feed on rotten wood and leaf litter. Entire life cycle takes two to three years. Adults are attracted to lights at night and may be locally abundant in or near riparian woodlands. Ontario to northern Georgia, west to Minnesota, Nebraska, and Texas. (1)

Triceratops Beetle *Phileurus truncatus* **(Palisot de Beauvois)** (32.0–38.0 mm) is a large, robust insect. Both males and females have large and distinct horns on the head. Adults are typically encountered at lights during the summer, but are seldom common. They occasionally enter homes through chimneys, which suggests that they may be associated with tree holes. The larval stages live in rotten, fungal infest wood, but have yet to be described; the pupae have been found under the bark of a rotting oak stump. Virginia south to Florida, west to Tennessee and southeastern Arizona. (2)

Phileurus valgus **(Olivier)** (17.0 to 28.0 mm) is shiny black, occasionally dark reddish brown. Head triangular with pair of sharp bumps in front of each eye and a single horn on pointed front margin. Pronotum has narrow pitted groove along middle with bump in front. Elytra deeply furrowed with areas between higher and wider. Tibiae of forelegs with four teeth. Adults and larvae found in rotting wood. Nocturnal adults active late spring and summer and attracted to light. Maryland to Florida, west to Indiana, Nebraska, and Texas; south to Argentina. (2)

Eastern Hercules Beetle *Dynastes tityus* **(Linnaeus)**
(40.0–60.0 mm) is a large, spectacular olive-green beetle
mottled with irregular black spots, sometimes completely
dark. Males with horn on head and three horns on
pronotum, largest horn projects over head; females lack
horns. Elytra smooth. Adults sometimes aggregate on ash
(*Fraxinus*) or in tree holes used as breeding sites. Larvae
feed on damaged rotten and crumbling heartwood of
various hardwoods, especially oaks, also pine; no harm is
done to living trees. Both sexes attracted to lights in summer,
but seldom in numbers. New York to Florida, west to
southern Illinois, western Arkansas, and eastern Texas. (1)

TOP RIGHT: *Dynastes tityus* male.
BOTTOM RIGHT: *Dynastes tityus* female.

Green June Beetle *Cotinis nitida* **(Linnaeus)** (15.0–
27.0 mm) is velvety green with tawny yellow borders;
variable tawny markings sometimes cover most of
elytra. Underside shiny metallic green mixed with tan, to
completely coppery. Adults eat leaves, sap, and ripening,
soft-skinned fruits of many plant species. Females fly,
sometimes in large numbers, over grassy areas, manure,
and other accumulations of plant material on warm, sunny
days in search of egg-laying sites. Root- and rhizome-
eating larvae occasionally become turf, vegetable, and
ornamental plant pests. New York and Connecticut south to
Florida, west to southern Illinois, Nebraska, and Texas. (2)

Euphoria areata **(Fabricius)** (10.5–11.5 mm) is robust,
sparsely to densely clothed in whitish or yellowish setae,
and black with distinct broad, irregular pale reddish-yellow
markings down sides of each elytron. Head with four sharp
teeth across front of clypeus. Pronotum coarsely punctured,
strongly narrowed at middle toward head, and clothed in
yellowish setae. Elytra with few punctures, fused along
suture, surface with scattered setae. All stages associated
with pocket gopher burrows in Florida. Adults active on
warm days in autumn and winter, found flying over sandy
soils. Atlantic and Gulf Coast states, from Connecticut to
Alabama. (8)

173

Euphoria fulgida (Fabricius) (13.4–19.8 mm) is mostly bright, shiny green or bluish. Head and pronotum typically brilliant green, latter margined with yellow. Pronotum and elytra lack setae. Elytra shiny green tinged with yellowish brown and sometimes with small chalky white spots or short, thin wavy bands; sides tinged with reddish brown. Legs reddish or yellowish brown and tinged with green. Pygidium always with four chalky white spots. Diurnal adults found flying or on flowers from spring through summer. Ontario and Québec south to Florida, west to Nebraska, Texas, and southeastern Arizona. (8)

Euphoria herbacea (Olivier) (12.0–16.0 mm) is dull green to brownish with scattered small white spots and thin lines on elytra. Head and pronotum often greener than elytra. Pronotum and elytra have scattered pale setae. Elytra with spots and lines sometime reduced, tips white or whitish. Pygidum lacks markings. Underside of abdomen deep metallic green with bronze reflections. Diurnal adults active in summer, on flowers and flying over grassy areas. New Jersey to Florida, west to South Dakota and Texas. (8)

174

Bumblebee Flower Beetle *Euphoria inda* (Linnaeus) (12.0–16.0 mm) have dull or shiny yellowish-brown elytra with variable black spots; head and pronotum mostly black. Adults often fly close to ground, especially over piles of grass, edges of haystacks, compost piles, manure, and other plant debris. They drink sap from wounds on tree trunks and exposed roots, or feed on various flowers and ripe fruits. Larvae develop in various accumulations of plant materials, rotten wood, and within the thatched nests of ants (*Formica*). Québec and Ontario, widespread in United States, except Nevada. (8)

Euphoria sepulcralis (Fabricius) (9.5–13.7 mm) is shiny, dark reddish brown to reddish black overall with faint metallic green or bronze reflections. Upper surface covered in small, pale hairs. Elytra have scattered, small chalky white spots and thin, irregular white lines across each elytron. Adults feed at sap flows on trees; eat a wide variety of flowers and fruits and may damage corn, roses, fruit tree blossoms. Larvae feed on plant detritus and roots in rich, organic or nutrient-poor soils. New Jersey to Florida, west to the Dakotas and Texas. Asian *Protaetia fusca* (Herbst) has tips of elytra produced into spines; Florida. (8)

Cremastocheilus harrisii **Kirby** (10.0–11.0 mm) is black and distinctly shiny. Pronotum shining with front angles delimited by finely impressed line, posterior angles with distinct patch of stiff setae (trichomes) near base and separated from rest of surface by moderately deep impression. Elytra densely punctate, punctures oval. Diurnal adults active in spring, found mating on bright, reflective substrates, such as coastal sand dunes and sandbars along river; overwinter in ant (*Formica*) nests. Massachusetts and New York to Florida, west to Michigan, Iowa, and Mississippi. (7) *Psilocnemis leucosticta* Burmeister with oval pronotum lacking pronounced angles and trichomes; Maryland to South Carolina. (1)

Maculate Flower Scarab *Gnorimella maculosa* **(Knoch)** (11.0–16.0 mm) has brown elytra variably mottled with dark brown or black; northern populations darker overall. Body and legs are black, while head, pronotum, scutellum, sides of abdomen, and pygidium are variously marked with cream or yellowish orange. Adults frequent wooded areas and are usually found buzzing around like bees near dogwoods (*Cornus*) or the fresh blooms of viburnum (*Viburnum*) and other flowers on hot spring days, but seldom in numbers; often collected in Lindgren funnel traps. Larvae feed in rotten wood, including hollow trunks of redbud (*Cercis canadensis*). Widespread from Nova Scotia and Ontario to Florida, and west to Wisconsin, Kansas, and Texas. (1)

175

Hermit Beetle *Osmoderma eremicola* **(Knoch)** (21.0–32.0 mm) is large, robust, somewhat flattened, smooth, dark chestnut brown to mahogany with polished luster. Pronotum with or without deep depressions bordered in front by raised line. Scutellum usually without punctures along middle and sides. Elytra with rows of fine punctures, shallow punctures, spaces between with smaller scattered punctures becoming denser at sides. Larvae develop in rotten wood and tree holes. Adults active in summer, found in wooded habitats on tree trunks, in tree holes, exude a leathery odor; occasionally attracted to light. Nova Scotia and New England south to Georgia, west to Ontario, Minnesota, Iowa, and Indiana. (2)

Osmoderma scabra **(Palisot de Beauvois)** (14.5–20.3 mm) is blackish to black. Pronotum with metallic greenish or coppery luster. Elytra flat or weakly convex, moderately to coarsely sculptured, sometimes with a coppery sheen. Larvae develop in decaying deciduous logs and hollow centers of living trees. Nocturnal adults are active in summer, found at sap flows, in or under bark; attracted to light. Maritime Provinces and Québec to Georgia, west to Ontario, Minnesota, Iowa, Kansas, and Tennessee. (2)

Trichiotinus affinis **(Gory & Percheron)** (7.0–10.0 mm) with elytra reddish and variably brownish and blackish, ridges only slightly convex, spaces between white lines on sides dull, suture not flanked by white lines. Abdomen with pygidium densely setose, without markings underneath. On flowers in spring and summer. New Hampshire and Ontario to Georgia, west to Indiana and Alabama. *Trichiotinus assimilis* (Kirby) elytra usually with distinct, pale lines obliquely crossing surface and flanking tip of elytral suture, even intervals densely punctate; Maritime Provinces and Northeast, also in West. (7)

Trichiotinus bibens **(Fabricius)** (7.0–11.5) is shiny brown, usually with bright green luster. Pronotum bright metallic green. Elytra metallic green or reddish yellow-brown, without white markings. Pygidium with pair of white marks on sides absent or partly obscured by dense setae. Adults are found on flowers in spring and summer. Larvae develop in rotting wood. New York to northern Georgia, west to Michigan, Indiana, and Alabama. (7)

Trichiotinus lunulatus **(Fabricius)** (7.0–11.5) is bright, shiny green (southern populations) or reddish yellow-brown with green luster (northern populations). Elytra with a pair of small white oblique lines on each side. Pygidium with pair of white marks not obscured by dense setae. Adults active in late spring and early summer, found on flowers, especially Queen Anne's lace (*Daucus carota*). Larvae develop in rotting wood. Southern Maryland to Florida, west to eastern Tennessee and Texas. *Trichiotinus viridans* (Kirby) usually with white markings underneath; Michigan to Missouri, west to Minnesota, Nebaska, and Kansas. (7)

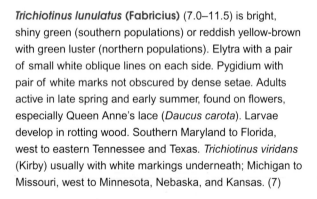

Trichiotinus piger **(Fabricius)** (7.0–12.4 mm) with head and pronotum blackish with greenish hue. Elytra variable, ranging from mostly black to mostly light brown, with intervals 2 and 4 densely punctate, less shiny, 3 and 5 distinctly raised, convex, shiny; sloped sides of each elytron dull between and behind white bands. Pygidium without setae, nonwhite portions indistinctly wrinkled only at middle. Adults found on flowers in spring and summer. Larvae develop in rotting wood. Ontario and Michigan to Florida, west to Minnesota, Nebraska, and Texas. *Trichiotinus rufobrunneus* (Casey) with pygidium setose with widely separated wrinkles all across; Florida. (7)

Trigonopeltastes delta (**Forster**) (8.1–12.9 mm) has dull orange elytra and legs and black pronotum with distinct golden yellow or whitish triangle. Male front tibiae tridentate, female bidentate. Larvae develop in oak (*Quercus*) stumps and accumulations of plant debris. Adults active late spring through summer, found on various flowers, especially Queen Anne's lace (*Daucus carota*) and New Jersey tea (*Ceanothus americanus*). New Jersey and Pennsylvania south to Florida, west to southeastern Kansas and eastern Texas. Scrub palmetto scarab beetle, *Trigonopeltastes floridana* (Casey) (6.0–8.6 mm) with V-shaped mark on pronotum, front of triangle faint; scrub habitat; central Florida. (2)

Valgus canaliculatus (**Fabricius**) (4.0–6.0 mm) usually appears reddish or yellowish in both sexes. Male abdomen densely clothed in overlapping yellow and cream-colored setae. Female has long, smooth-sided spine on tip of pygidium. Eggs, larvae, pupae, and adults are frequently found in galleries of the eastern subterranean termite, *Reticulitermes flavipes*. Adults eat pollen of various flowers in spring and early summer. Delaware and Pennsylvania south to Florida, west to Illinois, Missouri, southeastern Oklahoma, and northeastern Texas. (3)

177

Bristly Necked Valgus *Valgus seticollis* (**Palisot de Beauvois**) (6.0–8.0 mm) male elytra usually brownish, female elytra dark reddish brown. Underside of male's abdomen moderately clothed in nonoverlapping tawny setae. Female lacks spine on pygidium. Adults commonly feed on pollen of flowers, especially dogwood (*Cornus*), Queen Anne's lace (*Daucus carota*), New Jersey tea (*Ceanothus americanus*), and viburnum (*Viburnum*). Mating and all life stages occur in galleries of eastern subterranean termite (*Reticulitermes flavipes*) chewed in logs and stumps of pines and hardwoods. Massachusetts south to Georgia, west to Nebraska and northeastern Texas. *Valgus hemipterus* (Linnaeus) (8.0–9.0 mm) larger, elytra blackish in both sexes, male with distinct patches of white scales on elytra and pygidium, female pygidial spine serrate. Southern Ontario and Michigan to northern Virginia. (3)

TOP RIGHT: *Valgus seticollis* male.
BOTTOM RIGHT: *Valgus seticollis* female.

PLATE-THIGH BEETLES, FAMILY EUCINETIDAE
(YOU-SIH-*NET*-IH-DEE)

The common family name for these beetles is derived from the distinctively large coxal plates at the bases of the hind legs. When disturbed, plate-thigh beetles are capable of jumping. The fungus-feeding adults are typically found in association with decaying wood and leaf litter. They sometimes occur in aggregations, along with the larvae, under bark of decaying logs, where they feed on slime molds (*Eucinetus*) or basidiomycete fungi (*Nycteus*, some *Eucinetus*). *Eucinetus* adults have chewing mouthparts for grinding, while those of *Tohlezkus inexpectus* Vit are of the piercing-sucking type. The clubbed and compact antennae of *Tohlezkus* are similar to those of some other beetles that live with ants.

FAMILY DIAGNOSIS Adult eucinetids are elongate-oblong, brownish yellow to black, sometimes with tips of elytra reddish. Head small, partially visible from above (*Tohlezkus*) or not, with mouthparts strongly directed downward and backward and resting on bases of forelegs. Serrate antennae with 11 antennomeres gradually expanding toward tips. Prothorax short, broad, with coxal cavities open, not completely surrounded by cuticle, open behind. Elytra completely cover abdomen with surface punctate, sometimes with punctures arranged in fine transverse lines rather than rows (*Eucinetus*), folded under portion of side margin (epipleuron) is short (*Eucinetus*, *Nycteus*) or runs along entire length of elytron (*Tohlezkus*). Tarsi 5-5-5, middle and hind tarsomeres tipped with rings of dark spines, hind legs with coxal plates large and oblique, partially covering legs and first abdominal sternite, femora short, and tibiae tipped with pair of long spurs. Abdomen with six ventrites.

SIMILAR FAMILIES Plate-thigh beetles resemble species in several other families that are compact and elliptical in outline, but the combination of their enlarged hind coxal plates and ability to jump are distinctive.

COLLECTING NOTES Look for adults beneath bark of decaying logs or in fungi; they also fly to light and into Malaise traps.

178

FAUNA 11 SPECIES IN FOUR GENERA (NA); SIX SPECIES IN THREE GENERA (ENA)

Eucinetus morio LeConte (2.5–3.0 mm) is oval, reddish brown, blackish, or black with fine wrinkles across elytra. Head and pronotum sometimes lighter, reddish. Elytra crossed with very fine and dense lines. Hind tibiae with two spurs on tip. Larvae develop in fruiting bodies of slime molds. Adults active in late spring and summer in deciduous woodlands and coniferous forests. Found under bark in association with slime mold, including *Arcyria*, *Stemonitis*, *Fuligo*, and *Tubifera*; specialist feeders on spores; also in Malaise traps. Maritime Provinces and New England to Florida, west to Wisconsin and Texas. (3)

Nycteus oviformis (**LeConte**) (4.0 mm) is broadly oval in front and abruptly tapered in rear. Head not visible from above. Elytra mostly densely punctate, widest just behind base. Abdomen with six ventrites. Adults active spring through fall, associated with basidiomycete fungi (*Coniophora*) associated with brown rot; found by sweeping vegetation or in Lindgren funnel traps. Maritime Provinces and New York to North Carolina, west to Michigan and Illinois. (3)

MINUTE BEETLES, FAMILY CLAMBIDAE
(*CLAM*-BIH-DEE)

Very little is known about the natural history of minute beetles. Adults and larvae are found in leaf litter and other accumulations of decomposing plant debris, where they probably feed on microfungi. Some species are found on the fruiting bodies of sac fungi, mushrooms, and slime molds, where they feed on hyphae and spores. Adults are sometimes seen flying above the forest floor at dusk.

FAMILY DIAGNOSIS Adult clambids are very small, oval, convex, yellowish brown to black, and capable of partially rolling up into a ball; surface of pronotum and elytra clothed in pubescence. Head with eyes partially or completely divided. Abruptly clubbed (capitate) antennae with 10 antennomeres attached closely to eyes, 9–10 forming clubs. Pronotum short, broader than head, sides spread out and flattened (explanate), and slightly overlapping elytra. Elytra at widest point slightly wider than prothorax, completely covering abdomen, flight wings fringed with setae. Legs with hind coxal plates expanded, partially covering hind legs, femora swollen, tibiae and tarsi slender, tibia without apical spurs, tarsal formula 4-4-4, and claws simple. Abdomen with five ventrites.

SIMILAR FAMILIES
- pill beetles (Byrrhidae) – antennae with 11 antennomeres; cannot roll up into ball; tarsal formula 5-5-5 (p.195)
- shining fungus beetles (Phalacridae) – ball-rolling ability more developed; antennal club with three to five antennomeres; hind coxae not enlarged; tarsal formula 5-5-5 (p.290)
- *Cybocephalus* (Cybocephalidae) – head almost as wide as pronotum; antennal club with three antennomeres; hind coxae not enlarged (p.304)
- minute fungus beetles (Corylophidae) – cannot roll up into ball; antennal club usually with three antennomeres; hind coxae not enlarged; tarsal formula 5-5-5 (p.320)

COLLECTING NOTES Look for adult clambids in rotting vegetation or flying in wooded areas at dusk, or at light.

FAUNA 12 SPECIES IN THREE GENERA (NA); SIX SPECIES IN ONE GENUS (ENA)

Clambus **species** (0.9–1.1 mm) are very small, moderately to very convex, shiny, with or without pubescence above, and brownish, sometimes with lighter margins. Head broad, with side margins dividing eyes. Antennae attached close to eyes, with 10 antennomeres, first and last two enlarged. Scutellum well developed. Underside of both sexes with five abdominal ventrites. Adults and larvae found in decaying plant matter feeding on fungal spores, especially those of slime molds (Myxogastria) and sac fungi (Ascomycota). Widely distributed in eastern North America. (6)

MARSH BEETLES, FAMILY SCIRTIDAE
(SIR-TIH-DEE)

Adult marsh beetles are terrestrial, short-lived insects commonly found on vegetation growing near marshes, ponds, streams, rivers, and other wetlands. Species of *Ora* and *Scirtes* have greatly enlarged hind femora and are capable of jumping. *Cyphon* species are drab and difficult to identify. Scirtid larvae are found in flowing and standing waters. *Elodes* larvae are found in small streams and clear ponds, while those of *Cyphon* and *Sacodes* are associated with aquatic plants growing along margins and shallows. *Scirtes* larvae prefer to feed and develop in water-filled tree holes. The larvae are quite active and feed on vegetable detritus (*Sacodes*), dead leaves and insects (*Prionocyphon*), or duckweed (*Scirtes*). Pupation occurs in cells in damp soil and among dead moss and leaves, while *Scirtes* pupae are attached to aquatic vegetation. This family is very much in need of revision.

FAMILY DIAGNOSIS Adult scirtids are elongate-oval to nearly circular, somewhat convex, black, brown, yellowish brown to pale yellow, sometimes with red or orange markings. Head large with bulging eyes on sides and usually concealed by pronotum with mouthparts directed downward and backward. Antennae filiform or subserrate with 11 antennomeres. Pronotum always very short, sides flattened and spread out. Scutellum triangular. Elytra punctate, covering abdomen, tips rounded. Legs with hind femora sometimes enlarged (*Ora*, *Scirtes*), tarsal formula 5-5-5 with fourth tarsomere bilobed and claws simple. Abdomen with five ventrites, first two sometimes fused togther.

SIMILAR FAMILIES

- plate-thigh beetles (Eucinetidae) – hind coxae expanded (p.178)
- ptilodactylid beetles (Ptilodactylidae) – scutellum heart-shaped (p.204)

- shining mold beetles (Phalacridae) – antennae clubbed (p.290)
- sap beetles (Nitidulidae) – antennae distinctly clubbed, club with three antennomeres (p.295)
- some lady beetles (Coccinellidae) – antennae slightly clubbed (p.311)
- minute fungus beetles (Corylophidae) – antennae clubbed (p.320)
- hairy fungus beetles (Mycetophagidae) – antennae clubbed; pronotum longer, often with a pair of pits near posterior margin (p.323)
- flea beetles (Chrysomelidae) – head clearly visible from above (p.429)

COLLECTING NOTES Adult scirtids are swept or beaten from herbaceous vegetation, shrubs, and trees growing near swamps ponds, streams, canals, ditches, damp areas, and other wetland habitats. They are also attracted to light in these habitats and are sometimes captured in light traps in large numbers.

FAUNA 50 SPECIES IN EIGHT GENERA (NA); 21 SPECIES IN EIGHT GENERA (ENA)

Cyphon collaris **(Guérin-Ménèville)** (3.5–4.0 mm) is elongate, oval, shiny reddish to blackish to black with reddish markings and appendages. Front of head, pronotum, antennomeres 1–4 or 1–5, and legs reddish yellow. Antennomeres 2–3 each long, combined length long as or longer than 11. Pronotum nearly three times wide as long, sparsely and indistinctly punctate, with side margins distinctly flattened and nearly as wide as elytra. Legs with hind femora enlarged. Adults found resting on vegetation in spring and summer. Massachusetts to Georgia, west to Indiana and Tennessee. (8)

Cyphon padi **(Linnaeus)** (1.80–2.2 mm) is small, oval, reddish to blackish with pair of clearly defined yellowish spots at apical third; lighter individuals sometimes with spot vaguely defined and extended forward as irregular stripe. Appendages mostly pale, femora blackish. Pronotum finely and sparsely punctured. Elytra finely and densely punctured. Legs with hind femora not enlarged. Adults most active spring and summer, found on vegetation, in leaf litter; attracted to light. Maritime Provinces and New England to Florida, west to Indiana; also Utah, Washington. (8)

Cyphon ruficollis **(Say)** (3.5–4.0 mm) is oblong-oval, blackish to black with red to blackish pronotum. Appendages mostly paler, femora darker. Head with few punctures, antennomeres 2–3 short, 3 narrower than 2, each about half length of 4. Pronotum almost three times wide as long, densely punctate, punctures coarser at sides, narrower than elytra. Elytra coarsely, densely punctate. Legs with hind femora not enlarged. Adults active spring and summer, found on wetland vegetation; attracted to light. Atlantic Canada to Georgia, west to Kansas. (8)

Elodes maculicollis **Horn** (4.0–4.5 mm) is elongate, oval, and black with pronotum yellow along sides. Pronotum somewhat circular in outline, moderately convex, and not densely punctate. Elytra more coarsely and densely punctate. Legs with hind femora not enlarged. Adults active spring and summer; found on vegetation and inside beaver dams. Atlantic Canada and New England to South Carolina, west to Ontario. (1)

181

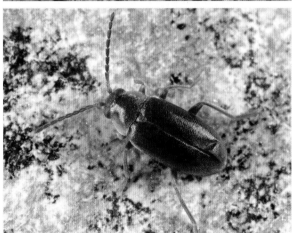

Ora troberti **(Guérin-Ménèville)** (6.0–8.6 mm) is oval and moderately convex. Elytra slightly pubescent, and pale yellowish with long brown stripes, those near suture tend to be long, while lateral stripes shorter. Bases of hind legs in contact only in front, hind femora enlarged for jumping, apical tibial spurs long. Adults attracted to light. Virginia to Florida, west to Texas. Elytral stripes form three irregular transverse bands in similarly distributed *O. texana* Champion; elytra of *O. hyacintha* Blatchley unicolorous: South Carolina to Florida. (3)

Prionocyphon limbatus (LeConte) (4.0–5.0 mm) is oval, moderately convex, yellowish brown. Antennomeres 4–11 dusky and simple in both sexes. Prosternal process dilated, spear-shaped at apex. Elytra each with variable, diffuse dusky spot sometimes covering almost entire surface. *Prionocyphon discoideus* (Say) (3.5–4.5 mm) with antennomeres yellow, 4–11 bipectinate in male, simple in female. Prosternal process not dilated. Elytra each with variable spot distinctly black. Both species widely distributed in eastern North America. *Prionocyphon* adults inhabit deciduous woodlands and coniferous forests; attracted to light in summer, also Lindgren funnel traps. Larvae live in standing water with leaves on bottom, and in water-filled tree holes. (2)

Sacodes pulchella (Guérin-Ménèville) (3.5–5.0 mm) is broadly oval, width greater than half of length, and yellowish orange with black spots on elytra. Elytra with basal spots smaller, apical spots sometimes joined at suture. Underside with tip of abdomen slightly concave (male) or straight (female). Tarsomere 1 of middle legs flat above and finely margined on sides, hind femora not enlarged. Adults active spring and summer in deciduous hardwoods and coniferous forests, found on tree trunks and vegetation; attracted to light, also Lindgren funnel traps. New Brunswick and Ontario to Florida, west to Indiana and Texas. (2)

Sacodes thoracica (Guérin-Ménèville) (2.5–3.7 mm) is broadly oval with blackish head and elytra. Pronotum pale yellowish brown, occasionally with a diffuse dark patch in center. Appendages mostly yellow, femora and ventral surface brown to blackish. Larvae develop in tree holes. Adults found in late spring and summer on tree trunks; also attracted to light. Ontario and Québec to Georgia, west to Illinois and Kansas. (2)

Sarabandus robustus (LeConte) (5.0 mm) is oblong-oval, somewhat shiny brown with sparse pubescence. Head with antennomeres 2–3 small, combined length equal to 4. Pronotum with front margin slightly upturned and extended over head. Elytra with groove along suture and three ridges down middle very faintly indicated. Middle legs narrowly separated at base by process, first tarsomeres flat above and finely margined on sides, and hind femora not enlarged. Adults active spring and summer; attracted to light and found in Lindgren funnel traps. Nova Scotia and New York to South Carolina. (1)

182

Scirtes orbiculatus (Fabricius) (2.5–3.0 mm) is broadly oval, shiny, blackish to black, sparsely clothed in setae, enlarged hind femora, and one hind tibial spur. Head, pronotum finely punctate, elytra more densely so. Pronotum with sides pale. Elytra with short, red stripe along suture at middle. Femora dark, remaining leg segments and antennae pale. Larvae are aquatic, feed on submerged vegetation, and pupate on land. Adults found on vegetation in wetlands in summer; also attracted to light. Québec and Maine to Florida, west to Minnesota and Texas. (4)

Scirtes ovalis Blatchley (3.0–3.5 mm) is broadly oval, slightly flattened, uniformly dull reddish-to-yellowish brown, and clothed in long, reclining yellowish setae. Pronotum wider than long, with fine, dense setae-bearing punctures. Elytral surface appears rough with coarse, setae-bearing punctures. Legs with femora darker, tibiae and tarsi lighter, hind femora enlarged, hind tibiae with one spur at tip nearly as long as adjacent tarsomere. Adults active in summer, found on vegetation near water; attracted to light. Virginia to Florida. (4)

CICADA PARASITE BEETLES, FAMILY RHIPICERIDAE
(RIP-IH-*SAIR*-IH-DEE)

Rhipicerid beetles are also known as cedar beetles. Little is known about the biology of these beetles, with the exception of *Sandalus niger* Knoch. This species gathers in mating aggregations in late summer on the trunks of American elm (*Ulmus americanus*), shingle oak (*Quercus imbricarius*), and other hardwoods. Males and females are found crawling or copulating on the bark, resting on nearby grass, or flying nearby. Females lay large numbers of eggs in the holes and cracks of bark, preferably in areas where there are plenty of cicadas, with an ovipositor that is nearly as long as their body. The subterranean larvae develop by hypermetamorphosis. After hatching, the highly active triungulin makes its way through the soil in search of young cicada nymphs. The larval stages between the triungulin and pupa are unknown. A single pupa with a shed larval exoskeleton of *S. niger* was found inside the hollowed-out exoskeleton of a cicada nymph. The remains of the larval exoskeleton revealed a more sedentary, grublike larva. Several undescribed species of *Sandalus* occur in the Southeast.

FAMILY DIAGNOSIS Adult rhipicerids are long, convex, coarsely and deeply punctured, reddish brown to black beetles. Head with mouthparts directed somewhat downward (hypognathous). Antennae with 11 antennomeres distinctly fan-shaped (flabellate) in males, more or less serrate in females. Pronotum narrowed behind head, becoming wider behind, but narrower than base of elytra. Scutellum visible. Elytra long, completely concealing abdomen, surface vaguely ribbed and coarsely pitted. Legs with tarsal formula 5-5-5, each tarsomere distinctly heart-shaped and padded, and claws equal and simple. Abdomen with five ventrites.

SIMILAR FAMILIES The fan-shaped antennae of the male, elongate body form, and lobed and padded tarsi are distinctive.

COLLECTING NOTES Look out for adult rhipicerids on tree trunks. They can also be spotted on the wing in spring and early summer or fall; occasionally individuals can be captured in Malaise traps.

FAUNA FIVE SPECIES IN ONE GENUS (NA); THREE SPECIES IN ONE GENUS (ENA)

Sandalus niger Knoch (17.0–25.0 mm) is blackish or black, sometimes with reddish brown elytra. Antennae bright reddish brown or black. Prothorax cone-shaped, uniformly narrowed from base to front, with keel along sides weakly developed, most evident at basal third. Pronotum and elytra coarsely, densely punctate. Elytra at base much wider than pronotum, each with ridge faintly indicated or absent. Adults active summer and early fall. Southern Ontario to Florida, west to Colorado and Texas (3)

Sandalus petrophya Knoch (12.0–18.0 mm) is uniformly blackish or brownish, sometimes bicolored with elytra brown and rest of body dark. Sides of pronotum distinctly ridged and somewhat angled behind middle. Adults active from midsummer through fall and are found flying or on tree trunks, especially hardwoods such as beech (*Fagus*), elm (*Ulmus*), and oak (*Quercus*), in late summer and early fall, sometimes in large numbers. New York to Florida, west to Illinois, Missouri, and Texas. (3)

184

METALLIC WOOD-BORING OR JEWEL BEETLES, FAMILY BUPRESTIDAE
(BOO-*PRESS*-TIH-DEE)

The common name of this family is an apt description of the beautiful, iridescent colors that often adorn many buprestids. Some of these beetles are brightly marked with orange, yellow, or red bands and spots. Their rigid and streamlined bodies resemble those of click beetles, but their serrate antennae and metallic colors underneath will distinguish them from the elaterids. Adults are most active on hot, sunny days and feed on foliage, pollen, or nectar; flower visitors are likely to play a role in pollination. Many are strong fliers and readily take to the air, often with a loud buzzing noise, when threatened. Females are often seen running rapidly over tree trunks and branches, stopping briefly to probe the bark and wood with their ovipositors extended in preparation for laying eggs. Eggs are laid in crevices on trunks and branches or, among leaf miners, glued to leaves of their host plants. Although a few of the wood-boring species attack healthy trees, most prefer to breed in trees or shrubs weakened by drought, fire, injury, or infestations by other insects. Emerging adults leave behind distinctive elliptical or oval emergence holes in trunks and branches. Despite the fact that buprestids are among the most destructive of borers in managed timber regions, they are an important link in the recycling of dead trees and downed wood. The usually flattened and always legless larvae often have broad and flat thoracic segments that gives them a "square nail" look. Many mine the sapwood of branches, trunks, and roots, whereas others bore extensively into the heartwood; some species work both. Their galleries are relatively wide and flat and form long linear or meandering tracts beneath the bark or in the heartwood and are usually tightly packed with dust and frass. This material is frequently arranged in finely reticulate ridges that resemble fingerprints. Their wood-boring activities can hasten the death of already weakened trees. A few species will attack seasoned wood (*Buprestis*). The tunneling activities of *Agrilus* larvae that breed in living plant tissues produce knotty swellings, or galls, while girdlers construct spiral galleries around small stems, killing the terminal end of the branch. Still other species (*Brachys, Pachyschelus, Taphrocerus*) are stem and leaf miners of herbaceous and woody plants.

FAMILY DIAGNOSIS Adult buprestids are elongate, broadly flattened or narrowly cylindrical, and have rigid bodies; usually metallic, or black with yellow markings above, and usually iridescent underneath. Head tucked inside slightly broader prothorax with mouthparts directed downward (hypognathous). Antennae serrate with 11 antennomeres. Scutellum visible or not. Elytra smooth, ribbed, or sculptured and usually almost completely conceal abdomen. Legs with tarsal formula 5-5-5, claws equal in size and simple, lobed, or notched. Abdomen with five ventrites, first two fused together.

SIMILAR FAMILIES

- false click beetles (Eucnemidae) – never metallic; body distinctly flexible between prothorax and elytra (p.210)
- click beetles (Elateridae) – body distinctly flexible between prothorax and elytra (p.213)
- lizard beetles (Erotylidae) – antennae clubbed (p.278)

COLLECTING METHODS Buprestids are most active during the hottest parts of the day and often found resting on tree trunks or flowers and foliage of plants in which their larvae feed and develop. Woodland species (*Chalcophora, Chrysobothris, Dicerca*) are sometimes found sunning themselves on dead or dying tree trunks and limbs. Still other species are attracted to freshly cut wood, especially recently felled trees and slash cut by logging operations. *Acmaeodera* are commonly attracted to a variety of flowers but especially the yellow blooms of composites and mustards, and they are frequently attracted to yellow pan traps. Beating and sweeping vegetation during the early morning hours is also very productive. Using an aspirator will allow sucking up specimens quickly and easily from the beating sheet. As the heat of the day increases, dislodged beetles will fall on the sheet and quickly fly away before they can be captured. Rearing jewel beetles from infested wood is also productive.

185

FAUNA 788 SPECIES IN 53 GENERA (NA); 189 IN 30 GENERA (ENA)

Acmaeodera ornata (**Fabricius**) (8.5–11.0 mm) is elongate, robust, convex, somewhat cylindrical, sparsely clothed in black setae, shiny bluish black with yellow markings. Pronotum wider than long, coarsely punctured, without markings. Scutellum hidden. Elytra fused along sutured, shiny blue-black, with rows of coarse, close-set punctures, and variably marked with yellow spots and short dashes. Underside black with sparse long white setae. Adults active spring and early summer, found on flowers, e.g., cinquefoil (*Potentilla*), rose (*Rosa*), serviceberry (*Amelanchier*), coreopsis (*Coreopsis*), dogwood (*Cornus*), purple coneflower (*Echinacea*), sunflower (*Helianthus*), blackberry (*Rubus*), coneflower (*Rudbeckia*), and viburnum (*Viburnum*). Pennsylvania south to Florida, west to Missouri, Arkansas, and Mississippi. (3)

Flat-headed Bald Cypress Sapwood Borer
Acmaeodera pulchella **(Herbst)** (6.0–10.4 mm) is
elongate, robust, convex, somewhat cylindrical, and
bronze and black with yellow markings. Scutellum hidden.
Pronotum bronze, wider than long, coarsely punctured, with
long yellow spot just before the hind angles. Elytra fused
along suture, with one or two transverse bands before
tip broken at suture. Larva occasional pest, develops in
dead and dying bald cypress (*Taxodium distichum*), also
hackberry (*Crataegus*) and honeylocust (*Gleditsia*). Adults
active late spring and summer, found on flowers, including
New Jersey tea (*Ceanothus americanus*) and coneflower
(*Rudbeckia*). New Jersey and Pennsylvania to Florida, west
to Ontario, Montana, Wyoming, and eastern Texas. (3)

Acmaeodera tubulus **(Fabricius)** (5.0–7.0 mm) is
blackish bronze with two rows of usually eight irregular
yellow spots on each elytron. Adults active in spring and
early summer and feed on the petals of many flowers.
Larvae develop in dead twigs and small branches of
various deciduous hardwoods, including hawthorn
(*Crataegus*), hickory (*Carya*), hackberry (*Celtis*),
honeylocust (*Gleditsia triacanthos*), black walnut
(*Juglans nigra*), eastern hophornbeam (*Ostrya
virginiana*), willow (*Salix*), and slippery elm (*Ulmus
rubra*). Ontario and Delaware to Florida, west to
Nebraska and Texas. (3)

Mastogenius crenulatus **Knull** (2.0–3.0 mm) is small,
somewhat cylindrical, robust, and uniformly shiny black.
Pronotum wider than elytra, evenly convex. Elytra shinier
than pronotum, with slightly larger punctures, except along
suture. Larvae develop in branches of hickory (*Carya*),
redbud (*Cercis*), persimmon (*Diospyros*), and oak (*Quercus*).
Adults active in summer, found on leaves of trees and shrubs,
including maple (*Acer*) and willow (*Salix*). Pennsylvania to
Florida, west to Iowa, Missouri, and Texas. (3)

Mastogenius subcyaneus **(LeConte)** (2.0–3.0 mm)
is small, elongate, somewhat cylindrical, robust, and
bluish black. Pronotum punctate, without setae, sides
slightly curved, with base straight and closely abutting
elytra. Elytra with deep bluish or bluish-violet reflections.
Larva develops in oak (*Quercus*) branches. Adults active
in summer, found on leaves of trees and shrubs, including
oak and dogwood (*Cornus*). Rhode Island and New York
to Florida, west to Illinois, Missouri, and Texas. (3)

186

Flat-headed Redbud Borer *Ptosima gibbicollis* (Say)
(4.7–8.0 mm) has a row of rasplike grooves along base of
pronotum, a visible scutellum, and elytra not fused. Elytra
shiny blue-black with variable yellow markings; always with
subapical band broken at suture. Adults found primarily on
foliage of redbud (*Cercis canadensis*). Larvae feed and
develop in redbud; pupae transform into adults in fall and
remain in pupal cells until spring. Pennsylvania to Florida,
west to Kansas and Texas. (3)

Chalcophora liberta (Germar) (19.0–24.0 mm) is
elongate, robust, coppery or brassy yellow with appendages
and raised lines on pronotum and elytra blackish. Pronotum
wider than long, sides round, with three broad raised lines,
middle line not broken at base. Elytra with groove along
entire length of suture, with depressions finely, densely
punctate, not rough, sides next to rounded tips weakly
serrate. New Brunswick and New England to Connecticut,
west to Manitoba, Wisconsin, and Texas. (4)

Chalcophora virginiensis (Drury) (20.0–33.0 mm) is
elongate, oblong, robust, and dull black or dark bronze
with brassy reflections. Pronotum broader than long. Elytra
with dark or shiny elevations and rough brassy or grayish
depressions. Larva develops in injured, dying, and dead
pine (*Pinus*) snags, logs, and stumps. Adults active in
late spring and summer, found sunning on pine trunks.
Maritime Provinces and Québec to Florida, west to Ontario,
Minnesota, Missouri, Oklahoma, and Texas. (4)

Hardwood Heartwood Buprestid *Texania campestris*
(Say) (22.0–25.0 mm) is elongate-oval, uniformly shiny
grayish-green bronze above, coppery underneath.
Pronotum wider than long, coarsely, deeply, and roughly
punctate with deep channel down middle and sides
roughly, deeply impressed. Elytra each with four interrupted
and narrow ridges, spaces between rough, with slightly
impressed spots before and after middle, and sides serrate
along apical third. Larvae develop in maple (*Acer*), beech
(*Fagus*), sycamore (*Platanus*), and willow (*Salix*). Adults
beaten from many deciduous trees. Pennsylvania and
Ontario to Florida, west to Michigan, Kansas, and Texas. (2)

Divergent Beech Beetle *Dicerca divaricata* **(Say)**
(15.0–22.0 mm) is long, strongly convex, golden coppery to brassy green, with strongly extended elytral tips truncate, slightly divergent, and distinctly coppery; last abdominal segment of female with three teeth. Antennomere 2 subequal to 3. Pronotum widest at middle with channel down middle faintly indicated. Breeds in various dead or dying deciduous trees, including maple (*Acer*), birch (*Betula*), *Prunus*, and American beech (*Fagus grandifolia*). Adults found on tree trunks and in Malaise and Lindgren funnel traps from spring through fall. Atlantic Provinces to Georgia, west to Manitoba, North Dakota, and eastern Texas. (14)

Dicerca lurida **(Fabricius)** (12.0–20.0 mm) is brassy to coppery, with raised smooth areas on pronotum and elytra feebly indicated. Pronotum with side margins nearly parallel from base to beyond middle, then narrowed toward head, surface evenly and densely punctate. Elytra with tips not strongly produced, each with two teeth. Underside with plates in front of hind coxae without triangular tooth on outside of indistinct notch. Larvae develop in deciduous trees, e.g., alder (*Alnus*) and hickory (*Carya*). Adults active spring and summer, on hickory and oak (*Quercus*). Québec to Florida, west to Minnesota, and Texas. (17)

Dicerca obscura **(Fabricius)** (13.0–20.0 mm) is elongate, moderately convex, brassy to coppery above and below. Pronotum with sides converging from base. Elytra with small, inconspicuous raised black areas, each tipped with a pair of teeth. Male with middle tibiae simple. Underside with hind coxal plate notched with tooth on outer side of notch, last abdominal ventrite of female with three teeth. Larvae develop in common persimmon (*Diospyros virginiana*) and staghorn sumac (*Rhus typhina*). Adults active spring and summer, on hickory (*Carya*) and oak (*Quercus*); overwinter under loose bark of hardwoods and conifers. Massachusetts to Florida, west to Kansas, and Texas. (17)

Poecilonota cyanipes **(Say)** (10.4–16.0 mm) is elongate, dark coppery gray with tips of elytra bronzed. Head finely, sparsely pubescent, densely punctate with groove down middle, antennal base coppery. Pronotum widest at middle with smooth raised line down middle, sides coarsely, densely punctate. Scutellum short, wide, straight behind with angles distinct. Elytra with distinct rows of irregular punctures, spaces between with irregular smooth spots, tips prolonged with small teeth or finely saw-toothed (serrulate) on edges. Underside bronze. Larva in cottonwood (*Populus*) and willow (*Salix*). Nova Scotia, New Brunswick, and Québec to Louisiana, west to Yukon Territory and Arizona. (4)

Actenodes acornis **(Say)** (10.0–13.0 mm) is broadly oblong, somewhat flattened, densely and coarsely punctured, uniformly brassy black above, without green or coppery markings. Eyes separated on top by half their own widths at widest part, antennae short, antennomere 4 triangular, nearly twice as wide as 3, 5–11 wider than long. Pronotum twice as wide as long. Elytra broader than pronotum, roughly sculptured with wrinkles across surface, and no depressions or ridges. Tarsomere 3 extended on each side into a long, divergent spine extending beyond 4. Larvae develop in maple (*Acer*), hickory (*Carya*), beech (*Fagus*), and oak (*Quercus*). Connecticut to Florida, west to Iowa, Kansas, and Texas. (4)

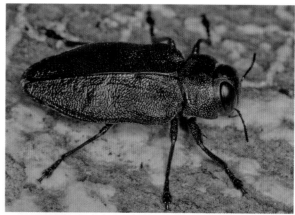

Agrilaxia flavimana **(Gory)** (3.8–5.0 mm) is very slender, black with blue, green, or blue-green, head convex, not impressed down middle, and clypeus elongate and narrow. Antennae blackish green (male) or black (female). Pronotum wider than long, widest in front. Hind coxal plate nearly straight, not broadly notched in front. Elytra long, strongly convergent and sinuate after middle, and side of abdomen exposed. Larvae develop in small branches and twigs of oak (*Quercus*) and pine (*Pinus*). Adults active spring and summer, found on flowers and foliage of many shrubs in mixed forests and woodlands. New York to Florida, west to southern Ontario, Colorado, and Arizona. (8)

189

Anthaxia quercata **(Fabricius)** (3.8–5.3 mm) is elongate, stout, and mostly bright, shiny green with yellow and copper. Head uniformly green (male) or blue-green to purple-blue with bronzy or yellow-green (female). Pronotum with side arched in front half and nearly parallel behind, with large impression near each hind angle. Elytra shining, densely and minutely wrinkled, and sides sinuate just before middle. Claws toothed at base. Larvae develop in hardwoods and some conifers. Adults found on flowers and vegetation. New Hampshire and New York to Florida, west to Iowa and Texas. (9)

Lined Buprestis *Buprestis lineata* **(Fabricius)** (12.0–17.0 mm) is light chocolate-brown to shiny brassy black. Front of head red-orange or yellow. Brick red, cream, or yellow stripes on elytra distinctive, stripes sometimes broken into small specks and streaks. Adults found resting on dead or dying pines (*Pinus*) in spring and summer. Larvae breed in longleaf (*P. palustris*), loblolly (*P. taeda*), pitch (*P. rigida*), shortleaf (*P. echinata*), and Virginia (*P. virginiana*) pines. Nova Scotia to Florida, west to Missouri and Texas; introduced to West Indies. (12)

Red-legged Buprestis *Buprestis rufipes* (Olivier) (12.0–28.0 mm) has a green pronotum with yellow sides. Each elytron with yellow stripe from humerus to middle followed by two yellow spots (sometimes connected), and yellow tip. Legs and last three abdominal sterna reddish brown. Adults are active in spring and summer. Larvae develop in deciduous hardwoods, including honeylocust (*Gleditsia triacanthos*), beech (*Fagus*), maple (*Acer*), hickory (*Carya*), tulip tree (*Liriodendron tulipifera*), and slippery elm (*Ulmus rubra*). New York to Florida, west to Kansas and Texas. (12)

Buprestis salisburyensis (Herbst) (10.0–15.0 mm) is variable in color. Elytra green with suture and side margins bright coppery or brassy, green with purple or blue stripe with coppery margins, or entirely dark coppery with side margins dull and darker. Adults are found in spring and summer on pine branches. Larvae develop in pine (*Pinus*). Ontario and Massachusetts to Georgia, west to Wisconsin and Oklahoma. (12)

Buprestis striata (Fabricius) (13.0–20.0 mm) is uniformly dull coppery brown to brilliant green or blue with side margins copper. Pronotum with front angles not visible from above. Elytra with four or five broad rows of coarse punctures separated by narrowly raised and sparsely punctate ridges, and usually with a pair of short ridges behind scutellum. Front tibiae without notches or spine or tooth on tip. Larva develops in sound or rotten pine (*Pinus*). Adults active in spring, found on needles or in beach drift, overwinter under bark. Maritime Provinces and New England to Florida, west to Ontario, Missouri, and Texas. (12)

Chrysobothris azurea LeConte (5.5– 9.0 mm) ranges from bright violet-blue to purple. Pronotum with sides sinuate. Elytra each with three broad depressions bright blue or yellowish. Larva develops in many trees and vines, e.g., oak (*Quercus*), birch (*Betula*), alder (*Alnus*), hickory (*Carya*), maple (*Acer*), sumac (*Rhus*), grape (*Vitis*), and wisteria (*Wisteria*). Adults active in summer, found on dogwood (*Cornus*), hawthorn (*Crataegus*), and willow (*Salix*), among others. Across Canada and widely distributed in eastern United States. (20)

***Chrysobothris chrysoela* (Illiger)** (7.0–9.5 mm) is broadly elongate, moderately convex, coarsely and deeply punctured, and very shiny reddish purple to purplish black. Head bronzy green to bronzy black (male), or uniformly greenish black (female). Pronotum twice as wide as long, widest at base. Elytra each with five golden green spots. Larvae develop in both hardwoods and conifers, including button magnolia (*Conocarpus erectus*), bald cypress (*Taxodium distichum*), persimmon (*Diospyros virginiana*), oak (*Quercus*), and ash (*Fraxinus*). Adults beaten from oak, wax myrtle (*Morella cerifera*), or found on stems of persimmon in spring and summer. District of Columbia to Florida, west to Texas. (20).

Flat-headed Apple Tree Borer *Chrysobothris femorata* (Olivier) (7.0–16.0 mm) is elongate-oblong, slightly flat, black with coppery or bronze reflections, and indistinctly marked with dull spots and irregular bands. Head with clypeus sharply notched at middle with round sides, male with bright green face. Larvae feed and develop in many species of hardwoods, including maple (*Acer*), apple (*Malus*), pear (*Pyrus*), peach (*Prunus*), willow (*Salix*), oak (*Quercus*), and elm (*Ulmus*); a pest in orchards already in poor condition. Adults found in late spring and summer on sunlit tree trunks, under bark; also in Malaise traps. Throughout North America. (20)

191

***Melanophila acuminata* (De Geer)** (7.0–13.0 mm) is somewhat dull, blackish, and elytra without any markings. Pronotum with surface coarsely punctate and granulate, widest just in front of middle, sinuate at base. Elytra uniformly dark, with pointed tips. Larva typically develops in conifers, including pine (*Pinus*), fir (*Abies*), spruce (*Picea*), cedar (*Cupressus*), and arborvitae (*Thuja*). Adults often common around forest fires and scorched timber; occasionally attracted to light. Holarctic; widespread in coniferous forests across North America. Uncommon *Melanophila notata* (Laporte & Gory) similar with six to eight yellow spots on elytra. (2)

***Phaenops fulvoguttata* (Harris)** (8.0–12.0 mm) is black with bronze luster, usually with three small yellow spots on each elytron. Antennae reaching hind angles of pronotum, antennomere 3 twice as long as 2 and longer than 4. Pronotum with surface distinctly and finely wrinkled, widest in front of middle. Elytra without ridges, with many fine, short setae, sides weakly divergent to front two-thirds, tips broadly rounded. Tarsomeres with fine setae only on rear margins. Larvae develop in conifers, e.g., fir (*Abies*), tamarack (*Larix*), spruce (*Picea*), pine (*Pinus*), and hemlock (*Tsuga*). Transcontinental, in east from Atlantic Canada to South Carolina, west to Ontario, Michigan, and Tennessee. (5)

Spectralia gracilipes (Melsheimer) (10.0–11.0 mm) is elongate, somewhat cylindrical, and black to violet bronze above and more bronze below. Head with distinct, ridged cavities at antennal bases, antennae with well-defined pits on most antennomeres. Scutellum small, distinct. Elytra each with bases smooth, tips not extended beyond abdomen. Larva develops in dead branches of ash (*Fraxinus*), hophornbeam (*Ostrya*), and oak (*Quercus*). Adults found on oak, hophornbeam, hawthorn (*Crataegus*), and flowers of goldenrod (*Solidago*). New England and Southern Ontario to South Carolina, west to Kansas and Texas. (1)

Xenorhipis brendeli LeConte (3.7–6.7 mm) is elongate, metallic blue and copper (black or brown after death), and coarsely punctate; antennae and tarsi brown. Antennae of male pectinate, female serrate. Head and pronotum densely punctate, metallic. Pronotum wider than long, hind angles sharp, base sinuate. Elytra long, parallel-sided, covering abdomen, with long, indistinct white spot extending from basal angle almost to suture at basal third. Larvae develop in dead branches of hickory and pecan (*Carya*) and oak (*Quercus*). Adults active in summer, found on larval hosts, also locust (*Gleditsia*). Massachusetts and New York to Florida, west to Iowa, Missouri, and Texas. (1)

192

Two-lined Chestnut Borer *Agrilus bilineatus* **(Weber)** (6.0–12.0 mm) is black with a bluish, sometimes greenish caste with distinct yellowish or whitish stripes of setae. Pronotum with pair of stripes on sides. Elytra with pair of stripes on sides not reaching tips, sometimes reduced to patches on humeri. Sides of abdomen below densely clothed in setae. Larva mines primarily oak (*Quercus*) and beech (*Fagus*); American chestnut (*Castanea dentata*) was primary host. Adults active late spring and summer, feed on leaves of larval hosts. Widespread in eastern North America. (64)

Agrilus cyanescens (Ratzeburg) (5.5–6.3 mm) is robust, slightly convex, feebly shining, and uniformly dark to greenish blue. Antennae with apical antennomeres 4–11 serrate, 7–11 as long as wide. Pronotum without depression down middle or ridges near basal angles. Scutellum not crossed with ridges. Elytra at base slightly wider than pronotum, surface sculpted like roof shingles, tips not pronolonged. Pygidium without distinct ridge. Underside shiny black to bluish black, suture between first two abdominal ventrites barely visible at sides, if at all. Adults found on blackberry (*Rubus*), coralberry (*Symphoricarpos orbiculatus*), viburnum (*Viburnum*), and other deciduous trees. Europe; established from Ontario to Virginia, west to Illinois and Missouri. (64)

Agrilus obsoletoguttatus Gory (4.7–8.0 mm) is elongate, slender, somewhat flat on top, moderately shiny brass, copper, and bronze. Head bronzy to golden green to coppery brown. Pronotum and elytra bronzy or olive-black, sometimes with purplish tinge. Elytra each with three or four whitish yellowish pubescent spots sometimes vague. Underneath shiny brassy or coppery. Legs more greenish. Larvae develop in buckeye (*Aesculus*), birch (*Betula*), hickory (*Carya*), beech (*Fagus*), honeylocust (*Gleditsia*), hophornbeam (*Ostrya*), and oak (*Quercus*). Adults active spring and early summer, found on many deciduous trees and shrubs. Widespread in eastern North America. (64)

Red-necked Cane Borer *Agrilus ruficollis* **(Fabricius)** (4.0–8.0 mm) is elongate, nearly cylindrical, and feebly shining, bluish or velvety black. Head dark and brassy. Pronotum usually bright coppery red, sometimes golden, brassy, or blue. Elytra slightly wider behind middle, tips rounded and finely saw-toothed (serrate). Adults found on flowers and stems of wild and cultivated blackberries, raspberries, and dewberry bushes (*Rubus*) in late spring and summer. Spiral boring of larve under bark of woody stems produce galls, especially in raspberry canes. Québec and Ontario to Florida, west to Manitoba, Nebraska, and Texas. (64)

Alder Gall Buprestid *Eupristocerus cogitans* **(Weber)** (6.5–8.0 mm) is elongate, robust, and black with head and pronotum dull reddish copper. Pronotum with broad depression at hind angles, sides bright. Elytra with rough granular surface sculpturing, widest at apical three-quarters with vague bands of scattered pale setae. Larva produces galls on alder (*Alnus*) and birch (*Betula*). Adults active in late spring and summer, found on larval hosts and in Malaise traps. Maritime Provinces and New England to Florida, west to Ontario, Ohio, Kentucky, and Mississippi. (1)

Brachys aerosus Melsheimer (4.0–6.3 mm) is broadly ovate, triangular, and clothed in gray and reddish or yellowish pubescence. Scutellum small. Elytra blue, sometimes blackish with brassy or purplish luster, without single broad white band. Abdomen underneath with tip of last ventrite straight in both sexes. Larva mines leaves of oak (*Quercus*) and many other deciduous trees. Adults active late spring and summer, found on leaves of many hardwoods. Widespread across Canada and eastern United States. (5)

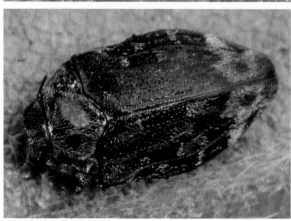

Brachys floricolus Kerremans (4.0–5.5 mm) is broadly ovate, slightly convex, with golden red pubescence. Head without prominent bumps above eyes. Elytra with rows of large, coarse punctures and three narrow, irregular bands of white setae, without tufts. Last abdominal ventrite of female with deep notch fringed with setae. Adults active spring and early summer, found on oak (*Quercus*) and blueberry (*Vaccinium*). Virginia to Florida, west to Mississippi. (5)

Brachys ovatus (Weber) (3.0–5.8 mm) is broadly ovate, triangular. Elytra with irregular golden or silvery bands bordered with white setae, apical half with broad space lacking setae. Abdomen with notch on tip of ventrite fringed with long setae (female) or not (male). Larva mines leaves of oak (*Quercus*) and many other deciduous trees. Adults active late spring and summer, found on leaves of many hardwoods. Widespread in eastern United States to Ontario and Québec. (5)

Pachyschelus purpureus (Say) (2.5–3.5 mm) is broadly ovate, triangular, shiny, black with purple elytra marked with whitish pubescent. Head and pronotum black. Pronotum widest at base, tapering toward head. Scutellum large, triangular, smooth. Elytra with white lines before tips. Underside smooth, male with two projections on last abdominal ventrite, each with three, rarely four teeth. Larva mines leaves of ticktrefoil (*Desmodium*) and lespedeza (*Lespedeza*). Adults active spring and early summer, and late summer, beaten or swept from vegetation in marshy places. In east from Québec to South Carolina, west to Ontario, Minnesota, Missouri, Oklahoma, and Texas. (6)

Taphrocerus nicolayi Obenberger (3.0 mm) is elongate, slender, and shiny black with brassy luster. Head with broad shallow impression in front, sides with fine scattered punctures. Pronotum wider than long, narrowed in front, smooth and shiny on top with scattered punctures on sides. Elytra with narrow bands of fine white setae on apical half sometimes rubbed off or absent. Larvae mine leaves of sedges, e.g., *Carex* and *Rhynchospora*. One or two generations are produced annually. Adults feed on sedge leaf margins in late spring and summer; swept from sedges growing along wetland edges, roadsides, and ditches, also in Malaise traps. Eastern North America. (11)

PILL OR MOSS BEETLES, FAMILY BYRRHIDAE
(*BEER*-IH-DEE)

Both adult and larval byrrhids feed primarily on mosses and occasionally on liverworts. The larvae burrow through the tissues and underlying substrate, while the adults are strictly surface grazers. Beetles are primarily nocturnal, but will feed during the day in conditions of low light or under the cover of debris. Most species have grooves underneath their bodies into which they can withdraw their legs when disturbed. Remaining motionless with their legs withdrawn, pill beetles strongly resemble seeds. Species capable of flight take to the air in spring and early summer and are sometimes found washed up among lines of shore debris.

FAMILY DIAGNOSIS Adult byrrhids are broadly oval, convex above and below, compact, upper surface often with scales, setae, or bristles. Head often concealed from above, with mouthparts directed downward. Gradually (clavate) or abruptly (capitate) clubbed, or somewhat threadlike (subfiliform) antennae with 11 antennomeres. Elytra cover abdomen. Underside usually with depressions to receive legs. Tarsi 4-4-4, 5-5-5, tarsomeres usually increasingly larger from 1 to 3, 4 small, 5 long, simple or with pads underneath; claws simple. Abdomen with five ventrites, first two fused.

SIMILAR FAMILIES

- round fungus beetles (Leiodidae) – dorsal surface without setae or scales (p.118)
- wounded-tree beetles (Nosodendridae) – flattened fore legs (p.244)
- some dermestid beetles (Dermestidae) – have ocelli and distinctly clubbed antennae (p.246)
- death-watch beetles (Ptinidae) – antennal club lopsided (p.252)
- minute fungus beetles (Corylophidae) – underside flat (p.320)
- *Hyporhagus* (Zopheridae) – mouthparts directed forward, upper surface without setae or scales, antennal club distinct (p.343)
- some darkling beetles (Tenebrionidae) – bases of antennae hidden from above (p.344)
- seed beetles (Chrysomelidae: Bruchinae) – usually with short beak on head, pygidium visible (pp.430–2)
- small fungus weevils (Anthribidae) – usually with short, broad beak, pygidium visible (p.458)

195

COLLECTING NOTES These infrequently collected beetles are most often found along lake beaches in drift, beneath debris, in moss, under bark, or among the roots of grasses growing in sandy or moist habitats. Some species are occasionally attracted to light.

FAUNA 57 SPECIES IN 15 GENERA (NA); 18 SPECIES IN 7 GENERA (ENA)

Byrrhus americanus **LeConte** (7.0–9.5 mm) is oval, very convex, black, shining, with coarse punctures, and densely clothed in fine grayish pubescence. Head with punctures coarse and merging together, apical antennomeres slightly enlarged. Pronotal punctures small, slightly larger in diameter than base of seta, and separated by more than their own diameters. Elytra not fused, each with three or four interrupted velvety black lines and a gray, narrow, sinuous band across middle often forming crescent. Tarsi simple. Adults and larvae burrow through dense mats of moss and graze on their surfaces. Nova Scotia and Labrador to New Jersey, west to Manitoba, South Dakota, and Iowa. (5)

Cytilus alternatus (Say) (4.0–6.5 mm) is oblong-oval, convex, black and gray with bronze luster. Head, pronotum, and underside finely punctate, reddish-brown to golden setae almost lying on surface. Scutellum with golden pubescence. Elytra with 11 fine grooves, surface finely, densely roughly punctate, with black and grayish pubescence and patches of black or golden pubescence, often with alternating stripes appearing bronze, sometimes metallic green or blue-green at base. Semiaquatic larvae eat filamentous and feathery mosses in bogs and seeps and along streams, cascades, and shorelines. Adults found along streamsides and lakeshores, or in ocean drift. In east from Atlantic Canada and New England to Pennsylvania, west to Manitoba and Ohio; also Europe. (2)

Chaetophora spinosa (Rossi) (0.9–2.1 mm) is strongly oval, convex, and clothed only above in distinctly clubbed bristles. Head tucked under prothorax. Antennae short and distinctly clubbed. All legs completely capable of being withdrawn into special grooves on underside of thorax. Adults associated with mosses and algae in moist and disturbed habitats. Europe; established in east from Maritime Provinces and Québec to Maryland, west to Ontario and Ohio; also British Columbia and Idaho. (1)

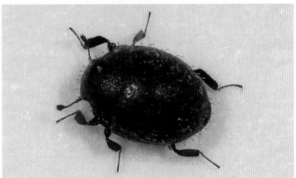

196

RIFFLE BEETLES, FAMILY ELMIDAE
(*EL*-MIH-DEE)

Riffle beetles typically live among the rocks and cobble of shallow rapids (riffles) of streams and rivers. Although they may be present in large numbers, elmids are largely inconspicuous. Larvae and adults are usually found together crawling over, under, and between submerged substrates; a few species are associated with aquatic mosses. The presence of elmids is recognized as an indication of good water quality because of their preference for living in clean and permanent streams. Adults usually emerge at dusk on warm summer nights; fully winged species fly only once to disperse and are often attracted to lights. They are completely covered with a dense layer of short setae called a plastron that envelops them in a silvery blanket of air. Once submerged, elmids seldom, if ever, need to go to the surface or leave the water. Adults are long-lived and it is not unusual to find them caked in mineral and organic deposits, or covered with small aquatic organisms. Mature larvae crawl out of the water to pupate in small cells in moist sand beneath rocks, under loose bark, in wet moss, or in other protected sites near the water's edge.

FAMILY DIAGNOSIS Adults elmids are elongate or oval, with long legs and large claws and underside clothed in thick silvery gray pile; some species have faint or distinct yellowish or reddish markings on elytra. Head with mouthparts directed downward, often hidden from above. Antennae long, filiform or clavate, with 8–11 antennomeres. Prothorax broader than head, broadly pointed in front, often notched or slightly serrate toward sides, with ridges on top. Scutellum small, suboval, triangular, or pentagonal.

Elytra pitted, rough, sometimes ribbed, and completely conceal abdomen. Legs generally long and not modified for swimming; tarsal formula 5-5-5, first tarsomere nearly subequal to remaining tarsus, with large and equal claws sometimes toothed. Abdomen with five ventrites.

SIMILAR FAMILIES

- minute moss beetles (Hydraenidae) – maxillary palps long; antennae short (p.114)

- long-toed water beetles (Dryopidae) – antennae short, most antennomeres wider than long (p.198)
- travertine beetles (Lutrochidae) – antennae short with articles 1–2 long and broad (p.200)
- minute marsh-loving beetles (Limnichidae) – body covered with colorful scales (p.201)
- water penny beetles (Psephenidae) – strongly oval in form; antennae flabellate or serrate; elytra soft (p.203)

COLLECTING NOTES Elmids are found year-round. Look for them on vegetation and debris in the riffle areas of small gravelly and rocky streams. Stir up the bottom of these habitats by overturning or kicking rocks so the current will wash the dislodged beetles into a net or screen placed immediately downstream. Dump the net's contents into a shallow, light-colored pan so the small, dark-colored larvae and adults are easily seen. Beetles are also extracted from submerged plant debris by using a Berlese funnel. Adults attracted in large numbers to lights near streams.

FAUNA 99 SPECIES IN 26 GENERA (NA); 39 SPECIES IN 9 GENERA (ENA)

Ancyronyx variegata (**Germar**) (3.0–3.5 mm) is elongate, narrowed on both ends, with bright yellow or orange markings and long legs. Antennae filiform, with 11 antennomeres. Pronotum with pair of depressions in front, front and rear margins yellowish. Elytra each with slender mark from basal angle to suture and across to sides, and a short stripe just before tip. Bases of hind legs globular, with all tibiae yellowish. Adults found year-round on submerged wood and plants festooned with algae in creeks, streams, and rivers; attracted to light. New England and Québec to Florida, west to Ontario, Wisconsin, Kansas, and Texas. (1)

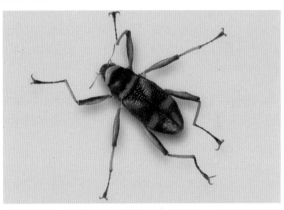

197

Dubiraphia vittata (**Melsheimer**) (2.5–3.0 mm) is elongate, yellowish brown or blackish, with two broad reddish yellow-brown elytral stripes. Pronotum with anterior margin pale, sides not margined, somewhat parallel at basal two-thirds. Elytra with seven rows of large punctures, stripes not sharply defined (difficult to see in dark specimens), and narrow just before tip. Legs with front tibiae with fringe of short, matted woolly setae, tarsi lighter than tibia and femora. Adults found year-round on roots in sandy-bottomed streams, ponds, and lakes. Nova Scotia and Québec to Florida, west to Manitoba and Texas. (5)

Optioservus trivittatus (**Brown**) (1.6–2.2 mm) is broadly oval, not noticeably humped when viewed from side, distinctly tapered at apical third of elytra, dark reddish brown to black with distinct brownish-yellow to yellow stripes on elytra. Antennae with 11 antennomeres, 9–11 enlarged. Pronotum with sides evenly curved and slightly serrate, with golden pubescence becoming denser at middle. Elytra with stripe from basal angle almost to tip. Tarsi yellowish brown. Adults found year-round in riffles and narrow chutes with gravel bottoms in small, brown-stained acidic streams. Maritime Provinces and New England to Georgia, west to Ontario, Wisconsin, and Louisiana. (6)

Stenelmis mera **Sanderson** (2.3–3.2 mm) is small, elongate, somewhat convex, and brown and gray, with each elytron marked with two yellowish brown spots or a stripe. Pronotum longer than wide, widest behind middle, deep groove down middle, sides sinuate, dark gray with light gray and blackish stripes. Elytra brown, wider than pronotum, widest behind middle, each with a sharp ridge from basal angle almost to tip, stripe or spot extending over basal angle, and rows of deep punctures. Femora gray with yellowish-brown tips, tarsomere 5 with tip flat, shorter than 1–4 combined. Adults active in summer, found in rocky areas in streams and rivers; attracted to light. Québec to Georgia, west to Michigan, Arkansas, and Alabama. (20)

Macronychus glabratus **Say** (2.5–3.5 mm) is elongate, mostly dark brown to black, and leggy. Antennae short, with seven antennomeres, 1, 2, 7 wider than rest. Pronotum narrowed in front, sinuate on sides. Elytra have vague grooves most conspicuous on sides and tips, with ridge just before sides bordered by a distinctive golden or silvery band. Some individuals capable of flight, most are not. Larva develops in submerged wood. Long-lived adults typically found on submerged coarse woody debris on sandy bottoms of streams and rivers; also at light. Nova Scotia and Québec to Florida, west to Ontario, North Dakota, and Texas. (1)

198

LONG-TOED WATER BEETLES, FAMILY DRYOPIDAE
(DRY-*OH*-PIH-DEE)

Dryopids live in both shallow rapids and riffles of streams and in slow-moving water. Their common name is derived from their unusually long claws, or "toes." Adult *Helichus* live underwater and walk about on aquatic vegetation and submerged debris, while the larvae live in moist sand several feet from the edge of streams where they probably feed on roots or decaying vegetation. Adult *Helichus* have a plastron, a dense layer of short setae that covers their body and traps a silvery blanket of air. *Pelonomus* lacks a plastron, but is very pubescent. Female flight muscles become reduced or disappear altogether as they age. They have well-developed egg-laying tubes with blades that enable them to place their eggs in the soil or in plant tissues. Larval development may require two or more years and pupation takes place on land. *Helichus* pupae have special structures on the abdomen called gin-traps that probably serve to anchor the pupae within the cast skin of the last larval instar to help facilitate adult emergence. Newly emerged adults fly or crawl to running water.

FAMILY DIAGNOSIS Adult dryopids are elongate, oval, dull dark gray, brown, or nearly black, and densely clothed in coarse or fine setae; upper surfaces often encrusted with minerals. Head hypognathous and distinctly retracted into prothorax. Antennae short with 11 antennomeres, 2 greatly expanded into an earlike process that nearly covers rest of antenna (*Helichus*) or not (*Pelonomus*), 4–11 expanded sideways to form a loose club. Pronotum wider than head, without broad projection in front. Elytra completely conceal abdomen. Legs long, slender, not modified for swimming, tarsal formula 5-5-5, last tarsomere long with unusually long and simple claws. Abdomen with five ventrites.

SIMILAR FAMILIES

- minute moss beetles (Hydraenidae) – maxillary palps elongate (p.114)

- riffle beetles (Elmidae) – antennae long, with most antennomeres longer than wide (p.196)
- travertine beetles (Lutrochidae) – small, oval, antennae short with antennomeres 1–2 long and broad (p.200)
- minute marsh-loving beetles (Limnichidae) – body covered with short, scalelike hairs (p.201)
- water penny beetles (Psephenidae) – oval; antennae flabellate or serrate; elytra soft (p.203)

COLLECTING NOTES *Helichus* is usually found clinging to logs and debris in stream riffles. *Pelonomus obscurus* is found on aquatic plants and debris in ditches, swamps, and ponds. Specimens are collected by stirring up the bottom of riffles or submerged plant debris and letting the current wash the dislodged beetles into an aquatic net or screen placed just downstream. Dump the net's contents into a shallow, light-colored pan where the dark-colored adults will stand out against the light background. Another method is to search stream pools for active adults at night with a flashlight. Dryopids are also extracted from plant debris using a Berlese funnel. Recently emerged adults in both genera are attracted to lights placed near these habitats at night.

FAUNA 13 SPECIES IN FIVE GENERA (NA); FIVE SPECIES IN TWO GENERA (ENA)

Pelonomus obscurus **LeConte** (4.5–6.8 mm) is elongate-oval and brown with uniformly dense, long, bristly yellowish setae. Antennomeres 1 and 2 broad and form a shield, 3–11 each with platelike extensions. Pronotum wider than long, narrowed in front, and side slightly sinuate. Elytra with sides parallel, each with series of faint ridges. Adults active spring and summer, found on plants and debris in standing waters, e.g., ditches, ponds, swamps, and lakes; attracted to light. Québec to Florida, west to Illinois, Kansas, and Texas. (1)

199

Helichus lithophilus **(Germar)** (5.0–5.5 mm) is oblong, somewhat convex, brown, and uniformly clothed in dense, silky pubescence. Pronotum wider than long, convex, with front and hind angles sharp. Last abdominal ventrite reddish and lacks pubescence. Adults found under rocks or on submerged wood in creeks and streams. Ontario and Québec to Florida, west to Wisconsin, Iowa, and Texas. (4)

TRAVERTINE BEETLES, FAMILY LUTROCHIDAE
(LU-*TROCK*-IH-DEE)

Both adults and larvae are aquatic and found on calcareous deposits (travertine) along the edges of fast-flowing warm springs and streams. They feed on algae and waterlogged wood. The larvae overwinter and pupation occurs in protected sites just above water level. One generation is produced annually.

FAMILY DIAGNOSIS Adult lutrochids are oval and strongly convex, yellowish, and densely pubescent and punctate. Head broad, with mouthparts directed downward. Antennae short, with 11 antennomeres, 1–2 broad, conspicuously setose, and subequal to combined length of remaining antennomeres. Pronotum wider than head, but narrower than base of elytra. Elytra densely punctate and setose, and completely cover abdomen. Legs with femora grooved to receive tibiae, tarsal formula 5-5-5, last tarsomere long, and claws simple. Abdomen with five ventrites.

SIMILAR FAMILIES

- minute moss beetles (Hydraenidae) – maxillary palps elongate (p.114)

- riffle beetles (Elmidae) – antennae long, with most antennomeres longer than wide (p.196)
- minute marsh-loving beetles (Limnichidae) – body covered with short, scalelike setae (p.201)
- water penny beetles (Psephenidae) – oval; antennae flabellate, serrate; elytra soft (p.203)

COLLECTING NOTES Adults of *Lutrochus laticeps* are found in small to large warm travertine streams at or just above the waterline on the downstream side of rocks or wood projecting from water riffles. They are sometimes found in large numbers in these habitats and are quick to fly when disturbed.

FAUNA THREE SPECIES IN ONE GENUS (NA); ONE SPECIES, *LUTROCHUS LATICEPS* CASEY (ENA)

200

Lutrochus laticeps Casey (2.9–3.6 mm) is elongate-oval, convex, and shiny black with greenish or brassy luster; appendages brownish. Head broad, about two-thirds width of pronotum. Pronotum twice as wide as long, base notched on either side of scutellum. Elytra convex and slightly wider than pronotum. together narrowed toward tip. Larvae found on submerged calcareous incrustations on rocks. Adults found at or just above waterline on downstream side of emergent rocks and logs among rapids and riffles; attracted to light. Pennsylvania and District of Columbia to Michigan and Illinois, south to Alabama and Oklahoma. (1)

MINUTE MARSH-LOVING BEETLES, FAMILY LIMNICHIDAE
(LIM-*NICK*-IH-DEE)

Little is known about the biology and natural history of limnichids. Most adults are found on wet sand beaches or among well-vegetated edges along the margins of lakes and streams, while others are found on emergent vegetation and wood. They are also found in trash washed up on shore by floodwaters. Larvae live in damp soil or debris near ponds and streams where they probably feed on decaying plant materials. Pupation occurs in larval habitats.

FAMILY DIAGNOSIS Adult limnichids are oval, convex, uniformly brownish to blackish, or colorful and clothed in fine grayish pubescence or scalelike setae. Head small, hypognathous, retracted deep inside prothorax, with eyes visible from above (*Limnichites*) or not (*Eulimnichus*). Antennae short and clavate, with 11 antennomeres, most antennomeres broad, 2 large, 3–8 smaller and nearly moniliform, 9–11 gradually larger and forming loose club (clavate). Pronotum convex with sides sharply margined and converging toward head. Elytra punctate and completely covers abdomen, setae uniform (*Eulimnichus*, *Limnichites*), or mixed with reclining and erect setae (*Limnichoderus*). Legs slender, tarsal formula 5-5-5. Abdomen with five ventrites.

SIMILAR FAMILIES
- some small water scavenger beetles (Hydrophilidae) – maxillary palps conspicuous (p.105)
- minute moss beetles (Hydraenidae) – maxillary palps elongate (p.114)
- moss beetles (Byrrhidae) – antennae clubbed; strongly convex (p.195)
- riffle beetles (Elmidae) – antennae long, with most antennomeres longer than wide (p.196)
- travertine beetles (Lutrochidae) – small, oval, antennae short, antennomeres 1–2 long, broad (p.200)
- water penny beetles (Psephenidae) – oval; flabellate or serrate antennae (p.203)
- some small lady beetles (Coccinellidae) – antennae clubbed; tarsi 4-4-4 or 3-3-3 (p.311)

COLLECTING NOTES Look for adult limnichids in riparian habitats on streamside plants, on emergent vegetation and wood, or in debris along the shore. Most individuals will drop into the water or take to the air when disturbed. Beating and sweeping riparian vegetation is also productive. Most adults fly to light.

FAUNA 28 SPECIES IN SIX GENERA (NA); EIGHT SPECIES IN THREE GENERA (ENA)

Limnichites punctatus **(LeConte)** (1.8 mm) is oval, black, with scalelike setae. Head broad, narrower than prothorax, with eyes prominent and visible from above. Prothorax without grooves to receive antennae, pronotum evenly convex and broadest a base. Elytra with setae of uniform size, epiplurae flat or slightly concave and coarsely punctate. Underside of thorax with grooves to receive legs. Difficult to sex; males with densely punctate and pubescent triangle on last abdominal ventrite more developed. Québec and Maine to Georgia, west to Manitoba, Minnesota, and Texas. *Limnichites olivaceus* LeConte (> 2.0 mm) has deeply concave, obscurely punctate epiplurae. (2)

VARIEGATED MUD-LOVING BEETLES, FAMILY HETEROCERIDAE
(HET-ERO-*SAIR*-IH-DEE)

Heterocerids are small, flat, and distinctively shaped beetles, often with a zigzag pattern on the elytra. Both adults and larvae live in galleries dug in sand or mudflats along the shores of ponds, lakes, and streams. They push forward through the sediment consuming algae, zooplankton, and other organic debris that washes up on shore. The rakelike forelegs of the adults are equipped with rows of heavy spines that are used to clear sediment away from the head and rake it to the sides and rear as they plow through the substrate. Heterocerids prefer to dig their own tunnels but will sometimes inhabit cracks and crevices that occur naturally in the soil. Adult burrows are often marked by chimneylike piles of soil. The adults are fast on their feet and fly readily, but only for short distances. They leave their shoreline burrows after dusk during the summer and are often attracted to light in enormous numbers. Their relatively stationary larvae are much more likely to succumb to dehydration or inundation than the highly mobile adults. Young larvae initially use the tunnels dug by the adults, but soon construct their own. They pupate within a sealed chamber and emerge as adults in about three to six days. Heterocerids are an important prey item for birds and frogs, and apparently play a significant role in seed dispersal and burial in sandy soils. The 10 genera previously recognized in North America were recently reduced to three: *Augyles*, *Heterocerus*, and *Tropicus*.

FAMILY DIAGNOSIS Adult heterocerids are long, robust, somewhat flattened, usually dark (*Tropicus pusillus* is pale), covered with dense silky pubescence, and often with contrasting dark and light zigzag markings on elytra. Head prognathous with prominent, flattened mandibles, especially males. Antennae short, usually with 11 antennomeres (9 in *Tropicus*), 5–11 form an oblong and serrate club. Pronotum broader than head and narrower or equal to base of elytra. Scutellum visible. Elytra completely cover abdomen, with (*Heterocerus*) or without (*Tropicus*) three irregular bands. Legs, especially front pair, with rakelike rows of spines, tarsal formula 4-4-4, claws large, slender, and simple. Abdomen with five ventrites, first ventrite with distinctly curved lines (*Augyles auromicans* [Kiesenwetter]) or not (*Heterocerus*, *Tropicus*) behind the hind coxae.

SIMILAR FAMILIES The protruding mandibles, flattened body, zigzag patches of setae on the elytra, and spiny, rakelike legs are distinctive.

COLLECTING METHODS Adults are sometimes found in large numbers along the muddy banks of streams, ponds, and lakes during the warmer months and commonly attracted to light near the shoreline. Splashing water onto sandy banks may drive the beetles from their underground galleries into plain view; this technique is of limited value on muddy shores.

FAUNA 33 SPECIES IN THREE GENERA (NA); 18 SPECIES IN THREE GENERA (ENA)

Heterocerus (formerly *Neoheterocerus*) *fenestratus* (Thunberg) (3.5–5.3 mm) is elongate, distinctly blotched, and blackish brown with dense setae. Antennae with 11 antennomeres, 5–11 forming oblong serrate club. Pronotum distinctly pale, finely punctate, and basal margin finely notched. Elytra with distinct and elongate pale blotches, some reaching pale margins, turned-under rim pale. Tarsi pale. Adults active in summer; attracted to light. Widespread in North America. (5)

Heterocerus (formerly *Lanternarius*) *mollinus* **Kiesenwetter** (3.9–5.6 mm) is dark with three distinct reddish-brown zigzag bands across each elytron, bands sometimes forming spots or are vague in older specimens. Front angles of pronotum pale or blackish. Lines behind bases of middle legs present and in contact with bases. Males with mandibles elongate, clypeus long in some specimens. Adults attracted to lights. This species occurs from Québec to Florida, west to Manitoba and Arizona. (3)

Tropicus pusillus **(Say)** (2.0–3.0 mm) is small and uniformly dull yellow to pale sooty brown and densely clothed in short yellowish pubescence, sometimes with a broad darker band running down middle from head to elytral apices. Mandible of male with process that overlaps labrum. Antennae with nine antennomeres. Elytra smooth and without transverse spots or markings. Epiplurae and legs pale. Adults sometimes attracted to light in very large numbers along drainage ditches, sandy ponds, and intermittent creeks. Québec, Ontario, and throughout United States to Central America; also Caribbean. *Tropicus nigrellus* King & Lago is entirely black, rarely collected; Coastal Plain, North Carolina to Florida to Mississippi. (2)

WATER PENNY BEETLES, FAMILY PSEPHENIDAE
(SEH-*FEN*-IH-DEE)

Water pennies are so named because the distinctly oval, flat, and often golden brown larvae resemble small, segmented pennies. They are aquatic and make their living on or under submerged stones and wood in riffles of slow to moderately rapid streams and rivers with good water quality. Water pennies scrape off and eat algae from the upper surfaces of submerged objects mostly at night and spend their days hiding under rocks. While most mature larvae leave the water to construct pupal chambers in moist soils along the streamside, others actually pupate underwater inside air-filled chambers. Pupation occurs under the protective cover of the last larval exoskeleton. Adult psephenids are relatively short-lived and seldom feed, if they eat at all. They are usually found on rocks and vegetation along side streams. After mating, females enter the water to lay their eggs on the surfaces of submerged rocks beneath the water, sometimes for days. Their oxygen supply is in the form of a layer of air trapped within the "hairy" body surface.

FAMILY DIAGNOSIS Adult psephenids are oval, slightly flattened, brownish to blackish. Head partly retracted inside prothorax, with mouthparts directed somewhat downward and mandibles concealed. Antennae long with 11 moniliform, serrate, or pectinate antennomeres. Scutellum visible. Elytra soft and leathery, completely covering abdomen. Tarsal formula 5-5-5, with claws equal in size and simple, toothed, or notched at tip. Abdomen with five to seven ventrites.

SIMILAR FAMILIES

- marsh beetles (Scirtidae) – tarsi with fourth tarsomere deeply lobed (p.180)
- ptilodactylid beetles (Ptilodactylidae) – larger, elongate; antennae inserted below eyes (p.204)

COLLECTING NOTES Adult *Psephenus* are found during the day in riffles on exposed rock surfaces as they search for mates in summer. *Ectopria* are nocturnal and sometimes attracted to light in large numbers. They spend their days on vegetation near the water, usually on the undersides of leaves of trees and shrubs and are captured by beating or sweeping vegetation. *Dicranopselaphus variegatus* Horn is rarely collected.

FAUNA 16 SPECIES IN FIVE GENERA (NA); FIVE SPECIES IN THREE GENERA (ENA)

Ectopria leechi **Brigham** (2.8–4.9 mm) is somewhat pear-shaped with elytra widest behind middle. Elytra light brown with distinct dark brown lines that run together toward apex. Appendages light brown or yellowish brown. Males with antennae distinctly serrate. Adults found resting on vegetation along shores of streams and rivers. Connecticut to Virginia, west to Illinois and Arkansas. (3)

Psephenus herricki **(DeKay)** (3.5–6.3 mm) is oval, somewhat flattened, and dull brownish black or blackish, and head visible from above. Head with front margin round; maxillary palp about half length of antenna; black in females. Antennae serrate, longer than combined lengths of head and pronotum. Pronotum with anterior margin half as wide as smooth posterior margin. Males have six abdominal ventrites, females five. Short-lived adults found resting on vegetation above running water and on rocks in or near water. Limpet-like larvae cling to submerged rocks in flowing water. Found along Atlantic Seaboard from New Brunswick to Georgia, west to Ontario, Wisconsin, Missouri, and eastern Oklahoma. (1)

204

PTILODACTYLID BEETLES, FAMILY PTILODACTYLIDAE
(TIE-LO-DACK-*TIL*-IH-DEE)

Adult ptilodactylids are terrestrial and thought to feed on microfungi growing on leaf surfaces. Their larvae are terrestrial, semiaquatic, or aquatic and feed on decaying vegetation and wood. *Ptilodactyla* larvae are terrestrial and live in moist habitats, while those of *Anchytarsus* are truly aquatic. The larvae of *Paralichus* are found in small, shallow seeps in sandy substrates containing fine and coarse bits of detritus and other debris. Species in all these genera pupate on land. Adults of *Ptilodactyla* are similar in size and color and best identified to species by examining the male genitalia; females cannot be identified unless they are associated with males. A single undescribed species of *Lachnodactyla* is known from Florida. It resembles a species of *Ptilodactyla*, but is distinguished by the enlarged tips of the maxillary palps.

FAMILY DIAGNOSIS Adult ptilodactylids are elongate-oblong, nearly parallel-sided, uniformly yellowish brown to brown or partly blackish (*Anchytarsus*, *Ptilodactyla*) or bicolored (*Paralichus*), and moderately clothed in dense setae. Head distinctly hypognathous, mostly concealed from above, with bulging eyes. Antennae with 11 antennomeres, pectinate (male *Ptilodactyla*), filiform (female *Ptilodactyla*, all *Anchytarsus*), or serrate (*Paralichus*). Pronotum broad at base with margin finely notched, narrowed and rounded toward head, with sides rounded (*Anchytarsus*), partially (*Ptilodactyla*), to completely (*Paralichus*) margined. Scutellum somewhat triangular, basal margin simple or finely notched. Elytra punctostriate or not, never ribbed, rounded apically, and completely covering abdomen. Legs slender, tarsal formula 5-5-5, fourth tarsomere small and hidden by lobe on third (*Ptilodactylus*) or not, and claws simple or pectinate (*Paralichus*). Abdomen with five ventrites.

SIMILAR FAMILIES

- some death-watch beetles (Ptinidae, *Eucrada*) – base of pronotum not carinate (p.254)
- comb-clawed beetles (Tenebrionidae: Alleculinae) – tarsal formula 5-5-4; antennae filiform (pp.351–4)

COLLECTING NOTES Look for ptilodactylids in the immediate vicinity of riparian, semiaquatic, and aquatic habitats. Adults of *Anchytarsus* and *Ptilodactyla* are usually found at light, but also beaten from vegetation in and near wetlands. *Paralichus* is rarely collected on vegetation surrounding wetlands. Species in all genera are captured in Malaise traps.

FAUNA 19 SPECIES IN FIVE GENERA (NA); NINE SPECIES IN FOUR GENERA (ENA)

Paralichus trivittus **(Germar)** (8.0–9.0 mm) is elongate, more or less straight-sided, dull blackish, clothed in erect dark and pale setae. Head with prominent eyes and mandibles. Pronotum convex, reddish yellow with two large black spots. Elytra with narrow stripe of gray setae along suture and continuous with side margins, four rows of punctures between suture and a pair of close-set gray stripes down middle of each elytron. Larva develops in small, shallow spring seeps with sandy substrates consisting of fine and coarse bits of detritus and other organic debris. Adults active in early summer; males sometimes collected in large numbers in Malaise traps. Pennsylvania to Georgia, west to Michigan and Ohio. (1)

Ptilodactyla **species** (3.0–6.0 mm) are oblong, light to dark brown with appendages sometimes lighter. Antennae of male pectinate, female filiform. Pronotum hoodlike, narrowed toward front, with basal margin finely toothed in front of scutellum. Scutellum heart-shaped with notch in front. Elytra with feebly impressed grooves of variable punctures. Legs with front coxae large, tarsomere 3 with large ventral lobe, 4 very small. Larvae aquatic. Adults found on streamside vegetation during day; attracted to light. Males are best identified by examination of genitalia, while females are usually identified by association with males. Throughout eastern North America. (6)

CHELONARIID BEETLES, CHELONARIIDAE
(KEY-LO-NAR-*EE*-IH-DEE)

Approximately 300 species of chelonariids are known worldwide. Of these, only one genus and described species, *Chelonarium lecontei*, is found in North America and is restricted to southeastern United States. The larva of *C. lecontei* is unknown. Once thought to be aquatic, the larvae of other species are now known to occur under bark, or in dry to moist detritus and leaf litter.

FAMILY DIAGNOSIS Chelonariids are oval, compact, shiny, hard-bodied, red-brown to dark brown, and seedlike in appearance, with the basal margin of the pronotum finely notched, or crenulate. Head concealed within pronotum. Antennae with 11 antennomeres, 1–4 small, 2–3 enlarged, 5–10 serrate, 11 broad; basal antennomeres received in grooves underneath prothorax. Pronotum with sharp and continuous lateral and anterior margins, with anterior margin extending over head, and posterior margin finely notched (crenulate). Scutellum small, crenulate in front. Elytra tightly cover abdomen, with surface punctate. Legs capable of tightly retracting against body in thoracic depressions; front tibiae broad, flat, tarsal formula 5-5-5, tarsomeres 1–2 pubescent underneath, 3 broadly lobed, 4 small and somewhat concealed. Abdomen with five ventrites.

SIMILAR FAMILIES The body form and antennal and pronotal characters of adult chelonariids are distinctive, including the finely crenulate basal margin of the prothorax.

COLLECTING NOTES Adults are infrequently collected at lights, on vegetation at night, in Berlese funnel extractions of leaf litter samples, and in Malaise traps.

FAUNA ONE DESCRIBED SPECIES, *CHELONARIUM LECONTEI* THOMAS (NA); ADDITIONAL UNIDENTIFIED SPECIES IN FLORIDA AND GULF STATES

Turtle Beetle *Chelonarium lecontei* Thomson (7.0–8.0 mm) is shiny, oval, compact, with patches of white setae scattered on elytra. It looks remarkably seedlike when head is retracted within pronotum and legs are tightly tucked against body. Posterior margin of pronotum finely and distinctly notched (crenulate). Adults are attracted to lights at night, taken in Malaise traps or by beating and sweeping vegetation at night; they are sometimes found inside tree holes. Larvae are unknown. Virginia to Florida, west to Tennessee and Texas. (1)

CALLIRHIPID BEETLES, FAMILY CALLIRHIPIDAE
(CAL-LIH-*RIP*-IH-DEE)

Very little is known about the natural history of the single North American callirhipid, *Zenoa picea* (Palisot de Beauvois). The larvae occur in punky, rotten wood infested with white rot and may take as long as two years to complete their development. Adults are short-lived, nocturnal, and attracted to lights in late spring and summer.

FAMILY DIAGNOSIS Adult callirhipids are elongate, somewhat convex, and uniformly blackish or dark reddish brown. Head with thickened ridge between eyes and distinct mandibles directed downward (hypognathous). Antennae with 11 antennomeres, strongly serrate (female) or pectinate (male), and attached to a prominence on head between large eyes. Prothorax about one-third wider than long, narrower in front, posterior margin sinuate, not as wide as elytra; surface with a distinct or vague pit and depression on either side of midde. Scutellum round. Elytra long, straight-sided, extending beyond outline of abdomen; each elytron rounded at tip, surface vaguely ridged, spaces between ridges coarsely and irregularly punctate. Legs with trochanters long, triangular; tarsal formula 5-5-5, tarsomeres without pads; claws simple and equal. Abdomen with five ventrites, 1–3 fused.

SIMILAR FAMILIES
- cicada parasite beetles (Rhipiceridae) – male antennae flabellate; tarsi padded underneath (p.183)
- rare click beetles (Cerophytidae) – smaller (5.4–8.5 mm); hind trochanters nearly as long as femora; tarsi padded underneath (p.209)

COLLECTING NOTES Look for callirhipids, especially males, at light near mature forests. Specimens are occasionally collected beneath logs and under bark in dry upland woods. Mostly females are found in or reared from rotten wood.

FAUNA ONE SPECIES, *ZENOA PICEA* (PALISOT DE BEAUVOIS) (NA)

Zenoa picea **(Palisot de Beauvois)** (11.0–17.0 mm) is elongate, oblong, somewhat shining and uniformly reddish brown or blackish brown; appendages and underside lighter in darker individuals. Mandibles short, broad. Antennae serrate, male more so. Pronotum strongly narrowed toward head, disk with a small round indentation on each side of middle. Elytra with four ridges on each elytron, inner two coalescing at apical third. Larvae develop in wood decaying with white-rot fungi. Nocturnal adults apparently short-lived and attracted to light. Pennsylvania to Florida, west to Illinois, Kansas, and Texas. (1)

ARTEMATOPODID BEETLES, FAMILY ARTEMATOPODIDAE
(AR-TEH-MAH-TO-*POD*-IH-DEE)

Very little is known about the biology and natural history of these small beetles. Adults are usually found resting on understory growth in wooded habitats. The larvae probably tunnel into the rhizoids of mosses growing in mats on boulders.

FAMILY DIAGNOSIS Adult artematopodids are elongate, strongly convex, clothed in erect setae, and somewhat resemble click beetles (Elateridae). Head lacks distinct ridge along front margin. Antennomeres 2–4 very short and combined not longer than 5 (*Macropogon*), or 2–3 short and combined equal to 4 (*Eurypogon*). Prothorax with backward directed process and corresponding mesothoracic groove weakly developed. Elytra each tipped with a tonguelike process underneath. Tarsal formula 5-5-5, two or more tarsomeres lobed beneath, claws simple. Abdomen with 4–5 connate, or fused ventrites.

SIMILAR FAMILIES

- ptilodactylid beetles (Ptilodactylidae) – males with pectinate antennae (p.204)
- rare click beetles (Cerophytidae) – hind trochanters very long (p.209)
- throscid beetles (Throscidae) – antennae clavate (p.211)
- click beetles (Elateridae) – forebody loosely attached to rest of body; rear angles of pronotum directed backward (p.213)
- fruitworm beetles (Byturidae) – tarsomeres 2–3 lobed underneath (p.274)

COLLECTING NOTES Artematopodid beetles are collected by beating or sweeping vegetation along streams, rivers, and other bodies of water. They are also attracted to light and found in flight intercept and Malaise traps.

FAUNA EIGHT SPECIES IN THREE GENERA (NA); THREE SPECIES IN TWO GENERA (ENA)

Eurypogon niger **(Melsheimer)** (3.5–4.5 mm) is black and clothed in dense, erect, dark and pale setae; appendages dark brown, tarsi sometimes lighter. Antennae somewhat serrate, antennomeres 2–3 short, combined length almost equal to 4; 5 subequal to 4, which is at least 1.5 times longer than 3. Elytra with rows of fine, deep punctures, spaces between rows narrow, somewhat convex. Front and middle legs with basal tarsi lacking comblike setae underneath. Larva probably feeds on mosses. Adults active late spring and summer, found on vegetation; also attracted to light. Maine and Québec to Georgia, west to Indiana, Kansas, and Tennessee. (2)

RARE CLICK BEETLES, FAMILY CEROPHYTIDAE
(SAIR-O-*FYE*-TIH-DEE)

Extant rare click beetles are represented by only one genus (*Cerophytum*) with 10 species found in North America, Europe, and the Neotropical region. Of the two species found in North America, only one occurs in the east. Very little is known about the natural history of these uncommon beetles. The known larvae of European species are associated with layers of decaying xylem of deciduous hardwoods. Like other "clicking" beetles (Elateridae, Throscidae, Eucnemidae), adult rare click beetles have the ability to "jump"; however, unlike the thoracic clicking mechanisms of these other families, the clicking mechanism of cerophytids is very poorly developed and their jumping ability is not well understood.

FAMILY DIAGNOSIS Adult cerophytids are elongate, somewhat convex, and moderately clothed in dark setae. Head with mouthparts directed downward (hypognathous), bulging between eyes, deeply set inside prothorax and partly visible from above. Antennae with 11 antennomeres, strongly serrate (female) or pectinate (male), bases narrowly separated on bulge between eyes. Prothorax convex and loosely connected to body. Scutellum small and triangular. Elytra long, straight-sided with rows of deep and rectangular punctures; abdomen completely covered. Legs do not retract into grooves; hind trochanters very long, almost as long as femora; tarsal formula 5-5-5, tarsomeres 2–4 with pads underneath, 3 shallowly and 4 deeply notched; claws comblike. Abdomen with five ventrites, 1–4 fused.

SIMILAR FAMILIES Cerophytids are superficially similar to the following families but easily distinguished by their body form and long hind trochanters:
- artematopodid beetles (Artematopodidae) (p.208)
- false click beetles (Eucnemidae) (p.210)
- throscid beetles (Throscidae) (p.211)
- click beetles (Elateridae) (p.213)
- death-watch beetles (Ptinidae) (p.252)

COLLECTING NOTES Adult cerophytids are seldom collected. They occur in forested habitats and are usually found at light or in Malaise trap samples. Individuals are also encountered on the wing, under bark, in decaying wood, or swept from vegetation. Additional specimens are also sifted from leaf litter and other plant debris on the ground.

209

FAUNA TWO SPECIES IN ONE GENUS (NA); ONE SPECIES, *CEROPHYTUM PULSATOR* (HALDEMAN) (ENA)

- -

Eastern Rare Click Beetle *Cerophytum pulsator* **(Haldeman)** (5.4–8.5 mm) is dark reddish black to black; appendages and underside usually lighter. Body clothed in fine, erect, yellowish setae. Elytra somewhat dull, deeply grooved, and finely and densely punctured. Adults active mostly at night during spring in mature, mostly deciduous forests; also collected at black light, in Malaise and Lindgren funnel traps, and by sweeping understory foliage and searching rotten wood and bark, or in leaf litter. Capable of clicking and jumping to escape danger. Pennsylvania to Florida, west to Illinois and Alabama. (1)

FALSE CLICK BEETLES, FAMILY EUCNEMIDAE
(YUKE-*NEM*-IH-DEE)

Most "false" click beetles can "click" as well as elaterids, while a few species have enough flexibility between the prothorax and elytra that they are capable of flipping themselves into the air. The clicking mechanism of eucnemids is the same as that of the Elateridae and likewise is thought to startle predators. Adults are active in spring and summer and found resting on vegetation or on tree trunks during the day. Although little is known of their habits, eucnemids probably play an important role in the interactions between trees, fungi, and forest regeneration and could be used as important indicators of forest diversity. Eucnemid larvae lack legs, have mandibles with their grinding surfaces on the outside, and resemble the larvae of metallic wood-boring beetles because the first thoracic segment is wider than the rest of the body. They are sometimes called "cross-cut borers" because they typically mine across the wood grain. Although some species (*Hylis, Melasis*) prefer coniferous trees, most prefer to attack decaying hardwoods infected with fungi that causes white rot. They apparently feed on fungus, not wood, and are able to at least partially digest their food before swallowing it.

FAMILY DIAGNOSIS Adult eucnemids are long, convex, sometimes nearly cylindrical, brownish to blackish beetles. Head partially retracted inside prothorax, with mouthparts directed strongly downward (hypognathous). Antennae with 11 antennomeres and moniliform, filiform, or with last seven or eight antennomeres serrate or pectinate. Prothorax broader than head and elytra. Scutellum visible, oval to broadly oval, or triangular. Elytra parallel-sided, rows of punctures with smooth spaces between, rounded at tips, and completely cover the abdomen. Tarsal formula 5-5-5, tarsomere 4 sometimes lobed, with claws equal, simple, toothed, or comblike. Abdomen with five fused ventrites.

SIMILAR FAMILIES
- metallic wood-boring or jewel beetles (Buprestidae) – most shiny or metallic underneath (p.184)
- rare click beetles (Cerophytidae) – hind trochanters very long (p.209)
- throscid beetles (Throscidae) – antennal club usually with three antennomeres (p.211)
- click beetles (Elateridae) – labrum visible; abdomen with three, four, or five fused ventrites (p.213)
- lizard beetles (Erotylidae) – antennae clubbed (p.278)

COLLECTING NOTES Eucnemids are seldom as common as click beetles. Some species are beaten or swept from vegetation, whereas others are found beneath loose bark of their host trees. A few species can be netted on the wing at dusk or are attracted to light. Flight intercept and Malaise traps will also produce a few specimens.

FAUNA 85 SPECIES IN 37 GENERA (NA); 50 SPECIES IN 31 GENERA (ENA)

Isorhipis obliqua **(Say)** (4.2–8.5 mm) elongate, narrow, bicolored. Head, pronotum, underside mostly dark brown or black, appendages lighter. Antennomeres 4–10 flabellate in male, serrate in female. Pronotum with narrow groove limited to basal half. Elytra with distinct and punctate rows, yellowish with sides and tips dark brown. Abdomen with ventrite 6 pointed at middle, 7 with a toothlike process at middle. Larvae develop in dry, hard heartwood of decaying hardwoods. Adults active in summer, found on trunks of hardwoods, including maple (*Acer*) and beech (*Fagus*); captured in Malaise traps. Nova Scotia and Québec to Georgia, west to Manitoba, Minnesota, and Texas. (3)

Deltometopus amoenicornis **(Say)** (2.7–4.8 mm) is black with appendages partly or entirely pale yellowish brown. Antennomeres 4–5 always about equal to 6–7, male's antennae pectinate, female's serrate. Prothorax bell-shaped, underside with grooves for antennae. Elytral epipleurae punctate, not grooved at base. Protibia with one apical spur, meso- and metatibiae with single spur on sides, all claws simple. Adults beaten from vegetation, especially in damp locations, and reared from decaying logs. Larvae develop in many kinds of hardwoods, and possibly conifers. Most common eucnemid in eastern North America. Nova Scotia to Florida, west to Ontario, Minnesota, Colorado, Oklahoma, and Texas. (1)

Onichodon orchesides **Newman** (8.0–17.0 mm) is elongate, somewhat cylindrical, uniformly pale to dark brown and sparsely clothed in almost erect yellowish setae. Antennae reaching just past hind angles, slightly serrate, more so in male. Pronotum slightly wider than long, densely punctate with hint of groove down middle flanked by faint, round depressions, sides mostly evenly curved to front. Elytra shallowly grooved, spaces between shiny and sparsely to densely punctate. First tarsomere of foreleg without comb of spines at base. Larva develops in rotting hardwood logs, including yellow birch (*Betula allegheniensis*), red spruce (*Picea rubens*), and American beech (*Fagus grandifolia*). Nocturnal adults active in summer, attracted to light. Maritime

Provinces and New England to North Carolina, west to North Dakota, Illinois, Oklahoma, and Arkansas. (4)

THROSCID BEETLES, FAMILY THROSCIDAE
(*THROSS*-IH-DEE)

Throscids resemble very small and stout click beetles (Elateridae) with rigid bodies. Very little is known about their natural history. Adults are commonly found on flowers and vegetation on warm days in spring and early summer; they are also attracted to light. The larvae live and develop in decaying logs in association with fungi. When disturbed, adults will retract their legs and antennae in special grooves on the underside of the thorax and remain motionless. In spite of their rigid bodies, throscids do possess a clicking mechanism similar to that of click beetles and are capable of propelling themselves several inches into the air.

FAMILY DIAGNOSIS Adult throscids are oblong to somewhat elongate, moderately convex, reddish brown to black, and covered with fine, pale pubecscence. Head with mouthparts directed downward (hypognathous), deeply inserted in prothorax, with eyes coarsely faceted and deeply notched to nearly divided, labrum distinct. Antennae with 11 antennomeres, narrowly expanded to loosely clubbed, or clavate, antennae received by grooves on underside of prothorax. Prothorax narrowed toward head, pronotum tightly fitted against elytra, posterior angles directed backward. Scutellum small, triangular. Elytra shallowly grooved and punctured, rounded at tips, and completely covering abdomen. Underside of metathorax smooth on sides (*Trixagus*), or with deep oblique grooves to accommodate middle tarsi (*Aulonothroscus*). Legs tightly retracting against body, tarsal formula 5-5-5, tarsomere 4 lobed, claws equal and simple. Abdomen with five ventrites all fused together.

SIMILAR FAMILIES

- metallic wood-boring beetles (Buprestidae) – usually larger; antennae usually serrate; metallic ventrally (p.184)
- false click beetles (Eucnemidae) – usually larger; generally widest at prothorax; antennae never clubbed (p.210)
- click beetles (Elateridae) – prothorax loosely hinged to rest of body (p.213)
- fruitworm beetles (Byturidae) – tarsi lobed (p.274)
- false skin beetles (Biphyllidae) – posterior pronotal angles not extended (p.276)
- silken fungus beetles (Cryptophagidae) – posterior pronotal angles not extended (p.283)

COLLECTING NOTES Beating and sweeping flowers and foliage of oaks (*Quercus*) and other deciduous hardwoods along roads and trails in wooded areas is the best way to collect adults. Additional specimens are attracted to light traps, captured in Malaise traps, or collected in Berlese samples. Others have been found in moss and leaf litter on the forest floor.

FAUNA 20 SPECIES IN THREE GENERA (NA); 11 SPECIES IN TWO GENERA (ENA)

Aulonothroscus constrictor **(Say)** (2.0–3.3 mm) is oblong, robust, and brownish black (female) or reddish (male) with coarse setae. Head without ridges, eyes entire, and antennomeres 9–11 forming a club. Pronotum distinctly impressed on base at middle and coarsely punctured, underneath with process between legs with long distinct grooves along sides. Pronotum and elytra coarsely punctured. Elytra with rows of deep, widely separated punctures separated by one or two rows of coarse punctures. Underside of thorax with distinct, deep oblique grooves to receive middle tarsi. Legs with tarsomere 4 lobed. Adults active spring and summer, found resting on vegetation; attracted to light. Maritime Provinces to Florida, west to Manitoba, Minnesota, and Arkansas. (9)

Trixagus carinicollis **(Schaeffer)** (2.1–3.3 mm) is oblong-oval, dull reddish to black with long yellowish or grayish pubescence. Head with a pair of parallel ridges, eyes divided by a narrow depression, and antennomeres 9–11 forming a club. Pronotum wider than long with hind angles distinct, projecting backward, and each bearing a narrow ridge. Elytra with dense fringe of long setae on sides just behind middle (male) or not (female). Underside of thorax without distinct grooves to receive middle tarsi. Legs with tarsomere 4 lobed. Adults active spring and summer, found resting on vegetation; attracted to light. Maritime Provinces to Virginia, west to Ontario, Iowa, and Kentucky; also Pacific Northwest. (2)

CLICK BEETLES, FAMILY ELATERIDAE
(EL-UH-*TARE*-IH-DEE)

Click beetles are commonly found on vegetation, under bark, or at light. Most species are active during the day; others are nocturnal. Adults feed on rotting fruit, flowers, nectar, pollen, fungi, and sapping wounds on shrubs and trees. Some prey on small invertebrates, especially wood-boring insects and plant hoppers. The clicking sound, which inspired the common family name, is produced when adults tuck the forebody down and backward to snap the prosternal spine into the mesosteral groove on the underside of the thorax. Both sound and behavior may be intended to startle predators or to propel the insect away from danger. When stranded on their backs, click beetles also use their clicking behavior to flip into the air to right themselves. Small species can propel themselves up to 10 inches into the air; larger species, such as eyed click beetles (*Alaus*), may flip only a few inches. The larvae, most of which are tough and wiry, are called "wireworms." They are found in soil, rich humus, or decaying plant materials, especially rotten wood. They feed on liquids and have the ability to partially digest solid food before swallowing it. Some wood-dwelling species prey on small invertebrates, while others scavenge fungi. Soil-dwellers are opportunistic predators and/or root-feeders. Herbivorous larvae of *Agriotes*, *Limonius*, *Melanotus*, and *Selatosomus* attack sprouting seeds and roots of young grasses. The larvae of some species are economically important and damage the seeds and roots of a variety of crops and garden plants. Three to five molts and up to three years may be required to reach maturity. Both adults and larvae overwinter in the ground, under bark, or in rotten wood.

FAMILY DIAGNOSIS Adult elaterids are long, somewhat flattened, and mostly brownish or black, although many are quite colorful, sometimes with distinct markings, or with a metallic upper surface (*Chalcolepidius, Nitidolimonius*); often clothed in setae or scales; prothorax is large and loosely hinged to rest of body. Head with mandibles exposed or not, clypeus absent, and labrum distinct. Antennae with 11 antennomeres serrate to pectinate and attached near eyes. Prothorax flattened and ridged on sides with sharp, backward-pointing posterior angles, occasionally with grooves or depression underneath to accommodate antennae and legs; sometimes with pair of light organs on pronotum (*Deilelater*). Scutellum visible. Elytra smooth, ribbed, usually with hairlike setae or scaly, always concealing the abdomen. Legs with tarsal formula 5-5-5, tarsomeres simple or lobed, claws equal and simple, toothed, or pectinate (*Glyphonyx, Melanotus*). Abdomen with five ventrites, 1–4 fused together.

SIMILAR FAMILIES
- metallic wood-boring or jewel beetles (Buprestidae) – body rigid; most species shiny or metallic underneath (p.184)
- false click beetles (Eucnemidae) – labrum not visible; abdomen with 5 fused ventrites (p.210)
- throscid beetles (Throscidae) – antennae clubbed, rarely serrate (p.211)
- lizard beetles (Erotylidae: Languriinae) – antennae capitate (p.278)
- some false darkling beetles (Melandryidae) – tarsi 5-5-4 (p.329)
- synchroa bark beetles (Synchroidae) – clypeus visible; tarsi 5-5-4 (p.359)

COLLECTING NOTES Forests and woodlands in multiple stages of succession and woodland/wetland edges harbor the greatest diversity of click beetles. Sweep and beat vegetation in these and other habitats for adults. Many species are found beneath the bark of snags, logs, and stumps. Others are found beneath stones, boards, or debris, or in riparian sand or gravel, especially in spring. Most nocturnal species that are frequently beaten from vegetation are also attracted to light. Additional species are captured in Malaise, flight intercept, and Lindgren funnel traps.

FAUNA 965 SPECIES IN 91 GENERA (NA); 71 GENERA (ENA)

Selonodon medialis **Galley** (11.0–14.0 mm) is elongate, dull light reddish brown to brown, flying male smaller than flightless female. Mandibles sharp, clearly visible. Antennomeres long, 4–10 broadly triangular, 3 longer than 2 (male), or short, 4–11 small (female). Pronotum moderately convex, nearly wide as long, with sides almost parallel. Elytra cover abdomen entirely (male), or with two tergites exposed (female); flight wings developed in both sexes. Legs with front tibiae slender, middle and hind tibial spurs long and distinct. Adults active after rain in sandy habitats in late spring; males attracted to light. Southern Alabama and Louisiana. (16)

Danosoma brevicorne **(LeConte)** (13.0–16.0 mm) is dull reddish brown with irregular blotches of tan scales. Pronotum densely, coarsely punctured, broadly and deeply impressed at base near middle and at sides near midlength, hind angles divergent, rounded, and depressed; underneath with antennal grooves only. Elytra densely, coarsely, and irregularly punctured. Claws without basal setae. Predatory larva develops under bark. Adults found under bark in summer in coniferous forests and mixed woodlands. Across Canada, and montane western North America; in east from Maritime Provinces and New England to Massachusetts, west to Minnesota. (1)

Lacon discoideus **(Weber)** (8.0–11.0 mm) is elongate-oblong, slightly flattened, dull black with head and sides of pronotum covered with thick golden or orangish scales. Pronotum with a deep groove down middle; tarsal grooves on prosternum faint and somewhat parallel to antennal grooves. Elytra densely covered with coarse, irregular punctures. Adults are found under loose bark of stumps and logs in winter and early spring or resting on vegetation in spring and early summer. Ontario, eastern United States. (6)

Lacon marmoratus **(Fabricius)** (14.0–17.5 mm) is blackish or dark reddish brown, with surface closely, deeply punctured and covered with irregular patches of black and dull yellow or whitish scales. Pronotum long as wide, somewhat convex, with a deep median groove; tarsal grooves on prosternum deep, joining antennal grooves at base. Elytra densely covered with coarse, irregular punctures. Tarsal grooves present on prosternum. Adults found under bark in colder weather, on vegetation, and at light in spring and summer. Ontario, Québec, and New York to Florida, west to Indiana and Texas. (6)

214

Alaus myops **(Fabricius)** (19.0–42.0 mm) has brownish or grayish pubescence and small, narrow, eyelike spots on prothorax indistinctly margined with pale scales. Predatory adults and larvae found in spring and summer beneath loose bark of dead pine stumps and logs infested with wood-boring beetles; sometimes found in Lindgren funnel and Malaise traps. Québec to Florida, west to Minnesota, Manitoba, Kansas, and Texas. (3)

Eyed Click Beetle *Alaus oculatus* **(Linnaeus)** (24.0–44.0 mm) is covered with black and white or yellowish-white scales. Eyelike spots on prothorax distinctly margined with white scales. Adults are found on trees or under loose bark of logs and stumps infested with wood-boring beetle larvae year-round, especially in spring and summer. They are sometimes attracted to solvents and freshly painted surfaces. Predaceous larvae found in decaying stumps and logs with beetle larvae. Québec, Ontario, and eastern United States west to the Dakotas, Colorado, and Texas. (3)

Chalcolepidius viridipilis **(Say)** (18.0–30.0 mm) is elongate, narrow, straight-sided, dark brown or black, and sparsely covered with metallic green-olive or bluish-green scales, or both. Antennae reaching hind angles of pronotum, pectinate (male) or serrate (female). Elytra with rows of indistinct punctures. Adults active in summer, found on sapping wounds on trunks of ash (*Fraxinus*) and oak (*Quercus*) in summer. New Jersey and Pennsylvania to Florida, west to Ohio, Missouri, and Texas; Mexico. (1)

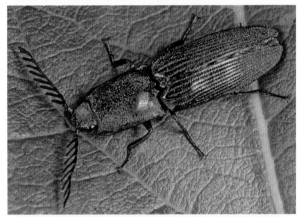

Pherhimius fascicularis **(Fabricius)** (14.0–25.0 mm) has flabellate antennae and is brown except for yellowish elytra marbled with reddish-brown sinuous bands. Body covered with yellowish-white setae, pubescence on pronotum arranged in small circles. Legs with tibial spurs absent. Adults attracted to light in summer. Pennsylvania to Florida, west to Kansas and Texas, south to South America. (1)

Flat wireworm *Aeolus mellilus* **(Say)** (5.0–8.0 mm) is orangish brown with distinct black markings and short, pale setae; appendages lighter. Head black with front margin raised and projected over labrum. Pronotal stripe sometimes a spot, with hind angles long, sharp, and extended backward. Scutellum black, raised and cone-shaped. Elytra with distinct rows of pits separated by shiny and convex rows between, each elytron with long black spot before middle and V-shaped band before tip, marks sometimes connect. Tarsomere 4 with setose pad below, claws slender and simple, without setae at base. Adults active on soil spring and early summer; attracted to light. Widespread in eastern North America. (3)

Conoderus bellus **(Say)** (3.5–4.5 mm) is oblong, subconvex, and golden brown above with variable amounts of blackish markings. Pronotum with narrow or broad stripe down middle. Underside of prothorax pale, pterothorax and abdomen dark. Legs pale with tarsomere 4 narrowly lobed underneath. Adults found under debris in moist habitats and are pests of tobacco; often abundant at light. Ontario to Florida, west to Indiana and Texas, Arizona, California. Neotropical *Conoderus pictus* (Candeze) similar, but with small tubercle at base of pronotum. (10)

Conoderus lividus **(De Geer)** (11.0–17.0 mm) is light tan to medium brown with pale legs and antennae and covered with dense whitish pubescence, giving it a velvety look. Tarsomere 4 broadly lobed underneath. Adults are active from late spring to early fall and are beaten from vegetation, found in corn fields, and attracted to lights. Omnivorous larvae prey on insects and feed on roots. Very common from Québec and New York to Florida, west to Indiana and Texas. (10)

Peanut wireworm *Conoderus scissus* **(Schaeffer)** (9.0–11.0 mm) is elongate, nearly parallel-sided, and pale brown with yellowish legs. Pronotum moderately, coarsely punctate, hind angles short with single ridge above. Elytra with tips slightly sinuate or notched. Tarsomere 4 narrowly lobed underneath. Larva eats roots of many plants, sometimes an agricultural pest, especially of sweet potato, peanut, cowpea, and corn. Adults prefer sandy habitats; attracted to lights. Virginia to Florida, west to Louisiana. (10)

Conoderus suturalis **(LeConte)** (6.0–7.0 mm) is elongate and clothed in fine, sparse, gray pubescence, and dull reddish brown with brown stripe down middle of pronotum and elytra, underside mostly dark; appendages pale brownish yellow. Head completely margined in front. Pronotum one-half longer than wide, sides broadly rounded, hind angles sharp, divergent, and weakly ridged, coarsely punctate. Elytra with grooves indistinctly punctate, spaces between with fine punctures, and sutural line, if present, expanded at apical third. Tibiae with spurs on tips, tarsomere 4 with broad, membranous lobe underneath. Adults at light in spring and summer. Virginia to Georgia, west to Indiana and Texas. (10)

Tobacco Wireworm *Conoderus vespertinus* **(Fabricius)** (7.0–10.0 mm) is elongate, variable in color, usually dark reddish brown above and yellowish below, and clothed in yellow pubescence. Pronotum one-fourth longer than wide with a broad stripe on each side, and narrowed toward head. Elytra with broad line along suture from base to broad expansion at apical two-thirds, humeri and apices paler. Legs with tarsomere 4 narrowly lobed. Larvae pests of tobacco, corn, potatoes, and other truck crops. Adults active in summer; attracted to light. Connecticut to Florida, west to South Dakota and Arizona. (10)

Gulf Wireworm *Heteroderes amplicollis* **(Gyllenhal)** (6.0–10.0 mm) is uniformly blackish with appendages reddish brown. Pronotum somewhat flat at center, with punctures of two sizes, sides almost parallel at middle, with hind angles short, stout, each with single ridge on top diverging away from margin toward head. Elytra with rows of punctures. Tibiae with spurs on tips, tarsomere 4 with membranous lobe underneath, and claws with basal setae. Commonly collected at lights. Larvae attack roots of various crops, including sweet potatoes (*Ipomoea batatas*). Caribbean; established from Virginia to Florida, west to California. (3)

Southern Potato Wireworm *Heteroderes falli* **(Lane)** (6.0–9.0 mm) is usually somewhat shiny brown, occasionally blackish, with sparse pubescence; appendages tan. Pronotum wider than long, widest in rear, with punctures of two sizes, hind angles short, stout. Elytra with rows of punctures and faint markings often not visible without magnification. Legs with tibiae with spurs on tips, tarsomere 4 with broad, membranous lobe underneath, and claws with basal setae. Subterranean larva eats seeds, roots, stems, and tubers of crops. Adults active spring and summer, found during day under debris; attracted to light. Neotropical; established from Virginia to Florida, west to California. (3)

Lanelater sallei (**LeConte**) (22.0–30.0 mm) is large, uniformly and somewhat shining dark brown, and clothed in sparse, fine brown pubescence that is sometimes rubbed off. Antennae received in long, deep grooves on underside of prothorax. Pronotum long with hind angles diverging and distinctly double-ridged. Elytra with rows of fine, shallow, punctures. Legs with claws setose at base. Larvae live in sand or decaying wood and prey on other beetle larvae and sea turtle eggs. Adults active in spring, often found at light (especially males) or under driftwood and other debris in sandy coastal habitats. New York to Florida, west to Louisiana. (2)

Deilelater physoderus (**Germar**) (15.0–20.0 mm) is elongate, dull reddish brown with moderately sparse grayish setae, and light-producing organs. Antennomeres 2–3 nearly equal in length, combined length equal to 4, 3 somewhat triangular; antennae of male long, extending three antennomeres beyond hind angle of pronotum. Pronotum with punctures moderate in size and simple, not ringed, with side margins narrow, not flattened, and light-producing organs at hind angles. Elytra with tips combined rounded. Adults active in summer; attracted to light. Georgia and Florida west to Arizona. (2)

218

Oestodes tenuicollis (**Randall**) (7.0–10.0 mm) is elongate, slender, yellowish brown with pale legs to shiny black with blackish legs. Head without carinae over antennal bases. Antennae longer than head and prothorax (male) or just reaches hind angles (female), antennomere 3 triangular and twice as long as wide in both sexes. Prothorax with hind angles each with two ridges and slightly divergent, underside with process between legs appearing cut-off in front, not covering mouthparts. Elytra with rows of distinct punctures, spaces between flat with small punctures. Claw with broad tooth at basal third. Adults active in damp areas in summer; attracted to light. Maritime Provinces and New England to Georgia, west to Ontario and Ohio. (1)

Pityobius anguinus **LeConte** (25.0–30.0 mm) is large, elongate, blackish brown to black, and clothed in short yellow pubescence. Antennae of male bipectinate, female somewhat serrate. Pronotum coarsely sculpted with navel-like punctures, distinct groove down middle, and sharp and diverging hind angles. Elytra with rows of deep coarse punctures, spaces between convex, rough, punctured. Larva develops in pine (*Pinus*), a voracious predator of insect larvae and pupae, especially those of longhorn beetles (Cerambycidae). Adults found under bark; at light. Maritime Provinces and New England to Florida, west to Alberta and eastern Texas. (1)

Melanactes morio **(Fabricius)** (19.5–30.5 mm) is large, elongate, robust, shiny black above, tibae and tarsi slightly redder; females larger than males. Head with ridge between eyes and over antennal bases depressed and indistinct near midline. Antennae serrate. Prontotum with posterior margin uneven; underside of prothorax with large lobe projecting toward head. Scutellum straight at base. Punctured grooves (punctostriae) on elytra deep and distinct with spaces between convex. Tarsi simple, without lobes or pads. Adults attracted to lights in summer. New York to Florida, west to Oklahoma, Arkansas, and Alabama. (4)

Melanactes piceus **(De Geer)** (20.5–33.0 mm) is large, elongate, slightly flattened, robust, appearing smooth and very shiny reddish black to black, without conspicuous setae, with appendages reddish black; females larger and heavier bodied than male. Head with ridge between eyes and over antennal bases depressed and indistinct near midline. Pronotum longer than wide, irregularly punctate. Elytra as wide as base of pronotum, not grooved, with rows of very fine shallow punctures most evident at base, spaces between flat. Adults active spring and summer, especially May and June, found on tree trunks in wooded habitats. New York to North Carolina, west to Nebraska, and Texas. (4)

Athous acanthus **(Say)** (7.1–11.0 mm) is uniformly dark or light brown, pronotum sometimes darker or bicolored. Head with triangular impression on frons with distinct ridge in front clearly above clypeus. Antennae long, reaching past posterior angles of pronotum, three to five antennomeres in male, two or three in female; middle antennomeres with sides nearly parallel. Pronotum sometimes with dark spot on center margined in reddish brown. Prosternal suture single and not excavated in front. Claws simple and without setae at bases. Adults active late spring through summer, found on dead branches and vegetation; also at light. Very similar to *Athous neacanthus* Becker. Maritime Provinces to North Carolina, west to Wisconsin, Iowa, and Tennessee. (16)

Athous cucullatus **(Say)** (9.5–15.0 mm) is uniformly brown to reddish brown. Head with triangular impression on frons with distinct ridge in front clearly above clypeus. Scutellum with anterior margin prominent, straight, and elevated above surface of elytra that overhangs rest of scutellum. Pronotum longer than wide, hind angles with ridges and side margins converging at angle. Prosternal suture single and not excavated in front. Claws simple and without setae at bases. Adults active in late spring and summer; attracted to light. Maritime Provinces to Florida, west to Ontario, eastern North Dakota, Nebraska, and Texas. (16)

Athous neacanthus **Becker** (5.7–8.7 mm) is brown to dark brown, pronotum typically lighter with dark median spot touching apical and basal margins. Head with triangular impression on frons with distinct ridge in front clearly above clypeus. Antennae shorter than *A. acanthus*, reaching past posterior angles of pronotum, two or three antennomeres in male, one or two in female; middle antennomeres triangular, especially in male. Pronotum sometimes uniformly brown, hind angles without ridges above. Prosternal suture single, not excavated in front. Claws simple and without setae at bases. Adults on vegetation in late spring through summer; attracted to light. Québec to Georgia, west to Ohio and Alabama. (16)

Denticollis denticornis **(Kirby)** (9.0–16.0 mm) has pronotal and elytral markings resembling those of fireflies (Lampyridae). Head with triangular impression on frons and distinct ridge above clypeus. Front of head, sides and middle of pronotum, and a thin line down each elytron pale yellowish brown; rest of body brown. Adults found on vegetation in coniferous and deciduous forests, and at light in late spring and early summer. Predatory larvae found in forest litter and decaying wood. Nova Scotia and Prince Edward Island to North Carolina, west to Alberta, Michigan, and Tennessee. (3)

Hemicrepidius nemnonius **(misspelled as** *memnonius***) (Herbst)** (12.0–22.0 mm) is elongate, oblong, robust, pale to dark brown with yellowish pubescence. Head with front depressed, same plane as labrum. Pronotum with base distinctly notched just inside ridged angles, shining and longer than wide (male) or dull and wider than long (female). Elytra with rows of deep, coarse close-set punctures, spaces between somewhat convex and densely punctate. Tarsomere 1 long as 2–3 combined, 2–3 lobed, claws simple, without setae at base. Adults active in summer, found under loose bark and rocks; attracted to light. Maritime Provinces and New England to Florida, west to Alberta and Missouri. (10)

Limonius basilaris **(Say)** (5.1–6.2 mm) is elongate, black, with yellowish hind pronotal angles and pale pubescence. Head black, coarsely punctate, with clypeal margin raised and broadly, shallowly notched, without triangular impression on frons. Antennae mostly black, antennomere 1 pale, 2–3 combined equal to 4. Pronotum convex with brassy luster. Elytra with rows of fine, deep punctures, spaces between slightly convex with coarse, irregular, setose punctures. Legs yellowish or orange, tarsomeres unlobed, sequentially shorter from first, claws simple. Adults found resting on vegetation in spring and early summer; also at light. Québec to Florida, west to Wisconsin, Iowa, and Texas. (19)

Limonius griseus **(Palisot de Beauvois)** (10.5–14.5 mm) is brown or black above and clothed with yellowish setae, with underside reddish; sides of prothorax, abdominal and elytral margins, and appendages reddish yellow. Head distinctly margined in front and above labrum, without triangular impression on frons. Antennomeres 3–4 equal in length, each longer than 2. Pronotum coarsely, densely punctate with sides of posterior angles parallel. Elytral grooves indistinct with large punctures, areas between flat and densely punctate. Legs with claws and tarsi simple. Ontario to Florida, west to Wisconsin, eastern Kansas, Oklahoma, and Louisiana. (19)

Limonius quercinus **(Say)** (5.5–6.4 mm) is elongate, with pale setae. Head black with clypeal margin raised and broadly notched, without triangular impression on frons. Antennae dark brown to black with yellow bases, antennomeres 2–3 longer than 4. Pronotum black. Elytra dark brown to black, with rows of deep punctures, spaces between flat with dense yellow setae. Tarsomeres beginning with 1 becoming shorter, claws and tarsomeres simple. Adults active spring and early summer, found on vegetation; attracted to light. Maine and New York to Florida, west to Ontario, Wisconsin, and Texas. (19)

Limonius stigma **(Herbst)** (6.5–10.3 mm) is elongate, black with bicolored elytra. Head black with clypeal margin elevated and straight, without triangular impression on frons. Antennae black, antennomeres 2–3 long as 4. Elytra black, basal third orange, with rows of fine punctures, spaces between with deep punctures separated by their own width, and covered with fine yellow setae. Legs light to dark brown, tarsomeres beginning with 1 becoming shorter, claws simple. Rare, adults active spring and early summer, found on vegetation (possibly a canopy species); attracted to light. Québec and Ontario to Georgia, west to Indiana. (19)

Actenicerus cuprascens **(LeConte)** (13.0–17.0 mm) is elongate, robust, brownish bronze to purplish reddish brown, with irregular patches of dense greyish pubescence often rubbed off. Head with ridge between eyes and over antennal bases depressed and indistinct near midline. Pronotum with coarse punctures. Elytral grooves deep, punctured, areas between closely punctate at base, becoming rough behind middle. Adults active late spring through summer, swept from vegetation in wet habitats such as bogs, meadows, and swamps. Europe; established from New Brunswick to New Jersey, west to Ontario and New York. (2)

Anostirus (formerly *Ctenicera*) *vernalis* (Hentz) (8.0–10.0 mm) is weakly convex and shiny black and orange. Head with ridge between eyes (over antennae) depressed and indistinct near midline. Pronotum convex, narrowed in front, and sinuate just before hind angles without carina. Elytra yellow-orange to orange, each with two large black spots and common black patch around scutellum, surface deeply grooved with coarse punctures. Rarely collected. Adults active in spring in orchards, deciduous woodlands, and mixed forests; possibly found on flowers, in Lindgren funnel trap. Maritime Provinces to North Carolina, west to Michigan, and Tennessee. (1)

"Ctenicera" pyrrhos (Herbst) (15.0–23.0 mm) is slender and uniformly dull brown or reddish brown with sparse yellow pubescence. Head with ridge between eyes (over antennae) depressed and indistinct near midline. Pronotum very long, convex, sparsely coarsely punctate on middle and more so on sides, with disintct front angles and divergent hind angles. Elytra with punctured grooves, punctures coarse. Adults found on walnut, hickory, and other trees in summer; also at light. Will be moved to another genus. Ontario and Massachusetts to Georgia, west to Indiana and Tennessee.

Eanus estriatus (LeConte) (5.9–6.1 mm) is elongate, robust, blackish with a brassy luster and base of elytra and margins yellowish. Base of antennae pale, antennomere 3 slightly narrower and almost equal in length to 4. Head with ridge between eyes and over antennal bases depressed and indistinct near midline. Pronotum wider than long, constricted near front angles, side margins broadly rounded, and hind angles diverging. Elytra and sides pale about basal fifth, without spots. Adults found on flowers and vegetation. In east from Atlantic Canada and New England to New York, west to Ontario and Michigan. (3)

Hadromorphus inflatus (Say) (8.0–12.0 mm) is moderately elongate, shallowly convex, blackish with brassy reflections and densely clothed in pale setae. Antennae do not reach posterior pronotal angles. Head with ridge between eyes and over antennal bases depressed and indistinct near midline. Pronotum slightly wider than long, distinctly convex, with posterior angles somewhat sharp, diverging, and ridged. Scutellum somewhat straight in front. Elytra with grooves distinctly punctate, spaces between coarsely punctate. Legs reddish yellow, femora sometimes darker, tarsi without setose pads or lobes, and claws simple. Alaska and Canada, eastern United States to Georgia and Texas. (1)

Hypoganus sulcicollis (**Say**) (15.0–24.0 mm) is uniformly reddish to dark brown with very sparse short brown pubescence. Head with ridge between eyes and over antennal bases depressed and indistinct near midline. Pronotum longer than wide with a line down middle, surface very finely wrinkled coarsely and evenly punctured, widest just behind front, sides sinuate just before sharp, ridged, slightly divergent angles. Elytra with rows of deep, coarse punctures, spaces between finely punctate. Adults active in late spring and summer, found on tree trunks and under bark; also at light. In east from Nova Scotia and New England to Georgia, west to Ontario and Illinois. (1)

Pseudanostirus hamatus (**Say**) (9.0–11.0 mm) has yellowish elytra, each with triangular or hooklike dark brown spot on apical third. Head, prothorax, underside, and appendages reddish brown to blackish. Head with ridge between eyes (over antennae) depressed and indistinct near midline. Head and pronotum with dense yellow pubescence. Elytra yellowish, grooved with coarse, deep punctures. Adults active in spring and summer, found on oaks (*Quercus*) and other deciduous trees and shrubs; attracted to light. Maritime Provinces and New England to Georgia, west to Ontario and Indiana. (4)

Pseudanostirus hieroglyphicus (**Say**) (10.0–13.0 mm) is black with antennae, pronotal hind angles, and legs reddish. Head with ridge between eyes (over antennae) depressed and indistinct near midline. Elytra yellowish with irregular black bands behind scutellum and middle; bands sometimes joined with elongate blotch. Adults found in spring and summer in both deciduous and coniferous forests on trees, shrubs, other undergrowth, and at light. Nova Scotia west to Manitoba, and throughout central and eastern United States. (4)

Pseudanostirus triundulatus (**Randall**) (6.3–12.0 mm) is black with yellow or reddish-orange elytra bearing two black zigzag bands and dark crescent or triangle at tips. Head with ridge between eyes (over antennae) depressed and indistinct near midline. Elytra with finely impressed and punctate grooves. Adults active spring and summer, found on conifers. Across Canada, New England, Rhode Island; also Rocky, Cascade, and Sierra Nevada Mountains. (4)

Selatosomus pulcher **(LeConte)** (10.0–14.0 mm) is elongate, moderately convex, with distinct blackish to black, yellow, and reddish-yellow markings, and very sparse, fine, pale setae above. Head black, area near antennal bases reddish, antennae brown, with ridge between eyes and over antennal bases depressed and indistinct near midline. Pronotum black with broad reddish stripes of varying widths down each side. Scutellum black. Elytra yellow, with humeral and sutural stripes and middle band blackish. Underside mostly black. Legs red or reddish brown. Adults active in summer, found on trees and shrubs in cool deciduous forests; also at light. Maritime Provinces and New England to New Jersey, west to Ontario and New York. (7)

Paradonus pectoralis **(Say)** (1.5–2.0 mm) is small, elongate, somewhat flat, and dull yellowish. Head dark. Pronotum wider than long, convex, closely punctured and very finely wrinkled, with hind angles short, stubby, and ridged. Elytra without distinct grooves or rows of punctures, clothed in erect yellow setae, often with faintly darker areas around scutellum and band behind middle, rarely entirely blackish. Claws simple. Adults active in summer, attracted to light. Nova Scotia to North Carolina, west to British Columbia, Illinois, Nebraska, and Arkansas. (6)

Agriotes collaris **(LeConte)** (10.0–11.0 mm) has a distinctly bicolored pronotum. Pronotum between punctures shiny, less so in females. Prosternal suture notched in front. Underside of pro- and mesothorax reddish along sides. Scutellum broadly arched in front. Elytra reddish brown and somewhat pointed at apex. Legs with tarsomeres, claws simple. Adults and larvae found under decaying deciduous and coniferous stumps. Adults active in spring and summer, found on vegetation or hiding under debris. Maritime Provinces and New England to New Jersey, west to Ontario, New York, and Pennsylvania. (15)

Lined Click Beetle *Agriotes lineatus* **(Linnaeus)** (8.0–10.0 mm) is robust, brownish, clothed in fine yellowish setae, and elytra sometimes paler with uneven elevation of spaces between paired grooves; appendages light brown. Head with frontal ridge extending completely between antennal bases. Pronotum with sides rounded then parallel at posterior third, angles ridged, slightly divergent. Pronotosternal suture notched in front. Scutellum broadly arched in front. Legs with tarsomeres, claws simple. Larvae are root feeders, developing in soil. Adults found under boards, stones, and other debris around edges surrounding fields. Europe; in east established in Maritime Provinces and New England; Pacific Northwest. (15)

Idolus (formerly *Agriotella*) *bigeminata* (Randall) (4.0–5.3 mm) is bicolored black and reddish yellow; appendages brownish yellow or reddish yellow. Head with complete semicircular frontal ridge covering bases of antennae and not protruding over clypeus; antennomeres 2–4 all about equal in length. Head and pronotum moderately, coarsely punctate. Pronotum entirely black with two large, variable reddish-yellow spots that do not touch side or sutural margins; apical spots somewhat rectangular. Adults active on rocky hills in late spring and summer; found on pine (*Pinus*); also in table-mountain pine heath in Great Smoky Mountains. Maritime Provinces and New England to Rhode Island, west to Manitoba, and Tennessee. (1)

Ampedus areolatus (Say) (4.0–5.0 mm) is elongate, oblong, somewhat convex, blackish or dark reddish brown with pair of oblique yellowish spots near base of elytra. Antennae serrate, anntenomere 3 slender, twice as long as 2, equal to triangular 4. Elytra weakly grooved with large punctures, areas between with punctures sparse, sometimes with additional pale spots that merge at tips. Adults active spring and summer, found on low vegetation; attracted to light. Nova Scotia to Florida, west to Ontario, South Dakota, Missouri, and Texas. (31)

Ampedus collaris (Say) (6.0–9.0 mm) is oblong, slender, somewhat convex, clothed in grayish setae, and bicolored. Head, underside of prothorax at middle, and elytra black. Pronotum and underside of prothorax along sides red. Elytra with weakly impressed rows of coarse punctures. Appendages dark brown to blackish; claws simple. Adults active in late spring and summer, found under bark and on flowers. Nova Scotia and New Brunswick to Georgia, west to Québec and Illinois. (31)

Ampedus linteus (Say) (8.0–11.0 mm) is elongate, black with mostly pale yellow elytra, and clothed in yellowish setae. Head with frontal margin extending over clypeus. Pronotum shining and densely punctate. Elytra shining with rows of deep punctures; pale with suture and tip black. Legs dark with tarsi and claws simple, claws without setae at base. Adults found in spring and summer under bark, on vegetation, and at light. Québec and Ontario to Florida, west to South Dakota, Nebraska, Texas. (31)

Ampedus nigricollis **(Herbst)** (8.5–12.0 mm) has a black head, prothorax, scutellum, and underside, with pale yellowish elytra and pale reddish legs. Head with complete frontal margin extending to labrum. Antennae dark with first two antennomeres paler, second antennomere shorter than third. Elytra paler at base and outer margins and shallowly grooved with coarse punctures. Adults found under loose hardwood bark nearly year-round in moist woods. Maritime Provinces and Ontario to Florida, west to South Dakota and Louisiana. (31)

Ampedus rubricollis **(Herbst)** (fomerly *A. verticinus* [Palisot de Beauvois]) (12.0–14.0 mm) is elongate, bicolored, and clothed in yellowish setae. Top of head and most of pronotum reddish, while pronotal margins, elytra, and most of underside black. Legs mostly black with brown tarsi, tarsi and claws simple, claws without setae at base. Larvae develop in rotten stumps and logs of conifers and hardwoods. Adults active in late spring and early summer under bark or in Malaise and Lindgren funnel traps. Maine and Québec to Florida, west to Ontario, Indiana, and Florida. (31)

Ampedus rubricus **(Say)** (7.0–9.0 mm) is mostly black with yellowish pubescence, and distinctly bicolored pronotum; appendages mostly blackish, basal antennomeres lighter. Antennae serrate, 3 half as long as 2, nearly as long as 4. Pronotum bright red at base and sides, with sides straight at base and hind angles slightly divergent. Elytra with rows of deep punctures, spaces between rough and finely punctate. Adults active late spring and summer, found on vegetation; attracted to light. Maritime Provinces and New England to North Carolina, west to Manitoba, Wisconsin, and Indiana. (31)

Ampedus xanthomus **(Germar)** (9.0 mm) is elongate, bicolored, dark shiny black with orange-red or red patches, and clothed in black setae. Head with complete frontal margin extending to labrum. Pronotal punctures fine, sparse. Elytra roughly sculptured with rows of deep punctures. Legs black with tarsi and claws simple, claws without setae at base. Massachusetts and New York to North Carolina, west to Ohio. (31)

Anchastus binus **(Say)** (7.0–8.0 mm) is elongate, oblong, clothed in dense yellow pubescence, and black or blackish with each elytron bearing a pair of reddish-yellow spots; appendages yellow. Antennae serrate, antennomere 3 larger than 2, smaller than each of 4–11. Pronotum longer than wide, densely punctured, hind angles sharp and ridged. Elytra with rows of deep punctures, spaces between densely and roughly punctate, each with large basal spot extending almost to middle, another spot on apical quarter. Tarsomere 3 lobed below. Adults active in late spring and summer; attracted to light. Virginia to Florida, west to Indiana, Missouri, and Texas. (6)

Dicrepidius palmatus **Candéze** (12.0–15.0 mm) is elongate, slender, and shiny dark reddish brown to blackish with sparse pale pubescence. Front margin of head sharp, projecting over labrum, merging with pair of oblique ridges below at middle. Antennae of male pectinate, female serrate. Pronotum longer than wide, sides parallel, coarsely and sparsely punctate, base deeply notched near sides, hind angles sharp and ridged. Elytra with rows of deep punctures, spaces between slightly convex and sparsely punctate. Tarsomeres 2 and 3 with membranous lobes, claws simple. Adults active spring and summer; attracted to light. Pennsylvania to Florida, west to Indiana and Texas. (2)

Elater abruptus **Say** (15.0–22.0 mm) is somewhat elongate and convex, clothed in fine reddish-brown setae reclining backward, shining dark brown to black; mandibles, legs, and underside lighter. claws simple, without setae. Antennae serrate, about two-thirds length pronotum (female) or long (male). Pronotum slightly wider than long, abruptly narrowed toward front at apical fourth. Elytra very faintly grooved, with irregular setose punctures. Adults active in summer; in hollow trees, attracted to light. Maritime Provinces and New England to Virginia, west to Manitoba and Kansas. (1)

Orthostethus infuscatus **(Germar)** (25.0–35.0 mm) is large, elongate, uniformly dark reddish or grayish brown, and densely clothed in recumbent yellowish setae. Antennae serrate, shorter than pronotum, with antennomere 2 less than half length of 3, which is shorter and much narrower than 4. Pronotum longer than wide with posterior angles long, sharp, ridged, and divergent. Elytra weakly grooved, more densely punctured than pronotum. Legs with tarsal claws simple, without setae. Adults common at light in summer. New York to Florida, west to Ohio, Kansas, and southern Arizona. (1)

Megapenthes limbalis (Herbst) (8.0–16.0 mm) is dull, densely punctured, usually with distinctly bicolored reddish yellow and black males that resemble fireflies (Lampyridae), sometime uniformly tannish; females black. Antennomeres 2–3 as long as wide, their combined lengths equal to 4. Front margin of prothorax notched at suture underneath. Tarsomeres simple, not lobed. Adults found resting on vegetation in late spring and summer. Massachusetts to Florida, west to Illinois. (8)

Melanotus species (5.2–12.6 mm) are usually uniformly yellowish brown to dark reddish brown with comblike claws. Head with coarse hexagonal punctures separated by less than their own diameters, distinct margin across front, usually with two oblique ridges underneath merging with middle of frontal ridge; antennae with 11 antennomeres, 1 long and cylindrical, 2 spherical, 3 variable, 4–7 triangular. Prothorax underneath without grooves to receive antennae. Elytra each with nine punctate grooves. Legs with apical tibial spurs and tarsi without lobes underneath, claws pectinate. Adults commonly found on flowers and vegetation in spring and early summer (night and day), under bark in fall and winter. Widespread and abundant in eastern North America. (38)

Cardiophorus cardisce (Say) (6.0–8.0 mm) is elongate, black, and thickly clothed in yellow pubescence. Pronotum strongly convex, finely and densely punctate, with hind angles oblique and appearing cut off. Scutellum is heart-shaped. Elytra with rows of coarse punctures, spaces between convex, finely punctate, each with two variable yellow spots present or not. Adults active in spring and summer, found in burrows associated with dune grasses and under debris along sandy lakeshores and coastlines. New England and Québec to Florida, west to Alberta, South Dakota, and Texas. (9)

Cardiophorus convexus (Say) (8.0–10.0 mm) is shiny blackish or black, clothed in very fine yellowish setae, with legs and bases of antennae reddish; sometimes basal pronotal angles and base of elytra reddish. Pronotum convex, widest at middle, side margins not marked by a sharp ridge, hind angles evident, each with a short ridge; underside with shallow, broadly curved groove beginning at hind angle, but not reaching front angle. Scutellum heart-shaped. Elytra sometimes pale at base with lines of punctures more or less distinct. Legs uniformly reddish, tarsomeres not lobed underneath. Adults active in late spring and summer, found on foliage of deciduous trees and shrubs; also attracted to light. Québec and Ontario to Florida, west to Illinois, Kansas, and Texas. (9)

Horistonotus curiatus (Say) (4.0–4.5 mm) is elongate-oblong, somewhat convex, and clothed in slender setae. Pronotum with sides sharply margined only at base, posterior margin distinctly uneven. Scutellum shallowly notched at base, elytra with rows of punctures (punctostriate), dark yellow with dark marks on posterior half of each elytron. Appendages dull reddish yellow; tarsi simple, claws with basal tooth, without setae. Adults are active from early spring through fall and found on vegetation; also attracted to light. Ontario to Florida, west to Indiana and Texas. (3)

NET-WINGED BEETLES, FAMILY LYCIDAE
(*LIE*-SIH-DEE)

Lycids are typically soft-bodied and lethargic beetles that are often conspicuously marked with black and red or orange. They fly with their elytra spread and slowly flutter mothlike through the air. The short-lived adults are believed to feed on nectar. Most species are found resting on vegetation, sometimes in large numbers. Smaller species with mostly dark, straight-sided elytra and brightly colored pronota resemble fireflies (Lampyridae) and are abundant in the vicinity of moist woodlands. The soft, leathery wings of net-winged beetles are punctuated with long, brittle, and hollow ridges that rupture easily to release noxious fluids. When attacked or roughly handled, they will also produce fluids from the leg joints. As a result, net-winged beetles are mimicked not only by other beetles (e.g., Cleridae, Chrysomelidae, and Cerambycidae) but also by moths and other insects. Lycid larvae live under bark and in decaying wood and feed on fluids and soft tissues associated with fungal infestations.

229

FAMILY DIAGNOSIS Adult lycids are soft-bodied and flattened, with coarsely sculptured and loose-fitting elytra black and often marked with red or orange markings. Head with sometimes beaklike (*Lyconotus*) mouthparts directed downward and partially covered by pronotum. Antennae with 11 flattened antennomeres, weakly to strongly serrate or pectinate (*Caenia*). Pronotum flattened, bell-shaped, margins distinct, concealing head from above. Elytra nearly straight-sided or expanded past the middle and extend beyond outline of abdomen; surface with network of long ridges connected by less distinct cross-ridges. Legs with basal segments (coxae) widely separated; tarsal formula 5-5-5, tarsomeres 1–4 with dense pubescence underneath, claws simple and equal. Abdomen with seven (female) or eight (male) ventrites.

SIMILAR FAMILIES
- reticulated beetles (Cupedidae) – head exposed (p.60)
- glowworms (Phengodidae) – elytra without ridges; antennae plumose; mandibles distinct (p.233)
- fireflies (Lampyridae) – elytra without ridges; abdomen sometimes with two or three yellow and bioluminescent ventrites (p.234)
- soldier beetles (Cantharidae) – elytra without ridges; head clearly visible from above (p.238)
- some leaf beetles (Chrysomelidae: Cassidinae) – hard-bodied; antennae short, weakly clubbed (p.429)

COLLECTING NOTES Sweeping and beating vegetation during the day in spring and summer will produce net-winged beetles. Pupae and freshly eclosed adults are sometimes found under the loose bark of snags, stumps, and logs. Look for species of *Calopteron* resting on vegetation or feeding on nectar at flowers during the day in late spring and summer. *Dictyoptera* is usually found on or under tree bark in early spring. Other species are usually found in summer flying or resting on vegetation during the day, attracted to lights at night, or captured in Malaise traps.

FAUNA 76 SPECIES IN 19 GENERA (NA); 37 SPECIES IN 12 GENERA (ENA)

Dictyoptera aurora **(Herbst)** (6.5–11.0 mm) is elongate, somewhat flattened, straight-sided or weakly widened toward tip, black with pronotal margins and elytra red or reddish orange. Antennae black, those of male more than half length of body, female's shorter. Underside black. Adults found in early spring on and under bark of decaying stumps and on tree trunks in deciduous woodlands and mixed forests; also in Malaise traps. Newfoundland and Labrador to Florida, west to Manitoba, Minnesota, and Arkansas; also in Pacific Northwest and Europe. (2)

Dictyoptera munda **(Say)** (6.0 mm) is elongate, somewhat flattened, and bright scarlet red or orange above. Antennae black with first two antennomeres scarlet. Pronotum without dark central area. Underside of thorax red. Abdominal sternites black. Tarsi dusky. Diurnal adults found in spring on tree trunks and foliage of shrubs in deciduous woodlands and mixed forests; also in Malaise traps. Pennsylvania to Georgia, west to Kentucky and Louisiana. (2)

Caenia dimidiata **(Fabricius)** (8.5–13.5 mm) has pectinate antennomeres in both sexes; branches on 4–10 longer and attached at base of the antennomeres in male, but shorter and arising near tip of antennomeres in female. Labial palps tipped with broadly triangular palpomeres. Fan-shaped elytra are broadly expanded toward apices. Adults are found in later spring and early summer on vegetation during the day or at lights. Québec to Florida, west to Wisconsin, Missouri, and Mississippi. (1)

Calopteron discrepans **(Newman)** (9.0–14.5 mm) is somewhat triangular, flattened, and bright orange and black. Second antennomere brown and underside of thorax with reddish-brown patch. Elytra not undulate in profile and even-numbered ridges more strongly elevated than odd-numbered ridges. Adults found on flowers and vegetation, especially near water, in late spring and summer. Québec to Florida, west to Manitoba, Colorado, and Texas. (3)

Calopteron reticulatum **(Fabricius)** (9.5–18.0 mm) is somewhat triangular, flattened, and bright orange and black. Antennae black, flat, saw-toothed, with antennomere 2 entirely and several beyond underneath partially reddish brown. Pronotum half again as wide as long. Elytra divergent to about apical fourth, not undulate in profile, with even ridges more strongly elevated than odd, median band usually present, with or without narrowing extension along suture to scutellum. Underside with middle thoracic segment reddish brown in front. Adults active late spring and summer, found on flowers and vegetation, especially near water. New England and Ontario to Florida, west to Minnesota, South Dakota, and Texas; southern Mexico. (3)

Calopteron terminale **(Say)** (8.5–16.0 mm) is somewhat triangular, flattened, and bright orange and black, with black elytral bands shiny with distinct bluish tinge. Elytra with ridges of equal height throughout entire length and are distinctly undulate when viewed in profile; median band, if present, does not extend along elytral suture toward base. Adults found in spring and summer on flowers and vegetation, especially near water. Québec to Florida, west to Manitoba and Oklahoma. (3)

Leptoceletes basalis **(LeConte)** (6.5–9.0 mm) is black with sides of pronotum, small triangular patches on elytral angles, and portions of leg bases reddish brown. Antennae of male pectinate with branches arising from base of antennomere; female's flat and serrate. Pronotum triangular and pointed in front with narrow ridge down middle. Elytral somewhat straight-sided, surface with four distinct ridges. Adults active late spring and summer, attracted to light. Nova Scotia and New Brunswick to Florida, west to Saskatchewan, South Dakota, Arkansas, and Mississippi. (1)

Calochromus perfacetus **(Say)** (6.0–10.5 mm) is elongate, flattened, black with sides of pronotum reddish brown. Head without rostrum. Antennae somewhat serrate, antennomere 2 as long as wide, longer in male than female. Pronotum distinctly narrowed in front, with uniformly narrow groove down middle, without ridges, underneath with coxae touching or nearly so. Elytra uniformly pubescent, with feeble ridges, and gradually expanded behind middle. Legs with tibial spurs similar in shape. Adults active in summer, found on vegetation. Maritime Provinces to Florida, west to Michigan and New Mexico. (1)

Eropterus trilineatus **(Melsheimer)** (4.0–7.0 mm) is elongate, slightly widened at rear, and black with upturned portions of sides and outer front margin reddish yellow. Antennae weakly serrate, narrowly separated at base, more than half as long as body in male. Pronotum broadly arched in front, widest at base, with single short ridge down middle of front and oblique ridges joining on sides near basal fourth. Elytra each with rows of somewhat squarish punctures, three outermost ridges most distinct. Abdomen underneath with tip broadly notched in male. Tibiae with small, sharp spurs. Nova Scotia and New England to Florida, west to Ontario and Texas. Species best identified using male genitalia. (4)

Eros humeralis **(Fabricius)** (6.0–9.5 mm) is elongate, slender, somewhat flattened, and blackish with partly reddish pronotum and elytra. Head slopes down, without points or ridges, and antennal bases almost in contact with each other. Pronotum mostly black with narrow to very broad reddish margins, with two or more less distinct longitudinal ridges with central cell open in front. Elytra black with variable reddish patches on humeri extending to apical third. Adults found under pine (*Pinus*) bark in early spring or on vegetation; in Malaise and light traps. Nova Scotia and New England to Florida, west to Ontario, Michigan, Illinois, and Texas. (1)

Erotides **(formerly *Platycis*) *sculptilis* (Say)** (5.0–8.0 mm) is black with pronotum entirely black or reddish brown with black patch. Pronotum wider than long, somewhat rectangular with front margin broadly curved, usually with ridge down middle that divides central rectangular cell in half, cell connected to each side by ridge, posterior half with distinct ridges at middle. Elytron with four distinct ridges, spaces between filled with irregular cells. Femora of male with broad setose pit near base. Larva develops in rotting pine (*Pinus*) logs and feeds on fluids. Nocturnal adults active in summer, taken in Malaise and light traps. New Brunswick and Québec to Florida, west to Ontario, Michigan, Illinois, Tennessee, and Mississippi. (1)

Lopheros fraternus **(Randall)** (6.5–11.5 mm) is elongate, somewhat straight-sided, slightly wider toward rear, black, with reddish-yellow spot on middle of pronotum. Antennae of male flat, serrate, second antennomere small. Pronotum with single, fine ridge running down entire middle often crossed at middle by another ridge that angles back at sides. Each elytron with four strong ridges. Larva develops in very wet red-rot logs. Adults active in summer; likely found on vegetation during day. Maritime Provinces and New England to North Carolina, west to Ontario, Ohio, and Tennessee. (2)

Lyconotus lateralis (Melsheimer) (8.0–10.0 mm) is fan-shaped, black or brownish black, with sides of pronotum and humeral areas of elytra orange; elytral spots variable. Head prolonged into a slender beak, antennomere 3 almost as long as 4. Pronotum with trace of short median ridge on front, without oblique ridges on sides. Elytra expanded well beyond sides of abdomen. Abdomen with seven (male) or eight (female) ventrites. Legs of male with coxae spinose and hind tibiae strongly curved. Diurnal adults found in spring and early summer on vegetation and flowers, including Queen Anne's lace (*Daucus carota*). Maine to Florida, west to Illinois, Kansas, and Texas. (1)

Plateros species (3.5–10.5 mm) are elongate, almost parallel-sided, slightly wider at rear, dull black, and pronotum reddish brown with spot on middle and front of head very short and mouthparts directed downward; appendages only weakly flattened. Pronotum without ridge down middle or oblique ridges on sides, front margin and angles broadly rounded, widest at base. Elytra with ridges all of similar height. Species most reliably distinguished by examination of male genitalia; females best identified by capture in copula with male. Adults active early spring and summer; attracted to light. Throughout eastern North America. (20)

233

GLOWWORMS, FAMILY PHENGODIDAE
(FEN-GO-DIH-DEE)

Phengodes is the sole representative of this family in eastern North America. The soft-bodied males resemble fireflies (Lampyridae) and soldier beetles (Cantharidae), but have feathery antennae, conspicuous mandibles, and short, paddle-shaped elytra. Adult females are larviform and may reach 40.0–65.0 mm in length when fully extended. Larviform females have compound eyes, while the larvae have simple eyes, or stemmata. The eggs, larvae, and larviform females are bioluminescent and produce a continuous greenish light; adult males are also weakly bioluminscent. Males use highly sensitive chemical receptors on their elaborate, plumose antennae to detect pheromones released by larviform females. Once in her immediate vicinity, a male zeros in on the light she emits. Adult phengodids are not known to feed. The larvae live in forest leaf litter or hide beneath loose bark, logs, or other debris on the ground where they hunt for much larger millipedes. Upon finding a millipede, the *Phengodes* larva runs alongside its victim for a short distance before coiling itself around the front of the millipede's body (Fig. 18, p.24). The larva then reaches under the millipede's head and uses its sicklelike mandibles to deliver a lethal dose of digestive enzymes that also instantly paralyze the millipede to prevent it from secreting its defensive fluids. The millipede soon dies and the digestive enzymes liquefy its internal tissues. The larva pushes its way into the millipede's body cavity, ingests its contents, and leaves its hollowed-out exoskeleton behind as a series of disarticulated rings.

FAMILY DIAGNOSIS Male *Phengodes* are elongate, flattened, pale orangish or orangish brown, with conspicuous sickle-shaped mandibles, plumose antennae, and short elytra. Head distinct, with mouthparts directed forward (prognathous) and narrower than prothorax. Antennae with 12 antennomeres, 4–11 bipectinate, each with two long and curled appendages. Pronotum flat, narrowed toward head, and sharply margined or keeled on each side. Scutellum visible. Elytra smooth, short with three or more abdominal segments exposed, paddle-shaped, broadest at base and strongly narrowed toward tips. Tarsal formula 5-5-5, claws equal and simple. Abdomen with seven ventrites.

SIMILAR FAMILIES

- net-winged beetles (Lycidae) – antennae with 11 articles, never bipectinatet; head and mandibles not conspicuous; elytral ridges usually connected by less conspicuous cross veins (p.229)
- fireflies (Lampyridae) – antennae with 11 articles, serrate; mandibles not visible (p.234)
- false soldier beetles (Omethidae) – antennae with 11 articles, simple (p.237)

- soldier beetles (Cantharidae) – antennae with 11 articles, never bipectinate; mandibles not visible (p.238)
- *Dendroides* (Pyrochoridae) – male antennae with 11 articles, pectinate; elytra cover abdomen; tarsi 5-5-4 (p.374)

COLLECTING NOTES Males are readily attracted to lights in summer in various wooded habitats. Raking moist soil from underneath plants where millipedes are active sometimes reveals larvae. Larvae also seek shelter under boards and other flat objects deliberately placed on the ground. Covered pitfall traps set against logs or used in conjunction with drift fences also produce specimens.

FAUNA 23 SPECIES IN SIX GENERA (NA); FOUR SPECIES IN ONE GENUS (ENA)

Phengodes laticollis **LeConte** (14.0–20.0 mm) male with head usually dark, lighter in front; some with paler heads and dark margins along eyes. Front of labrum broadly concave, middle smooth with a line impressed down middle. Distinctly banded larviform female distinguished from larva by presence of compound eyes. Males attracted to lights in summer. Larvae found in leaf litter and under objects where millipedes occur. New York to Florida, west to Wisconsin and Louisiana. (4)

FIREFLIES, LIGHTNINGBUGS, AND GLOWWORMS, FAMILY LAMPYRIDAE
(LAM-*PEER*-IH-DEE)

Lampyrids are soft-bodied beetles that are mostly tropical and subtropical in distribution. The adult females of some species are larviform and are called glowworms. Nocturnal, light-producing species spend their days hiding beneath bark, in leaf litter, or resting on leaves. Fireflies with weak or no light-producing organs (*Ellychnia, Lucidota, Pyropyga*) are active during the day and are generally found on flowers, streamside vegetation, or feeding at sapping wounds on tree trunks. The feeding habits of adult fireflies are poorly known and many species appear not to feed at all, while the larvae are predators. They paralyze, kill, and liquefy the tissues of snails, slugs, earthworms, and small insects with the aid of chemicals pumped through channeled mandibles. Steroidal compounds called lucibufagins chemically protect fireflies by making them distasteful to predators. Whether the adults glow or not, all known egg, larval, and pupal stages of fireflies are bioluminescent, which serves as an aposematic warning to potential predators of their distastefulness; glowing adults no doubt benefit from this defensive strategy as well.

FAMILY DIAGNOSIS Lampyrids are soft-bodied and flattened, with the head covered by the pronotum that is nearly as wide as elytra. Head with mouthparts directed downward and eyes relatively large, especially in male.

Antennae with 11 antennomeres threadlike (filiform) or saw-toothed (serrate). Pronotum flattened and distinctly margined or keeled on sides. Scutellum visible. Elytra with surface sometimes weakly ridged, with side margins nearly parallel, widest at middle, and almost or completely conceal abdomen. Tarsal formula 5-5-5, tarsomere 4 heart-shaped; claws equal in size and usually simple (exceptions being the anterior half of claw is cleft in *Photuris* and *Micronaspis*). Abdomen with seven (female) or eight (male) ventrites.

SIMILAR FAMILIES

- net-winged beetles (Lycidae) – elytral ridges usually connected by distinct but less conspicuous cross veins (except in *Calochromus*) (p.229)
- adult male glowworms (Phengodidae) – head exposed; sicklelike mandibles visible; elytra short (p.233)

- false soldier beetles (Omethidae) – labrum distinct; antennae separated by nearly twice diameter of antennal pits; abdomen without light-producing organs (p.237)
- soldier beetles (Cantharidae) – head exposed, not covered by pronotum (p.238)

COLLECTING METHODS Bioluminescent lampyrids, mostly males, are captured at night by hand or with a net as they are flashing; flashing females, both winged and wingless, are generally found on foliage or on the ground. Adults are sometimes found during the day resting on vegetation where they are collected by beating or sweeping. Species that are not bioluminescent are usually found under bark, drinking sap from freeze cracks on tree trunks, resting on vegetation, or flying during the day. Lampyrids are only occasionally attracted to light.

FAUNA 126 SPECIES IN 17 GENERA (NA); 81 SPECIES IN 13 GENERA (ENA)

Pyractomena dispersa **Green** (8.0–12.5 mm) is elongate-oval. Head, antennae, and legs black. Pronotum with distinct ridge down middle, black stripe down middle triangular and regularly narrowed toward head, markings along side margins narrow and faint. Scutellum dark, pale at tip. Elytra black, suture pale and extending around scutellum, and lateral margins slightly narrowed apically; setae sparse, pale, and most conspicuous on apical quarter to third. Associated with wetland habitats in summer; larvae probably feed on snails. Male flash pattern consists of four or five bursts; females remain stationary. Maine to Alabama, west to southern Alberta, Michigan, Iowa, and Missouri; also Colorado, Idaho, and Utah. (14)

Winter Firefly *Ellychnia corrusca* **(Linnaeus)** (10.0– 14.0 mm) is oblong-oval, dull black to black, sides of pronotum with reddish and yellow stripes. Antennomere 1 longer than 3, 2 short and long as wide. Elytra finely granulate, sparsely covered with fine, yellowish setae, margins dark; each elytron with three or four indistinct ridges. Diurnal adults on tree trunks, especially at sap flows on maple (*Acer*) trunks in spring; also nectar on maple flowers; adults nectaring on flowers (*Solidago*) in fall needs corroboration. Adults are diurnal and nonluminous. Likely a complex of several closely related species. Maritime Provinces to northern Florida, west to Manitoba, North Dakota, and Louisiana. (3)

235

Lucidota atra **(Olivier)** (8.0–11.0 mm) is elongate-oblong, dull black, with broad orangish borders on sides of pronotum narrower in front. Antennomeres thick, broadly triangular and flattened, 1 longer than 3, 2 very short and wider than long. Pronotum triangular, rounded in front. Elytral surface granular with faint raised lines mostly at base. Adults are diurnal and nonluminous. Diurnal adults fly slowly in shady places, or rest on low herbaceous growth and tree trunks in wet habitats in summer. Threatened beetles readily exude a disagreeable fluid from sides of abdomen. Eastern North America. (3)

Big Dipper Firefly *Photinus pyralis* **(Linnaeus)** (9.0–15.0 mm) is elongate-oblong. Head completely hidden by pronotum. Pronotum pinkish on middle with variable dark spot usually narrowing toward rear and not reaching base. Elytra brown or blackish, sutural and broader side margins pale. Abdomen with part of one (female) or two full (male) luminous segments. Legs with front and middle claws simple. Males emit long, distinctive J-shaped flash at dusk while flying in vertical looping pattern along edges in gardens, parks, and woods; females respond from nearby vegetation. New York to northern Florida, west to South Dakota and Texas. (47)

Pyropyga nigricans **(Say)** (4.2–8.5 mm) is elongate-oval and blackish to black. Antennae delicate, flattened, first antennomere shorter than third, second very short and wider than long. Pronotum semicircular, pale with broad black stripe down middle, margins usually black, sometime faintly so. Female elytra shorter than male in some populations. Adults are diurnal and nonluminous. Maritime Provinces to Virginia, west Manitoba and Illinois; widespread in West. *Pyropyga decipiens* Harris (4.5–7.3 mm) similar; Northeast. *P. minuta* (LeConte) (3.0–5.5 mm) with pronotal margins pale; Southeast to Kansas and Arizona. Species best determined by examining male genitalia. (3)

Pennsylvania Firefly *Photuris pennsylvanica* **(De Geer)** (8.0–10.0 mm) is elongate, with head and pronotum dull yellow. Head partly exposed. Pronotum with broad black central cloud flanked by reddish-brown spots. Elytra usually with short or moderate oblique pale stripes sometimes absent, or nearly extending length of elytron. Front claws similar in size. Near wetlands; males emit two greenish flashes in a dot–dash configuration; females remain in vegetation, also fly while luminescent. Maritime Provinces and Québec to Georgia, west to Ontario, North Dakota, Iowa, Illinois, and Kentucky. Species best identified using male genitalia and flash patterns. (~50)

FALSE SOLDIER AND FALSE FIREFLY BEETLES, FAMILY OMETHIDAE
(OH-*MEETH*-IH-DEE)

The family Omethidae consists of 8 genera and 33 species distributed in eastern Asia and North America. Larval omethids are unknown, as are the feeding habits of the adults. Adults emerge in spring and summer, are predominately diurnal, and short-lived. Two genera and species are found east of the Mississippi River. *Blatchleya gracilis* (Blatchley) is known only from Indiana and Ohio, while *Omethes marginatus* LeConte is found throughout much of eastern United States.

FAMILY DIAGNOSIS Adult omethids are elongate and soft-bodied. Head with labrum distinct and hardened. Antennae are either simple (*Omethes*) or modified with two antennomeres enlarged and excavated (*Blatchleya*). Tarsi 5-5-5, tarsomeres 3–4 bilobed. Abdomen with 7–8 ventrites, above with tergites lacking paired glandular openings, below without luminous organs.

SIMILAR FAMILIES
- net-winged beetles (Lycidae) – elytra with network of raised ridges (p.229)
- glowworms (Phengodidae) – antennae of male distinctly plumose; females larviform (p.233)
- fireflies (Lampyridae) – head partially or completely covered above by pronotum (p.234)
- soldier beetles (Cantharidae) – clypeus membranous, not hard or distinct; only tarsomere 4 bilobed (p.238)

COLLECTING NOTES Omethids are seldom collected. The short-lived adults are usually swept from herbaceous vegetation near woods in May and June, or are found in Malaise and purple traps used for monitoring the emerald ash borer.

237

FAUNA 10 SPECIES IN SEVEN GENERA (NA); TWO SPECIES IN TWO GENERA (ENA)

Omethes marginatus LeConte (4.0–5.0 mm) is elongate, parallel-sided, clothed in long, reclining yellowish setae, coarsely punctured, and bicolored. Head, antennomeres 4–11, and most of elytra dark brown; antennomeres 1–3, pronotum, sutural and side margins of elytra, and appendages reddish brown. Head with surface rough, not deeply excavated on top, antennae filiform, antennomeres 4–5 simple, not enlarged or scooped out, and partly covered by front margin of pronotum. Elytra with fine, somewhat indistinct ridges. Tarsomeres 3 and 4 lobed underneath. Adults active in May and June, found on vegetation; occasionally in Malaise traps. Connecticut to Georgia, west Indiana and Arkansas. (1)

SOLDIER BEETLES, FAMILY CANTHARIDAE
(CAN-*THAR*-IH-DEE)

The biology and natural history of most cantharids are poorly known. The adults are short-lived and frequently encountered on flowers and foliage during the day, or at lights at night. They feed on pollen or high-nutrient liquids drawn from nectar or nectar-feeding insects (e.g., aphids). The larvae, pupae, and adults of some species produce defensive secretions from their abdominal glands. The contrasting color patterns of the adults warn potential predators of their bad taste. Beetles in other families mimic the color patterns of distasteful soldier beetles to discourage attacks by predators. When disturbed, some cantharids will quickly withdraw their legs, drop to the ground, and become lost in the tangle of plants and debris below. Dead and contorted soldier beetles with their mandibles embedded in stems or leaf edges are likely infected by fungal pathogens (e.g., *Eryniopsis lampyridum*, *E. lampyridarum*, *Zoophthora radicans*) that also attack other insects. The open wings and contorted bodies of the fungal victims have been dubbed "violent deaths" in the literature and are thought to enhance dispersal of spores of the killer fungus. Goldenrod soldier beetles, *Chauliognathus pensylvanicus* (De Geer) are popular research subjects for scientists studying mating behavior, color polymorphism, dispersal, and genetics. The nocturnal larvae develop under bark or in damp areas beneath stones, logs, or other debris. They are either predatory and attack earthworms, slugs, caterpillars, maggots, and grasshopper eggs, or somewhat ommivorous and graze on grasses and other plant materials. Numerous genera are in need of revision; many species of *Podabrus* will eventually be transferred to *Dichelotarsus*.

FAMILY DIAGNOSIS Adult cantharids are long, soft-bodied beetles, many of which resemble fireflies (Lampyridae), but their head is not completely concealed under the pronotum. Head with mouthparts directed forward (prognathous). Head with labrum membranous or hidden under clypeus. Antennae long, usually filiform, sometimes serrate or pectinate, with 11 antennomeres. Pronotum flat, sharply margined or keeled along sides, usually broader than head, and partially conceals head (e.g., *Chauliognathus*, *Pacificanthia*, *Rhagonycha*) or not (e.g., *Dichelotarsus*, *Podabrus*); sides sometimes notched or otherwise distinctly modified (*Ditemnus*, *Silis*). Soft elytra are short (*Malthinus*, *Trypherus*), or long, parallel-sided, and nearly or completely conceal abdomen. Tarsal formula 5-5-5, tarsomere 4 deeply notched and heart-shaped, claws equal in size, and simple, toothed, or lobed. Abdomen with seven (females, some males), or eight (most males) ventrites, and always without bioluminescent organs.

SIMILAR FAMILIES
- net-winged beetles (Lycidae) – labrum evident; elytral ridges connected by distinct but less conspicuous cross veins (except in *Calochromus*) (p.229)
- adult male glowworms (Phengodidae) – antennae plumose; mandibles distinct, sickle-shaped (p.233)
- lightningbugs, fireflies (Lampyridae) – head covered by pronotum, labrum evident; abdomen sometimes with bioluminescent organs (p.234)
- false soldier beetles (Omethidae) – labrum distinct; tarsomeres 3 and 4 lobed; abdomen without glandular openings (p.237)
- false blister beetles (Oedemeridae) – prothorax without distinct side margins, tarsi 5-5-4 (p.362)
- blister beetles (Meloidae) – bodies more cylindrical; head with neck; tarsi 5-5-4 (p.365)
- some longhorn beetles (Cerambycidae) – tarsi appearing 4-4-4, but are 5-5-5 (p.388)

COLLECTING NOTES Cantharids are found feeding on flowers and resting among foliage during the day and easily handpicked or collected by sweeping. They are sometimes especially abundant on vegetation in meadows and riparian habitats. Species in several genera are attracted to light.

FAUNA 473 SPECIES IN 23 GENERA (NA); 14 GENERA (ENA)

Atalantycha bilineata **(Say)** (6.0–9.0 mm) is oblong, robust, and moderately clothed in short, pale setae. Head and most of antennae black. Pronotum dull, roughly punctured, wider than long, narrowed in front, broadly margined, dull reddish yellow with two sometimes oblong black spots, with distinct impression down middle. Elytra black with sides narrowly pale. Underside reddish yellow with pterothorax dark. Legs with femora reddish yellow, tips of femora, tibiae, and tarsi darker, and only outer claws toothed. Diurnal adults found on flowers or resting on low vegetation in spring; also in Malaise traps, occasionally at lights. Nova Scotia to Florida, west to Minnesota and Oklahoma. (3)

Atalantycha dentigera **(LeConte)** (8.0–10.0 mm) is oblong, mostly dusky black, coarsely punctured, and moderately clothed in short, gray setae. Pronotum dull, roughly punctured, wider than long, yellowish pink with dark, angular spot across middle, with distinct impression down middle; elytra blackish with dull yellowish borders. Underside and legs mostly dusky brown. All claws toothed. Adults found on vegetation in spring; attracted to light. Ontario and Québec to Virginia, west to Wisconsin, Iowa, and Texas. (3)

Atalantycha neglecta **(Fall)** (8.0–10.0 mm) is oblong, blackish, clothed in fine pubescence. Head between antennal bases all or mostly dark. Antennae not quite reaching midlength of body, antennomeres 4–10 three times longer than wide. Pronotum smooth, shining, wider than long, slightly constricted in front, front margin rounded, median impression most evident in front and rear, with a broad pinkish border around a triangular black mark. Elytra long, coarsely and roughly punctate, without trace of ridges. Tip of last ventrite with a broad V-shaped notch. Tarsomeres lobed underneath, all claws distinctly toothed in both sexes. Attracted to light. Ontario to Virginia, west to Minnesota and Oklahoma. (3)

Pacificanthia rotundicollis **(Say)** (12.0–14.0 mm) is elongate and reddish yellow with grayish-brown elytra. Eyes large, dark; antennomeres 3–11 mostly dusky, pale at bases. Pronotum shiny, slightly longer than wide, front rounded, sides parallel, and grooved along base. Elytra faintly ridged, surface with short, dense pale setae. Legs uniformly reddish yellow, tarsomere 4 widened and expanded underneath 5, and middle tibiae of male with spine. Adults active in summer; attracted to light. Underside dusky, rarely blackish. Maritime Provinces to Virginia, west to Minnesota and Illinois. (2)

Podabrus brevicollis **Fall** (10.5–12.5 mm) with yellowish-brown area in front of eye smooth, area between and behind eyes and neck dark, coarsely punctured; antennomeres 1–2 partly dark, remainder dark. Pronotum nearly twice as wide as long, side margins wide, smooth, broadly rounded, yellowish brown overall with coarsely punctured black spot narrowed in front and not or scarcely reaching front margin. Elytra dark with suture and side margins narrowly pale. Legs with femora yellowish brown, except for black tips, tibiae, and tarsi. Ontario to North Carolina, west to Ohio. (107 NA)

Podabrus brimleyi **(Green)** (7.0–10.0 mm) is blackish with mouthparts, top of head, and prothorax reddish brown, and margins of elytra narrowly brownish yellow. Back of head, center of pronotum, and elytra densely and coarsely punctured. Head of male nearly as wide as pronotum, female's distinctly narrower. Pronotum not much wider than long; male with dark spot closer to posterior margin, female without spot. Antennae and legs black except for pale bases. Adults are found late spring and summer on shrubs and vines; also attracted to light. New Jersey to Georgia, west to Indiana and Texas. (107 NA)

240

Podabrus rugosulus **LeConte** (7.0–8.0 mm) is elongate, mostly black with front of head and sides of pronotum yellow. Head shiny with coarse punctures becoming denser on neck. Pronotum with sides narrowed at middle to front, slightly notched at base, distinct narrow groove down middle, and broadly flattened yellow side margins. Elytra rough, widest at last third, with fine setae on surface and faint ridges. Tarsomere 4 deeply lobed, claws deeply notched. Underside, except mouthparts and sides of prothorax, black. Adults found on flowers and vegetation in spring. Maritime Provinces to Georgia, west to Minnesota and Kansas. (107 NA)

Rhagonycha longula **(LeConte)** (5.0–6.5 mm) is nearly or entirely pale yellowish brown. Head not constricted behind eyes, sometimes black behind. Antennae brown or black, first article pale, following articles paler at base, tip dusky. Elytra sometimes with faint oblique stripe from humerus to apex. Abdomen with posterior margin of seventh ventrite entire, not deeply notched. Tarsi, tibiae, and tips of femora dusky, third tarsomere simple, not notched at tip with fourth inserted apically, tibial spurs present; male protarsi broader, claws incised in both sexes. Adults active in late spring and early summer in wooded areas on flowers and vegetation; also attracted to light. Virginia to Florida. (34)

Rhagonycha mollis (Fall) (4.2–5.8 mm) is elongate, blackish, with brownish elytral margins and appendages. Head extended in front of eyes, especially in female, antennae more than half body length in both sexes, with middle antennomeres at least three times longer than wide. Prothorax entirely orange. Elytra long, sutural stripe broad at base, narrowed at tips. Tarsomere 3 simple, not notched or bilobed, with 4 inserted at tip, protarsal claws narrowly cleft, inner and outer blade separate at tips. Adults found on flowers and vegetation; attracted to light. Maritime Provinces to North Carolina, west to Ontario. (34)

Rhaxonycha carolina (Fabricius) (9.0–13.0 mm) is elongate, finely pubescent , black with pronotum pinkish or reddish along sides. Pronotum somewhat convex, smooth, sides narrowly flattened, black spot with sides straight, unbroken, converging toward head. Tarsomere 3 broadly notched, 4 attached before tip; claws deeply cleft. Adults prey on aphids, plant bugs, and other small foliage-visiting insects, also eat pollen and nectar; attracted to light. New England and Québec to Florida, west to Ontario, Minnesota, and Texas. *Rhaxonycha bilobata* (McKey-Fender) with pronotal spot narrowly lobed at sides; Québec to North Carolina, west to Minnesota and Oklahoma. (2)

Polemius laticornis (Say) (6.0–8.0 mm) is elongate-oblong, finely setose, black with pinkish-orange pronotal margins. Antennae serrate, longer in male. Head with suture between front and clypeus absent (male). Pronotum slightly wider than long, front angles apparent, side margins finely and shallowly notched just before middle, margins narrower in front. Elytra roughly sculptured, each with three faint ridges. Penultimate ventrite with deep, U-shaped notch. Outer claws with broad basal tooth, middle and hind outer claws not finely notched on tips. Adults found on low herbaceous vegetation in moist habitats in summer; at light. Pennsylvania to Florida, west to Illinois and Texas. Genus infrequently collected, needs revision. (3)

Silis bidentata (Say) (3.0–3.5 mm) is black with a reddish prothorax. Pronotum with impression in middle. Hind lobe on side margin of thorax evident before hind angles, distinct, somewhat rectangular in shape, and barely wider than front lobe. Adults found on low herbaceous growth during day from late spring through summer; attracted to light. Nova Scotia and Maine to Florida, west to Ontario, Ohio, and Mississippi. (1)

Tytthonyx erythrocephala **(Fabricius)** (3.5–4.0 mm) is mostly dull black and somewhat flattened. Head with front, back, and underside yellowish red. Antennae serrate, nearly as long as body. Prothorax wider than long, anterior margin straight, and posterior margin broadly rounded. Elytra half as long as abdomen. Adults are found from late spring through summer resting on foliage of various shrubs. New Jersey to Georgia, west to Indiana and Kansas. *Tytthonyx flavicollis* Blatchley and *T. furtiva* Blatchley both endemic to Florida. (4)

Malthinus occipitalis **LeConte** (2.5–3.5 mm) is long, slender, with short elytra tipped in lemon yellow. Head dark with mandibles and bases of antennae paler, rest of antennae dark. Pronotum wide as long, uniformly yellowish or with darker area in middle. Elytra short, about four times length of pronotum. Underside of body yellowish with legs paler. Incredibly agile adults found on oak leaves and grasses in low, moist habitats from spring through early summer. Massachusetts to Florida, west to Ohio and Texas. (4)

242

Malthodes fuliginosus **LeConte** (3.5–4.0 mm) is blackish with tips of clypeus and mandibles yellowish; scutellum, elytral tips, and legs sometimes lighter. Eyes large, antennae stout and reaching elytral tips, with antennomeres 1–2 yellowish brown. Pronotum dark with narrowly pale on front and rear margins, sometimes almost entirely yellow. Elytra short, sides straight before converging to tips, surface finely punctate at base, becoming coarser toward straight and oblique tips. Abdomen with tip rounded (male) or narrowly elongate (female). Adults found in spring on shrubs. Females best identified by association with males. Maritime Provinces and New England to North Carolina, west to Ontario, Michigan, and Tennessee. (21)

Margined Leatherwing *Chauliognathus marginatus* **(Fabricius)** (7.0–11.0 mm) is elongate, slender, parallel-sided, has an orange head with thick V-shaped mark. Pronotum longer than wide, side margins narrowly extended, with broad black stripe down middle reaching both apical and basal margins. Elytra with dark spots on apical half sometimes extending to base. Adults found on flowers or resting on vegetation in late spring and early summer. Massachusetts to Florida, west to Illinois and Texas. (2)

Goldenrod Soldier Beetle *Chauliognathus pensylvanicus* **(De Geer)** (9.0–12.0 mm) is elongate, slender, parallel sided, and a black head. Pronotum wider than long, side margins broadly extened, with black patch at basal half. Elytra with dark elytral spots on apical half sometimes extending to base. Adults feed on pollen from various flowers, especially goldenrod (*Solidago*), growing in gardens, parks, fields, and meadows and along roadsides and woodland edges in late summer and early fall. Often used as research subjects by scientists studying mating behavior, color polymorphism, dispersal, and genetics. Nova Soctia and New Brunswick to Florida, west to Ontario, Colorado, and Texas. (2)

Trypherus latipennis **(Germar)** (6.0–7.0 mm) is elongate, slender, and black with pronotal margins and elytral tips yellow. Pronotum slightly wider than long. Elytra short, about twice length of pronotum. Legs with tibial spurs. Tip of abdomen trilobed (female) or with asymmetrical plates (male). Adults active spring and early summer, found on flowers, e.g., catnip (*Nepeta*) and red haw (*Crataegus chrysocarpa*), herbaceous foliage in the understory of deciduous woodlands, and along streams, damp habitats. New York to North Carolina, west to Kansas, and Alabama. (5)

243

TOOTH-NECK FUNGUS BEETLES, FAMILY DERODONTIDAE
(DARE-OH-*DONT*-IH-DEE)

Derodontids generally inhabit moist, cool forests. Both adults and larvae of *Derodontus* feed on the fruiting bodies of basidiomycete fungi; *Laricobius* is not a fungivore, but a predator of adelgid aphids that feed on conifers. The European *Laricobius erichsoni* Rosenhauer and *L. nigrinus* Fender, a species native to western North America, were introduced into eastern North America for biological control of the balsam woolly adelgid (*Adelges picea*) and hemlock woolly adelgid (*A. tsugae*), respectively.

FAMILY DIAGNOSIS The combination of a pair of ocelli on head, antennae with loose club with three antennomeres, and serrate pronotal side margins (*Derodontus*), coarse surface sculpturing, rows of large and close-set punctures on elytra, and open middle coxal cavities are characteristic of adult derodontids. Abdomen with five ventrites free (*Derodontus*) or with 1–2 fused (*Laricobius*).

SIMILAR FAMILIES
- fruitworm beetles (Byturidae) – lack distinct rows of punctures on elytra (p.274)
- silken fungus beetles (Cryptophagidae) – lack ocelli and squarish elytral punctures (p.283)
- minute bark beetles (Cerylonidae) – antennae captitate (p.307)
- hairy fungus beetles (Mycetophagidae) – lack ocelli (p.323)

COLLECTING NOTES Derodontids are infrequently collected. *Derodontus* is usually found on fungi, under loose bark, and in Lindgren funnel traps during cool seasons of the year. *Laricobius* adults are found overwintering at the base of conifers infested with adelgids, or beaten from the branches of coniferous trees in spring and early summer.

FAUNA NINE SPECIES IN THREE GENERA (NA); FIVE SPECIES IN TWO GENERA (ENA)

Derodontus esotericus **Lawrence & Hlavac** (1.8–2.7 mm) is yellowish brown to dark reddish brown with variable dark markings and clothed in short, fine setae. Pronotum edged with five to eight straight toothlike projections. Elytra with 11 rows of squarish punctures, margins finely saw-toothed (serrulate). Legs short, hind tibiae tipped with pair of spurs, tarsi 5-5-5, tarsomeres 1–3 slender. Adults and larvae active in fall and spring, inhabit cool and humid forests, and feed on or just below surface of fresh or rotting fruiting bodies of basidiomycete fungi. Ontario to Alabama, west to Iowa and Texas. *Derodontus maculata* (Melsheimer) with sides of pronotum with prominent tooth directed backward at about apical third. (2)

Laricobius rubidus **LeConte** (2.0–2.5 mm) is clothed in long, erect setae, with reddish elytra margined in black. Pronotum without toothlike projections on margins. Elytra with 10 rows of round punctures, margins smooth. Legs short, hind tibiae tipped with setal comb, tarsi 4-4-4, tarsomeres distinctly lobed underneath. Adults and larvae inhabit cool, humid forests, and prey on conifer-feeding adelgids; adults also consume adelgid eggs and fungal hyphae and spores. Inhabits cooler, humid forests. Maritime Provinces to District of Columbia, west to Michigan. *Laricobius nigrinus* Fender is uniformly brownish or black, while *L. erichsoni* Rosenhauer has coarser elytral punctation. (3)

244

WOUNDED-TREE BEETLES, FAMILY NOSODENDRIDAE
(NO-SO-*DEN*-DRIH-DEE)

Adults and larvae of *Nosodendron unicolor* Say develop in fermented flows of hardwood sap teeming with microorganisms known as slime flux. Wounds oozing with slime flux are typically marked by black stained bark.

FAMILY DIAGNOSIS Adult nosodendrids are oval, compact, convex, black, with ability to retract appendages tightly against the body, flattened front legs with tibiae held in front of femur at rest, and distinct club with three antennomeres protected in cavities underneath the prothorax between the prolegs and sides. Abdomen with five ventrites not fused.

SIMILAR FAMILIES
- round fungus beetles (Leiodidae) – antennae loosely clavate (p.118)
- marsh beetles (Scirtidae) – antennae filiform to weakly serrate (p.180)
- pill beetles (Byrrhidae) – antennae filiform or clavate; dorsal surface scaled (p.195)
- *Chelonarium* (Chelonariidae) – mouthparts elongate; elytra with patches of setae (p.206)
- death-watch beetles (Ptinidae) – antennae longer, club asymmetrical (p.252)
- pleasing fungus beetles (Erotylidae) – elytra with rows of punctures (p.277)
- sap beetles (Nitidulidae) – elytra short with abdominal tergites exposed; front tibiae not expanded (p.295)
- *Hyporhagus* (Zopheridae) – elytra with rows of punctures (p.343)

COLLECTING NOTES Look for *Nosodendron* in slime flux flows on the trunks of deciduous hardwoods; also check below these trees in the leaf litter and sap-soaked soil.

FAUNA TWO SPECIES IN ONE GENUS (NA); ONE SPECIES, *NOSODENDRON UNICOLOR* SAY (ENA)

Nosodendron unicolor Say (5.0–5.7 mm) is rounded-oval, strongly convex, uniformly and densely punctate, compact with retractable appendages, and somewhat shiny black; clubbed antennae paler. Head underneath with mouthparts hidden under plate (mentum). Pronotum short, wide, with grooves underneath to receive antennae and front legs. Elytra with rows of short, erect, yellowish setae, not grooved. Front legs large, flat, covering mouthparts when retracted. Adults active spring and summer, found on slime flux on wounded deciduous trees and in sap-soaked soil below. Widespread in eastern North America. (1)

JACOBSONIID BEETLES, FAMILY JACOBSONIIDAE
(JAY-KOB-SOHN-*EE*-IH-DEE)

These beetles are very small and usually collected by specialized techniques; therefore, it is likely that they are more common and widely distributed than currently known. Only two species in one genus, *Derolathrus*, are known to occur in the United States. In other regions, adults and larvae are found under bark and in decaying wood, leaf litter, fungi, and bat guano. The sole described species from the United States, *Derolathrus cavernicolus* Peck, is associated with bat guano and leaf litter in subtropical and warm temperate forests.

245

FAMILY DIAGNOSIS Jacobsoniids are very small, elongate, narrow, yellowish brown, with an elongate pronotum narrowed behind and no visible scutellum, mesosternum as long or slightly longer than combined length of all five abdominal ventrites, and a tarsal forumula of 3-3-3.

SIMILAR FAMILIES The combination of small size, lack of visible scutellum, long mesosternum, and tarsal formula are characteristic of adult jacobsoniids and distinctive.

COLLECTING NOTES Adult *Derolathrus* have been collected in flight intercept traps, from leaf litter extractions, under bark, and on fungal fruting bodies and rotten palm trunks. In Florida, specimens of *D. cavernicolus* were extracted from bat guano collected in a cave and in a flight intercept trap in a hardwood hammock

FAUNA TWO SPECIES (INCLUDING ONE UNDESCRIBED SPECIES) IN ONE GENUS (NA)

Derolathrus cavernicolus Peck (0.8–0.9 mm) is very small, elongate, and yellowish brown, with head and pronotum with large, scattered seta-bearing punctures. Head oval, bent down, with Y-shaped or somewhat triangular impression on top. Prothorax longer than wide, slightly wider than head, narrowed in rear, with deep linear depression down middle. Elytra broadest at middle, each with pit at base followed by groove along suture, and tips somewhat blunt. Southern Florida. (1)

SKIN BEETLES, FAMILY DERMESTIDAE
(DER-*MESS*-TIH-DEE)

Most adult and larval dermestids are largely scavengers of protein and often associated with fur, feathers, and organic debris in animal nests, or on carcasses. A few species feed on cork, seeds, grains, and other cereal products. Adults, especially *Orphilus*, feed largely on pollen and nectar. Some species (*Anthrenus, Attagenus*) will enter homes and other buildings in spring and summer to lay their eggs, where their larvae damage woolen materials, carpets, silk products, dried meats, and museum specimens including insect collections. Household reinfestations may stem from undetected natural reservoirs immediately outside, such as bird, mammal, or paper wasp nests. Indoors, dead insects in spider webs, windowsills, and light fixtures may become dermestid breeding grounds. Some species (*Dermestes*) are used by natural history museums around the world to clean animal skeletons for use in research collections and exhibits.

FAMILY DIAGNOSIS Adult dermestids are usually oblong or oval, compact, robust, and clothed in black, brown, tan, and white setae or scales, and have a single simple eye (ocellus) between the compound eyes. Head retracted within prothorax, with or without (*Dermestes*) ocellus, and mouthparts directed downward. Antennae with 11 (nine in *Dearthrus*) antennomeres, 9–11, sometimes more, forming loose or compact club, or not (*Thylodrias*). Pronotum broader than long, narrowed to head, underside with grooves to receive antennae. Elytra clothed in setae or scales, and completely covering abdomen, or absent (female *Thylodrias*). Hind legs with coxae excavated to receive femora, tarsal formula 5-5-5, claws equal in size and simple. Abdomen with five or seven (*Thylodrias*) ventrites.

SIMILAR FAMILIES No beetles similar in form have an ocellus.

- plate-thigh beetles (Eucinetidae) – antennae filiform, not clubbed (p.178)
- marsh beetles (Scirtidae) – antennae not clubbed (p.180)

- wounded-tree beetles (Nosodendridae) – front tibia broad, flat (p.244)
- death-watch beetles (Ptinidae) – antennae long, if clubbed then antennomeres lopsided (p.252)
- *Hyporhagus* (Zopheridae) – elytra with rows of punctures, tarsi 5-5-4 (p.343)
- seed beetles (Chrysomelidae: Bruchinae) – head elongate with short rostrum; pygidium exposed (p.429)

COLLECTING NOTES *Orphilus* and other small, flower-visiting dermestids are commonly hand-collected or swept from plants with dense clusters of flowers, such as yarrow (*Achillea*), spirea (*Spiraea*), New Jersey tea (*Ceanothus*), hydrangea (*Hydrangea*), and various species in the carrot family (Apiaceae). Species of *Anthrenus* and *Attagenus* are found indoors on windowsills of homes and other buildings with infested animal products. All stages of *Dermestes* are found on or underneath carcasses, whereas the adults are occasionally taken at lights.

FAUNA 117 SPECIES IN 17 GENERA (NA); 50 SPECIES IN 13 GENERA (ENA)

Dermestes caninus **Germar** (5.5–8.5 mm) is elongate-oblong, black, with dense black, gray, and reddish-brown pubescence on pronotum and elytra. Head without ocellus. Pronotum completely covered with pubescence, with three small white spots across middle. Abdomen with whitish pubescence and black spots on sides. Middle and hind femora with a white ring. Adults and larvae found on caracasses in various habitats; adults attracted to light. Widely distributed in southern Canada and United States. (13)

Larder Beetle *Dermestes lardarius* **Linnaeus** (5.0–9.0 mm) is oblong, black, clothed in setae, with basal three-fifths of each elytron with dense grayish setae enclosing three dark broad spots; underside and legs black, clothed in fine yellowish pubescence. Head without ocelli, antennae clubbed. Pronotum dark, plain, without sharp ridges along sides, and completely clothed in dark pubescence. Bases of front legs large and touching; hind femora clearly received in coxal groove. Adults and larvae found on carrion, and in bird and wasp nests; pest of stored animal products such as pet foods, dried meats, and hides; preys on eggs masses of gypsy moth (*Lymantria dispar*). Eastern North America. (13)

Orphilus ater Erichson (2.3–2.8 mm) is small, somewhat oval, compact with retractable appendages, and shiny black with upper surface coarsely punctate; clubbed antennae reddish brown. Head with a simple eye on top, inserted into prothorax. Scutellum large and oval. Pronotum at base as wide as elytra, with basal margin lobed at middle. Elytra with surface rough, base more coarse and dense. Underside of body somewhat convex. Larvae found in dead wood and probably feed on fungi. Adults active spring and summer, found on flowering plants and shrubs. New Hampshire and Québec to Florida, west to Ontario, Wisconsin, and Arkansas. (1)

247

Odd Beetle *Thylodrias contractus* **Motschulsky** (2.1–5.2 mm) is aptly named and the most physically aberrant of dermestid beetles. Both sexes have antennae with nine antennomeres, seven abdominal ventrites, and a simple eye between the compound eyes. Most males have reduced flight wings; females lack all wings. Strictly associated with humans. They feed on skins, hides, fur, feathers, silk, and wool and are minor pest in homes, markets, butcher shops, and insect collections. Rare; collections usually consist of larvae or individual males.Asia; probably established throughout North America. (1)

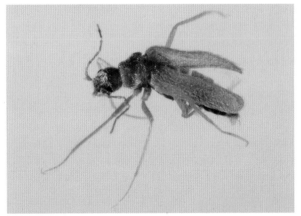

Anthrenus pimpinellae (*Fabricius*) (2.0–3.0 mm) is broadly oval, with sides of elytra distinctly rounded and covered with white, golden, and dark golden brown to nearly black scales. Antennae with 11 antennomeres, 9–11 forming club. Pronotum flanked by oval patches of dark scales surrounded by white scales. Elytra usually with white band at basal third narrower at suture than lateral margin and golden brown suture extending from basal third or middle to apex. Larvae develop in bird nests outdoors; also in woolens and insect collections indoors in Europe. Adults found on flowers in spring. Northeastern United States. (8)

Anthrenus verbasci (**Linnaeus**) (2.0–3.0 mm) is oblong-oval, moderately convex, with variable patterns of long, narrow scales. Antennae with antennomeres 9–11 forming club. Most individuals covered with white, yellowish, and dark brown to black scales; occasionally with few or no yellow scales or with mostly white and golden scales. Elytral bands, if present, include yellowish scales and patches of white scales. Infests insect collections and insect remains in spider webs, an occasional pest in alfalfa leaf-cutting bee nests; sometimes preys on gypsy moth eggs; also reared from mud dauber wasp nests. Adults eat pollen. Widespread in North America. (8)

Cryptorhopalum **species** (2.0–3.0 mm) are small, ovate, evenly convex, sparsely pubescent, blackish or black, with retractable appendages. Head underneath with mouthparts mostly covered by prothoracic process. Antennal club with two antennomeres. Pronotum punctate on either side of basal lobe, underneath with deep grooves for accepting antennae bound in rear by thin ridge. Hind coxae excavated to receive femora. Adults feed on pollen and nectar and are collected on many flowering plants and shrubs. Females best identified through association with males. Widespread in eastern North America. (4)

Trogoderma glabrum (**Herbst**) (2.0–3.5 mm) is oblong-oval, dark brown or black, coarsely pubescent, with narrow golden brown and white pubescent bands across elytra. Head with eyes emarginate in front and ocellus on front of head. Antennae with 11 articles, 3–10 gradually wider in male, with 3 less than half as wide as 2. Band at base of elytron looped or appearing as vague humeral spot, middle band often uninterrupted and expanded at suture. Legs with first hind tarsomere long as second. Once a major pest of granaries, now kept in check by a parasitic wasp, *Mattesia trogodermae*. Europe; widely established in North America. (8)

Trogoderma ornatum (**Say**) (1.9–3.6 mm) is oblong-oval, shining black, with variegated patterns of coarse and erect black, reddish brown, and white setae on dorsal surface, underside with ashy gray pubescence; appendages blackish to light brown. Head with eyes oval and ocellus on front of head. Antennae with 11 articles, 5–10 serrate in male with 2–4 subequal in size. Elytra punctate with irregular patches and bands of setae. Legs with first hind tarsomere long as second. Adults occasionally found in homes and museums; larvae develop mostly outdoors on dead insects; sometimes feed on spider eggs. Québec and Ontario to Florida, west to Minnesota, Nebraska, and Texas. (8)

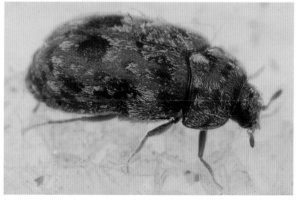

ENDECATOMID BEETLES, FAMILY ENDECATOMIDAE
(EN-DEH-KAH-*TOE*-MIH-DEE)

This family is represented in North America by one genus, *Endecatomus*, previously placed in the Bostrichidae. Adults and larvae bore into the fruiting bodies of various bracket fungi, including *Phellinus gilvus*, *Bjerkandera adusta*, and *Fomes fomentarius*.

FAMILY DIAGNOSIS Adult endecatomids are oblong, convex, and somewhat cylindrical; dorsal surface smooth with scattered miscroscopic bumps, each bearing a stout seta, and the side margins of pronotum flattened and fringed with stiff setae.

SIMILAR FAMILIES
- hide beetles (Trogidae) – antennae lamellate (p.147)
- twig and branch borers (Bostrichidae) – side of pronotum not expanded; elytral surface not smooth with scattered setose bumps (p.250)
- some death-watch beetles (Ptinidae) – antennae long (p.252)

COLLECTING NOTES Look for *Endecatomus* on bracket fungi and on dead or dying trees at night; also attracted to light.

FAUNA TWO SPECIES IN ONE GENUS (NA)

Endecatomus rugosus (Randall) (3.0–5.0 mm) is uniformly dark reddish brown to black, upper surface densely covered with small bumps bearing yellowish curled and nearly erect setae. Pronotum convex, with side margins somewhat flattened and fringed with stiff setae. Elytra with side margins bearing row of long, curved setae. Adults found at night in late spring and summer on snags infested with polypore fungi (*Polyporus*); larvae develop within fungi. Maine to Florida, west to Manitoba and Texas. *Endecatomus dorsalis* Mellié (4.5–5.0 mm) with setae along sides of elytra short and straight; southern Illinois to Alabama, west to Oklahoma and Texas. (2)

BOSTRICHID BEETLES, FAMILY BOSTRICHIDAE
(BAW-*STRICK*-IH-DEE)

Bostrichids, also known as twig or branch borers and powder-post beetles, develop in dead branches, living trees, or fire-killed wood. Some species prefer old wood, whereas others attack cut and seasoned wood. The tunneling activities of some larvae are particularly damaging to old dwellings and furniture. Others mine living limbs of weakened cultivated trees or tunnel through green shoots of living plants. Because of their tendency to bore into wood products, bostrichid beetles are widely distributed around the world through commerce. Some species (*Rhyzopertha*) cause considerable damage to stored products, especially dried roots and grains. The feeding galleries of adults and larvae of many species are filled with coarse dust mixed with waste and wood fragments. The fine "post" of powdery frass left behind in the tunnels of some species (*Lyctus, Trogoxylon*) suggested the common name powder-post beetles. The closely placed round exit holes of some species inspired another common name, "shot hole borers." Many bostrichids maintain intracellular bacteria in special organs called mycetomes located inside the midgut that aid in the digestion of wood. Larval bostrichids are especially tolerant of extremely low-moisture environments.

FAMILY DIAGNOSIS Most adult bostrichids are distinguished from other beetles in eastern North America by their narrow to broadly cylindrical bodies, strongly convex and hoodlike pronotum, and downward-deflected head not visible from above. Powder-post beetles (*Lyctus, Trogoxylon*) have completely exposed heads with a somewhat flattened prothorax with distinctly margined or keeled sides. Head with mandibles exposed and clubbed antennae with 11 antennomeres, those of club often enlarged on one side. Hoodlike pronotum sometimes rough, toothed, or with hornlike projections in front. Elytra parallel-sided, coarsely or finely punctate, with rows of punctures or ridges, sharp bumps or spines on tips, and completely concealing abdomen; tips may or may not appear abruptly cut off. Tarsal formula 5-5-5, claws equal in size, toothed. Abdomen with five ventrites.

SIMILAR FAMILIES

- endecatomid beetles (Endecatomidae) – sides of pronotum expanded; elytra surface smooth with scattered setose bumps (p.249)
- some death-watch beetles (Ptinidae) – antennae serrate or flabellate (p.252)
- minute tree fungus beetles (Ciidae) – antennae with symmetrical club (p.326)
- cylindrical bark beetles (Zopheridae: Colydiinae) – mandibles concealed; tarsi 5-5-4 (p.340)
- bark or ambrosia beetles (Curculionidae) – antennal club compact (p.469)

COLLECTING NOTES Adult bostrichids are commonly found at lights, netted on the wing, or occasionally beaten from infested dead branches. Wood- and bark-feeding species are best found by gathering infested materials and storing them in rearing chambers. Check wooden furniture for exit holes and powdery residue. Bostrichids emerging indoors are attracted to sunny windows and found dead on windowsills.

FAUNA 77 SPECIES IN 26 GENERA (NA); 32 SPECIES IN 16 GENERA (ENA)

Apple Twig Borer *Amphicerus bicaudatus* (Say) (6.0–13.0 mm) is elongate, cylindrical, and uniformly reddish brown, chestnut, brownish black, or black. Dorsal surface sparsely clothed in short, recumbent, yellowish setae. Males have a pair of forward-projecting hornlike tubercles on pronotum and a small tubercle on tip of each elytron. Larvae develop in dying or diseased wood of deciduous trees and will tunnel in cut and dying branches and exposed roots. Adults occasionally tunnel in healthy wood to seek shelter, overwinter in larval galleries; at light in spring and early summer. Eastern North America. (2)

Lichenophanes bicornis (**Weber**) (7.0–12.0 mm) is elongate, cylindrical, dark reddish brown, with antennae and tarsi sometimes lighter. Head much narrower than pronotum. Antennae with 10 antennomeres. Pronotum widest near middle, with two hooklike processes, surface with small, round bumps at basal half becoming rasplike at front. Elytra with small bumps and distinct inner ridge extending from base to apical slope. Adults attracted to light in summer. Larve develop in dead twigs and branches of various hardwoods. Widespread in eastern North America, northeast to Cape Breton Island, Nova Scotia. (4)

Red-shouldered Bostrichid *Xylobiops basilaris* (**Say**) (3.3–7.0 mm) is brownish black to reddish brown with bases of elytra reddish yellow to brownish yellow; tips of each elytron with three conspicuous teeth. Adults bore into bark and sapwood, and are attracted to light in summer. Larvae develop in branches and twigs of a variety of deciduous hardwoods, shrubs, and vines; conifers sometimes attacked. Southeastern Canada and New York to Florida, west to Kansas and Texas. (1)

Prostephanus punctatus (**Say**) (4.0–5.0 mm) is elongate, cylindrical, pale reddish brown to brownish black with appendages paler. Head partly covered by prothorax. Pronotum evenly convex, without distinct side margins, with vague groove down middle, sides with rows of small teeth, widest at basal third. Elytra with long reclining setae, with tips appearing cut off and flat, and each usually with one or two short bumps. Front tibiae each with one spur on tip, tarsomere 1 long and equal in length to 2. Larva develops in roots and stumps of oak (*Quercus*) and pecan (*Carya*). Adults active in summer; attracted to light. Widespread in eastern North America. (1)

Rhyzopertha dominica (**Fabricius**) (2.0–3.0 mm) is elongate, cylindrical, clothed in yellowish setae, shining, and uniformly dark reddish brown to brownish black; appendages sometimes lighter. Head slightly convex, partly covered by prothorax, not visible from above. Pronotum distinctly and uniformly convex, widest near middle, front half with arched rows of broadly rounded teeth, those nearest front forming a raised and notched ridge, rear half with flattened granules. Elytra at base almost equal in length to pronotum, with rows of coarse, deep punctures. Adults and larvae infest stored grains and various vegetable foods, especially cereals. Cosmopolitan. (1)

Southern Lyctus Beetle *Lyctus planicollis* LeConte (2.5–6.0 mm) is elongate, slender, somewhat straight-sided, and clothed in fine, reclining setae. Head visible, slightly pointed downward, narrower than pronotum, antennal club stout, antennomere 10 wider than long. Pronotum shallowly punctate, slightly wider than long, narrower than elytra, with sharply defined side margins, interstriae distinct hind angles, and a deep groove down middle at base. Elytra grooved, interstriae with two rows of punctures. Larva develops in dead oak (*Quercus*), hickory (*Carya*), and ash (*Fraxinus*) branches; also attacks hardwood flooring, cabinets, and tool handles. Southern Canada and United States. (6)

Trogoxylon parallelopipedum (Melsheimer) (2.5–5.0 mm) is elongate, slender, somewhat parallel-sided, sparsely clothed in yellowish pubescence, and dull reddish brown. Pronotum slightly wider than long, slightly narrowed behind, with surface faintly impressed, coarsely punctate, front margin broadly arched, angles sharp, and hind angles distinct. Elytra irregularly punctate, punctures fine and dense, with sides slightly widened toward rear. Hind femora enlarged. Larvae develop in branches and trunks of honeylocust (*Gleditsia*), persimmon (*Diospyros*), hickory (*Carya*), oak (*Quercus*), and osage orange (*Maclura*); also wood products. Throughout eastern United States, Ontario. (3)

252

DEATH-WATCH AND SPIDER BEETLES, FAMILY PTINIDAE
(*TIN*-IH-DEE)

The family Ptinidae includes the group formerly known as Anobiidae. The name used for one species, the "death-watch" beetle, is based on the behavior of the European furniture beetle, *Anobium punctatum* (De Geer), where the males strike their heads against the pronotum to produce a series of audible clicks often heard during hushed, deathbed vigils. Important ptinid pests of stored products include the cigarette beetle, *Lasioderma serricorne* (Fabricius), and the drugstore beetle, *Stegobium paniceum* (Linnaeus). They cause considerable economic damage by infesting drugs, tobacco, seeds, spices, cereals, and leather. Larval ptinids attack hardwoods and softwoods, boring into bark, dry wood, twigs, seeds, woody fruits, and galls. A few species feed on woody fungi or puffballs or attack young stems and shoots of growing trees. Some species store symbiotic yeastlike organisms in special pouches in their midgut that aid the digestion of wood. Spider beetles have inflated elytra conspicuously wider than the pronotum, giving them a spiderlike appearance. Most spider beetles feed on accumulations of plant and animal materials, especially in nests. This includes pollen in the nests of solitary bees or in animal dung. They are sometimes household pests, infesting stored flour, cereal products, wool, and other similar dried plant or animal materials.

FAMILY DIAGNOSIS Adult ptinids are short with head strongly pointed down and a hoodlike prothorax, or spiderlike with head directed somewhat downward, head and prothorax either narrower than elytra or about the same width, very convex elytra, and long legs and antennae; legs often fit in grooves on underside. Antennae usually with 11 antennomeres; club, if present, lopsided, especially in male. Often clothed in fine scales or setae. Elytra with surface smooth or rough, with grooves or rows of punctures present or absent. Tarsal formula 5-5-5, claws equal and simple. Abdomen usually with five ventrites.

SIMILAR FAMILIES

- skin beetles (Dermestidae) – antennae with symmetrical club (p.246)
- endecatomid beetles (Endecatomidae) – sides of pronotum expanded; elytra surface smooth with scattered setose bumps (p.249)
- bostrichid beetles (Bostrichidae) – antennae short with compact club (p.250)
- minute tree fungus beetles (Ciidae) – antennae with symmetrical club (p.326)
- bark beetles (Curculionidae: Scolytinae) – antennae with symmetrical club (p.469)

COLLECTING NOTES Death-watch beetles are usually collected in small numbers, either at lights, or by beating and sweeping vegetation, or rearing from infested wood and fungus. Spider beetles living indoors are found in stored organic products or in related debris. Outdoors a few might be taken with similar techniques used for death-watch beetles as well as in pitfall traps, animal nests, or dried dung.

FAUNA 471 SPECIES IN 61 GENERA (NA); 110 SPECIES IN 32 GENERA (ENA)

Smooth Spider Beetle *Gibbium aequinoctiale* **Boieldieu** (1.7–3.2 mm) is shiny reddish brown to nearly black, humpbacked, with short, dense, yellowish setae on legs. Head, thorax, and elytra completely bare. Elytra more than twice as wide as four abdominal ventrites when viewed from underneath. Larva develops in woolens and dried animal products. Adults found in homes, hotels, warehouses. Adults and larvae eat cereals, stored grains, stale bread, dry pet food, and many other stored food products. Widely distributed Mediterranean species found on all continents except Antarctica. (1)

Northern Spider Beetle *Mezium affine* **Boieldieu** (2.3–2.5 mm) is shiny dark red with head, pronotum, base of elytra, and appendages densely setose. Pronotum with broad shallow groove down middle becoming wider toward elytra. Elytra with setose base or collar entire, not broken or interrupted. Hind legs with trochanter about one-third length of hind femur. Abdomen with five ventrites. Adults associated with seeds, dead insects, and decaying animal and plant matter. North African; now established Southeastern Canada and northeastern United States. (2)

White-marked Spider Beetle *Ptinus fur* **Linnaeus** (2.0–4.3 mm) is elongate and slender (male) or stout and oval (female), and pale to dark reddish brown. Eyes large, especially in male. Prothorax distinctly constricted posteriorly, without distinctly shining areas, with pair of dense rows of yellowish setae, rows not raised above surface, often forming a U or V. Elytra with angles prominent, punctures in elytral grooves bearing setae; female flightless. Legs of male longer, more slender than female. Found year-round in homes, granaries, warehouses, and museums. Europe; widely established in North America. (14)

Ptinus quadrimaculatus **(Melsheimer)** (3.0–3.8 mm) is mostly reddish black with pale reddish appendages. First antennomere thick, second smallest, and 3–11 long and nearly equal in length; male antennae as long as body. Pronotum narrower than elytra. Elytra elongate and somewhat straight-sided; clothed in scales and both erect and reclining setae with broad black band at middle interrupted at suture. Adults are found in spring and summer on dead branches and at light. Massachusetts to Georgia, west to Ohio and Texas. (14)

Eucrada humeralis **(Melsheimer)** (4.0–6.5 mm) is elongate, oblong, dull black, with center of pronotum and basal elytral angles orangish. Head with gray or yellow setae, male with antennae pectinate, female serrate. Pronotum wider than long, sides without keeled margins. Elytra with rows of close-set punctures, spaces between narrow, barely convex and pubescent. Larva bores into the bark and wood of oak (*Quercus*). Adults found on bark of oaks. Maine and Québec to South Carolina, west to Ontario, Iowa, and Kentucky. (1)

Ernobius granulatus **LeConte** (2.3–4.3 mm) is elongate, reddish brown with elytra becoming yellowish at tip. Head without narrow ridge over antennal bases in front of eyes, eyes large and convex in male, last three antennomeres long, antennomere 5 nearly equal in length to 4 and much shorter than 3. Prothorax with distinct margin along entire side, pronotum with narrow impression down middle lacking setae. Elytra coarsely punctate, with front edge of puncture raised to give surface a granular appearance, becomes sparser and finer at tip. Legs with tarsi shorter than tibiae, bases of front legs touching. Larvae generally develop in pine cones (*Pinus*). Adults found under bark, attracted to light. Massachusetts to Florida, west to Pennsylvania and Texas. (7)

Furniture Beetle *Anobium punctatum* **(De Geer)** (2.7–4.0 mm) is elongate, clothed in short yellowish-gray pubescence lying on surface, and reddish brown to blackish brown. Antennae filiform, antennomeres each long and cylindrical. Head deeply inserted in prothorax, with prominent bump on top, and mandibles not directed back under body. Pronotum with sides sharply margined or keeled and raised behind, underneath with surface concave and bases of forelegs widely separated. Elytra with grooves deeply punctate. Abdomen underneath with grooves much more visible at sides than middle. Claws simple. Adults and larvae found in many hardwoods and conifers; also infests beams, flooring, furniture. Europe, widely distributed in North America. (1)

Hadrobregmus notatus (Say) (3.2–4.0 mm) is elongate, subcylindrical, dark brown with distinct pattern on elytra. Upper surface covered with short, fine, somewhat reclining pubescence. Adults are found on dead branches and are attracted to lights in late spring and summer. Larvae develop in dead and rotten wood, including oak (*Quercus*), ash (*Fraxinus*), pine (*Pinus*), and pine boards. Nova Scotia to North Carolina, west to Ontario, Ohio, and Mississippi. (1)

Hemicoelus carinatus (Say) (3.5–6.5 mm) is oblong, somewhat cylindrical, reddish black to brownish black. Pronotum slightly narrower than elytra, side margins completely keeled, surface coarsely punctate, granulate, with low conelike hump on middle near base. Elytra with rows of deep and close-set punctures. Adults active in spring and summer, found on decaying logs of maple (*Acer*), beech (*Fagus*), and other deciduous hardwoods. Maritime Provinces and New England to North Carolina, west to Manitoba, Iowa, and Missouri. (5)

Drugstore Beetle *Stegobium paniceum* (Linnaeus) (2.0–3.5 mm) is oblong, reddish to reddish brown. Head concealed from above by pronotum. Antennal club longer than preceding antennomeres combined, 9–11 each somewhat elongate and slightly expanded at tips. Prothorax with side margins distinctly keeled, underneath with sides concave. Elytra long with distinct rows of elongate punctures. Bases of front legs widely separated. Common pest in homes, commercial food-distribution and processing facilities. Adults and larvae infest a variety of stored food products and dried plant and animal materials, including museum specimens. Cosmopolitan; widely distributed in North America. (1)

Trichodesma gibbosa (Say) (4.5–6.8 mm) is densely covered with long white setae; tufts on pronotum and elytra partly brownish yellow to reddish brown. Adults found on foliage of various deciduous trees and shrubs in summer; also attracted to light. Larvae bore into twigs and branches of various hardwoods; occasionally infest structural timbers in historic buildings made of sweetgum (*Liquidambar styraciflua*). Québec to Florida, west to Wisconsin and Texas. *Trichodesma klagesi* Fall (5.7–6.7 mm) with tufts of setae on pronotum and elytra uniformly dark brown; Pennsylvania to Virginia, west to Ohio and Kentucky. (2)

Ptilinus ruficornis **Say** (2.8–5.0 mm) is cylindrical, blackish or black and clothed in short, fine, appressed setae; antennae and legs reddish yellow, femora sometimes darker. Third antennomere elongate and cylindrical; males with antennomeres 4–10 with long flat branches, branch of fourth antennomere six or seven times longer than antennomere, female antennae pectinate. Pronotum with side margin defined and even throughout. Elytra not wider than thorax. Abdomen with distinct ridge just before tip of last tergites. Adults found mostly in spring and summer on dead branches of oak (*Quercus*), maple (*Acer*), and other hardwoods; larvae burrow, feed, and develop in these branches. Nova Scotia to Florida, west to Alberta and Alabama. (3)

TOP RIGHT: *Ptilinus ruficornis* male.
BOTTOM RIGHT: *Ptilinus ruficornis* female.

256

Euvrilletta harrisii **Fall** (3.7–5.5 mm) is elongate, robust, reddish brown with moderately dense yellow pubescence that is not erect. Antennomeres 9–11 about equal in length to 5–8. Pronotum with sides distinctly rounded, keeled margins broadly upturned. Elytra deeply and narrowly grooved, spaces between slightly convex. Southeastern Canada and northeastern United States. Massachusetts and New Hampshire to New Jersey, west to Michigan, Indiana, and Kentucky. (4)

Cigarette Beetle *Lasioderma serricorne* **(Fabricius)** (1.8–3.0 mm) is oval, uniformly light yellowish brown to reddish brown, and humpbacked with serrate antennae and smooth elytra. Body clothed in short, dense, yellowish pubescence. Elytra with faint rows of erect pubescence. Front legs with tibiae distinctly widened and flattened toward tips. Larvae and adults found in various dried plant products, including tobacco products, herbarium specimens, flour, spices, grains, cereals, etc. Larva pupates in silken cocoon. Cosmopolitan. (4)

Byrrhodes incomptus LeConte (2.0–2.5 mm) is oval, somewhat elongate, shiny brown or blackish, with recumbent yellowish-gray setae; head, pronotum, underside, and legs sometimes reddish with antennae and tarsi lighter. Head with eyes slightly notched, antennae with 10 antennomeres, 8 and 9 triangular. Elytra each with only two distinct grooves from apices to back legs, surface with rows of fine, close-set punctures separated by lines of smooth areas, and grooves along sides distinct only from base to hind legs. Massachusetts to Florida, west to Illinois. (8)

Caenocara oculata (Say) (1.8–2.3 mm) is nearly circular, very convex, shiny black, sparsely and coarsely punctate, with nearly erect yellowish setae. Head and pronotum more or less reddish, appendages reddish brown. Eyes similar in both sexes, deeply notched and nearly divided. Outer margins of elytra with two nearly complete grooves with a third inner groove barely reaching middle. Adults are found in late spring and summer on low vegetation and shrubs in damp habitats, as well as in puffballs (*Calvatia*, *Lycoperdon*, *Sclerodema*) where the larvae develop. Disturbed beetles tuck in their heads and appendages, resembling small, bristly seeds. Nova Scotia and New Brunswick to North Carolina, west to Minnesota, Kansas, and Arizona. (8)

257

Dorcatoma pallicornis LeConte (2.6–3.2 mm) is elongate-oval, shining black, with scattered recumbent pubescence on upper surface and reddish legs. Head and pronotum finely punctured. Head with 10 antennomeres, 8–10 enlarged, more so in male. Prothorax short, surface underneath with grooves on each side to receive antennae. Elytra with humeri prominent, punctures confused, two grooves on each side nearly complete, a short groove visible at base. New Hampshire to Georgia, west to Michigan, Kansas, and Lousiana. (3)

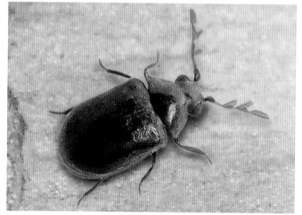

Protheca hispida LeConte (1.5–2.5 mm) is oblong-oval, dull reddish brown to brown, with rather dense, dull yellow and uniformly bristling pubescence. Head above with two sizes of punctures and excavated underneath to receive antennae, antennae with 11 antennomeres, 9–11 greatly enlarged to form club. Pronotum most convex behind middle when viewed from side, and finely punctate, punctures denser at sides. Elytra with vague rows of large punctures, spaces between with dense, obscure punctures variable in size becoming more conspicuous at sides. Abdominal sutures at least apparent at sides and middle. New York to Florida, west to Kentucky and Arkansas. (2)

Priobium sericeum **(Say)** (4.9–6.2 mm) is somewhat elongate, reddish brown to brown, with surfaces granular and clothed in short, appressed, moderately dense yellowish setae. Head convex, deeply withdrawn into prothorax; antennomeres 3–7 distinctly saw-toothed, 8–10 less so, 11 narrow and elongate, 9–11 not longer than preceeding 5. Pronotum with faint groove to just behind middle. Elytral grooves with deep, squarish punctures. Abdomen underneath with sutures between segments distinct at sides, weak at middle, middle with large seta-bearing ring-shaped punctures with shiny centers. Bases of front legs separated. Develops in dead branches of hardwoods, may damage flooring, furniture, and other woodwork. Eastern United States. (4)

Tricorynus **species** (1.6–3.9 mm) are oblong, convex, compact, shining or dull light reddish brown to reddish black, with sparse to dense yellowish or grayish pubescence often rubbed off in patches; appendages paler. Head slanted back, eyes not deeply notched, and antennae clubbed, with 10 antennomeres, antennal bases in front of each eye and far apart. Sides of pronotum sharp, complete. Elytra grooved only at sides near tips. Underside with bases of front legs hidden, front of metasternum grooved to receive middle legs, hind legs capable of tucking between raised posterior margin of thorax and abdomen. Difficult to identify without careful examination of appendages. Adults active in spring and summer; attracted to light. Widespread in eastern North America. (27)

258

SHIP-TIMBER BEETLES, FAMILY LYMEXYLIDAE
(LIE-MEH-*ZYE*-LIH-DEE)

The larvae of lymexylids bore and develop in sapwood and heartwood of dead hardwoods, especially oak (*Quercus*). The chestnut timberworm, *Melittomma sericeum* (Harris) was once a destructive pest of chestnut logs when chestnut trees were common. *Elateroides lugubris* larvae, commonly known as sapwood timberworms, feed in the sapwood of various deciduous hardwoods, especially freshly cut *Populus* logs. Both species are thought to feed on symbiotic fungi growing on the walls of their tunnels and originally deposited by the egg-laying female. Adults of both species are found on tree trunks or under bark.

FAMILY DIAGNOSIS Adult lymexylids are elongate, narrow, and nearly cylindrical (*Melittomma*) or somewhat flattened (*Elateroides*), with short filiform or serrate antennae, expanded and fanlike maxillary palps (male), and long, cylindrical, and projecting prothoracic coxae. Elytra long, without grooves, sometimes weakly ridged, loose-fitting, with parallel sides, and covering most of abdomen. Tarsal formula 5-5-5, tarsi slender, claws equal in size and simple. Abdomen with five (*Melittomma*, male *Elateroides*) or six (female *Elateroides*) ventrites.

SIMILAR FAMILIES

- some fireflies (Lampyridae) – antennae long, filiform (p.234)
- some soldier beetles (Cantharidae) – antennae long, filiform (p.238)
- some blister beetles (Meloidae) – antennae long, filiform; tarsi 5-5-4 (p.365)
- some longhorn beetles (Cerambycidae: Lepturinae) – antennae long, filiform (p.388)

COLLECTING NOTES These seldom-collected beetles are sometimes attracted to lights. Peeling bark of decaying logs or examining boles at night may produce additional adults.

FAUNA TWO SPECIES IN TWO GENERA (NA)

Sapwood Timberworm *Elateroides lugubris* (Say) (10.0–12.0 mm) is elongate, slender, uniformly dark reddish brown to black, sometimes with base of elytra paler; upper surfaces punctate with short setae. Appendages and abdomen pale, outer antennomeres darker. Top of head with small, deep line down middle. Maxillary palp ornate in male, simple in female. Abdomen with six (male) or seven (female) ventrites. Larvae bore into heartwood of poplar (*Populus*), birch (*Betula*), oak (*Quercus*), and elm (*Ulmus*); found in association with *Ascoides* fungi growing on tunnel walls. Adults active in summer, found in decaying wood, under bark, and running on tree trunks. Maritime Provinces to New York, west to Ontario and Indiana. (1)

Chestnut Timberworm *Melittomma sericeum* (Harris) (11.0–15.0 mm) is elongate, slender, somewhat cylindrical, clothed in fine pale pubescence, and brown or blackish brown with downward-pointed head. Eyes large, mouthparts comblike (male) or simple (female), antennae half combined length of head and pronotum. Pronotum longer than wide, round in front, sides sharply margined, and sloped down toward head. Elytra long, parallel-sided, densely and irregularly punctate. Appendages and underside paler. Larva develops in decayed oak (*Quercus*), elm (*Ulmus*), and chestnut (*Castanea*). Nocturnal adults active in summer, found under bark; attracted to light. Maine to North Carolina, west to Illinois, Missouri, and Tennessee. (1)

259

BARK-GNAWING BEETLES AND CADELLES, FAMILY TROGOSSITIDAE
(TRO-GO-*SIT*-IH-DEE)

Trogossitids are found under the bark of dead trees, logs, and stumps. Longer, slender, and cylindrical species (*Airora*) are specialist predators of bark beetles (Curculionidae), while larger and somewhat flatter species (*Temnoscheila*, *Tenebroides*) prey on all kinds of wood-boring beetles and their larvae. Both adults and larvae of the cadelle, *Tenebroides mauritanicus* (Linnaeus), are cosmopolitan pests of stored grains and cereals. Broad, oval, and flat (*Calitys*, *Grynocharis*, *Peltis*) or convex (*Thymalus*) species are generally associated with fungi, as are their larvae. The adventive *Lophocateres pusillus* (Klug), a minor grain pest, also eats both living and dead insects and other detritus.

FAMILY DIAGNOSIS Some adult trogossitids are elongate, parallel-sided, and somewhat convex to slightly flattened (*Temnoscheila*, *Tenebroides*), or cylindrical (*Airora*) with head and prothorax narrowly and loosely attached to the rest of the body, while others are oblong or oval and flattened (*Calitys*, *Grynocharis*, *Peltis*), or round and convex (*Thymalus*). Head with mandibles directed forward or slightly down. Clubbed antennae with 11 antennomeres, 9–11 forming lopsided club. Prontum wider than head, squarish, or wider than long. Elytra completely covers abdomen. Tarsal formula 5-5-5, tarsomere 1 usually very small, with claws equal in size and simple. Abdoment with five ventrites not fused.

SIMILAR FAMILIES

- some ground beetles (Carabidae) – antennae filiform, ventrite 1 divided by metacoxae (p.63)

- cylindrical bark beetles (Zopheridae) – tarsal formula 4-4-4 (p.340)

COLLECTING NOTES Look for bark-gnawing beetles during the day beneath bark of dead conifers and broadleaf trees, where some species (*Calitys*, *Peltis*) are associated with fungus. Other species are found crawling on dead branches, logs, and stumps at night. *Airora*, *Temnoscheila*, and *Tenebroides* are occasionally attracted to light.

FAUNA 59 SPECIES IN 14 GENERA (NA); 28 SPECIES IN 11 GENERA (ENA)

Grynocharis quadrilineata **(Melsheimer)** (4.9–10.4 mm) is oblong, somewhat flat, and blackish to black. Elytral sides narrowly turned up, each elytron with four distinct ridges, spaces between with four irregular rows of small punctures. Adults found mainly under bark of fungal-infested hardwoods, e.g., poplar (*Populus*) in spring and summer. Maine to Virginia, west to Manitoba, Wisconsin, and Iowa. (2)

Lycoptis americana **(Motschulsky)** (1.9–2.2 mm) is oblong-oval, somewhat flattened, coarsely punctured, moderately pubescent, and reddish brown. Head not concealed by pronotum, clubbed antennae with seven antennomeres, 7 expanded into club. Pronotum wider than long, front broadly notched, sides rounded with margins finely serrate. Elytra broader than pronotum, each with prominent basal angle, sutural, and five fine ridges, spaces between regular in width with two rows of large, shallow punctures, with sides narrowly flattened and almost parallel. Tarsi and claws simple. Adults collected under bark. Maryland to Georgia. (1)

Peltis septentrionalis **(Randall)** (6.8–12.3 mm) is broadly oval, somewhat flattened, uniformly shiny dark reddish brown above, paler below; side margins of pronotum and elytra flat. Head coarsely punctate. Pronotum much wider than long. Elytra longer than broad, with seven long ridges without bumps. Adults found under bark of conifers in association with red banded (*Fomitopsis pinicola*) and brown staining cheese (*Oligoporus fragilis*) polypores. Across Canada and northern United States; in eastern North America south to New York and Minnesota; Eurasia. *Peltis columbiana* (Casey) (6.0–9.7) has pronotal and elytral margins distinctly upturned. (2)

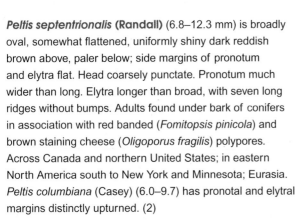

Thymalus marginicollis Chevrolat (4.3–6.2 mm) resembles a small, hairy tortoise beetle; broadly oval, evenly convex, smooth, shiny, and pale to dark brown with margins and underside paler. Upper surface with long, erect setae. Antennae clubbed. Margins of pronotum and elytra reddish, flattened, and slightly turned up. Elytra more coarsely punctate than pronotum. Larvae and adults found on bracket fungi (*Polyporus betulinus*, *Daedalea*). Adults active late spring through summer. Across Canada and United States; in east from Maritime Provinces and New England to South Carolina, west to Minnesota, Iowa, and Arkansas. (1)

Calitys scabra (Thunberg) (6.6–12.2 mm) is somewhat flat, oval, dorsal surfaces roughly sculptured with small bumps or tubercles, and dark brown to black, mostly brown in the east. Sides of pronotum and elytra expanded, flattened, and serrate. Each elytron with two ridges topped with small, buttonlike tubercles. Found under pine (*Pinus*) bark in association with polypore fungi. Northern Hemisphere, across Canada and northern and western United States; in east, south to Maryland, Pennsylvania, Michigan, Wisconsin, and Minnesota. (2)

261

Airora cylindrica (Audinet-Serville) (4.5–14.6 mm) is elongate, cylindrical, reddish black to black. Anterior prosternal and pronotal margins not continuous, interrupted by pronotal angle. Outer margins of tibiae with spines. Adults prey on wood-boring beetles and are found year-round under bark of hardwoods and conifers, on tree trunks at night, and at light in spring and summer. Ontario and Massachusetts to Florida, west to Missouri and eastern Texas. (1)

Corticotomus parallelus (Melsheimer) (3.3–4.5 mm) is elongate, somewhat convex, blackish with reddish area along sides of elytra at base. Head flat with mandibles extended forward. Pronotum convex, sides parallel. Elytra with rows of punctures and distinct impressions behind humeri. Adults found under bark of conifers, e.g., pine (*Pinus*). New England to North Carolina, west to Illinois. (3)

Temnoscheila virescens **(Fabricius)** (8.6–17.8 mm) is elongate, somewhat convex, and shiny metallic green, blue, or purple. Head densely, finely punctate; pronotum similarly sculptured. Elytra finely punctate, striae and intervals flat, with interval punctures slightly smaller than strial punctures. Adults and larvae found in pines infested with bark beetles and are important predators of *Dendroctonus*. Adults prey on adult bark beetles, while their larvae consume *Dendroctonus* eggs and larvae. Eastern North America east of Great Plains. (3)

Tenebroides collaris **(Sturm)** (4.5–8.1 mm) is oblong, very flat, and dull black with orange-red head and pronotum; pronotum and elytra broadly margined. Antennomere 8 cylindrical, smaller than 9. Pronotum with basal bead broadly interrupted at middle. Elytra with rows of fine shallow punctures except along sides. Underside orange-red. Adults active in summer, found under bark of pine (*Pinus*) in association with bark beetles; also attracted to light. New England and Ontario to Florida, west to Michigan and Texas. (12)

Tenebroides laticollis **(Horn)** (4.5–9.7 mm) is somewhat flat and dark reddish brown to blackish. Antennomere 8 much smaller than 9 and cylindrical, with sensory patches on each club antennomere occupying more than one-third of surface. Elytra grooved, with three outermost grooves distinctly punctured. Sides of pronotum somewhat flattened and gradually converging to base. Adults are collected beneath bark of dead hardwood trees, including oak (*Quercus*) and occasionally attracted to light at night. Ontario to Florida, west to Minnesota, Kansas, and Texas. (12)

CHECKERED BEETLES, FAMILY CLERIDAE
(KLAIR-IH-DEE)

Both adult and larval clerids prey on insects, especially beetles. Many species associated with dead wood (*Cregya, Enoclerus, Madoniella, Monophylla, Neorthopleura, Placopterus, Priocera, Thanasimus*) are often found on branches or under bark in tunnels and galleries where they attack the immature stages of bark (Curculionidae), longhorn (Cerambycidae), and metallic wood-boring beetles (Buprestidae). The larvae of *Trichodes* and *Lecontella* develop in the nests of bees and wasps, while others are found on carcasses and dried meats (*Necrobia*) infested with insects and mites. Still others (*Isohydnocera, Phyllobaenus*) are associated with galls, twigs, and stems that support developing insects. The larvae and adults of *Zenodosus sanguineus* (Say) prey on small wood-boring beetles attacking conifers east of the Rockies. The cosmopolitan *Thaneroclerus buquet* Lefebvre occurs in stored products, where it preys on insects infesting spices, drugs, and tobacco. *Ababa tantilla* (LeConte) has been reared from *polypore* fungi inhabited by ciids. *Trichodes* are generalist predators found on various flowers. They prey on various flower-visiting insects and pollen. Their hairy bodies suggest that they may also play a role in pollination. The alternating light-and-dark pattern at the middle of the elytra gives some species a "wasp-waist" appearance. Some species appear to be part of mimicry rings that involve other clerids, as well as Buprestidae, Elateridae, Lycidae, Lampyridae, Cantharidae, and Meloidae.

FAMILY DIAGNOSIS Adult clerids are typically elongate, narrow, somewhat cylindrical, robust, covered in bristly setae, and have broad heads with bulging eyes and a pronotum narrower than elytra, and elytra that are sometimes brightly or distinctly marked. Head with mouthparts directed downward, wide as or wider than prothorax. Antennae with 9–11 antennomeres that may be gradually and loosely to abruptly and compactly clubbed, filiform, serrate, pectinate, flabellate, or spatulate. Pronotum usually longer than wide, narrower than base of elytra. Elytra almost or completely concealing abdomen. Tarsal formula 5-5-5, setal-bearing pad between claws present, with claws equal in size and simple or toothed. Abdomen with five or six ventrites.

SIMILAR FAMILIES
- *Micromalthus* (Micromalthidae) – antennae moniliform (p.61)
- small soldier beetles (Cantharidae) – antennae filiform (p.238)
- soft-winged flower beetles (Melyridae) – pronotum margined; antennae usually serrate (p.271)
- *Pedilus* (Pyrochroidae) – head with neck; not bristly (p.373)
- narrow-waisted bark beetles (Salpingidae) – head prognathous (p.376)
- antlike flower beetles (Anthicidae) – head with neck (p.377)
- antlike leaf beetles (Aderidae) – head with neck (p.382)

COLLECTING NOTES Flower-visiting clerids are easily collected by hand or gathered in a sweep net. Search trunks, limbs, and twigs of trees infested with or dead or dying from wood-boring and bark beetles day and night. Look under loose bark of living and dead conifers and hardwoods. Also beat infested branches of trees and shrubs and sweep grasses and other soft herbaceous plant growth. Examine caracasses and infested dried meats and meat products for *Necrobia*. Adults of several genera are readily attracted to light or collected in Malaise and Lindgren funnel traps. *Zenodosus sanguineus* (Say) and *Ababa tantilla* (LeConte) are attracted to Lindgren funnel traps baited with turpentine or alpha-beta pinene and ethanol.

FAUNA 243 SPECIES IN 37 GENERA (NA); 65 SPECIES IN 25 GENERA (ENA)

Zenodosus sanguineus (Say) (4.5–6.5 mm) has a reddish-brown head and pronotum with bright red elytra and abdomen. Pronotum with posterior side margins not serrate. Adults found in spring and summer on recently cut logs or trunks of recently dead or dying pines and other conifers; also under loose bark of dead or dying conifers and hardwoods infested with small wood borers. Also attracted to Lindgren funnel traps. Maritime Provinces to North Carolina, west to North Dakota, Colorado and Arkansas. (1)

Cymatodera bicolor (Say) (5.5–10.0 mm) has a reddish or yellowish pronotum with anterior and posterior margins black, or dark with only lighter spot on prosternum. Legs brownish yellow except for tips of femora. Basal antennomeres pale (uniformly or gradually darkening in *C. inornata* [Say]). Elytra black to bluish black, sometimes with faint white transverse band at middle. Adults on shrubs and trees infested with bark beetles in spring and summer; also at light. Dark forms resemble *C. inornata*, while typical individuals resemble smaller and more elongate *C. collaris* (Say) (<7.0 mm). Nova Scotia to Florida, west to Wisconsin and Arizona. (5)

264

Cymatodera inornata (Say) (7.0–11.0 mm) is densely clothed in long yellowish setae, more or less uniformly shiny dark brown. Head coarsely punctate, eyes coarsely faceted. Pronotum longer than wide. Elytra widest at apical third, with rows of coarse punctures becoming faint at broadly rounded tips. Legs mostly brown, bases and tarsi lighter. Adults active late spring and summer, found on birch (*Betula*), hickory (*Carya*), hackberry (*Celtis*), and redbud (*Cercis*) branches infested with bostrichids, anobiids, eucmenids; attracted to light. Commonly confused with more coarsely punctate *Lecontella* and dark *C. bicolor*. Maine and Québec to Florida, west to Utah and Arizona. (5)

Cymatodera undulata (Say) (9.0–12.0 mm) is elongate, narrow, and shining dark brown to black with light band across middle of elytra. Head convex, coarsely punctate, eyes coarsely faceted, with antennomere 11 oval and pointed at tip. Pronotum longer than wide, constricted at front and behind middle, with sparse small punctures. Elytra with rows of coarse punctures becoming indistinct toward broadly rounded tips and variable pale patches at base and apical third. Legs pale. Adults active late spring and summer, found on dry branches of deciduous trees and shrubs infested with bostrichids, eucmenids, and buprestids; attracted to light. Ontario, widespread in United States. (5)

Lecontella brunnea **(Melsheimer)** (8.0–15.0 mm) is elongate, coarsely punctured, brown, with last antennomere longer than 9. Pronotum longer than wide, constricted in front and just behind middle, finely and densely punctate. Elytra at base wider than head and pronotum, with rows of coarse punctures reaching tip. Larvae develop in nests of solitary bees (Megachilidae) and wasps (Eumenidae, Sphecidae, Vespidae). Adults found dead in or reared from hymnenopteran nests; attracted to light. Sometimes confused with less coarsely punctate *Cymatodera inornata*. Maine to Florida, west to Kansas and Arizona. (1)

Monophylla terminata **(Say)** (4.0–8.4 mm) is elongate, narrow, and mostly shining black with distinctive last antennomere long, flat. Head densely punctate, last antennomere one-quarter (female) or half (male) length of elytra. Pronotum longer than wide with variable black spot margined in red. Elytra widest behind middle, coarsely punctate with narrow brownish-yellow stripe on sides. Adults active late spring and early summer, found on conifers infested with bark beetles and hardwood trees hosting wood-boring beetles. Southern Ontario to Florida, west to Illinois, Kansas, and Texas. (1)

Isohydnocera curtipennis **(Newman)** (3.5–5.0 mm) is elongate, narrow, black or bluish black with yellow-brown appendages; front and sides of head often pale yellow. Pronotum cylindrical, constricted near front, about twice as long as wide. Elytra mostly pale to dark, about one-half length of abdomen, distinctly punctate, side margins nearly straight to apex, apical margins minutely saw-toothed (serrulate), with tips variably dark. Legs long with simple claws (*Phyllobaenus verticalis* (Say) claws bifid). Adults found on vegetation from late spring and summer. Larvae thought to parasitize larvae of solidago gall moth (*Gnorischema gallesolidaginis*). Dark form resembles *I. tabida* (LeConte), which has longer elytra and legs usually more orange. Nova Scotia and New Brunswick to Florida, west to Ontario, Minnesota, Kansas, and Texas. (6)

Phyllobaenus humeralis **(Say)** (3.5–5.5 mm) is black to bluish black with reddish humeri sometimes reduced or absent. Head short, with eyes broader than prothorax. Antennae, mouthparts, tarsi, and front tibiae usually pale brown. Pronotum wider than long, constricted in front and at base. Elytra broader than prothorax at base, coarsely punctate, widest at apical third, and covering abdomen. Larvae develop in oak (*Quercus*) and hickory (*Carya*). Adults are found in spring and summer on sunlit foliage of oaks in open habitats, also flowers; attracted to light. Maritime Provinces to Florida, west to Ontario, Illinois, and Texas. (12)

Phyllobaenus pallipennis (Say) (3.5–5.0 mm) is mostly dark with broad head. Yellow-brown elytra short with variably dark humeri, suture, apices, and medial band. Appendages pale, claws each bearing a broad basal tooth. Larvae develop in trunks and limbs of oaks (*Quercus*) and hickory (*Carya*). Adults reported on oak foliage in mid- and later summer feeding on soft-bodied insects, especially aphids, also found on flowers, herbaceous plants, and tree trunks and limbs; attracted to light. Nova Scotia, Prince Edward Island, and New Brunswick to Florida, west to Ontario, Indiana, and Texas. (12)

Phyllobaenus unifasciatus (Say) (3.5–4.5 mm) is metallic blue or green with pale band sometimes very faint across middle of elytra, and clothed in erect yellowish setae; appendages partly or entirely brownish yellow. Prothorax slightly wider than long with a bump on each side. Elytra entirely covering abdomen, coarsely punctured, usually with narrow pale bar with long, appressed white setae at middle interrupted at suture. Larvae in trunks and branches infested with wood-boring beetles, also insect galls. Adults are found late spring and summer on living and dead branches of hardwood trees and shrubs, especially infested oak (*Quercus*) and hickory (*Carya*). Eastern North America. (12)

266

Wolcottia pedalis (LeConte) (3.5–4.0 mm) is short, narrow, clothed in long pale pubescence, mostly black with brownish-yellow front legs and mouthparts. Head with small punctures, antennomere 3 about as long as wide. Pronotum wide as long, widest in front of middle with weak tubercles on sides, mostly convex with broad depression across front with scattered punctures, and no tubercles on sides. Elytra short. Claws simple. Adults found on grasses, flowers of many herbaceous plants, and oak (*Quercus*). Confused with much hairier *Phyllobaenus pubescens* (LeConte), which has weak pronotal tubercles. New Jersey to Virginia, west to Wisconsin, Kansas, and Texas. (1)

Enoclerus ichneumoneus (Fabricius) (8.0–11.0 mm) is a large, reddish velvet ant (Mutillidae) mimic. Prothorax ranging from red to black underneath. Scutellum long, triangular. Elytra coarsely punctured at base, each with stout tubercle, basal fourth reddish margined by incomplete narrow black band, middle half paler than base, apical fourth with broad black and narrower white bands, and black tips. Adults on trees infested with bark beetles during summer; hibernate under bark in winter. Pennsylvania south to central Florida, west to Wisconsin, Illinois, and Kansas. Similar to the northeastern species *Enoclerus muttkowski* (Wolcott) that lacks basal elytral tubercle. (10)

Enoclerus nigripes **(Say)** (5.0–7.0 mm) is dull reddish brown with appendages darker, sometimes blackish overall with usual elytral markings or darker with base of elytra only reddish brown. Elytra in reddish-brown individuals with apical two-thirds black and sinuate band of white pubescence across middle; apices also white. Adults found in late spring and early summer on conifers infested with bark beetles and weevils (Curculionidae), and other wood-boring beetles; overwinter under loose bark or in litter at base of trees. New England to Florida, west to Manitoba, Wisconsin, Missouri, and Tennessee; additional subspecies west to California. (10)

Enoclerus quadrisignatus **(Say)** (8.0–12.0 mm) is dull reddish brown, clothed in recumbent and erect setae, appendages dark brown to black. Dorsal surface coarsely punctate, especially elytral bases. Pronotum long as wide with faint transverse and sinuate groove in front of middle. Elytra wider than pronotum, widest as apical third, with broad white or light-colored band across the middle and just before tips broken by suture, each surrounded by dark brown to black. Nocturnal adults are active in summer and found on hickory (*Carya*) branches infested with bark beetles; also attracted to light. New Jersey to Georgia, west to Colorado, Arizona, and southern California; Mexico. (10)

Enoclerus rosmarus **(Say)** (3.5–7.0 mm) has a reddish-brown head, prothorax, and basal half of elytra with appendages sometimes darker; abdomen black. Elytra with pale median bands on apex not reaching suture. Underside of thorax and legs red, abdomen black. Adults active in late spring and summer on flowers, e.g., milkweed (*Asclepias*) and goldenrod (*Solidago*) and other herbaceous growth, as well as dead branches of shrubs (*Sumac*); generalist insect predators. Also attracted to Lindgren funnel traps baited with turpentine and ethanol. Ontario and Maine to Florida, west to Nebraska and Texas. (10)

Placopterus thoracicus **(Olivier)** (5.2–7.3 mm) is elongate with dark brown appendages and elytra, and clothed in pale and dark erect setae. Head mostly black except for yellow stripe underneath. Prothorax wider than head, widest at middle, reddish orange except for central black spot on pronotum that sometimes reaches front margin. Elytra shiny and finely wrinkled, wider at base than prothorax. Adults found on small branched shrubs infested with bark beetles and weevils (Curculionidae), longhorns (Cerambycidae), and metallic wood-boring beetles (Buprestidae) in spring and summer, also reared from mud nests and galls of wasps; attracted to light. Widespread in eastern North America. (3)

Priocera castanea (Newman) (5.0–10.0 mm) is elongate, narrow, and shining dark brown with tricolored elytra. Head with coarsely faceted eyes, antennae serrate. Pronotum convex, shiny, longer than wide, widest in front, sides without projection or tubercle. Elytra with rows of coarse punctures becoming indistinct toward tips, base reddish brown, followed by two pairs of offset pale spots, a brown band sometimes extended forward on sides, and pale apical quarter. Legs with femora thick. Adults found under bark on deciduous and coniferous logs infested with lymexylids and bark beetles; attracted to light. Maine and to Florida, west to Michigan, Kansas, and Texas. (1)

Thanasimus dubius (Fabricius) (7.5–9.0 mm) is sparsely clothed in long, erect setae, reddish with two sinuate bands of white pubescence across mostly black elytra; antennae and tibiae dark. Head, prothorax, and base of elytra bright reddish brown, with eyes notched in front and finely granulate, and loose and gradually expanded antennal club. Pronotum barely longer than wide with narrow Y-shaped depression across front and down middle, latter sometimes faint. Elytra coarsely punctured at base. Larva preys on larval bark beetles in their galleries. Adults found on dead and dying spruce (*Picea*), pine (*Pinus*), and elm (*Ulmus*) infested with wood-boring beetles. Widespread in North America. (4)

Trichodes apivorus Germar (7.0–15.0 mm) is large, elongate, robust, clothed in reddish-brown setae, dark metallic blue or green to black, antennae dark and mouthparts light brown, and bicolored elytra. Antennae clubbed, tips flat, appearing cut off. Pronotum slightly longer than wide, widest at middle. Elytra red with coarse scattered punctures, two broad blue-black bands sometimes interrupted at suture, and blue-black tips. Larvae are predators in nests of bees. Adults active in late spring and summer, found on flowers, especially Asteraceae and Apiaceae, feeding on pollen. New Hampshire and New York to Florida, west to Colorado and New Mexico. (2)

Trichodes nuttalli (Kirby) (8.0–10.0 mm) is elongate, robust, sparsely clothed in light-colored setae, metallic blue or green, antennae and mouthparts brown, and bicolored elytra. Antennae clubbed, tips flat, appearing cut off. Pronotum slightly longer than wide, widest at middle. Elytra sparsely and finely punctate, each with a red C-shaped mark from base to middle and narrow band near tips. Larvae are predators in nests of bees and wasps. Adults active in late spring and summer, found on flowers feeding on pollen. New England and Québec to Virginia, west to Alberta, Montana, Colorado, and Kansas. (2)

268

Madoniella dislocata **(Say)** (3.0–6.0 mm) is elongate, narrow, coarsely punctured with erect setae, and dark brown to black with variable tan markings. Head and pronotum dark brown, coarsely punctate. Antennomeres before club combined longer than club and sparsely setose. Pronotum slightly longer than wide, widest behind middle. Elytra convex, mostly dark, each with close set rows of coarse punctures and three variable tan markings at base, middle, and tips. Diurnal adults usually found on dead coniferous and deciduous tree and shrub branches infested with wood-boring beetles; also in baited Lindgren funnel traps and at light. Maritime Provinces to Georgia, west to Manitoba, Colorado, and Texas. (3)

Chariessa pilosa **(Forster)** (7.5–13.0 mm) resembles a firefly (Lampyridae) with a reddish-yellow pronotum and two wide black stripes converging at base. Head with eyes finely granular, tips of palps strongly triangular. Pronotum with two thick black stripes somewhat parallel. Elytra soft, dull, sometimes with margins and suture pale. Adults and larvae live on hardwoods infested with wood-boring larvae, including bark beetles (*Scolytus*), weevils (*Magdalis*) (Curculionidae), and *Xylotrechus* (Cerambycidae). Diurnal adults emerge in late spring and are active throughout summer; attracted to light. Ontario and Québec to Florida, west to Kansas and Texas. *Chariessa floridana* Schaeffer has thin, arched pronotal stripes; Florida Keys. (2)

269

Cregya oculata **(Say)** (4.0–6.5 mm) has dark brown to black elytra with pale brown-orange margins and suture. Mouthparts, antennal bases, prothorax, portions of legs also pale brown-orange. Antennae with 10 antennomeres. Pronotum angled on sides. Adults found in spring and summer on trees and shrubs infested with larvae of bark beetles and weevils (Curculionidae) and longhorns (Cerambycidae); also attracted to light. Ontario and Massachusetts to Florida, west to Kansas and Texas. *Cregya mixta* Spinola is similar in form, elytra pale with black patches at base and apical quarter; Virginia to Florida, west to Texas. (3)

Red-shouldered Ham Beetle *Necrobia ruficollis* **(Fabricius)** (4.0–6.2 mm) is oval with upper surface metallic blue or greenish and brownish red. Front of head and apical three-fourths of elytra metallic blue. Base and underside of head and thorax, and base of elytra reddish brown. Elytra with rows of fine punctures. Antennae and abdomen dark brown. Legs with claws toothed at base. Adults found on carrion, where they scavenge tissues and prey on insects. Cosmopolitan; across southern Canada and United States. (3)

Red-legged Ham Beetle *Necrobia rufipes* **(De Geer)**
(3.5–6.0 mm) is oval and uniformly metallic blue or green
with legs and antennal bases red. Antennae mostly dark
brown. Pronotum wider than long with sides broadly
rounded. Elytra convex, with rows of find and widely
separated punctures, spaces between finely punctured.
Adults scavenge carrion and prey on other insects in spring
and summer, sometimes found in stored grains and other
foods where it feeds on insect pests. Cosmopolitan; across
southern Canada and United States. (3)

Black-legged Ham Beetle *Necrobia violacea*
(Linnaeus) (3.2–4.5 mm) is oval, uniformly metallic green
or blue, with dark brown to black appendages. Head and
pronotum densely and finely punctate. Elytra with rows
of coarse punctures, spaces between broad with dense,
minute punctures. Adults active in spring and summer
and scavenge on carrion and prey on other insects.
Cosmopolitan; across southern Canada and United
States. (3)

270

Neorthopleura thoracica **(Say)** (3.0–14.0 mm) is
somewhat cylindrical, usually black with a red pronotum.
Head with eyes notched and 11 antennomeres, club two-
thirds (male) or one-half (female) of total antennal length.
Pronotum with dark margins, sometimes all black, with
sides not keeled. Elytra sometimes with faint and narrow
crossbar (fascia). Adults found in spring and summer
at night on dead, dying, and recently cut hardwoods,
especially oaks (*Quercus*), infested with buprestids,
cerambycids, and weevils (Curculionidae); also at light.
Québec to Florida, west to Iowa and Texas. (1)

Pelonides quadripunctatus **(Say)** (5.0–6.6 mm) is
elongate-oval, shiny black with bright red elytra, each
with two variable, round black spots; head and pronotum
sometimes partly or wholly red in Texas. Head finely
and densely punctate. Pronotum cylindrical, almost wide
as long, widest at middle, narrower than elytra at base.
Scutellum broadly rounded behind. Elytra densely, finely
punctate, widest behind middle with sides strongly divergent
from base to middle, tips broadly rounded. Larvae reared
from branches of black walnut (*Juglans nigra*). Diurnal
adults found on flowers, e.g., hawthorn (*Crategus*). Ohio to
Mississippi, west to Kansas and Texas. (1)

Pelonium leucophaeum (**Klug**) (6.0–11.0 mm) has notched eyes, antennae with 11 antennomeres, rough pronotal surface, and broad pale band across elytra. Pronotum longer than wide, widest at middle, sides angulate, with constriction near base. Elytra with pale, semierect setae and coarse irregular punctures; cryptic pattern thought to resemble lichens. Larvae develop in small trees and branches of bald cypress (*Taxodium distichum*) and juniper (*Juniperus*) infested with larvae of longhorn beetles (Cerambycidae). Adults found on various trees and shrubs, also in Malaise, baited Lindgren funnel, and various fruit fly traps; also at light. Pennsylvania to Florida, west to Ohio and Texas. (1)

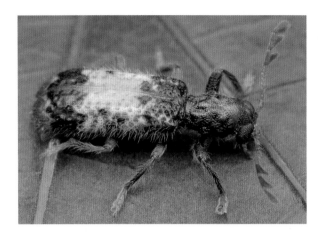

SOFT-WINGED FLOWER BEETLES, FAMILY MELYRIDAE
(MEH-*LEER*-IH-DEE)

Melyrids feed on both plant and animal materials. Adults of some species gather in large aggregations on conifers or flowering plants as they feed on pollen and look for mates. Some species (*Collops*, *Malachius*) feed on pollen and nectar, or prey on small arthropods. Recent studies of the genus *Collops* suggest that they might be important predators of crop pests in alfalfa, cotton, and sorghum fields. Species of *Collops* and *Malachius* often sport bright aposematic, or warning colors. They have eversible vesicles, balloonlike structures that expand like air bags, that are normally hidden under the prothorax and abdomen. These structures are thought to produce odors that deter predators. The biology of larval soft-winged flower beetles is poorly known. The scant information available suggests that they live in leaf litter or under bark, probably feeding on detritus, fungi, and the eggs and larvae of various small arthropods. Some *Malachius* larvae live under bark in association with the galleries of wood-boring beetles; those of Old World species are found on plant stems inhabited by tumbling flower beetles (Mordellidae). All the genera treated here are in need of study.

271

FAMILY DIAGNOSIS Adult melyrids in eastern North America are typically blue, black, or green with red, yellow, or orange markings. Head broad with bulging eyes, more or less hidden under pronotum. Filiform antennae appear to have 10 antennomeres, but actually have 11, 2 partially hidden within 1 (*Collops*), or distinctly with 11 antennomeres. Prothorax wider than long, with sides sharply margined or keeled. Elytra soft, loose fitting, and almost always widest at rear. Tarsal formula 5-5-5 (male *Collops* 4-5-5), with claws equal and simple or toothed. Abdomen with five or six ventrites, sometimes with eversible vesicles along sides.

SIMILAR FAMILIES

■ *Micromalthus* (Micromalthidae) – antennae moniliform; prothorax not margined or keeled on sides (p.61)

■ *Ditemnus*, *Silis* (Cantharidae) – antennae filiform; sides of prothorax notched; tarsi 5-5-5 (p.241)

■ checkered beetles (Cleridae) – antennae usually clubbed, occasionally serrate or filiform; prothorax not margined or keeled on sides (p.263)

■ some leaf beetles (Chrysomelidae) – antennae filiform; sides of prothorax not distinctly margined or keeled on sides; tarsi appear 4-4-4, but actually 5-5-5 (p.429)

COLLECTING NOTES Although a few species fly to lights at night, most melyrids are collected by hand from flowers or beaten and swept from trees, shrubs, grasses, and other herbaceous vegetation.

FAUNA 520 SPECIES IN 58 GENERA (NA); 47 SPECIES IN 13 GENERA (ENA)

Anthocomus equestris (Fabricius) (2.5–3.0 mm) is small and black with a bluish or greenish luster with orange-red elytra. Antennae dark, serrate. Elytra covering abdomen, with dark spots of variable size and shape behind middle that may or may not reach margins and suture, tips appearing pinched in male. Legs dark, variably with tips of femora and tibia lighter. Adults active in spring, found in homes walking on walls and near windows; also on roses (*Rosa*) and other vegetation. Europe, established in eastern North America from Maine and Québec to North Carolina. (3)

Attalus circumscriptus (Say) (3.0 mm) has a black head with dull yellowish labrum. Pronotum reddish yellow with black stripe down middle. Elytra black with margins narrowly pale. Abdomen black. Legs dusky yellow; front tarsomere 2 with distinct lobe. Adults found in spring and early summer on vegetation. Virginia to Florida, west to Indiana and Arizona. (19)

Attalus scincetus (Say) (3.0 mm) is yellowish or reddish yellow with back of head, broad spot or stripe on middle of pronotum, and elytral suture blackish; lateral margins of elytra sometimes dark. Underside of thorax and abdomen usually black. Appendages mostly reddish yellow. Adults found on flowers, including cherry (*Prunus*), hawthorn (*Crataegus*), dogwood (*Cornus*), elderberry (*Sambucus*), and rose (*Rosa*) in spring and early summer. Massachusetts and New York to Florida, west to South Dakota, Kansas, and Texas; also Mexico. (19)

Collops quadrimaculatus (Fabricius) (4.0–6.0 mm) is so named because of four distinct blue or bluish-black spots on elytra. Appendages blackish or black, except basal antennomeres and mouthparts pale. Head and abdomen black. Antennae appear to have 10 antennomeres, but actually have 11; second antennomere hidden in first, third (apparent second) enlarged with slender appendage at base in male. Pronotum, and elytral margins and suture reddish. Last tarsomere with two membranous lobes. Predatory adults found on flowers, grasses, and other vegetation in wet habitats; in cotton fields. Québec and Ontario to Florida, west to Montana, Utah, and Arizona. (9)

Hypebaeus apicalis (Say) (1.7–2.5 mm) is blackish with bluish tinge, pronotum broader than long and black or yellow, and yellowish legs and antennal bases. Elytra wider at base than pronotum and slightly expanded at tips; male with extended tips yellowish with cup-shaped processes opening upward, in female rounded and black. Legs with five tarsomeres. Adults found on leaves of trees and shrubs in spring and early summer. Ontario and Québec to Florida, west to Indiana. (2)

Scarlet Malachite Beetle *Malachius aeneus* **(Linnaeus)** (6.0–8.0 mm) is broadly oblong, mostly dull, metallic green and clothed in long, dark setae; eversible yellow sacs present behind head and next to hind legs. Head in front of antennae yellow. Pronotum with anterior angles reddish. Elytra brownish red, except for broad margin at base and extending along suture to apical quarter, and widest at tips. Adults active in late spring and summer, found among cereal crops where they likely prey on other insects. Europe; established from Atlantic Provinces and New England to Rhode Island, west to Ontario and Great Lakes region; also British Columbia, Alberta, Pacific Northwest, and Colorado. (1)

Temnopsophus bimaculatus Horn (2.0–2.2 mm) is antlike, blackish with bases of antennae, pronotum, and elytra yellowish brown; mouthparts and legs pale; pubescence pale, sparse, and inconspicuous. Basal antennomere of male hooked. Pronotum longer than wide, narrowed at base. Elytra oval, narrow at base, inflated apically; flight wings reduced in both sexes. Legs with tarsal formula 4-5-5 (male) or 5-5-5 (female) Adults found by sweeping herbaceous growth in meadows and along shores of lakes and streams. Widely distributed in eastern United States. *Temnopsophus impressus* Schwarz has strongly depressed elytral bases and pale markings not reaching humeri; Florida. (2)

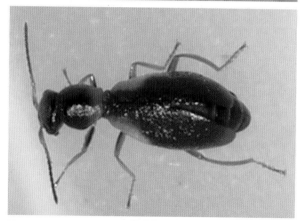

Melyrodes basalis (LeConte) (2.2–2.5 mm) is elongate-oval, moderately convex, mostly brownish black with pair of spots on each elytron. Pronotal half as long as wide, margins finely toothed (serrulate). Elytra wider than pronotum, coarsely and densely punctured, with sparse pubescence barely noticeable, and pale reddish marks at bases and just before tips. Adults found in spring on hardwood flowers and vegetation. Virginia to Florida, west to Texas. *Melyrodes cribrata* (LeConte) more common, uniformly dark, pronotum abruptly narrowed toward front, pubescence inconspicuous, Southeast; *M. floridana* (Casey) (1.7–1.8 mm) also dark, pubescence conspicuous, Florida. (3)

FRUITWORM BEETLES, FAMILY BYTURIDAE
(BY-*TUR*-IH-DEE)

The sole representative of this species in eastern North America is the raspberry fruitworm, *Byturus unicolor* Say. Adults emerge from subterranean pupae in spring and feed on leaves and flowers of various plants. After mating, females probably lay eggs on or near buds, flowers, and developing fruits of avens (*Geum*), blackberry (*Rubus*), and possibly spotted geranium (*Geranium maculatum*). Specific larval hosts are documented for this species in the Pacific Northwest, but not for populations in eastern North America. When mature, the larvae drop to the ground to pupate.

FAMILY DIAGNOSIS Adult byturids are robust with platelike lobes on the second and third tarsomeres and clubbed antennae, moderately clothed in long and dense setate, and are usually uniformly yellowish, reddish brown, to blackish. Head inserted to eyes inside prothorax with mouthparts directed downward (hypognathous). Antennae 11 antennomeres, 9–11 forming club. Prothorax wider than head and almost equal in width to base of elytra. Scutellum small. Elytra with scattered punctures, straight-sided, uniformly colored or sometimes with faint and oblique bands, and completely cover abdomen. Legs with femora moderately swollen, tibiae slender; tarsal formula 5-5-5 with tarsomeres 2–3 broadly lobed beneath, 4 small, and claws equal with large tooth at base. Abdomen with five ventrites, first ventrite without lines, all sutures visible.

274

SIMILAR FAMILIES
- throscid beetles (Throscidae) – hind angles of pronotum extended backward; tarsi not lobed (p.211)
- tooth-neck fungus beetles (Derodontidae) – elytra grooved; tarsi not lobed (p.243)
- skin beetles (Dermestidae) – tarsi not lobed (p.246)
- false skin beetles (Biphyllidae) – tarsomeres 2–3 with slender lobes; ventrite 1 with lines converging between legs; prognathous (p.276)
- silken fungus beetles (Cryptophagidae) – tarsi not lobed (p.283)
- hairy fungus beetles (Mycetophagidae) – tarsi not lobed (p.323)
- comb-clawed beetles (Tenebrionidae) – claws pectinate (pp.351–3)

COLLECTING NOTES Adults are handpicked, beaten, or swept from foliage of flowering blackberries, avens, and other plants in spring.

FAUNA TWO SPECIES IN TWO GENERA (NA); ONE SPECIES, *BYTURUS UNICOLOR* SAY (ENA)

Raspberry Fruitworm *Byturus unicolor* Say (2.7–4.8 mm) is oblong, somewhat convex, usually uniformly yellowish to reddish brown to blackish, sometimes with prothorax and or underside of pterothorax darker, with seta-bearing punctures. Antennal club with three antennomeres. Pronotum wider than long. Elytra with very faint, fine ridges topped with fine seta-bearing punctures, spaces between with one or two irregular rows of larger seta-bearing punctures. Legs with tarsomeres 2–3 lobed. Adults active in spring, found on leaves of berry shrubs (*Rubus*). Atlantic Canada and Ontario, south to Georgia and Texas. (1)

CRYPTIC SLIME MOLD BEETLES, FAMILY SPHINDIDAE
(*SFIN*-DIH-DEE)

Adult and larval sphindids feed on spores and other structures inside sporocarps of slime molds growing on dead trees, logs, and stumps. Although the adults may have broad tastes in fungus, they may be more selective when it comes to breeding.

FAMILY DIAGNOSIS Adult sphindids are cylindrical, parallel-sided, with head partially visible from above, antennae with 10–11 antennomeres with gradual club (clavate) with two or three pubescent antennomeres, pronotum convex and wide as elytra, elytra with rows of large, deep punctures. Tarsal formula 5-5-5 (female) or 5-5-4 (male). Abdomen with five distinct ventrites.

SIMILAR FAMILIES
- branch and twig borers (Bostrichidae) – antennal club lopsided (p.250)
- death-watch beetles (Ptinidae) – antennal club lopsided (p.252)
- minute tree fungus beetles (Ciidae) – elytra usually without grooves or rows of punctures (p.326)
- bark and ambrosia beetles (Curculionidae; Scolytidae) – antennal club ball-like with one antennomere (p.469)

COLLECTING NOTES Cryptic slime mold beetles are not often collected, but they can be locally abundant on slime molds growing on dead trees, logs, stumps, and leaf litter. They are best extracted from these substrates by applying mild heat. Adults are occasionally attracted to lights and found in flight intercept and Malaise traps.

FAUNA NINE SPECIES IN FOUR GENERA (NA); SEVEN SPECIES IN FOUR GENERA (ENA)

Sphindus americanus **LeConte** (1.5–2.5 mm) is small, elongate-oval, straight-sided, somewhat shining, blackish or brownish, and sparsely pubescent. Head with several grooves adjacent to each eye; antennae with 10 antennomeres, club with 2. Pronotum lacks fine ridge down middle, side margin without teeth. Elytra sometimes lighter than head and pronotum, with humeri prominent. Appendages reddish brown. Adults active in summer, found on fruiting bodies of slime molds such as *Fuligo* and *Stemonitis* growing on old trees and logs; also attracted to light. Nova Scotia and Québec to Florida, west Ontario, Wisconsin, Iowa, Kansas, and Texas. (2)

FALSE SKIN BEETLES, FAMILY BIPHYLLIDAE
(BI-*FIL*-LIH-DEE)

This small family is represented in eastern North America by two species in the genus *Diplocoelus*. Adults of *D. brunneus* LeConte are sometimes found on dead oak (*Quercus*) infested with *Hypoxylon*, a genus of ascomycete fungus that causes cankers and white rot in dead hardwoods. The beetles seem to prefer standing trunks (snags) over those lying on the ground (logs). *Diplocoelus rudis* (LeConte) is found under bark of fungal-infested oak, hickory (*Carya*), and conifers, but seems to prefer logs on the ground and not standing snags.

FAMILY DIAGNOSIS Adult biphyllids are oblong-oval, somewhat convex, strongly pubescent with a mixture of setae on dorsal surface that lie flat on body surface or stand more erect in rows on pronotum and elytra, slender lobes on tarsomeres 2 and 3, and oblique lines on first abdominal ventrite that converge between hind legs; light brown to blackish brown. Head with mouthparts directed forward and inserted in prothorax to base of eyes. Antennae with 11 antennomeres with 9–11 forming club, attached in front of eyes. Prothorax broad, wider than head, slightly narrower than elytra at base, with a pair of ridges along each side (*D. brunneus*) or not (*D. rudis*). Scutellum partly exposed and broad. Elytra with rows of punctures, sides slightly rounded, and completely cover abdomen. Legs slender; tarsal formula 5-5-5, tarsomeres 2–3 with slender and pubescent lobes, 4 short, 5 longer than remaining tarsomeres combined, and claws equal and simple. Abdomen with five distinct ventrites.

SIMILAR FAMILIES

- comb-clawed beetles (Tenebrionidae) – claws pectinate (pp.151–3)
- throscid beetles (Throscidae) – hind angles of pronotum extended backward; tarsi not lobed (p.211)
- tooth-neck fungus beetles (Derodontidae) – elytra grooved; tarsi not lobed (p.243)
- skin beetles (Dermestidae) – tarsi not lobed (p.246)
- fruitworm beetles (Byturidae) – tarsomeres 2–3 with broad lobes; first abdominal ventrite without lines; head hypognathous (p.274)
- silken fungus beetles (Cryptophagidae) – tarsi not lobed (p.283)
- hairy fungus beetles (Mycetophagidae) – tarsi not lobed (p.323)

COLLECTING NOTES Look for *Diplocoelus* under the bark of snags, logs, and fallen branches infested with fungi, especially when there is moisture; also attracted to light.

FAUNA THREE SPECIES IN TWO GENERA (NA); TWO SPECIES IN ONE GENUS (ENA)

Diplocoelus rudis (**LeConte**) (2.0–3.0 mm) is elongate-oval, pubescent, coarsely punctured, and dark shiny brown. Head with long setae on eyes, more than twice diameter of facet. Pronotum wider than long, edges somewhat serrate, without ridges along sides, underneath with coxal cavities closed. Elytra with rows of punctures not separated by ridges. Hind femora slender and similar, tarsal formula 5-5-5, tarsomeres 2–3 lobed, 1–3 short, each similar in length, 4 shorter, 5 longer than 1–4 combined. Abdomen with ventrite 1 bearing pair of distinct converging lines forming triangle with rear margin. Adults found under bark of pine (*Pinus*), oak (*Quercus*), and hickory (*Carya*). Eastern North America. (2)

276

PLEASING FUNGUS AND LIZARD BEETLES, FAMILY EROTYLIDAE
(ERO-*TIL*-IH-DEE)

Adult and larval pleasing fungus beetles are usually found on large basidiomycete fungi under the bark of rotten wood or in the soil on fungi associated with roots. They feed on the fruiting bodies of mushrooms (*Panus, Pleurotus*), as well as soft (*Hapalopilus, Inonotus, Oxyporus, Piptoporus, Polyporus*) and woody bracket fungi (*Ganodermus, Phellinus*) growing on logs. Both adults and larvae often have contrasting red or yellow markings that serve as aposematic (warning) colors that may be associated with the production of defensive chemical compounds that make them distasteful to predators. Eggs are usually laid on the fungal host of larvae. The larvae feed either by burrowing through fungal tissues or by grazing the surface. Adults of some species are mostly diurnal, while others are primarily nocturnal. Lizard beetles are frequently found on flowers and feed on pollen and leaves. Their larvae bore within the stems of plants, especially asters (Asteraceae) and legumes (Fabaceae). Their feeding activities seldom kill the plant, but do reduce its vitality by weakening stems and causing them to break off. One widespread North American species, the clover stem borer, *Languria mozardi* Latreille, is a minor pest of alfalfa in the west and red clover in the east.

FAMILY DIAGNOSIS Adult erotylids are elongate-oval, broadly oval, or slender and straight-sided, reddish brown or black, sometimes with contrasting colors and markings. Head retracted inside pronotum with mouthparts directed downward (hypognathous). Antennae with 11 antennomeres, with last three or four to five (lizard beetles) forming a club. Pronotum variable in shape and distinctly margined. Scutellum visible. Elytra smooth, sometimes with rows of pits, and completely conceal abdomen. Legs with tarsal formula 5-5-5, with fourth tarsomere sometimes reduced, appearing 4-4-4, first three tarsomeres are more or less broad with brushy pads below, claws are equal in size and simple. Abdomen with five distinct ventrites.

SIMILAR FAMILIES
- metallic wood-boring or jewel beetles (Buprestidae) – usually metallic; antennae not clubbed, and metacoxae with grooves to receive hind femora (p.184)
- false click beetles (Eucnemidae) – antennae usually serrate; with clicking mechanism (p.210)
- click beetles (Elateridae) – antennae usually serrate; with clicking mechanism (p.213)
- short-winged flower beetles (Kateretidae) – elytra usually short, abdomen partially exposed (p.293)
- sap beetles (Nitidulidae) – elytra usually short, abdomen partially exposed (p.295)
- handsome fungus beetles (Endomychidae) – front angles of pronotum distinct, extended forward; tarsi 4-4-4, appear 3-3-3 (p.308)
- lady beetles (Coccinellidae) – antennae not distinctly clubbed; tarsi 4-4-4, appear 3-3-3 (p.311)
- *Hyporhagus* (Zopheridae) – antennae fit into grooves under prothorax; tarsi 5-5-4 (p.343)
- some darkling beetles (Tenebrionidae) – antennae not distinctly clubbed; tarsi 5-5-4 (p.344)
- some leaf beetles (Chrysomelidae) – antennae filiform or clavate (p.429)

COLLECTING NOTES Look for pleasing fungus beetles on or near woody and soft fungi on snags and logs, or beneath loose bark of fungal-infested logs in moist woodlands. *Dacne, Tritoma,* and *Triplax* are found on the fruiting bodies of mushrooms and soft bracket fungi growing on logs. *Ischyrus* is found on soft bracket fungi, including *Oxyporus latemarginatus* and *Phellinus gilvus*, and is also attracted to light. Other erotylids, such as *Megalodacne* and *Microsternus*, prefer woodier fungi, such as *Ganoderma* and *Phellinus*, respectively. Species are also sifted from moist duff beneath trees or extracted by placing leaf litter samples in a Berlese funnel. Some species are captured in Malaise and light traps. Lizard beetles are found on various flowers and vegetation, especially those species that serve as larval food plants; *Toramus* is frequently attracted to light.

FAUNA 82 SPECIES IN 20 GENERA (NA); 40 SPECIES IN 15 GENERA (ENA)

Acropteroxys gracilis **(Newman)** (6.0–12.0 mm) is narrow, strongly tapered at rear, shiny greenish black with variably colored and marked pronotum. Head as broad as pronotum with raised ridge along inside margin of eye. Pronotum longer than wide, entirely orangish red or black, or orangish red with variable dark marking reaches basal and/or anterior margin. Elytra with spaces between rows of punctures with small, shallow punctures. Larva mines stems of annual ragweed (*Ambrosia artemisiifolia*). Adults active late spring and summer, found on larval hosts, flowers, and other vegetation. Québec and Ontario to South Carolina, west to Saskatchewan, Idaho, Colorado, Arizona; Central America. (2)

Clover Stem Borer *Languria mozardi* **Latreille** (4.0–9.0 mm) has antennal club with five antennomeres. Head, pronotum, and at least the last two or three abdominal ventrites red. Adults found on various flowers and vegetation in spring and summer. Larvae develop in stem of red clover (*Trifolium pratense*). Widespread in southern Canada and United States. (8)

Languria taedata **LeConte** (9.0–11.0 mm) is large, robust, elongate. Head usually dark, antennal club with five antennomeres. Pronotum more deeply and densely punctate than head, appears greasy with ill-defined dark spot on middle. Elytra uniformly blackish with rows of deep punctures, spaces between faintly punctured, and tips rounded. Legs with front tarsi large and setose underneath. Abdomen red, sometimes with tip blackish. Larvae develop in stems of cordgrass (*Spartina*). Adults active in summer. Atlantic and Gulf Coast states. (9)

Toramus pulchellus **(LeConte)** (1.3–1.6 mm) is elongate-oval, smooth and shiny, brownish yellow to blackish; appendages mostly paler, antennal club dark. Antennae long, extending past pronotum. Pronotum wider than long, sides broadly, irregularly arched, broadly lobed at base and narrower than elytra, underneath with coxal cavities open behind, not surrounded by thoracic plate. Elytra without grooves, almost without setae, with large spots behind humeri and broad crossbar just before tips often narrowly interrupted at suture. Adults active spring and summer, found on limbs; attracted to light. Québec and Ontario to Florida, west to Illinois and Louisiana. (4)

Dacne quadrimaculata (Say) (2.4–3.5 mm) is blackish with yellowish-red appendages, abdomen, and elytral spots. Head with last maxillary palpomeres cylindrical. Pronotum with base finely margined. Elytra with humeral and apical spots. Legs with tarsomeres 3 and 4 subequal. Overwintering adults found under bark and on oyster mushroom (*Pleurotus ostreatus*) and other fungi in late spring and summer. Nova Scotia to North Carolina, west to Manitoba and Texas. (1)

Megalodacne fasciata (Fabricius) (9.0–15.5 mm) is oblong-ovate, with shiny black head and pronotum, and reddish-orange crossbars on elytra. Head and pronotum black, smooth and shiny. Pronotum broad with narrow side margins. Elytra with rows of fine punctures, with red band near base not reaching suture. Adults active spring and summer, found under bark and on fungus growing on stumps and decaying logs; attracted to light, often overwinter in groups. Québec and Ontario to Florida, west to Minnesota, Iowa, Kansas, and Texas; also California, Colorado. (2). *Microsternus ulkei* (Crotch) (3.8–4.9 mm) is a rare species that resembles a very small *Megalodacne* with lines of elytral punctures. (1)

279

Megalodacne heros (Say) (14.0–22.0 mm) is oblong-oval, and shining black and reddish orange; females larger. Pronotum wider than long. Elytra with two broad orange-red bands, basal band surrounds two round humeral spots and nearly encloses a short black band just behind scutellum; no punctures on black areas. Adults and larvae eat shelf fungus (*Ganoderma*); larvae feed, develop, and pupate within fungus. Adults active in spring and summer, found on logs in moist woods during day, or hiding in cracks of logs and under loose bark; sometimes form large wintering aggregations. Ontario and Québec to Florida, west to Minnesota, Illinois, and Texas. (2)

Ischyrus quadripunctatus (Olivier) (4.8–8.1 mm) is elongate, oval, convex, pale to reddish yellow with black spots and bands. Head entirely black. Pronotum with row of four round spots. Base of elytra with large, somewhat rectangular spot at middle sometimes merging with spots on sides, irregular band across middle, and elongate spot on each tip. Underside black with sides of abdomen yellow. Larvae develop in fungus. Adults active in spring and summer, found on soft polypore fungi (*Oxyporus latemarginatus, Phellinus gilvus*) and under bark of various dead trees; frequently attracted to light. Ontario and Québec to Florida, west to Minnesota and Texas. (2)

Triplax frontalis Horn (3.9–5.9 mm) is oblong oval, black with reddish-yellow pronotum. Head mostly black with base narrowly reddish yellow. Antennae black, except at very base with antennomere 10 no more than twice as wide as 7. Pronotum with small punctures about same size as those in rows on elytra. Elytra black, somewhat shiny with spaces between rows flat. Underside with oblique suture from base of middle leg to side; legs yellowish. Adults found under bark in association with fungus. New Jersey and Pennsylvania to Georgia and northwestern Florida, west to Michigan, Iowa, Nebraska, and Texas. (8)

Triplax thoracica Say (3.0–5.6 mm) is oblong oval and reddish yellow with black antennal clubs, scutellum, and elytra. Head with tips of maxillary palpi three times wider than long. Elytra not distinctly margined along bases. Underside completely yellow or reddish yellow. Adults found under bark in association with fungus growing under bark, including oyster mushroom, *Pleurotus ostreatus*. In east from New Brunswick to Florida, west to North Dakota and Texas. *Triplax flavicollis* Lacordaire (3.3–5.1 mm) Lacordaire is similar, but with underside of mesothorax, methathorax, and abdomen black. (8)

Tritoma biguttata biguttata **(Say)** (2.6–4.5 mm) is elongate, oval, convex, reddish yellow underneath, usually with bicolored elytra. Head mostly black, antennal club reddish. Punctures on head and pronotum small, becoming larger at sides. Pronotum, scutellum, and elytra black. Most of underside and somewhat variable triangular patch, limited to basal third of each elytron, reddish yellow. Adults active late spring and summer on fungus. New Hampshire and Québec to North Carolina, west to Michigan and Indiana. *Tritoma b. affinis* Lacordaire has a reddish-yellow head, pronotum, scutellum black; southern North Carolina to Florida, west to Iowa and Texas. Intergrades have pale forebodies and reduced or absent elytral patch. (11)

Tritoma mimetica **(Crotch)** (3.1–4.4 mm) is broadly oval with reddish-yellow elytra with dark side markings. Most of head, mouthparts below, antennal clubs, entire prothorax, undersides of remaining thorax, abdomen, and trochanters are blackish or black. Adults are active in spring and summer and collected on the mushroom *Collybia radicata*. New York to Georgia, west to Kansas and Arkansas. (11)

ROOT-EATING BEETLES, FAMILY MONOTOMIDAE
(MO-NO-*TOME*-IH-DEE)

Most monotomids are found under bark or in decomposing plant materials. *Europs* is found under bark of dead trees, associated with cultivated plants, and attracted to light. *Hesperobaenus rufipes* LeConte lives under the bark of oak (*Quercus*) and maple (*Acer*), where it presumably feeds on fungus. *Monotoma* adults feed on mold in association with decaying plant material. They occupy compost heaps, haystacks, fouled stored food products, and ant nests. *Rhizophagus* lives under tree bark where it eat fungus and scavenges dead insects. In Europe, some species prey on bark beetles.

FAMILY DIAGNOSIS Adult monotomids are elongate, narrow, parallel-sided, with last abdominal segment exposed beyond tip of elytra. Antennae with 10 antennomeres, last one or two forming antennal club. Abdomen with five ventrites.

SIMILAR FAMILIES
- sap beetles (Nitidulidae) – clubbed antennae with 11 antennomeres, club with 3 antennomeres (p.295)
- palmetto beetles (Smicripidae) – mandibles clearly visible; clubbed antennae with 11 antennomeres, club with 3 antennomeres (p.305)
- zopherid beetles (Zopheridae) – tip of abdomen not exposed (p.340)

COLLECTING NOTES Look carefully for monotomids in rotting wood or under stones. Species that frequent decomposing plant debris may be found in stacks of hay and compost heaps. Some species living in wooded habitats are attracted to molasses traps. A few species are attracted to light.

FAUNA 56 SPECIES IN 11 GENERA (NA); 25 SPECIES IN 8 GENERA (ENA)

Rhizophagus cylindricus **LeConte** (2.0–5.0 mm) is long, narrow, dark reddish brown. Head of male with long mandibles and palps, and small eyes with coarse facets and distinctive bulges (temples) behind; females with normal mouthparts, slightly larger eyes, and shorter, less pronounced temples; eye facets coarse; tip of antennal club rounded, antennomere 11 not enclosed in 10, 3 shorter than 4–6 combined. Pronotum longer than wide, with sides sinuate (male) or not (female) at middle. Abdomen with last ventrite without depression. Bases of front legs wide. Adults are found under pine (*Pinus*) bark. New York to Georgia, west to Ohio, Oklahoma, and Alabama. (8)

Rhizophagus remotus **LeConte** (2.0–2.5 mm) is elongate, somewhat flat, and uniformly blackish or brownish yellow with appendages reddish yellow. Head with bulge (temple) behind eye not swollen, about half the vertical diameter of eye. Antennomere 3 shorter than combined length of 4–6, antennomere 11 not enclosed inside 10, tip of club rounded. Pronotum slightly wider than long. Abdomen with last ventrite without depression. Bases of front legs wide. Adults found under bark of pine (*Pinus*), aspen and cottonwood (*Populus*), also bracket fungi. Across Canada; in east from Maritime Provinces and New England to North Carolina, west to Manitoba and Indiana. (8)

Monotoma bicolor Villa & Villa (1.9–2.5 mm) is elongate and reddish brown to blackish, with head and pronotum darker than elytra. Antennal club with one antennomere, 3 as long as 2. Pronotum elongate, coarsely punctate with shallow dual impressions, and blunt protruding front angles. Elytra with paired rows of punctures somewhat confused at very base and tip, not covering abdomen and exposing one (female) or two (male) abdominal ventrites. Abdomen underneath with first ventrite longer than rest. Adults active in summer, found in decaying vegetable matter. Europe; in east from New Brunswick to North Carolina, west to Iowa, Kansas, and Oklahoma. (11)

Monotoma producta LeConte (2.5–3.2 mm) is uniformly reddish brown to blackish. Head lacks longitudinal impressions and pronotal disk with two shallow depressions; head and pronotum with large, deep, closely placed punctures. Pronotum distinctly elongate with its sides diverging toward rear, anterior angles blunt, while posterior angles marked by large protuberances. Adults found by sifting beach wrack and under boards and other debris on beaches. Atlantic Coast, from New Brunswick to Florida. (11)

Bactridium species (2.0 mm) are elongate, somewhat flattened, shining reddish brown to blackish. Head wide as long, side parallel and not narrowed at base; antennal club with one antennomere. Pronotum flat to convex. Elytra with rows of distinct punctures. Abdomen with visible first ventrite long and crossed oblique bead from each coxa, 2–4 each with transverse row of large, oblong punctures. Adults found under bark of dead trees. Eastern North America. (7)

Europs pallipennis (LeConte) (2.8 mm) is blackish with mostly dull yellowish elytra. Head not longer than wide, without antennal grooves, antennal club with two antennomeres. Pronotum shiny, as long as wide with curved impression at base, with sparse punctures becoming denser toward sides. Elytra with rows of fine setose punctures, downturned side margins with three rows, darker at tips. Abdomen of male with fifth ventrite plain. Adults active in summer; reared from pine cones (*Pinus*). Connecticut and New York to Florida, west to Texas. (3)

SILKEN FUNGUS BEETLES, FAMILY CRYPTOPHAGIDAE
(KRYPT-O-*FAJ*-IH-DEE)

Cryptophagids feed on hyphae, spores, conidia, and other fungal materials. Species are typically found in association with mold, moldy stored food products, and other substrates that foster mold growth, such as beneath the bark of dead or dying trees and in decaying vegetation. Some species are scavengers in bee and wasp nests. Several species in the region await scientific description.

FAMILY DIAGNOSIS Adult cryptophagids are elontate-oval to oval, robust, with surface frequently clothed in long, silky setae. Antennal club loose, with three antennomeres. Pronotum sometimes with irregular margins on sides and often with a pair of depressions along base. Elytra with irregular punctures and lack grooves or rows of punctures. Tarsal formula 5-5-5, sometimes 5-5-4 in males. Abdomen with five ventrites, first ventrite longer than remaining four.

SIMILAR FAMILIES

- round fungus beetles (Leiodidae) – club with five antennomeres, 8 usually small (p.118)
- tooth-neck fungus beetles (Derodontidae) – elytra with distinct squarish punctures (p.243)
- fruitworm beetles (Byturidae) – abdominal ventrites all of equal length, tarsomeres 2–3 lobed underneath (p.274)
- false skin beetles (Biphyllidae) – sublateral lines present on the pronotum, with postcoxal lines on abdomen (p.276)

- minute bark beetles (Cerylonidae) – antennal club with two antennomeres; usually without setae above (p.307)
- hairy fungus beetles (Mycetophagidae) – most species distinctly bicolored, abdominal ventrites all of equal length (p.323)
- polypore fungus beetles (Tetratomidae) – antennae weakly clavate if clubbed at all, abdominal ventrites all of equal length (p.327)
- zopherid beetles (Zopheridae) – antennal club with two antennomeres, tarsi 4-4-4 (p.340)

COLLECTING NOTES Cryptophagids are usually found in association with mold or moldy substrates, on fungus, and in decaying vegetation. Look under bark of dead trees, in decaying wood and other vegetable debris, or accumulations of plant materials in abandoned animal nests. Some species are swept or beaten from vegetation, or attracted to yellow pan traps.

283

FAUNA 145 SPECIES IN 16 GENERA (NA); ~43 SPECIES 12 GENERA (ENA)

Antherophagus ochraceus **Melsheimer** (4.0–5.0 mm) is uniformly yellowish brown and clothed in dense, appressed yellowish pubescence. Antennae and base of tibiae dark in males. Prothorax broader than long with fine, dense punctures and sides nearly straight and somewhat parallel. Elytra wide as pronotum and very finely and densely punctate. Adults on flowers, such as wild hydrangea (*Hydrangea arborescens*), Queen Anne's lace (*Daucus carota*), Virginia rose (*Rosa virginiana*), and common milkweed (*Asclepias syriaca*) in summer; possibly found in bumble bee nests. Across southern Canada to North Carolina, west to Minnesota, Indiana, and Tennessee. (2)

Cryptophagus **species** (1.6–3.5 mm) are small, oblong, reddish brown to black with distinct and irregular serrate margins on sides of pronotum. Head without groove before clypeus. Pronotum with sides lacking narrow parallel grooves before margins, margins each with broad angle in front and small, distinct toothlike projection at middle. Elytra punctate, without grooves or rows of punctures, and distinctly clothed in setae. Adults and larvae occur in habitats promoting fungal growth, some species associated with mammal nests or occasionally infest stored products. Widespread in eastern North America. (23)

Henotiderus obesulus (Casey) (1.5–1.8 mm) is short, oval, very convex, clothed in long setae, shiny black and mostly reddish elytra with black around scutellum and tips; appendages yellowish brown. Antennal bases widely separated. Pronotum wider than long, anterior angles projecting forward, with small irregular teeth on sides, a fine ridge along each side, and pair of pits along base lobed at middle. Elytra at base wide as pronotum, becoming much wider before middle, with two ill-defined rows of punctures. Middle of femora black. Adults found in leaf litter or on fungi of forested habitats. Massachusetts and New York to South Carolina, west to Alaska and Rocky Mountains. (2)

Telmatophilus americanus LeConte (2.5–3.0 mm) is oblong-oval, convex, dark reddish brown to blackish with fine gray pubescence and reddish-brown appendages. Male with external flangelike expansion at base of hind tibiae. Last abdominal ventrite of male with pit near tip. Adults found in summer on flowers of bur-reed (*Sparganium*) and arrow arum (*Peltandra virginicum*). Across Canada south to Colorado, Indiana, and New York. (2)

Caenoscelis basalis Casey (2.2–2.5 mm) is elongate, oval, and uniformly reddish brown with pronotum half or more wider than long. Eyes large with many facets. Antennae attached closely together in middle, space between with a ridge, club with three antennomeres. Pronotum coarsely, deeply punctate with sides distinctly ridged and almost parallel, narrower than elytra. Elytra coarsely, closely punctate, two-thirds longer than wide, and distinctly rounded at apex. Adults found in spring and summer under loose bark. Newfoundland and Nova Scotia to New England, west to Québec and New York. (4).

Atomaria distincta Casey (1.4-1.5 mm) is narrowly oval, convex, shiny, pubescent, and distinctly bicolored . Head reddish brown with suture behind clypeus present, bases of antennae closer to eyes than each other. Prothorax, except for area near coxae, reddish brown, with process underneath narrow, flat, and not bearing parallel lines. Scutellum black. Elytra black at base, reddish brown at apical two-fifths to one-half extending forward slightly along suture. Adults and larvae found in accumulations of plant debris with fungus. Nova Scotia, New Brunswick, and Québec to District of Columbia. (10 NA)

SILVANID FLAT BARK BEETLES, FAMILY SILVANIDAE
(SIL-*VAN*-IH-DEE)

The biologies of silvanids that are of no economic importance are mostly unknown. Most species are found under loose tree bark (*Cathartosilvanus, Silvanus, Uleiota*), on plants (*Cryptamorpha, Telephanus*), or under plant debris (some *Ahasverus*) where they probably eat fungi. Several genera (*Ahasverus, Cathartus, Oryzaephilus, Nausibius*) contain species that are pests of stored grains, grain products, nuts, and spices.

FAMILY DIAGNOSIS Adult silvanids are small, elongate, parallel-sided to slightly oval in outline, and somewhat flattened with the sides of the pronotum distinctly margined, wavy, or toothed; most lack conspicuous setae. Head broad, with mouthparts directed forward, usually distinctly narrowed behind eyes. Antennae with 11 antennomeres, usually long and mostly filiform (*Telephanus, Uleiota*), or shorter with moniliform antennomeres and distinct club (*Cathartosilvanus, Nausibius, Oryzaephilus, Silvanus*). Prothorax longer than wide. Elytra long, distinctly pitted or rough, and cover abdomen completely. Tarsal formula is 5-5-5 (4-4-4 in *Uleiota*), with claws equal and simple. Abdomen with five distinct ventrites.

SIMILAR FAMILIES
- root-eating beetles (Monotomidae) – antennae with 10 antennomeres, club with one or two (p.281)
- flat bark beetles (Cucujidae) – more flattened; antennae not clubbed; pronotum usually wider than long to almost square; tarsi 5-5-4 in males (p.288)
- lined flat bark beetles (Laemophloeidae) – head and pronotum with distinct lines or ridges along sides (p.291)
- *Adelina* (Tenebrionidae) – bases of antennae hidden from above by rim (p.354)

COLLECTING NOTES Look for silvanids on plants, under loose bark, in decaying plant materials, especially rotting fruit, and in infested stored products.

285

FAUNA 32 SPECIES IN 14 GENERA (NA); 21 SPECIES IN 13 GENERA (ENA)

Dendrophagus cygnaei Mannerheim (5.0–7.0 mm) is elongate, flat, straight-sided, and reddish yellow-brown to dark brownish black with appendages, especially tarsi, paler. Antennae long, filiform, without obvious club. Prothorax with sides smooth and front angles rounded, pronotum densely punctured, underneath with coxal cavities open behind. Tarsi 5-5-5, tarsomeres not lobed underneath. Southern Canada and northern United States; in east from Maritime Provinces and New England to Connecticut and New York, west to Ontario and Indiana. (1)

Uleiota dubius (Fabricius) (4.0–6.0 mm) is long, straight-sided, and flat with long antennae. Body mostly brownish black, legs, elytral margins, sometimes head and pronotum paler. Pronotum with front angles prominent and toothed, margins distinctly serrate. Male's mandibles armed with slender, curved horn, tips of elytra more squared off and expanded than in female. Adults found year-round under loose bark of snags, logs, and stumps. Widespread in northeastern North America. *Uleiota debilis* (LeConte) (5.0–5.5 mm) is blackish with appendages and elytral margins paler; front angles of pronotum less prominent; tips of male elytra not expanded. (2)

TOP RIGHT: *Uleiota dubius.*
BOTTOM RIGHT: *Uleiota debilis.*

Telephanus atricapillus Erichson (4.0–4.5 mm) is elongate, slender, mostly yellowish brown, with dense erect setae on elytra. Head black, densely punctured, without grooves, and slender antennae without club. Pronotum densely punctured, pronotal margin with small bumps bearing setae. Scutellum small, not crossed by distinct groove. Elytra broader than pronotum with rows of deep punctures, and apical third sometimes with broad dark band. Legs with tarsomere 3 simply lobed and setose underneath. Adults found in late spring and summer on vegetation, under bark, beneath stones and other debris. Québec and Ontario to Florida, west to Iowa, Kansas, and Arizona. (1)

Ahasverus rectus (LeConte) (1.8–2.2 mm) is elongate, ovate, somewhat flat, and pale reddish brown. Antennae clubbed, antennomere 9 equal in width to 10, 11 rounded at tip. Pronotum widest toward front, front angles weakly lobed, and side margins smooth, not toothed. Elytra with rows of deep punctures. Tarsomere 3 expanded. Adults active primarily spring through summer, found in forest floor leaf litter; also flight intercept traps, attracted to light. North Carolina to Florida, west to Arizona. (3)

Cathartosilvanus imbellis (LeConte) (2.4–2.8 mm) is moderately shining. Head wider than long and coarsely punctured, distance between eyes less than that between front angles on pronotum. Antennae clubbed. Pronotum longer than wide, with front angles poorly developed, slightly undulate sides more or less parallel, a pair of slight depressions toward base. Tarsi not lobed. Adults active in summer, found under bark of hardwoods, e.g., oak (*Quercus*); attracted to light. In east from Québec and Ontario to Florida, west to Iowa, Kansas, and Texas. (1)

Nausibius major Zimmerman (3.9–5.1 mm) is elongate, somewhat convex, not obviously parallel-sided. Antennae without cavities or grooves at base, club appears composed of four antennomeres. Pronotum is more or less uniformly punctate, with sides distinctly undulate, not toothed, and crescent-shaped depression at base; underneath with coxae completely surrounded by thoracic plate. Tarsal formula 5-5-5 in both sexes, tarsomere 1 longer than 2, 3 simple and not lobed. Adults found under bark or in association with slime flux on oak (*Quercus*); attracted to light. New York to Florida, west to Colorado, Oklahoma, and Texas. (4)

Merchant Grain Beetle *Oryzaephilus mercator* **(Fauvel)** (2.2–3.1 mm) is elongate, flattened, and uniformly brown. Head with surface less coarsely and closely punctate in front of eyes, sides behind eye less than one-third length of eye and sharply and narrowly angular. Sides of pronotum each with six sawlike teeth. Elytra ridged, between with rows of coarse and close-set punctures. Hind femora each with (male) or without (female) a tooth. Adults and larvae are common pantry pests and associated with cereals, dried fruits, and nuts; adults not cold-tolerant. Old World, cosmopolitan. (2)

Saw-toothed Grain Beetle *Oryzaephilus surinamensis* **(Linnaeus)** (2.1–3.2 mm) is elongate, flattened, and uniformly brown. Head with surface close-set coarse punctures throughout and sides behind eye at least half length of eye and not narrow and sharp, club antennomeres squarish. Sides of pronotum each with six sawlike teeth. Elytra ridged, between with rows of coarse and close-set punctures. Hind femora each with (male) or without (female) a tooth. Adults and larvae associated with cereals, dried fruits, and nuts, especially in food processing centers; adults cold-tolerant, sometimes found under tree bark. Old World, cosmopolitan. (2)

FLAT BARK BEETLES, FAMILY CUCUJIDAE
(KOO-*KOO*-JIH-DEE)

The red flat bark beetle, *Cucujus clavipes* Fabricius, is thought to be predatory based on the remains of insects and other arthropods found in the intestinal tract of the larvae. The larvae of *C. clavipes* are the subjects of numerous studies focusing on the cold tolerance of insects and other ectothermic animals. Although both the larvae and adults overwinter, the larvae are better adapted for surviving cold temperatures and generally more common under loose bark during the winter months. Individuals avoid freezing by seeking out favorable microenvironments and eliminating water from their tissues. They also produce high levels of "antifreeze" in their blood and combine it with special compounds that encourage survivable ice crystal formation between cells, rather than lethal crystal formation inside cells.

FAMILY DIAGNOSIS Adult cucujids are strongly flattened and somewhat rectangular in outline. Head is broad and triangular, with mouthparts directed forward (prognathous). Antennae with 11 antennomeres, moniliform. Pronotum shorter than wide or squarish. Scutellum is small. Elytra straight-sided and completely conceal abdomen; surface flat and finely punctured. Tarsal formula of male is 5-5-4, female 5-5-5; claws equal and simple. Abdomen with five ventrites.

SIMILAR FAMILIES

- silvanid beetles (Silvanidae) – less flattened; antennae clubbed or filiform; pronotum usually longer than wide; tarsi 5-5-5 in both sexes (p.285)
- parasitic flat bark beetles (Passandridae) – pronotum longer than wide; tarsi 5-5-5 in both sexes (p.289)
- lined flat bark beetles (Laemophloeidae) – head and pronotum with a distinct line or fine ridge near sides (p.291)

COLLECTING NOTES Look for adult and larval cucujids under the loose bark of recently dead or decomposing pines and deciduous hardwoods.

288

FAUNA THREE SPECIES IN TWO GENERA (NA); TWO SPECIES IN TWO GENERA (ENA)

Red Flat Bark Beetle *Cucujus clavipes clavipes* Fabricius (10.0–13.0 mm) is strongly flattened and mostly bright red, sometimes with dark infusions on elytra. Head distinctly triangular and bulging behind eyes. Antennae, eyes black, legs black with red femora. Adults and distinctly segmented larvae flat, and are both found under loose bark of deciduous trees. Newfoundland to Florida, west to Manitoba and Texas; adventive in Italy. The western subspecies, *C. c. puniceus* Mannerheim, is restricted to states and provinces west of the Great Plains. (1)

Pediacus subglaber LeConte (3.3–4.0 mm) is elongate, somewhat parallel-sided, flattened, coarsely punctured, and shiny reddish brown. Head not expanded sideways behind eyes, antennae distinctly clubbed. Pronotum with distinct impressions. Tarsomeres not lobed, tarsi 5-5-4 (male) or 5-5-5 (female). Adults and larvae usually found underneath conifer bark, mainly in montane or boreal habitats. Québec and Ontario to Georgia, west to Michigan, Illinois, and Tennessee. *Pediacus fuscus* Erichson is dull, without pronotal impressions; Atlantic Canada and New England west to Alaska, British Columbia, and Wisconsin. (2)

PARASITIC FLAT BARK BEETLES, FAMILY PASSANDRIDAE
(PAS-*SAN*-DRIH-DEE)

The feeding habits of adult passandrids are unknown. Larval passandrids appear to be ectoparasites of other wood-boring insects, especially the pupae of longhorn beetles (Cerambycidae) and braconid wasps. *Catogenus rufus* (Fabricius) is associated with the pupa of a longhorn beetle, *Anelaphus parallelus* (Newman), while a larva of *Taphroscelidia linearis* (LeConte) was found in the galleries of a bark beetle, *Pityophthorus concentralis* Eichoff.

FAMILY DIAGNOSIS Adult passandrids are elongate, strongly flattened (*Catogenus*) or nearly cylindrical in cross section (*Taphroscelidia*), dark reddish brown, with more or less distinct punctate elytral grooves. Head with mouthparts directed forward (prognathous), rounded plates (genae) that conceal maxillae, and distinct lines and grooves; underside with gular sutures confluent. Moniliform antennae with 11 antennomeres. Pronotum longer than wide, slightly narrower at base than elytra. Scutellum small, visible. Elytra long, straight-sided, with punctate grooves, and completely covering abdomen. Legs stout, tarsal formula 5-5-5 in both sexes, tarsomeres not lobed underneath, claws simple and equal. Abdomen with five ventrites.

SIMILAR FAMILIES

- wrinkled bark beetles (Carabidae) – pronotum with deep grooves (p.63)
- silvanid beetles (Silvanidae) – antennae not moniliform (p.285)
- flat bark beetles (Cucujidae) – flattened; pronotum somewhat quadrate; males 5-5-4 (p.288)
- lined flat bark beetles (Laemophloeidae) – flattened; distinct lines along sides of head and prontoum (p.291)
- cylindrical bark beetles (Zopheridae) – antennae abruptly clubbed (pp.341–3)
- some darkling beetles (Tenebrionidae) – antennal insertions hidden from above (p.344)

COLLECTING NOTES Look for passandrids under bark and at lights. They are sometimes found in Malaise and flight intercept trap samples.

289

FAUNA THREE SPECIES IN TWO GENERA (NA); TWO SPECIES IN TWO GENERA (ENA)

Parasitic Flat Bark Beetle *Catogenus rufus* (Fabricius) (4.0–13 mm) is elongate, strongly flattened, and uniformly dark reddish brown. Head with deep groove across base. Elytra with deep punctate grooves. Hind tibial spurs longer than first tarsomere. Adults are found under bark of recently dead or dying hardwoods and conifers; they are also attracted to lights in summer. Larvae are external parasitoids of pupae of wood-boring longhorn beetles (Cerambycidae) and wasps (Braconidae). Ontario and Québec to Florida, west to Illinois and Texas; also south to Costa Rica. (1)

Taphroscelidia linearis (LeConte) (4.4–7.1 mm) is elongate, somewhat cylindrical, and uniformly reddish brown. Head without deep groove across base. Elytra with punctate grooves. Hind tibial spurs shorter than first tarsomere. Larvae might be ectoparasitic on wood-boring insects, possibly bark beetles (Curculionidae); one individual found in galleries of *Pityopthorus concentralis* in Florida poison tree (*Metopium toxiferum*). Adults found at light in summer. Illinois to Florida, and Texas; also the Carribean, Mexico, Central and South America. (1)

SHINING FLOWER AND SHINING MOLD BEETLES, FAMILY PHALACRIDAE
(FUH-*LACK*-RIH-DEE)

Phalacrids are round, strongly convex beetles with flat undersides and have the ability to foil predators by tucking in their appendages. Their form and behavior not only shield them from attacks, but also allow them to escape danger by rolling off leaves and taking to the air, or simply falling to the ground. Adults feed on either pollen or fungal structures. Adult and larval phalacrids associated with fungi that cause diseases in vascular plants, including those that cause ergot, rusts, and smuts, are apparently important natural control agents of these diseases, because any spores they ingest become unviable; however, their use as biological control agents for these fungal diseases in crops must await further study. The pollen-feeding species of *Olibrus* are commonly found on composite flowers in late summer, including *Aster*, *Bidens*, *Cirsium*, *Chrysopis*, *Eupatoria*, *Solidago*, *Vernonia*; their larvae develop in the flower heads on a diet of plant fluids. *Acylomus* adults feed on saprophytic fungi on dead or dying plant structures, especially leaves, seedpods, and woody floral structures. *Stilbus* nibbles on molds growing on plant surfaces, especially grasses, and in piles of moldy grass thatch. *Phalacrus* is associated with the spores of smut fungi. *Acylomus* is found on ergot fungus or molds growing on clusters of drying leaves, dead legume pods, and cotton bolls; they also occur on Spanish moss (*Tillandsia usneoides*).

FAMILY DIAGNOSIS Adult phalacrids are small, broadly oval to nearly circular, and have a continuous body outline, very convex above and flat below, shiny brownish or black without dorsal hairs. Head with eyes not prominent, surface smooth, and visible from above with mouthparts directed downward (hypognathous). Antennae with 11 antennomeres, 9–11 forming elongate club, 11 largest. Scutellum somewhat large, triangular. Elytra completely cover abdomen, one or two grooves near suture or absent, and tips rounded. Legs with tarsal formula 5-5-5, 1–3 broad and hairy underneath, 4 small and obscure, claws with tooth or broadly expanded at base. Abdomen with five ventrites, surfaces smooth, and sutures distinct. Examination of male genitalia is usually required for species identification.

SIMILAR FAMILIES
- water scavenger beetles (Hydrophilidae) – usually more than 3 mm; mouthparts long (p.105)
- round fungus beetles (Leiodidae) – antennal club with three to five antennomeres; tibia usually shiny, expanded, spiny (p.118)
- minute beetles (Clambidae) – can partially roll up (p.179)
- marsh beetles (Scirtidae) – antennae not clubbed (p.180)
- pleasing fungus beetles (Erotylidae) – rarely as convex; usually black with red, yellow, or orange (p.277)
- sap beetles (Nitidulidae) – antennal club ball-shaped (p.295)
- lady beetles (Coccinellidae) – antennae short, club with three to six antennomeres; often clothed in hairs (p.311)

COLLECTING NOTES Adult phalacrids are best collected by beating and sweeping grasses and shrubs, or by searching moldy vegetation, plants infected with smut, and fungus on decaying logs in forested habitats. Check tree branches broken off by summer storms for clumps of dried leaves that might harbor adult and larval phalacrids within wilted and curled surfaces. Cutting branches of hardwood trees, bundling them up, and then hanging them in shady places will duplicate this microhabitat. Hibernating adults are sometimes sifted from leaf litter or found under boards and stones in open fields and under beach drift from late fall through early spring. Malaise and UV light traps will also produce additional specimens.

FAUNA 122 SPECIES IN 12 GENERA (NA); ~60 SPECIES IN 11 GENERA (ENA)

Olibrus **species** (1.4–2.8 mm) are oblong-ovate, shiny reddish brown to blackish, underside paler. Bases of antennae at sides of front of head above mandibles and visible from above, upper margin of clypeus above bases sinuate, and antennomeres 9–11 forming long club, 11 largest. Elytra each with one or two rows of punctures, with or without distinct markings. Legs with hind tarsomere 1 shorter than 2. Larvae develop in flower head of composite flowers such as goldenrod (*Solidago*). Adults active in spring and summer, found on flowers feeding on pollen. Widespread in eastern North America. (8)

Stilbus apicalis **(Melsheimer)** (1.6–2.3 mm) is relatively elongate, oval, convex, polished brown to black with apical third of elytra, underside, and appendages yellowish to yellowish brown. Head about half as wide as prothorax, antennal bases visible from above. Pronotum more than twice as wide as long. Elytra each with single groove along suture that disappears before reaching scutellum. Legs with tibial spurs small, inconspicuous, hind tarsi short with first tarsomere shorter than and not fused to second. Adults associated with smutted fall panicgrass (*Panicum dichotomiflorum*); attracted to light. Males collected only rarely. Maritime Provinces and New England to Florida, west to Ontario, Illinois, Kansas, and Louisiana; also western North America. (22)

291

LINED FLAT BARK BEETLES, FAMILY LAEMOPHLOEIDAE
(LEE-MO-*FLO*-IH-DEE)

Little is known about the biology of most laemophloeids. Both adults and larvae are found beneath the bark of logs, usually hardwoods such as oak (*Quercus*). Some feed on fungal spores and hyphae in leaf litter or under bark and in the galleries of bark beetles (Curculionidae), while others have been found on the fruiting bodies of ascomycete fungi. *Narthecius* is found in galleries under bark and apparently preys on bark beetles. A few species (*Cryptolestes*) found outside of eastern North America are of economic importance and attack stored grains or prey on scale insects. The elongate, flattened larvae of this family are unique among the Coleoptera in producing silk from a pair of prothoracic glands to form a cocoon in which they pupate.

FAMILY DIAGNOSIS Adult laemophloeids are usually flattened or somewhat cylindrical (*Narthecius*) with a pair of fine lines or grooves along sides of pronotum and usually on head (absent in *Lathropus*). Head broad with sides bordered by carina or groove, widest across round or oval eyes, mandibles stout to elongate, directed forward (prognathous) and sometimes visible from above. Antennae usually filiform with 10 antennomeres. Scutellum broad to triangular. Elytra usually with ridge running from humerus, with side margins (epipleural fold) moderate to broad and complete from base to tip. Legs with tarsal formula in females 5-5-5, mostly 5-5-4 in males; first tarsomere shortest; claws simple. Abdomen with five distinct ventrites.

SIMILAR FAMILIES

- wrinkled bark beetles (Carabidae) – prothorax with deep grooves (p.76)
- powder-post beetles (Bostrichidae: Lyctinae) – antennae short, club with two antennomeres (p.250)
- silvanid beetles (Silvanidae) – first tarsomere longer than second (p.285)
- flat bark beetles (Cucujidae) – first antennomere short; tarsi lobed (p.288)
- parasitic flat bark beetles (Passandridae) – maxillae hidden; elytra, not pronotum with distinct lines; tarsi 5-5-5 in both sexes (p.289)
- cylindrical bark beetles (Zopheridae) – antennal club distinct (pp.341–3)
- *Adelina* (Tenebrionidae) – no grooves or ridges on head or pronotum (p.354)

COLLECTING NOTES Adults are found under bark of oak and other deciduous hardwoods, beaten from dead branches, or attracted to light at night.

FAUNA 52 SPECIES IN 13 GENERA (NA); 25 SPECIES IN 10 GENERA (ENA)

Charaphloeus convexulus LeConte (1.7–2.4 mm) is slightly convex, and dark brown to blackish. Head with elongate mandibles in male. Head and pronotum finely punctate. Pronotum wider than long, widest toward front, with front angles sharp and sides rounded, not angulate. Elytra more finely punctate, without ridges at humeri, with cells absent or poorly expressed. Legs with tarsomere 1 as long as or longer than penultimate tarsomere, male tarsal formula 5-5-4. Adults found under bark; also in flight intercept traps and at lights. Nova Scotia and New England to Florida, west to Michigan, Iowa, and Oklahoma. (3)

Rusty Grain Beetle *Cryptolestes ferrugineus* (Stephens) (2.0 mm) is slightly convex and uniformly reddish brown. Antennae of both sexes about equal in length. Males with outer mandible surface expanded at base with tooth. Pronotum distinctly constricted near base, especially in male. Pronotum with one line parallel to side margin, basal angles distinct. Elytra with spaces between first two ridges from suture with four rows of setae, outer spaces with three rows. Legs with tarsi 5-5-4. Pest in stored products. Cosmopolitan. (4)

Laemophloeus biguttatus (Say) (1.9–3.3 mm) is elongate, flat, and blackish with pair of small oval pale spots on elytra; upper surface is densely punctate. Adults and larvae feed on ascomycete fungal tissues and spores. Adults active in spring and summer, found under bark; attracted to light. Widely distributed in eastern North America. (4)

Laemophloeus fasciatus **Melsheimer** (2.1–3.1 mm) is elongate, flat, and blackish or black with pair of triangular pale patches on elytra. Adults active spring and summer, found under bark. In east from Maritime Provinces and New England to Florida, west to Ontario, Iowa, Kansas, and Texas. (4)

Placonotus modestus **(Say)** (1.4–2.2 mm) has elytral apices truncate exposing most of last abdominal tergite (propygium). Elytra with distinct rows of punctures. Adults are found under bark of dead hardwoods, especially oak (*Quercus*), in association with ascomycete fungi; also attracted to lights. New York to Florida, west to Arizona; also Mexico to Panama. (4)

SHORT-WINGED FLOWER BEETLES, FAMILY KATERETIDAE
(KAT-ER-*ET*-IH-DEE)

293

Both adult and larval kateretids are plant feeders and associated with flowers. Adults eat petals and pollen, while the larvae develop in seed capsules.

FAMILY DIAGNOSIS Adult kateretids are somewhat elongate, oval, with maxilla with two lobes (galea, lacinia) and weak antennal club with three antennomeres. Tarsal formula 5-5-5. Abdomen with five ventrites.

SIMILAR FAMILIES

- water scavenger beetles (Hydrophilidae) – long maxillary palps, clavate antennal club (p.105)
- clown beetles (Histeridae) – antennae elbowed; elytra short, lined with rows of punctures and cover all but last two abdominal tergites (p.110)
- round fungus beetles (Leiodidae) – elytra grooved; antennomere 8 small (p.118)
- some rove beetles (Staphylinidae) – antennae usually not distinctly clubbed; elytra with rows of punctures or distinctly ridged (p.124)
- marsh beetles (Scirtidae) – antennae filiform or serrate; elytra completely covering abdomen (p.180)
- pill beetles (Byrrhidae) – antennae filiform or clavate, club with three to seven antennomeres (p.195)

- wounded-tree beetles (Nosodendridae) – tibiae broadly expanded; elytra covering abdomen (p.244)
- skin beetles (Dermestidae) – body usually covered with scales or hairs (p.246)
- some bark-gnawing beetles (Trogossitidae) – antennal club loose, side margin of pronotum sharp, tarsal claws long (p.261)
- pleasing fungus beetles (Erotylidae) – elytra completely covering abdomen (p.277)
- shining flower beetles (Phalacridae) – dorsal surface shiny; antennal club less compact (p.290)
- minute fungus beetles (Corylophidae) – head often not visible from above (p.320)
- hairy fungus beetles (Mycetophagidae) – body with short hairs; antennal club less compact (p.323)
- tortoise beetles (Chrysomelidae: Cassidinae) – head not visible from above; antennae filiform or clavate (pp.434–6)

COLLECTING NOTES Adult kateretids are found on flowers and swept from vegetation.

FAUNA 11 SPECIES IN SEVEN GENERA (NA); FIVE SPECIES IN FIVE GENERA (ENA)

Brachypterolus pulicarius **(Linnaeus)** (1.8–2.5 mm) is oval, convex, coarsely punctate, shiny black with appendages pale to blackish. Antennomeres 9–11 forming feeble club. Pronotum with hind angles rectangular. Tarsi 5-5-5, claws with distinct tooth at base. Larvae develop in toadflax (*Linaria*). Adults active in spring and early summer, found on flowers, e.g., dandelion (*Taraxacum*), buttercup (*Ranunculus*), wild mustard (*Sinapis*), clover (*Trifolium*), apple (*Malus*), and dogwood (*Cornus*); injurious to strawberry (*Fragaria*). Europe, established from Maritime Provinces and New England to Delaware, west to Ontario, Wisconsin, and Iowa. (1)

Brachypterus urticae **(Fabricius)** (1.5–2.0 mm) is oval, convex, and shining brownish or black with sparse pubescence, sometimes with brassy tinge. Head narrower than pronotum. Pronotum nearly as wide as elytra, sides broadly arched, with hind angles obtuse, not rectangular. Legs with claws toothed at base. Adults active in summer, found on the flowers of various plants, including aster (*Aster*), joe pye weed (*Eutrochium*), ash (*Fraxinus*), laportea (*Laportea*), goldenrod (*Solidago*), and nettle (*Urtica*) in mesic hardwood forests. Across southern Canada, south to Virginia, Missouri, and Colorado. (1)

Heterhelus **(formerly *Boreades*)** *abdominalis* **(Erichson)** (2.0–3.0 mm) is oval, convex, deep metallic blue-green with abdomen and legs reddish. Antennae reddish with dark clubs. Legs with claws simple. Adults active in spring and summer, found on flowers, including elderberry (*Sambucus*), apple (*Malus*), pear (*Pyrus*). New Brunswick and New England to Georgia, west to Manitoba, Nebraska, Kansas, and Texas. (1)

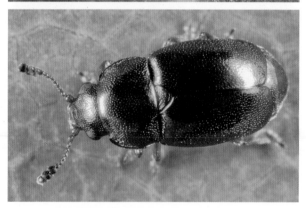

294

SAP BEETLES, FAMILY NITIDULIDAE
(NIH-TIH-*DEW*-LIH-DEE)

Nitidulids are small, mostly compact beetles that are found in a wide variety of habitats. Many species (*Carpophilus, Colopterus, Cryptarcha, Epuraea, Lobiopa, Glischrochilus*) are found around sap flows in forests and woodlands; some of these are known or suspected to carry fungal diseases of plants. Other species are found on flowers or in association with decaying wood, rotting fruit, carrion, and fungi; a few species (*Aethina, Carpophilus, Epuraea*) inhabit bee nests, while others (*Amphotis*) spend at least part of their lives with ants. Some species of *Carpophilus* are pests of dried fruits and other stored products. The product is not only contaminated by adult and larval waste, these insects also inoculate the product with molds and other organisms that further hasten its decomposition. Larvae of some species have modified glands that secrete a mucous-like substance that is believed to act as a deterrent to predators.

FAMILY DIAGNOSIS Adult nitidulids are elongate and robust or broadly oval and hemispherical or slightly flattened, with distinctly clubbed antennae with the clubs usually ball-shaped and often short elytra exposing one to three abdominal tergites. Head with mouthparts directed forward. Clubbed antennae with 11 antennomeres, usually 9–11 forming club. Pronotum wider than long, front margin deeply and broadly notched, with side sharply margined or keeled. Elytra usually short and without grooves, tips appear cut off or individually rounded at tips. Tarsal formula 5-5-5, with tarsomeres broad, 4 small. Abdomen with five ventrites.

SIMILAR FAMILIES

- water scavenger beetles (Hydrophilidae) – long palps, clavate antennal club (p.105)
- clown beetles (Histeridae) – antennae elbowed; elytra short, lined with rows of punctures and cover all but last two abdominal tergites (p.110)
- round fungus beetles (Leiodidae) – antennomere 8 small (p.118)
- some rove beetles (Staphylinidae) – antennae usually not distinctly clubbed; elytra with rows of punctures or distinctly ridged (p.124)
- marsh beetles (Scirtidae) – antennae filiform to serrate; elytra covering abdomen (p.180)
- pill beetles (Byrrhidae) – antennae filiform or clavate, club with three to seven antennomeres (p.195)
- wounded-tree beetles (Nosodendridae) – tibiae broadly expanded; elytra completely covering abdomen (p.244)
- skin beetles (Dermestidae) – body usually covered with scales or hairs (p.246)
- some bark-gnawing beetles (Trogossitidae) – antennal club loose, side margin of pronotum sharp, tarsal claws long (p.261)
- pleasing fungus beetles (Erotylidae) – elytra completely covering abdomen (p.277)
- shining flower beetles (Phalacridae) – dorsal surface shiny; antennal club less compact (p.290)
- short-winged flower beetles (Kateretidae) – maxilla with two lobes (galea, lacinia) antennal club less compact, elytra always short and exposing at least two abdominal tergites (p.293)
- cybocephalid beetles (Cybocephalidae) – tarsi 4-4-4 (p.304)
- minute fungus beetles (Corylophidae) – head often not visible from above (p.320)
- hairy fungus beetles (Mycetophagidae) – body covered with short hairs; antennal club less compact (p.323)
- tortoise beetles (Chrysomelidae) – head not visible from above; antennae filiform or clavate (pp.434–6)

COLLECTING NOTES Look for nitidulids in flowers and leaf litter, at sap flows on tree trunks, and on decaying fruits and fungi, and under loose bark and carcasses in the advaced stages of decay. Several species are attracted to light. Pitfall traps baited with fermenting malt or molasses are also effective for species known to occur on fungi, including subterranean species. Place about a quarter-inch of malt or molasses in a metal or plastic container and add enough water so that the mixture is about an inch deep. Add a couple pinches of yeast to the solution. Many species are collected in Malaise and flight intercept traps placed in forests and woodlands.

FAUNA 173 SPECIES IN 33 GENERA (NA)

Epuraea aestiva (**Linnaeus**) (2.5–3.5 mm) is somewhat oval, moderately shining, reddish to reddish yellow-brown, with short yellowish-brown pubescence. Head densely punctured, mouthparts prognathous, antennae with enlarged terminal antennomere. Pronotum wider than long. Elytra each usually with a dark elongate spot. Middle tibiae slender in both sexes, first three tarsomeres bilobed. Adults active spring and summer, found at sap, in compost, on flowers of trees and shrubs; attracted to light. Holarctic; widely distributed in North America. (19)

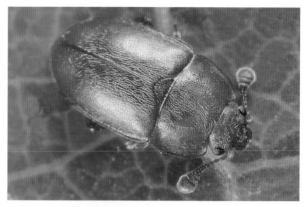

Epuraea flavomaculata **Mäklin** (2.5–3.4 mm) is broadly oblong-oval, sparsely pubescent, shiny brown to blackish with pale markings. Head with mouthparts directed forward. Pronotum nearly twice as wide as long, margins pale. Elytra each with pair of spots and side margins pale, surface more coarsely and sparsely punctate than pronotum. Adults active spring and summer, found in moist woods; attracted to baited traps. Maritime Provinces and New England to Massachusetts, west to Manitoba and Wisconsin; also western North America. (19)

Carpophilus discoideus **LeConte** (2.2–3.0 mm) is somewhat oval and flat, reddish black to blackish with mostly pale elytra. Head and pronotum moderately punctate. Pronotum wider than long. Elytra short, exposing two abdominal tergites, without setae along sides, each with large pale spot, punctures similar to pronotum, becoming finer at tips. Legs pale. Adults active in spring and summer. Widely distributed in United States; in east north to Ontario. (13)

Dried Fruit Beetle *Carpophilus hemipterus* (**Linnaeus**) (2.0–4.0 mm) is oblong, somewhat flattened, weakly shining, dark reddish brown to blackish. Head narrower than pronotum, with few punctures, and large eyes. Pronotum one-third wider than long, sides weakly curved, hind angles obtuse. Elytra together wider than long, more finely punctate than pronotum, short, exposing three abdominal tergites, with humeral patches and irregular areas on tips yellowish brown. Adult minor pest of stored products and dried fruits, attracted to decaying corn, nuts, apples, melons, citrus, and other fruits and vegetables; also under rotten logs, oak wilt mycelial mats. Nearly Cosmopolitan; widespread in North America. (13)

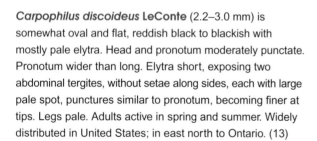

Carpophilus melanopterus Erichson (3.2–4.5 mm)
is bright reddish brown with dark or black elytra. Adults
found on flowers of yucca (*Yucca*) in late spring and early
summer. Larvae mine base of calyx and corolla before
pupating in soil. Adults emerge within weeks of pupation,
but remain in earthen pupal cells until following spring. New
York to Florida, west to Wisconsin and Texas; Mexico. (13)

Carpophilus sayi Parsons (3.0–4.5 mm) is oblong,
somewhat oval, and blackish; appendages mostly dull
dark reddish, antennal clubs dark. Head densely punctate.
Pronotum wider than long, margins and basal angles of
elytra often paler, sometimes reddish. Elytra somewhat flat,
more sparsely punctate than pronotum. Tip of abdomen
beyond elytra with distinct blunt ridge (female) or not (male).
Adults active spring and summer; found on flowers, rotting
fruit, and sap flows; also associated with oak wilt mycelial
mats on oak (*Quercus*). Maritime Provinces and Québec to
Virginia, west to Ontario, Wisconsin, and Missouri. (13)

Amphicrossus ciliatus (Olivier) (3.5–4.5 mm) is oval,
convex, yellowish brown with obscure yellowish markings
to dark reddish black. Pronotum wider than long with paler
sides and spot along base at middle. Elytra more or less
sparsely and finely punctate, male with stiff pair of bundled
setae at middle near suture. Legs paler. Adults active spring
and summer, found on sapping hardwoods, including poplar
(*Populus*), maple (*Acer*), and oak (*Quercus*); also attracted
to flowers, fungus, traps baited with fermenting fruit, and light.
Ontario to Florida, west to Wisconsin, Missouri, and Texas. (1)

Fabogethes (formerly *Meligethes*) *nigrescens*
(Stephens) (1.8–2.0 mm) is oblong-oval, moderately
convex, shining black, and sparsely pubescent. Head
densely punctate with clypeus nearly square, labrum
distinct. Prothorax twice as wide as long, narrowed;
sides more rounded in front. Elytra together one-fourth wider
than long, surface densely punctate, completely covering
abdomen. Legs with outer edges of middle and hind tibiae
with a row of spines, claws simple. Larva develops in flowers
of clover (*Trifolium*) and other plants in pea family (Fabaceae).
Pollen-feeding adults found in spring and summer on flowers
in various open habitats. Eurasia; established across
Canada, New England to Maryland and Ohio; Oregon. (1)

Small Hive Beetle *Aethina tumida* Murray (5.0–7.0 mm) is oval, reddish brown, dark brown, or black. Head with labrum distinct and eyes with conspicuous setae. Pronotum wider than long, widest at middle. Elytra long, covering all but last abdominal tergite, and slightly narrower than pronotum. Legs with outer edges of middle and hind tibiae with two rows of spines, tarsal formula 5-5-5. Larvae are serious pests of beehives, ruining combs and contaminating honey. Adults active spring and summer, feed on honey and pollen, usually found in association with beehives. Subsaharan Africa: widespread in eastern United States. (1)

Amphotis schwarzi Ulke (5.0–5.2 mm) is elongate-oval, somewhat convex, and yellowish brown to reddish black. Head with front lobed over antennal bases. Pronotum with margins broadly flattened, nearly as wide as elytra, underneath with antennal grooves parallel. Elytra each with eight long ridges Adults found with ants in spring and on decaying fungi in fall. Virginia to Florida, west to Mississippi. *Amphotis ulkei* LeConte (6.0–7.5 mm) similar but larger, more oval, paler, with six ridges on each elytron; found with ants in spring, decaying fungi in fall. Massachusetts to South Carolina, west to Texas. (2)

Cychramus adustus Erichson (3.0–4.5 mm) is oval, convex, pubescent, and partly or wholly reddish brown. Head with eyes not setose and mouthparts directed downward. Pronotum not margined across base. Elytra with rows of fine punctures, uniformly reddish brown, with sides and posterior halves blackish, or entirely blackish, and covering all but tip of abdomen. Legs with all tibiae simple, not sinuate or toothed, middle and hind tibiae with two rows of small marginal spines, tarsal formula 5-5-5, and all tarsi equal in length. Adults active late spring and summer, found in fungi and flowers. New Brunswick and New England to Georgia, west to Michigan, Nebraska, and Texas. (2).

Lobiopa insularis (Laporte) (5.0–6.5 mm) is oval, flattened, coarsely punctate, finely and sparsely pubescent, and variably dark reddish brown with centers of pronotum and elytra blackish with reddish spots. Lateral margins of pronotum and elytra broadly flattened. Eyes longer than pronotal margin. Elytra with broad, pale band behind middle not reaching sides. Adults found at sap or under bark in spring and summer. Virginia to Florida, west to Texas; Mexico and West Indies to South America. (5)

Lobiopa undulata (Say) (3.6–5.3 mm) is oval, not twice as long as wide, flat, and brown or blackish with margins yellowish brown. Head with front margin lobed over antennal bases, bare eyes shorter than depth of pronotal front margin notch. Pronotum twice as wide as long, narrowed toward front, base with distinct margin, underneath with antennal grooves parallel, process between legs not extended backward. Elytra long and completely covering abdomen, not distinctly ridged, with several zigzag spots across. Outer edges of middle and hind tibiae with two rows of marginal spines, tarsi not greatly widened. Adults active in spring and summer, found under bark, at sap flows; attracted to light. New Brunswick and New England to Florida, west to Manitoba, Iowa, and Texas. (5)

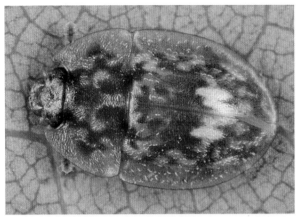

Nitidula bipunctata (Linnaeus) (3.0–5.0 mm) is broadly oval, moderately convex, densely clothed in short setae, and brown to black with pale, occasionally orange circular spot on each elytron. Head broad, along with pronotum more distinctly punctate than elytra. Pronotum wider than long, sides arched and usually broadly upturned, with rectangular hind angles, and underneath with short antennal grooves. Adults active spring and early summer, associated with carrion and fungi. Alaska, across Canada, to North Carolina, west to Minnesota, Iowa, and Texas. (3)

299

Nitidula carnaria (Schaller) (1.6–3.0 mm) is oblong-oval, and blackish with a pair of pale spots on each elytron, sometimes faint or absent. Head broad. Pronotum wider than long and narrowly upturned, hind angles obtuse, underneath with short antennal grooves. Adults active spring and summer, associated with carrion and fungi. Europe; widely distributed across southern Canada and northern United States. (3)

Omosita colon Linnaeus (2.0–3.5 mm) is elongate oval, somewhat flattened and blackish with pronotal margins, spots on base of elytra reddish brown. Apical half of each elytron mostly light yellowish brown that may or may not enclose a black dot. Adults are found on flowers, beneath carcasses, and on dry fungi from spring through early fall. Widespread in North America and Europe, sometimes known in New World as *Omosita nearctica* Kirejtshuk. (1)

Pallodes pallidus **(Palisot de Beauvois)** (3.0–4.0 mm) is oval, moderately convex, faintly iridescent, pale or dark yellow-brown without setae. Labrum and frons fused to clypeus, eyes without setae. Pronotum without margin along base and dark central spot if elytra are dark. Elytra completely covering abdomen, sometimes dark. Pterothorax with protuberances. Front legs with process projecting toward rear, middle legs narrowly separated at base, outer edges of middle and hind tibiae with two rows of spines, tarsal formula 5-5-5 with hind tarsi longest of all. Adults associated with fleshy fungi. Massachusetts to Florida, west to Michigan and Texas. *Pallodes austrinus* Leschen very similar, pronotum never with spot, faintly iridescent with magnification; Southeast. (2)

Phenolia grossa **(Fabricius)** (6.5–8.0 mm) is elongate-oval, somewhat convex, coarsely and sparsely punctate, weakly shiny black with indistinct reddish spots on elytra. Head large, front not lobed over antennal bases. Pronotum twice as wide as long, front deeply and broadly emarginate, slightly narrower than base, sides broadly flattened, margins somewhat curved and sinuate before hind angles. Elytra wide as pronotum, sides flattened and reddish, each with six or seven spots, weak ridges topped by short, reddish, scalelike setae, spaces between with two or three irregular rows of large punctures. Adults found year-round under bark and on fungi. Widespread in eastern North America. (1)

Prometopia sexmaculata **(Say)** (4.5–6.5 mm) is broadly oval, flattened, somewhat shining, sparsely and finely pubescent, with spots on elytra. Pronotum twice as wide as long, with mixed coarse and fine seta-bearing punctures. Elytra coarsely punctured, each puncture bearing a seta. Adults found in wooded habitats in spring and summer on sap and under bark of hardwoods in association with fungus, including oak wilt fungus mycelial mats; also at light, flight intercept and Lindgren funnel traps. Québec to Florida, west to Ontario, Wisconsin, Kansas, and Texas. (1)

Strawberry Sap Beetle *Stelidota geminata* **(Say)** (2.0–3.0 mm) is oval, convex, sparsely punctate, narrower behind, and somewhat shiny yellowish brown to reddish black with indistinct pale spots on elytra. Pronotum with deeply concave front margin, broadly flat before evenly curved margins, widest at base. Middle tibiae of male strongly curved, abruptly expanded at tips. Elytra with rows of round punctures separated by narrow ridges. Adults most active in spring, found at sap flows, under leaves, at rotten fruit; occasionally attracted to light. New England to Florida, west to Wisconsin and Texas, south to South America. (4)

Stelidota octomaculata (Say) (2.2–3.5 mm) is oval, convex, sparsely punctate, narrower behind, and somewhat shiny yellowish brown to reddish black with indistinct pale spots on elytra. Pronotum with deeply concave front margin, broadly flat along sides with margins widest just before base. Elytra with rows of oval punctures with spaces between almost flat. Middle tibiae of male not curved or abruptly expanded at tips. Adults most active in spring, found at sap flows, under leaves, at rotten fruit; occasionally attracted to light. Nova Scotia and Québec and New England to Florida, west to Ontario, Wisconsin, and Arizona. (4)

Thalycra carolina Wickham (2.8–4.6 mm) is oval, convex, somewhat shining and pubescent, and yellowish brown to chestnut. Foretibia with no teeth or two indistinct teeth apically, apical margin prolonged, lateral margin with two distinct teeth. Adults found in early spring and fall in sandy habitats, especially among stands of loblolly pine (*Pinus taeda*) in association with underground basidiomycete fungi (*Rhizopogon*), but are also collected on flowers, at sap under bark, and at lights; attracted to malt traps, occasionally light. Coastal Plain pine belt, from Maryland to Florida. (3)

Brachypeplus glaber LeConte (3.3–4.0 mm) is elongate, flat, straight-sided, reddish brown with blackish abdomen. Head slightly narrower than rectangular pronotum. Pronotum nearly as broad as elytra, with posterior angles nearly right-angled. Elytra short, together longer than wide, exposing two abdominal tergites and distinctly punctured pygidium. Abdomen above more finely and sparsely punctate than pronotum. Adults active in spring and summer in sabal palm (*Sabal*) inflorescence sheaths. Coastal, from North Carolina to Mississippi. (1)

Colopterus truncatus (Randall) (1.5–2.7 mm) is oblong-oval, very flat, sparsely pubescent, and reddish yellow-brown to blackish with an oblique pale spot on each elytron; darker specimens have brownish antennae and reddish legs, paler individuals with yellowish-brown appendages. Head coarsely punctate. Pronotum almost twice as wide as long and sparsely punctate. Elytra densely punctate. Tarsi with claws simple. Adults active spring and summer, found on fungus, also probably under bark. Maritime Provinces and New England to Florida, west to British Columbia and southern California; south to South America, also Caribbean. (5)

Conotelus obscurus Erichson (3.5–4.5 mm) is elongate, somewhat flattened, dull black with tibiae, tarsi, and all but antennal club paler. Resemble rove beetles (Staphylinidae), but are easily distinguished by distinctly clubbed antennae. Pronotum finely wrinkled between punctures. Elytra short, together long as wide, with surface finely granulate and with shallow irregular punctures. Abdomen with sides rounded, tapering toward tip, and last three tergites not covered by elytra; male with tip sharply notched. Legs short and pale. Adults found in summer on flowers, especially dogwoods (*Cornus*). Maritime Provinces to Georgia, west to Manitoba, Colorado, and Arkansas. (3)

Cryptarcha ampla Erichson (4.5–7.8 mm) is oblong-oval, broader in front, somewhat convex, weakly shining, yellowish brown to blackish, with sparse setae on elytra sometimes absent. Elytra gradually narrowing toward rear, tips broadly rounded. Adults attracted to tree sap of maple (*Acer*), hickory (*Carya*), oak (*Quercus*), and willow (*Salix*) in spring and summer; also associated with fungus and attracted to light. Nova Scotia and Maine to Florida, west to British Columbia, Wisconsin, Colorado, California, and Texas. (3)

Cryptarcha strigatula Parsons (2.7–3.5 mm) is ovate, moderately convex, blackish, surfaces finely wrinkled, and sparsely pubescent. Head large, broad. Pronotum as wide as elytra, margined at base, and slightly overlapping elytra. Elytra with two irregular pale bands, basal band sometimes broken at suture, each with seven indistinct rows of setae, and completely covering abdomen. Front legs with bases widely separated, plate surrounding base open toward rear. Adults active spring and summer at sapping tree wounds; attracted to light. Widespread in eastern United States. (3)

Picnic Beetle *Glischrochilus fasciatus* (Olivier) (4.0–7.0 mm) is oblong, moderately convex, shiny black with four orange or reddish-yellow patches shaped like jigaw puzzle pieces; underside black. Adults attracted to anything sweet-smelling; found on fungi, flowers, ripening fruit; associated with oak wilt fungus mats. They are well-known pests of crops (corn, raspberries, strawberries, and tomatoes) as well as making nuisances of themselves at picnics and other outdoor gatherings with food. Across southern Canada and eastern United States west to Oregon, Kansas, and New Mexico. (7)

Glischrochilus obtusus (Say) (7.3–12.5 mm) is robust, oblong, shining black, with somewhat circular red or orange elytral spots. Elytra with basal spots larger and equidistant between suture and sides, spots behind middle smaller and closer to suture, with tips slightly more oblique in female than male. Underside of thorax and abdomen black. Adults active late spring and summer, found under bark near sap flows, at banana traps, and in Lindgren funnel traps baited with fruit. New York to Florida, west to Minnesota and Arkansas. (7)

Four-spotted Sap Beetle *Glischrochilus quadrisignatus* **(Say)** (4.0–7.0 mm) is oblong, convex, somewhat shiny black with a pair of yellowish or reddish spots on each elytron. Head large, broad. Pronotum with sides narrowly but distinctly upturned. Elytra with basal spots further from suture than spots behind middle. Adults active spring and summer, attracted to decaying and stored fruit and vegetables and other sweet odors; also attracted to light. Maritime Provinces to Florida, west to Iowa, Utah, and Texas. (7)

303

Glischrochilus sanguinolentus (Olivier) (4.5–6.2 mm) is oblong-oval, with red and black elytra. Elytra red with basal two-thirds red and humeri, spots just before middle, and apical third black; some with elytra black with basal band and middle spot red. Underside black with metathorax and abdomen red. Legs black, tarsi paler. Adults active spring through fall, found on sap flows of maple (*Acer*) and other hardwoods and in association with fungi; also attracted to sweet, fermenting baits. Maritime Provinces to Florida, west to Ontario, Wisconsin, and Texas. (7)

Glischrochilus vittatus (Say) (3.5–6.0 mm) is elongate, oval, convex, shining black with long, pale yellowish spots. Elytra with spots arranged in a row approximately parallel to suture, spots sometimes joined, other spots sometimes present near sides and tips; tips rounded (male) or produced (female). Adults found almost year-round, most common in spring, often found under bark of pine (*Pinus*). In east from Nova Scotia and New Brunswick to North Carolina, west to Ontario, Wisconsin, and Missouri. (7)

CYBOCEPHALID BEETLES, FAMILY CYBOCEPHALIDAE
(SYE-BO-SEH-*FAL*-IH-DEE)

The Cybocephalidae were once considered a subfamily of the Nitidulidae. The family consists of seven genera worldwide, but only *Cybocephalus* occurs in North America. They are capable of tightly tucking their head and appendages in against the body so that their mandibles rest on the underside of the thorax. Unlike their nearest relatives, the sap beetles (Nitidulidae), cybocephalids are exclusively predators, primarily of armored scales (Diaspidae) and occasionally whiteflies (Aleyrodidae), as well as mealybugs (Pseudococcidae) and citrus red mites (*Panonychus citri*). Several species have been released in various parts of the world as biological control agents of scale insects. For example, *C. nipponicus* Endrody-Younga was released in Florida to control scale insects on sago palms (*Cycas*) and has been introduced into other states to prey on additional scale insect species.

FAMILY DIAGNOSIS Adult cybocephalid beetles are ovate, very convex, black or bicolored, and capable of contracting all appendages tight against body. Head broad and deflected down. Antennae with 11 antennomeres, longer than width of head, antennal club flat with antennomeres. Pronotum with sides short, margined base covering base of elytra. Underside of thorax impressed to receive middle and hind legs. Scutellum large, triangular. Elytra long, nearly covering tip of abdomen. Legs with tibiae simple, tarsal formula 4-4-4, with each tarsomere slightly expanded underneath, second and third tarsomeres bilobed, and claws simple. Abdomen with five ventrites.

SIMILAR FAMILIES
- *Agathidium* (Leiodidae) – tarsi 5-5-4 (male), 5-4-4 (female) (p.119)
- minute beetles (Clambidae) – antennal club with two antennomeres; clypeus completely covers mouth; hind coxae enlarged (p.179)
- shining flower and mold beetles (Phalacridae) – tarsi 5-5-5; antennal club elongate (p.290)
- lady beetles (Coccinellidae) – head long, inserted in prothorax; tarsi 4-4-4, appear 3-3-3 (p.311)

COLLECTING NOTES Adults are collected by beating or sweeping plants infested with armored scales, such as southern magnolia (*Magnolia grandifolia*), Fraser fir (*Abies fraseri*), and sago palm (*Cycas*), or in Malaise traps.

FAUNA FIVE SPECIES IN ONE GENUS (NA); THREE SPECIES IN ONE GENUS (ENA)

Cybocephalus nipponicus **Endrody-Younga** (1.0–1.3 mm) is elongate-oval, strongly convex, capable of rolling up, mostly shiny black with pronotum black with sides pale (female), or yellow or tan (male). Head nearly broad as pronotum, bent downward. Antennomere 3 slightly shorter than 4 and 5 together, club smaller than eye, with serrate margins. Scutellum with sides convex. Front legs and antennae of female yellow, remaining legs in both sexes brownish. Introduced from Southeast Asia for biocontrol of several scale insects, including euonymus, San Jose, and elongate hemlock scales. Massachusetts and New York to Virginia; Florida, Texas. *Cybocephalus nigritulus* LeConte is black, with antennal club serrate, scutellum convex, and front femora and antennae pale. (3)

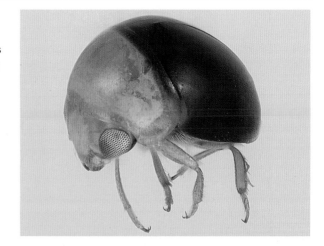

304

PALMETTO BEETLES, FAMILY SMICRIPIDAE
(SMICK-*RIP*-IH-DEE)

Very little is known about the biology and natural history of palmetto beetles. Adults are found in decaying flowers, leaf litter, and under bark. In Florida, *Smicrips palmicola* LeConte is commonly found on cabbage palmetto (*Sabal palmetto*).

FAMILY DIAGNOSIS Adult smicripids are small, elongate, parallel-sided, and flattened, with last of five abdominal ventrites equal in length to that of previous ventrites combined. Head not narrowed behind eyes, antennae with 11 antennomeres, 9–11 forming distinct club, maxilla with single lobe (lacinia), plate surrounding bases of front legs open behind, and elytra short and exposing last two abdominal segments, including pygidium.

SIMILAR FAMILIES
- rove beetles (Staphylinidae) – antennae filiform (p.124)
- root-eating beetles (Monotomidae) – antennal club consisting of one or two antennomeres (p.281)
- sap beetles (Nitidulidae) – last abdominal ventrite not longer than previous two ventrites combined (p.295)

COLLECTING NOTES Look for *Smicrips* on palmetto. Pitfall and flight intercept traps in areas with palmettos are also productive.

FAUNA TWO SPECIES IN ONE GENUS (NA)

Smicrips palmicola **LeConte** (1.0–2.0 mm) is small, elongate, parallel-sided, flattened, and reddish brown. Head with distinct groove between front and clypeus curved, mandibles well developed in male, antennae clubbed, with antennomeres 9–11 forming club. Pronotum slightly wider than head. Elytra short, twice as long and barely wider than pronotum, sides broadly rounded, with pygidium exposed. Legs with last tarsomere longer than rest of tarsus. Larvae found in decaying leaf litter near near adult plant host. Adults found in inflorescences of cabbage palmetto (*Sabal palmetto*). Georgia to Florida; California. (2)

BOTHRIDERID BEETLES, FAMILY BOTHRIDERIDAE
(BAW-THRIH-*DARE*-IH-DEE)

Most larval bothriderids are external parasites on the larvae and pupae of wood-boring beetles. Although bothriderid larvae are currently of little or no economic importance, studies on their parasitic habits may encourage their use as biocontrol agents of wood-boring beetles in managed forests. For example, the larvae of *Bothrideres geminatus* (Say) parasitize the larvae and pupae of *Chrysobothris* species (Buprestidae), while *Sosylus* species prey on ambrosia beetles (Curculionidae). Adults are typically found at the base of long dead and dry trees. More or less flattened species (*Bothrideres, Annomatus*) live under bark, whereas more cylindrical species (*Oxylaemus, Sosylus*) generally inhabit the tunnels of their beetle hosts.

FAMILY DIAGNOSIS Adult bothriderids are long and narrow and somewhat flattened or cylindrical, or oblong-oval and somewhat convex (*Prolyctus*) and nearly three times longer than wide. Head broad and flattened with mouthparts directed forward (prognathous). Antennae with 10 (*Oxylaemus*) or 11 antennomeres, club with one (*Oxylaemus*) or two antennomeres; attachment point of antennae visible from above. Prothorax longer than wide. Scutellum visible. Elytra punctured, with ridges (*Bothrideres, Proclytus*) or without (*Annomatus, Oxylaemus*). Legs with tarsal formula 4-4-4. Abdomen with five distinct ventrites.

SIMILAR FAMILIES

- wrinkled bark beetles (Carabidae) – antennae moniliform; tarsi 5-5-5 (p.63)
- powder-post beetles (Bostrichidae: Lyctinae) – head hypognathous; tarsi 5-5-5 (p.250)
- small bark-gnawing beetles (Trogossitidae) – mandibles prominent in front; tarsi 5-5-5 (p.259)
- cylindrical bark beetles (Zopheridae: Colydiinae) – antennal insertions hidden from above; tarsi 4-4-4 (p.340)
- small darkling beetles (Tenebrionidae) – antennal insertions hidden from above; tarsi 5-5-4 (p.344)

COLLECTING NOTES Peeling back bark of hardwoods and conifers is the most productive method for collecting bothriderids. Standing dead trees dry out from the top down, forcing many wood-boring species down the trunk; therefore searching for predatory bothriderids at the bases and in the roots is often productive. Some bothriderids are occasionally associated with fire scars or collected at light.

FAUNA 18 SPECIES IN EIGHT GENERA (NA); SEVEN SPECIES IN FIVE GENERA (ENA)

Bothrideres geminatus (**Say**) (2.0–5.0 mm) is oblong, somewhat flat and shining, dark brown, and clothed in long, pale setae. Pronotum longer than wide, depressions usually indistinct, becoming narrow behind. Elytra with single row of large punctures on each side of suture, spaces between more or less equal in height, raised area at shoulder with two scattered rows of punctures; tip blunt, upturned (male) or more pointed, downturned (female). Adults found year-round under dry bark of various hardwoods, occasionally pines (*Pinus*), infested with buprestid larvae (*Chrysobothris*); rarely attracted to light. Ontario to Florida, west to Illinois and Texas. (2)

Sosylus costatus LeConte (3.8–4.1 mm) is elongate, slender, cyclindrical, and dark brown to blackish without pubescence. Antennae with 11 antennomeres, 10–11 forming large, abrupt club. Pronotum half again long as wide, widest near apical quarter, strongly convergent to base. Elytra each with four ridges between suture and side margins, sutural and outermost ridges joined at tip, spaces between irregularly punctate, shallow, nearly round. Adults active spring and summer, found under bark; also attracted to light. Virginia to Florida, west to Arkansas and Texas. (2)

MINUTE BARK BEETLES, FAMILY CERYLONIDAE
(SAIR-EE-*LON*-IH-DEE)

Cerylonid beetles are small and usually collected by mass extraction methods. As a result, little is known of their specific food preferences or life cycles. Both adults and larvae eat fungi. They are unusual among beetles in that all known larvae and some adults have piercing-sucking mouthparts. *Cerylon*, *Philothermus*, and *Mychocerinus* live under bark, while *Mychocerus* is commonly found in leaf litter. *Hypodacne punctata* LeConte is an apparent myrmecophile and is associated with carpenter ants (*Camponotus*). One species, the cosmopolitan *Murmidius ovalis* (Beck), is found in stored grain products in granaries and warehouses.

FAMILY DIAGNOSIS Adult cerylonids are elongate, robust, somewhat flattened, often oval, and mostly smooth and shining. Antennae usually with 10 antennomeres, last one or two forming a distinct club. Elytra almost always grooved with rows of punctures. Legs with tarsal formula 4-4-4, rarely 3-3-3, tarsi simple.

SIMILAR FAMILIES
- round fungus beetles (Leiodidae) – antennomere 8 small (p.118)
- powder-post beetles (Bostrichidae) – sides of body nearly parallel (p.252)
- root-eating beetles (Monotomidae) – tip of abdomen exposed beyond elytra (p.281)
- small handsome fungus beetles (Endomychidae) – antennal club with three antennomeres (p.308)
- hairy fungus beetles (Mycetophagidae) – pronotum with basal pair of grooves; antennal club usually with three antennomeres (p.323)
- zopherid beetles (Zopheridae) – antennal bases concealed from above by frontal margin (p.340)

COLLECTING NOTES Minute bark beetles are best collected by using a Berlese funnel to extract them from sifted decayed wood and leaf litter. Also look for them under bark.

FAUNA 19 SPECIES IN 10 GENERA (NA); 12 SPECIES IN 9 GENERA (ENA)

307

Hypodacne punctata LeConte (2.0–2.5 mm) is convex, shining, uniformly dark reddish brown with appendages paler. Antenna with penultimate antennomere asymmetrical, almost as wide as last. Pronotum sparsely punctate, widest at base, sides curved. Elytra widest at basal fourth and narrowed to rounded tips, with punctures coarse, sparse, and irregular. Front coxal cavities closed and tarsi not lobed underneath. Adults found under bark of oak (*Quercus*) and other hardwoods, sometimes in galleries of carpenter ants (*Camponotus*), and beaten from vegetation; Ontario to Florida, west to Indiana, Kansas, and Texas. (1)

Murmidius ovalis (Beck) (1.2–1.4 mm) is oval, strongly convex, shiny brown, and clothed in inconspicuous, sparse, short, fine, recumbent setae. Head with eyes large and finely faceted, antennae with 10 antennomeres, cavities for receiving antennae visible from above. Pronotum twice as wide as long, widest at base, with dorsal cavities along sides to receive antennae clearly visible. Elytra with rows of distinct punctures. Tarsi 4-4-4. Adults found in packages of seeds, rice, and other stored products, also in cut grass, hay, leaves, and other decomposing vegetation. Cosmopolitan; widespread in United States. (1)

Cerylon unicolor (Ziegler) (1.8–2.4 mm) is elongate, somewhat convex, somewhat parallel-sided, shiny dark reddish brown. Head without suture across front, antennae with 10 antennomeres, club with one antennomere, 3 more than 1.5 times longer than 4. Pronotum with surface distinctly punctured, nearly wide as long with sides somewhat parallel, slightly divergent at base (male) or convergent in front and parallel at base (female); no grooves underneath to receive antennae. Elytra with distinct rows of punctures at base, spaces between with very fine punctures. Adults found in association with fungi under bark of rotten hardwood and conifer logs; attracted to light. (2)

Philothermus glabriculus LeConte (1.9–2.3 mm) is elongate-oval, somewhat flattened, shining, and dark reddish brown. Antennae with 11 antennomeres, 10–11 forming club. Pronotum with entire side margins evenly smooth and visible from above, underside without antennal grooves. Elytra with rows of coarse punctures becoming less distinct at tips. Abdomen underneath with last ventrite finely notched along tip. Adults active in late spring and summer, found under bark of conifers and hardwoods, and in rotten logs, leaf litter, and tree holes. New England and Ontario to northern Florida, west to Oklahoma and Texas. (2)

308

HANDSOME FUNGUS BEETLES, FAMILY ENDOMYCHIDAE
(EN-DOE-*MY*-KIH-DEE)

Endomychids are typically found in decaying wood, beneath logs, or under bark where they feed on the spores and microhyphae of fungi. Some species reflex-bleed when alarmed, secreting a noxious fluid from the leg joints as a defensive measure, much like lady beetles (Coccinellidae). Endomychids are seldom of any economic importance, but at least one species, the hairy cellar beetle, *Mycetaea subterranea* (Fabricius), is a minor pest in granaries and warehouses where it infests moldy stored grain products.

FAMILY DIAGNOSIS Adult endomychids are distinguished by a pair of distinct basal grooves that flank the midline of the pronotum. They are broadly rounded, oval, or elongate-oval, and sometimes moderately flattened. Clubbed antennae with 11 antennomeres, 9–11 forming loose club. Elytra are irregularly punctured, sometimes setose, and completely conceal abdomen. Tarsal formula appears 3-3-3, but is actually 4-4-4, tarsomeres 1–2 strongly bilobed beneath. Abdomen with five or six ventrites.

SIMILAR FAMILIES
- pleasing fungus beetles (Erotylidae) – front angles of pronotum not extended forward; elytra with rows of punctures; tarsi appear 5-5-5 (p.277)
- minute bark beetles (Cerylonidae) – never black; last palpomere small or pointed; elytra almost always with rows of punctures (p.307)
- lady beetles (Coccinellidae) – antennae not as distinctly clubbed; pronotal grooves lacking (p.311)
- some leaf beetles (Chrysomelidae) – tarsi apparently 4-4-4, but actually 5-5-5 (p.429)

COLLECTING NOTES Look for handsome fungus beetles in fungi and under bark, or by sifting through rotten wood and leaf litter; a few species are attracted to light.

FAUNA 45 SPECIES IN 22 GENERA (NA); 26 SPECIES IN 20 GENERA (ENA)

Phymaphora pulchella **Newman** (3.0–3.8 mm) is elongate, somewhat oval, bicolored with reddish yellow or orangish yellow and black. Head blackish, antennal club modified with antennomeres greatly (male) or somewhat (female) expanded. Pronotum with central and variable dark cloud. Scutellum blackish. Elytra with narrow dark suture and broad, black bands across middle and tips. Adults found on birch polypore (*Piptoporus betulinus*) and *Climacodon pulcherrima*; occasionally attracted to light. Maritime Provinces and New England to North Carolina, west to Manitoba, Wisconsin, Missouri, and Louisiana. (1)

Rhanidea unicolor **(Ziegler)** (2.0–2.5 mm) is elongate, somewhat straight-sided, shining, typically dark reddish brown (sometimes lighter or darker), and sparsely punctate. Pronotum wider than long, widest before middle, sides round before middle, then straight and converging behind, and basal two-thirds with pair of lines down middle, each flanked by a pit before angle. Elytra usually darker, sometimes with angles and tips broadly reddish. Adults found with fungus, including *Irpex lacteus*. New Brunswick and Ontario to Florida, west to Wisconsin and Texas. (1)

309

Endomychus biguttatus **Say** (3.5–4.2 mm) is oblong-oval and mostly black with distinctive red elytra with black spots. It occurs commonly in moist deciduous forests. Adults often found overwintering under bark and among forest debris. Reproductive peaks occur in spring and fall. Both adults and larvae occur on sporocarps of basidiomycete fungi, including split-gill fungus (*Schizophyllum commune*), jelly ear (*Auricularia auricula*), and birch polypore (*Piptoporus betulinus*). A defensive milky yellowish fluid is released from the "knee" joints. Nova Scotia and New Brunswick to Florida, west to Ontario, Iowa, and Texas. (1)

Danae testacea **(Ziegler)** (3.5–4.0 mm) is elongate, oblong, distinctly and sparsely pubescent, and shiny pale to dark reddish brown; appendages darker. Antennae with 11 antennomeres, 9–11 darker and forming distinct club. Pronotum wider than long, widest at apical third, with membrane at middle on front margin, broad raised side margins, hind angles prominent, and distinct groove along base at middle. Elytra with irregular rows of fine punctures. Tarsi appearing 3-3-3, actually 4-4-4. Adults active in late spring and summer, found in Lindgren funnel and pitfall traps; attracted to cantharidin. Nova Scotia and New England to Florida, west to Ontario, Wisconsin, and Louisiana. (1)

Stenotarsus hispidus (**Herbst**) (3.5–4.5 mm) is broadly oval, densely clothed in erect and nearly erect setae, and orangish or reddish brown with elytra indistinctly brown or black at middle. Antennal club loose with three antennomeres, 6–11 dark. Pronotum wider than long with broad flat side margins delimited inside by long grooves and short curved grooves at base. Elytra coarsely punctured. Adults active in late spring and summer, found in Malaise and pitfall traps. Connecticut to Florida, west to Indiana and Louisiana. (2)

Aphorista vittata (**Fabricius**) (5.5–6.5 mm) is elongate, oblong, and orange or brownish red. Antennae dark, last antennomere paler. Pronotum with sides broadly margined, with or without a dusky spot on each side. Elytra with broad, tapering stripe down suture and long markings on sides black. Larvae and adults associated with wood-rotting fungus *Coniophora arida*; adults also attracted to light in summer. Québec and Ontario to Florida, west to Manitoba, Wisconsin and Texas. (1)

310

Lycoperdina ferruginea **LeConte** (4.5–6.0 mm) is oblong-oval, shiny dark reddish brown to nearly black, pronotum and elytra sometimes darker. Pronotum densely covered with minute cracks (alutaceous) and sparse, fine punctures. Antennae with last two antennomeres abruptly widened and flattened. Although sometimes found on other fungi and leaf litter, adults are specialist feeders on puffballs, *Morganella pyriforme* (Lycoperdales); also attracted to cantharidin traps. Nova Scotia to Georgia, west to Ontario, Iowa, Kansas, and Louisiana. (1)

Mycetina perpulchra (**Newman**) (3.5–4.0 mm) is oblong-oval, convex and shiny blackish to black. Head black. Pronotum somewhat flattened, wider than long with sides broadly and sharply margined, reddish yellow, and a dark spot on middle or at base. Elytra convex, black with four reddish-orange to orangish patches, patches near base usually larger. Larvae and adults found on the wood-rotting fungus *Coniophora arida*, boletes associated with dead pine (*Pinus*), and other soft species of Agaricales; adults occasionally attracted to light in late spring and summer. Nova Scotia and New Brunswick to Georgia, west to Ontario, Indiana and Arkansas. (1)

LADY BEETLES, FAMILY COCCINELLIDAE
(COX-SIN-*EL*-LIH-DEE)

Coccinellids, also known as ladybugs, are among the most familiar and beloved of all insects. They are surprisingly diverse in their habits as adults, ranging from insect predators and fungivores to plant feeders. A small number feed on molds, fungi, and pollen. The vast majority of species prey on plant pests, including aphids, scale insects, mealybugs, and even mites. These are generally considered among the most beneficial of insects and are commonly released as biological control agents. The bright contrasting patterns of spots or stripes of many coccinellids serve as aposematic or warning colors that advertise the presence of repellent chemicals in their bodies. Yellowish fluid released from their "knees" (femoro-tibial joints) is called reflex bleeding. This fluid contains toxic alkaloids that render these beetles distasteful to their attackers.

FAMILY DIAGNOSIS Many adult coccinellids are conspicuously marked in red and black and are typically oval and convex to strongly hemispherical in profile. Head shallowly or deeply inserted within prothorax. Antennae clavate with 7–11 antennomeres, ending in a loose or compact club. Prothorax convex, wider than long, distinctly margined or keeled along sides. Scutellum small, triangular. Elytra without grooves or rows of punctures, covering abdomen entirely. Underside flat. Tarsi usually 4-4-4, may appear 3-3-3. Abdomen with five to seven ventrites visible, first ventrite with at least one distinct line behind base of hind legs (absent in *Coleomegilla*).

SIMILAR FAMILIES

- round fungus beetles (Leiodidae) – antennae capitate; elytra often grooved (p.118)
- marsh beetles (Scirtidae) – antennae filiform or serrate (p.180)
- pleasing fungus beetles (Erotylidae) – antennae capitate (p.277)
- shining flower beetles (Phalacridae) – antennae capitate; tarsi appear 4-4-4, but are 5-5-5; no distinct markings on the elytra; abdomen without lines (p.290)
- handsome fungus beetles (Endomychidae) – front angles of pronotum distinctly pointed forward (p.308)
- minute fungus beetles (Corylophidae) – antennae capitate (p.320)
- leaf beetles (Chrysomelidae) – tarsi appear 4-4-4, but are 5-5-5 (p.429)

COLLECTING NOTES Search for lady beetles on flowering plants, especially those covered with sap-sucking aphids. Sweeping and beating trees, shrubs, and other woody vegetation as well as herbaceous will reveal a diversity of taxa. A few species are regularly attracted to lights.

FAUNA ~481 SPECIES IN 60 GENERA (NA)

Microweisea misella (**LeConte**) (0.9–1.5 mm) is small, slightly elongate, oval, convex, without pubescence on upper surface, completely dark brown or black; appendages slightly paler. Head finely wrinkled, not set deep inside prothorax, antennal club with three antennomeres. Pronotum strongly punctured with line just inside front angles. Flight wings present. Tarsi each with three tarsomeres. Adults active spring and summer, prey on armored scales (Diaspididae) on blueberry (*Vaccinium*) and other trees and shrubs. Across southern Canada and most of United States, except Southwest. (3)

Mealybug Destroyer *Cryptolaemus montrouzieri*
Mulsant (3.4–4.5 mm) is oval, convex, and bicolored with
head, prothorax, and tips of elytra reddish yellow, rest of
body black or blackish. Head underneath with mouthparts
and antennae covered by thoracic plate. Antennomeres
8–10 forming club. Legs with tibial spurs absent, tarsi 3-3-3,
claws with broad basal tooth. Abdomen underneath with
curved lines on first ventrite reaching sides. Adults and
larvae prey primarily on scale insects. Australia; established
in California and southern Florida, patchily distributed in
eastern United States. (1)

Diomus terminatus **(Say)** (1.5–1.9 mm) is elongate,
somewhat oval, hemispherical, clothed in short, reclining
setae, black with head, front angles of pronotum, and apical
fourth of elytra reddish brown or yellowish; area between
front legs with pair of fine ridges converging toward head.
Elytra widest at middle of elytra, with golden setae longer
than on pronotum. Legs and last four abdominal ventrites
reddish brown or yellowish. Metathorax with fine, curved
sutures from base of legs to first abdominal ventrite. Adults
and larvae probably prey on mealybugs, aphids, and
scales. Massachusetts and southern Ontario to Florida,
west to Iowa, Oklahoma, and Texas. (12)

Scymnus **species** (1.9–2.5 mm) are small, somewhat
elongate to oval, setose, and often bi- or tricolored. Head
with eyes large, separated by twice their own widths.
Antennae short, with 10–11 antennomeres, 1–2 not
enlarged, basal antennomeres of club uneven on lower
margins. Pronotum deeply and broadly notched in front,
rounded at base, underneath with distinct ridge completely
surrounding process between legs. Elytra dark, partially
reddish, spotted, or lighter at tips. Abdomen underneath
with curved lines on first ventrite reaching sides or not. Tarsi
4-4-4, inner claws larger than outer (male). Identification
may require examination of male genitalia. Widespread in
eastern North America. (24)

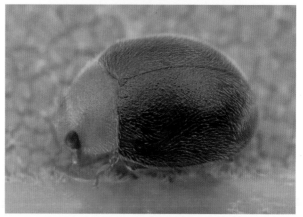

Hyperaspis octavia **Casey** (2.2–2.8 mm) is broadly oval,
convex, and shiny black with variable pattern of complete,
irregular stripes or three spots along sides; legs pale brown.
Antennae with 10 antennomeres. Pronotum with pale sides
narrower than basal angle spot on each elytron. Elytra each
with a central spot, punctures slightly larger than those on
pronotum. Maritime Provinces and Québec to Mississippi,
west to Ontario and Wisconsin. (33)

Hyperaspis proba (Say) (2.0–3.0 mm) is small, round, very convex, and shiny black. Antennae with 11 antennomeres. Pronotum of male with front margin and broad side margins yellow; female with smaller yellow or white patch on side margins. Elytral pattern distinctive and consistent, each elytron with three yellow or red spots. Adults and larvae prey on scale insects. Maine to South Carolina, west to South Dakota and Texas. (33)

Brachiacantha quadripunctata (Melsheimer) (2.5–4.0 mm) is round and hemispherical, with somewhat variable dorsal color pattern. Head pale (male) or black (female). Pronotum of male usually black with front angles and up to one-third of front pale. Elytron black with basal and apical spot (female), or additional basal angle spot merging with basal spot (male). Larva feeds on root-feeding soft scales (Coccidae) in nests of *Lasius* ants. Adults active spring and summer, prey on mealybugs and root-feeding soft scales and aphids. Southern New England to Virginia, west to Iowa, Kansas, and Arkansas. (11)

Two-stabbed Lady Beetle *Chilocorus stigma* (Say) (3.7–5.0 mm), is broadly oval, hemispherical, and completely black above, except for a red spot slightly in front of middle on each elytron. Elytral margins reflexed. Thorax underneath always dark, usually black, sometimes brown. Adults found in spring and summer on vegetation and trunks of trees infested with scales, mealybugs and, to a lesser extent, aphids. Nova Scotia to Florida, west to Alberta, Oregon, Nevada, and Arizona. (3)

Exochomus marginipennis (LeConte) (2.5–3.6 mm) is elongate, oval, slightly flattened. Front angle of pronotum and front leg yellow (male), or black or slightly pale with legs dark (female). Elytra with coarse, dense punctures, usually black with reddish-yellow spots or markings, suture with a pale area just behind middle. Abdomen with complete oblique curved lines on first ventrite merging with thorax. Legs with claws toothed at base. Adults active spring and summer and are aphid predators. Massachusetts to Florida, west Kansas, and Texas. (2)

Coccidula lepida LeConte (2.7–3.5 mm) is elongate-oval, clothed in dense setae lying on surface. Head mostly exposed and not deeply inserted into prothorax, eyes very coarsely faceted, antennae serrate, with 11 antennomeres, 9–11 forming club. Pronotum underneath with process between front legs delimited by curved ridge. Abdomen underneath with first ventrite with pair of complete C-shaped lines beginning and ending at leg bases. Tarsal claws with feeble tooth. Europe, established from Maritime Provinces to New Jersey, west to Alaska, British Columbia, and Colorado. (1)

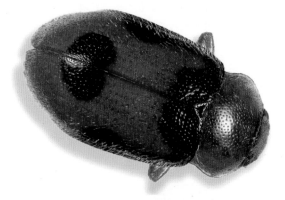

Adalia bipunctata (Linnaeus) (3.5–5.2 mm) is oval, weakly convex, with extremely variable color pattern. Pronotum wide, covering part of eyes, with M-shaped mark except in dark forms, base without fine groove or bead along margin. Abdomen underneath with first ventrite with complete C-shaped line behind each leg base. Underside with process between middle legs flat in front. Femora not extending beyond sides; middle and hind tibiae tipped with pair of spurs, tarsal claws each with a squarish basal tooth. Adults and larvae are aphid and adelgid predators. Throughout North America. (1)

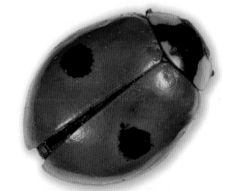

314

Fifteen-spotted Lady Beetle *Anatis labiculata* **(Say)** (7.2–9.5 mm) is a large, round, pale gray to dark brownish red with black markings. Elytral margins weakly flattened and expanded, not angulate at middle; dark spots never ringed with white or yellow. Adults prey on aphids on coniferous and deciduous trees in spring and summer; also attracted to light. New Brunswick and Maine to South Carolina, west to Ontario, North Dakota, Colorado, and Texas. *Anatis mali* (Say) (7.3–10.0 mm) is similar, with pale-ringed black elytral spots; across southern Canada and northern half of United States. (2)

Anisosticta bitriangularis **(Say)** (3.0–4.0 mm) is somewhat elongate, ovate, convex, and yellowish with variable black markings. Head black at base between eyes. Pronotum with two black triangular spots with sides or corners sometimes notched, base without a fine line or bead along margin. Elytra each black with two pale and sometimes deeply notched stripes down middle (northern), stripes, especially along sides, sometimes broken into larger or smaller spots (southern). Abdomen black with sides pale. Legs with middle and hind tibiae each with a single tibial spur at tip and claws simple. Labrador to New Jersey, west to Alaska and northern California. (2)

Calvia quatuordecimguttata (Linnaeus) (4.0–5.5 mm) is oval, not strongly convex, shiny, with extremely variable color pattern; bold dark spots on pale, or pale spots on dark background. Head with eyes partly covered in front with canthus, front corners of clypeus produced forward. Pronotum without any trace of finely wrinkled sculpturing, base without fine groove or bead along margin. Middle and hind tibiae tipped with pair of spurs, tarsal claws each with a squarish basal tooth. Adults and larvae prey on aphids and psyllids. Holarctic, Alaska, across Canada and northern half of United States. (1)

Seven-spotted Lady Beetle *Coccinella septempunctata* **(Linnaeus)** (6.5–7.8 mm) is broadly oval and convex. Head black with two distinct white spots. Pronotum black at middle of anterior margin with pale, somewhat triangular spots under anterior angles. Elytra red with seven black spots, including shared spot on scutellum. Adults found on vegetation and occasionally at light. Europe; widespread across southern Canada and throughout the United States. Nine-spotted Lady Beetle, *Coccinella novempunctata* Herbst (4.7–7.0 mm) is a seldom-seen native species, usually with four black spots on each elytron, plus shared spot. (9)

Coccinella trifasciata perplexa Mulsant (4.0–5.0 mm) is broadly oval and convex. Head pale with black band across base (male) or black with two pale spots (female). Pronotum usually with front margin pale, basal black spot broad and extended forward at middle. Elytra with three black bands, middle and rear band broadly broken at suture. Adults active spring and summer, and are aphid predators. Labrador to New Jersey, west to Alaska and California. (9)

Coleomegilla maculata lengi Timberlake (4.2–6.6 mm) is somewhat elongate and flattened. Pronotal spots large, triangular. Elytra pink or red with six black spots, median spot large, with post-median spots touching suture. Underside and legs black, except for prosternum and lateral abdominal margins. Adults on vegetation in spring and summer. New Hampshire to Georgia, west to Minnesota and eastern Texas. *C. m. fuscilabris* (Mulsant) has smaller, rounder spots on pronotum and elytral spots at tips not touching suture; along Atlantic and Gulf coasts, from South Carolina to Louisiana. (1)

Cycloneda munda (Say) (3.7–5.7 mm) is almost round, very convex, with shiny orange elytra without markings. Pronotum mostly black with pale lateral spot not entirely enclosed, or with isolated lateral black spot. Elytra sometimes with small white marks at base flanking scutellum. Legs with middle and hind tibiae each tipped with a pair of spurs, claws appendiculate, with somewhat squarish flange at base. Adults and larvae are aphid predators. Adults active spring and summer. Widespread in eastern North America, except Florida. (2)

Multicolored Asian Lady Beetle *Harmonia axyridis* **(Pallas)** (4.8–7.5 mm) is oval, convex, and incredibly variable in elytral color and pattern. Pronotum white with up to five black spots often joined to form an M-shaped mark or a solid trapezoid. Elytra red or orange, each with up to 10 black small or large spots in fully marked individuals, or black with two to four red spots, or some other variation, side margin distinctly beaded and not translucent. Sometimes considered a nuisance when they gather on or enter homes and outbuildings in late fall and winter. Adults found year-round on trees and shrubs; attracted to light. Eurasia; established throughout North America. (2)

316

Convergent Lady Beetle *Hippodamia convergens* **Guerin** (4.3–7.3 mm) is oval, somewhat elongate, with distinct markings on pronotum. Pronotum with convergent pale spots, pale borders along sides more or less even, and base not margined. Elytra each with six small, discrete spots usually present, sometimes reduced in number or absent; margins weakly reflexed along sides. Legs with femur visible beyond elytron and all claws narrowly notched or cleft. Adults active in spring and summer, found in wide variety of habitats on vegetation; sometimes found in summer or winter aggregations in mountains. Most common and abundant species of *Hippodamia*. Across southern Canada and United States. (7)

Hippodamia parenthesis (Say) (3.7–5.6 mm) is oval, somewhat elongate. Head black with variable pale spots. Pronotum with black spot nearly divided at base by white trapezoid spot. Elytra red with shared black triangular spot at scutellum, patches on humeri, and variable bold curved marks near tips sometimes reduced or broken into two spots. Adults active spring and summer. Widespread in North America, except for southeastern United States and Pacific Northwest. (7)

Hippodamia variegata (Goeze) (4.4–5.0 mm) is oval, somewhat elongate. Head whitish with black base (male) or a large spot (female). Pronotum black with front and side margins, and spot in each side pale (female) or with black area deeply notched in front an spots sometimes connected to front margin (male); both sexes with distinctive fine raised margin along base. Elytra orange, each with five to seven black spots, spots below humeri and immediately behind shared scutellar spot sometimes absent. Adults active spring and summer and are aphid predators. Old World: established in Maritime Provinces and New England west to Ontario. (7)

Mulsantina hudsonica (Casey) (3.5–5.0 mm) has a yellow head with pair of interrupted black lines connected to black top. Pronotum with variable and irregular black spots forming M-shaped pattern, plus a blotch on each side. Elytra dark suture with blotches on middle sometimes connected to stripe flanked by a spot at side behind middle. Across Canada; eastern United States from New England to Great Lakes region, south through Appalachian Mountains to Tennessee and North Carolina. (3)

Mulsantina picta (Randall) (3.3–5.3 mm) has an M-shaped pattern on pronotum and a stripe down each elytron. Head is yellow with pair black spots flanking clypeus, each narrowly connected to black top of head. Pronotum distinctively patterned with spot on each side connected to middle black M-shaped mark, all of which are sometimes broken up into smaller spots. Elytral markings vary from heavily marked to no marks at all. Across Canada and contiguous United States. (3)

Myzia pullata (Say) (6.5–8.0 mm) is brownish yellow to red; northern individuals with dark elytral spots. Pronotum dark brown or black in middle, broad white lateral margins with median dark spot sometimes connected to middle brown patch. Elytral border somewhat flattened. Adults on vegetation in spring and summer. Labrador to South Carolina, west to Alberta, Colorado, and Texas. (3)

Naemia seriata (Melsheimer) (4.0–6.7 mm) is orange with reddish margins and variable black spots. Head entirely black. Pronotum with central irregular black spot on basal half. Elytra with three distinct spots on suture and on each side, or more typically with all spots connected along sides and suture, these connected at tip. Larvae and adults probably prey on aphids. Coastal distribution suggests preference for humid habitats. Atlantic and Gulf coasts, from Massachusetts to Texas. (1)

Neoharmonia venusta (Melsheimer) (4.5–7.0 mm) is elongate, oval, somewhat flattened, with a distinct pattern. Elytra pink or reddish and black, pattern variable with spots across middle and shared A-shaped marking at base only sometimes present or absent entirely, or nearly all black with paler markings at sides behind middle. Middle and hind tibiae with apical spurs. Adults and larvae prey on larvae and pupae of willow leaf beetle, *Plagiodera versicolora* (Laicharting) (Chrysomelidae) (p.443), on wild and ornamental willow (*Salix*). New England and Ontario to Florida, west Michigan, Nebraska, and eastern Texas. (1)

Olla v-nigrum (Mulsant) (3.7–6.2 mm) is nearly circular in outline when viewed from above, very convex, and variably colored, including black with large pale spots on each elytron, or pale yellow with black spots; dark form predominates in east. Middle and hind tibiae each tipped with pair of spurs. Adults active spring and summer and prey on aphids in several genera. North America; also Mexico south to Argentina. (1)

Colour variation in *Olla v-nigrum*.
TOP RIGHT: Dark form.
BOTTOM RIGHT: Pale form.

Propylea quatuordecimpunctata (Linnaeus) (3.5–5.2 mm) is oval, convex, and yellow with black spots. Head with white (male) or black (female) clypeus. Pronotum yellow with irregular spots sometimes forming large irregular black spot on each side, underside grayish white (male) or black (female). Elytra yellow with distinctive irregular and variable black spots forming a checkerboard-like pattern. Adults active spring and summer and are aphid predators. Europe; established in Maritime Provinces and New England to New York, west to Québec. (1)

Twenty-spotted Lady Beetle *Psyllobora vigintimaculata* (Say) (1.7–3.0 mm) is small and pale. Pronotum with four dark spots. Elytral pattern variable, usually with nine spots on a pale background, sometimes with diffuse orange-yellow patch. Adults found on vegetation in spring and summer. Some species of *Psyllobora* feed on fungus, especially powdery mildews such as *Erysiphe*. Alaska and southern Canada throughout United States into Mexico. (3)

319

Mexican Bean Beetle *Epilachna varivestis* Mulsant (6.4–8.1 mm) is oval, somewhat convex, and pale brownish yellow to dark reddish yellow. Pronotum without spots. Elytra each with eight round spots, none in contact with suture. Adults and larvae are crop pests, damaging leaves of garden (*Phaseolus*) and field beans (*Vicia*), sometimes soybean (*Glycine*) and cowpea (*Vigna*). Widespread in east, from New Brunswick and New England to Florida, west to Wisconsin, Kansas, and Texas. (2)

European Alfalfa Beetle *Subcoccinella vigintiquatuorpunctata* (Linnaeus) (3.5–4.4 mm) is small, oval, brownish orange or reddish orange with variable black markings. First abdominal ventrite with line behind leg base not curved upward toward sides. Elytra widest in front of middle. Larvae and adults skeletonize undersides of leaves of bouncing bet (*Saponaria officinalis*) and many other plants in Caryophyllaceae, Chenopodiaceae, and Fabaceae. Adults active in spring and early summer on food plants; overwinter near hosts. Europe; established from New York to Maryland, west to Ohio and West Virginia. (1)

MINUTE HOODED AND FUNGUS BEETLES, FAMILY CORYLOPHIDAE
(KOR-EE-*LOAF*-IH-DEE)

The common name "minute hooded beetles" is derived from their small size and the broad, shelflike anterior rim of the pronotum projecting over the head and concealing it from view above. Most adult and larval corylophids eat the spores and hyphae of molds and other microfungi. They are typically found under bark, on leaf surfaces, and in accumulations of decaying plant material. *Orthoperus* and *Rypobius* adults feed on mold, while *Sericoderus* has been found on various gilled fungi. *Arthrolips* and *Orthoperus* have also been recorded feeding on bracket fungi. *Clypastraea* live among fungi and mold in rotten wood and under the bark of dead trees. *Gloeosoma* occur in leaf litter or mold at the base of plants.

FAMILY DIAGNOSIS Adult corylophids are very small, oval to almost circular in outline, with head often covered from above by sharp front margin of pronotum. Clubbed antennae with 9–11 antennomeres, last three forming distinct club. Front coxal cavities closed, bases of front legs completely surrounded by thoracic plate. Legs with tarsal formula 4-4-4. Abdomen with six ventrites, pygidium exposed.

SIMILAR FAMILIES Many families have species with similar body form, but none have the pronotum extending over the head *and* distinctly clubbed antennae.

COLLECTING NOTES Look for corylophids under bark, on flowers and foliage, and in accumulations of rotting vegetation, including leaf litter, hay stacks, cut grass, root masses, dead twigs and branches, and the moldy remains of eastern tent caterpillar nests.

FAUNA 61 SPECIES IN 10 GENERA (NA); 31 SPECIES IN 9 GENERA (ENA)

Orthoperus **species** (0.5–0.7 mm) are very small, oval, strongly convex, body uniformly shining black, sometimes with pale appendages. Antennae with nine antennomeres, last three forming elongate and loose club. Pronotum wider than long, front margin broadly emarginate. Elytra punctate or not. Flight wings fringed with setae. Mesosternum with femoral line and small median keel in males. Adults feed on fungus and found on leaves and flowers, also in nests of birds and caterpillars. Eastern North America. (5)

Arthrolips misellus **(LeConte)** (0.9–1.0 mm) is oblong-oval, shiny with head hidden under hoodlike and evenly arched front margin of pronotum, and uniformly blackish elytra. Pronotum pale with front rim somewhat flat, underside without grooves to receive antennae. Elytra long, smooth, widest part of body, surface with fine, distinct, and dense punctures, tips somewhat straight with abdomen only slightly exposed. Adults associated with ascomycete and basidiomycete fungi. Massachusetts and Pennsylvania to Virginia. (4)

Clypastraea lunata **(LeConte)** (1.0–1.3 mm) is somewhat elongate-oval, mostly shiny brownish black above, and widest across elytra, bearing a pair of yellowish spots just behind middle. Antennae with 11 antennomeres. Pronotum black with dull yellow margin across front broad, narrower along sides, with slots to receive antennae underneath. Elytra punctate and setose, with spots sometimes small or faint, tips pale and broadly rounded. Adults probably found in accumulations of plant material in association with fungus; flies at night and attracted to light. Nova Scotia and New England to Florida, west to Iowa and Missouri. (4)

Holopsis marginicollis **(LeConte)** (0.9–1.0 mm) is oval, strongly convex, shiny, blackish, with front margin of pronotum translucent; appendages pale. Pronotum short, wider than long. Elytra coarsely, yet sparsely punctate. Front legs with bases set in cavities open toward rear and front tarsi of male weakly expanded. Adults and larvae feed on fungi; larva reportedly develops on powdery mildew (*Uncinula flexuosa*). Adults active in spring and summer, found in leaf litter and on vegetation, often under leaves. Massachusetts and Ontario to Florida, west to Minnesota, and Texas. (3)

Rypobius marinus **LeConte** (1.0–1.2 mm) is evenly oval, strongly convex, upper surfaces finely wrinkled, and shiny brownish or blackish. Mandibles long, hooked at tips. Pronotum with sides not translucent, basal margin straight. Larvae are not known. Adults active in summer, found under beach drift and in salt marshes. All European species of *Rypobius* are found with mold at base of plants. Atlantic coast, from New Brunswick to Florida. (2)

Sericoderus lateralis **(Gyllenhal)** (0.9–1.0 mm) is oblong, dull pale yellow or pale reddish, and pubescent. Antennal club with three antennomeres. Front margin of pronotum with a vague dark spot. Legs with tarsi slender in both sexes. Adults and larvae are associated molds and fungus growing in damp situations under bark or in vegetable debris, such as *Mucor* (Zygomycota) and *Penicillium* (Ascomycota). Cosmopolitan; in eastern North America from Québec to Florida, west to Indiana. (3)

MINUTE BROWN SCAVENGER BEETLES, FAMILY LATRIDIIDAE
(LAT-RIH-*DIE*-IH-DEE)

Latridiids, both adults and larvae, feed on the reproductive structures of fungi (Zygomycota, Deuteromycota, Ascomycota), plant and animal materials, and slime molds. Several genera (*Cartodere, Corticaria, Corticarina, Dienerella, Enicmus, Latridius,* and *Thes*) include species regularly associated with stored products.

FAMILY DIAGNOSIS Adult latridiids are small, elongate-oval, usually widest at middle, somewhat convex, sometimes setose, with 10–11 antennomeres, the last two or three forming a gradual club, pronotum usually narrower than base of elytra, basal elytral angles often rounded, elytra grooved, and a tarsal formula of 3-3-3

SIMILAR FAMILIES
- tooth-neck fungus beetles (Derodontidae) – antennal club week; elytra with large punctures, not grooved (p.243)
- root-eating beetles (Monotomidae) – elytra shorter, exposing last abdominal tergite (p.281)

- silken fungus beetles (Cryptophagidae) – larger; pronotum as wide as base of elytra (p.283)
- minute bark beetles (Cerylonidae) – pronotum nearly as wide as base of elytra (p.307)
- hairy fungus beetles (Mycetophagidae) – larger; pronotum as wide as base of elytra (p.323)

COLLECTING NOTES Minute brown scavenger beetles are most commonly encountered during the rainy season. They are collected by sifting or applying Berlese techniques to leaf litter, or by sweeping dead, low-lying vegetation. Some species are found on dung and carrion, while others are attracted to light.

FAUNA 140 SPECIES IN 18 GENERA (NA); ~47 SPECIES IN 14 GENERA (ENA)

Corticaria serrata (Paykull) (1.7–2.3 mm) is oblong-oval, somewhat convex, dull reddish yellow to dark reddish brown, with grayish pubescence. Head and pronotum closely punctured, spaces between finely wrinkled. Bulge behind eye short. Pronotum wider than long, sides with small teeth, base at middle with deep round pit, narrower than elytra, underside with distinct pair of setose pits. Elytra coarsely punctate with faint rows of punctures. Adults feed on fungi, found in moldy plant debris and with stored foods in warehouses. Cosmopolitan; widespread in North America. (24)

Dienerella filum (Aubé) (1.2–1.6 mm) is elongate, somewhat straight-sided and flat, coarsely sculptured with areas without punctures on head and pronotum, shining, and uniformly reddish brown or yellowish brown. Head lacks paired ridges, eyes small with fewer than 20 facets, antennal club with two antennomeres, antennomere 3 not widest at base. Pronotum wider than long, sides broadest and expanded near front, with a broad, deep groove across base. Elytra each with seven rows of deep punctures. Mold-feeding larvae and flightless adults associated with fungal hyphae, slime molds, and accumulations of plant and animal material; also found in damp, moldy conditions and in buildings, basements, and warehouses. Widely distributed in North and South America, Europe, and North Africa. (9)

Enicmus aterrimus (Motschulsky) (1.6–1.9 mm) is dull blackish or reddish. Head with well-developed eyes with more than 70 facets and antennal club with three antennomeres. Head and pronotum densely punctate. Pronotum squarish with anterior angles lobed, sides somewhat parallel and sinuate before posterior angles, and broad, deep depression behind middle. Prothorax underneath with keeled process raised above coxae. Elytra each with eight rows of punctate grooves. Other species of *Enicmus* feed on spores of slime molds (Myxogastria). Europe; widely distributed in North America. (4)

Melanophthalma picta LeConte (1.3 mm) is oval, somewhat robust, dull reddish yellow, with short pubescence, and dark markings on elytra. Antennal club with two antennomeres. Pronotum slightly wider than head, punctured, without pits at base. Elytra wider than pronotum, oval, with dark band across middle and diffuse patches at base and tips, with surface finely grooved with sparse punctures, spaces between with very fine punctures. Adults active in late spring and early summer, found in damp leaves and tussock mounds associated with coastal and salt marsh habitats. Massachusetts to Florida, west to Indiana and Texas; also Pacific Northwest. (14)

323

HAIRY FUNGUS BEETLES, FAMILY MYCETOPHAGIDAE
(MY-SEE-TOE-*FAY*-JIH-DEE)

Adult and larval mycetophagids feed on fungi and are usually found under bark, on mushrooms and shelf fungi, and in moldy plant-based substrates. The cosmopolitan hairy fungus beetle, *Typhaea stercorea* (Linnaeus), is sometimes abundant indoors on stored products.

FAMILY DIAGNOSIS Most adult mycetophagids are oblong to somewhat ovate, slightly flattened, clothed in pubescence, and dark brown with orange or yellowish markings on elytra. Antennae clubbed, clubs gradual with up to five antennomeres. Pronotum with sides continuous with elytra, usually with a pair of depressions at base. Tarsal formula 4-4-4, sometimes 3-4-4 (males). Abdomen with five distinct ventrites.

SIMILAR FAMILIES
- small carrion beetles (Leiodidae) – weak antennal club with antennomere 8 small (p.118)
- variegated mud-loving beetles (Heteroceridae) – antennae filiform or serrate (p.202)
- fruitworm beetles (Byturidae) – color uniform; tarsomeres 2–3 distinctly lobed (p.274)
- false skin beetles (Biphyllidae) – color uniform; first ventrite with triangle behind legs (p.276)
- silken fungus beetles (Cryptophagidae) – colors different; pronotum usually widest at middle (p.283)
- *Clypastraea* (Corylophidae) – head covered by pronotum (p.321)
- minute brown scavenger beetles (Latridiidae) – prothorax narrower than elytra (p.322)
- *Tetratoma tessellata* (Tetratomidae) – loose, distinct antennal club of four antennomeres (p.327)
- *Prothalpia* (Melandryidae) – first hind tarsomere long; antennae not clubbed (p.332)

COLLECTING NOTES Look for hairy fungus beetles under fungal-bearing bark and in moldy plant debris. Some species are also attracted to light.

FAUNA 26 SPECIES IN FIVE GENERA (NA); 16 SPECIES IN FIVE GENERA (ENA)

Litargus tetraspilotus LeConte (1.8–2.0 mm) is blackish with two spots on each elytron. Head narrower than pronotum. Antennal club with three antennomeres. Pronotum lacks a pit near each distinct basal angle. Elytra with margins along sides at base (epipleura) concave, short, stiff pubescence on surface arranged in about 22 distinct rows with no setae between rows. Adults associated with moldy vegetation, with *Euvira micmac* Klimaszewski (Staphylinidae) in red oak galls in Nova Scotia; attracted to light. Maritime Provinces to Florida, west to Ontario, Kansas, and Texas. *Litargus sexpunctatus* (Say) with three spots on each elytron and 10 rows of longer setae. (5)

Mycetophagus flexuosus Say (3.0–4.6 mm) is oblong-oval, somewhat convex, bicolored, and clothed in stiff, reclining setae. Antennae gradually thickened toward tips, antennomeres 7–10 weakly serrate, 11 not longer than 9–10 combined. Elytra with pale markings reaching suture behind middle. Adults active in spring and summer, found under bark; also at light. New Brunswick and New England to Florida, west to Manitoba, Montana, South Dakota, and Louisiana. (8)

Mycetophagus melsheimeri LeConte (4.3–4.6 mm) is oblong-oval, somewhat convex, black above and yellowish brown underneath, and clothed in stiff, reclining setae. Antennae yellowish brown, club weak with five antennomeres. Pronotum deeply and uniformly punctured. Elytra twice as long as wide with side margins straight and parallel. Legs yellowish brown. Adults found in spring and summer under bark and at light. Pennsylvania to Georgia, west to Iowa and Texas. (8)

Mycetophagus obsoletus (Melsheimer) (4.9–5.3 mm) is oblong-oval, somewhat convex, black, and clothed in stiff, reclining setae. Antennal club with three antennomeres. Pronotum with side margins finely serrate, and pair of shallow pits at base. Elytra each with 11 rows of punctures, and large oblique Y-shaped yellowish spot not touching basal angle, small yellow spot on side at middle, broad zigzag spot across apical third, and yellow spot at tip. Abdomen underneath with first ventrite with brush of setae in male. Adults found under bark; attracted to light. New York to Florida, west to Indiana and Texas. (8)

324

Mycetophagus punctatus Say (4.5–6.5 mm) is oblong-oval, flattened, with blackish head and prothorax, and reddish-yellow elytra with black spots; large common spot surrounding scutellum and a small spot on each elytron confluent with margins; apical one-third dark. Antennae reddish, antennomeres 7–10 serrate, gradually increasing in size toward apex; last antennomere longer than preceding two antennomeres combined. Adults common under loose bark and on fungi; also attracted to lights in summer. Ontario to Georgia, west to Manitoba and Texas. (8)

Hairy Fungus Beetle *Typhaea stercorea* (Linnaeus) (2.2–3.2 mm) is oblong-oval, moderately convex, uniformly dull reddish yellow with black eyes, and moderately densely pubescent. Head across eyes narrower than pronotum, antennal club with three antennomeres. Pronotum widest across basal third with basal angles distinct. Elytra sometimes darker, with fine, erect, yellowish setae. Front tarsi with three tarsomeres in male, four in female. Adults and larvae found on moldly stored foods and other decaying organic materials. Adults attracted to light. Europe, nearly cosmopolitan; widely distributed in North America; Maritime Provinces and New England to Florida and westward. (1)

ARCHEOCRYPTICID BEETLES, FAMILY ARCHEOCRYPTICIDAE
(AR-KEY-OH-CRYP-*TISS*-IH-DEE)

Adults and larvae are usually found in leaf litter and other plant debris where they apparently feed on decaying plant material. Adults are collected in rotting flowers in Panama and from wood-rotting fungi in Australia. Only one species, *Enneboeus caseyi* Kaszab, is known from southeastern United States and is found in accumulations of leaves and other vegetable materials.

FAMILY DIAGNOSIS Adult archeocrypticids are very small, oval, strongly convex, and sparsely clothed in fine, recumbent setae. Antennae with 11 antennomeres, 9–11 forming a gradual club, with bases hidden from above. Underside of prothorax with process extending backward between coxae partially closing coxal cavities. Elytra with rows of fine punctures. Tarsal formula is 5-5-4, with claws simple. Abdomen with five ventrites, first two ventrites fused.

SIMILAR FAMILIES
- some pleasing fungus beetles (Erotylidae) – antennae abruptly clubbed (p.277)
- *Hyporhagus* (Zopheridae) – abdomen with first four ventrites fused (p.343)
- some darkling beetles (Tenebrionidae) – prothorax without process underneath partially closing coxal cavities (p.344)

COLLECTING NOTES *Enneboeus* are extracted from leaf litter and other vegetable debris using a Berlese funnel. They have also been found in second-year pine cones and at light.

FAUNA ONE SPECIES, *ENNEBOEUS CASEYI* KASZAB

Enneboeus caseyi **Kaszab** (1.7 mm) is elongate-oval, moderately convex, streamlined, and black with fine, dense, short pubescence; appendages dark reddish brown. Head set within prothorax. Pronotum twice as wide as long. Elytra with rows of fine punctures, sides and tips broadly rounded. Legs short. Both adults and larvae are found in leaf litter and other vegetative debris. Adults active spring and summer, also found in old pine cones (*Pinus strobus*) and rotten flowers. North Carolina to Florida, west to Kentucky and Texas; Mexico to Panama. (1)

MINUTE TREE-FUNGUS BEETLES, FAMILY CIIDAE
(*SEE*-IH-DEE)

Adults and larvae feed on the fruiting bodies or vegetative hyphae of woody or fibrous wood-rotting fungus growing on the logs and stumps of hardwoods, especially in jelly (*Auricularia*), polypore (*Fomes, Ganoderma, Phellinus, Trichaptum*), false turkey tail (*Stereum*), and turkey tail fungi (*Trametes*).

FAMILY DIAGNOSIS Adult ciids are small, elongate to oval, convex, cylindrical, with the head more or less hidden from above. Antennae short, with 8–10 antennmeres with last two or three forming a loose symmetrical club. Pronotum not or slightly narrower than elytra. Elytra not grooved and with erect setae. Tarsal formula 4-4-4. Abdomen with five ventrites.

SIMILAR FAMILIES
- branch and twig borers (Bostrichidae) – antennal club lopsided (p.250)

- death-watch beetles (Ptinidae) – antennal club lopsided (p.252)
- cyptic slime mold beetles (Sphindidae) – elytra with coarsely punctured grooves (p.275)
- bark beetles (Curculionidae) – antennal club large, apparently with one antennomere (pp.497–500)

COLLECTING NOTES Ciids are commonly found in tunnels chewed into their host fungi. They are easily reared from infested fungi.

FAUNA 84 SPECIES IN 13 GENERA (NA); 55 SPECIES IN 10 GENERA (ENA)

Octotemnus species (1.3–1.6 mm) are elongate oval, shining black, a few scattered minute and not readily visible setae. Antennae with eight antennomeres. Pronotum with front margin unmodified, sides smooth. Abdomen of male with first ventrite with posterior projecting triangular flap partly concealing pubescent pit. Legs with all tibiae spinose along outer edges; bases of front legs somewhat cone-shaped. Male of undescribed species has enlarged mandibles and horns on head, while *Octotemnus laevis* Casey does not. Adults found on various species of polypore fungi, including *Coriolus, Ganoderma, Lenzites, Stereum, Trametes*. Widespread in eastern North America. (2)

Strigocis opacicollis Dury (1.2–1.4 mm) is elongate, reddish brown or darker, clothed in sparse setae, and with pale appendages. Pronotal surface dull and elytral punctation coarse and separated by one diameter or less. Front margin of male pronotum produced into two angulate processes. Adults and larvae found in association with polypore fungi (*Coriolus*, *Lenzites*, *Pycnoporus*). Ontario to Florida, west to eastern Kansas and Arkansas; Mexico. (2)

POLYPORE FUNGUS BEETLES, FAMILY TETRATOMIDAE
(TET-TRA-*TOME*-IH-DEE)

Tetratomids differ substantially from one another in appearance and are challenging to characterize as a family. Both adults and larvae feed on the softer fruiting bodies of Hymenomycetes fungi growing on decaying wood, especially bracket fungi (Polyporaceae) and Tricholomataceae. The larvae bore into the tissues of fresh or decaying sporophores, while adults are usually found on the surfaces of fungi and dead wood. Adult *Penthe* have been collected on *Grifola berkeleyi*, *Polyporus squamosus*, *Piptoporus betulinus*, *Fomitopsis pinicola*, *Phaeolus schweinitzii*, and other polypore fungi.

FAMILY DIAGNOSIS Adult tetratomids are oblong to ovate, somewhat flattened, and pubescent with notched eyes. Antennal bases slightly hidden or visible from above. Bases of front legs separated by prosternal process. Tarsal formula 5-5-4, with tarsomeres not lobed underneath. Abdomen with five ventrites.

SIMILAR FAMILIES
- plate-thigh beetles (Eucinetidae) – hind coxal plates covering part of abdomen; elytra crossed with fine wrinkles; tarsi 5-5-5 (p.178)

- *Mycetophagus* (Mycetophagidae) – tarsi 4-4-4, 3-4-4 (p.323)
- false darkling beetles (Melandryidae) – middle tibia as long as femur or first tarsomere, if shorter then spurs at least one-third length of tibia (p.329)
- comb-clawed beetles (Tenebrionidae: Alleculinae) – claws pectinate (pp.351–3)

COLLECTING NOTES Look for tetratomids at night on fungi and on or under bark of fungus-ridden logs and stumps. They are sometimes attracted to light.

327

FAUNA 26 SPECIES IN 10 GENERA (NA); 17 SPECIES IN 9 GENERA (ENA)

Tetratoma truncorum LeConte (4.5–6.5 mm) is oblong-oval with black head, reddish-orange pronotum, legs, and underside, and metallic blue elytra. Antennae black. Pronotum wider than long, sides rounded, surface sparsely and deeply punctate, with a pair of deep, basal impressions on either side of middle. Elytral surface with punctures dense, deep, and scattered. Larvae and adults develop and feed within fruiting bodies of polypore fungi, e.g., *Spongipellis unicolor*. Adults active in fall, found under bark and in decaying wood of standing dead trees. Ontario and Québec to Virginia, west to Indiana and Oklahoma. *Tetratoma tessellata* Melsheimer (3.5 mm), pronotal margin unevenly notched, elytra with about 10 somewhat sinuous or confluent yellow spots. (3)

Penthe obliquata (Fabricius) (11.0–14.0 mm) is dull velvety black with densely punctured pronotum and elytra. Antennae mostly black, last antennomere reddish brown; antennomere 3 as long as combined lengths of antennomeres 4–5 and much longer than antennomeres 1–2 combined. Scutellum covered with long yellowish or orangish setae. Elytra each with 11 or more rows of deep punctures. Adults active spring and summer, found on tree trunks and fungus at night, also at light; overwinter under loose bark in winter. Widespread in eastern North America. (2)

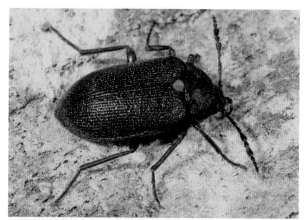

Penthe pimelia (Fabricius) (10.0–15.0 mm) is very similar to *P. obliquata* in form, habit, and distribution, but with a black scutellum. Antennae mostly black, last antennomere reddish brown; antennomere 3 as long as combined lengths of antennomeres 4–5 and much longer than antennomeres 1–2 combined. Elytra each with 11 or more rows of deep punctures. Adults overwinter under loose bark, found wandering on tree trunks and fungus on spring and summer evenings. Widespread in eastern North America. (2)

Hallomenus scapularis Melsheimer (4.0–5.0 mm) is elongate, oblong, densely clothed in yellowish setae, and dark reddish brown to blackish with legs and humeri of elytra yellowish or reddish yellow. Eyes with deep notches distant from antennal bases. Antennomeres short, slightly expanded outward, 3–10 almost equal in length. Pronotum densely punctured with a pair of deep depressions at base. Elytra not grooved. Legs with tibial spurs very short. Adults active in summer in coniferous and deciduous forests, found under bark of dead pine (*Pinus*), on pine strobili, and on polypore fungi, including *Piptoporus betulinus;* reproduces on *Perreniporia, Sparassa,* and *Tyromyces.* Nova Scotia and Québec to Georgia, west to Ontario, Indiana, and New Mexico. (3)

Eustrophopsis bicolor (Fabricius) (4.2–6.5 mm) is black, oblong-oval, convex, pubescent, and narrowed behind with legs and abdomen reddish brown. Head with eyes narrowly separated, nearly touching in front. Antennae black with antennomeres 1–4, 11 yellowish red. Pronotum nearly all black and broadly lobed on posterior margin. Elytra with rows of coarse punctures becoming smaller apically and flat intervals densely punctate. Middle and hind tibiae with numerous transverse ridges. Adults found under loose bark of fungal-infested conifer and hardwood logs, and on polypore fungi. Québec to Florida, west to Manitoba, Idaho, California, and Arizona; Mexico. (3)

Holostrophus bifasciatus (Say) (4.0–5.5 mm) is small, oval, convex, and distinctly tapered behind middle. Upper surface shining reddish brown and clothed in reddish pubescence. Elytra with fine, deep punctures and broad reddish bands at base and apical third both interrupted at suture. Eyes widely separated and notched, prosternal process widened at tip, middle and hind tibiae lack oblique ridges. Adults found in association with polypore fungi on various coniferous and hardwood tree, also beneath rotten logs, at lights, or in flight intercept traps from spring through summer. Eastern Canada to Florida, west to Minnesota and Texas. (1)

FALSE DARKLING BEETLES, FAMILY MELANDRYIDAE
(MEL-AN-*DRY*-IH-DEE)

Melandryids are found exclusively in forested habitats in association with fungi on dead or dying trees. The larvae of some species feed in fungal bodies, while others develop in soft or hard rotten wood infested with white-rot fungi. Some may prefer feeding on fungus developing in hardwoods or conifers. *Orchesia* larvae develop in sporophores, with each species having a definite feeding preference.

FAMILY DIAGNOSIS Adult melandryids are structurally diverse and difficult to characterize, and are elongate and slender or broad and oval. Antennal bases slightly visible from above. Middle tibia long as femur or first tarsomere, or shorter with long tibial spurs one-third or more of length of tibia. Tip of maxillary palp usually large and hatchet- or knife-shaped. Abdomen with five ventrites, first two fused.

SIMILAR FAMILIES
- ground beetles (Carabidae) – tarsi 5-5-5 (p.63)
- polypore fungus beetles (Tetratomidae) – tarsomeres not lobed underneath; procoxae separated by process (p.327)
- tumbling flower beetles (Mordellidae) – humpbacked; abdomen pointed (p.333)
- comb-clawed beetles (Tenebrionidae) – pronotum without pits; claws pectinate (pp.351–3)
- synchroa bark beetles (Synchroidae) – penultimate tarsomeres not lobed underneath (p.359)
- false flower beetles (Scraptiidae) – head not fitting into prothorax; sometimes with fine ridges across pronotum and elytra (p.384)

COLLECTING NOTES Adults are found under loose bark of snags and stumps. They are also found on fresh or decaying fungi or fungal-infested logs at night; some species are regularly attracted to lights. Take note of fungal masses, well-rotted tree holes, dying trees, and snags during the day and revisit these sites at night. Malaise and Lindgren funnel traps will also produce specimens.

FAUNA 50 SPECIES IN 24 GENERA (NA): 28 SPECIES IN 21 GENERA (ENA)

Orchesia castanea (Melsheimer) (4.0–5.8 mm) is elongate, convex, clothed in fine brown pubescence, and uniformly dark chestunut brown; appendages lighter. Eyes narrowly separated. Pronotum wider than long and more coarsely and densely punctured at base, basal impressions shallow. Elytra more densely punctured and pubescent at base. Legs with hind tibiae tipped with very long spurs at least one-third length of tibiae. Adults found on vegetation and logs infested with fungi; also at light. Will jump while attempting to escape. Newfoundland to South Carolina, west to Manitoba, Indiana, and Texas; also British Columbia. (3)

329

Dircaea liturata (LeConte) (7.0–12.0 mm) is elongate-oval, tapering behind middle, dark reddish brown to blackish with paler appendages, and distinct elytral markings. Prothorax slightly wider than long at base, anterior margin pale. Elytra each with irregular H-shaped yellowish spots at base and on apical third, coarse punctures at base becoming fine toward apex. Adults are found in late spring and summer on trees at night; also attracted to light. Based on European species of *Dircaea*, larvae may feed and pupate in beech (*Fagus*) logs. Nova Scotia and New Brunswick to Florida, west to Alberta, Minnesota, Arkansas, and Texas. (1)

Amblyctis praeses LeConte (10.0–12.6 mm) is elongate, convex, dull black, and finely pubescent with reddish-orange markings. Base and underside of head reddish orange. Antennae serrate with articles 3–10 broad and flat. Prothorax with two reddish-orange stripes on sides. Appendages black with mouthparts pale. Elytra with distinct ridges extending midway to apical third. A rare species collected in flight or reared from American beech (*Fagus grandifolia*). Ontario, Québec, New York, and Indiana. (1)

Enchodes sericea (Haldeman) (11.0–15.0 mm) is elongate, slender, tapering toward rear, densely clothed in fine yellowish pubescence, and uniformly brown; appendages paler. Pronotum about as wide as long, with side margins rounded, hind angles prominent, with shallow triangular depression on each side at base. Elytra smooth, shiny, without grooves, finely punctate, and evenly tapered from base to tip. Fleet-footed and nocturnal adults active in summer, found on dead, rotten conifer and hardwood limbs, snags, logs, and trunks, or beaten from dead limbs; also attracted to light. Maritime Provinces and Québec to Georgia, west to British Columbia, North Dakota, and Louisiana. (1)

Rushia longula (LeConte) (4.5–6.5 mm) is elongate and shining brown to chestnut-brown with appendages lighter. Antennomeres short and triangular. Nearly square pronotum slightly narrowed toward head, finely and densely punctate, with sides distinctly ridged. Elytra widest at middle, without grooves, and clothed in short, fine, yellowish setae. Hind tibia as long as femur or first tarsomere; tarsi cylindrical in cross section. Adults are active in summer and attracted to light. Maine to Florida. (1)

Spilotus quadripustulatus **(Melsheimer)** (3.0–3.5 mm) is elongate, slender, shiny, blackish, and sparsely covered with coarse seta-bearing punctures, setae fine, and two dull yellow spots on each elytron. Antennal articles pale yellowish at base, becoming darker. Pronotum wider than long, side margins rounded and sharp. Elytra more sparsely punctured than pronotum. Legs with femora dark, tibiae lighter, and tarsi pale. Adults found on vegetation, including leaves of walnut (*Juglans*), oak twigs (*Quercus*), or shoots of American basswood (*Tilia americana*); also attracted to light, in Malaise and Lindgren traps. Nova Scotia and Québec to Georgia, west to Ontario, Wisconsin, Missouri, and Louisiana. (1)

Hypulus simulator **Newman** (4.5–7.0 mm) is elongate, dull yellow with brownish-black to black markings on elytra and sometimes pronotum. Pronotum longer than wide, sides not keeled and somewhat parallel, surface near basal angles deeply depressed along sides to apical third, slightly narrower than elytra at base, and base with distinct raised line or bead. Elytra coarsely punctate with distinct humeri. Adults active late spring and summer in wooded habitats; attracted to light. Maritime Provinces and New England to Virginia, west to Ontario, Ohio, and Mississippi. (1)

Microtonus sericans **(LeConte)** (3.8–4.5 mm) is elongate, slender, convex, weakly shining brown, and sparsely clothed in short fine yellowish setae. Pronotum nearly square, wide as head, sides keeled, surface granulate, slightly narrower than base of elytra with hind angles sharp. Elytra slightly wider at base with surface coarsely and irregularly punctate. Adults found in late spring on vegetation, especially of deciduous shrubs and trees. Maine to Florida, west to Indiana and Texas. (1)

Symphora flavicollis **(Haldeman)** (3.0–3.5 mm) is elongate, somewhat convex, shining, clothed in fine pubescence, and bicolored. Head, prothorax, legs, and antennal bases reddish yellow; rest of body blackish. Pronotum wider than long, with sides not keeled and vague indentations near posterior angles. Adults active from late spring through early summer and found on foliage, limbs, and beneath bark in coniferous, hardwood, and mixed forests. Prince Edward Island and Nova Scotia to Florida, west to Indiana, Kansas, and Texas. (2)

Emmesa connectens **Newman** (7.0–11.5 mm) is blackish with tibiae and tarsi paler. Pronotum shining, wider than long, with front margin rounded, deep depression on sides at base, base slightly narrower than elytra. Elytra roughly punctured, with interrupted yellowish band across middle not quite reaching margins and a common apical spot; each elytron with trace of three ridges (costae) at base. Adults are attracted to lights and found in Malaise traps in summer. Associated with maple (*Acer*), beech (*Fagus grandifolia*), pine (*Pinus*), and red spruce (*Picea rubens*). Newfoundland and Nova Scotia to New York, west to Ontario and Michigan. (2)

Melandrya striata **Say** (7.0–15.0 mm) is elongate-oblong, shiny black, somewhat flattened with elytra striate. Head with eyes vaguely emarginate in front. Antennae reddish brown. Pronotum narrowed toward head with pair of depressions, posterior margin extending loosely over elytra. Elytra coarsely, with seta-bearing punctures, setae dark and recumbent, with at least seven raised intervals. Next to last tarsomere with short lobe underneath. Adults under bark and in Malaise, Lindgren, and flight intercept traps in summer. Larvae develop in deciduous logs. New Brunswick to South Carolina, west to Alberta, North Dakota, Iowa, Missouri, and Tennessee. (1)

Prothalpia undata **(LeConte)** (6.5 mm) is elongate, convex, light to dark reddish brown with distinct blackish or black markings on elytra; appendages pale brown. Head dark. Pronotum wider than long, depressions on sides short, confined to basal third, and base sinuate with distinct raised line or bead and loosely covering base of elytra. Elytra not grooved, moderately punctate, with dark triangular spot behind scutellum and other contrasting markings. Adults active spring and summer, found on fungi; attracted to light. Newfoundland and Québec to North Carolina, west to Wisconsin. (1)

Osphya varians **(LeConte)** (5.0–8.0 mm) resembles a firefly or soldier beetle. Antennae long, filiform. Pronotum slightly broader than long with side margins broadly rounded, reddish yellow with broad black stripe on either side of middle sometimes connected or largely joined. Elytra densely punctured, pale along suture. Penultimate tarsomeres distinctly lobed and extend toward claws, base of claws toothed. Adults found on vegetation and flowers of shrubs and trees in spring and early summer, especially elm (*Ulmus*), oak (*Quercus*), hawthorn (*Crataegus*), and tulip tree (*Liriodendron tulipifera*); also captured in light, Malaise, and boll weevil traps. Larvae probably feed in dead wood. Ontario to Florida, west to Iowa, Kansas, and Texas. (1)

TUMBLING FLOWER BEETLES, FAMILY MORDELLIDAE
(MOR-*DEL*-LIH-DEE)

Tumbling flower beetles are aptly named. When threatened, they rapidly kick their hind legs back and forth, causing them to bounce and tumble unpredictably, or quickly take flight. Mordellids are small, mostly black, sometimes distinctly patterned, wedge-shaped beetles commonly found on flowers, often in great numbers in spring and summer. Adults apparently feed on pollen and nectar of a variety of plants. There appears to be little relationship between adult feeding preferences and larval food plants. The larvae are adapted for boring into compact substrates and feed on rotten wood or inside the stems of numerous herbaceous plants and shrubs. Other species burrow into and feed on galls and shelf fungi. Of the more than 200 species of mordellids known in North America, nearly three-quarters are in the genus *Mordellistena*.

FAMILY DIAGNOSIS The humpbacked and wedge-shaped body form, long, narrow, pointed abdomen extending well beyond elytra, and jumping behavior of adult mordellids are distinctive. Adults are mostly black, sometimes with distinct patterns of setae. Head short, with mouthparts directed downward (hypognathous). Antennae with 11 antennomeres, antennomeres serrate, clavate, or filiform. Pronotum small, narrowed toward head, and distinctly margined. Scutellum visible. Elytra smooth and narrowed behind and completely conceal all but part of the last abdominal ventrite, surface clothed in fine hair and frequently patterned with lighter colored hair to form lines, bands, or spots. Hind legs long, tarsal formula 5-5-4, claws equal and toothed; outer surface of hind tibiae and first two or three tarsomeres often with distinct ridges. Abdomen with five ventrites.

SIMILAR FAMILIES
- wedge-shaped beetles (Ripiphoridae: *Macrosiagon*) – last abdominal ventrite blunt (p.339)
- false flower beetles (Scraptiidae) – abdomen not sharply pointed (p.384)

COLLECTING NOTES Mordellids are wary and escape easily, but they can be picked from flowers by hand, scooped into a container, or collected with a sweep net. Malaise and flight intercept traps produce the greatest diversity of species, especially those that do not visit flowers. A few species are sometimes attracted to lights or to baited Lindgren funnel traps.

333

FAUNA 189 SPECIES IN 17 GENERA (NA); 149 SPECIES IN 17 GENERA (ENA)

Glipa hilaris (**Say**) (10.0–12.0 mm) is large and black with narrow gray and broad brassy bands of setae. Pronotum patterned with gray bands, four black patches, two down middle and one either side at base. Scutellum with dense silvery gray setae. Elytra with irregular brassy band from just below base to basal quarter lined with gray. Legs black, no ridges except just before tips of hind tibiae, tibiae densely clothed in gray setae, front and middle tarsomere 4 deeply notched. Adults active late spring and early summer; captured with Lindgren and Malaise traps. Pennsylvania to Florida, west to Indiana and Texas. (3)

Glipa oculata (Say) (5.0–6.0 mm) typically has two large ashy pubescent patches at base of each elytron forming a broad band across elytra, patches sometimes golden or silvery; each patch surrounds a single black spot; variable hatchet-shaped marks behind middle, sometime appearing as a pair of spots. Last palpomere of maxillary palp triangular in both sexes. Elytra usually black, sometimes reddish brown. Penultimate tarsomeres of front and middle legs notched. Adults found on flowers and foliage of various shrubs, including New Jersey tea (*Ceanothus americanus*) in spring and summer. Pennsylvania and Ontario to Virginia, west to Illinois and Texas. (3)

Hoshihananomia octopunctata (Fabricius) (8.0–9.0 mm) is black with distinctive yellow, orange, or silver markings. Pronotum with setal pattern, including thin scalloped band across middle. Scutellum broadly rounded at tip. Legs with penultimate tarsomere of front and middle tarsi deeply notched. Hind tibiae without short spines along upper edge, outer surface lacks oblique ridges, save for short ridge just above tip. Underside with ashy setae, abdomen distinctly patterned. Larvae develop in dead wood, including in bark of dying American beech (*Fagus grandifolia*) and rotten oak logs (*Quercus*). Adults active in summer, found on flowers near woods, especially Queen Anne's lace (*Daucus carota*). New York to Florida, west to Minnesota, Kansas, and Texas. (2)

Mordella marginata Melsheimer (4.0–5.5 mm) is wedge-shaped and dull black with grayish pubescent pattern. Head with dense ash-colored pubescence. Pronotum wider than long, with narrow stripes of pubescence flanking middle, short line near hind angles, and spot or short, oblique line reaching sides at middle. Elytra with spots or blotches of pubescence, abbreviated lines, or both. Last abdominal ventrite with pubescence at base. Adults active in late spring and early summer on flowers. Maritime Provinces and New England to Florida, west to Manitoba, Colorado, and Arizona. (11)

Mordellaria serval (Say) (4.5–5.0 mm) is black or dark reddish brown with hairy eyes, fourth tarsomere of front tarsi not dilated or bilobed, and maxillary palpi elongate-oval. Hind tibiae with fine dorsal ridge; tibiae and tarsi without lateral ridges. Scutellum broadly rounded. Elytra with numerous spots of short yellowish or gray setae, a larger spot near base, a narrow band at apical third, and ash-colored apical margin. Adults are active in summer in mixed forests on flowers and foliage. Nova Scotia and New Brunswick to Virginia, west to Manitoba, Wisconsin, and Missouri. (5)

Tolidomordella discoidea (**Melsheimer**) (2.4–5.0 mm) is blackish with distinct yellowish markings. Head with last palpomere boat-shaped (male) or scalene (female). Pronotum brownish yellow with large triangular black spot. Elytra blackish, each with a pair of yellowish upside down 7s at base and broad patch behind middle. Pointed last abdominal ventrite reddish brown. Underside mostly blackish, black or yellow in south. Legs pale, hind tibia with fine dorsal ridge and short ridge parallel to tip; tarsomere 3 of front and middle legs deeply notched. Adults found on dead limbs of hardwoods; attracted to light. New York to Florida, west to Iowa and Texas. (1)

Tomoxia lineella (**LeConte**) (6.7–8.0 mm) is black or reddish brown with longitudinal lines of pubescence on both pronotum and elytra. Adults collected during summer on dead deciduous trees, such as elm (*Ulmus*), linden (*Tilia*), ash (*Fraxinus*), beech (*Fagus*), and hickory (*Carya*). Larvae and pupae were found under bark in sound wood of standing dead large-toothed aspen (*Populus grandidenta*) in Wisconsin. Nova Scotia to Virginia, west to Ontario, Wisconsin, and Kansas. (1)

Yakuhananomia bidentata (**Say**) (7.0–13.0 mm) is large, brownish black with variable gray spots and lines. Head with large mouthparts and antennae reddish brown. Pronotum wider than long. Scutellum wider than long with posterior margin broadly notched. Elytra only slightly narrowed to somewhat straight tips. Tibia without dorsal or lateral ridges, save for short ridge parallel to tip. Adults active primarily in late spring, found on boles of standing trees, e.g., hickory (*Carya*). Adults active late spring and summer. Maine to Georgia, west to Ontario, Michigan, Iowa, and Kansas. (1)

Falsomordellistena bihamata (**Melsheimer**) (3.0–5.0 mm) has small, oval eyes never indented (emarginate) behind antennae, last maxillary palpomere with sides unequal in length (scalene). Head and prothorax dark, pronotum with pale side and posterior margins. Antennae brown. Elytra dark brown with tan side and apical margins; each elytron with four elongate tan spots. Hind tibiae with three parallel, oblique ridges and distinct remnant of fourth; first and second tarsomeres with three and two ridges, respectively. New York and Pennsylvania to North Carolina, west to Indiana and Kentucky. (2)

Falsomordellistena pubescens (Fabricius) (3.0–5.0 mm) has a black head and body. Mouthparts and antennae pale. Pronotum with grayish pubescence not covering three well-defined spots; middle spot sometimes divided into two elongate spots. Elytra with humerus more or less reddish brown under certain light, sutural line gray, other markings variable, usually with curved gray line at base from humerus to suture, and bands across middle and tip. Front legs yellowish brown, middle femora dark and tibia and tarsi lighter, hind legs darker. Adults are active in summer and found on flower and vegetation near mixed hardwoods. Maine to North Carolina, west to Iowa, Kansas, and Texas. (2)

Mordellina pustulata (Melsheimer) (2.5–5.5 mm) is black with silvery gray pubescence; basal three or four antennomeres, palps, and front legs pale reddish brown. Eyes large, facets coarse, notched behind antennae. Elytra with numerous small silvery gray spots sometimes forming narrow broken bands. Larvae develop in stems of various plants, including great ragweed (*Ambrosia trifida*), calico aster (*Symphyotrichum lateriflorum*), lateflowering thoroughwort (*Eupatorium serotinum*), Jerusalem artichoke (*Helianthus tuberosus*), and rough cocklebur (*Xanthium strumarium*). Adults found on flowers from spring through summer; also in Malaise traps. Across southern Canada, northwestern and eastern United States. (5)

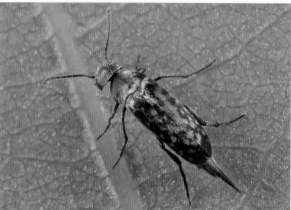

Mordellistena andreae LeConte (2.7–4.0 mm) has a yellowish (male) or black (female) head and thorax. Elytra dark, each with yellowish C-shaped mark variable in thickness. Hind tibiae with two oblique ridges across outer face before ridge at tip, tarsomere 1 with three ridges, 2 with two. Adults active in spring and early summer, found on foliage of black cherry (*Prunus serotina*), sparkleberry (*Vaccinium arboreum*), and wax myrtle (*Morella cerifera*). Virginia to Georgia and Alabama. (109)

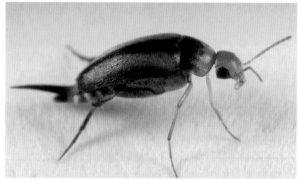

Mordellistena cervicalis LeConte (3.0–4.8 mm) is reddish orange and black with mostly reddish-brown pubescence. Head reddish orange with large black spot at base, clothed in pale gray pubescence, and antennae dark with 1–2 paler. Pronotum reddish orange with darker angles and basal spot at middle. Elytra black with pubescence similar to pronotum. Underside black. Hind tibiae with two parallel, oblique ridges on outer face before ridge at tip, tarsomere 1 with three or four ridges, 2 with two. Larvae develop in plant stems, e.g., common yarrow (*Achillea millefolium*) and fleabane (*Erigeron*). Maritime Provinces to Virginia, west to Manitoba, Minnesota, and Kansas. (109)

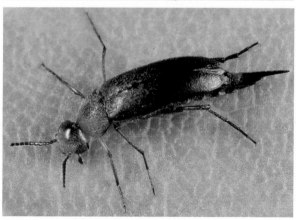

Mordellistena convicta LeConte (3.0–3.8 mm) is black with elytra clothed in four or five lines of brownish-gray pubescence. Antennae dark, 1–4 paler. Last abdominal ventrite short, abruptly pointed. Hind tibiae with three short, oblique ridges on outer face before ridge on tip, tarsomere 1 with three ridges, 2 with two. Larvae develop in stems of sneezeweed (*Helenium*), rosinweed (*Silphium*), aster (*Aster*), ragweed (*Ambrosia*), and goldenrod (*Solidago*). Maritime Provinces and New England to Maryland, west to Manitoba, Wisconsin, Kansas, and New Mexico. (109)

Mordellistena fuscipennis (Melsheimer) (5.0–6.5 mm) has reddish-brown elytra, usually with pale lateral borders. Hind tibia with three distinct and oblique parallel ridges, sometimes with small fourth ridge; first hind tarsomere with three ridges, second with two, third with one and sometimes with very small second ridge. Nova Scotia to Virginia, west to Ontario, Illinois, and Kentucky. (109)

Mordellistena liturata (Melsheimer) (3.4–4.5 mm) is reddish brown, or brownish yellow, with head and pronotum often paler than elytra. Antennae, mouthparts, and front and middle legs mostly pale. Elytra pubescent with two oblique bands darker, suture and apices pale; markings sometimes obscure. Abdominal ventrites densely covered with yellowish pubescence. Adults active late spring and summer, found on flowers and resting vegetation in hardwood forests; also found at light and in Malaise traps. Ontario and New York to Georgia, west to Wisconsin, Kansas, and Texas. *Mordellistena masoni* Liljeblad somewhat similar, with dark elytral bands speckled. (109)

Mordellochroa scapularis (Say) (4.0–5.8 mm) is dull black, elytra with yellow or reddish-yellow humeral spots not reaching scutellum. Femora black, while tibiae, tarsi, and last abdominal ventrite somewhat reddish yellow. Remaining abdominal ventrites reddish yellow to nearly black. Adults active during summer in woodlands, wet forests, and stands of red spruce (*Picea rubens*) and are found on flowers, such as hawthorn (*Crataegus*) and oaks (*Quercus*). New Brunswick and Maine to Virginia, west to British Columbia, Minnesota, Illinois, and Oklahoma. (1)

RIPIPHORID BEETLES, FAMILY RIPIPHORIDAE
(RIP-IH-*FOR*-IH-DEE)

Adult ripiphorids live for only a few days and information on their lives is fragmentary. They rest on low grasses or flowers and meet in mating swarms. The comblike antennae of the male presumably increase its ability to locate females emitting sexual pheromones. The mouthparts of adult *Macrosiagon* are greatly prolonged, suggesting they feed on nectar. Those of *Ripiphorus* are shorter and functional, but nothing is known of their dietary preferences. All species undergo hypermetamorphosis. Early instars feed internally on the larvae of other insects, whereas the later stages feed externally on their hosts. Species in the genus *Ripiphorus* lay eggs on flowers; the hatching triungulins attach themselves with their mandibles to solitary bees gathering pollen and are carried back to the bee's nest. *Macrosiagon* larvae parasitize wasps in several families, including Vespidae, Sphecidae, Crabronidae, and Tiphiidae. *Pelecotoma flavipes* Melsheimer (p.256) larvae attack the wood-boring larvae of the death-watch beetle *Ptilinus ruficornis* Say (Ptinidae). The larvae of an undescribed species of *Perhidius* in Florida are reputed to parasitize cockroaches.

FAMILY DIAGNOSIS Adult ripiphorids are elongate-oval (*Pelecotoma*), wedge-shaped (*Macrosiagon*) with black and orange, red, or yellow coloration, or flylike (*Pirhidius*, *Ripiphorus*). Head with mouthparts directed downward. Antennae with 11 antennomeres (10 in some *Ripiphorus* females), antennomeres flabellate, pectinate, or serrate; males typically have more elaborate antennomeres than females. Pronotum large, bell-shaped, narrowest behind head, and without lateral keeled margins. Scutellum visible (*Pelecotoma*), highly modified (*Perhidius*, *Ripiphorus*), or completely or partly covered by extended margin of the pronotum (*Macrosiagon*). Elytra smooth, without grooves; cover abdomen entirely (*Pelecotomus*, *Macrosiagon*), with apices sometimes pointed (*Macrosiagon*), scalelike (*Ripiphorus*), or short and soft (*Perhidius*). Legs slender, tarsal formula 5-5-4, hind tibiae never with ridges of spines before tip, claws equal, comblike or toothed. Abdomen usually with five ventrites (seven in *Perhidius*), last ventrite without apical spine.

SIMILAR FAMILIES
- twisted-winged parasites (Order Strepsiptera) – eyes stalked; elytra short and knoblike; abdomen pointed
- false darkling beetles (Melandryidae) – antennae filiform or slightly clubbed (p.329)
- tumbling flower beetles (Mordellidae) – elytra cover most of the abdomen; antennae filiform or serrate; last abdominal ventrite acutely pointed (p.333)

COLLECTING NOTES Ripiphorid beetles are rare in collections partly because of their short flight period, although they may be quite abundant locally. Collecting the fast-moving adults by hand can be challenging. Sweep or examine flowers and low vegetation closely in daytime during the warmer parts of the year, particularly those with blossoms attractive to bees and wasps. Malaise and flight intercept traps may yield additional specimens, especially of those species that do not frequent flowers.

FAUNA 51 SPECIES IN SIX GENERA (NA); ~16 SPECIES IN FOUR GENERA (ENA)

Pelecotoma flavipes Melsheimer (4.0–5.5 mm) is blackish with yellowish-brown appendages, portions of antennae darker. Head with eyes small, well-separated, kidney-shaped, and shallowly emarginate in front. Antennae with first three articles simple, pectinate in male, strongly serrate in female. Elytra long, covering abdomen, not separated at tip. Legs have claws with two very small teeth. Adults typically found in summer on exposed dead wood of maple (*Acer*), beech (*Fagus*), and oak (*Quercus*) infested with larvae of a wood-boring death-watch beetle, *Ptilinus ruficornis* Say (Ptinidae); *Pelecotoma* larvae parasitize larval *Ptilinus*. Ontario and Québec to North Carolina, west to Michigan. (1)

Macrosiagon cruentum (Germar) (5.0–8.0 mm) is variably red and black. Top of black head broadly rounded with front surface flat or only slightly concave. Pronotum black, without distinct depressions, and middle lobe on posterior margin not raised or cup-shaped. Elytra red with base and tips black to entirely red. Bases of front legs not separated by spine and nearly touching each other, second hind tarsomere longer than third. Abdomen of male usually black, while that of female is usually red; some individuals have a mixture of both colors. Adults on flowers. Virginia to Florida, west to Indiana and Texas. (~8)

Macrosiagon dimidiatum (Fabricius) (5.0–11.0 mm) is distinctly narrowed toward rear, mostly black, and elytra yellow with dark bases and tips. Head with front flat or convex, antennae orange-yellow and flabellate (male), or pectinate and blackish with reddish-brown bases (female). Basal pronotal margin at middle with distinct and concave lobe. Front coxae close, not separated by spine. Abdomen of female is black. Hind legs with tarsomere 2 longer than 3. Adults on flowers of mountain mint (*Pycnanthemum*) and joe pye weed (*Eutrochium*). New Hampshire to South Carolina, west to Indiana and Texas. (~8)

Macrosiagon flavipenne LeConte (7.0–11.0 mm) is mostly dull black with completely or part yellow elytra. Head and thorax black. Antennae yellow and flabellate (male) or black (female) with pale bases and tips, with antennomeres pectinate or conspicuously serrate. Pronotum with distinct broad basal process at middle flanked by two slight impressions. Elytra entirely yellow (male) or with narrow strip at base and apical half black (female). Abdomen black (male) or red (female). Legs with tibial spines sharp, bases of front legs nearly touching. Adults active in summer, found mainly on flowers. New York to California, south to Argentina. (~8)

Macrosiagon limbatum (Fabricius) (5.0–12.0 mm) is wedge-shaped and typically orange with black elytra and partly black appendages. Head with top black, antennae comblike (male) or serrate (female). Pronotum with variable black spot on top. Sides of mesothorax flat, not bulging. Elytra longer than abdomen, sometimes yellow with sides, suture, and base narrowly black. Underside sometimes variegated with black. Femora with black tips, front tibiae black, middle and hind tibiae with apical halves black or all black, and hind tarsomere 2 half length of 3, flat and shining above. Adults active in summer and regularly visit flowers, e.g., elderberry (*Sambucus*), thoroughwort (*Eupatorium*), beebalm (*Monarda*), and goldenrod (*Solidago*). New Hampshire and New York to Florida, west to Iowa, Kansas, and Texas. (~8)

Macrosiagon pectinatum (Fabricius) (3.5–7.5 mm) is red to black with reddish-yellow elytra variably marked. Head with front and top convex. Pronotum without any distinct excavations, lobe at middle of basal margin somewhat convex. Hind leg with tarsomere 2 shorter and thicker than 3. Adults active in summer, found on flowers. Massachusetts and New York to Florida, west to Kansas and Arizona; Mexico and Central America. (~8)

Ripiphorus species (2.5–8.0 mm) resemble wasps or flies more than beetles. Head with flabellate antennae attached above prominent and widely separated eyes. Most antennomeres each with one (female) or two (male) extensions. Pronotum bell-shaped, broad at base, strongly narrowed from base to head, and side margins rounded, not keeled, underside with spinelike process between legs. Elytra short, convex, scalelike, not extending beyond thorax, with flight wings and abdomen exposed. Abdomen becoming wide toward tip. Legs with claws comblike. Larvae are parasitoids of halictines and other bees. Adults found on flowers and vegetation. Genus is in need of revision. (6)

ZOPHERID BEETLES, FAMILY ZOPHERIDAE
(ZO-*FAIR*-IH-DEE)

Zopherid beetles are a diverse and challenging family. Both adults and larvae are associated with fungal-infested wood or decaying plant materials. Adults enter trees through preexisting insect tunnels or cracks as a result of injury or drying. Flattened species are usually found under bark or in dead wood, tunneling in rotten or sound logs and stumps of various conifers or hardwoods, where they feed on the fruiting bodies of tough, fleshy, or woody fungi. Adults of *Bitoma*, *Nanunaria*, and *Synchita* are collected on fruiting bodies of wood-rotting basidiomycetes. Zopherid larvae occur on rotten wood or ascomycete fungi. Early instars of *Lasconotus subcostulatus* Kraus feed primarily on fungi, but third-stage larvae prey on the larvae and pupae of *Ips* bark beetles (Curculionidae). Cylindrical species (e.g., *Aulonium*, *Colydium*) tend to follow the tunnels of bark and ambrosia beetles (Curculionidae) where the adults feed on rotten wood and cambial tissue. The larvae of *Alonium longulum* LeConte are considered predators of bark beetle (*Dendroctonus*) larvae, but European species have been reared on plant materials. Species of *Colydium* are recorded to prey on bark beetles, too, but more study is needed to confirm their predatory behavior.

FAMILY DIAGNOSIS Adult zopherids are elongate and cylindrical to flattened and parallel-sided or oval (*Hyporhagus*), usually brown or black with vestiture or not, occasionally with subtle patterns of yellow, red, or gray. Head visible from above with eyes shallowly or deeply notched and mouthparts directed forward (prognathous). Antennae with 9–11 antennomeres, bases concealed from above by front margin of head, are moderately to abruptly clubbed, club formed by two or three antennomeres. Pronotum square, elongate or transverse, margins expanded, smooth, finely toothed, or elaborately produced; procoxal cavities open or closed. Scutellum visible or not.

Elytra usually parallel-sided and completely conceal the abdomen, surface sculpturing with raised bumps, rows of deep pits, or sharp, well-defined ribs; smooth and oval in *Hyporhagus*. Legs slender, tarsal formula 4-4-4 or 5-5-4 (*Phellopsis*), claws equal and simple. Abdomen underneath with five ventrites; two, three, or four ventrites mostly fused and separated by indistinct sutures.

SIMILAR FAMILIES

- wrinkled bark beetles (Carabidae) – antennae moniliform (p.76)
- lyctine powder-post beetles (Bostrichidae) – mandibles prominent from above (p.252)
- root-eating beetles (Monotomidae) – elytra do not cover tip of abdomen (p.281)
- silvanid beetles (Silvanidae) – antennae filiform; tarsi 5-5-5 (p.285)
- bothriderid beetles (Bothrideridae) – antennal insertions exposed; tarsi 4-4-4 (p.305)
- minute bark beetles (Cerylonidae) – elytra smooth and without vestiture (p.307)
- some darkling beetles (Tenebrionidae) – defensive secretions; three fused abdominal ventrites (p.344)
- ambrosia beetles (Curculionidae) – antennal club spherical; tarsi 5-5-5 (p.500)

COLLECTING NOTES Zopherid beetles are found year-round beneath the bark of dead trees with fungal growth and are most numerous in the cambium during the earliest stages of decay when mold and fungi are just developing. Carefully peel bark off snags and logs, especially around the base where there is the most moisture. Use pine needles to coax individuals from wood-boring insect tunnels in bark. Other species are regularly found in the galleries of other wood-boring beetles in both the wood and bark. Some species are found only on hardwoods, while others are restricted to conifers. Many colydiine zopherids are active in early spring and are attracted to freshly cut and covered stumps of oak, hickory, locust, maple, sycamore, and elm. Other species are regularly attracted to UV lights. Beating large dead branches and young dead trees, especially those covered with fungal growth, is also productive.

FAUNA 109 SPECIES IN 39 GENERA (NA); 36 SPECIES IN 20 GENERA (ENA)

341

Colydium lineola Say (3.0–7.0 mm) is very elongate and slender, somewhat cylindrical, and shiny reddish brown or blackish. Head with tip of labrum and clypeus setose. Pronotum 1.5 times longer than wide, with narrow groove down middle, punctures elongate, and front wider than base. Elytra ridged, all but outermost ridges distinct all along their lengths. Adults found under bark and in tunnels of wood-boring beetles in hardwoods, occasionally pine (*Pinus*) and spruce (*Picea*), especially around base and exposed roots; sometimes attracted to light. In east from Ontario to Florida, west to Illinois and Texas. (3)

Colydium nigripenne LeConte (3.9–4.5 mm) is entirely reddish, except for blackish and ribbed elytra. Body is moderately shining and very long, slender, and nearly cylindrical. Prothorax much longer than wide with round pits and a deep line impressed down middle. Tip of clypeus and labrum hairy. Adults are found year-round beneath bark or in bore holes of other beetles on various trees, especially conifers; occasionally attracted to light. New Jersey to Florida, west to Illinois and Texas. (3)

Aulonium parallelopipedum (Say) (4.7–5.5 mm) has a flat head and reddish-black body. Male with anterior margin of pronotum lacking tubercles, but with a pair of raised areas separated by a shallow channel; female pronotum lacks raised areas. Adults found under bark of various hardwoods and conifers, including hickory (*Carya*), tulip tree (*Liriodendron tulipifera*), oaks (*Quercus*), and bald cypress (*Taxodium distichum*). New York to South Carolina, west to Michigan and Texas. (3)

Bitoma crenata (Fabricius) (2.6–3.5 mm) is somewhat flattened, black with four large red spots on elytra that reach basal, apical, and side margins. Antennal article 9 distinctly wider than 8. Pronotum widest just behind head. Elytral carinae low and rounded on disk. Adults found year-round under bark of dead hardwood and conifer logs infested with fungus, sometimes in large numbers. Europe; Ontario and New Hampshire to New York, west to Indiana; also Washington. (7)

342

Bitoma quadriguttata (Say) (1.7–2.8 mm) is elongate, somewhat flattened, dark, usually with two to four red spots on each elytron, spots sometimes larger and confluent. Eye facets moderately coarse. Antennae with 11 antennomeres, 8 and 9 subequal in width, 10–11 forming club. Pronotum ridged above with side margins finely serrate and lacks antennal grooves underneath. Elytra ridged with some pubescence. Adults usually found under bark of hardwoods, occasionally pine (*Pinus*), and on moldy lumber; also attracted to light and found in window intercept traps. Québec and Ontario to Florida, west to Indiana, and eastern Oklahoma and Texas. (7)

Endeitoma granulata (Say) (2.2–3.7 mm) is usually yellowish brown, rarely darker. Eyes prominent and coarsely faceted. Antennae with 10 antennomeres, 3 twice length of 4, club with one round antennomere. Pronotum with surface coarsely granulate, side margins toothed, narrowly flat, lighter, without antennal grooves underneath; freshly emerged specimens with waxy bluish-gray coating. Elytra with rows of punctures, spaces between with long granules, each bearing a seta. Adults found under loose bark of dead pine (*Pinus*) and hardwoods, including oak (*Quercus*) and southern magnolia (*Magnolia grandiflora*) near ground level in association with mold. Delaware to Florida, west to Oklahoma. (2)

Namunaria guttulata (**LeConte**) (3.5–5.0 mm) is elongate and oval, blackish with margins lighter. Head with prominent, finely faceted eyes. Antennae with 11 antennomeres, club with two. Pronotum strongly and evenly convex above, with wide, evenly rounded, and serrate margins widest at middle; short antennal grooves below. Elytra distinctly grooved with well-separated punctures, covered with both light and dark curved setae and tufts of white setae. Adults found in fungal growth under bark; also attracted to light. Ontario and New York to North Carolina, west to Ohio, Tennessee, Oklahoma, and Texas. (1)

Paha laticollis (**LeConte**) (1.8–3.0 mm) is elongate, oblong, somewhat flat, and dull dark brown to blackish, often with reddish spots on elytra. Antennae with 10 antennomeres, 3 not twice as long as 4, 10 forming club. Pronotum wider than long, granulate, with side margins not setose; front coxal cavities open behind. Elytra without pubescence, each with three ridges and variable reddish spots at base and near tip, sometimes reddish with margins, suture and apical two-thirds dark. Adults found year-round under bark of oak (*Quercus*) logs and stumps, especially near base. New York to Florida, west to Indiana and Oklahoma. (1)

Hyporhagus punctulatus Thomson (3.5–5.4 mm) is elongate-oval, convex, shining brownish black or blackish with appendages, and front and sides of pronotum brown. Head with eyes large, almost touching on top, antennal club with three antennomeres. Pronotum densely punctate, sides upturned and evenly curved, widest at base, underside with grooves to receive antennae. Elytra with rows of shallow punctures and fine lines, spaces between flat, filled with fine punctures. Front tarsi of male broad and pubescent below. Adults active spring and early summer, probably associated with decaying plant matter; also found in Malaise traps. Virginia to Florida, west to Texas. (1)

Phellopsis obcordata (**Kirby**) (11.0–22.0 mm) is large, elongate, parallel-sided, reddish brown to dark brown, and roughly, cryptically sculpted with small dark bumps. Antennae with 11 antennomeres. Pronotum distinctly sinuate on sides behind middle, procoxal cavities open. Elytra with large, very deep punctures, distinct swellings at base and tips, and thick, round ridges on sides. Adults found under bark of decaying hardwoods and conifers in association with polypore fungi (*Fomes*, *Piptoporus*) in dense boreal forests and at high elevation in Appalachian Mountains; larvae feed inside fungi. Newfoundland to southern Georgia, west to Michigan and Wisconsin. (1)

Pycnomerus sulcicollis LeConte (2.8–3.0 mm) is elongate-ovate, somewhat flattened, glabrous, dark reddish brown. Head with base of antennae and mandibles not separated by ridge. Antennae with 10 antennomeres, club with one. Pronotum slightly longer than wide, broadest near head and converging toward elytra, with pair of long, deep parallel depressions. Elytral intervals convex. Adults found under bark of decaying hardwood logs; also attracted to light. New Jersey to Florida, west to Indiana and Oklahoma. (3)

DARKLING BEETLES, FAMILY TENEBRIONIDAE
(TEN-IH-BREE-ON-IH-DEE)

Darkling beetles are usually hard-bodied and typically dull or shiny brown or black, although a few species are notably covered in pale scales, brightly marked in red, or distinctly metallic. They are incredibly diverse in form and adapted for living in sand, soil, decayed wood, fungi, and the nests of other animals, including ants. Soil-dwelling species hide in leaf litter or under rocks and other debris. Some species are adapted for life under harsh, dry conditions in shale barrens, sandy soils, and coastal beaches and dunes. Wood-associated species live under bark or in galleries created by the activities of wood-boring insects and are often dependent on fungi to break down wood into suitable food. The adults of some species nibble on the surface of polypore fungi, while their larvae bore within these woody fungi. The larvae of some species develop in dead wood and tree holes, especially in old growth forests. A few species are found on leaves and flowers, while others graze on algae or lichens. A few adventive species from the Old World are pests of stored food products.

FAMILY DIAGNOSIS Adult tenebrionids are incredibly diverse in form, ranging from elongate and somewhat cylindrical or slightly flattened, to oblong to strongly oval and strongly convex to nearly hemispherical. Head has strongly notched eyes and antennae that typically have 11 antennomeres and are moniliform or clavate, with bases that are hidden from above by the expanded rim on the front of the head. Procoxal cavities are closed. Elytra completely conceal the abdomen, sometimes fused together, and are smooth, pitted, bumpy, grooved, or ridged; flight wings fully developed, reduced, or absent. Species with elytra partially or completely fused have their flight wings reduced or absent. Legs are stout or slender, with a tarsal formula of 5-5-4, with claws equal in size, toothed or comblike. Abdomen with five ventrites, 1–3 fused.

SIMILAR FAMILIES
- ground beetles (Carabidae) – tarsi 5-5-5; first abdominal ventrite divided by hind coxae (p.63)
- pleasing fungus beetles (Erotylidae) – tarsi 5-5-5; antennae capitate; elytra sometimes with bright-colored markings (p.277)
- minute bark beetles (Cerylonidae) – very small, tarsi 4-4-4; antennae capitate (p.307)
- false darkling beetles (Melandryidae) – winged; pronotum often with two impressions at base (p.329)
- zopherid beetles (Zopheridae) – rough or ribbed elytra generally parallel-sided in outline; pronotum often with distinct grooves underneath to receive antennae with 9–11 antennomeres; abdomen usually with ventrites 2–4 fused (p.340)

COLLECTING NOTES Many less mobile species of darkling beetles are found during the day under stones and bark. Carefully inspect accumulations of decaying leaf litter at the bases of trees and shrubs or at the edges of rocky outcrops. Sift through debris washed up on the lake and ocean shores. Also carefully check soil and rock surfaces, tree trunks, and woody fungi at night. More active species are found by beating and sweeping flowers and vegetation and are also collected in light, Lindgren funnel, Malaise, and pitfall traps.

344

FAUNA ~1,184 SPECIES IN ~191 GENERA (NA); ~225 SPECIES IN ~71 GENERA (ENA)

Anaedus brunneus **(Ziegler)** (4.5–5.5 mm) is dark reddish brown, coarsely punctured, and sparsely clothed in long, yellow setae. Head and pronotum sparsely punctate. Prothorax twice as wide as long with side broadly rounded and abruptly straight just before sharp hind angles. Elytra with scattered, deep punctures forming a row only next to suture. Appendages light reddish brown. Adults found in leaf litter and occasionally under bark. New York to Florida, west to Wisconsin and Indiana. *Anaedus* is in need of revision. (5)

Paratenetus punctatus **Spinola** (3.0–4.0 mm) is light to dark reddish brown, appendages paler, and densely covered with long gray or yellow setae. Head and pronotum densely covered with punctures merging together. Prothorax with sides margined with five to seven teeth. Elytra with larger punctures not as dense. Adults found on dried up leaves and branches, especially on recently fallen trees; also under bark of dead trees. New York to Florida, west to Wisconsin and Indiana. *Paratenetus gibbipennis* Motschulsky (2.0–2.5 mm) is rounder; northeast. (2)

345

Arthromacra aenea **(Say)** (9.0–14.0 mm) is elongate, slender, cylindrical, metallic, blue, green, purplish green, or dark bronze, with pale antennae and tarsi. Antennae reddish brown, first and last antennomeres often darker; female with last antennomere equal in length to previous two. Eyes small, broad, notched, and coarsely faceted. Pronotum narrower than base of elytra, with surface usually wrinkled, coarsely punctate. Elytra coarsely punctured, without distinct grooves. Legs variably black and reddish brown, tibiae and portions of tarsi often lighter, with femora and tibiae slender. Adults active in late spring and early summer on vegetation; also in Malaise traps and at light. Five subspecies distinguished by relative lengths of last antennomere and variations in color and pronotal punctation. New England to Georgia, west to Manitoba, Wisconsin, Illinois, Missouri, and Kentucky. (3)

Color variation in *Arthromacra aenea.*
TOP RIGHT: Dark bronze form.
BOTTOM RIGHT: Purplish-green form.

Statira gagatina **Melsheimer** (6.5–8.8 mm) is shiny brown to black with reddish-brown appendages. Last antennomere of male equal to preceding 5.5–6.5, female with tarsal formula 3-3-3. Pronotum wide as long with sparse, fine punctures. Elytra distinctly grooved, with five or fewer setae between grooves, setae-bearing punctures distinctly larger than punctures in grooves. Base of front legs separated by raised process; all penultimate tarsomeres distinctly lobed and spongy beneath. Adults found on leaves of oak (*Quercus*) and other trees and shrubs. New England to South Carolina, west to Wisconsin, Kansas, and Alabama. (5)

Bothrotes canaliculatus canaliculatus **(Say)** (12.0–13.0 mm) is elongate-oval or parallel-sided, narrowed at both ends, convex, moderately clothed in short, pale setae, and uniformly blackish. Head longer than wide, eyes not bulging beyond sides. Pronotum of female with three distinct impressions, front margin broadly notched at impression, middle flanked by pair of lobes, and front and hind angles sharp and protruding; of male mostly convex; basal margin sinuate and narrowly rounded at middle. Elytra irregularly punctate, with faint ridges. Adults found on flowers, foliage, and grasses in sandy habitats. Central United States. *Bothrotes c. arundinis* LeConte is brown with coppery sheen, New York to Florida; *B. c. acutus* LeConte is darker, without metallic sheen, southern Florida. (2)

Epitragodes tomentosus **LeConte** (8.0–9.0 mm) has eyes scarcely bulging beyond sides of head. Upper surface mottled with scattered patches of setae. Prosternum narrow, pointed; mesosternum deeply excavated. Adults are found in cracks and crevices in bark, especially on deciduous trees, and are attracted to lights in summer. Larvae live under accumulations of leaf litter in pure sand along the seacoast and inland sand barrens. Atlantic and Gulf Coast states from Virginia to Florida and Alabama. (2)

Schoenicus puberulus **LeConte** (7.0–8.0 mm) is elongate-oval, narrowed at both ends, convex, sparsely clothed in short, fine setae, uniformly shiny, deep reddish brown with very short, pale setae. Head narrower than pronotum, eyes bulging beyond sides. Pronotom wider than long, more coarsely punctate toward side, side margins parallel at basal third, basal margin sinuate and narrowly rounded at middle. Elytra wider than pronotum, humeri distinct, with few vague rows of punctures, surface closely and irregularly punctate. Adults active in summer; found in sandy habitats; attracted to light. Atlantic states, New Jersey to Florida. (1)

Lesser Mealworm *Alphitobius diaperinus* **(Panzer)**
(5.8–6.3 mm) is shiny. Head widest in front of small eyes, eyes separated by more than three times their width, notched halfway across. Pronotum wider than long, front margin broadly notched, angles prominent, small punctures separated by greater distances than their own diameters, and middle flanked by pair of small impressions near base. Elytra with grooves finely punctured. Process between front legs flat, front tibiae broadly expanded at tips. In damp, moldy grains, stored products, and poultry litter; vectors of poultry pathogens and parasites; adults at light. Old World, cosmopolitan. (2)

Larger Black Flour Beetle *Cynaeus angustus* **LeConte**
(4.5–6.1 mm) is elongate-oval, flattened, parallel-sided, and dark brown to black. Head widest at slightly notched eyes, antennae not quite reaching base of pronotum, antennomeres gradually enlarged. Pronotum wider than long, convex, with fine punctures at middle becoming coarser at sides, a pair of pits near base, and basal margin slighty sinuate before angles. Elytra with punctate rows, spaces between convex. Adults active spring and summer, found on stumps, in plant debris, under driftwood, minor pest in stored grains in mills and poultry houses; at light. Widespread in eastern United States, Ontario, Québec. (1)

Meracantha contracta **(Palisot de Beauvois)** (11.0–14.0 mm) is elongate, broadly oval, globular, and shiny black with bronze luster. Pronotum wider than long, convex, coarsely punctured, widest at middle. Elytral grooves punctured, spaces between flat, finely punctured and wrinkled. Larvae develop in humus, soft decaying wood on soil, or rotten logs and stumps near ground. Nocturnal, flightless adults active in summer, found in leaf litter during day or climbing tree trunks and feeding on fungus, lichens at night in wooded habitats. Ontario to northern Florida, west to Wisconsin and Texas. (1)

Blapstinus metallicus **(Fabricius)** (4.0–4.8 mm) is long, somewhat oval and flattened and distinctly metallic, bronze. Head partially inserted inside pronotum with eyes completely divided. Base of pronotum bisinuate, scutellum triangular, protibiae straight and not produced dorsally at tip, and sides of body not lined with setae. Elytral punctures coarse, in sets of one to five punctures, giving surface a rough look. Adults found in spring and summer under leaf litter around bases of low plants in sandy habitats and sandbars along rivers; also attracted to light. Atlantic and Gulf coasts, Maritime Provinces to Louisiana, Great Lakes, and northern central states. Other *Blapstinus* species restricted to Florida. (7)

Bolitophagus corticola Say (6.5–8.5 mm) is dull black to brownish black, has antennae with 11 antennomeres, and completely divided eyes; both sexes lack horns on pronotum. Pronotum with sides round and widely flattened. Adults found under bark or on *Perenniporia* bracket fungi growing on decaying conifers, especially pine (*Pinus*); also attracted to lights in late spring and summer. Maritime Provinces to Florida, west to Wisconsin and Kansas. (1)

Horned Fungus Beetle ***Bolitotherus cornutus*** Panzer (10.0–12.0 mm) is dull black to reddish brown and roughly sculptured. Male with pair of fringed pronotal horns, female with distinct protuberances. Antennae with 10 antennomeres. Larvae feed and develop in burrows chewed in polypore fungi and oyster mushrooms (*Pleurotus ostreatus*) growing on hardwood logs. Nocturnal adults active spring and summer on fungi, under bark; fly to lights. Feign death when disturbed and live more than two years in nature. Maritime Provinces to Florida, west to Ontario, Wisconsin and Missouri, and Texas. (1)

Eleates depressus (Randall) (5.0–7.5 mm) is oblong, convex, and dull brown or black, with fine ridges on elytra. Head not deeply hidden in prothorax, eyes completely divided. Pronotum with front angles rounded, front margin not lobed at middle, and sides smooth, not finely serrate. Elytra finely ridged, spaces between with a row of coarse and uniformly distributed punctures. Adults found under bark in association with fungus in coniferous forests and mixed woodlands. New Brunswick and New England to Georgia, west to Manitoba, Wisconsin, and Ohio. (1)

Rhipidandrus paradoxus (Palisot de Beauvois) (2.0–2.8 mm) is short, oblong, robust, convex, coarsely and roughly punctate, dull dark brown to black, with yellowish or yellowish-brown appendages. Antennae pectinate (male) or somewhat serrate (female). Pronotum twice as wide as long. Elytra sharply ridged with spaces between rough and coarsely punctate. Adults active in late spring and early summer, found on fungi such as oyster mushroom (*Pleurotus ostreatus*) growing on trees. Québec and Ontario to Florida, west to Wisconsin, Kansas, and Texas. (2)

Centronopus calcaratus (Fabricius) (14.0–17.0 mm) is elongate, oblong, shiny, black with bluish or greenish luster. Head and pronotum densely punctured. Pronotum slightly broader than long, sides faintly curved, and widest just ahead of middle. Elytra with rows of small punctures, surfaces between rows minutely cracked and finely, sparsely punctate. Larva develops under bark in pithy decaying logs, mostly hardwoods. Adults found in summer under bark of decaying stumps and logs and on trees at night; also in Malaise and flight intercept traps. Maritime Provinces and Québec to Florida, west to Ontario, Wisconsin, Nebraska, Kansas, and Louisiana. (2)

Helops aereus Germar (7.0–9.0 mm) is somewhat pear-shaped and uniformly shiny black with faint purplish metallic luster. Elytral striae with closely spaced or fused punctures, interval feebly convex, smooth, with scattered and very fine punctures. Abdomen of males with median patches of golden setae on ventrites 1 and 2. Adults often encountered on tree trunks in open woodlands, gaps, and dry forest edges on spring nights. Connecticut to South Carolina, west to Arkansas and Mississippi. (3)

Tarpela micans (Fabricius) (12.0–19.0 mm) is elongate, blackish, with a distinctive oily rainbow appearance, especially on elytra. Pronotum coarsely, densely punctate. Elytra with rows of somewhat elongate punctures, space between flat and iridescent with scattered fine punctures, widest behind middle. Front tarsi conspicuously broad in male. Adults found under loose bark or in leaf litter at base of trees; attracted to light. Québec and Ontario to Georgia, west to Indiana and Alabama. (4)

Tarpela venusta Say (7.5–10.0 mm) resembles a small *T. micans*. Elongate, blackish, with a distinctive oily rainbow appearance, especially on elytra. Elytral grooves punctate with spaces between strongly convex. Adults active on tree trunks and flying day and night in deciduous woodlands and sandhill habitats during spring and summer. Atlantic and Gulf Coast states, from Virginia to Alabama. (4)

Ammodonus fossor **(LeConte)** (4.0–5.5 mm) is small, round and convex, pale, and speckled. Unable to fly, found walking over the dunes during the cooler parts of the day or sifted from accumulations of plant detritus that gathers in small depressions. Burrowing larvae found in association with this debris in the summer. Typically associated with bays on upper beach dunes from Ontario and New Jersey to South Carolina; it also occurs on widely isolated inland sites with open, flowing sand habitats in Alabama, Colorado, Kansas, Illinois, Indiana, Ohio, Texas, and Wisconsin. (1)

Alaetrinus minimus **(Palisot de Beauvois)** (8.5–11.0 mm) is somewhat flat, oval, dull black or dark brown. Pronotum coarsely punctured and elytra with rows of deep punctures. Adults found year-round in sandy habitats along roadsides, open woodlands, scrub, and coastal dunes in the southeastern coastal plain; often found running across open areas during the day in midsummer. Also found in open woodland gaps, barren slopes and crests, limestone outcrops, and cedar glades in Appalachians. Larvae develop in loose, sandy soil among dry plant debris. Massachusetts to Florida, west to Indiana and Texas. (2)

Idiobates castaneus **Knoch** (9.0–10.0 mm) is blackish or reddish brown; freshly emerged beetles lightly coated with waxy dust that is easily rubbed off. Prothorax nearly square, posterior margin straight, anterior margin nearly so, side margins wide and strongly reflexed. Elytral grooves deep, strongly punctate with areas between finely and sparsely punctate. Adults found year-round under loose bark of oak (*Quercus*) and elm (*Ulmus*) snags, logs, and stumps; gregarious in spring. Feigns death when disturbed. Ontario and New York to Florida, west to Wisconsin, Tennessee, and Arkansas. (1)

Neatus tenebroides **(Palisot de Beauvois)** (10.0–13.0 mm) is elongate-oval, shining dark reddish brown or black. Prothorax about one-third broader than long with sides broadly rounded and not expanded; pronotum with two sizes of punctures at sides. Elytral grooves densely punctate with somewhat convex intervals between distinct rows of punctures, intervals with dense, fine punctures. Tarsi underneath with spiny setae. Adults are found throughout the year under loose bark of dead trees and in dry tree holes. Ontario and Québec to Florida, west to British Columbia, Idaho, and Tennessee. (2)

Common or Yellow Mealworm *Tenebrio molitor* **Linnaeus** (12.0–18.0 mm) is elongate, oblong, weakly shining dark brown to black with distinctly grooved elytra. Pronotum wider than long, with large and small punctures, punctures not touching. Elytral grooves with punctures indistinct. Front tarsi with sharp edge above on apical half, tarsi underneath with sparse, dark setae. Adults and larvae are nocturnal and infest dark, undisturbed accumulations of grain and feed, especially if moist. Larvae commonly sold as pet food. European, now cosmopolitan. **Dark Mealworm** *Tenebrio obscurus* **Fabricius** similar in appearance and distribution, dull, pronotal punctures touching, front tibial edges rounded. (2)

Red Flour Beetle *Tribolium castaneum* **(Herbst)** (3.0–4.0 mm) is elongate and reddish brown. Head with eyes shallowly notched without ridge above, antennomeres 8–11 forming a distinct club, last antennomere rounded, not flat at tip, and underneath with eyes almost reaching base of maxillary palps. Head and pronotum sparsely, finely punctate. Pronotum wider than long, sides somewhat parallel, and hind angles distinct. Elytra with rows of small punctures, spaces between with scattered fine punctures and fine, raised lines. Cosmopolitan; most common across southern United States. Adults and larvae associated with stored grains and grain products, seeds, nuts, spices, dry pet food, and dried fruit. Southern Canada and northern United States. (3)

Uloma impressa **Melsheimer** (10.0–12.0 mm) is oblong-oval, convex, shiny dark reddish brown to almost blackish. Antennae moniliform, apical antennomere broadly rounded at tip. Pronotum about a third wider than long. Elytra with distinct grooves punctured, areas between with minute, sparse punctures. Front femora with broad, deep channel along entire length. Adults active spring and summer, commonly found under bark of rotting hardwoods, especially oak (*Quercus*). Massachusetts and New York to Florida, west to Wisconsin, southeastern Kansas, and Missouri. (4)

Andrimus murrayi **(LeConte)** (6.0–9.8 mm) is oblong-oval, dark brown, and clothed in fine setae almost lying on surface. Antennae longer and more serrate in male, with antennomeres broader and flatter. Head with eyes widely separated, inner margins rounded. Pronotum narrower than elytra at base, with basal angles prominent at sides. Elytra with distinct rows of punctures and clothed in long erect and shorter reclining setae, slightly parted along suture at apical third. Legs with tarsomeres never lobed, densely setose underneath in male. Adults active in spring in sandy coastal habitats; fly to light. Southeastern Virginia to Florida, west to Alabama. (1)

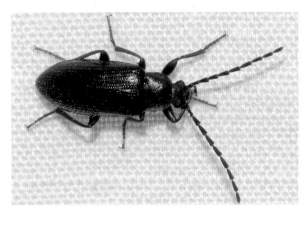

Androchirus erythropus (Kirby) (9.0–11.0 mm) is elongate, oval, convex, dull grayish black, and covered with fine, recumbent setae. Posterior angles of pronotum extended backward, especially in female. Legs uniformly reddish yellow or red (southern populations) with claws comblike; males with highly modified front tarsi. Adults found in late spring and summer in various wooded habitats, resting on decaying stumps and logs, flowers, and vegetation; also in Lindgren funnels and flight intercept traps. Maritime Provinces to Georgia, west to Wisconsin. (2)

Androchirus femoralis (Olivier) (9.0–10.0 mm) is oblong-oval, distinctly convex, clothed in dense and inconspicuous setae, and entirely dull black with bright reddish-orange femora. Head with eyes only slightly notched in front and long antennae. Legs long and slender with front tarsi of male curved and broadly expanded for grasping female during copulation; hind coxae divided by a transverse groove, rear part larger with a sharp edge. Adults found in spring and early summer on decaying logs and vegetation. Rhode Island to Florida, west to Ohio. (2)

Capnochroa fuliginosa (Melsheimer) (10.0–12.0 mm) is dark chestnut-brown to blackish with appendages paler; dorsal pubescence short, reclining and denser on prothorax. Antennomere 3 half as long as 4 in male, two-thirds as long or shorter in female. Prothorax twice as wide as long with sides parallel at base and converging toward head; basal angles rectangular. Elytra distinctly grooved, slightly wider at base than pronotum and gradually narrowing to basal third. Legs with tarsomeres not lobed underneath and claws comblike, or pectinate, well beyond middle. Adults attracted to light in summer, occasionally found on branches of shrubs. Widely distributed in eastern North America. (1)

Hymenorus obesus Casey (6.0–9.5 mm) is uniformly shiny above with pronotum coarsely, but not densely punctured. Head with distinctly notched eyes separated by a distance greater than their width, antennomeres 3 and 4 nearly equal in length. Pronotal margin rounded in front, areas underneath prothorax between sides and bases of legs coarsely wrinkled. Elytra with punctured grooves distinct at tips. Legs with tarsomere 4 lobed beneath, claws pectinate. Adults found in summer in various wooded habitats on stumps, beating vegetation, in Lindgren funnel and Malaise traps, and at light at night. New York to Florida, west to Wisconsin and Alabama. (34)

Isomira pulla (**Melsheimer**) (5.6–7.7 mm) is uniformly tan to dark brown with small eyes and moderately robust terminal maxillary palpomere, last palpomere with angle formed on inner and basal sides obtuse, inner side half as long as outer side. Elytra without grooves, finely and densely punctate. Adults found on vegetation and at light in late spring and summer. Québec and Ontario to Florida, west to Indiana and Mississippi. (8)

Isomira sericea (**Say**) (5.0–7.8 mm) is oval, convex, weakly shining, and uniformly pale brownish yellow; some individuals darker. Body is covered with short, fine pubescence. Head with eyes not particularly prominent, antennomere 3 subequal in length to 4, and clypeus with sides gradually tapered. Pronotum and elytra without grooves, finely and densely punctate. Adults found in late spring and early summer in various wooded habitats on flowers, including New Jersey tea (*Ceanothus americanus*) and common milkweed (*Asclepias syriaca*), and on vegetation of various deciduous trees and shrubs; collected by sweeping, found in flight intercept, Malaise, and Lindgren funnel traps, also at light. Nova Scotia and Ontario to Florida, west to Wisconsin and Mississippi. (8)

353

Lobopoda punctulata (**Melsheimer**) (8.0–11.0 mm) is long, oval, dark reddish brown to black, appendages reddish brown, and sparsely clothed in yellowish pubescence. Eyes of female separated by about half their width, male's nearly touching. Pronotum wider than long with straight sides converging toward head and pair of shallow pits on posterior margin. Elytra at base wide as pronotum, distinctly grooved. Fourth tarsomere distinctly lobed in both sexes; male with all front tarsomeres lobed. Adults found on dry branches and under bark in summer; also attracted to light and found in Malaise traps. New York to Florida, west to Wisconsin, Kansas, Texas. (4)

Mycetochara haldemani (**LeConte**) (3.5–5.0 mm) is elongate-oval, somewhat flattened, shiny dark reddish brown with oblique orangish patch just behind elytral humeri; underside and legs paler. Head usually not inserted within prothorax to eyes. Pronotum finely, sparsely punctate, underneath with coxae separated by a broad process that reaches same level, and equal in width to elytra. Elytra without rows of punctures, spaces between with irregular dense seta-bearing punctures, pubescence very short, scarcely longer than width of its puncture. Tarsi without lobes underneath, claws pectinate. Adults active spring and summer, found under bark; attracted to light. New York to montane North Carolina, west to Wisconsin and Illinois. (6)

Pseudocistela marginata (Ziegler) (10.0–13.5 mm) is long, broadly oval, somewhat convex, and mostly dull black. Antennae serrate, males with end of antennomeres produced. Prothorax pale reddish brown with variable black spot on pronotum. Posterior angles of pronotum sharp. Elytra with fine, complete grooves, sutural and lateral margins pale reddish brown. Legs and underside of abdomen sometimes partially pale. Adults found in late spring and summer in wooded areas on vegetation and at light at night. Connecticut and New York to Georgia, west to Tennessee. (3)

Gondwanocrypticus platensis (Fairmaire) (3.9–4.6 mm) is broadly oval, not more than twice as long as wide, and uniformly dull black; margins and sometimes pronotum lighter. Appendages reddish brown. Antennomeres 1–2 reddish at base, remaining dark, 2 much shorter than 3. Adults active in spring and summer, found in leaf litter, under beach wrack, sandy soil habitats, often associated with fire ants in Southeast. South American; widely established across southern United States. *Gondwanocrypticus obsoletus* (Say) (3.5–4.0 mm) similar, antennomeres 2–3 similar in size and color, coastal Delaware to eastern Texas; *G. pictus* Gebien, shiny brown with yellowish spots on apical half of elytra, Gulf Coast states. (3)

Poecilocrypticus formicophilus Gebien (2.6–2.8 mm) is elongate, oval, more than twice as long as wide, and bicolorous. Head dark brown to black. Pronotum reddish orange, wider than long. Elytra as wide as pronotum, with alternating rows of large and small punctures each bearing a seta, dark brown to black and yellowish brown, basal and apical dark areas connected by narrowly or broadly dark suture, squarish black patch at middle extends to side margin. Underside mostly yellowish orange, last two abdominal ventrites black. Legs yellowish, spiny, setose, with tibial spurs uneven; claws small, simple. Fast-running adults associated with exotic ants, including imported fire ant (*Solenopsis richteri*); also under leaf litter and grass clippings in disturbed habitats. Atlantic coast of South America; South Carolina to Florida to Texas. (1)

Adelina pallida (Say) (4.5–5.2 mm) is oblong, somewhat straight-sided, very flat, and shiny reddish brown. Head of male with two small triangular horns in front of eyes, each with smaller horn below. Antennomeres gradually enlarged toward tip. Pronotum with sides distinctly sinuate before hind angles and two short, deep lines near sides at base. Elytra with rows of punctures, spaces between sparsely punctate. Adults found in woodlands under bark; attracted to light. Virginia to Florida, west to Indiana. (3)

Diaperis maculata Olivier (4.7–7.2 mm) has one or two spots at base of elytra, while large blotches on posterior half sometimes coalesce to form a band across elytra (southern populations). Northern populations tend to have distinct black shoulder (humeral) spots that are sometimes faint or absent in the Deep South. Both adults and larvae feed on fleshy fungi, especially shelf fungi (Polyporaceae). Adults sometimes attracted to lights in summer; hibernating aggregations often found under bark in North. New Brunswick to Florida, west to Manitoba and Texas; also Caribbean. Elytra of *D. nigronotata* Pic have five black spots across base and a black band across tips. (2)

Neomida bicornis (Fabricius) (2.7–4.8 mm) is elongate, somewhat cylindrical, strongly convex, and shiny. Head black, male with thin, cylindrical, straight horns. Pronotum metallic green (northern populations) to red (southern populations); both color forms occur together in some areas. Elytra shiny metallic green, rarely blue. Adults found year-round under bark of fungal-infested snags, logs, and stumps and on woody bracket fungus (*Polyporus*) in spring and fall; also attracted to light. Nova Scotia to Florida, west to Minnesota and eastern Texas. Dorsal surface of *N. ferruginea* (LeConte) uniformly reddish brown, horns of male flat, curved; Gulf Coast. (2)

Platydema ellipticum (Fabricius) (4.4–7.7 mm) is elongate-oval, moderately convex, and dull brown to black with an irregular reddish spot on each elytron. Pronotum nearly twice as wide as long, sides evenly rounded. Elytra with sides nearly parallel, surface with rows of fine, widely spaced punctures in faint grooves, with reddish spots extending obliquely from humerus toward suture. In summer, both larvae and adults are associated with a woody shelf fungus (*Phellinus gilvus*) that commonly grows on dead hardwood logs. Groups of adults sometimes found overwintering under bark. Connecticut to Florida, west to Colorado, Wyoming, and Texas. (14)

Platydema flavipes (Fabricius) (3.6–5.4 mm) has the first three or four antennomeres lighter in color and entirely dark club, unlike all other *Platydema* in the region. Head without horns or tubercles, and dorsal surface uniformly dull black. Elytra with margins somewhat parallel. Legs reddish brown. Adults found under bark of pine (*Pinus*). Massachusetts to Florida, west to North Dakota and Texas. (14)

Platydema ruficorne **(Sturm)** (2.0–3.4 mm) is broadly oval, dull brownish black to black with light reddish-brown appendages. Antennae are uniformly light reddish brown. Adults usually found beneath bark of snags, stumps, and logs, and infrequently found in decomposing cereal products; "red-horned grain beetle" is of little or no economic importance. Québec and Ontario to Florida, west to Minnesota and Texas. (14)

Phaleria picipes Say (3.8–6.9 mm) is dull yellowish brown to black; populations from Virginia to Georgia are mostly black, while those in Florida usually mixed. Pronotum is finely yet distinctly grooved along posterior margin. Pygidium rounded. Front male tarsi spongy beneath, simple in female. Adults found year-round, sometimes in large numbers, beneath driftwood, seaweed, carrion, and other debris at or near high tide line; occasionally attracted to light. Atlantic coast from Maryland to Florida. (4)

Phaleria testacea Say (5.0–7.8 mm) varies from shiny brownish yellow to black; pale specimens may or may not have black spots on elytra. Eyes separated by at least the diameter of their lower surface when viewed underneath. Tip of the abdomen (pygidium) is broadly notched when viewed from above. Adults are found year-round beneath seaweed and other debris on upper beach. Along Atlantic and Gulf coasts of United States to Brazil, also Caribbean. (4)

Alobates morio **(Fabricius)** (17.0–20.0 mm) is oblong, somewhat dull dark brown to black. Underside of head with bright yellow clump of setae. Pronotum slightly wider than long, widest at middle, sides not sharply keeled. Elytra wider at base than prothorax, with rows of fine punctures, spaces between finely wrinkled with three irregular rows of very fine punctures. Adults sometimes found in large numbers, under bark of decaying hardwoods and on fungus; often associated with dead pine logs (*Pinus*) on dry bluffs and shoreline edges. New York to Florida, west to Wisconsin and Texas. (2)

Alobates pennsylvanica **(De Geer)** (20.0–23.0 mm) is oblong, somewhat dull dark brown to black. Underside of head without bright yellow clump of setae. Pronotum slightly wider than long, widest at middle, sides not sharply keeled. Elytra wider at base than prothorax, with rows of fine punctures, spaces between finely wrinkled with three irregular rows of very fine punctures. Adults found, sometimes in large numbers, under bark of decaying hardwoods, on fungus. Maritime Provinces and New England to Florida, west to Manitoba, Wisconsin, and Texas. (2)

Glyptotus cribratus **(LeConte)** (11.0–12.0 mm) is oblong and somewhat dull black. Head with deep groove above each eye. Pronotum evenly, finely, shallowly punctate, sides and base margined. Elytra with rows of deep punctures, surface between very finely wrinkled, and side margins narrowed at and overlapped by sides of abdominal ventrite 4. Underside with tip of abdomen margined. Larvae develop in rotten branches of living hardwoods, including live oak (*Quercus virginiana*). Adults found under bark and in tree holes; attracted to light. Virginia to Florida, west to Texas. (1)

357

Iphthiminus opacus **(LeConte)** (14.5–17.0 mm) is dull black with coarse sculpturing. Head and pronotum roughly punctate, pronotum with indistinct impression on each side of middle, sides coarsely serrate. Elytra with rows of long, deep punctures, surface between rough with fine punctures. Adults active spring and summer, found under bark. Atlantic Canada and New England to Rhode Island and Connecticut, west to Saskatchewan and Wisconsin. (1)

Merinus laevis **(Olivier)** (18.0–26.0 mm) is elongate, oval, robust, dull black with thickened femora. Head sparsely and finely punctate, more so on sides. Pronotum longer than wide, widest at front, sides broadly arched, with surface moderately punctured with fine, shallow punctures. Elytra with rows of fine punctures, spaces between coarsely and very finely wrinkled with fine, scattered punctures. Femora swollen, hind tibiae of male curved with tooth near tip. Larvae develop in decaying hardwood branches, e.g., cherry (*Prunus*), oak (*Quercus*), and maple (*Acer*). Adults found under bark on old live trees with lots of exposed wood. Québec and Ontario to northern Florida, west to Illinois, Missouri, and Alabama. (1)

Polopinus youngi Kritsky (13.2–20.0 mm) is elongate, oblong, and dull black, with elytra coarsely punctate. Head with upper lobe of kidney-shaped eye not surrounded by groove. Pronotum dull, somewhat convex, with basal margin distinctly sinuate. Elytral ridges poorly defined with shallow punctures. Adults active year-round, especially fall through spring, found under bark of oak (*Quercus*) in sand ridge habitats. Southern Florida. (3)

Polypleurus perforatus Germar (10.7–13.1 mm) is dull black with elytra distinctly ridged and coarsely punctate. Last antennomere wider than long. Pronotum with sides mostly round, sinuate behind middle to distinct, sharp hind angles. Elytron with broad ridges divided by double rows of deep punctures. Tarsi with pads of yellow setae. Long-lived and flightless adults found year-round on small, fallen branches and wood litter (where larvae develop) on dry ground in open undisturbed woodland gaps, shale barrens, rock outcrops, and sandhills. New Jersey and Pennsylvania to Florida, west to Missouri, Oklahoma, and Texas. (2)

Upis ceramboides (Linnaeus) (13.8–18.6 mm) is elongate with all but elytra dull black. Pronotum coarsely and irregularly punctate with apical angles rounded and depressed, basal angles obtuse, and basal margin sinuate. Elytra shining, with sides diverging to about apical third, with surface sculpted with large, coarse, irregular punctures. Adults found year-round in deciduous and mixed forests on or under bark of maple (*Acer*), aspen (*Populus*), and birch (*Betula*); capable of surviving very cold temperatures. Alaska, Canada, Pacific Northwest, Idaho, New England south to Wisconsin, Michigan, New York, and Connecticut; also Europe. (1)

Xylopinus saperdioides (Olivier) (12.0–16.0 mm) is elongate, somewhat straight-sided, convex, and black; freshly emerged adults coated with grayish waxy bloom. Prothorax nearly square, slightly narrowed in front and completely margined along base. Elytra with grooves closely and coarsely punctured, spaces between moderately convex. Legs black or red with cylindrical femora and setose pads on undersides of tarsi. Last abdominal ventrite grooved along apical margin. Adults found under bark, with polypore fungi, beaten from dead oak (*Quercus*) limbs, or at light. Nova Scotia to Florida, west to Wisconsin and Missouri. (2)

Strongylium crenatum Mäklin (7.4-10.8 mm) is elongate, somewhat cylindrical and shiny brown with metallic greenish reflections. Eyes large, almost touching on top in male. Antennomere 3 longer than 4. Pronotum short, broad, and coarsely punctured. Elytral grooves along entire length coarsely punctate, punctures set in broad pit almost equal in width to convex spaces between grooves; fully winged. Legs long, slender, tarsi cylindrical with fine, dense setae underneath. Last three ventrites separated by distinct membranes. Larvae tunnel and develop in decaying wood in living and standing dead hardwoods. Nocturnal adults active spring and early summer on tree trunks; also at light. Maryland to Florida, west to Iowa and eastern Texas. (6)

Strongylium tenuicolle (**Say**) (11.8–16.5 mm) is elongate, slender, and shiny brownish to black with antennomere 3 as long as or longer than 4. Pronotum with distinct side margins absent at middle when viewed above, surface punctures closely spaced, surface sometimes wrinkled. Elytra with rows of punctures in a continuous groove, not separate depressions. Abdomen with last three ventrites obviously separated by membranes. Legs with front tarsi strongly setose (male); sometimes reddish orange in southeastern populations. Larvae tunnel in standing dead hardwoods and rotten wood in live trees. Adults active spring and summer, found on tree trunks under bark; attracted to light, Lindgren funnel traps. Widespread in eastern United States to Ontario and Québec. (6)

359

SYNCHROA BARK BEETLES, FAMILY SYNCHROIDAE
(SIN-KRO-IH-DEE)

Both species of North American synchroids, *Synchroa punctata* Newman and the rarely encountered *Mallodrya subaenea* Horn, occur in eastern North America. They resemble click beetles (Elateridae) and have been traditionally included in the Melandryidae, but were placed in their own family based largely on the characters of the larvae. The larvae of *Synchroa* are found in cool, moist conditions under loose bark of decaying deciduous trees, especially wild cherry (*Prunus serotina*). Although they consume both woody and fungal materials, fungi are thought to be their primary source of nutrition. Pupation occurs under bark in an oval chamber of frass constructed by the larva.

FAMILY DIAGNOSIS Adult synchroids are elongate, narrow, and tapered on both ends like click beetles, but are distinguished by the antennal bases hidden from above, lack of thoracic clicking mechanism, possession of finely notched tibial spurs, and a 5-5-4 tarsal formula. Antennae filiform with 11 antennomeres. Prothorax slightly broader than head, widest at base, and equal to width of elytra. Elytra long and completely cover abdomen, with tips rounded. Legs slender, coxae of front legs widely separated (*Synchroa*) or nearly touching (*Mallodrya*), with first tarsomere longer than each of remaining tarsomeres. Abdomen with five ventrites, first two ventrites fused.

SIMILAR FAMILIES
- click beetles (Elateridae) – underside of thorax with clicking mechanism; tarsi 5-5-5 (p.213)
- false darkling beetles (Melandryidae) – antennal bases visible from above (p.329)

COLLECTING NOTES Look for *Synchroa punctata* on trunks of dead deciduous trees at night. They are also found in Malaise and Lindgren funnel traps, and are attracted to lights. *Mallodrya subaenea* has been found on the branches of dead honeylocust (*Gleditsia triacanthos*).

FAUNA TWO SPECIES IN TWO GENERA (NA, ENA)

Synchroa punctata **Newman** (7.0–13.0 mm) resembles a light or dark brown click beetle (Elateridae) with paler legs and antennae, but tarsal formula is 5-5-4 and clicking mechanism is absent. Bases of front legs (coxae) not prominent and widely separated. Entire body densely covered with long, curved, backward reclining setae. Elytra with fine, irregularly placed punctures; apical third of elytra deeply grooved. Adults are active in spring and summer. Larvae feed mostly on fungal material and decaying wood beneath the bark of conifers (*Abies*, *Picea*) and inside trunks and branches of deciduous trees (*Quercus*, *Prunus serotina*, *Toxicodendron radicans*). Nova Scotia south to Florida, west to Manitoba and Texas. (1)

FALSE LONGHORN BEETLES, FAMILY STENOTRACHELIDAE
(STE-NO-TRA-*KIL*-IH-DEE)

Little is known about the habits of this small family. Adults are somewhat rare, short-lived, and found on vegetation. Some species are found on flowers and their mouthparts are comparable to beetles in other families that feed on pollen and nectar. Known stenotrachelid larvae develop in decaying wood in deciduous and coniferous forests. *Nematoplus* larvae, and probably those of *Cephaloon*, are specifically associated with wood in the red-rot stage resulting from the presence of brown-rot fungi that destroy cellulose. The larvae of *Stenotrachelus aeneus* (Fabricius) are found under bark or in the wood of dead deciduous trees, including willow (*Salix*), poplar (*Populus*), alder (*Alnus*), and beech (*Fagus*).

FAMILY DIAGNOSIS Adult stenotrachelids are elongate, usually narrowed at both ends, and somewhat convex with usually fine vestiture. Head elongate and diamond or bell-shaped, narrowed gradually (*Cephaloon*) or abruptly (*Nematoplus*) behind eyes and with a neck with mouthparts directed forward; eyes notched. Antennae attached between eyes, with 11 antennomeres, usually filiform with apical antennomeres sometimes thickened. Pronotum elongate and narrowed to head (*Anelpistus*, *Cephaloon*, *Nematoplus*) or squarish (*Stenotrachelus*), side margins completely ridged or keeled (*Anelpistus*, *Stenotrachelus*), incompletely ridged (*Nematoplus*), or without distinct margins (*Cephaloon*); prothoracic coxal cavities open behind. Elytra gradually narrowed toward tips, vaguely ridged and irregularly punctate, and completely covering abdomen. Legs long, slender, with tarsomeres simple; tarsal formula 5-5-4, claws simple (*Anelpistus*, *Nematoplus*, *Stenotrachelus*) or pectinate with a membranous lobe beneath (*Cephaloon*). Abdomen with five ventrites.

SIMILAR FAMILIES
- false blister beetles (Oedemeridae) – pronotum widest toward head; last tarsomere wide, hairy underneath (p.362)
- blister beetles (Meloidae) – head broad, wider than pronotum; mouthparts directed downward (hypognathous) (p.365)
- fire-colored beetles (Pyrochroidae) – antennae serrate or plumose (p.373)
- *Retocomus*, *Stereopalpus* (Anthicidae) – head with neck; body clothed in setae (pp.377–8)
- longhorn beetles (Cerambycidae) – tarsi apparently 4-4-4, actually 5-5-5 (p.388)

COLLECTING NOTES Look for false longhorn beetles resting on flowers or vegetation in wooded habitats. They are collected by sweeping and beating vegetation, and are also attracted to light. Individuals are sometimes captured in Malaise and flight intercept traps.

360

Stenotrachelus aeneus **(Fabricius)** (11.0 mm) is elongate, black, punctate with silvery setae lying nearly flat on surface, with reddish-black appendages. Head exposed. Antennae filiform with article 3 elongate. Pronotum punctate, without granulations, and with distinct and complete margins along sides. Elytra irregularly undulate with traces of grooves. Adults attracted to light or found in flight intercept traps in late summer. Larvae develop in decomposing wood. Across Canada, south to New Hampshire and Michigan; also Scandinavia. (1)

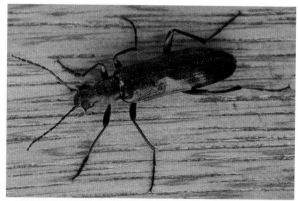

Cephaloon lepturides **Newman** (9.0–14.0 mm) varies from yellowish or reddish brown to nearly black, or combinations thereof. Head with sides gradually converging behind eyes. Antennae short with last three antennomeres distinctly thickened. Appendages of tarsal claws robust, straight, and blunt at tips. Adults found in late spring and early summer on vegetation, including flowers of viburnum (*Viburnum*) and alternate leaf dogwood (*Cornus alternifolia*). Maine, Québec, and Ontario south to Georgia, west to Minnesota and eastern Tennessee. (2)

361

Cephaloon ungulare **LeConte** (10.0–13.0 mm) is mostly yellowish brown with head and part of pronotum and underside dark. Head with sides gradually converging behind eyes. Filiform antennae nearly reaching midpoint of elytra, antennomeres 9–11 each long and cylindrical. Pronotum bell-shaped, with side margins not sharp or keeled and almost straight before hind angles. Ventral lobe of tarsal claws slender, curved, and sharp at tips. Adults active late spring and early summer, found on foliage. Maritime Provinces to Minnesota, south to Georgia through Appalachia. (2)

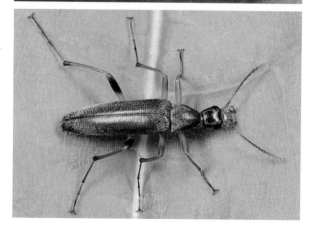

FALSE BLISTER BEETLES, FAMILY OEDEMERIDAE
(EE-DEH-*MARE*-IH-DEE)

Oedemerids have earned the name "false blister beetles" not only due to their resemblance to blister beetles (Meloidae), but also because some species have bodily fluids containing cantharidin, a chemical capable of producing blisters when the beetles are pinched or squashed against the skin. These blisters range from mild and painless to extremely painful wheals that are slow to heal. Many blistering species have contrasting warning or aposematic colors. False blister beetles are most abundant along the coast and in moist wooded habitats. Adults of some species are nectar and pollen feeders and often found on flowers. They are also found resting on foliage, in moist, rotten logs, or under driftwood. Oedemerid larvae develop in moist, decaying logs, stumps, roots of hardwoods and conifers, and driftwood. The larvae of the Old World species, *Nacerdes melanura* (Linnaeus), damage wharf pilings and are of minor economic importance.

FAMILY DIAGNOSIS Adult oedemerids are elongate, slender, and soft-bodied beetles, with colors ranging from black, brown, or gray to yellowish brown, sometimes with yellow, red, or orange pronotum or markings on elytra. Head with mouthparts directed downward (hypognathous). Antennae filiform, with 11 antennomeres. Pronotum with front margin slightly covering head, not keeled on sides, usually longer than wide, widest at front and narrowest at base. Elytra at base broader than pronotum, long, parallel-sided, and almost or completely conceal abdomen. Abdomen with five ventrites. Tarsal formula 5-5-4, next to last tarsomere wide and thickly setose underneath.

SIMILAR FAMILIES
- soldier beetles (Cantharidae) – pronotum keeled, tarsi 5-5-5 (p.238)
- blister beetles (Meloidae) – head usually wider than pronotum and with a distinct neck; pronotum not abruptly broader in the front than in back (p.365)
- longhorn beetles (Cerambycidae) – tarsi appearing 4-4-4, actually 5-5-5 (p.388)

COLLECTING NOTES Sweeping vegetation, especially flower heads and leaves, is productive for collecting adult false blister beetles. Check driftwood along beaches and shores of bays and large rivers. Many species in these habitats are attracted to light.

FAUNA 87 SPECIES IN 17 GENERA (NA); 24 SPECIES IN 10 GENERA (ENA)

Calopus angustus (LeConte) (15.0–21.0 mm) is elongate, large, brownish, with long antennae. Eyes deeply notched, antennae attached within notch. Antennae serrate, with 11 antennomeres, 2 small, remainder four times long as wide at middle, flat. Tips of mandibles notched. Pronotum as long as wide, scarcely widened in front, and roughly punctured. Elytra long, coarsely punctate, rounded at tips. Tarsi 5-5-4. Larvae develop in dead and living conifers and hardwoods. Adults active in summer, found under bark and in Lindgren funnel and flight intercept traps; attracted to light. Transcontinental, in east from Maritime Provinces and New England to Pennsylvania, west to Michigan. (1)

Wharf Borer *Nacerdes melanura* **(Linnaeus)** (10.0–12.0 mm) is yellowish orange with tips of elytra abruptly black. Eyes small, distance between twice length of single eye, and scarcely notched. Front tibiae tipped with only one spur. Larvae develop in damp and decaying driftwood along coast and major rivers, also in wharf pilings and old timber, and can survive tidal immersion. Adults active in late spring and summer, are short-lived, and do not feed. Cosmopolitan, widespread in eastern North America along coasts and rivers. (1)

Xanthochroa lateralis **(Melsheimer)** (8.0–10.0 mm) has an orange head with large eyes narrowly separated in front, moderately notched. Antennae black. Prothorax with a black mark on each side. Elytra black with pale margins. Legs mostly orangish with dark tarsi; protibiae each tipped with single spur. Last visible abdominal ventrite divided. Adults are found on flowers in spring and early summer; also at light. Virginia to Florida. (2)

Ditylus caeruleus **(Randall)** (13.0–17.0 mm) is robust, hard-bodied, black, coarsely and roughly punctate, and clothed in stiff whitish setae. Antennomeres 4–10 distinctly expanded toward their tips. Adults found in May through August among beach detritus along lakeshores, under wet logs, running over swampy ground, or on flowers of spirea (*Spiraea*); also collected in Malaise traps. Larvae found in old wet cedar logs and may take up to three years to complete their development. Maritime Provinces to New York, west to Manitoba and Minnesota. (1)

Asclera puncticollis **(Say)** (5.0–9.0 mm) has dull black head and weakly ridged elytra. Both mandibles notched at tips. Pronotum rough, orange, with central black spot of variable size. Claws toothed at base. Larvae found under bark of box elder (*Acer negundo*). Adults found in spring and early summer on shrubs and flowers, including autumn olive (*Elaeagnus umbellata*), and plum and cherry (*Prunus*). Maritime Provinces and Ontario to Florida, west to Wisconsin, Colorado, and Texas. (2)

Asclera ruficollis **(Say)** (5.0–9.0 mm) is similar to
A. puncticollis, but pronotum is unmarked and elytra
strongly ridged. Adults found in late spring and early
summer in hardwood forests on flowers and foliage of
shrubs, including willow (*Salix*), cherry (*Prunus*), wild pear
(*Amelanchier candadensis*), hawthorn (*Crataegus*), and
viburnum (*Viburnum*). Southeastern Canada to North
Carolina, west to Wisconsin, Nebraska, and Alabama. (2)

Hypasclera dorsalis **(Melsheimer)** (8.0–15.0 mm)
is elongate, slender, with pale yellow body, elytra, and
appendages, and clothed in fine pubescence. Head not
prolonged, with variable spot or stripe, tip of left mandible
a single point, right notched. Pronotum with a variable
dark spot or stripe down middle. Elytra covered with fine
bumps, each with a pair of faint ridges down middle and
brownish stripe down suture and middle. Front tibiae tipped
with pair of spurs, claws appendiculate with squarish
flange at bases. Adults active early summer through
fall along beaches and associated bays, found under
driftwood. Atlantic and Gulf coasts from Long Island to
Florida, west to Texas and south to Mexico. (7)

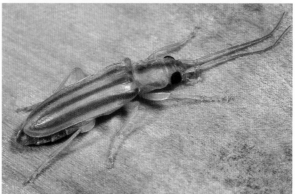

Oxacis taeniata **(LeConte)** (9.0 mm) has a broadly
sinuate stripe along elytral suture and large, distinct,
confluent punctures, and pale legs. Mandibles stout and
blunt, protibiae each tipped with single spur, and claws
simple. Adults found during the day on sea oats (*Uniola
paniculata*) and flowers of yucca (*Yucca*). Atlantic coast,
from Virginia south to Florida. The genus *Oxacis* is in need
of revision. (6)

Oxycopis mimetica **(Horn)** (6.0–11.0 mm) is elongate,
slender, with bicolorous pronotum and striped elytra. Head
not prolonged, front margin of eye not deeply notched
and near antennal base, antennae blackish, and mandible
tips with two points. Pronotum widest in front, orange or
reddish yellow with pale margins with a short, dark central
spot. Elytra blackish with narrow sutural stripe and broader
side margins yellow-brown. Front tibiae with two spurs on
tip, claws simple, not toothed. Adults active in summer;
attracted to light. New Jersey to Florida, west to South
Dakota, Iowa, Kansas, and Texas. (7)

Oxycopis thoracica (Fabricius) (7.0–9.0 mm) has a reddish-orange head and pronotum without any markings. Head with both mandibles incised at tips, short maxillary palps, and antennal base close to weakly notched eye. Elytra are uniformly black and smooth. Front tibiae with two spurs and all claws simple. Adults are found on flowers, including palmetto (*Sabal palmetto*), New Jersey tea (*Ceanothus americanus*), and aster (*Seriocarpus*). New Jersey and Pennsylvania to Florida, west to Arkansas and Texas. (7)

BLISTER BEETLES, FAMILY MELOIDAE
(MEH-*LO*-IH-DEE)

Blister beetles are of particular interest because of their medical, veterinary, and agricultural importance. They also exhibit exceptionally diverse courtship behavior, using chemical, tactile, and visual cues. Most species are diurnal, but a few are active at night. Nearly all species eat plants, especially in the families Asteraceae, Fabaceae, and Solanaceae, and sometimes gather in conspicuous feeding and mating aggregations. Most eat flowers and their associated tissues, but species of *Epicauta* prefer to eat leaves and are sometimes serious pests in gardens and field crops such as alfalfa, beets, potatoes, and tomatoes. Blister beetles are so named because their blood and soft tissues contain cantharidin, a caustic chemical released through leg joints (Fig. 34, p.30) that irritates and blisters sensitive tissues and deters predators. Antlike flower (Anthicidae) (Fig. 35, p.30) and fire-colored beetles (Pyrochroidae) use cantharidin for reproductive and defense purposes and are often attracted to living or dead meloids. The known larvae of meloids in eastern North America are parasitoids of ground-nesting bees and grasshopper eggs, and develop by a special type of metamorphosis called hypermetamorphosis.

FAMILY DIAGNOSIS Adult meloids are typically elongate, soft-bodied, black, gray, brownish, metallic blue or green, or a combination of black with yellow, orange, or red markings, with broad antlike head and short neck. Head with mouthparts directed downward (hypognathous). Antennae usually filiform or moniliform with 11 antennomeres; middle articles sometimes modified (male *Meloe*). Pronotum usually narrower than both head and base of elytra, rounded on sides. Elytra soft, leathery, rolled over abdomen along sides, and usually loosely cover most of abdomen; elytra short and overlap at base in *Meloe*. Legs long, tarsal formula is 5-5-4, tarsi simple with pads or bilobed, claws with dorsal and ventral blade, dorsal blade sometimes comblike, or pectinate. Abdomen with six ventrites.

SIMILAR FAMILIES
- soldier beetles (Cantharidae) – tarsi 5-5-5; elytra not rolled over abdomen (p.238)
- some darkling beetles (Tenebrionidae) – no neck; elytra not rolled over abdomen (p.345)
- false longhorn beetles (Stenotrachelidae) – head narrow; elytra not rolled over abdomen (p.360)
- false blister beetles (Oedemeridae) – head lacks neck; elytra not rolled over abdomen (p.362)
- fire-colored beetles (Pyrochoridae) – antennae serrate, pectinate; elytra not rolled over abdomen (p.373)
- some antlike flower beetles (Anthicidae) – elytra not rolled over abdomen (p.377)

COLLECTING NOTES Meloids are commonly found mating and feeding on flowers in spring and summer. They are carefully gathered by hand, or by beating and sweeping vegetation. Some are attracted to light, while flightless species are collected in pitfall traps. Avoid skin irritations by carefully washing after handling meloids.

365

FAUNA 424 SPECIES IN 21 GENERA (NA); 56 SPECIES IN 12 GENERA (ENA)

Pyrota germari **(Haldeman)** (10.0 mm) is elongate, cylindrical, and leggy with long antennae and striped elytra. Head black with large yellow patch on front. Pronotum reddish yellow with two dark spots. Elytra yellow with a broad, dark stripe down suture extending from base almost to tip. Legs black with bases of femora and tibiae yellow. Larvae probably parasitize brood of ground-nesting bees. Nocturnal adults active in summer, sometimes found on flowers; attracted to light. Maryland to Georgia. (7)

Epicauta atrata **(Fabricius)** (6.0–13.0 mm) is uniformly dark brown, grayish, or black; individuals with reddish heads are distinctive. Black individuals distinguished from *E. pensylvanica* by their wider, bulging eyes. Adults found on flowers of plants in the aster (Asteraceae), morning glory (Convolvulaceae), and mallow (Malvaceae) families from spring through fall, most active in summer. Larvae attack larvae of other *Epicauta* species. New York to Georgia, west to Manitoba, Montana, Wyoming, Kansas, and Texas. (22)

Margined Blister Beetle *Epicauta funebris* **Horn** (6.0–21.0 mm) has three color forms: gray, black, and black with grayish-white elytral margins. Antennae of males and females both filiform, all but first two antennomeres at least 2.5 times longer than wide; those of male lacking long, curved setae. Legs with hind tibial spurs in both sexes enlarged toward obliquely cut-off tips, outer spur much narrower. Adults active spring and summer, found on flowers of buttercup (*Ranunculus*) and ceanothus (*Ceanothus*); also on morning glories (*Convolvulus*), eggplant, potato, tomato (*Solanum*), clematis (*Clematis*), and pigweed (*Amaranthus*). New Hampshire to Florida, west to Iowa and Louisiana (margined); Iowa to Louisiana, west to South Dakota and Oklahoma (gray); Arkansas and Louisiana, west to Kansas and Texas (black). (22)

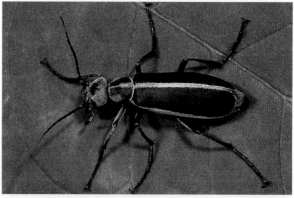

Black Blister Beetle *Epicauta pensylvanica* **(De Geer)** (7.0–15.0 mm) is dull black and uniformly clothed in short dark brown pubescence. Head with short, narrow reddish-brown line between eyes that are distinctly notched and not bulging. Hind tibiae with spurs truncate at tips. Adults active in summer and fall, found on goldenrod (*Solidago*), potatoes and tomatoes (*Solanum*), and many other kinds of flowers and vegetables. New Brunswick to Florida, west to Albert and Arizona; northern Mexico. (22)

366

Striped Blister Beetle *Epicauta vittata* **(Fabricius)** (9.0–18.0 mm) is brownish yellow with bold, black stripes. Head and pronotum with paired blackish markings. Antennomeres of male cylindrical, not flattened. Each elytron with two (northeast) or three (western, southeastern) black stripes, elytral suture pale; two-striped pattern sometimes with outer stripes partially split. Underside black. Adults active in summer, found in gardens and fields, sometimes in large numbers; attack tomato and potato (*Solanum*), bell peppers (*Capsicum*), and low-growing weeds; also attracted to lights. Maine and Québec south to Florida, west to South Dakota, Kansas, Oklahoma, and Louisiana. (22)

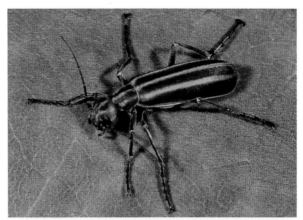

Lytta aenea **Say** (9.0–16.0 mm) is bright metallic brassy green, sometimes pure metallic green or blue, rarely purplish. Antennomeres nearly as wide as long, moniliform. Pronotum with hairlike setae. Legs mostly orange, tips of femora black, northern populations often with tibiae tipped with black. Larvae probably parasitize bees. Adults briefly active in spring, found feeding on flowers of plants in rose family, i.e., serviceberry (*Amelanchier*), hawthorn (*Crataegus*), cherry (*Prunus*), and apple (*Malus*). New England to Georgia, west to Missouri, Oklahoma, and Texas. (4)

Lytta polita **Say** (13.0–26.0 mm) has a shiny, brassy head, pronotum, and underside. Head with labral notch extending to middle. Antennomeres slightly longer than wide, moniliform. Pronotum lacks hairlike setae. Elytra duller. Femora orange and tipped with black, front and middle tibiae and tarsi black, hind tibiae orange with black bases and tips, black portions tinged with green; male front tibiae with single spur at tip. Adults active in spring, feed on pine pollen, fruits and flowers of orchard trees, especially those in the rose family (peach, plum, apple, and pear). Found on leaf litter or sandy paths at night; also attracted to light. Coastal Plain, southeastern Virginia to Florida, west to Louisiana. (4)

Lytta sayi **LeConte** (13.0–22.0 mm) is metallic green or blue. Head with labral notch not extending to middle. Antennomeres slightly longer than wide, moniliform. Orange femora black at tips; tibiae orange, with black base and tips, tarsi black; male front tibiae thickened and bowed. Abdomen of female with groove not strictly vertical on sixth sternite. Adults briefly active in spring, feed on flowers of willow (*Salix*), rose (*Rosa*), and locust (*Robinia*). Québec and Massachusetts to Ontario, Minnesota, and Iowa. *Lytta unguicularis* (LeConte) (17.0–25.0 mm) has similar antennae, is metallic green, with tibiae entirely orange, labral notch extending to middle, female abdomen with groove vertical; Alabama, Mississippi, South Carolina. (4)

Meloe impressus **Kirby** (6.0–17.0 mm) is brilliant metallic blue, violet, green, or black. Male antennae modified, antennomere 5 distinctly widened at tip. Pronotum with sides straight and converging toward elytra. Elytra overlapping, surface rough. Abdomen with pygidium subtrapezoidal, posterior margin straight or slightly rounded without flange; posterior margin of segment 6 of female distinctly notched. Larvae are bee parasitoids. Adults active summer and fall, found on ground or feeding on *Ranunculus* or *Clematis*. Widely distributed in North America; in east from New Brunswick to South Carolina, west to Manitoba, Minnesota, Iowa, Illinois, and Tennessee (mostly montane in southern part of range). (6)

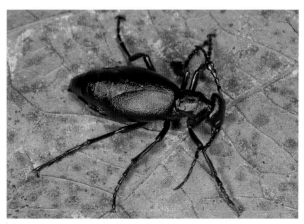

Nemognatha nemorensis **Hentz** (5.0–9.0 mm) is moderately shiny. Head varies from yellowish to reddish brown to black above and yellowish to yellowish brown below. Eyes, labrum, tips of mandibles, and remaining mouthparts black; mouthparts long, extending past bases of hind legs. Prothorax broadly oval. Scutellum black or yellow. Elytra rough, and moderately and uniformly clothed in fine, dark setae. Abdominal segments black or reddish brown underneath; male with tuft of setae on segments 3–5. Bases of legs usually pale, remaining leg segments pitchy or black, claws pectinate. Larvae associated with ground-nesting bees. Adults found from spring through summer on various flowers growing near wooded habitats. Québec and Ontario to Florida, west to Minnesota to Texas. (5)

Nemognatha piazata **(Fabricius)** (7.0–13.0 mm) ranges from shiny orange or orange and black, with or without black stripe down middle of each elytron. Head orange or black, with mouthparts very long, reaching past thorax to abdomen. Elytra broad, covering abdomen. Underside yellowish to blackish, with abdominal segments 4–5 of male concave. Hind tibial spurs similar and equal, all claws pectinate. Adults active spring and summer, found on thistle (*Cirsium*) and pineland nerveray (*Tetragonotheca helianthoides*). West Virginia to Florida, west to Mississippi. (5)

Pseudozonitis longicornis **(Horn)** (10.0–12.0 mm) is dull or feebly shining, with tarsi and antennae ringed with brown and yellow. Head reddish brown with pale spot between eyes, eyes separated underneath by a distance less than half that on top. Pronotum yellowish or pale yellowish brown with reddish spot in middle. Elytra mostly reddish brown or brown on margins with narrow pale yellow stripes on disk. Legs with femora pale on both ends and dark at middle. Adults found in spring and summer on vegetation and at light. Virginia to Florida, west to Illinois, Kansas, and Texas. (3)

368

Tricrania sanguinipennis (Say) (8.5–15.0 mm) is elongate, robust, convex, coarsely punctate, clothed in short setae, shiny blackish to black, with brick-red elytra. Antennae short, robust, with antennomeres moniliform. Pronotum as wide as head. Flight wings reduced. Larva a parasitoid of solitary ground-nesting bees (*Colletes*). Flightless adults found crawling on ground in late winter and spring, especially in sandy habitats where bees nest. Legs with upper blade of claws saw-toothed (serrate). New England and Québec to Florida, west to Wisconsin, Iowa, Kansas, and Texas; possibly Minnesota, South Dakota. (1)

Zonitis vittigera (LeConte) (7.0–12.0 mm) is somewhat shiny orangish with eyes, antennae, mouthparts, tips of femora, tibiae and tarsi, and elytral stripes blackish or black. Mouthparts long. Pronotum wider than head. Uniformly and somewhat densely punctate, with sides nearly parallel. Elytra orangish, often with dark stripe, and densely punctate at base; rarely entirely black. Adults active spring and summer, found on flowers, e.g., coneflower (*Rudbeckia*) and sunflower (*Helianthus*). Michigan to Florida, west to Minnesota, Nebraska, Kansas, and Louisiana. (4)

PALM AND FLOWER BEETLES, FAMILY MYCTERIDAE
(MIK-*TARE*-IH-DEE)

Little is known about the biology and natural history of mycterids. Larvae and adults of *Hemipeplus* are associated with grasses and palms, where the larvae are thought to feed, in part, on fungal spores of sooty molds. Adults of *Mycterus scaber* Haldeman are found on flowers. The specific habits of adult *Lacconotus punctatus* LeConte are unknown, but the larvae probably live under the bark of dead trees.

FAMILY DIAGNOSIS Adult mycterids are very diverse in appearance and difficult to characterize as a family. Head elongate with short rostrum (*Mycterus*) or not. Body elongate and flat (*Hemipeplus*), somewhat oval and slightly flattened (*Lacconotus*), or stout and convex (*Mycterus*). Antennae with 11 antennomeres, each antennomere short and moniliform or somewhat triangular (*Hemipeplus*), slightly elongate (*Lacconotus*), serrate, or vaguely flabellate (*Mycterus*). Underside of prothorax with sunken area in front of legs. Elytra with apical patch underneath sometimes visible on surface as a different color. Abdomen with five ventrites, 1–2 fused.

SIMILAR FAMILIES *Hemipeplus* species are similar to some silvanid flat bark (Silvanidae, p.285), flat bark (Cucujidae, p.288), and lined flat bark beetles (Laemophloeidae, p.291), but are distinguished by the tarsal formula of 5-5-4 in both sexes. *Lacconotus* and *Mycterus* differs from narrow-waisted bark beetles (Salpingidae, p.376) by their lateral pronotal margins not narrowed toward elytra.

COLLECTING NOTES Look for *Mycterus* on flowers, e.g., Queen Anne's lace (*Daucus carota*). Species of *Hemipeplus marginipennis* (LeConte) are found in the unopened bases of opened fronds of cabbage palmetto (*Sabal palmetto*) and everglades palm (*Acoelorraphe wrightii*).

FAUNA 12 SPECIES IN THREE GENERA (NA); SIX SPECIES IN THREE GENERA (ENA)

Mycterus scaber **Haldeman** (3.5–6.0 mm) is gray-black, densely and uniformly clothed in grayish pubescence, and black with reddish appendages. Head with distinct rostrum, and long as prothorax, antennomeres 4–10 distinctly produced sideways in male. Pronotum bell-shaped with front angles rounded, densely and coarsely punctate, at base same width as elytra. Elytra elongate-oval, widest at middle, without grooves, with dense and irregular punctures. Adults found in late spring and early summer on flowers, e.g., Queen Anne's lace (*Daucus carota*). Québec and Ontario to Florida. (3)

Lacconotus punctatus **LeConte** (4.4–5.8 mm) is elongate, blackish or black with sides of pronotum variably reddish orange. Antennae short, antennomeres 5–10 wider than long. Pronotum slightly wider than long, sometimes with reddish orange restricted to basal angles, posterior margin with pair of small, deep pits. Elytra flat, coarsely punctate, widest at apical third. First abdominal tergite with bare pale spot in male. Adults active spring and early summer, may be a high canopy specialist in wooded habitats; found in flight intercept traps. Maritime Provinces and Québec to Georgia, west to Ontario, Wisconsin, and Texas. (1)

Hemipeplus marginipennis (**LeConte**) (4.7–9.2 mm) is very elongate and slender, parallel-sided, distinctly flattened, and pale yellowish brown. Pronotum elongate, nearly parallel-sided, with elongate and oblique pits near basal angles. Elytral tips appear cut off, exposing pygidium. Adults and larvae are found year-round between the crevices of unopened fronds of cabbage (*Sabal palmetto*) and other palms; adults attracted to light. Georgia and Florida; adventive in California. (3)

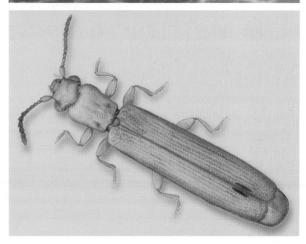

CONIFER BARK BEETLES, FAMILY BORIDAE
(*BOR*-IH-DEE)

Both North American species of borids occur in the east. Adults and larvae of *Boros unicolor* Say are found under the bark of dead pine (*Pinus*) boles or logs. *Lecontia discicollis* (LeConte) are also found on dead conifers, especially moist and decayed regions in the root systems of conifers killed by fire and bark beetles (Curculionidae).

FAMILY DIAGNOSIS Adult borids are distinguished by the hidden antennal bases from above and abrupt antennal club with three antennomeres, distinct ridge or keel along sides of prothorax, and lack of any conspicuous setae on the upper surface of the body. Body elongate, parallel-sided, and distinctly punctate. Antennae with 11 antennomeres, 9–11 each with kidney-shaped sensory patch. Elytra long and completely cover abdomen. Abdomen with five ventrites, 1–2 fused.

SIMILAR FAMILIES
- some false darkling beetles (Melandryidae) – antennal bases visible from above (p.329)
- dead log beetles (Pythidae) – pronotum with distinct pair of impressions (p.372)
- fire-colored beetles (Pyrochroidae) – head usually with distinct, narrow neck (p.373)
- narrow-waisted bark beetles (Salpingidae) – abdomen with five ventrites not fused (p.376)

COLLECTING NOTES Look for the conifer bark beetles under bark of standing and fallen dead pine and in forest litter. They are also found in Lindgren funnel traps.

FAUNA TWO SPECIES IN TWO GENERA (NA)

Boros unicolor **Say** (11.0–13.0 mm) is elongate, slender, somewhat cylindrical and slightly flattened dorsally, shiny, and uniformly dark brown to blackish. Head abruptly narrowed behind eyes. Pronotum oval with keeled sides evenly rounded and not joining posterior margin. Head and pronotum coarsely, densely punctate, elytra more finely punctured. Elytra without trace of grooves. Adults and larvae found beneath loose bark of dead pine (*Pinus*) snags and stumps; adults overwinter. Across southern Canada; in east from New Brunswick and Nova Scotia to North Carolina, west to Ontario and Indiana. (1).

Lecontia discicollis **(LeConte)** (12.0–23.0 mm) is elongate, somewhat convex, and blackish. Head with mandibles distinctly protruding from beneath labrum, sides behind eyes somewhat parallel, and moniliform antennae with last three antennomeres broad. Pronotum flattened on top and concave on sides, widest in front, with side margins keeled and joining basal margin. Elytra each with five indistinct grooves, spaces between slightly convex and with scattered coarse punctures. Adults and larvae found under bark of fire-killed conifers. In east from New Brunswick and New England to Rhode Island, west to Ontario, Minnesota, and Kansas. (1)

DEAD LOG BEETLES, FAMILY PYTHIDAE
(PYTH-IH-DEE)

Adult pythids are found on and beneath the loose bark of logs. Their mandibular structure suggests they are predators. The larvae live in the wood within the fungal-infested cambial-phloem layer (*Pytho*) or the sapwood of red-rotten coniferous logs (*Priognathus*). Both adults and larvae of *Pytho* are used in studies examining the physiology of cold tolerance and possess relatively high supercooling temperature points.

FAMILY DIAGNOSIS Adult pythids are elongate, about three times longer than wide, somewhat cylindrical or flattened, the dorsal surface with punctures of various depths. Head nearly square, slightly elongate, with small bulging eyes and mouthparts directed forward (prognathous). Antennae with 11 antennomeres, antennomeres moniliform except long third antennomere, and last three or four antennomeres slightly enlarged. Pronotum rounded or somewhat square, wider than long and widest at middle, surface evenly convex (*Priognathus*) to slightly flattened with vague or distinct pair of depressions (*Pytho*) with side margins rounded; front coxal cavities open between and behind. Scutellum small, triangular. Elytra elongate, more or less straight-sided, completely or nearly covering abdomen, with surface irregularly punctate (*Priognathus*) or weakly ridged (*Pytho*). Legs slender, tarsal formula 5-5-4, tarsomeres slender and simple, claws equal and simple. Abdomen with five distinct ventrites.

SIMILAR FAMILIES
- ground beetles (Carabidae) – tarsi 5-5-5 (p.63)
- comb-clawed beetles (Tenebrionidae) – claws pectinate (pp.351–3)
- conifer bark beetles (Boridae) – pronotum convex, elytra not distinctly grooved (p.371)

COLLECTING NOTES Look for dead log beetles year-round under the bark of dead conifers such as fir (*Abies*), larch (*Larix*), spruce (*Picea*), pine (*Pinus*), and hemlock (*Tsuga*). Large trees that have been dead for at least three or four years with loose but intact bark, not greatly decayed heartwood, and a large amount of cambium-phloem (inner bark) are the most productive. Beetles are sometimes swept or beaten from foliage.

FAUNA SEVEN SPECIES IN FOUR GENERA (NA); FIVE SPECIES IN TWO GENERA (ENA)

Pytho americanus **Kirby** (7.1–14.8 mm) has a pronotum with side margins weakly rounded and widest just in front of middle. Elytra reddish, blackish, or black with a weak violet sheen or slightly to strongly metallic green or blue luster. Abdomen orangish red to blackish. Legs reddish, tibiae and tarsi darker than femora. Adults found fall through spring under bark of dead conifers and disperse in summer. Widespread in North America, found in east from Nova Scotia to northern Georgia, west to Ontario, Minnesota, and Arkansas. (4)

Pytho niger **Kirby** (10.0–12.0 mm) is entirely dark brown to black and not metallic and entirely black. Pronotum with sides evenly rounded. Larvae develop in decaying pine (*Pinus*), spruce (*Picea*), and fir (*Abies*) logs. Adults found under bark. Alaska and across Canada south to New England, New York, Wisconsin, and Minnesota. (4)

Priognathus monilicornis (Randall) (8.0–11.0 mm) is reddish brown or blackish with appendages and abdomen paler, and upper surface coarsely punctate, elytra more so in vague rows. Antennae moniliform with antennomeres 8–11 forming indistinct club. Pronotum almost as long as wide, evenly convex. Larvae develop in sapwood and red-rotten conifer logs; adults found under bark. Maritime Provinces and New England to West Virginia, west to Michigan; also mountainous regions of western North America. (1)

FIRE-COLORED BEETLES, FAMILY PYROCHROIDAE
(PI-RO-*KRO*-IH-DEE)

Dendroides and *Neopyrochroa* adults are largely nocturnal and spend their days resting on vegetation; males of *D. concolor* (Newman) are sometimes found flying at dusk. The straight flat larvae of these genera are commonly found under loose tree bark of rotting hardwood and conifer logs in cool, moist conditions. They eat bits of fungi and fungal-infested wood and, depending on conditions, may take several years to develop. *Neopyrochroa* larvae prefer the cooler and wetter underside of logs, while *Dendroides* are found wherever there is sufficient fungus and moisture. *Pedilus* adults are diurnal and found on flowers and vegetation of mayapples (*Podophyllum*), horseweed (*Conyza*), willows (*Salix*), maples (*Acer*), buckeyes (*Aesculus*), alders (*Alnus*), and other plants growing in damp areas. The known larvae develop under the bark of rotting trees. *Schizotus* larvae are found in and around decaying wood and under moss growing on logs. Some adult male fire-colored beetles (*Neopyrochroa*, *Schizotus*, and many *Pedilus*) are attracted to cantharidin, a chemical compound produced by blister beetles (Meloidae) and some false blister beetles (Oedemeridae); *Pedilus* has been observed with meloids (Fig. 35, p.30).

373

FAMILY DIAGNOSIS Adult pyrochorids are elongate, weakly to moderately flattened, soft-bodied, and yellowish brown to black, often with reddish or orange pronotum. Head somewhat hypognathous, abruptly narrowed behind kidney-shaped eyes with distinct neck, eyes of males with distinct pits (*Neopyrochroa*, *Schizotus*) or not. Antennae long, with 11 antennomeres, mostly filiform to pectinate (females) to serrate or plumose (males). Prothorax narrower than elytra, elliptical in outline (*Pedilus*), or somewhat oval, without sharp side margins. Elytra usually dark and completely cover abdomen. Legs long, slender, tarsal formula 5-5-4, claws simple or distinctly toothed at base (*Pedilus*). Abdomen with six ventrites.

SIMILAR FAMILIES
- glowworms (Phengodidae: *Phengodes*) – antennae of males bipectinate, mandibles conspicuous, tarsi 5-5-5 (p.233)
- soldier beetles (Cantharidae) – antennae not pectinate; tarsi appear 4-4-4, actually 5-5-5 (p.238)

- false blister beetles (Oedemeridae) – pronotum widest in front of middle (p.362)
- blister beetles (Meloidae) – antennae filiform or moniliform, sometimes kinked in middle (p.365)
- antlike flower beetles (Anthicidae) – pronotum widest in front; eyes not kidney-shaped (p.377)
- some longhorn beetles (Cerambycidae) – no neck; tarsi appear 4-4-4, actually 5-5-5 (p.388)
- orsodacnid leaf beetles (Orsodacnidae) – no neck; tarsi appear 4-4-4, actually 5-5-5 (p.429)

COLLECTING NOTES Look for fire-colored beetles from late spring through midsummer in wooded habitats. Searching under bark, beating foliage of trees and shrubs during the day, and checking lights at night are the most effective ways of collecting adults; chunks of fruit under bark of decaying trees is also productive. *Neopyrochroa* are attracted to fermenting baits made with beer and molasses at night. Males of *Neopyrochroa*, *Schizotus*, and *Pedilus* are drawn to cantharidin bait traps. Some species are also attracted to light.

FAUNA 50 SPECIES IN SEVEN GENERA (NA): 15 SPECIES IN FOUR GENERA (ENA)

Pedilus lugubris **(Say)** (6.0–8.0 mm) is mostly black with a red or black pronotum. First two antennal articles, palps, tarsi, and labrum reddish brown. Male with tips of elytra slightly swollen, less punctured, and deeply indented, appearing pinched; female indistinguishable from those of *Pedilus elegans* (Hentz). Diurnal adults found on flowers and vegetation growing in damp habitats in spring; also associated with blister beetles (*Epicauta* species). Nova Scotia and New Brunswick to Virginia, west to Ontario and Ohio. (10)

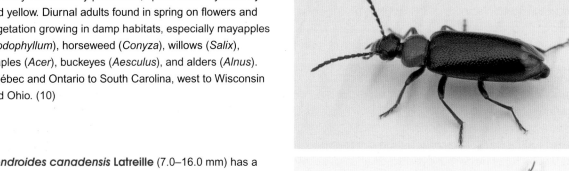

Pedilus terminalis **(Say)** (5.0–8.0 mm) has a black head, elytra, and abdomen and red pronotum in both sexes. Elytra coarsely and densely punctured; tips of male elytra hairy and yellow. Diurnal adults found in spring on flowers and vegetation growing in damp habitats, especially mayapples (*Podophyllum*), horseweed (*Conyza*), willows (*Salix*), maples (*Acer*), buckeyes (*Aesculus*), and alders (*Alnus*). Québec and Ontario to South Carolina, west to Wisconsin and Ohio. (10)

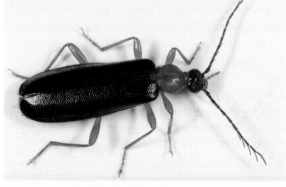

374

Dendroides canadensis Latreille (7.0–16.0 mm) has a pale yellowish to reddish-brown head and pronotum; elytra are black. Underside and legs reddish yellow-brown. Antennae pectinate, article appendages much longer in male. Adults are active in late spring and summer and found on vegetation during the day and at lights at night. Flattened larvae commonly found under loose bark of deciduous logs. Most commonly encountered pyrochroid. Nova Scotia south to Florida, west to central Manitoba and Kansas. (2)

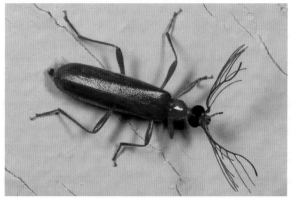

Dendroides concolor **(Newman)** (9.0–17.0 mm) is uniformly yellowish brown, save for its black mandibles. Upper surfaces of pronotum and elytra are equally and deeply punctured, and apical third of flight wings with weakly developed yellowish-brown patches. Antennae pectinate, article appendages much longer in male. Adults active in summer and hide beneath the foliage of trees and shrubs in forested habitats during the day; also attracted to light. Newfoundland and Nova Scotia south to North Carolina, west to Ontario, northern Illinois, Kansas, and eastern Tennessee. (2)

Neopyrochroa femoralis **(LeConte)** (11.0–19.0 mm) is easily distinguished from the only other large pyrochroid in eastern North America, *N. flabellata*, by its black and orange legs. Male *N. femoralis* have branched (pectinate) antennae, but lack a head horn. Adults are found in woodlands under bark, on vegetation during the day, or at lights at night in spring and summer. Larvae feed in underside of fungal-infested decaying logs. Ontario and Québec south to Georgia, west to eastern Nebraska and Texas. (2)

Neopyrochroa flabellata **(Fabricius)** (13.0–19.0 mm) with head, first two antennomeres, pronotum, underside of the last two thoracic segments, legs, most or all of abdomen yellow to yellow-orange. Male with branched (pectinate) antennae and wide pit across head largely covered by short, broad horn. Primarily nocturnal adults found under bark, on vegetation in daytime, and at lights during spring and summer. Flattened larvae are primarily fungivores and work fungal-infested decomposing wood, mostly in underside of log where decay advances more quickly. Ontario and Québec to South Carolina, west to Nebraska and Texas. (2)

375

Schizotus cervicalis **Newman** (5.5–9.0 mm) is mostly black with reddish-orange markings. Head with mouthparts pale, males with a pair of pits behind eyes. Antennae black, serrate in females, weakly pectinate in males. Elytra black with yellow or yellowish-orange margins. Leg black. Adults are found in boreal habitats under bark and by sweeping vegetation; they are not attracted to light. Larvae typically found in association with decaying wood and under moss on logs. New Brunswick and Maine to Maryland, west to Manitoba, Minnesota, South Dakota, and Indiana; also British Columbia and Alberta. (1)

NARROW-WAISTED BARK BEETLES, FAMILY SALPINGIDAE
(SAL-*PINJ*-IH-DEE)

Adult salpingids are usually found on flowers and foliage, or on decaying twigs and under the bark of logs. The few known larvae are associated with decaying twigs and logs. The larvae and adults of *Aglenus brunneus* Erichson are found in caves and are apparently scavengers of plant and animal tissues.

FAMILY DIAGNOSIS Adult salpingids are difficult to characterize as a family and are elongate and convex or very flat (*Inopeplus*). Head with rostrum (*Rhinosimus*) or without, eyes usually present (absent in *Aglenus*). Antennae filiform with 11 antennomeres, or clavate. Elytra long and cover abdomen, or short (*Inopeplus*) with three or four abdominal tergites exposed. Abdomen with five ventrites not fused.

SIMILAR FAMILIES
- rove beetles (Staphylinidae) – antennae not clubbed (p.124)
- zopherid beetles (Zopheridae: Colydiinae) – eyes present (p.340)
- *Mycterus* (Mycteridae) – shiny and metallic; pronotum narrow at base (p.369)

COLLECTING NOTES Look for narrow-waisted bark beetles on flowers and under bark, or find them by sweeping or beating foliage and decaying twigs. *Inopeplus* is attracted to light.

FAUNA 20 SPECIES IN EIGHT GENERA (NA); SIX SPECIES IN FIVE GENERA (ENA)

Inopeplus immunda **(Reitter)** (2.6–4.0 mm) is uniformly yellowish brown to brownish black, shining, flattened, with short elytra; antennae, palps, tibiae, and tarsi lighter. Head broad, eyes large and convex, not strongly constricted behind, and equal in width to prothorax. Prothorax broadest behind head, side somewhat straight, distinctly narrowed toward elytra. Elytra rounded apically, last three abdominal tergites completely exposed. Abdomen short, broad. Adults and larvae probably found under bark of decaying logs; adults attracted to light in summer. Maryland to Florida. (2)

Rhinosimus viridiaenus **(Randall)** (2.5–4.5 mm) is shiny black with metallic greenish luster and no setae; appendages and tip of rostrum reddish yellow. Rostrum nearly twice as long as wide at base. Pronotum with front angles rounded, widest just behind head, and narrowed toward elytra. Elytra with rows of fine punctures, spaces between flat and every other one with single row of distinct punctures. Diurnal adults active in spring and early summer, found in dead leaves and moss, or under lichens associated with dead branches of hardwoods including red alder (*Alnus rubra*) and big leaf maple (*Acer macrophyllum*); also found under bark. Widely distributed across Canada and northern United States; in east, south to South Carolina and Indiana. (1)

ANTLIKE FLOWER BEETLES, FAMILY ANTHICIDAE
(AN-*THISS*-IH-DEE)

In spite of their common name, only species in a few anthicid genera (*Ischyropalpus*, *Retocomus*, *Stereopalpus*) are actually found on flowers where they feed on pollen and nectar. Many scavenge plant, fungal, and animal materials, and sometimes prey on small arthropods. They are found on foliage or are associated with decaying vegetation on the ground, or crawling over areas of exposed soil in riparian habitats with nearby ground-hugging vegetation, bits of debris, stones, or clumps of litter under which to hide. Species of *Anthicus* and *Notoxus* are scavengers of dead insects and attracted to the cantharidin in the bodies of dead blister beetles (Meloidae) and false blister beetles (Oedmeridae). Adults of *Amblyderus*, *Malporus*, and *Mecynotarsus* spend their days burrowed into sandy soils or hiding under objects and debris along the coast or along the margins of marshes, lakes, and rivers. The omnivorous larvae live in soil in association with decayed vegetation on the ground, where they generally have the same feeding habits as the adults.

FAMILY DIAGNOSIS As their common name implies, adult anthicids are antlike in appearance. Head distinct, with neck. Antennae with 11 antennomeres, usually filiform, serrate, or weakly clubbed. Pronotum constricted or narrowed at base, sides not margined or keeled, with base narrower than base of elytra; *Mecynotarsus* and *Notoxus* have a single prominent horn that projects over head. Elytra covered with short hairs and nearly or completely cover abdomen. Tarsal formula 5-5-4, tarsi slender, penultimate tarsomeres narrowly lobed beneath, claws simple to appendiculate. Abdomen with five ventrites.

SIMILAR FAMILIES
- antlike stone beetles (Staphylinidae) – antennal club loosely formed with three or four antennomeres; abdomen with six ventrites; tarsi 5-5-5 (p.134)
- spider beetles (Ptinidae) – antennae clubbed; tarsi-5-5-5 (p.252)
- checkered beetles (Cleridae) – antennae clubbed; tarsi 5-5-5 (p.263)
- fire-colored beetles (Pyrochroidae) – pronotum round (p.373)

- antlike leaf beetles (Aderidae) – eyes notched next to antennal insertion; first two abdominal ventrites fused (p.382)
- orsodacnid leaf beetles (Orsodacnidae) – tarsi appear 4-4-4, but are 5-5-5 (p.429)
- leaf beetles (Chrysomelidae) – tarsi appear 4-4-4, but are 5-5-5 (p.429)

COLLECTING METHODS Look for antlike flower beetles crawling on exposed ground in riparian habitats or along shores and beaches with scattered prostrate plants, stones, and debris, or clumps of litter under which they can hide; wet spots in otherwise dry areas, especially under debris and mats of algae are particularly productive. Beating and sweeping vegetation, especially oaks (*Quercus*), willows (*Salix*), and grasses are the most effective methods for collecting *Notoxus* adults. *Anthicus*, *Mecynotarsus*, *Notoxus*, and *Vacusus* are attracted to cantharidin traps left in shaded areas, especially in the morning and late afternoon. These traps consist of boxes with recently killed or pinned blister beetles, or small containers of alcohol in which blister beetles have been soaked. Many species of anthicids are attracted to light, especially in riparian habitats with suitable substrates.

FAUNA 229 SPECIES IN 32 GENERA (NA); 60 SPECIES IN 16 GENERA (ENA)

Retocomus murinus **(Haldeman)** (7.5–12.0 mm) is somewhat cylindrical and uniformly reddish brown with irregularly placed clumps of pale setae. Eyes only slightly notched near antennal bases, tips of maxillary palps hatchet-shaped, and antennae filiform. Pronotum with front margin flanged, not collarlike and protruding over head, widest in front, underside with coxal cavities at sides. Elytra coarsely, irregularly, and deeply punctate. Adults active in late spring, probably found on flowers; attracted to light. Pennsylvania to Georgia, west to Oklahoma and Alabama. (2)

Stereopalpus mellyi LaFerté-Sénectère (7.0–9.0 mm) is elongate, somewhat cylindrical, uniformly grayish brown or reddish brown and densely clothed in yellowish-brown pubescence. Head with neck broad, roughly sculptured, eyes shallowly notched at base of antennae, last antennomere shorter than combined length of preceding two. Pronotum bell-shaped, widest in front of middle, about wide as long, front margin with curved flange over neck, and densely punctate surface with distinct line down middle. Elytra convex, densely and coarsely punctate, sometimes slightly paler. Legs often reddish brown. Adults active late spring and summer; attracted to light. New York and Ontario to South Carolina, west to Illinois. (3)

Macratria confusa (Fabricius) (2.0–4.5 mm) is elongate, slender, blackish and densely covered with fine pale setae. Head with smooth, narrow neck, without suture delimiting clypeus, and last maxillary palpomere flat and hatchet-shaped. Last three antennomeres each longer than rest. Pronotum with prominent rim in front, longer than wide, slightly wider than head. Elytra convex, with rows of shallow close-set punctures, and thin grooves along sides at base. Some legs partly pale, base of middle legs narrowly separated, tibiae each tipped with pair of spurs, and hind tarsomere long. Adults active in summer, found on vegetation near water; attracted to light. Eastern North America. (3)

Acanthinus argentinus (Pic) (2.6–3.2 mm) is distinctly antlike, with sparse stout setae on sides, and mostly reddish brown with appendages paler. Pronotum with basal part distinctly humped at middle. Elytra indistinctly pale across base, rest mostly dark, with sharply defined tips; sometimes with obscure pale band across middle. Fast-running adults active spring and summer; attracted to light. Brazil, Paraguay, and Argentina; established from Florida to Louisiana. (3)

Amblyderus pallens LeConte (3.1–4.2 mm) is robust, clothed in surface-hugging setae, and yellow to light yellowish brown. Head triangular. Pronotum widest near front, with broad neck at base short. Elytra dull, densely pubescent, and long, leaving only tip of abdomen exposed, grooves evident only on apical half; flight wings reduced. Flightless adults active mostly in late spring and summer, found in sand beneath sprawling plants, among roots in dunes, and beneath debris washed up on sandy beaches. Atlantic Canada to Florida, west to Alberta, Dakotas, and Arizona. (2)

Anthicus cervinus **LaFerté-Sénectère** (2.5–3.3 mm) is yellowish to reddish brown, with head somewhat straight across base and darker than prothorax, and elytra darker at apical two-fifths. Prothorax stout and not deeply constricted. Elytra with strongly curved setae only at base; pale spot on each elytron at apical third sometimes poorly marked. Adults common under debris, especially in sandy habitats, from spring through fall; adults overwinter. Widespread across southern Canada and United States to southern Mexico. (~17)

Ischyropalpus nitidulus **(LeConte)** (2.6–3.3 mm) is somewhat stout, densely pubescent, and shiny reddish to black with appendages paler. Head with neck thin and smooth. Tip of maxillary palps large, triangular. Pronotum with front collarlike, sides rounded in front half, then straight and parallel behind. Elytra impressed across basal fourth, without grooves. Adults found on flowers, e.g., milkweed (*Asclepias*); prey on mites on pine (*Pinus*) in west. Widespread in North America. (4)

Malporus formicarius **(LaFerté-Sénectère)** (3.4-4.1 mm) is very antlike, mostly orange to dark brown, and with setae lying flat on head and pronotum. Head with punctures as large as eye facets. Front half of head and last two-thirds of elytra darker. Elytra with straight yellowish band across depression near base broken at suture, apices dark or indistinctly lighter. Adults are found in coastal dunes, under debris washed up on beaches and lakeshores, and along salt marsh margins; occasionally attracted to light. Atlantic Provinces to Virginia, west to Saskatchewan and Kansas. (3)

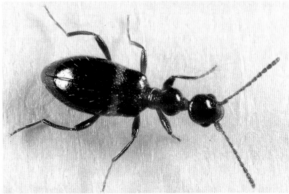

Omonadus formicarius **(Goeze)** (3.0–3.5 mm) is usually reddish with last three-quarters of elytra darker. Head broad, somewhat box-shaped, and straight along base, deeply grooved, with large, prominent eyes. Pronotum lacks bumps in front. Side margins of mesosternum nearly straight and lacking a fringe of appressed setae. Adults found in coastal dunes and in association with decaying vegetation; also collected at light. Old Word species now cosmopolitan; throughout southern Canada and United States. (2)

Sapintus species (3.0–4.0 mm) are usually uniformly pale to dark brown. Head short. Prothorax very small, without horn, sides sinuate before middle. Elytra lacking thin grooves along sides at base, with two layers of setae, longer directed backward, shorter more appressed. Adults swept or beaten from vegetation, attracted to light. Eastern North America. (7)

Stricticollis (formerly *Stricticomus*) *tobias* (Marseul) (2.6–3.1 mm) is reddish with yellowish appendages. Head with basal margin slightly rounded with notch in middle. Pronotum and elytra flat. Elytra clothed in moderately fine and reclining pubescence, reddish-brown to blackish area extending from basal third or quarter to apex, suture entirely pale, and faint pale spot before tip of each elytron. Middle East and India, widespread in North America. (1)

Vacusus vicinus (LaFerté-Sénectère) (2.3–2.8 mm) is mostly blackish with indications of paler markings. Head with base wide, almost straight without notch, with neck thin and smooth. Mouthparts with maxillary palps curved, not angular. Pronotum with narrow collarlike margin in front and no horn, side margins straight, evenly converging from middle to base, underside with short fringe of setae just in front and outside of middle coxae. Elytra convex with long and short erect setae, covering all but tip of abdomen. Adults active in late spring and summer; attracted to light. Virginia to Florida, west to Arkansas and southeastern Texas. (1)

Notoxus desertus Casey (2.8–4.2 mm) is elongate and tan with dark markings on elytra. Pronotal horn with pits underneath clearly defined margins, base without short, sharp ridge down middle. Elytral setae long, irregular dark band behind middle. Abdomen with ventrite 5 broadly rounded (male) or rounded-triangular (female). Adults found on various trees, shrubs, and grasses; attracted to light and cantharidin; overwinter in leaf litter. New Jersey and Pennsylvania to Virginia and South Carolina, west to Michigan, Nebraska, and Texas; Arizona, Pacific states. (9)

Notoxus monodon **(Fabricius)** (2.7–3.6 mm) has reddish-brown head and pronotum with light brown to orange elytra with dark brown band behind middle. Margins of pronotal horn distinct, finely notched (crenulate), with row of pits on underside of margin, and without a median ridge on top. Posterior margin of last abdominal ventrite of male broadly rounded, broadly triangular in female. Adults found year-round, especially in spring and summer on vegetation and at light. Virginia to Florida, west to Arkansas and Texas. (9)

Notoxus murinipennis **(LeConte)** (2.9–3.9 mm) is horned with uniformly colored elytra. Head reddish brown, with short, slender neck and fringed with setae. Pronotum tan or orangish with narrow collarlike margin, sides converging to base, clothed in whitish setae; horn extending over head with margin finely notched. Elytra blue-brown to brown, convex and smooth, without ridges or grooves, and clothed in whitish pubescence. Adults active spring through summer, found on flowers and vegetation of trees and shrubs, including oak (*Quercus*), maple (*Acer*), and hickory (*Carya*); attracted to light. Pennsylvania to Florida, west to Illinois, Kansas, and Texas. (9)

381

Tomoderus **species** (2.5–3.0 mm) are robust, convex, often uniformly pale or dark. Head with neck slender, smooth; eye facets coarse; antennae thick, antennomeres moniliform, slightly wider than wide toward tips. Pronotum with collar or rim in front, constricted at sides and across middle. Elytra sometimes paler at base. Abdomen of male with semicircular and flat pygidium. Legs with femora thick, club-shaped, penultimate tarsomeres bilobed. Adults found in spring and fall under rocks and debris along coastal and riparian habitats. Species identification is best accomplished through examination of male genitalia. Massachusetts to Florida, west to Indiana, Kansas, and coastal Texas. (4)

ISCHALIID BEETLES, FAMILY ISCHALIIDAE
(ISS-KA-*LEE*-IH-DEE)

The unusual genus *Ischalia* was originally placed in the family Pedilidae, now a subfamily of the Pyrochroidae. Based on characters of the larvae, it was later moved to the Anthicidae; however, it is very different from other antlike flower beetles and has been placed by some coleopterists in its own family, while others still consider it a subfamily of anthicids. The adults and larvae of the western *I. vancouverensis* Harrington feed on fungal mycelia associated with decaying stumps and logs; the sole eastern species, *I. costata* (LeConte), probably has similar feeding habits.

FAMILY DIAGNOSIS Adult *Ischalia* are characterized by a pronotum with three angles along the base and distinct ridges along the rim and above the sides of each elytron, with the space between nearly vertical; flight wings are reduced. Antennae filiform. Pronotum with side margins ridged or keeled. Tibial spurs lacking. Abdomen with five distinct ventrites.

SIMILAR FAMILIES The pronotal and elytra characters are unique.

COLLECTING NOTES Adults are found year-round by sifting leaves and other decaying vegetation and by searching under boards.

FAUNA THREE SPECIES ON ONE GENUS (NA); ONE SPECIES, *ISCHALIA COSTATA* (LECONTE) (ENA)

Ischalia costata (**LeConte**) (4.0–6.5 mm) is dull brownish yellow or orangish and brownish black. Pronotum bell-shaped with ridges extending beyond basal margin and ridged elytra distinctive. Flightless adults collected year-round by sifting through leaves and other decaying plant material, and by searching in rotten white wood and under boards. Québec to South Carolina, west to Indiana and Tennessee. (1)

ANTLIKE LEAF BEETLES, FAMILY ADERIDAE
(A-*DARE*-IH-DEE)

Little is known of the biology and natural history of aderids. Adults are found on vegetation, especially on the underside of leaves, and flowers. Known larvae are found in leaf litter, under bark, and in rotten wood, especially that in the red-rot stage of decay. Some possibly scavenge dead insects or eat fungi. The immature stages of a species that occurs in southcentral United States, *Vanonous balteatus* Warner, were found in the subterranean nests of solitary bees (Apidae) in Chiapas, Mexico. They were apparently opportunistically feeding on fungi growing on masses of old, decaying provisions and dead bees.

FAMILY DIAGNOSIS Adult aderids are small and antlike in form, with broad head bent downward and constricted at base, and eyes coarsely faceted, notched, hairy. Antennae filiform, clavate, or comblike (some males pectinate), with 11 antennomeres. Tarsi appear 4-4-3, actually 5-5-4, tarsomere 1 long, penultimate tarsomeres very short, third from last tarsomeres lobed underneath, claws simple. Abdomen with five ventrites, 1–2 fused.

382

SIMILAR FAMILIES

- *Pedilus* (Pyrochroidae) – larger (p.373)
- antlike flower beetles (Anthicidae) – eyes not notched; abdominal ventrites 1–2 not fused (p.377)
- false flower beetles (Scraptiidae) – not antlike; abdominal ventrites not fused (p.384)
- orsodacnid leaf beetles (Orsodacnidae) – larger, tarsi 5-5-5 (p.429)
- some leaf beetles (Chrysomelidae: Criocerinae) – larger, tarsi 5-5-5 (p.429)

COLLECTING NOTES Antlike leaf beetles spend their days on the undersides of leaves and are collected by sweeping and beating the foliage of shrubs and trees, especially deciduous hardwoods such as oak (*Quercus*). They are often collected in Malaise and flight intercept traps. Some species are attracted to light.

FAUNA 48 SPECIES IN 11 GENERA (NA); 37 SPECIES IN 11 GENERA (ENA)

Zonantes fasciatus **(Melsheimer)** (2.4 mm) is robust, mostly dark brown to black with yellowish appendages; hind coxae and femora sometimes darker. Elytra with triangular reddish-yellow patches on either side of scutellum and reddish-yellow apices. Adults found on vegetation and at light in late spring and summer. Québec to Florida, west to Michigan, Oklahoma, and Alabama. (10)

Zonantes subfasciatus **(LeConte)** (1.5 mm) is somewhat oval, convex, dull reddish yellow to pale brown with a dark head bearing large, coarsely granulated eyes. Elytra pale with distinct broad band just before middle and broken at suture; band sometimes broken into two elongate spots on each elytron, lateral spot just behind medial spot. Hind femora dusky in some individuals. Adults found on vegetation and at light in late spring and summer. New Hampshire to Florida, west to Wisconsin and eastern Texas. (10)

Emelinus melsheimeri **(LeConte)** (2.2 mm) is slender, pubescent, and mostly tan with dark zigzag pattern on elytra; antennae, tibiae, and tarsi dull yellow. Head dark with eyes large, coarsely faceted, antennomeres 4–11 each with long appendage (male) or not (female). Pronotum dark. Elytra with three dark uneven bars. Underside dark. Legs with femora dark. Adults active spring and summer, found on vegetation. Massachusetts to Florida, west to Illinois and eastern Arizona; also Mexico. (1)

Elonus basalis (LeConte) (2.8–3.0 mm) is robust, blackish, with notched eyes, red humeri, and elytra clothed in intermixed short and long setae. Appendages mostly dark, tarsi and antennal tips lighter. Elytra with deep, flat-bottomed punctures and clothed in moderately long, erect setae and laterally directed setae between; fresh individuals with narrow border of gray pubescence along suture and in weakly developed patch behind middle. Adults on foliage of deciduous shrubs in spring and early summer; attracted to light. Québec and Ontario to Florida, west to Minnesota and eastern Oklahoma. (2)

Vanonus piceus (LeConte) (1.4–1.7 mm) is somewhat elongate and straight-sided, sparsely pubescent, uniformly dull dark brown, with reddish-brown appendages. Head darker in pale individuals, with front flat (male) or convex (female). Elytra long, coarsely punctured with sides abruptly vertical. Hind femora each with long setal brushes in both sexes. Adults active spring and summer, found on vegetation, especially undersides of leaves on trees and shrubs; attracted to light. Ontario and New Hampshire to Florida, west to Wisconsin, Oklahoma, and Alabama. (13)

FALSE FLOWER BEETLES, FAMILY SCRAPTIIDAE
(SCRAP-*TEE*-IH-DEE)

This family of beetles consists of two very different subfamilies (Scraptiinae, Anaspinae) and is difficult to characterize. Its members have been variously placed in other families. Adults are mostly diurnal and commonly encountered on foliage and flowers. The few known larvae of scraptiids are found under the bark of dead snags, in decaying logs, or on lichens.

FAMILY DIAGNOSIS Adult scraptiids are mostly soft-bodied, sometimes distinctly clothed in setae, and have deeply notched eyes. Body elongate, parallel-sided to somewhat ovate, slightly flattened to moderately convex, with or without distinct vestiture on supper surface. Head not retracted within pronotum, with mouthparts directed downward. Antennae with 11 antennomeres beadlike or filiform, with or without distinct club. Prothorax widest at front, side margins often sharpest toward rear, sometimes with pair of small depressions near posterior margins, surface sometimes with fine transverse lines (*Anaspis, Diclidia, Pentaria, Sphingocephalus*). Elytra elongate to somewhat ovate with punctures (*Allopoda, Canifa, Scraptia*) or fine transverse lines (*Anaspis, Diclidia, Pentaria, Sphingocephalus*) and cover entire abdomen. Legs slender with femora slightly swollen midlength, tarsal formula 5-5-4,

penultimate tarsomere with or without fleshy lobes; claws simple or toothed. Abdomen with five ventrites, those of male *Anaspis* with short movable appendages.

SIMILAR FAMILIES
- False darkling beetles (Melandryidae) – head retracted within pronotum (p.329)
- Tumbling flower beetles (Mordellidae) – last abdominal ventrite long, sharply pointed (p.333)
- Comb-clawed beetles (Tenebrionidae: Alleculinae) – claws pectinate (pp.352–4)

COLLECTING NOTES Look for false flower beetles in forests and adjacent open habitats on vegetation and flowers, especially those in the carrot (Apiaceae) and rose (Rosaceae) families. Hand-collecting, sweep-netting, and beating foliage the most productive collecting techniques; additional specimens are found in Malaise traps and at light. *Anaspis* and *Canifa* are especially common on flowers and leaves in open areas; *Canifa* are also encountered on foliage in woods. *Pentaria* are sometimes abundant inside unopened ears of corn.

FAUNA 46 SPECIES IN 13 GENERA (NA); 13 SPECIES IN SEVEN GENERA (ENA)

Allopoda lutea (Haldeman) (3.0–3.5 mm) is elongate, somewhat flat, uniformly dull brownish yellow to reddish yellow with appendages paler; margins and tips of elytra sometimes darker. Antennomeres simple and cylindrical. Tip of maxillary palp triangular. Pronotum wider than long, sides broadly rounded, surface finely punctate and granular, with three broad, shallow depressions across base. Elytra with punctation sparser and coarser than pronotum. Legs with tarsomere 1 shorter than others combined, hind tarsomere 3 not lobed underneath. Larva probably develops under loose bark. Adults active in spring on flowers and foliage of various trees, shrubs, and undergrowth; attracted to light. New York to Florida, west to Indiana and Texas. (1)

Canifa pallipes (Melsheimer) (2.0–2.5 mm) is slender, parallel-sided, dark brown, and densely clothed in fine yellow pubescence. Head darker with antennae slightly more than half body length; articles 2–3 short, equal in length. Pronotum punctate with pair of distinct impressions at base. Elytra punctate. Legs dull yellow. Adults found on foliage of shrubs and trees in spring and early summer. Southern Canada and eastern North America. (4)

Scraptia sericea (Melsheimer) (4.0–5.5 mm) is small, elongate and straight-sided, uniformly brownish yellow, and sparsely clothed in fine yellow pubescence with appendages paler. Antennae about two-thirds length of body; third to last tarsomere of all tarsi lobed. Pronotum with three broad, shallow impressions at base, middle impression reaching to middle. Adults found in late spring and summer on flowers and foliage. Québec and Ontario to Florida, west to Indiana and Texas. (1)

Anaspis flavipennis Haldeman (2.5–3.0 mm) has a dark head and pronotum, reddish-brown elytra, mostly paler appendages, and fine lines across upper surfaces. Antennae with first four articles filiform and reddish yellow, remaining articles darker and nearly moniliform. Abdomen of male with long, movable appendages on third ventrite, female ventrites plain. Common in wooded areas on flowers on late spring and summer days; also attracted to light. Prince Edward Island, Nova Scotia, and Maine to Virginia, west to Minnesota and Illinois. (3)

Anaspis nigrina (Csiki) (2.5–3.0 mm) is blackish with fine lines across upper surfaces. Tibiae, mouthparts, and antennal bases lighter. Male with prothorax about as long as wide and a pair of short appendages on the middle of third abdominal ventrite; female prothorax wider than long, abdomen without appendages. Adults are found in coniferous forests and mixed woodlands in late spring and summer on flowers and vegetation during the day; also attracted to lights. Newfoundland and Nova Scotia to Virginia, west to Ontario, Wisconsin, and Indiana. (3)

Anaspis rufa Say (3.0–4.0 mm) is mostly yellowish brown with fine, transverse lines across upper surfaces. Antennae with first four articles filiform and reddish yellow, remaining articles darker and nearly moniliform. Pronotum wider than long. Elytra broader at middle than prothorax. Abdomen with underside black, ventrites 3 and 4 each with pair of movable appendages, those on fourth shorter. Common on late spring and early summer days on flowers and vegetation in forests and edges; also attracted to light. Maritime Provinces and Maine to Virginia, west to Ontario, Idaho, and Kansas. (3)

Pentaria trifasciata (Melsheimer) (3.0–4.0 mm) is narrowed on both ends, finely clothed in yellowish pubescence, and finely wrinkled across upper surfaces, with spotted elytra. Head, antennomeres 1–5, base of pronotum, legs, and elytral spots before middle and tips yellowish brown; rest of body pale to dark brown or blackish. Pronotum wider than long, with sides evenly rounded from front to sharp hind angles. Elytra at base nearly as wide as pronotum, not covering tip of abdomen, with spots sometimes connected across suture. Adults active late spring and early summer, found on flowers of trees and shrubs including dogwood (*Cornus*), hydrangea (*Hydrangea*), and black haw (*Viburnum*); Malaise traps. Widespread in North America, in east from Québec and Ontario to Virginia, west to Iowa and Kansas. (1)

DISTENIID LONGHORN BEETLES, FAMILY DISTENIIDAE
(DIS-TEN-*EE*-IH-DEE)

Disteniid longhorns resemble lepturine longhorn beetles and were once considered a subfamily of the Cerambycidae; however, their mouthparts and larval characters indicate that they are more closely related to leaf beetles (Chrysomelidae). The family is primarily southern in distribution with only one species, *Elytrimitatrix unduta* (Fabricius), found in eastern North America.

FAMILY DIAGNOSIS Adult *Elytrimitatrix* are elongate, slender, dark brown to blackish, and densely covered with short gray pubescence. Head is extremely short in front of large, coarsely faceted eyes, clypeus and frons distinct and not in same plane, and mouthparts directed forward with mandibles strongly bowed and chisel-shaped. Antennae filiform, with 11 antennomeres usually bearing batches of long setae underneath, 3 more or less equal to 1. Pronotum with both raised calluses and distinct projections on sides. Elytra broadest at humeri, long and covering all of abdomen, each tipped with two sharp spines. Tarsal formula 5-5-5, apparently 4-4-4, tarsomere 4 very small and enveloped by 3. Abdomen with five ventrites.

SIMILAR FAMILIES
- longhorn beetles (Cerambycidae) – clypeus and frons in same plane; mandibles not strongly bowed and narrowed at tips (p.388)

COLLECTING NOTES Look for disteniids at night on dead branches of oak (*Quercus*), locust (*Robinia*), hickory (*Carya*), and redbud (*Cercis*); also attracted to light and traps baited with fermenting fruit.

FAUNA ONE SPECIES, *ELYTRIMITATRIX UNDATA* (FABRICIUS) (NA)

Elytrimitatrix undata (Fabricius) (16.0–26.0 mm) is elongate, slender, dark brown to blackish and densely covered with short gray pubescence. Mouthparts prognathous. Pronotum with prominent tubercle on each side. Elytra strongly tapered with a dark zigzag band of darker pubescence at base, front of middle, and apical third; each elytron tipped with pair of spines. Larva develops in recently killed oak (*Quercus*), hickory (*Carya*), and other deciduous trees. Adults active in summer and attracted to light and fermented fruit traps. Connecticut and Pennsylvania to Florida, west to Iowa, Missouri, and Texas. (1)

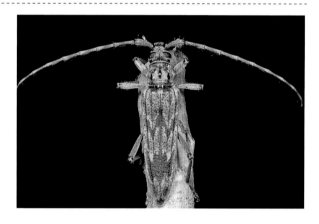

LONGHORN BEETLES, FAMILY CERAMBYCIDAE
(SAIR-AHM-*BISS*-IH-DEE)

Cerambycids are particularly conspicuous in wooded areas, where they are attracted to freshly painted surfaces, cut wood, flowers, or lights at night. They are commonly found in dead or damaged tree material, twigs, and small branches of woody plants. Diurnal flower visitors tend to be brightly or contrastingly colored and sometimes look and behave like stinging wasps. Nocturnal species are mostly dull black or brown and spend their days hiding beneath logs and bark, emerging at dusk or in the evening to search for food and mates. Some are cryptically marked, allowing them to hide out in the open during the day, camouflaged against the bark of trees. Wood feeders consume twigs, bark, and bast (fibrous inner bark), while plant feeders eat leaves, needles, cones, fruits, and sap. Flower visitors consume pollen, stamens, and nectar. The plump and cylindrical larvae are often called roundheaded borers. They almost always feed internally, attacking dead and decaying wood or living trees and shrubs by chewing their way into branches, trunks, stems, roots, and cones. Some species girdle twigs, while the feeding activities of others may induce galls and other abnormal tissue growths. Others burrow in the soil and feed on roots from the outside. Adults and larvae play a beneficial role by recycling dead and dying trees, reducing them to humus; however, some species are serious pests in managed timber killed or weakened by storms, fires, or severe infestations of other insects. Stressed or injured shade and ornamental trees are particularly susceptible to attack by larvae.

FAMILY DIAGNOSIS Adult cerambycids are extremely variable in shape. They are usually robust, broad across base of elytra, with antennae at least half as long as body, eyes usually notched around antennal bases, and tarsi usually appearing 4-4-4, but actually 5-5-5 with tarsomere 4 small and tucked between lobes of heart-shaped 3. Abdomen with five ventrites.

SIMILAR FAMILIES
- stag beetles (Lucanidae) – antennae with lopsided club (p.142)
- soldier beetles (Cantharidae) – tarsi distinctly 5-5-5: body and elytra soft (p.238)
- false longhorn beetles (Stenotrachelidae) – claws comblike; tarsi 5-5-4 (p.360)
- false blister beetles (Oedemeridae) – pronotum broadest in front; tarsi 5-5-4 (p.362)
- orsodacnid leaf beetles (Orsodacnidae) – antennae short; pronotum widest in front (p.429)
- some leaf beetles (Chrysomelidae) – antennae and body short, or pronotum broadest in front, or elytra broadest at tips (p.429)

COLLECTING NOTES Look for longhorn beetles on flowers or resting on nearby vegetation. Nocturnal species are attracted to light, especially if placed in an opening surrounded by woods. Be sure to check the shadows just beyond the light's glow. Beating and sweeping branches and leaves of larval host plants is also productive. Check downed logs and freshly cut wood day and night. Beetles will often take cover under green branches placed on freshly cut stumps. Some species are attracted to fermenting molasses and watermelon rinds, while conifer feeders are attracted to fresh paint, turpentine, and other solvents. Another very productive method is to collect sections of larvae-infested wood and place them in a rearing container from which emerging adults cannot escape.

FAUNA 958 SPECIES IN 306 GENERA (NA); ~400 SPECIES IN 167 GENERA (ENA)

Pole Borer *Neandra* (formerly *Parandra*) *brunnea* **(Fabricius)** (8.0–21.0 mm) resembles a shiny reddish-brown stag beetle (Lucanidae). Head with moniliform antennae and notched eyes; mandibles more developed in male. Pronotum with sides with narrowly expanded rim in front. Tarsi lack setae-bearing pad between claws. Larvae feed and develop in moist, rotting heartwood of many deciduous trees; sometimes found in cavities of living trees and damaging wooden structures in contact with soil. Adults attracted to light in summer. New Brunswick to Florida, west to Ontario, Minnesota, Colorado, and Alabama. (1)

Parandra polita **Say** (10.0–25.0 mm) is elongate, parallel-sided, smooth, shiny pale brown to reddish brown with short antennae and conspicuous mandible. Head large, punctures fine, eyes oval without notch, antennomeres moniliform. Pronotum widest in front, sides without expanded rim in front, with very small punctures. Elytra with surface sparsely punctate and rounded tips. Legs short, tarsi distinctly 5-5-5, claws with conspicuous pad tipped with pair of setae between. Larva develops in heartwood of deciduous trees, including beech (*Fagus*), hickory (*Carya*), and tulip tree (*Liriodendron*). Adults active in summer; attracted to light. Virginia to Florida, west to Colorado and Texas. (1)

389

Live Oak Root Borer *Archodontes melanoplus* **(Linnaeus)** (33.0–57.0 mm) is large, elongate, broad, somewhat flattened and straight-sided, dark brown to black, with prominent mandibles. Head with eyes coarsely faceted and weakly notched, with antennae reaching basal third of elytra. Mandibles nearly vertical, one tooth internally. Pronotum with sides serrate, and converging toward head. Elytra wrinkled and with rounded tips. Adults active late spring through summer; attracted to light. Larvae bore into roots of oaks, especially live oak (*Quercus virginiana*) and other deciduous trees. Virginia to Florida, west to Arkansas and Texas. (1)

Hardwood Stump Borer *Mallodon dasystomus* **(Say)** (20.0–50.0 mm) is large, elongate, somewhat flattened, and reddish brown to dark brown. Head large, very coarsely punctured, mandibles directed forward. Antennae slender, reaching basal third (male), or shorter (female). Mandibles nearly horizontal. Pronotum with sides lined with many small teeth, surface of male with shiny raised areas often merging toward base. Elytra long, smooth, with fine shallow punctures. Larvae burrow into heartwood of living and recently dead hardwood trees. Adults active spring and summer; attracted to light. Virginia to Florida, west to Arizona. (1)

Hairy Pine Borer *Tragosoma harrisii* **(LeConte)** (18.0–36.0 mm) is long, slender, and shiny brown to dark brown. Antennae slender. Prothorax with single spine on sides, pronotum densely hairy in male, female less so. Elytral surface feebly wrinkled with scattered, moderate punctures to strongly wrinkled. Larvae feed and develop in sapwood of decaying logs. Adults attracted to lights in coniferous forests at higher elevations in summer. Adults attracted to light in summer. Québec and Ontario to Pennsylvania, west to Minnesota; also montane western North America and Europe, Russia. (1)

Derobrachus thomasi Santos-Silva (35.2–52.5 mm) is elongate, parallel-sided, shiny brown. Mandibles long, directed forward. Pronotum finely punctate and densely pubescent on top, sharp side margins adorned with three sharp teeth on each side. Antennae reaching apical fourth (male) or middle (female) of elytra, antennomere 3 distinctly longer than 1–2 combined and about as long as 4–5 together. Elytra with tips flattened (male) or rounded (female). Larvae develop in oak (*Quercus*). Adults active in summer; attracted to light. Southern Florida. *Derobrachus brevicollis* Audinet-Serville (31.9–40.0 mm) similar, antennae of male to apical third of elytra, pronotum mostly bare; North Carolina to northern Florida and Alabama. (2)

Orthosoma brunneum **(Forster)** (24.0–50.0 mm) is light brown and somewhat flattened. Antennae slender, filiform, with third antennomere subequal to first and second combined and distinctly shorter than combined lengths of 4 and 5. Prothorax with three sharp spines on sides and narrower than elytra at base. Elytra with three fine ridges on each elytron. Breeds in long dead, moist, decaying hardwood and coniferous logs; poles, structural timbers; lumber in contact with ground also utilized. Adults attracted to light in summer. Québec and Nova Scotia to Florida, west to Ontario, Minnesota, Kansas, and Texas. (1)

Tile-horned Prionus *Prionus imbricornis* **(Linnaeus)** (24.0–50.0 mm, without mandibles) is large, robust, and shiny dark reddish brown with large mandibles. Antennae thick, with 18–20 antennomeres and reaching middle of elytra (male), or thinner, reaching basal third, with 16–18 (female). Pronotum as wide as base of elytra, three sharp teeth on sides. Larvae feed externally or bore into the roots of deciduous trees, shrubs, and woody vines, oak (*Quercus*) and pecan (*Carya*); also fruit trees. Nocturnal adults active in summer, hide during the day in litter at tree bases; attracted to light. Connecticut to Florida, west to Nebraska and Texas. (6)

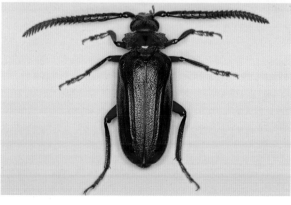

390

Broad-necked Root Borer *Prionus laticollis* **(Drury)** (22.0 to 32.0 mm) is dark brownish black, sometimes with obscure reddish cast. Antennae with 12 overlapping antennomeres, and eyes widely separated above. Pronotum armed with three blunt teeth, wide as elytra at base. Elytra wrinkled. Metathorax of male pubescent underneath, female bare. Males attracted to light in summer. Heavy-bodied females flightless, found at night or early morning on ground, sometimes containing up to 300–400 eggs. Larvae feed externally on living roots of trees and shrubs, including fruit trees and grapevines. Québec and Maine to Florida, west to Minnesota and eastern Texas; more common in northern part of range. (6)

Sphenostethus taslei **(Buquet)** (20.0–29.0 mm) is shiny black, sometimes with brown elytra, with appendages reddish brown or black. Pronotum smooth, with distinct punctures becoming coarser at sides, sides roughly margined or keeled, and widest at base and nearly as wide as elytra. Elytra without pubescence, each tipped with small, sharp teeth. Larvae tunnel in dead, dry tops of various hardwoods, including oak (*Quercus*), beech (*Fagus*), and redbud (*Cercis*). Adults active in summer, found flying during day; also in Malaise and sticky traps. New Jersey to Florida, west to Indiana, Missouri, and Texas. (1)

391

Elderberry Borer *Desmocerus palliatus* **(Forster)** (18.0–27.0 mm) is elongate, somewhat cylindrical, brilliant metallic blue or violet and yellow to yellowish orange. Adults emerge in spring and early summer and feed on flowers of wild and ornamental subspecies of black elderberry (*Sambucus nigra*); larvae tunnel and feed in pithy stems. Mature larvae bore into roots and pupate at or just below soil surface. Life cycle takes one year in Deep South, up to three years further north. Québec and Maine to North Carolina, west to Wisconsin, eastern Kansas, and Arkansas. (1)

Oak Bark Scaler *Encyclops caerulea* **(Say)** (7.0–11.0 mm) is slender, parallel-sided, bright metallic green or purplish with yellowish-brown legs. Pronotum coarsely punctured with broad tubercles on each side. Female slightly more robust. Adults found on vegetation and flowers (e.g., *Cornus*, *Rubus*) in late spring and summer. Larvae develop in the outer bark of various living deciduous hardwoods, such as oak (*Quercus*), maple (*Acer*), walnut (*Juglans*), ash (*Fraxinus*), and hickory (*Carya*). Widespread in eastern North America. (1)

Analeptura lineola (Say) (6.0–12.0 mm) is slender with dark, dorsally arched pronotum topped with fine golden setae often forming shiny spot, antennae banded toward tip, and yellowish-red legs. Elytra variably marked, usually with marginal and median stripes; median stripes sometimes lost or broad and fused with lateral stripes. Adults found on various flowers from early spring through summer and are attracted to lights at night. Larvae develop in beech (*Fagus*), hophornbeam (*Ostrya*), hornbeam (*Carpinus*) and pine (*Pinus*). Maritime Provinces to Florida, west to the Midwest. (1)

Anastrangalia sanguinea (LeConte) (7.0–13.0 mm) is elongate, somewhat cylindrical, weakly convex, tapered, with both sexes black with shining, dark yellowish-brown to reddish-brown or brown elytra. Head short, margins behind eyes nearly parallel, with somewhat silky antennae. Elytra densely punctate, those at base larger than punctures on pronotum. Elytra narrowly dark at tips, each with two vague ridges down middle. Larva develops in pine (*Pinus*). Adults active in summer, found on flowers, e.g., viburnum (*Viburnum*), dogwood (*Cornus*), and blackberry (*Rubus*). Western North America; in east from Maritime Provinces and Maine to Massachusetts, west to Ontario. (1)

Anthophylax attenuatus (Haldeman) (12.0–17.0 mm) is shiny black with shiny yellowish-brown elytra mottled with irregular, dense patches of pale, appressed setae. Pronotum, legs, and underside clothed in fine pale setae. Antennae reaching just beyond apical third of elytra in male, about middle in female; antennomere 3 longer than 4, nearly equal to 5. Elytral tips blunt. Middle legs of male with distinct spurlike structure between spines on tips. Larva develops in wet, decaying logs of maple (*Acer*), beech (*Fagus*), and cottonwood (*Populus*), also in living branches of spruce (*Picea*); pupates in soil. Adults active late spring through summer, found on male pine (*Pinus*) strobili. Maritime Provinces to northern Virginia, west to Ontario and Wisconsin. (4)

Anthophylax cyaneaus (Haldeman) (11.0–16.0 mm) is bright shining metallic green or bluish with orangish-brown femora. Pronotum and elytra coarsely punctate. Larva develops in alder (*Alnus*), beech (*Fagus*), and common serviceberry (*Amelanchier arborea*); may also use conifers. Adults active late spring and summer, found on flowers of mountain maple (*Acer spicatum*) and dogwood (*Cornus*), also on strobili of eastern white pine (*Pinus strobus*). New Brunswick and Nova Scotia to Georgia, west to Ontario, Michigan, Pennsylvania. (4)

***Bellamira scalaris* (Say)** (20.0–26.0 mm) is long, slender, strongly tapered, and reddish brown; male with expanded abdominal tip. Head short, broad, with eyes notched. Pronotum lacks spines or bumps on sides, with deep impressions behind head and at base, and sharp hind angles. Elytra constricted behind middle, with variable dark markings. Larvae develop in various hardwoods, including maple (*Acer*), alder (*Alnus*), hickory (*Carya*), beech (*Fagus*), cottonwood (*Populus*), willow (*Salix*); also pine (*Pinus*). Adults collected on various flowers in spring and summer; occasionally attracted to light. Nova Scotia and New Brunswick to Florida, west to Manitoba, Minnesota, South Dakota, and Texas. (1)

***Brachyleptura champlaini* Casey** (8.0–12.0 mm) is short, stout, usually with uniformly reddish or brownish elytra or sometimes dark with reddish or brownish stripes along sides; tips rounded and distinct at apical third. Antennomeres 1–5 black, remaining antennomeres with pale bands at base. Pronotum convex, strongly punctate. Hind tibiae of male not flattened or modified. Adults are found in late spring and early summer on various flowers, including New Jersey tea (*Ceanothus americanus*), spirea (*Spiraea*), aruncus (*Aruncus*), chestnut (*Castanea*), and beebalm (*Monarda*). Prince Edward Island and Nova Scotia to Florida, west to Ontario and Tennessee. (4)

***Brachyleptura vagans* (Olivier)** (8.0–12.0 mm) is similar to dark form of *B. champlaini*, with reddish humeral patches sometimes absent; reddish form with dark elytral suture. Pronotal punctation is less dense than that of *B. champlaini*, punctures separated by more than their own diameters. Males with hind tibiae bowed, flattened, and polished on inner surface. Adults on flowers in late spring, early summer; larvae develop in decaying hardwoods. Eastern North America. (4)

***Brachysomida bivittata* (Say)** (7.0–11.0 mm) is variable. Head light or dark. Pronotum orange with dark spots, sometimes all orange or black, with midline and margins sometimes densely punctate; pubescence absent to moderately dense. Elytra coarsely punctate, sometimes with finer punctures, orange with broad black stripes, or all black, sometimes with narrow yellow margins. Legs orange or black, with spurs on tips of tibiae. Larvae feed in oak (*Quercus*), hickory (*Carya*), and dogwood (*Cornus*). Adults found on flowers, including dogwood, viburnum (*Viburnum*), sweetclover (*Melilotus*), and anemone (*Anemone*). Nova Scotia and New Brunswick to South Carolina, west to Alberta and Mississippi. (1)

Evodinus monticola **(Randall)** (8.0–13.0 mm) has eyes
shallowly notched. Pronotum longer than broad, sides
with feeble projections, and constricted base with dense
golden setae. Elytra with basal margins not raised around
scutellum, mostly pale with variable black markings, each
with three or four sometimes connected black spots and
black tips. Tibiae with spurs on tips, hind leg with tarsomere
3 notched to base. Larvae develop in larch (*Tsuga*), fir
(*Abies*), spruce (*Picea*), and pine (*Pinus*). Diurnal adults
active in late spring and summer, found on tree and shrub
flowers such as dogwood (*Cornus*), rose (*Rosa*), elderberry
(*Sambucus*), and viburnum (*Viburnum*). Atlantic Canada to
North Carolina, west to Manitoba. (1)

Gaurotes cyanipennis **(Say)** (9.0–13.0 mm) is easily
distinguished by its brilliant metallic bluish or greenish
elytra and bulging process between middle legs. Head and
prothorax shiny black. Appendages reddish yellow. Eggs
are laid on bark of dying deciduous trees in early summer.
Larvae develop beneath bark, reaching maturity in fall.
Pupation occurs in spring inside earthen cells at base of
food plant. Adults emerge in spring and early summer and
are found on flowers of various trees and shrubs. Québec
and Maine to northern Georgia, west to Ontario, Minnesota,
Iowa, and Tennessee. (2).

Grammoptera haematites **(Newman)** (4.0–7.0 mm).
Head black with reddish clypeus, antennal bases, and
forelegs. Eyes with front margins touching base of mandibles.
Pronotum with faint impressed line down middle, usually
reddish, occasionally blackish. Male with tip of last ventrite
narrowly rounded, female without tubercle. Adults found on
flowers (*Viburnum, Aruncus, Cornus, Crataegus, Spiraea,
Ceanothus*) in spring and early summer. Larvae develop in
various shrubs. Occurs in New Brunswick to North Carolina,
west to Saskatchewan, Iowa, Missouri, and Mississippi. (3)

Grammoptera subargentata **(Kirby)** (5.0–8.0 mm) is
black, occasionally with legs, antennal bases, and clypeus
partly reddish; pronotal and elytral pubescence shiny,
dark or silvery, never pale. Head inflated behind eyes;
front margins of eyes narrowly separated from bases of
mandibles. Pronotum black with line of backward-directed
setae. Elytra finely punctate. Last ventrite rounded without
tubercle (female), narrowly rounded (male). Adults in spring
and summer on flowers. *Grammoptera haematites* has eye
margins contiguous with mandible bases, more closely and
coarsely punctate elytra; *G. exigua* (Newman) with ventrite
tuberculate (female) or broadly notched (male). Boreal
North America; in east to North Carolina. (3)

Idiopidonia pedalis **(LeConte)** (8.0–11.0 mm) is elongate, uniformly black, and parallel-sided. Head short in front with small eyes. Pronotum dull, pubescent, midline narrow and shining, widest at distinctly expanded posterior margin. Hind leg with metatibia distinctly longer than metafemur, first tarsal segment longer than remaining segments combined. Larval host is unknown. Seldom collected adults active in summer and found on flowers of azalea and rhododendron (*Rhododendron*), viburnum (*Viburnum*), spirea (*Spiraea*), and pear (*Pyrus*). Atlantic Canada through Appalachian mountains to northwestern Georgia. (1)

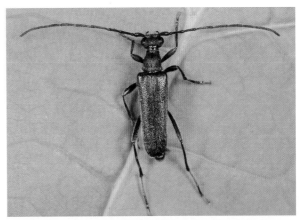

Judolia cordifera **(Olivier)** (8.0–12.0 mm) is robust with yellow elytra, each with a variable black spot and tipped with black. Antennae are not serrate and extend past middle (female) or nearly reaching elytra tips (male). Pronotum wider than long, convex, densely and minutely punctate and distinctly pubescent, with posterior angles sharp. Elytra with surface densely and minutely punctate and narrowly rounded black tips. Hind tibiae of male each with row of small teeth. Larvae develop in hickory (*Carya*). Diurnal adults found on flowers and vegetation in late spring and summer. New England to Georgia. (2)

395

Judolia montivagans **(Couper)** (7.0–12.0 mm) is black with yellow elytra with three variable black bands just behind base and middle, and apex. Pronotum convex, appearing dull, coarsely punctate with punctures running together, sparsely pubescent with sharp hind angles. Scutellum notched at tip. Elytral apices black, broadly rounded. Metatarsi uniformly dark. Larvae develop in conifers. Adults active in summer, found on flowers. Alaska, across Canada, New England; also Rocky Mountains south to New Mexico. (2)

Leptorhabdium pictum **(Haldeman)** (9.0–17.0 mm) is slender, nearly straight-sided, with head and pronotum darker, distinct tubercles on sides of prothorax, and stripes on elytra; appendages reddish brown. Eyes notched and coarsely faceted. Mouthparts with tips of palpi expanded. Antennae slightly longer (male) or shorter (female) than body. Pronotum somewhat constricted just inside front and base. Elytra with long, narrow stripes and dark spot on sides just behind middle, dense and coarse punctures at base finer and sparser toward rounded tips. Larvae develop in birch (*Betula*), dogwood (*Cornus*), oak (*Quercus*), and hickory (*Carya*). Adults active late spring and early summer, found on flowers of trees and shrubs; occasionally at light. Connecticut and New York to Georgia, west to Ohio and Louisiana. (1)

Lepturobosca (formerly *Cosmosalia*) *chrysocoma* **(Kirby)** (10.0–20.0 mm) is bright yellow with shiny golden-yellow setae on pronotum. Elytral surface usually yellow, sometimes with blackish tinge with usually dense pubescence lying flat and directed away from suture. Larva develops in pine (*Pinus*), spruce (*Picea*), aspen (*Populus*), and alder (*Alnus*). Adults active in summer on flowers. Across southern Canada and northeastern United States; also Cascades, Sierra Nevada, and Rocky Mountains to New Mexico. (1)

Lepturopsis biforis **(Newman)** (12.0–16.0 mm) is brownish with two dark spots at middle of elytra. Pronotum about as wide as long, sides rounded, strongly constricted in front and rear, hind angles not produced, and a deeply impressed line down middle. Elytra with bases lobed around scutellum, sides sinuate, moderately punctate. Legs slender, hind femora not extending beyond tips of elytra. Larvae develop in hardwoods and conifers. Adults active in summer, found on flowers of Queen Anne's lace (*Daucus carota*), hydrangea (*Hydrangea*), and spirea (*Spiraea*). New Brunswick to North Carolina, west to Ontario, Michigan, and Ohio. (1)

Metacmaeops vittata **(Swederus)** (6.0–8.0 mm) usually has an orange head and prothorax, sometimes darker. Margins of eyes entire, not notched. Antennae banded black and orange. Elytra yellowish with a dark stripe down middle of each elytron. Legs orange; male with toothlike projections on front tibiae. Adults found on flowers of dogwood (*Cornus*), hydrangea (*Hydrangea*), lily of the valley (*Mianthemum*), New Jersey tea (*Ceanothus americanus*), aruncus (*Aruncus*), and spirea (*Spiraea*) in late spring and early summer. Larvae develop in hardwoods, including tulip tree (*Liriodendron*). Québec and Ontario to Alabama, west to Michigan. (1)

Pidonia ruficollis **(Say)** (6.0–9.0 mm) is elongate, slender, shiny, and varies in color from all black to striped. Head large, black, sparsely punctured; antennae long, filiform in both sexes, with antennomere 3 longer than 1. Pronotum sparsely punctured, black or red. Elytra black or yellowish brown with black stripes down suture and sides. Abdomen with last ventrite notched with outside angles produced (male) or rounded (female). Adults active late spring and early summer, found on flowers such as elderberry (*Sambucus*), viburnum (*Viburnum*), dogwood (*Cornus*), and pear (*Pyrus*). Maritime Provinces and New England to northwest Georgia, west to Ontario and Indiana. (3)

***Pseudostrangalia cruentata* (Haldeman)** (8.0–12.0 mm)
is black with markings on sides and bases of hind femora
red. Pronotum shiny, wider than long with sides sinuate and
all angles distinct. Elytra broad with bases raised on
either side of scutellum, a long red spot on each side, and
tips distinctly diverging from each other. Larva unknown.
Adults active late spring and early summer, found on
flowers of dogwood (*Cornus*), buckeye (*Aesculus*),
rose (*Rosa*), hackberry (*Celtis*), oak (*Quercus*), cow
parsnip (*Heracleum*), and goatsbeard (*Tragopogon*);
attracted to light. New England and Québec to New York,
west to Ontario, Iowa, and Texas. (1)

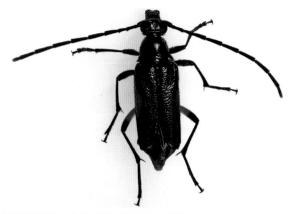

Stenelytrana* (fomerly *Leptura*) *emarginata
(Fabricius) (25.0–35.0 mm) is large, robust, black with
mostly bright reddish-orange elytra clothed in thick setae.
Antennae stout, somewhat serrate, extending past middle
of elytra (male) or to basal third (female). Elytra broader
at base than pronotum, smooth, with tips dark and broadly
notched. Larva develops in rotting hardwoods, including
beech (*Fagus*), elm (*Ulmus*), tulip tree (*Liriodendron*), tupelo
(*Nyssa*), and maple (*Acer*). Diurnal adults active spring and
summer, found on flowers and sap flows. Massachusetts to
Florida, west to Michigan, Kansas, and Texas. (1)

***Stenocorus cinnamopterus* (Randall)** (10.0–16.0 mm) is
elongate, narrow, dull reddish yellow-brown to brownish, and
strongly tapered to elytral tips. Female more densely clothed
in golden pubescence. Head broad with large, broadly
notched, and coarsely faceted eyes. Antennomere 3 distinctly
longer than 4. Pronotum densely punctate and pubescent.
Elytra smooth. Larvae feed in hydrangea (*Hydrangea*), black
cherry (*Prunus serotina*), and running strawberry bush
(*Euonymus obovatus*). Adults active spring through early
summer, found on hydrangea, plum (*Prunus*), and spindletree
(*Euonymus*); attracted to light. Massachusetts to Florida,
west to Iowa, Kansas, and Texas. (4)

***Stenocorus schaumii* (LeConte)** (17.0–30.0 mm) is light
to dark brown, finely pubescent, with dark gray or black
elytra and mostly black appendages. Head with eyes
broadly and shallowly notched, antennomere 3 longer
than 4. Pronotum shiny on top, with a prominent and
pointed bump on each side. Elytra dull and rough, with
humeri prominent. Legs with femora orange at center.
Larvae develop in ash (*Fraxinus*), beech (*Fagus*), maple
(*Acer*), and serviceberry (*Amelanchier*). Adults active late
spring and early summer, likely found feeding on flowers.
Québec and Massachusetts to Virginia, west to Manitoba,
Wisconsin, and Iowa. (3)

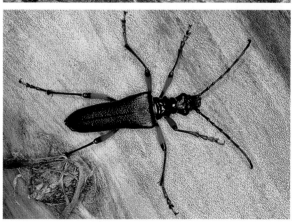

Stictoleptura canadensis (Olivier) (11.0–24.0 mm) is large with rounded pronotal angles, apically and basally impressed, subserrate antennae usually with yellow rings, and sharp elytral apices. Pronotum and elytra coarsely punctate. Elytra usually red and black, occasionally uniformly reddish. Larvae develop in fir (*Abies*), hemlock (*Tsuga*), pine (*Pinus*). Adults active in summer and found on flowers. Newfoundland to Pennsylvania, west to Ontario and Minnesota. (1)

Strangalepta abbreviata (Germar) (10.0–14.0 mm) sometimes has wholly black or mostly yellowish elytra, but most individuals have a pale stripe running down middle of each elytron. Pronotum somewhat globose, without restriction, or "collar," behind head. Males with small tubercle on inside of hind tibia. Larvae develop in various decaying conifers and hardwoods. Diurnal adults are found on flowers or resting on vegetation from late spring through summer. New Brunswick to Georgia, west to Ontario, Wisconsin, and Arkansas. (2)

Strangalia acuminata (Olivier) (8.0–12.0 mm) is very slender, tapered behind, with head, antennae, and prothorax all black. Elytra vary from mostly brownish with black margins in the north to all black in southern populations, more than three times as long as broad. Adults are found on spring flowers. Larvae develop in ninebark (*Physocarpus*), alder (*Alnus*), viburnum (*Viburnum*), hornbeam (*Carpinus*), and hophornbeam (*Ostrya*). Widespread in eastern United States to Ontario. (8)

Strangalia bicolor (Swederus) (11.0–15.0 mm) is elongate, slender, strongly tapered behind base angles of elytra, with head, appendages, and pronotum reddish, eyes and usually elytra all black. Antennae with distal antennomeres slender, not thicker than those at base. Elytra rarely dark only along side margins. Abdomen with last ventrite elongate and deeply notched. Legs of male with hind tibiae ridged along inside margins. Larvae develop in maple (*Acer*) and oak (*Quercus*). Adults active in early summer, found on flowers of New Jersey tea (*Ceanothus americanus*), rose (*Rosa*), hydrangea (*Hydrangea*), grape (*Vitis*). Eastern North America. (8)

***Strangalia famelica* Newman** (10.0–17.0 mm) is elongate, slender, and yellowish with dark markings. Antennae black, antennomeres uniformly slender. Pronotum bell-shaped with two long dark stripes and distinctly sharp hind angles. Elytra with two black spots along margin (male) or on top (female) at middle and tip. Abdomen with tip expanded, especially in male, and notched underneath, reddish in female. Legs with hind tibiae ridged along inside (male), or not (female). Larvae develop in oak (*Quercus*) and beech (*Fagus*). Adults active late spring and early summer, found on flowers of New Jersey tea (*Ceanothus americanus*), Queen Anne's lace (*Daucus carota*), dogwood (*Cornus*), hydrangea (*Hydrangea*), and rose (*Rosa*). East of Appalachian Mountains, from Massachusetts to Florida. (8)

***Strangalia luteicornis* (Fabricius)** (9.0–14.0 mm) is slender with body and antennae mostly pale, usually yellow or yellowish brown; females are more robust than males. Black spots on each side of head and two black bars on pronotum. Pronotum longer than wide, broadest at base. Elytra attenuated with tips obliquely truncate, each four variable bands or spots. Legs long, hind femora dark at tips. Larvae develop in wood of various shrubs and hardwood trees. Adults found on flowers in late spring and summer; occasionally attracted to lights. Ontario to Florida, west to Minnesota, Kansas, Arkansas, and Texas. (8)

***Strangalia sexnotata* Haldeman** (8.0–13.0 mm) is less elongate with body and antennae mostly yellowish or reddish and six black spots on on bristly pubescent elytra. Mid-Atlantic coast form with dark appendages, southeastern form sometimes with only antennal bases dark and pale legs. Females more robust than males. Adults active late spring and summer, found on flowers such as coneflower (*Rudbeckia*), goldenrod (*Solidago*), rubberweed (*Hymenoxys*), rose (*Rosa*), aster (*Aster*), honeycombhead (*Balduina*), false goldenaster (*Heterotheca*), thistle (*Cirsium*), and cliffrose (*Cowania*). North Carolina to Florida, west to Missouri and Arizona. (8)

Chestnut Bark Borer *Strophiona nitens* (Forster) (10.0–15.0 mm) is boldly marked in black and yellow, resembling *Typocerus*. Pronotum clothed in metallic yellow setae and distinctly constricted toward base with posterior angles more rounded than in *Typocerus*. Larvae feed and develop in living or dead hardwoods, including beech (*Fagus*), hickory (*Carya*), maple (*Acer*), and oak (*Quercus*). Adults found at light in late spring and early summer. Nova Scotia to Florida, west to Manitoba, Colorado, and Kansas. (1)

Trachysida mutabilis (Newman) (8.0–15.0 mm) has antennae inserted well away from eyes and in front of notch. Head, thorax, and abdomen coarsely punctured, with those on elytra evenly spaced. Color variable, ranging from all black to black with brownish elytra. Eggs deposited under bark and in cracks on decaying hardwoods, including maple (*Acer*), alder (*Alnus*), birch (*Betula*), beech (*Fagus*), poplar (*Populus*), oak (*Quercus*), and willow (*Salix*). Diurnal adults are found on flowers or resting on vegetation of a variety of shrubs from spring through midsummer. Prince Edward Island to Georgia, west to Alberta, Minnesota, Iowa, and Missouri. (2)

Trigonarthris minnesotana (Casey) (15.0–18.0 mm) is stout and has a densely pubescent and inflated pronotum lacking bumps, or tubercles, on the sides. Last abdominal sternite feebly emarginate in male, feebly and longitudinally ridged in female. Larvae develop in decaying branches of conifers and hardwoods. Adults found on flowers and leaves of shrubs in summer. Maritime Provinces and Québec to Florida, west to Manitoba, Minnesota, and Missouri. (3)

400

Typocerus acuticauda acuticauda Casey (9.0–14.0 mm) is elongate, robust, similar to *T. velutinus*, but usually with pale elytral bands restricted to base and tip. Antennae reaching apical fourth (male) or just past middle (female) of elytron. Pronotum wider than long, surface with scattered large and small punctures concealed by long, yellowish, almost erect setae, and a fine bare midline. Elytra finely and densely punctate, each with four light spots often missing, tips oblique and sharply pointed. Adults active late spring and early summer, found on flowers, e.g., spirea (*Spiraea*). Nova Scotia and New England to Georgia, west to Iowa. *Typocerus a. standishi* Knull is darker with yellow bands; Mississippi to Kansas and Texas. (9)

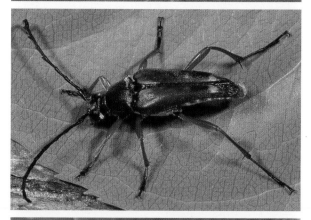

Typocerus velutinus (Olivier) (10.0–16.0 mm) is elongate, slender, tapered behind humeri of banded elytra. Antennae black. Pronotum pubescent, with densely pubescent bands of golden setae along anterior and posterior margins. Elytra reddish brown with variably reduced yellow bands and spots, apices obliquely truncate. Adults visit flowers in late spring and summer. Larvae develop in deciduous hardwoods, including oak (*Quercus*), hickory (*Carya*), beech (*Fagus*), and cottonwood (*Populus*). Nova Scotia to Florida, west to Saskatchewan, Minnesota, Kansas, and Mississippi. (9)

Typocerus zebra (Olivier) (10.0–16.0 mm) is elongate, robust, and black with distinct yellow markings on elytra. Antennae extending to apical fourth (male) or just past middle (female). Pronotum is coarsely punctate and bordered on all sides with dense golden setae. Elytra narrow posteriorly, with four yellow bands broken at suture, yellow marks at base triangular. Legs mostly black, tarsi light brown. Larvae develop in decaying pine (*Pinus*) logs and stumps. Adults active late spring and early summer, found on many flowers including New Jersey tea (*Ceanothus americanus*), Queen Anne's lace (*Daucus carota*), dogwood (*Cornus*), hydrangea (*Hydrangea*), and rose (*Rosa*). New Jersey to Florida, west to Ohio and eastern Texas. (9)

Xestoleptura octonotata (Say) (11.0–14.0 mm) is slender, shining, and black, with four yellow triangular spots on each elytron. Pronotum convex, about as wide as long, narrower in front than at base, with sides broadly rounded, and depressions across front and rear margins. Elytral markings sometimes reduced in size or middle spots joined. Hind tarsi pale. Adults active in late spring and early summer, found on flowers. Massachusetts to South Carolina, west to Ontario, Wisconsin, Iowa, and Mississippi. (1)

401

Rhagium inquisitor (Linnaeus) (9.0–21.0 mm) is variable in color and size, but short antennae, produced side margins of pronotum, and strongly ridged elytra are distinctive. Eggs deposited in bark crevices in spring and larvae bore through bark and into cambium of various conifers, especially pine (*Pinus*); development take two years. Pupation occurs in ring of coarse wood fibers under bark. Adults overwinter in pupal rings or under loose bark in winter and early spring; on pine logs in spring and summer. Often collected in Lindgren funnel traps. Northern Hemisphere; widespread in North America. (1)

Arhopalus foveicollis (Haldeman) (14.0–30.0 mm) is elongate, robust, brownish to black. Antennae reaching apical third (male) or basal fourth (female) of elytra. Head with mandibles not prominent, eyes shallowly notched. Antennomere 2 long. Pronotum wider than long, with sides rounded and not sharply margined, and a pair of sharp, curved impressions. Elytra long, slightly narrowed toward rounded tip, and faint ridges. Front tibia tipped with only one spur, hind tarsomere 3 deeply notched for about half its length. Larvae develop in dead pine (*Pinus*) and spruce (*Picea*). Nocturnal adults active in summer; attracted to light. Widespread in central and eastern North America. (2)

Asemum striatum **(Linnaeus)** (10.0–18.0 mm) is dull black and brown with surface densely, finely pubescent. Eyes with finely granulated facets. Subapical antennomeres short with second antennomere subequal to or slightly shorter in length than ninth. Elytral surface with faint ridges. Larvae develop in conifers, including pine (*Pinus*), larch (*Larix*), and fir (*Abies*). Adults are found under bark and at the bases of conifer trunks at night from spring through midsummer; also attracted to light at night. Across southern Canada, widespread in United States, except for the Great Plains. (2)

Small Cedar-bark Borer *Atimia confusa* **(Say)** (6.0–9.0 mm) is short, robust, and black with short gray pubescence lying on surface; legs brown with tarsi darker. Eyes notched, partly surrounding antennal bases. Pronotum wider than long, with four bare stripes. Elytra with bare spots without punctures forming irregular patterns and tips broadly notched. Larvae develop under bark of dead or dying redcedar (*Juniperus*), cypress (*Cupressus*), bald cypress (*Taxodium*), arborvitae (*Thuja*), and cedar (*Chamaecyparis*). Adults active spring and fall; attracted to light. Widespread in eastern North America. (1)

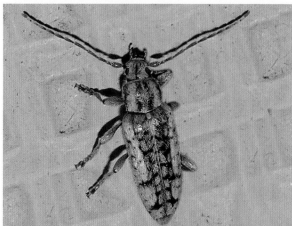

Neospondylis upiformis **(Mannerheim)** (8.0–20 mm) is elongate, robust, coarsely punctate, and shining black. Head with weakly notched eyes, long mandibles, and short antennae; antennae of female not reaching base of pronotum. Prothorax widest toward front, without keeled margins along sides. Elytra with two or more faintly raised ridges. Legs short, with front tibiae expanded, tarsi distinctly 5-5-5, tarsomere 4 small. Larvae probably develop in pine (*Pinus*) or fir (*Abies*). Adults fly during day, sometimes attracted to shiny surfaces. In east from Ontario, Québec, and Great Lakes region; also West. (1)

Scaphinus muticus **(Fabricius)** (13.0–18.0 mm) is elongate, robust, reddish brown to brown, and coarsely punctate. Head with mandibles sharp, longer than head, and antennae barely reaching (female) or surpassing (male) middle of pronotum. Pronotum with irregular and indistinct polished areas. Elytra with three more or less distinct ridges, with tips together broadly rounded. Larvae develop in pine (*Pinus*). Adults active in summer, one record on bald cypress (*Taxodium distichum*); attracted to light. Virginia to Florida, west to Arkansas and Louisiana. (1)

Necydalis mellita (Say) (12.0–22.0 mm) is long, very slender, wasplike in flight, reddish or blackish, with short elytra. Antennae slender, long as body. Pronotum somewhat cylindrical, longer than wide, and narrower than head. Elytra nearly flat. Appendages, elytra, and abdomen partially or completely dull reddish yellow-brown. Legs long and slender. Larva develops in sound, dead heartwood of oak (*Quercus*). Adults active spring through summer. Ontario to Florida, west to Iowa and Mississippi. (1)

Achryson surinamum (Linnaeus) (10.0–23.0 mm) is elongate, almost cylindrical, and yellowish brown with undulating black marks and spots. Head slightly narrower than prothorax, antennomeres not armed with spines. Prothorax longer than wide, sides broadly rounded. Elytra coarsely punctate and somewhat granulate. Larvae prefer woody legumes as hosts, including locust (*Robinia*); also elm (*Ulmus*) and hackberry (*Celtis*). Adults active spring through summer; attracted to light. Atlantic coast and southwestern United States and Caribbean to Argentina; also recorded from Midwest. (1)

403

Cabbage Palm Longhorn *Osmopleura chamaeropis* (Horn) (19.0–22.0 mm) is elongate, narrowed at both ends, with white stripes on head and pronotum. Elytra much wider at base than pronotum, reddish brown, suture darker, with long pale pubescence, surface without bands or spots, and tips rounded. Abdomen with fifth ventrite shorter (male) or longer (female) than fourth. Larvae develop in cabbage palmetto (*Sabal palmetto*). Seldom-collected adults sometimes locally abundant, active in May and June, usually found near bases of living stems on larval host plants in pine-palmetto woodlands. Georgia, Florida, Texas. (1)

Cyrtophorus verrucosus (Olivier) (7.0–11.0 mm) is antlike with varying amounts of red. Basal portion of antennae usually reddish; those of female reach basal third of elytra. Black pronotum strongly convex. Elytra with pronounced knobs at base, a pair of oblique white lines of setae in front of middle, and a thin, white transverse line just behind middle. Larvae develop mostly in hardwoods, also in pine (*Pinus*). Adults found on spring flowers; attracted to light and bait traps in spring through early summer. Across southern Canada and eastern United States to Florida and Kansas. (1)

Tilloclytus geminatus **(Haldeman)** (5.0–7.0 mm) is small, antlike, and blackish or reddish with apical half of elytra and abdomen blackish. Antennomere 4 shorter than 3 or 5. Pronotum strongly convex, domelike, with short, parallel stripes of white setae at base. Elytra each with a tubercle at base and narrow oblique bands lacking any setae outlined with single row of white setae in basal fourth and at rounded tips. Larvae mine dead branches of deciduous hardwoods; also pine (*Pinus*). Adults active spring and early summer, found on larval host plants. Ontario to Florida, west to Ohio, Missouri, and Texas. (1)

Plinthocoelium suaveolens suaveolens **(Linnaeus)** (29.0–38.0 mm) is metallic green, blue, or bronze and tinted with bronze or coppery luster, especially on pronotum. Legs always with red or reddish-orange femora and black tibiae and tarsi. Larva develops in trunks and roots of gum bully (*Sideroxylon lanuginosum*), also water tupelo (*Nyssa aquatica*) and mulberry (*Morus*). Diurnal adults active late spring and summer, found on trunks of larval host plants and sapping hickory (*Carya*); attracted to fermenting baits. Delaware to Florida, west to Missouri and eastern Texas. (1)

Meriellum proteus **(Kirby)** (10.0–16.0 mm) is elongate, flattened, somewhat parallel, and black with bronze, bluish, or violet tints. Antennae shorter than body in both sexes, antennomere 2 twice as long as broad, remainder not expanded. Pronotum wider than long, constricted at base, with sides rounded, smooth with sides finely (male) or coarsely (female) punctate. Elytra with yellow ridges variable, most conspicuous at base. Legs wholly or partly yellow-brown, tips of femora and tibiae often dark. Larvae develop under bark of dead spruce (*Picea*) and pine (*Pinus*). Adults active in early summer. Alaska, across Canada and northern United States. (1)

Phymatodes amoenus **(Say)** (5.0–7.0 mm) is reddish brown with darker mouthparts, antennae, and tibiae, bright shiny blue elytra, and pale pubescence. Antennae shorter than body in both sexes, antennomere 2 less than twice as long as broad. Eyes deeply divided, upper and lower portions connected by one or two rows of facets. Sides of pronotum rounded. Antennae and tibiae often blackish. Legs with femora clubbed, first tarsomere of hind leg slender, twice as long as broad. Larva develops in dead grapevines (*Vitis*), tightly packing their mines with frass. Adults active late spring and early summer. Eastern Canada to Florida, west to Minnesota and Oklahoma. (5)

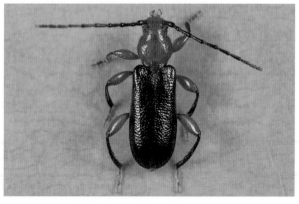

Tanbark Borer *Phymatodes testaceus* **(Linnaeus)**
(8.0–17.0 mm) is elongate, somewhat flattened, shining,
unmarked, and with yellowish-brown or reddish yellowish-
brown body. Antennae shorter than body in female,
second antennomere half or more as long as third. Eyes
moderately notched, upper and lower lobes connected
by more than three rows of facets. Pronotum with distinct
raised swellings, punctate, and smooth between punctures.
Antennae shorter than body in both sexes, antennomere 2
less than twice as long as broad. Elytra yellowish brown or
blue, very finely punctate. Larva develops in oak (*Quercus*),
beech (*Fagus*), apple (*Malus*), cherry (*Prunus*), and hickory
(*Carya*). Adults active spring and summer, attracted to light.
Europe; widely established in eastern North America. (5)

Pronocera collaris **(Kirby)** (9.0–14.0 mm) is black with
reddish pronotum, with weakly notched eyes barely
surrounding antennal bases, and slender femora. Pronotum
smooth, shiny, wider than long. Elytra with bluish or
greenish luster, densely punctured, and evenly clothed in
long, erect, pale setae. Larva develops in spruce (*Picea*)
and pine (*Pinus*). Adults active in summer on flowers.
Alaska, Canada, Pacific Northwest, Rocky Mountains
to New Mexico, New England to North Carolina, west to
Minnesota. (1)

Ropalopus sanguinicollis **(Horn)** (10.0–17.0 mm) is
clothed in black pubescence, coarsely punctured, and dull
black with broad, red pronotum. Antennae reaching apical
fifth (male) or middle (female) of elytra. Pronotum twice as
wide as long, coarsely punctured, and sparsely clothed in
setae on top, more densely so on sides. Legs with femora
swollen, club-shaped. Larvae mine under the bark of living
wild cherry (*Prunus*); two years required to complete life
cycle. Adults active in early summer. Maritime Provinces and
New England to Virginia, west to Manitoba and Ohio. (1)

Calloides nobilis **(Harris)** (19.0–24.0 mm) is robust,
dull, and dark brown with variable yellow markings rarely
absent. Antennae extending to middle of elytra (male), or
shorter (female), antennomeres without spines. Pronotum
convex, smooth, wider than long, widest at middle, sides
broadly rounded, not sharply margined or keeled. Elytra
parallel-sided with tips rounded. Larvae develop in stumps
and bases of recently dead or dying ash (*Fraxinus*), oak
(*Quercus*), and chestnut (*Castanea*). Adults active late
spring and early summer. New England and Québec to
Georgia, west to Manitoba, Illinois, and Missouri. (1)

Clytus marginicollis **Laporte & Gory** (6.0–10.0 mm) is elongate, robust, dark brown or black, hairy and wasplike with distinctive color pattern. Pronotum nearly round, finely and roughly punctate. Elytra paler at base, with four reddish-yellow crossbands, and rounded at tips. Legs light brown. Larva feed under bark of recently broken or cut pine (*Pinus*) and spruce (*Picea*) branches. Adults active spring and early summer. Maritime Provinces and Québec to Florida, west to Ohio and Mississippi. (2)

Clytus ruricola **(Olivier)** (10.0–15.0 mm) is black and boldly marked with yellow bands and spots, including a U-shaped band on middle of elytra. Front of head without ridges and basal antennomeres without spines. Pronotum convex, densely punctured, without ridges, and rounded on sides. Adults are found resting on vegetation in late spring and early summer. Legless larvae develop in decaying hardwoods, especially maple (*Acer*). Nova Scotia and New Brunswick to South Carolina, west to Manitoba, Wisconsin, and Tennessee. (2)

Sugar Maple Borer *Glycobius specious* **(Say)** (19.0–28.0 mm) is large, robust, and brilliant black and yellow. Head bright yellow. Pronotum black with two yellow bands broken at middle. Elytra with five dark yellow bands, middle band W-shaped, with two black dots near tips. Legs yellow. Larvae take two years to develop in maple (*Acer*) and are important pests of sugar maple. Tunneling activities impair maple syrup production, often girdling or killing smaller branches and younger trees; healed wounds leave unsightly ridges and swellings on branches that survive. Adults active in summer, found on maple trunks. Historical range Maritime Provinces to mountains of North Carolina, west to Ontario, Minnesota, eastern Kansas, and Missouri; now extirpated from much of Midwest. (1)

Megacyllene decora **(Olivier)** (12.0–25.0 mm) is elongate with contrasting black and dark yellow to almost orange markings and variable broad bands across elytra; appendages brown or reddish black, or with no bands. Pronotum with middle band, if present, not reaching sides. Elytra each with prominent, shining ridge along suture, bands not joined on sides, usually with broad yellow band across basal one- or two-thirds followed by black bands of medium thickness, sometimes with finer bands along entire length. Adults active in summer. New York to Florida, west to Alberta, South Dakota, Kansas, and New Mexico. (3)

Locust Borer *Megacyllene robiniae* **(Forster)** (11.0–28.0 mm) is very wasplike in appearance and marked with yellow elytral bands narrower than black bands. Anterior pronotal margin with distinct band of yellow pubescence; sides of last thoracic segment mostly yellow. Larvae develop in black locust (*Robinia pseudoacacia*). Adults found on goldenrod (*Solidago*) in daytime during September and October. Maritime Provinces to Florida, west to Québec, Ontario, and Great Plains. (3)

Neoclytus mucronatus **(Fabricius)** (7.5–23.0 mm) is boldly marked, elytra and tips of hind femora both with distinct spines. Pronotum with many ridges across surface, margined at apex and base with thin line of yellow pubescence, but without band of pubescence across middle. Larvae develop in dead or dying hickory (*Carya*), briefly feeding beneath bark before moving into heartwood. Adults active in summer and attracted to light at night. Ontario to Florida, west to Nebraska, and Texas. (8)

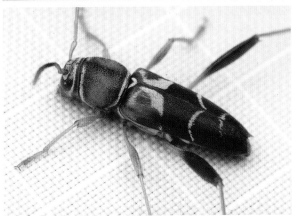

Sarosesthes fulminans **(Fabricius)** (12.0–22.0 mm) has a distinctive eyespot on the pronotum and angulate bands on elytra. Larvae tunnel under bark and in sapwood of hardwoods, especially chestnut (*Castanea*), oak (*Quercus*), and walnut (*Juglans*). Adults are attracted to light and bait traps in late spring and summer. Québec and Ontario to North Carolina, west to Minnesota, Iowa, and Kansas. (1)

Gall-making Maple Borer *Xylotrechus aceris* **Fisher** (10.0–14.0 mm) has pronotum and underside of thorax with white patches of pubesence and anterior pronotal margin with pubescent patch extended to lateral margin. Adults attracted to lights in summer. Larvae develop in the trunks of living maples, especially red maple (*Acer rubra*). Southeastern Canada to Georgia, west to Michigan and Mississippi. (9)

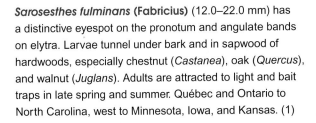

Xylotrechus colonus (Fabricius) (8.0–15.0 mm) has elytra with broad, pale markings; humerus enclosed in a narrow yellow band, and apices obliquely truncate. Pronotum with patches of yellow pubescence, surface sometimes reddish. Larvae develop in many species of deciduous hardwoods. Adults occasionally attracted to lights in spring and summer. Maritime Provinces to Florida, west to Ontario, Minnesota, and eastern Texas. (9)

Xylotrechus sagittatus (Germar) (12.0–25.0 mm) is brownish with pale pubescence mainly along elytral suture. Sides of pronotum evenly rounded. Larvae feed and develop in coniferous trees, such as pine (*Pinus*), fir (*Abies*), and spruce (*Picea*). Adults are found under bark of dead trees or at lights. Québec and Maine to Florida, west to Manitoba, Minnesota, Colorado, and Arizona. (9)

Maple Dryobius *Dryobius sexnotatus* Linsley (20.0–26.0 mm) is elongate, robust, and dark brown or black with golden yellow bands across head, pronotum, and elytra. Larvae take two to three years to develop in heartwood of mature living, dying, or solid standing dead sugar maple (*Acer saccharum*), sometimes using beech (*Fagus*), elm (*Ulmus*), or basswood (*Tilia*). Diurnal adults most active in summer, found on or under bark of larval host. Species appears to be in decline. Pennsylvania to Virginia, west to Michigan, Kansas, and Louisiana. (1)

Eburia quadrigeminata (Say) (12.0–24.0 mm) is elongate, robust, sparsely pubescent with punctures visible, and mostly light brown. Head with eyes deeply notched, antennae extended beyond (male) or reaching tips (female) of elytron. Pronotum coarsely punctate, with two dark calluses, sides each with single spine. Elytra long, coarsely and densely punctured, each with two raised elongate ivory spots at base and middle connected by a faint pair of ridges, and tips with two spines. Larvae develop in dry heartwood of oak (*Quercus*), hickory (*Carya*), ash (*Fraxinus*), maple (*Acer*), and honeylocust (*Gleditsia*). Adults attracted to light in summer. Ontario to Florida, west to Kansas and Texas. (5)

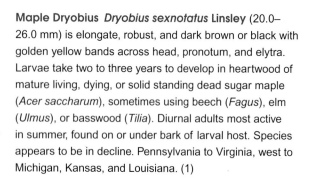

Oak Twig Pruner *Anelaphus parallelus* (Newman) (8.0–20.0 mm) is elongate, very slender, and dark brown with pubescence on elytra appearing striped. Antennomeres 3–4 with short spines and about equal in length. Pronotum with sides only weakly expanded at middle and a short shiny raised callus down middle, male slightly broader and more granulate than female. Elytra with narrow lines lacking pubescence, and tips each with two sharp spines. Larvae develop in twigs of many deciduous hardwoods. Adults active spring and summer; attracted to light. Maritime Provinces and New England to Florida, west to Manitoba, Kansas, and Texas. (5)

Twig Pruner *Anelaphus villosus* (Fabricius) (12.0–20.0 mm) is slender, reddish brown, and sparsely and evenly mottled with small patches of off-white setae. Antennomere 3 longer than 4. Pronotum as long as broad with sides weakly rounded. Elytra each tipped with pair of spines. Tip of abdomen rounded. Larvae hatch from eggs laid on branch tips of oak (*Quercus*) and other deciduous trees and shrubs and mine down stems. Adults attracted to light in late spring and summer. Maritime Provinces and New England to Florida, west to Manitoba, Wisconsin, and Texas, Arizona. (6)

409

Spined Bark Borer *Elaphidion mucronatum* (Say) (13.0–20.0 mm) is elongate, brown to dark brown, and irregularly clothed in dense brown pubescence. Antennae extend past tips of elytra (male), or not (female), spined antennomeres with single spine, spine of antennomere 3 usually about half length of 4. Elytra not striped, with some patches of exposed exoskeleton, and tips each with two sharp spines. Legs with tips of middle and hind femora spined. Larvae develop in dead branches of deciduous trees and shrubs, also bald cypress (*Taxodium distichum*). Adults active spring and summer; attracted to light. Widespread in eastern North America. (5)

Red Oak Borer *Enaphalodes rufulus* (Haldeman) (15.0–28.0 mm) is uniformly reddish brown and densely clothed in golden setae; patches of setae sometimes rubbed off. Antennomeres 3–5 each with single spine; male antennae twice as long as body, female's about as long. Pronotum much wider than head, sides broadly rounded. Elytra each tipped with pair of spines. Larvae mine living oak (*Quercus*) and are serious pests of managed timber; sometimes attack maple (*Acer*); two years required to complete life cycle. Adults nocturnal, attracted to light at night in summer; occasionally found at sapping wounds. New England and Québec to Florida, west to Ontario, Minnesota, Oklahoma, and Texas. (4)

Parelaphidion aspersum **(Haldeman)** (14.0–21.0 mm) has spines on antennae and tips of elytra. Pronotum with long, shiny callus in middle tapering toward head. Males with antennae long and extending about three articles beyond elytra, fourth article shorter than scape, and articles 6–9 each as long as third; female antennae long as body. Larvae develop in hickory (*Carya*) and oak (*Quercus*). Adults found at night on standing dead trunks of beech (*Fagus*), hackberry (*Celtis*), and oak in summer through early fall; also attracted to light and traps for wood-boring insects. Québec and Ontario to Florida, west to Iowa and Texas. (2)

Branch Pruner *Psyrassa unicolor* **(Randall)** (7.5–13.0 mm) is long, slender, and uniformly brownish yellow. Antennae extend past elytra, antennomeres not ridged, spines on tips of 2 and 3 nearly equal. Pronotum smooth, shining, longer than broad, and widest at middle. Elytra clothed in short setae. Legs with middle and hind femora gradually expanded at tips. Larvae develop in deciduous trees and shrubs, including oak (*Quercus*), hickory (*Carya*), walnut (*Juglans*), beech (*Fagus*), mulberry (*Mora*), and redbud (*Cercis*); girdle branches at or near node. Nocturnal adults active in summer and attracted to light. Québec and Ontario to South Carolina, west Minnesota, Kansas, and Texas. (2)

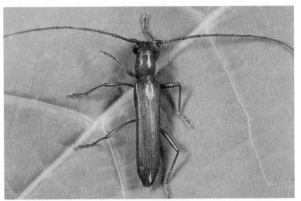

Round-necked Romulus Longhorn Beetle *Romulus globosus* **Knull** (29.0–35.0 mm) is elongate, robust, dark reddish brown with head and pronotum darker; antennomeres and elytral tips without spines. Prothorax smooth, round, convex, with sharp depression down middle at base flanked by slight elongate pubescent depressions. Elytra at base wider than prothorax, with tips broadly notched. Legs thick. Larval plant hosts unknown. Adults active May through July, probably in sandhill scrub habitats; attracted to light; seldom collected. Peninsular Florida. (1)

Stenosphenus notatus **(Olivier)** (9.0–16.0 mm) has a red pronotum with black spot (sometimes nearly absent) and shiny black elytra clothed in short white setae. Larvae breed in dead limbs of hickory and pecan (*Carya*), sometimes hackberry (*Celtis*). Adults found on vegetation and at light in late spring and early summer. Québec and Ontario to Florida, west to Minnesota and Texas. (1)

Hesperophanes pubescens (Haldeman)
(15.0–22.0 mm) is elongate, robust, pale light brown
without spines or other prominent surface features.
Antennae extended past elytral tips (male) or not (female).
Pronotum with pubescence uniformly pale in vaguely
whorled pattern. Elytra long, coarse punctures at base
becoming finer at tips, with sides somewhat straight and
parallel, and tips rounded. Larval habits unknown. Adults
uncommon, active in summer; attracted to light. Québec
to Georgia, west to Ontario, Minnesota, Missouri, and
Alabama. (1)

Tylonotus bimaculatus **Haldeman** (9.0–18.0 mm)
is elongate, somewhat broad, flattened, and dark brown
to blackish. Antennae reach middle (female) or about as
long as body (male). Pronotum rounded on sides, surface
dull, with three elevated and smooth ridges, and sparsely
covered in fine pale setae. Elytra each usually with pale
areas in front of middle and near tips, coarsely punctate.
Legs with femora mostly pale, darker at tips. Larvae feed
and develop living and dead ash (*Fraxinus*) and privet
(*Ligustrum*); also elm (*Ulmus*), hickory (*Carya*), walnut
(*Juglans*), and birch (*Betula*). Adults active late spring
and summer. Québec to Florida, west to Minnesota,
Kansas, and southeastern Arizona. (2)

Heterachthes quadrimaculatus **Haldeman**
(7.0–12.0 mm) is elongate, slender, and very shiny yellowish
brown to reddish brown, without ridges on antennae or
tibiae. Eyes coarsely faceted. Pronotum almost twice as
long as wide, almost cylindrical. Elytra with a pair of pale
spots at basal third and usually at apical third. Femora
straight, gradually expanded outward. Larvae develop
in hickory and pecan (*Carya*), tulip tree (*Liriodendron*),
and oak (*Quercus*). Adults active in summer. Québec and
Ontario to Florida, west to Iowa, Kansas, and Louisiana. (3)

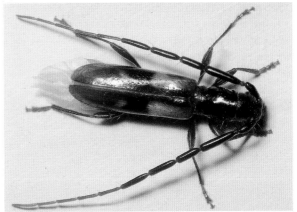

Methia necydalea (Fabricius) (5.0–9.0 mm) is
elongate, very slender, brown with short partly or wholly
yellowish-brown elytra and long antennae. Eyes deeply
notched, almost completely divided. Pronotum coarsely
punctate, slightly wider than long, widest at middle, with
constriction at base. Elytra about 4.5 times longer than
pronotum and clothed in pale pubescence. Larva develops
in bald cypress (*Taxodium*), oak (*Quercus*). Adults active
late spring and summer; attracted to light. Virginia to
Florida, west to Arkansas and Texas; Caribbean. (1)

Molorchus bimaculatus bimaculatus Say (4.0–12.0 mm) is small, slender, with short, bicolored elytra with black margins. Head and thorax black. Pronotum elytra coarsely, closely punctate. Legs with slender femora clubbed at tips. Larvae mine branches of various plants, including common hackberry (*Celtis occidentalis*), redbud (*Cercis canadensis*), and silver maple (*Acer saccharinum*). Adults found on various flowering shrubs, including dogwood (*Cornus*), and attracted to lights in spring and early summer. Eastern North America. *Molorchus b. celti* Knull larger, more slender, pronotum more finely punctate, northeast; *M. b. corni* Haldeman with reddish prothorax; *M. b. semiustus* (Newman) mostly reddish brown-yellow, abdomen partly or mostly dark, Gulf states. (1)

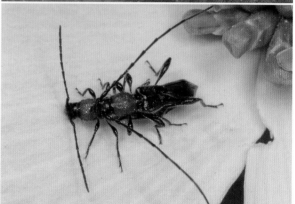

TOP RIGHT: *Molorchus b. bimaculatus.*
BOTTOM RIGHT: *Molorchus b. corni.*

412

Obrium maculatum (Olivier) (4.0–8.0 mm) is shiny pale yellowish brown with distinctive brown markings on elytra. Pronotum strongly constricted at base. Larvae develop in branches of many hardwood trees and shrubs, including oak (*Quercus*), pecan (*Carya illinoiensis*), hawthorn (*Crataegus*), river birch (*Betula nigra*), black cherry (*Prunus serotina*), and hackberry (*Celtis*). Nocturnal adults active spring through early fall and attracted to light. New York to Florida, west to Iowa, Missouri, and southern California; Mexico to El Salvador. (3)

Oeme rigida (Say) (6.0–20.0 mm) is long, slender, and uniformly pale yellowish brown to blackish. Head coarsely punctate, about as wide as pronotum, with long, slender antennae clothed in bristly setae. Pronotum is strongly constricted at base. Elytra about as wide at base as at middle, with three weak ridges and mostly uniform pubescence with very few suberect setae. Larva usually develops in juniper (*Juniperus*) and bald cypress (*Taxodium distichum*), rarely pine (*Pinus*). Nocturnal adults are uncommonly encountered in summer and attracted to light. Connecticut to Florida, west to Ohio, Missouri, and eastern Texas. (1)

Callimoxys sanguinicollis (Olivier) (7.0–12.0 mm) has distinctive, tapering, paddle-shaped elytra only partially covering abdomen, and slender club-shaped femora. Pronotum of male mostly black, usually red in female. One or more pairs of legs bicolored; hind tibiae of male with many teeth on outer margin. Larvae develop in hickory (*Carya*), oak (*Quercus*), cherry (*Prunus*), and probably walnut (*Juglans*). Adults active in spring and early summer, found on flowers of *Ceanothus*, dogwood (*Cornus*), and other vernal blooming trees and shrubs. Québec and Ontario to Florida, west to Michigan, Kansas, and Texas. (1)

Rhopalophora longipes (Say) (6.0–9.0 mm) is very distinctive, with a long, slender body and legs. Head and appendages black. Pronotum longer than wide, reddish with faint stripes of white pubescence on sides. Elytra grayish and distinctly punctured. Legs with femora club-shaped. Larvae feed and develop in small branches of redbud (*Cercis canadensis*) and dogwood (*Cornus*). Adults found on flowers and vegetation in spring. Pennsylvania to Florida, west to Michigan, Kansas, and Texas. (1)

Smodicum cucujiforme (Say) (7.0–10.0 mm) is small, pale, and extremely flat. Adults are found under bark and at lights in summer. Eggs laid in exposed wood crevices of deciduous trees, including locust (*Robinia*), hickory (*Carya*), oak (*Quercus*), beech (*Fagus*), hawthorn (*Crataegus*), willow (*Salix*), and cottonwood (*Populus*). Larvae chew meandering galleries in heartwood and pack them with fine granular frass; stored lumber and cabins are sometimes damaged. Adults attracted to light in summer. Ontario and Massachusetts to Florida, west to Wisconsin, Iowa, and Texas. (1)

Euderces picipes (Fabricius) (5.0–9.0 mm) is usually entirely black in northern populations, sometimes reddish. Eyes nearly divided, lobes connected by thin line. Pronotum distinctly grooved. Pale elytral bars appear as raised ridges. Larvae mine under the bark of various hardwoods, including hickory (*Carya*), black walnut (*Juglans nigra*), chestnut (*Castanea*), oak (*Quercus*), elm (*Ulmus*), redbud (*Cercis canadensis*), locust (*Robinia*), and dogwood (*Cornus*). Adults visit flowers or rest on vegetation in late spring and early summer. Ontario and Québec to Florida, west to Minnesota, Nebraska, and Texas. (2)

Euderces pini (Olivier) (6.0–9.0 mm) is pale reddish brown with apical third of elytra and abodomen blackish or black, rarely all blackish with pale reddish-brown antennae. Eyes completely divided. Antennae and legs reddish. Male antennae longer than body by two to three antennomeres; antennae reach apical third of elytra in female. Pronotum distinctly grooved. Larvae develop in pecan (*Carya illinoiensis*), flowering dogwood (*Cornus florida*), osage orange (*Maclura pomifera*), western soapberry (*Sapindus saponaria drummondii*), mescal bean (*Sophora secundiflora*), and winged elm (*Ulmus alata*). Adults on flowers and tree trunks in spring. New Jersey and Pennsylvania to Georgia, west to Kansas and Texas. (2)

Banded Hickory Borer *Knulliana cincta cincta* (Drury) (15.0–30.0 mm) is dull reddish brown with pale bands on elytra. Pronotum, femora, and elytra with distinct spines. Male antennae much longer than elytra, female's barely reach tips. Elytra faintly ridged, each tipped with pair of spines. Middle and hind femora tipped with spines. Larvae mine dry, dead branches and limbs of hickory (*Carya*), walnut (*Juglans*), apple (*Malus*), oak (*Quercus*), and willow (*Salix*); two or three years required to complete development. Québec and Ontario to Georgia, west to Minnesota, Kansas, and Texas. *K. c. spinifera* (Fabricius) (Florida to Mississippi) similar, but darker without elytral markings. (1)

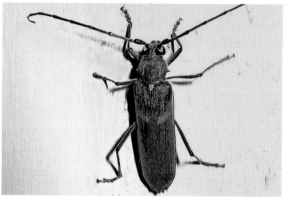

Ancylocera bicolor (Olivier) (8.5–12.3 mm) is elongate, somewhat cylindrical, parallel-sided, and blackish or reddish black with bright red elytra and abdomen. Head coarsely punctate, antennae of male exceeding elytral tips by at least four antennomeres. Prothorax longer than wide, cylindrical, finely punctate with irregularly placed larger punctures. Elytra nearly three times longer than wide. Legs slender with femora clubbed at tips, hind femora each armed with a spine. Larvae develop in hickory (*Carya*) and oak (*Quercus*). Adults active spring and summer and early summer. Virginia to Florida, west to southern Texas. (1)

Batyle suturalis (Say) (7.0–9.0 mm) is slender, parallel-sided, and shiny red with mostly black appendages. Antennae black, reaching tips of elytra (male) or not (female). Pronotum wider than long, convex with sides rounded, and constricted at base. Elytra with coarse, well-separated punctures and rounded tips, occasionally black along suture. Legs with femora red with black tips. Larvae develop in dead twigs and branches of hickory (*Carya*) and oak (*Quercus*). Adults active spring and summer, found on flowers. Connecticut to Florida, west to Saskatchewan, Montana, Nebraska, Texas. (2)

Elytroleptus floridanus **(LeConte)** (8.0–11.0 mm) is elongate, flat, and black with stripes on pronotum; humeri and side margins of elytra reddish orange. Elytra each with three ridges, spaces between coarsely and roughly punctured, with sides straight or slightly divergent toward rounded tips and turned-under margin narrow and extending to tips. Larva develops in oak (*Quercus*). Adults found on oaks in late spring and early summer; mimic and predator of net-winged beetle (*Lyconotus lateralis*), possibly to obtain lycid's defensive chemicals. Maine and southern Ontario to Florida, west to Oklahoma and Texas. (1)

Purpuricenus axillaris **Haldeman** (10.8–18.5 mm) is robust, cylindrical, sparsely pubescent, and black, with basal third of elytra red. Pronotum convex, wider than long, front narrower than base, surface punctured and weakly callused, middle callus without polished line in front, and sides with small, but distinct bumps. Elytra finely and sparsely punctate at base, with faintly indicated ridges, and sutural angles at tips weakly or not toothed. Larvae develop in hickory (*Carya*). Adults active late spring and summer, attracted to fermenting bait traps. Massachusetts to Florida, west to Missouri and Oklahoma. (3)

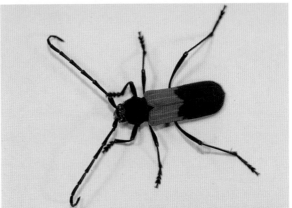

415

Trachyderes mandibularis **(Dupont)** (17.0–32.0 mm) is large, distinctive, shiny black or reddish brown and yellow with very long, banded antennae. Base color for Florida Keys population reddish brown, mainland population black. Head with mandible large (male) or smaller (female). Diurnal adults active in October and November, found on spathes of traveller's palms (*Ravenala madagascariensis*), at sapping wounds of small-leaf arrowwood (*Viburnum obovatum*), and resting on other trees and shrubs. Restricted to Florida east of Mississippi River; long established on Key West, Stock Island, and Fleming Key; more recent introduction in Manatee County. (1)

Acanthocinus nodosus **(Fabricius)** (18.0–28.0 mm) is easily distinguished by its gray body with black markings. Male with dense apical tuft on fourth antennomere, female with long egg-laying tube (ovipositor). Larvae feed on the bark of dead or dying pitch pine (*Pinus rigida*). Adults active spring through early fall and are attracted to lights. Pennsylvania to Florida, west to Texas. (3)

Acanthocinus obsoletus **(Olivier)** (7.0–13.0 mm) has long antennae and variable dark spots on the elytra; four bands are usually visible to naked eye on each elytron, second band just before middle often irregular and interrupted under magnification. Elytra with punctures on apical half and without erect setae. Tibiae with two pale rings, tarsi always dark. Female with broad, extended pygidium. Larvae develop in several species of pine (*Pinus*). Adults are active year-round and attracted to lights or found on pine bark. Québec and Ontario to Florida, west to Minnesota and Texas. (3)

TOP RIGHT: *Acanthocinus obsoletus* male.
BOTTOM RIGHT: *Acanthocinus obsoletus* female.

416

Astyleiopus variegatus **(Haldeman)** (7.0–11.0 mm) is variably mottled with distinctive oval dark and light spot on last third of each elytron; dark spots behind middle sometimes reduced. Antennae long with alternating short pale and long dark bands at base. Pronotum broader than long with small bumps on side before depression at base, with three dark bumps, or calluses on top, middle callus long. Larvae develop in wide variety of deciduous hardwoods, including maple (*Acer*), buckeye (*Aesculus*), hackberry (*Celtis*), walnut (*Juglans*), locust (*Robinia*), and elm (*Ulmus*). Adults attracted to light in summer. Eastern North America west to North Dakota and Arizona. (1)

Astylidius parvus **(LeConte)** (5.0–7.0 mm) is small, broad, with round prominent tubercles on sides of pronotum, greenish pubescence, and dark pubescent ridges at base of elytra. Antennae 1.5 times longer than body in male, shorter in female. Pronotum with three large calluses and a few large, deep punctures along base. Elytra with a dark chevron sometimes faint just behind middle. Legs stout, femora swollen. Larva feeds in branches of hardwoods, shrubs, and vines, including maple (*Acer*), hawthorn (*Crataegus*), persimmon (*Diospyros virginiana*), mulberry (*Morus*), and elm (*Ulmus*). Adults fly to light in late spring and summer. Mid-Atlantic states to Minnesota and Texas. (1)

Astylopsis sexguttata **(Say)** (6.0–10.5 mm) has highly variable mottled gray, brown, and black pubescence; dark coloration of pronotum, underside, and appendages also varies. Pronotum densely punctate with five moderate calluses, two on each side and one on middle. Elytra lack dark sides, but have black-tufted tubercles, especially at base, and two conspicuous pale spots on suture just behind middle. Females similar to males, more robust. Larvae bore into conifers, including larch (*Larix*), spruce (*Picea*), and pine (*Pinus*). Nocturnal adults active spring and summer. Québec to Florida, west to Manitoba and Texas (5)

Soybean Borer *Dectes texanus* **LeConte** (5.0–11.0 mm) is somewhat cylindrical, reddish to black, and uniformly clothed in dense grayish pubescence. Antennomere 2 distinctly as long as broad. Pronotum longer than wide, with a spine on each side. Elytra with short, almost erect setae. Legs with femoral and tibial tips black. Larvae are stem borers of many herbaceous plants, including soybeans (*Glycine*), sunflower (*Helianthus*), cotton (*Gossypium*), ragweed (*Ambrosia*), cocklebur (*Xanthium*), and caltrop (*Kallstroemia*). Adults found on stems of larval host plants in late spring and summer. New York to Florida, west to North Dakota, Colorado, and Arizona. (2)

Eutrichillus biguttatus **(LeConte)** (6.0–11.0 mm) has a sharp spine on each side of prothorax. Elytra mostly uniform brown with long, dark spots past middle of elytra usually interrupted by weak pale lines; these markings sometimes poorly defined. Elytra, legs, and dorsal surface of antennal scape with erect setae. Female with long pygidium. Larvae develop in pine (*Pinus*). Adults are attracted to lights from spring through summer. Eastern United States, west to Wisconsin and Mississippi. (1)

Graphisurus **(formerly *Urographis*) *fasciatus* (De Geer)** (9.0–15.0 mm) has elytra with variable and irregular spots, lacking dark band around scutellum, and notched tips. Antennae very long in male; antennomere 3 longer than 1 in both sexes. Females similar to males, except for greatly elongated last abdominal pygidium and antennae extending only three antennomeres past elytra. Larvae mine many different deciduous trees and shrubs. Nocturnal adults attracted to light from spring through summer. Maritime Provinces and New England to Florida, west to Ontario, Wisconsin, Iowa, Missouri, and Texas. (3)

Graphisurus (formerly *Urographis*) *triangulifer* **(Haldeman)** (12.0–17.0 mm) is robust, dark brown, with long erect setae on elytra, and dark, distinctive markings on pronotum and base and sides of elytra. Antennomere 3 shorter than 4. Pronotum sparsely punctate. Elytra with dark marking surrounding scutellum and elsewhere on surface. Female with tip of abdomen long and broad. Larvae develop in hackberry (*Celtis*) and maple (*Acer*). Adults active spring and summer. New Jersey to Florida, west to Ohio and Louisiana. (3)

Hyperplatys aspersa **(Say)** (4.5–9.5 mm) is small, somewhat flat, and clothed in very fine light gray pubescence. Antennae dark. Pronotum broader than long, four spots across front half, no spots on basal half, and a long sharp spine on each side just before base. Elytra each with more than 10 small black round spots, a ridge from basal angle almost to tip, and vertical part of sides between ridge and margin not dark. Femora swollen and club-shaped in male, weakly so in female. Larvae develop in many hardwoods, also moonseed (*Menispermum*) and burdock (*Arctium*). Adults active spring and summer. In east from southeastern Canada to Virginia and Kansas. (3)

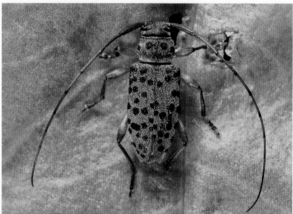

Hyperplatys maculata **Haldeman** (4.5–7.5 mm) is small, somewhat flattened, pale to dark reddish brown, clothed in fine whitish to dark brown setae, and has small irregular spots on pronotum and elytra. Elytra with steep sides, distinct blackish line behind humeri, faint white lines, two large spots at apical third, and tips each with two short spines; lines and spots sometimes reduced or absent. Legs orangish brown, with tips of distinctly swollen femora, tibiae, and tarsi dark. Nocturnal adults active late spring through early fall and attracted to light. Maritime Provinces to North Carolina, west to Manitoba, North Dakota, and Texas. (3)

Leptostylopsis planidosus **(LeConte)** (8.5–13.0 mm) is clothed with short, dense, grayish, pale, and dark setae. Pronotum wider than long, with five shallow tubercles and sides shallowly, broadly tuberculate behind middle. Elytra mottled grayish and brownish, tapering at about apical fourth, each with oblique narrow to broad grayish band behind middle, tips truncate. Legs robust, mottled with pubescence and small glabrous spots, tibiae each with two dark rings, tarsi dark. Larvae develop in river birch (*Betula nigra*), eastern redbud (*Cercis canadensis*), laurel oak (*Quercus laurifolia*), and probably grape (*Vitis*). Adults at light in summer. Maryland to Florida, west to Oklahoma. (4)

Leptostylus asperatus (Haldeman) (9.0–13.0 mm) is robust, variable in both size and appearance, with mottled surface mostly roughly sculpted. Elytra mostly white with dark contrasting areas. Hind legs with bases (trochanters) spined. Larvae bore in oak (*Quercus*) and sumac (*Rhus*). Adults attracted to lights from spring through early fall. Atlantic and Gulf coasts, Maryland to Texas. (2)

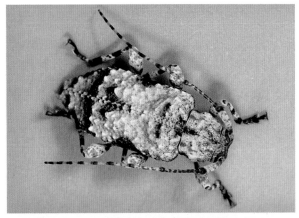

Leptostylus transversus (Gyllenhal) (6.0–14.0 mm) is robust, variable in both size and appearance, generally blackish brown with rough, mottled pattern of short gray or white pubescence. Elytra mostly dark with narrow light band before tip. Larvae develop in deciduous trees, shrubs, and vines, also conifers. Adults active spring and summer; attracted to light. Québec and Ontario to Florida, west to South Dakota, Kansas, and Arizona; Mexico. (2)

419

Lepturges pictus (LeConte) (8.0–11.0 mm) is small, slightly flattened on top, clothed in fine pubescence lying on surface, and brown with distinct dark brown markings on elytra. Antennae long. Pronotum wider than long, sides tapering toward front, and broadly impressed across base between distinct angles on sides. Elytra without dark markings on sides from humerus to apical third. Larvae develop in hardwoods, especially hackberry (*Celtis*). Adults active in spring and summer; attracted to light. Pennsylvania to Georgia, west to Iowa, Missouri, and Mississippi. *Lepturges symmetricus* (Haldeman) (6.0–9.0 mm) similar, elytral markings lighter, sides dark from humerus to apical third. (6)

Sternidius mimeticus (Casey) (5.0–9.0 mm) is robust with dense grayish pubescence. Elytra with oblique dark marks at apical third; dark patches along sides never reaching elytral bases sometimes absent, individuals without patches always with dark spots on top of elytral humeri. Hind tarsi with first tarsomere shorter than tarsomeres 2 and 3 combined. Larvae develop in a variety of deciduous trees. Adults are attracted to lights from spring through early fall. Virginia to Florida, west to Kansas and Texas. (4)

Styloleptus biustus (LeConte) (4.5–9.0 mm) is small, somewhat flattened, and varies from grayish with dark markings to brownish with dark spots. Pronotum wider than long, rounded on sides with broad bumps near base. Legs with femora strongly club-shaped, tarsi short, middle and hind legs with tibiae ringed with pale pubescence and tarsi dark, and hind tarsomere 1 shorter than 2–3 combined. Larvae develop in various hardwoods. Adults active spring and summer; attracted to light. Virginia to Florida, west to Iowa and Texas. (1)

Urgleptes signatus (LeConte) (4.5–8.0 mm) is dark reddish brown with underside and appendages yellowish. Pronotum with sharp, backward projecting spines just before hind angles, and a broad groove across entire base with a row of large, deep punctures. Elytra with basal markings U-shaped, narrow bands behind middle broader at suture than sides, front margin of band oblique and mostly straight, with tips not entirely dark. Larvae develop in branches of deciduous hardwoods, e.g., maple (*Acer*), hickory (*Carya*), mulberry (*Morus*), dogwood (*Cornus*), oak (*Quercus*), and basswood (*Tilia*). Adults active late spring and early summer. Québec and Ontario to Florida, west to Minnesota and Mississippi. (4)

Acanthoderes quadrigibba (Say) (9.0–16.0 mm) is robust, dark, often somewhat shining, thickly clothed in yellowish-brown pubescence and with white bands on elytra. Each elytron with short, longitudinal crest at middle of base and distinctive white zigzag band just in front of middle. Legs robust, with femora oval, tibiae narrowly ringed in white at middle, front tarsi fringed underneath (male), or not (female). Larva develops in many deciduous trees, including maple (*Acer*), redbud (*Cercis*), elm (*Ulmus*), linden (*Tilia*), hickory (*Carya*), and beech (*Fagus*). Adults active late spring and summer; at light. Ontario to Florida, west to Indiana and Texas; northeastern Mexico. (1)

Aegomorphus modestus (Gyllenhal) (10.0–16.0 mm) is variably mottled with strong spines on sides of pronotum and distinct M-shaped markings on elytra; Florida specimens often more grayish with bold black punctures and markings. Larva develops primarily in various deciduous trees, including oak (*Quercus*), elm (*Ulmus*), hickory (*Carya*), alder (*Alnus*), beech (*Fagus*), and maple (*Acer*); one record from loblolly pine (*Pinus virginiana*) in Virginia. Adults active late spring and summer; attracted to light. New England and Québec to Florida, west to Ontario, North Dakota, Kansas, and Texas. (3)

Hippopsis lemniscata (Fabricius) (7.0–15.0 mm) is elongate, slender, reddish brown, with short grayish pubescence, with alternating dark and yellowish stripes. Head projecting forward. Antennae at least twice as long as body in both sexes. Pronotum longer than wide, cylindrical. Elytra long, becoming narrow at tips. Legs short, finely pubescent. Larvae develop in stems. Adults active spring through early fall, especially midsummer, found feeding on annual ragweed (*Ambrosia artemisiifolia*), coreopsis (*Coreopsis*), sunflower (*Helianthus*), and other Asteraceae. New York to Florida, west to southern Ontario, Kansas, and Texas; south to South America. (1)

Cyrtinus pygmaeus (Haldeman) (2.3–3.5 mm) is smallest longhorn in region, egg-shaped, antlike, and shiny reddish brown. Antennomeres often pale at bases so antennae appear "ringed." Each elytron with prominent spine at base surrounded by coarse punctures and oblique patches of white setae. Larva develops in dry branches of many hardwoods, especially oak (*Quercus*), maple (*Acer*), hickory (*Carya*), dogwood (*Cornus*), walnut (*Juglans*), redbud (*Cercis*), hawthorn (*Crataegus*), and locust (*Robinia*). Adults active spring through summer, found in woodlands running antlike on branches of larval host plants. Ontario to Florida, west to Ohio, Missouri, and Texas. (1)

Eupogonius tomentosus (Haldeman) (5.0–10.0 mm) is shiny reddish brown with small triangular patches of appressed pubescence and scattered black setae. Larvae burrow under bark (first season) then into the wood to form a U-shaped pupal cell in same plane as grain (second season). Host trees include pine (*Pinus*), spruce (*Picea*), and the introduced Deodar cedar (*Cedrus deodara*). Adults attracted to lights spring through summer. New England and Québec to Florida, west to Ontario, Illinois and Texas. (4)

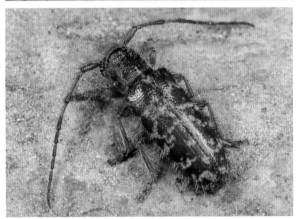

Currant-tip Borer *Psenocerus supernotatus* (Say) (4.0–8.0 mm) is elongate, somewhat cylindrical and straight-sided, dark reddish brown to black with white markings. Head and pronotum coarsely, densely punctate. Pronotal outline round. Scutellum and pair of oblique curved bands on elytra white, basal band before middle more slender than band at apical third. Pronounced blunt tubercle at base of each elyton distinctive. Larva develops in various deciduous trees and shrubs. Adults active spring through summer; attracted to light. New England and Québec to Georgia, west to Manitoba, Dakotas, Kansas, and Texas. (1)

Dorcaschema cinereum (**Olivier**) (8.0–13.0 mm) is elongate, slender, cylindrical, and black with surface obscured by uniformly dense light gray pubescence. Head ridged on top, antennae very long in both sexes, extending five (male) or four (female) antennomeres past elytral tip. Pronotum about as long as wide, with a bare black stripe down middle. Elytra with densely and coarsely punctate surface visible through pubescence, sides somewhat parallel, and tips narrowly rounded to somewhat pointed. Larvae develop in dead hickory (*Carya*), walnut (*Juglans*), osage orange (*Maclura*), hackberry (*Celtis*), linden (*Tilia*), maple (*Acer*), and mulberry (*Morus*). Adults found resting on vegetation in late spring and summer. Pennsylvania to Florida, west to Wisconsin, Nebraska, and Oklahoma. (4)

Hemierana marginata ardens (**LeConte**) (6.0–10.5 mm) is elongate, somewhat parallel-sided, black with dull orange on head, pronotum, and elytral angles; appendages black. Pronotum wider than long, sides rounded, widest at base, and broadly impressed at base on either side of middle, with broad dark stripe down middle. Elytra with coarse scattered punctures, with sides and tips rounded, without ridge or stripes of pubescence. Larvae develop in ironweed (*Vernonia*). Adults active spring and summer. Massachusetts to Georgia, west to Kansas and Texas. *Hemierana m. marginata* (Fabricius) has dense elytral pubescence along sides and suture; Florida. (1)

Hickory Borer *Goes pulcher* (**Haldeman**) (18.0–27.0 mm) is robust, cylindrical, and brown with light and dark brown pubescence. Head coarsely punctured, antennae extending three antennomeres beyond (male) or just reaching (female) elytral tips. Pronotum wider than long, sides with sharp tubercle. Elytra brown at base with broad dark brown band just behind middle. Larvae mine heartwood of living hickory and pecan (*Carya*), possibly walnut (*Juglans*); oak (*Quercus*) and elm (*Ulmus*) reported, but doubtful. Adults found on tender twigs, leaf petioles, and midribs in late spring and early summer; attracted to light. Massachusetts to Florida, west to Wisconsin, Kansas, and Texas. (7)

White Oak Borer *Goes tigrinus* (**De Geer**) (22.0–44 mm) is elongate, robust, dark brown with irregular and dense patches of white pubescence. Antennae extending beyond tips of elytra in both sexes, shorter in heavier-bodied female. Elytra with dark areas at base and just behind middle. Larva develops in living oak, especially white (*Quercus alba*) and overcup oaks (*Q. lyrata*). Adults active spring and summer, feed on leaves and twigs; attracted to light. New York to Florida, west to Michigan and Texas. (7)

Microgoes oculatus **(LeConte)** (8.0–12.0 mm) is short, slender, parallel-sided, and black with grayish pubescence. Head finely punctured, with antennae extending six (male) or four (female) antennomeres beyond elytral tips. Pronotum convex, lightly and densely punctured, wider than long, and sides with sharp bump at middle. Eytra often reddish, densely and coarsely punctured, slightly rough at base, irregular patches of white pubescence, each with round patch of black pubescence behind middle. Legs short, stout. Larvae develop under bark of dead hardwoods, including dogwood (*Cornus*), beech (*Fagus*), and sourwood (*Oxydendrum*); also pine (*Pinus*). Maritime Provinces and New England to Georgia, west to Wisconsin, Illinois, and Mississippi. (1)

Monochamus carolinensis **(Olivier)** (15.0–23.0 mm) is dark reddish brown with less distinctly mottled reddish, brown, and grayish patches of pubescence, dark brown patches raised. Antennae very long (male) or just passing tips of elytra (female). Pronotum with sharp tubercles on sides and sparsely clothed in pubescence. Scutellum with white and yellow pubescence. Elytra densely and closely punctate, mostly mottled, and weakly toothed at suture. New Brunswick and New England to Florida, west to Ontario, Wisconsin, and Texas. (5)

Northeastern Borer *Monochamus notatus* **(Drury)** (23.0–35.0 mm) is reddish brown, surfaces mostly clothed in dense grayish pubescence, and scutellum with off-white setae. Pronotal tubercles white or off-white at base. Elytra densely pubescent with scattered small patches of black-brown pubescence; tips angled at suture. Larva develops in dead and dying conifers, especially pine (*Pinus*), but also fir (*Abies*), spruce (*Picea*), and Douglas-fir (*Pseudotsuga*). Adults active late spring through summer. Across southern Canada, south to South Carolina, west to Montana. (5)

White-spotted Sawyer *Monochamus scutellatus* **(Say)** (13.0–40.0 mm) is mostly very dark reddish brown to black, sometimes with brassy luster, with white scutellum. Antennae extend beyond elytra in both sexes, shorter in female. Elytra with a few dense patches of white setae present (female) or absent (male), apical half coated with dense and inconspicuous gold pubescence, and rounded tips. Larvae develop in injured or recently cut conifers, especially eastern white pine (*Pinus strobus*), also other pines, fir (*Abies*), larch (*Larix*), and spruce (*Picea*). Adults active spring and summer, feed on needles and young bark; attracted to light. In east from Atlantic Canada to North Carolina, west to Ontario, Minnesota, Illinois and Tennessee. (5)

423

Southern Pine Sawyer *Monochamus titillator*
(Fabricius) (17.0–31.0 mm) is reddish brown with variegated
pattern of pubesence. Antennae of male two or three times
longer than body. Prothorax without strong spines on sides.
Elytra mottled in white, yellow, gray, and dark brown, finely
and sparsely punctate, with sutural margins usually tipped
by sharp spines. Larvae develop in conifers, including pine
(*Pinus*), fir (*Abies*), and spruce (*Picea*). Adults emerge
primarily in spring and remain active through summer;
attracted to light. Ontario and Massachusetts to Florida,
west to North Dakota and Texas. (5)

Neoptychodes trilineatus (Linnaeus) (19.0–31.0 mm)
is large with smooth-sided pronotum tapered toward front,
and with distinctive dense grayish pubescence, brown-
orange spots, and white stripes. Head with eyes deeply
notched, mouthparts directed downward. Pronotum long as
wide, widest at base, without distinct spines or bumps on
sides. Elytra tapered toward rear, with markings, especially
sutural stripe, sometime expanded at middle and spined
tips. Larvae develop in fig (*Ficus*), alder (*Alnus*), mulberry
(*Morus*), willow (*Salix*), and hackberry (*Celtis*). Adults active
in summer and fall, found on trunks of larval hosts. Florida
west to Arizona. (1)

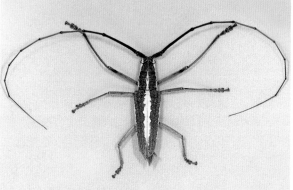

424

Cottonwood Borer *Plectrodera scalator* (Fabricius)
(25.0–40.0 mm) is elongate, robust, somewhat cylindrical,
and shiny black with irregular and contrasting markings of
white pubescence; appendages mostly black. Pronotum
with patches of black on top and sides. Elytra each with
two variable and irregular rows of shiny black rectangular
patches. Larvae develop in poplar and cottonwood
(*Populus*) and willow (*Salix*); one to two years required
for development. Adults active in summer, feed on leaf
petioles, found on larval plant hosts. New Jersey to Florida,
west to Dakotas, Colorado, and Texas; mostly Midwest and
Mississippi River Valley to Michigan. (1)

Twig Girdler *Oncideres cingulata* (Say) (11.0–20.0 mm)
is elongate, robust, and cylindrical. Head broad, as wide
as pronotum. Antennomeres clothed in fine and appressed
pale setae and line of large setae down one side, and
extending much (male) or slightly (female) past elytral tips.
Pronotum as wide as long, sides without bumps or spines.
Elytra with slightly pale band across middle and mottled
with faint orange spots. Sometimes a pest; female girdles
branches of many species of hardwood trees and shrubs,
larvae develop above girdle. Adults active spring through
fall; attracted to light. Connecticut and Florida, west to
Minnesota, Kansas and Texas. (1)

Mecas cineracea Casey (6.0–11.0 mm) is elongate, parallel-sided, and uniformly clothed in dense grayish pubescence. Antennae long, slender, antennomere 3 longer than 1. Pronotum wider than long, with sides rounded, surface without polished black calluses. Legs with femora black and tooth on all inner claws small. Larvae develop in live stems of sneezeweed (*Helenium*) and other composites (Asteraceae). Adults active spring and summer; found by sweeping larval hosts, composites, and other plants. Virginia to Florida, west to Colorado and Arizona. (5)

Oak-sprout Oberea *Oberea gracilis* (Fabricius) (10.0–15.0 mm) is long, slender, reddish orange, and lacks small black spots or calluses on pronotum. Antennae dark. Elytra three times longer than wide with coarse punctures and distinct dark stripes on sides. Legs reddish orange with dark tarsi and outer portions of tibiae. Larvae develop in oak (*Quercus*). Adults attracted to lights in spring and early summer. Massachusetts to Florida, west to Ohio and Mississippi. (12)

425

Dogwood Twig Borer *Oberea tripunctata* (Swederus) (8.0–14.0 mm) is long, slender, body never mostly covered with gray pubescence. Head mostly dark. At least outer antennomeres pale at bases producing a "ringed" appearance. Pronotum with two raised calluses and dark median spot in front scutellum, underside nearly completely dark. Elytra yellowish brown to smoky gray-brown with blackish tinge, usually with dark stripes. Underside of abdomen mostly dark. Legs yellow, each claw appendiculate at base. Larva develops in living branches of various deciduous trees and shrubs. Adults active in late spring and summer, attracted to light. New Brunswick and Québec to Florida, west to Manitoba, North Dakota, Kansas, and Texas. (12)

Ecyrus dasycerus (Say) (4.0–10.0 mm) is variable in size and color, with light and dark variants; dark curved band across base of elytra distinctive, sometimes faint. Elytra coarsely punctate with grayish pubescence. Larva develops in many deciduous hardwoods, including maple (*Acer*), hackberry (*Celtis*), locust (*Robinia*), elm (*Ulmus*), and oak (*Quercus*). Adults active spring and summer; attracted to light. New England and Québec to Florida, west to Ontario, Michigan, Iowa, Oklahoma, and Texas. (1)

Ataxia crypta (**Say**) (11.0–18.0 mm) is elongate, robust, dark brown, and clothed in brown, gray, and white pubescence. Head coarsely punctured, antennae shorter than (female) or extending beyond (male) elytra. Pronotum wider than long, sides rounded, each with single bump, and broad depression across base. Elytra coarsely punctate at base, irregularly marked with lighter pubescence along suture, oblique tips with outer angles sharp. Larvae develop in dead branches of hardwoods, including oak (*Quercus*) and necklacepod (*Sophora*). Adults active late spring and summer, play dead; attracted to light. Pennsylvania to Florida, west to Kansas and Texas. (3; 2 restricted to Florida)

Poplar Borer *Saperda calcarata* (**Say**) (18.0–33.0 mm) is elongate, somewhat robust, reddish brown to black and clothed in dense, grayish pubescence mottled with pale brown. Head, three pronotal stripes, scutellum, and some lines and spots on elytra with orange-yellow pubescence. Elytra with distinct spines on tips. Larvae develop in poplars, including quaking aspen (*Populus tremuloides*), eastern cottonwood (*P. deltoides*), and balsam poplar (*P. balsamifera*); also willow (*Salix*). Life cycle takes two to five years. Adults active late spring and summer and feed on foliage, bark, and young shoots. Across North America; in east from Maritime Provinces to Florida, west to Ontario, Dakotas, Kansas, and Texas. (14)

Round-headed Apple Tree Borer *Saperda candida* **Fabricius** (10.0–21.0 mm) is elongate, robust, somewhat cylindrical, and brownish, with broad white stripe on each side from head to elytral tips. Head not impressed between antennae. Pronotum longer than wide. Elytra with tips rounded. Underside white. Larvae attack many deciduous hardwoods, including orchard and ornamental trees. Adults active late spring and summer; attracted to light. Maritime Provinces to Florida, west to Saskatchewan, North Dakota, Oklahoma, and Louisiana. (14)

Hickory Saperda *Saperda discoidea* **Fabricius** (10.0–16.0 mm) male is uniformly brown or black and sparsely covered with gray pubescence that forms light gray lines on pronotum. Females more robust, with head, prothorax, and scutellum densely clothed in dull yellow setae. Elytra distinctly punctured, female's with grayish pubescence along outer and apical margins and in crescent-shaped patches at middle. Legs reddish. Larvae develop primarily in hickory (*Carya*), as well as other deciduous trees. Adults attracted to lights in summer. Québec and Ontario to Florida, west to South Dakota and Oklahoma. (14)

Alder Borer *Saperda obliqua* Say (14.0–19.0 mm)
is distinctively brown or reddish brown, pubescent, with
darker oblique elytral bands. Elytra with many punctures,
darker oblique depressions less pubescent, and long
spine at each tip. Larvae develop in living alder (*Alnus*)
and beech (*Fagus*). Adults active in summer, found on
upper branches of host tree; attracted to light. Maritime
Provinces to Georgia, west to Manitoba, Wisconsin, Iowa,
Missouri, Oklahoma, and Mississippi. (14)

Woodbine Borer *Saperda puncticollis* Say
(8.0–12.0 mm) is distinctly marked with four black spots
on a yellow pronotum and yellow margins on elytra. Larvae
develop in dead, dying, or otherwise weakened vines of
creeper (*Parthenocissus*), grape (*Vitis*), and poison ivy
(*Toxicodendron*). Adults are attracted to lights during
summer. Widely distributed in eastern North America
from Ontario and Québec to Mississippi, west to
Minnesota and Texas. (14)

427

Elm Borer *Saperda tridentata* Olivier (10.0–17.0 mm)
is elongate, robust, brown, and densely clothed in variable
gray and orange-red pubescent stripes. Antennae reaching
apical sixth (female), or longer than elytra (male). Elytra
coarsely and densely punctate, with sides parallel, tips
rounded. Larvae develop in elm (*Ulmus*). Adults active
spring and summer; attracted to light. Maritime Provinces
and New England to Florida, west to Manitoba, Dakotas,
and eastern Texas. (14)

Tetraopes melanurus Schönherr (7.5–11.0 mm) is
elongate, robust, somewhat cylindrical, sparsely pubescent,
and red, usually with distinct oblique black or dark gray
markings just before middle and at apical third. Eyes
completely divided. Antennae thick, uniformly black, without
white rings, tapered, and usually not quite reaching elytral
tips (male) or extending to abdominal ventrite 3 (female).
Elytral markings are sometimes reduced, especially in
front. Larvae feed on roots of butterfly milkweed (*Asclepias
tuberosa*). Adults active in late spring and summer, found on
larval host plants. New England to Florida, west to Michigan
and Mississippi. (4)

Red Milkweed Beetle *Tetraopes tetrophthalmus* **(Forster)** (8.0–15.0 mm) is bright red with bold black markings. Eyes completely divided. Antennae uniformly dark. Pronotum with broad, weakly raised hexagonal callus surrounded by four black spots. Elytra with distinct black spots, spots below humeri present and often large. Larvae develop in roots of milkweeds (*Asclepias*) and dogbane (*Apocynum*). Adults active late spring and summer, found on host plants. Québec and Ontario to Georgia, west to North Dakota, Colorado, Oklahoma, and Texas. (4)

MEGALOPODID LEAF BEETLES, FAMILY MEGALOPODIDAE
(MEG-AH-LO-*PO*-DIH-DEE)

Megalopodid beetles are represented in North America by the single genus *Zeugophora*. Both the adults and larvae are leaf feeders. The adults feed externally, while their legless and flattened larvae chew tunnels inside the leaves and form large, dark, and blotchy mines. Little is known of their host plant preferences in the Nearctic, but several species feed on willow (*Salix*) and poplars (*Populus*).

FAMILY DIAGNOSIS The antennae of adult *Zeugophora* are short and not directed backward or set on bumps, attached low on head between mandibles and eyes, and all tibiae tipped with a pair of spurs. Antennae with 11 antennomeres, 5–11 almost serrate. Pronotum with sides distinctly angled at middle. Elytra covering abdomen, rounded at apices. Abdomen with five distinct ventrites, 1–4 each somewhat equal in length, 5 longer.

SIMILAR FAMILIES
- orsodacnid leaf beetles (Orsodacnidae) – prothorax with broadly rounded sides (p.429)
- leaf beetles (Chrysomelidae) – tibiae without or with inconspicuous spurs, or spurs only on hind legs (p.429)

COLLECTING NOTES Adults are swept or beaten from the foliage of willows, poplars, and other trees and shrubs.

FAUNA SIX SPECIES IN ONE GENUS

Poplar Black-mine Beetle *Zeugophora scutellaris* **Suffrian** (3.5–4.0 mm) is elongate-oblong, convex, coarsely punctured, sparsely pubescent, shining. Head, prothorax, and legs reddish orange; elytra, metasternum, and abdomen black. Antennae half length of body, antennomeres 1–4 pale, 5–11 somewhat serrate and dark. Pronotum longer than wide, strongly convex, sides each with prominent bump. Elytra broader than pronotum, humeri distinct. Tibiae each tipped with pair of spurs. Feeding activities of larvae inside leaves result in blotchy black mines. Adults active spring and early summer, found on stems of poplar (*Populus*) and willow (*Salix*). Widespread in Canada and northern United States; in east, south to Maryland and Missouri. (6)

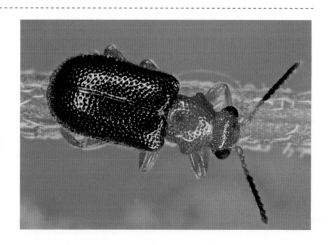

ORSODACNID LEAF BEETLES, FAMILY ORSODACNIDAE
(OR-SO-*DACK*-NIH-DEE)

Only one species of orsodacnid occurs in North America, *Orsodacne atra* (Ahrens). Adults feed on the floral parts of many different kinds of trees and woody shrubs and are among the first phytophagous beetles to emerge in spring. The larvae are unknown, but they are suspected to be external root feeders.

FAMILY DIAGNOSIS Adult *Orsodacne* strongly resemble a leaf beetle (Chrysomelidae), but their antennae are short, attached low on head between mandibles and eyes, and are not directed backward or set on bumps, and all tibiae are tipped with a pair of spurs. Head with distinctly square labrum. Antennae filiform, with 11 antennomeres. Pronotum with sides rounded from above and not margined or keeled. Elytra covering abdomen, rounded at apices. Abdomen with 5 distinct ventrites, each somewhat equal in length.

SIMILAR FAMILIES
- megalopodid leaf beetles (Megalopodidae) – prothorax distinctly angled at middle (p.428)
- leaf beetles (Chrysomelidae) – tibiae without or with inconspicuous spurs, or spurs only on hind legs (p.429)

COLLECTING NOTES Adult *Orsodacne* are handpicked, swept, or beaten from blooming shrubs and trees in spring.

FAUNA ONE SPECIES, *ORSODACNE ATRA* (AHRENS) (NA)

Orsodacne atra (Ahrens) (4.0–7.0 mm) is elongate, narrow, somewhat convex, and variably black, dark red, or brownish yellow; sometimes with stripes or spots. Head is broad as pronotum. Pronotum with sides not keeled and narrower than base of elytra. Larvae are unknown, but may be external root feeders. Adults found in early spring feeding on a wide variety of flowers of deciduous trees and shrubs. Most of Canada and all but southernmost United States. (1)

LEAF AND SEED BEETLES, FAMILY CHRYSOMELIDAE
(KRY-SO-*MEL*-IH-DEE)

Chrysomelids are the fourth-largest family of beetles in North America. Most species are small to very small and many are conspicuously colored, possibly warning of their distastefulness to predators. Both adults and larvae attack many kinds of flowering plants, eating the bark, stems, leaves, flowers, seeds, and roots, but a few species prefer conifers, ferns, and their allies. The majority of chrysomelids are specialists, feeding only on a single species of plant or groups of closely related plants. Some species feed solely on aquatic plants, with adults grazing on leaves and other vegetative structures above the water surface and larvae consuming submerged plant tissues. Many species of chrysomelids, both as adults and as larvae, are of economic importance. Garden and crop pests damage plants directly through defoliation, leaf mining, or root boring, or by infecting them with disease. Some seed beetles attack leguminous crops such as alfalfa, beans, lentils, and peas, while others infest stored and dried seeds.

FAMILY DIAGNOSIS Adult chrysomelids are extremely variable in shape and difficult to characterize as a family. They are long and cylindrical, or compact, square or oval, convex to almost hemispherical, or flattened. Head with mouthparts directed downward, sometimes forward. Antennae with 11 antennomeres usually filiform, sometimes serrate, plumose, flabellate, or clavate. Pronotum triangular or rectangular, broader than head, usually keeled on sides, sometimes broadly flattened and expanded on sides. Elytra conceal abdomen (leaf beetles) or not (seed beetles). Hind legs sometimes enlarged for jumping. Tarsi appear 4-4-4, but are actually 5-5-5, tarsomere 4 small and hidden between lobes of heart-shaped 3, claws usually equal in size, simple or with broad tooth. Abdomen with five usually distinct ventrites.

SIMILAR FAMILIES
- checkered beetles (Cleridae) – antennae clubbed; tarsi distinctly 5-5-5 (p.263)
- soft-winged flower beetles (Melyridae) – antennae serrate; tarsi distinctly 5-5-5 (p.271)
- pleasing fungus beetles (Erotylidae) – antennae with distinct, flat clubs (p.277)
- handsome fungus beetles (Endomychidae) – tarsi appear 3-3-3, but are 4-4-4 (p.308)
- lady beetles (Coccinellidae) – tarsi appear 3-3-3, but are 4-4-4 (p.311)
- darkling beetles (Tenebrionidae) – tarsi 5-5-4 (p.344)
- antlike flower beetles (Anthicidae) – head with neck (p.377)
- longhorn beetles (Cerambycidae) – pronotum not parallel-sided, widest at middle or behind (p.388)
- leaf-rolling weevils (Attelabidae) – antennal club with three antennomeres (p.462)
- weevils (Curculionidae) – snout usually longer; antennae elbowed with distinct, antennal club with three antennomeres (p.469)

COLLECTING NOTES Look for chrysomelids on the foliage and flowers of trees, shrubs, vines, and herbaceous growth in all kinds of habitats. Handpick adults in gardens, crops, and other sensitive habitats to avoid damaging plants; beating and sweeping are generally more efficient methods of collection elsewhere. Seed beetles are best obtained by collecting seeds and seedpods and placing them in a secure container until the adults emerge.

FAUNA 1,869 SPECIES IN 218 GENERA (NA)

Amblycerus robiniae **(Fabricius)** (3.8–7.3 mm) is oblong-oval, weakly convex, dark red, and clothed in grayish-yellow pubescence. Eyes weakly notched around base of antennae. Pronotum convex, nearly semicircular with front margin straight. Elytra broadest at middle, with rows of punctures and small black dots of setae arranged in five irregular bands. Middle tibiae with a pair of movable and unequal apical spurs, hind legs with base wider than femur and tibiae without ridges. Larvae develop in seedpods of honeylocust (*Gleditsia triacanthos*) and water locust (*G. aquatica*). Adults active spring and summer; attracted to light. New Hampshire and New York to Florida, west to Alberta, the Dakotas, and Texas. (5)

Bruchidius villosus **(Fabricius)** (2.4–3.2 mm) is black except for reddish-brown antennomeres 1–4. Body uniformly clothed in white setae with golden sheen above and white below. Hind femora with tooth on inner lower margin very small, obscure; tibiae slightly bent at base. Larvae develop in pods of shrubs and Scotch broom (*Cytisus scoparius*) and other leguminous trees and shrubs; adults found on larval host plants. Europe; established from Nova Scotia and Ontario to Florida. (1)

Bruchus brachialis **Fåhraeus** (2.5–2.9 mm) is black and clothed in black and brown setae and rows of white spots. Antennae reddish (male) or bicolored (female). Front legs mostly reddish orange. Pronotum with hind angles white. Tergite beyond elytra whitish with two black spots. Hind femora broadly angulate underneath, not toothed, middle tibiae of male with apical spines finely notched. Larvae develop in seedpods of pea (*Lathyrus*) and vetch (*Vicia*). Adults active in late spring and summer, found on Queen Anne's lace (*Daucus carota*). Europe; established in east from Ontario to Florida, west to Indiana, Kansas, and Texas. (3)

Megacerus cubiculus **(Casey)** (2.5 mm) is mostly reddish brown with top of head, underside, and most of hind femora black. Head yellowish with white patch above each eye; antennae with last four or five antennomeres usually dusky black, pectinate in male, serrate in female. Front and middle legs reddish brown. Pronotum with two squarish spots. Scutellum white. Elytra alternately marked with black and yellow stripes, with black spot on shoulders (humeri) and near each apex, and variably marked elsewhere with black spots. Larvae develop in seeds of morning glory (*Ipomoea*), while adults are found on flowers in spring and early summer. Maryland to Florida, west to Oklahoma and Texas. (6)

Megacerus discoidus **(Say)** (2.6–3.6 mm) is mostly black, with reddish infusion on hind legs and spot on each elytron. Head, middle of pronotum, and elytra with sparse, white pubescence; sides of pronotum with denser pubescence; antennae pectinate in male, serrate in female. Elytra each with two large reddish spots not reaching base or suture. Abdomen underneath with black spot on each side margin of abdominal ventrite 5, pygidium with four black spots. Larva develops in seeds of false bindweed (*Calystegia*) and morning glory (*Ipomoea*). Adults found on flowers in spring and early summer. Widely distributed in eastern North America. (6)

Acanthoscelides alboscutellatus **(Horn)** (1.1–2.3 mm) is black with prominent white scutellum and white mottling on elytra; antennomeres 1–4 reddish brown underneath. Pronotum with scales more dense on sides than down middle. Elytra with regular rows of patches of white setae. Abdomen with pygidium slightly mottled. Larvae develop in seedpods of licorice (*Glycyrrhiza*) and primrose-willow (*Ludwigia*). Adults found on flowers, including Queen Anne's lace (*Daucus carota*). New York to Florida, west to Colorado, Kansas, and Texas. (18)

Gibbobruchus mimus **(Say)** (2.3–3.5 mm) has elytral patterns of dark brown, orange, white, and yellow with velvety v-shaped patch near base; occasionally all red. Male pygidium yellow with bare patch near tip, female's with large, dark heart-shaped spot. Legs of both sexes mostly reddish, tarsi and antennae reddish yellow; antennal club sometimes dusky; hind femur with serrate ridge underneath at middle, including a large tooth followed by a gap and three small teeth. Adults found on flowers of numerous hardwoods. Larvae develop in seeds of redbud (*Cercis*) and texasplume (*Bauhinia lunarioides*). Maryland to Florida, west to Nevada and Arizona; Mexico. (1)

Meibomeus musculus **(Say)** (1.6–2.7 mm) is black with grayish-white scales. Antennae entirely yellow (male) or partly dark (female). Pronotum with sides more densely pubescent. Elytra with a dense spot on middle. Pygidium with three basal spots and line down middle to tip. Legs with tarsi, front legs, and middle tibiae yellow, hind femora yellow (male) or partly darkened (female). Larvae develop in seeds of tick trefoil (*Desmodium*) and lespedeza (*Lespedeza*). Adults active spring and summer, found by sweeping vegetation. Québec and Ontario to Florida, west to Minnesota, Kansas, and Texas. (2)

432

Sennius abbreviatus **(Say)** (2.1–3.0 mm) is black with distinct red patches on elytra. Antennae with antennomeres 1–4 reddish orange, 5–11 reddish orange to black. Pronotum bell-shaped and uniformly convex. Elytra each with reddish-orange spots extending from side margins to first or second row of punctures out from suture and not reaching base. Abdomen with pygidium black. Legs dark brown to black, hind legs with femora toothed underneath and tibiae ridged. Larvae develop in seedpods of cassia (*Cassia*) and senna (*Senna*). Adults found on various flowers spring and summer. New York to Georgia, west to Illinois, Missouri, and Texas. (3)

Donacia **species** (5.0–9.0 mm) are elongate, metallic or dark brown, with head and pronotum much narrower than elytra, appearing broad-shouldered. Elytra without spines at apices, suture with elytral edges (beads) uniformly narrow along entire length. Hind legs long, with femora of most species with one or two teeth underneath just before apex, and tarsomere 5 on all legs shorter than 1–4 combined. Adults active in late spring and summer, found mostly on sedges; they are alert and fly quickly when disturbed. Some species difficult to identify without examination of male genitalia. Widespread in eastern North America. (31)

Plateumaris **species** (5.5–8.6 mm) are elongate, shiny and metallic, with head and pronotum much narrower than elytra, appearing broad-shouldered. Head with eyes small, round. Elytra each with apices individually rounded, suture with elytral edges (beads) becoming wider behind middle. Hind legs long, with hind femora of males more strongly toothed. Species variable in color, shape, and sculpturing. Eggs laid above or below water surface, on or within plant tissues. Adults active in late spring and summer, found mostly on sedges; they are alert and fly quickly when disturbed. Widespread in eastern North America. (15)

Asparagus Beetle *Crioceris asparagi* **(Linnaeus)** (4.7–6.6 mm) has a dark metallic blue head as wide as pronotum. Prothorax light orange to reddish orange with variable dark spots sometimes absent, narrower than elytra, with sides rounded not margined and appear bowed from above. Elytra mostly dark metallic blue with light markings, variable dark spots, orange sides and apices, and broad, dark suture; completely cover abdomen. Claws separate at base with tips divergent. Both adults and larvae are severe pests of asparagus (*Asparagus*). Europe; widely established in North America. (2)

Scarlet Lily Beetle *Lilioceris lilii* **(Scopoli)** (6.3–7.3 mm) is bright, shiny red, with unmarked pronotum and elytra. Head, appendages, and underside black, pronotum and elytra red. Pronotum longer than wide, narrower than elytra, and distinctly constricted. Adults and larvae are pests of lilies (*Lilium*). Europe; Maritime Provinces and Québec to Connecticut, west to Ontario; Washington. (1)

Three-lined Potato Beetle *Lema daturaphila* **Kogan & Goeden** (5.7–8.0 mm) is yellow to yellow-orange with three black stripes on elytra. Head yellow with a pair of bumps between eyes. Antennae, outer half of tibiae, tarsi, and sometimes metasternum black. Pronotum slightly wider than long, constricted at middle, with a pair of spots sometimes merging to form large patch. Each elytron white with shared stripe down suture and stripe just above side margins, surface distinctly punctate. Adults and larvae feed on nightshade (*Solanum*), jimsonweed (*Datura*), ground-cherry (*Physalis*), and belladonna (*Atropis*). Adults active spring and summer. Southeastern Canada and United States. (4)

Lema solani Fabricius (4.8–6.7 mm) is mostly black with bicolored elytra. Head usually black, sometime reddish at base. Elytra mostly black with red band more often expanded to base than reduced, side margins pale except at base, with next to last row of punctures before sides complete, not broken. Legs with tarsal claws touching at base. Adults and larvae found on nightshade (*Solanum*). Delaware to Florida, west to Texas. (7)

Neolema sexpunctata (Olivier) (4.8–6.2 mm) is orange to orange-red, shiny, with antennae, most of legs, spots on elytra, sides of pterothorax, and first abdominal ventrite black. Head with orange clypeus. Pronotum narrower than elytra. Elytra each with three black spots; ninth elytral striae with a gap of 8–11 punctures. Legs with tarsal claws touching at base. Females usually larger than males. Adults overwinter. Adults and larvae feed on Asiatic (*Commelina communis*) and Virginia dayflowers (*C. virginica*). New Jersey and Pennsylvania to Florida, west to Kentucky and Texas. (4)

434

Cereal Leaf Beetle ***Oulema melanopus*** (Linnaeus) (4.6–5.3 mm) is shiny blue-black with mostly reddish-orange legs, and black head and antennae. Head with antennae half as long as body, without tubercles between antennae and mouthparts. Pronotum convex with sides rounded and constricted at base. Elytra with nine rows of distinct punctures, humeri smooth. Pterothorax and abdomen shiny blue-black. Legs with bases, apices of tibiae, and tarsi black. Adults and larvae feed on grasses (Poaceae). This Old World species is established from Nova Scotia and New Brunswick to Georgia, west to Ontario, Wisconsin, Kansas, and Texas. (12)

Agroiconota bivittata (Say) (4.5–6.0 mm) is broadly oval, convex, dull yellow with dark brown to black stripes on elytra. Pronotum pale yellowish brown with darker brown triangular patch at base, sides and front broadly flattened and translucent. Elytra yellowish with suture and two stripes on each side dark brown or black, and rows of coarse, deep punctures, and punctures along sides black. Underside and legs black. Adults and larvae found on plants in the morning-glory family (Convolvulaceae). Widespread in eastern United States, also Ontario and Québec. (1)

Thistle Tortoise Beetle *Cassida rubiginosa* Müller (6.0–8.0 mm) is uniformly bright green, sometimes with yellow margins, and black underneath; color fades after death. Adults and larvae feed on a variety of plants, but prefer thistles (*Arctium*, *Carduus*, *Cirsium*). Used as biological control agent against pest thistles, especially Canada thistle (*Cirsium arvense*) and nodding plumeless thistle (*Carduus nutans*). A European immigrant first reported in North America in 1902; established from Nova Scotia and New Brunswick to Virginia, west to Alberta, Wisconsin, and South Dakota. (1)

Charidotella purpurata (Boheman) (5.4–6.5 mm) is broadly oval and shiny; appendages mostly yellow with antennomeres 6–11 dark. Pronotum smooth, front pale, translucent, rest yellowish brown, with basal margin briefly straight across middle. Elytra convex with rows of fine punctures down middle with partially translucent sides delimited by diffuse dark "C," and remainder yellowish brown. Claws appendiculate at base, male with middle claws simple. Adults and larvae attack hedge false bindweed (*Calystegia sepium*), field bindweed (*Convolvulus arensis*), and man of the earth (*Ipomoea pandurata*). Southern Canada and United States, except Southwest. (3)

435

Golden Tortoise Beetle *Charidotella sexpunctata bicolor* (Fabricius) (5.0–7.0 mm) with head completely concealed by pronotum. Underside of pronotum not grooved. Legs with some claws toothed, front claws with broad extension at base. Elytra with front margins smooth, never striped, and very shiny; turns brown after death. Adults active late spring and summer. Both adults and larvae feed on undersides of leaves of sweet potato (*Ipomoea*), bindweed (*Calystegia*), and other morning glories (Convolvulaceae). Larvae carry cast skins and waste on "anal fork" held over body. Eastern North America, west to Iowa and Texas. (3)

Mottled Tortoise Beetle *Deloyala guttata* (Olivier) (5.3–6.8 mm) is broadly oval, convex, with pronotal and elytral margins broadly flattened and brilliant metallic colors. Pronotum and elytra with central black patterns surrounding irregular patches of brilliant metallic green or gold. Prothorax underneath with ridged antennal grooves. Elytra with front margins finely notched. Legs with projections on tarsomere 5 that cover simple tarsal claws. Larvae hide under shield of cast exoskeletons and feces. Adults found on bindweed (*Convolvulus*), false bindweed (*Calystegia*), sweet potato (*Ipomoea*), and other morning glories (Convolvulaceae). Southern Canada, eastern United States. (2)

Eggplant Tortoise Beetle *Gratiana pallidula* (Boheman) (5.4–6.1 mm) is oval, not very convex, and mostly pale green-yellow (fades to yellowish brown after death), with pronotal and elytral margins wide and completely translucent. Head hidden from above, antennae short and thick with last three or four antennomeres black. Pronotum without punctures. Elytral bases strongly sinuate and surface with rows of coarse, deep punctures. Spiny pale green larva feeds on nightshade (*Solanum*) and carries a defensive fecal shield over its back. Adults found in spring and summer on larval host plant. New York to Florida, west to Nebraska, and California. (1)

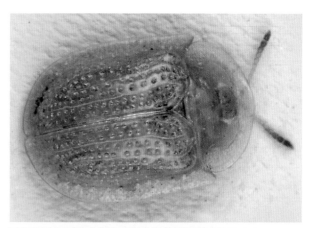

Plagiometriona clavata (Fabricius) (7.0–7.7 mm) is broadly oval with broadly flattened and translucent elytra margins, except at corners. Head, appendages, and underside yellow, while tips of antennae are brown. Pronotum smooth and sinuate at base, with anterior margin broadly flattened and translucent. Elytra brown, except on sides and apices, roughly sculptured at center with prominent bump at base. Adults and larvae found on pepper (*Capsicum*), jimsonweed (*Datura*), nightshade and tomato (*Solanum*). Widespread in eastern North America. (1)

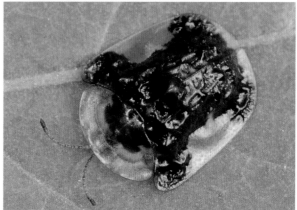

436

Stenispa metallica (Fabricius) (5.3–5.6 mm) is elongate, shining and uniformly black with dull, brassy luster and sides nearly straight. Antennae thickened, blackish brown to black. Elytra slightly shinier than pronotum. Legs black, femora thick, apices of tibiae and especially broad tarsomeres pilose. Larva feeds at base of developing leaves of green bulrush (*Scirpus atrovirens*); damage consists of long, parallel lines between veins. Adults active in summer, found on sedges (*Carex*), and bluestem (*Andropogon*) and cordgrass (*Spartina*). Massachusetts and New York to Georgia, west to Wisconsin, Missouri, and Texas. (2)

Baliosus nervosus (Panzer) (4.5–7.0 mm) is wedge-shaped and yellowish red with darker spots. Clypeus usually yellow, rarely black. Antennae dark reddish brown with 11 antennomeres. Elytra with 10 distinct ridges and rows of punctures, first ridge branched. Adults feed on leaves of various trees and shrubs, while larvae mine leaves of various deciduous trees. Adults overwinter in leaves and other debris on plants and emerge in spring to feed and mate; next generation of adults emerges in summer. Nova Scotia and New Brunswick to Florida, west to Ontario, Minnesota, Colorado, and New Mexico. (1)

Chalepus bicolor (**Olivier**) (6.3–7.6 mm) is elongate, straight-sided, coarsely sculptured, and black with red pronotum. Head with clypeus black, coarsely punctured. Pronotum usually with black spots. Scutellum red. Elytra black, ridged, with five to eight rows of punctures reduced to three rows at middle. Underside red. Legs with basal half of femora red. Larvae eat deer-tongue (*Dichanthelium clandestinum*), cypress panicgrass (*D. dichotomum*), and Heller's rosette-grass (*D. oligosanthes*). Adults found on larval host plants in late spring and summer. New York and Ontario to Florida, west to Kansas, Oklahoma, and Texas. (3)

Microrhopala floridana **Schwarz** (3.4–4.9 mm) is somewhat slender and uniformly black or metallic blue. Pronotum with lateral margins only slightly narrowed toward head. Width of elytral humeri about twice that of base of head. Larvae feed on narrowleaf silkgrass (*Pityopsis graminifolia*). Adults found on stems of larval host plant, also lupine (*Lupinus*) in spring and early summer. District of Columbia to Florida, west to Alabama. Similar to *Microrhopala excavata* (Olivier) that has pronotal margins strongly narrowed toward head and width of humeri more than twice width of base of head; southeast. (9)

437

Microrhopala vittata (**Fabricius**) (5.0–7.0 mm) has a reddish head with small eyes separated from mouth by distance equal to length of third antennomere and black or sometimes reddish antennae. Pronotum reddish with sides narrowed toward head and front margin narrowly transparent. Elytra with sides undulate or not, never finely saw-toothed (serrulate). Adults feed on flowers and leaves of goldenrod (*Solidago*), while the larvae mine the leaves. This species is widely distributed across southern Canada and United States. (9)

Microrhopala xerene (**Newman**) (3.6–4.9 mm) has large eyes with punctures behind either confused or arranged in double row. Frons distinctly angled. Anterior margin of pronotum lacks slender, transparent strip of cuticle. Adults and larvae feed on various plants in the Asteraceae; larvae mine leaves of goldenrods (*Solidago*), asters (*Aster*), and ragweeds (*Ambrosia*). New Brunswick to Florida, west to British Columbia, Nevada, and Arkansas; also Cape Breton Island, Nova Scotia. (9)

Octotoma plicatula (Fabricius) (3.8–4.8 mm) is wedge-shaped, with darker head and elytra. Head with groove on top, eight antennomeres, 1 thick, 2 cylindrical, 1–3 each nearly equal in length. Elytra with ridges and punctures in a network, not lines, sides somewhat parallel, then diverging just before apices. Legs with front tibiae flat. Underside infused with red and black. Larvae form tent-shaped mines in leaves of trumpet creeper (*Campis radicans*). Adult active spring and summer, found on buckeye (*Aesculus*), clover (*Lespedeza*), ash (*Fraxinus*), privet (*Ligustrum*), and fringe-tree (*Chionanthus*). Maryland to Florida, west to Michigan, Kansas, and Texas. (1)

Locust Leaf Miner *Odontota dorsalis* (Thunberg) (5.5–7.0 mm) is wedge-shaped with orange-yellow pronotum and elytra; elytra with black sutural stripe expanding to apex. Overwintering adults emerge in spring to feed on unfolding leaves of black locust (*Robinia pseudoacacia*) and other trees, skeletonizing foliage. Larvae mine leaflets. Large populations of locust leaf miners cause noticeable damage. Mines usually occur at tip and include up to two-thirds of leaflet; fresh mines are greenish, older mines brownish with brittle leaflets. One generation is produced annually. New Brunswick to Florida, west to Manitoba and Oklahoma. (6)

Odontota scapularis (Olivier) (6.3–7.8 mm) has an orange-red pronotum with middle and margins black. Elytra black with orange humeri, margins finely serrate. Head, antennae, and abdomen black. Underside of prothorax orange, remaining surface black. Front femora orange-yellow at bases. Adults found on a wide variety of plants in spring and summer. Larvae mine the leaves of groundnut (*Apios americana*), tick trefoil (*Desmodium*), and honeylocust (*Gleditsia triacanthos*). Ontario to Florida, west to Wisconsin and Texas. (6)

Sumitrosis inaequalis (Weber) (3.4–4.2 mm) has a small groove in middle of head, plus a small depression on either side near eye. Elytra with third elytral ridge not flared out at apex, outside apical angles evenly rounded, becoming wider at apices. Adults are found on various plants, while the larvae mine leaves of various Asteraceae, including asters (*Aster*), baccharis (*Baccharis*), joe pye weed (*Eutrochium*), sunflower (*Helianthus*), coneflowers (*Rudbeckia*), and goldenrod (*Solidago*). Maritime Provinces to Florida, west to British Columbia, Montana, Colorado, Wyoming, and Texas. (4)

***Hemisphaerota cyanea* (Say)** (4.6–5.6 mm) is oval and deep, shining metallic blue. Head with antennae short, thick, mostly yellow, and swollen at tips. Pronotum with front margin broadly emarginated with head clearly visible from above, front angles each with seta-bearing puncture, and sides more coarsely punctured than middle. Elytra with rows of large, deep punctures. Legs with thick, yellow pads under tarsi. Adults and larvae feed on palmetto (*Sabal*). Larvae hide under strands of their own feces coiled over their bodies; pupation occurs in these fecal shelters on leaf surface. North Carolina to Florida, west to Texas. (1)

***Physonota helianthi* (Randall)** (7.5–12.0 mm) is oval, convex, and has three color phases. Freshly emerged adults are dingy white, then turn black and white for about 3 weeks before reaching maturity as a brilliant metallic green beetle; pale yellow to brownish gray after death. Head completely covered by pronotum. Pronotum with three, occasionally five distinct spots. Elytra with base finely notched, side margins broadly flattened, but not thickened. Legs with tarsal claws simple. Adults and larvae feed on underside of sunflower (*Helianthus*) leaves. Québec and Ontario to Georgia, west to Manitoba, South Dakota, Nebraska, and Kansas. (3)

439

Color variation in *Physonota helianthi.*
TOP RIGHT: **Immature adult.**
BOTTOM RIGHT: **Mature adult.**

Argus Tortoise Beetle *Chelymorpha cassidea* (Fabricius) (8.5–12.0 mm) is oblong oval, convex, and brick red (teneral specimens yellow) with black spots. Bases of antennae red, remainder of antennomeres, legs, and rest of body black. Pronotum finely, sparsely punctate, elytra more coarsely punctate, punctures not in rows, and with four black spots across and two more behind. Elytra with five or six spots and a shared spot on suture behind scutellum. Both adults and larvae feed on bindweed (*Convolvulus*) and morning glories (*Ipomoea*). Larvae carry fecal shields over their backs. Adults most active in spring and early summer, early fall. Southern Canada and widespread across United States; also West Indies. (3)

Calligrapha alni **Schaeffer** (7.0–8.5 mm) is oval, convex. Prothorax entirely dark, surface sculpted with minute cracks. Each elytron with irregular spots and pair of stripes next to, not in contact with suture, and diffuse reddish-brown coloration; turned under edge dark. Legs yellowish red. Adults and larvae on alder (*Alnus*) in summer. Canada south to Minnesota, Wisconsin, Michigan, Ohio, West Virginia, and New Jersey. (28)

Calligrapha philadelphica **(Linnaeus)** (7.0–9.0 mm) is oval, convex. Pronotum entirely dark. Elytra pale with slender green stripes, long spots, and dots, long stripes parallel to, but not in contact with suture; underside of outer margins (epiplurae) mostly as pale as surface. Red legs with divergent tarsal claws. Adults and larvae feed primarily on redosier dogwood (*Cornus sericeus*). Widespread in eastern North America, ranging from Nova Scotia and New Brunswick to Georgia, west to Indiana, Nebraska, and Mississippi. (28)

440

Calligrapha rowena **Knab** (6.5–8.5 mm) is oval, very convex, with an entirely dark pronotum and elytral suture. Pronotum black with greenish luster. Underside of elytral rim pale, sutural stripe usually not connected to nearby spots on apices of elytra, and blackish markings with greenish hue. Legs reddish. Adults and larvae found on dogwood (*Cornus*). New Brunswick and Nova Scotia to Georgia, west to Manitoba, Minnesota, Kansas, and Missouri. (28)

Chrysomela interrupta **Fabricius** (6.0–8.4 mm) has a greenish-black head with antennomeres 1, 7–11 dark, 2–6 pale. Pronotum greenish black on disk delimited by a broad groove on each side, and brownish yellow along sides. Elytra red in living beetles with scattered punctures and seven dark spots sometimes joined into irregular bands. Underside and legs greenish black, tibiae partly brownish yellow, rest of tibiae and tarsi dark. Adults found in spring and early summer on alder (*Alnus*). Pennsylvania and Rhode Island to Florida, west to West Virginia, Kentucky, and Texas. (6)

Chrysomela mainensis Bechyné (5.5–7.8 mm) has greenish reflections on head and on dark area on pronotum, and sometimes on elytral spots. Pronotum pale with distinct broad grooves along each side of dark area. Elytra reddish orange, each with seven dark spots, middle pair never elongate but sometimes merge to form irregular band. Adults and larvae on alder (*Alnus*) in spring. Canada south to New Jersey and Michigan. (6)

Cottonwood Leaf Beetle *Chrysomela scripta* **Fabricius** (5.4–10.0 mm) has a greenish-black head with antennomeres 1, 7–11 dark and 2–6 reddish or dark. Pronotum greenish black at middle and reddish yellow outside of broad, distinct groove along each side. Elytra yellowish with distinct black markings and reddish-yellow margins. Underside and appendages various colors, legs with claws simple. Larvae and adults feed on species of cottonwood (*Populus*) and willow (*Salix*). Adults active spring through summer; attracted to lights at night. Widely distributed in North America, except West Coast of United States. (6)

441

Green Dock Beetle *Gastrophysa cyanea* **Melsheimer** (4.0–5.3 mm) is oval, somewhat convex, and entirely brilliant metallic blue or green, sometimes with bronze luster. Pronotum and elytra moderately punctured, punctures irregularly scattered. Pronotum lacks groove at base. Abdomen of egg-bearing female may be greatly enlarged. Legs with tibiae sharply angled at apices, hind femora not swollen, and claws simple. Larvae and adults feed on dock (*Rumex*), knotweed (*Polygonum*), and rhubarb (*Rheum*). Adults overwinter, emerge in early spring to feed and mate through early summer. Throughout southern Canada and United States. *Gastrophysa polygoni* (Linnaeus) is more northern, prothorax and legs reddish. (2)

American Aspen Beetle *Gonioctena americana* **(Schaeffer)** (5.0–6.2 mm) is not metallic, usually with pronotum marked and elytra spotted; appendages brown. Head reddish brown with clypeus pale and base black; antennomere 10 not longer than wide. Pronotum reddish brown and black at base. Elytra red with rows of punctures, spaces between finely punctate. Adults and larvae found on aspen (*Populus*). Adults briefly active in late spring, overwinter in leaf litter at base of host. Alaska and Canada south to Washington, Wyoming, Minnesota, Indiana, Michigan, Pennsylvania, and New England. (2)

Swamp Milkweed Beetle *Labidomera clivicollis* (Kirby) (8.0–11.0 mm) is distinctly robust and humpbacked with a blue-black head, pronotum, underside, and legs. Black pattern on yellow or orange elytra variable with mostly black individuals known in northeastern part of range; pattern wholly absent in some beetles. Both larvae and adults feed exclusively on milkweeds (*Asclepias*). Nova Scotia south to Florida, west to Manitoba, Idaho, and Texas; also occurs in Mexico. (1)

Colorado Potato Beetle *Leptinotarsa decemlineata* **(Say)** (9.0–11.5 mm) is oval, very convex, pale yellow to yellowish brown, with distinctive stripes on elytra. Head and pronotum with dark markings. Elytra each with four black stripes, each stripe bordered by irregular double row of coarse punctures, second and third stripes out from suture joined at apex. Plump reddish, pinkish, or orangish larvae are humpbacked with pairs of black spots on sides of abdomen. Adults and larvae found on potatoes and eggplant (*Solanum*) and many other relatives of nightshade (Solanaceae). Widespread in North America. (2)

442

False Potato Beetle *Leptinotarsa juncta* **(Germar)** (8.0–12.0 mm) has two outermost elytral stripes joined near elytral apex. Elytral suture pale with stripes bordered by a single row of regular punctures. Outer surface of femora with distinct dark spot. Both adults and larvae are found on solanaceous plants (Solanaceae), especially horse nettle and nightshade (*Solanum*), as well as on ground-cherry (*Physalis*). Pale, plump, almost white humpbacked larvae have distinct black spots on sides and feed on the leaves for about three weeks before entering the soil to pupate. Pennsylvania to northern Florida, west to Illinois, Kansas, Missouri, and eastern Texas. (2)

Yellow-margined Leaf Beetle *Microtheca ochroloma* **Stål** (4.2–6.0 mm) is dark brown, bronze, or black with elytra margined in dull yellow; each elytron with four rows of deep punctures. Adults and larvae feed on plants in the mustard family, including mustard and turnip (*Brassica*), pepperweed (*Lepidum*), watercress (*Nasturtium*), and radish (*Raphanus*). South America; established from Virginia to Florida, west to Oklahoma and Texas. (2)

Imported Willow Leaf Beetle *Plagiodera versicolora* **(Laicharting)** (3.3–4.5 mm) is oval, convex, and dark metallic blue, purple, or green. Head finely punctured, with antennae mostly black with basal antennomeres reddish. Pronotum finely punctured, a few larger punctures at sides. Elytra with punctures larger, more dense, sometimes lighter than head or pronotum. Underside and most of legs black; tarsi reddish, tarsomere 3 heart-shaped. Adults and larvae feed on quaking aspen (*Populus tremuloides*) and willow (*Salix*). Europe; established from Nova Scotia, New Brunswick, and Québec to South Carolina, west to Manitoba, Minnesota, Iowa, and Tennessee. (1)

Zygogramma suturalis **(Fabricius)** (5.0–7.0 mm) is almost hemispherical, uniformly brown except for whitish elytra with distinct and uninterrupted dark lines. Head with tips of maxillary palps truncate. Pronotum with moderate punctures on middle becoming larger at sides. Elytra with three to five stripes, including sutural stripe; each elytron with a single wide or two slender stripes joined at apices not reaching base; epipleuron finely setose at apices. Legs with third tarsomeres broad, slightly notched, with tips of claws divergent and bases fused. Québec and Ontario to Florida, west to Dakotas, Colorado, Kansas, and New Mexico. (2)

443

Alligator Weed Flea Beetle *Agasicles hygrophila* **Selman & Vogt** (4.3–5.1 mm) is elongate and black with somewhat irregular yellow stripes on elytra. Pronotum wider than long, without impressions before base. Elytra dull, with punctures scattered, not aligned in rows, yellow stripes along side and sutural margins usually joined at apices, sometimes broken into spots. Front coxal cavities open behind and hind femora enlarged for jumping. Introduced into United States to control alligator weed (*Alternanthera philoxeroides*). South America; established from North Carolina to Florida, west to Tennessee and Texas. (1)

Grape Flea Beetle *Altica chalybea* **(Illiger)** (4.0–5.5 mm) is oval, somewhat robust, shiny metallic blue, sometimes coppery or greenish; underside and appendages black. Basal half of antennae metallic, antennomeres 2–4 successively longer. Pronotum wider than long, with small punctures and deep impression across base reaching from side to side. Adults active spring and summer, found on grape (*Vitis*) and Virginia creeper (*Parthenocissus quinquefolia*). Widespread in eastern North America to Ontario and Québec. (39)

Blepharida rhois (Forster) (5.0–7.7 mm) is oval, very convex, with head and pronotum orangish or yellowish with elytra mottled or irregularly striped red and white. Antennal bases widely separated. Elytra with rows of coarse, widely separated punctures. Underside and legs reddish brown, hind tibiae grooved, and tips of claws finely split. Adults active spring and summer, found on smoke-tree (*Cotinus*), sumac (*Rhus*), and poison sumac (*Toxicodendron vernix*). In east from Ontario to Florida, west to Minnesota, South Dakota, Kansas, and Texas. (1)

Capraita sexmaculata (Illiger) (2.8–4.0 mm) is oval, somewhat flattened, and deeply and coarsely punctate. Head dark or reddish brown, pronotum dull yellow-brown with dark or reddish markings, and elytra with irregular zigzag markings. Adults found in summer on ash (*Fraxinus*) and fringe-tree (*Chionanthus*); also at light. Connecticut, New York, and southern Ontario to Florida, west to South Dakota and Texas. (14)

Capraita subvittata (Horn) (3.5–5.0 mm) is broadly oval, barely convex, somewhat shiny yellowish brown, with pronotal and elytral side margins flat, pale. Head usually with dark spot. Pronotum pale, wider than long, finely and sparsely punctate. Elytra with irregularly placed deep coarse punctures, sides broadly rounded. Underside dark. Hind legs with last tarsomere swollen. Adults active spring and summer, found on aster (*Eurybia*). In east from Maritime Provinces and New England to Georgia, west to Ontario, Wisconsin, Missouri, Arkansas, and Mississippi. (14)

Disonycha caroliniana (Fabricius) (5.0–6.5 mm) is oblong-oval, somewhat shiny, and mostly red. Head without punctures except for pit between eyes, antennae dark. Pronotum with pair of dark spots near front. Elytra each with three dark stripes, including shared sutural stripe, not joined at apices, red stripes flanked by whitish stripes, and margins pale. Legs with tibiae and tarsi dark, hind femora swollen, and hind tarsi with last tarsomere normal, not swollen. Adults most active spring and summer, found on various plants. New England to Florida, west to Colorado, Kansas, and Texas. (23)

Passionflower Flea Beetle *Disonycha discoidea*
(Fabricius) (6.5–7.8 mm) is red (yellow in preserved
specimens) with antennae, most of elytra, tibiae, and tarsi
black; black elytral spot distinctive, somewhat variable in
size, never reaching side or apical margins. Adults and
larvae feed on passionflower (*Passiflora*). Pennsylvania and
Rhode Island to Florida, west to Illinois and Texas. (23)

Disonycha pensylvanica **(Illiger)** (5.0–6.0 mm) is
elongate-oval, shiny, with sides of elytra pale, each elytron
with three black stripes, including shared stripe down
suture. Head mostly dark, except at antennal bases, with a
deep pit next to each eye surrounded by coarse punctures.
Pronotum twice as wide as long, with slight depression on
middle at base. Elytra with punctures indistinct, female with
three or four pronounced ridges. Hind tarsomeres normal,
not inflated. Larvae feed on smartweed (*Polygonum*).
Adults active spring and summer on larval host plants; also
attracted to light. Québec and Ontario to Florida, west to
Michigan, Kansas, and Texas. (23)

445

Spinach Flea Beetle *Disonycha xanthomelas*
(Dahlman) (4.5–5.8 mm) is elongate, oval, somewhat shiny
red and black or bluish black. Head black, smooth or with
a few large punctures between eyes, and antennae mostly
dark with light bases. Pronotum red, wider than long. Elytra
black, finely and sparsely punctate, sometimes with bluish
or brassy luster. Abdomen partly or completely red. Femora
often pale at base. Adults active spring and summer, found
on many kinds of plants. Widespread in eastern North
America. (23)

Southern Tobacco Flea Beetle *Epitrix fasciata*
Blatchley (1.6 mm) is small, mostly brownish, and clothed
in nearly erect setae. Head and pronotum dull reddish brown.
Pronotum with coarse, deep punctures and distinct groove
in front of base; underside of prothorax and appendages
dull yellowish brown. Elytra punctured with dull yellowish
brown with broad and diffuse brownish mark across middle
that narrows at brownish suture. Adults active in spring
and summer and feed on plants in the nightshade family
(Solanaceae), including tobacco (*Nicotiana tabacum*),
ground-cherry (*Physalis*), nightshade (*Solanum*), also
mustard (*Brassica*) and gourd (*Cucurbita*). Maryland to
Florida, west to Texas; likely found in other states. (8)

Epitrix fuscula Crotch (1.8–2.5 mm) is small, robust, and slightly shiny. Upper surfaces and femora blackish, while appendages reddish yellow-brown, tips of antennae sometimes darker. Pronotum with coarse, deep punctures, and shallow groove in front of base almost obscured by punctures. Elytra grooved, grooves with deep punctures (punctostriate) and narrower at base than spaces between. Adults active in spring and summer and feed on plants in the nightshade family (Solanaceae), including jimsonweed (*Datura stramonium*), tobacco (*Nicotiana tabacum*), husk tomato (*Physalis pubescens*), and nightshade (*Solanum*). New York and New Jersey to Florida, west to Illinois, Nebraska, and Texas. (8)

Kuschelina gibbitarsa (Say) (5.0–7.5 mm) has a red and black head and pronotum, pronotum with or without two to five dark spots sometimes united in a broad band. Elytra shining greenish, bluish, or purplish. Femora red, tibiae and tarsi dark or reddish. Adults found on Canada germander (*Teucrium canadense*) and mint (*Mentha*) in spring and summer; also at light. Ontario to Florida, west to South Dakota and Texas. (18)

446

Waterfern Flea Beetle *Pseudolampsis guttata* **(LeConte)** (2.0 mm) is robust, dorsal surface clothed in appressed setae with golden or brassy reflections on underside and appendages yellowish brown. Head reddish yellow, coarsely punctate, with bulging eyes. Pronotum shiny dark brown, straight-sided, and closely punctured, underneath with coxal cavities open behind. Elytra lighter brown, twice as wide as pronotum, with prominent "shoulders" (umbones), and with punctures in distinct rows. Legs with hind femora and last tarsomeres swollen. Larvae and adults feed on Carolina mosquitofern (*Azolla caroliniana*). Adults active in spring and summer, often common at light near water. Maryland to Florida, west to Missouri, Oklahoma, and Texas. (1)

Elongate Flea Beetle *Systena elongata* **(Fabricius)** (3.2–4.2 mm) is elongate, oval, moderately punctate, and shiny black with brassy luster and broad yellowish stripe down each elytron. Appendages mostly yellowish brown, antennal bases and femora darker. Prothorax below with legs bases completely surrounded by plate, process extending back between legs clearly visible. Legs with hind femora expanded. Larvae feed externally on roots of many plants, pest on sweet potato (*Ipomoea*). Adults found nearly year-round, feed on many plants; attracted to light. Widespread in United States; Manitoba. (8)

Systena marginalis (Illiger) (3.5–4.7 mm) is elongate, oval, somewhat flat, and dull pale yellowish with dark margins. Pronotum wider than long with side margins usually narrowly brown. Elytra broader than pronotum, with side margins usually narrowly brown, sometimes with small brown spot on rounded humeri, surface densely and coarsely punctate. Adults active in summer and early fall, feed on many plants, including bald cypress (*Taxodium*), pine (*Pinus*), and oak (*Quercus*); attracted to light. Québec and Ontario to Florida, west to South Dakota to Texas. (8)

Trichaltica scabricula (Crotch) (2.5–4.0 mm) is oblong-oval, nearly parallel-sided, somewhat convex, and reddish brown with dull metallic green or bluish-green elytra. Head with two distinct, sharp bumps in front and blackish antennae. Pronotum more than half again as long, with deep impression with ends bent backward. Elytra wider at base than pronotum, each with 10 rows of deep, close-set pits, spaces between narrower with short, erect setae. Larvae feed on fringe-tree (*Chionanthus*), ash (*Fraxinus*), and privet (*Ligustrum*). Adults active spring and early summer. Ohio to Tennessee, west to Kansas and Texas. (1)

Water Leaf Beetle *Galerucella nymphaeae* (Linnaeus) (4.5–6.0 mm) is somewhat oblong, dull. Head brown, black across top. Pronotum wider than long, reddish brown with three blackish spots, sides each with broad, deep, punctate depression. Elytra brown, suture and sides reddish brown. Bases of front legs not quite touching, narrowly separated by prosternal process; tibiae without spurs. Adults and larvae found on floating aquatic plants, where they chew irregular trenches on leaf surfaces. Hosts includes watershield (*Brasenia schreberi*), pond-lily (*Nuphar*), and smartweed (*Polygonum*). Adults active spring through early fall; attracted to light. Europe; widely established in North America, except Southwest. (1)

Larger Elm Leaf Beetle *Monocesta coryli* (Say) (11.2–15.4 mm) is the largest leaf beetle in North America. Elytra soft, distinctly and broadly widened apically. Living beetles bright yellow or yellowish orange with dark or pale brown markings on elytra that may or may not have a metallic blue or blue-green luster; sometimes with broad brown band across elytral apices and a dark brown spot at base; basal spots sometimes connected to form basal band. Ohio and West Virginia populations with dark or light markings, light basal and dark apical markings, or no markings at all. Adults and larvae feed on the leaves of elm trees (*Ulmus*). Pennsylvania to Florida, west to Indiana, Kansas, Oklahoma, and Louisiana. (1)

447

Black-margined Loosestrife Beetle *Neogalerucella calmariensis* **(Linnaeus)** (3.6–5.6 mm) is elongate, brown with dark markings on pronotum and elytra. Pronotum brown with black triangle or broad stripe down middle. Scutellum black. Elytra with dark stripes not sharply defined, reaching from base to apical third. Abdominal ventrite 4 partly or wholly dark. Legs with bases of forelegs not separated by prosternal process, bases of middle legs narrowly separated. and all femora mostly black. Introduced as a biological control of purple loosestrife (*Lythrum salicarium*). Larvae eat stems and leaves, reducing plant growth and preventing development of seeds. Overwintering adults emerge in spring to feed on developing plants and reproduce. Europe; broadly established in northeastern United States. (4)

Ophraella conferta **(LeConte)** (4.2–5.5 mm) is oblong oval and yellowish. Head with black spot. Elytra setose with distinct and complete stripes, dark stripes narrower with two punctures across basal width of stripe along suture, sides nearly parallel. Adults and larvae on goldenrod (*Solidago*). In eastern North America from Nova Scotia to Florida, west to Ontario, Wisconsin, and Louisiana. (8)

Pyrrhalta viburni **(Paykull)** (4.0–5.0 mm) is yellowish brown above with black spot on top of head, and densely clothed in yellowish pubescence; appendages and underside yellowish brown. Head nearly as wide as pronotum. Pronotum finely, densely punctate with weak dark lines on sides and midline. Elytra with humeri dark. Adults and larvae found on viburnum (*Viburnum*). Eurasia; established from Maritime Provinces and New England to Pennsylvania, west to Ontario. (1)

Cherry Leaf Beetle *Tricholochmaea cavicollis* **(LeConte)** (4.2–5.0 mm) is oval, somewhat flattened, coarsely punctate, and somewhat shiny bright red. Antennae, tibiae, tarsi, and sometimes portions of underside blackish. Pronotum almost twice as wide as long, narrowed in front, sides flattened and thickened, without markings. Elytra broadest just behind middle with margins flattened and thickened. Adults active late spring and summer on pin cherry (*Prunus pensylvanica*) and black cherry (*P. serotina*). Across Canada, in eastern United States from New England to Georgia, west to Minnesota and Iowa. (8)

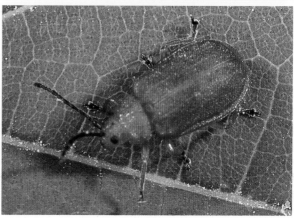

Trirhabda bacharidis (Weber) (7.5–12.0 mm) has a single black spot on back of head and three black spots across pronotum. Antennomere 3 shorter than 4. Pronotum no more than twice as wide as long, with punctures similar to those of elytra. Elytra with dark lateral and sutural stripes joined just behind middle, or with pale stripe distinctly narrowed behind middle. Hind femora not particularly enlarged, claws each with two teeth. Both adults and larvae feed on eastern baccharis (*Baccharis halimifolia*). Québec to Florida, west to Texas. (6)

Striped Cucumber Beetle *Acalymma vittatum* **(Fabricius)** (4.5–5.9 mm) is distinctly striped with yellow and black. Head dark brown or black. Antennomere 2 as long as 3, 1–4 mostly yellow, 5–11 mostly dark brown. Pronotum yellow. Elytra distinctly wider than pronotum at base, yellow, each elytron with two black stripes including those along suture; sutural stripe narrower than adjacent pale stripes. Legs yellow with apices of femora and both ends of middle and hind tibiae dark; claws notched. Abdomen black. Adults and larvae of this garden and crop pest devour all plant structures of cucurbits; also transmit bacterial wilt. Widespread in North America, except southwestern United States. (3)

449

Bean Leaf Beetle *Cerotoma trifurcata* **(Forster)** (4.2–6.0 mm) is oval, widest just behind middle, dull red to yellow, with dark triangular mark over scutellum. Head and most of underside black. Antennomeres 1 and 3 much longer than 4. Elytral markings variable with two or three spots along pale or dark suture. Underside of prothorax and bases of femora yellowish. Tips of femora and most of tibiae dark brown, tarsi light brown, tarsomere 1 as long as 2–5 combined. Adults and larvae injurious to beans and peas, but seldom so in the South. Québec to Florida, west to Manitoba, Minnesota, Kansas, and New Mexico. (2)

Northern Corn Rootworm *Diabrotica barberi* **Smith & Lawrence** (5.0–5.5 mm) is elongate and pale green without black markings. Pronotum wider than long with a pair of deep pits near base, some with large central pit near front. Scutellum pale or dark. Elytra each with six sinuate rows of punctures. Adults and larvae attack corn (*Zea mays*). Adults active in late spring, late summer and early fall; attracted to light. New Brunswick and Québec to Georgia, west to Saskatchewan, Colorado, Kansas, and Texas. (5)

Diabrotica cristata **(Harris)** (4.2–5.3 mm) is elongate and shiny with entirely black elytra. Head without punctures. Pronotum orange or black, nearly without punctures, with two large pits. Elytra very finely wrinkled and moderately punctate, each with two conspicuous ridges, one running from basal angle to apex and parallel to side, another from basal to sutural angle sinuate. Adults found on grasses, e.g., bluestem (*Andropogon*), brome (*Bromus*), panicgrass (*Panicum*), and bristlegrass (*Setaria*) as well as goldenrod (*Solidago*). New England to Georgia, west to Saskatchewan, Colorado, and Arizona. (5)

Spotted Cucumber Beetle *Diabrotica undecimpunctata howardi* **Barber** (4.6–7.7 mm) is oval, moderately shiny, and mostly greenish yellow with bold, black spots. Head black with basal antennomeres pale. Pronotum plain, sometimes different shade than elytra. Elytra each with three pairs of spots. Underside with prothorax and abdomen yellow, remainder black. Legs yellow with tibiae, tarsi, and apices of femora black. Larva feeds on roots, attacking cucumbers and relatives (Cucurbitaceae), and sweet potatoes (*Ipomoea batatas*). Adults consume all aboveground parts of larval hosts and transmit bacterial wilt; attracted to light. Ontario and Québec, widespread in United States. (5)

450

Clay-colored Leaf Beetle *Anomoea laticlavia laticlavia* **(Forster)** (6.6–9.0 mm) is nearly cylindrical, robust, orange with elytral margins narrowly to broadly black; ventral surface and legs variably orange and black. Legs with claws simple, front legs elongate with tibiae curved in male. Adults active spring and summer, found on albizia (*Albizia*), tick trefoil (*Desmodium*), honeylocust (*Gleditsia*), lespedeza (*Lespedeza*), black locust (*Robinia*), and mimosa (*Mimosa*). Widespread in eastern North America. *A. l. angustata* Schaeffer has black elytra with broad orange margins; Georgia and Florida. (3)

Babia quadriguttata **(Olivier)** (2.5–5.5 mm) is robust, cylindrical, and shiny black with four red-orange to dark red spots on elytra. Antennae serrate, antennomere 1 inflated, 2 offset and not attached to tip of 1. Elytra widest near apices, each with spot over basal angle and apex, and nine rows of punctures. Adults active spring and summer, feed on sumac (*Rhus*), oak (*Quercus*), hickory (*Carya*), hazelnut (*Corylus*), walnut (*Juglans*), and New Jersey tea (*Ceanothus americanus*). Ontario, widespread in eastern United States. (1)

Coleothorpa dominica franciscana **(LeConte)** (4.0–7.0 mm) is small, cylindrical, uniformly clothed in silvery setae, and almost entirely black with pronotal margins somewhat flattened. Head mostly densely setose, labrum yellow. Antennae serrate with antennomere 1 large and round, 2 attached off to side, 3 black and bare. Pronotum twice as wide as long. Bases of front legs separated by distinct process. Elytra (and body) widest at base. Larvae associated with ants. Adults active spring and summer, found on many plants. Widespread in eastern United States. *C. d. dominica* (Fabricius) has elytral pubescence limited to elytral base and apices. (2)

Saxinis omogera **(Lacordaire)** (2.5–5.5 mm) is robust, cylindrical, and somewhat shiny and metallic black, deep blue, or bluish green. Head is densely punctate, rough. Pronotum very convex, with sides and middle of hind margin flat. Elytron with red spot over basal angle, spots continuous along undersides of margins, coarse punctures arranged mostly in irregular series. Abdominal ventrite 5 shallowly depressed (male), or with a round pit (female). Adults active spring and early summer, feed on many plants. Vermont and Ontario to Georgia, west to Illinois, Oklahoma, and Texas. (1)

Bassareus detritus **(Olivier)** (4.6 mm) has a smooth and uniformly dull or shiny reddish or reddish-brown pronotum. Appendages brownish or orangish brown, last seven antennomeres and tarsi sometimes darker. Anterior margin of prothorax with small, but prominent tooth next to eye at each junction of side margins, becoming sinuate ventrally; posterior margin of pronotum finely notched. Elytra with rows, some irregular, of punctures with broad red bands across middle broken at suture and a pair of apical spots. Male with front tarsomere 1 not broader than 2. Atlantic and Gulf Coast states, New York to Alabama. (8)

Bassareus mammifer **(Newman)** (3.5–4.6 mm) has a shiny black or red pronotum, sometimes with yellowish spots. Antennae brownish, last seven antennomeres and tarsi sometimes darker. Anterior margin of prothorax with small but prominent tooth next to eye at each junction of side margins, becoming sinuate ventrally; posterior margin of pronotum finely notched. Elytra shiny with rows, some irregular, of punctures, dark reddish brown to black. Each elytron with two medial and two apical spots often merging. Legs black with tarsi brown; male with front tarsomere 1 distinctly broader than 2. New England and Québec to Florida, west to Manitoba, Minnesota, South Dakota, Kansas, and Texas. (8)

Cryptocephalus guttulatus Olivier (3.9–6.0 mm) is compact, somewhat cylindrical, with fine notches along base of pronotum. Pronotum light orange to reddish with yellow humeri, sometimes with light margins and spots across base. Elytra black, red, or dark orange, each with eight somewhat equal, usually oval, creamy yellow or dull orange spots, and eight rows of punctures with rows 6–7 confused. Adults found on honeylocust (*Gleditsia triacanthos*), cotton (*Gossypium*), and okra (*Abelmoschus*). Québec and Ontario to Florida, west to Wisconsin, Kansas, and Texas. (28)

Cryptocephalus leucomelas Suffrian (4.0–6.0 mm) is short, compact, somewhat cylindrical, with fine notches along base of pronotum. Pronotum creamy yellow to orange with four distinct red, brown, or black stripes. Elytra creamy yellow to orange with red, brown, or black markings, outer rows of punctures irregular, inner and outer rows joined at apices. Adults active late spring and summer, found on poplar and cottonwood (*Populus*) and willow (*Salix*). New Jersey and Ontario to Florida, west to South Dakota, Colorado, and Arizona. (28)

Cryptocephalus quadruplex Newman (2.9–4.0 mm) is dark brown to black, sometimes with a bluish luster. Side of prothorax beside head straight, not toothed or sinuate; anterior pronotal margin of both sexes broadly and evenly rounded; basal margin finely wrinkled (crenulate). Each elytron with two orange spots, larger spot at base not quite reaching suture, smaller spot at apex. Adults are found on many plants in spring and summer. Nova Scotia to Georgia, west to Manitoba, Montana, Kansas, and New Mexico. (28)

Griburius scutellaris (Fabricius) (4.0–6.0 mm) is robust, oblong, cylindrical, and black with orange or yellow markings. Base of antennae, pronotal margins, scutellum, and legs orange or yellow. Head with antennae long, filiform, extending beyond elytral umbones. Pronotum black, not spotted, with base margined, not finely notched; prothorax underneath flat in front, depressed behind. Scutellum raised at posterior tip. Elytra marked with yellow or orange broken transverse band and apical spots. Adults found in spring and early summer on ceanothus (*Ceanothus*), tick trefoil (*Desmodium*), and oak (*Quercus*). New York to South Carolina, west to Illinois and Texas. (4)

Pachybrachis bivittatus **(Say)** (3.9–5.0 mm) is yellow above. Basal half of antennae pale, antennomere 10 three times long as wide. Pronotum with indistinct black or reddish M-shaped mark, or completely dark, base with smooth, distinct margin. Elytra each with two stripes down middle, black or brown, one just above side often broken into three spots, one or more spots sometimes absent. Fifth abdominal ventrite with pit (female) or not (male). Ventral surface mostly black, tip of abdomen yellow. Legs reddish brown, tarsi darker. Adults active in summer on poplar (*Populus*) and willow (*Salix*). Widespread in North America. (37)

Pachybrachis subfasciatus **(LeConte)** (2.8–3.2 mm) is dull black with sides of pronotum and elytra reddish. Head wide as pronotum; sometimes variegated reddish. Pronotum coarsely and unevenly punctate, elytral sculpturing coarser, sometimes variegated reddish, slightly narrower than base of elytra; basal margin smooth, distinct. Elytra with punctured grooves at sides and apices, with broad, irregular band across middle often interrupted at suture, each elytron with a small spot at apex. Underside and appendages black. Adults active in late spring and summer, found on black walnut, *Juglans nigra*. Ontario to Georgia, west to Manitoba, Michigan, Illinois, Kansas, Oklahoma, and Louisiana. (37)

453

Neochlamisus bebbianae **(Brown)** (3.2–4.1 mm) is dark brownish bronze, sometimes bright reddish bronze, very coarsely pitted with sharp bumps, widest at elytral base, and resembles a caterpillar dropping. Antennae yellowish to light brown, sometimes becoming darker at tips. Pronotum with irregular and fine grooves on sides at base. Pygidium moderately, coarsely punctate. Abdomen with obscure large pits. Middle and front tibiae with one and two spines, respectively (male), or both with single spines (female). Adults and larvae feed on willow (*Salix*), alder (*Alnus*), maple (*Acer*), and beech (*Fagus*). Maritime Provinces to Florida, west to Minnesota and Texas. (14)

Western Grape Rootworm *Bromius obscurus* **(Linnaeus)** (4.0–5.5 mm) is robust, black, brown, or black and brown, and densely clothed in pale pubescence. Pronotum rounded on sides and much narrower than elytra. Minor grape (*Vitis*) pest; larvae feed externally on roots, while adults chew long, linear cuts in leaves. North American populations reproduce sexually, while European populations are parthenogenetic. Widely distributed in North America; in east from Maritime Provinces to North Carolina, west to Manitoba, Illinois, and Kansas. (1)

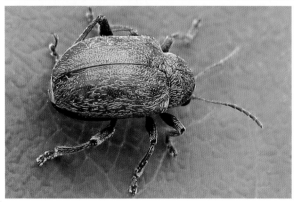

Demotina modesta **Baly** (2.8–3.1 mm) is short, broad, and dull yellowish brown to reddish brown; darker individuals with a pair of blackish spots on elytra. Body covered with short, pale scales; elytral scales curved. Pronotum one-third wider than long, broadly curved side margins finely serrate, and hind angles broadly rounded. Elytra wider than pronotum, humeri distinct, and side margins nearly straight-sided. Adults are found on oak (*Quercus*) and are attracted to light in late spring and summer. European; established from Virginia to Florida, west to Tennessee and Texas. (1)

Grape Rootworm *Fidia viticida* **Walsh** (5.5–7.0 mm) is oblong, convex, and light or dark reddish brown with long grayish setae. Head wider than pronotum. Pronotum longer than wide, sides without margins, wider than elytra. Elytra with rows of deep punctures. Legs long, uniformly colored. Subterranean larva eats roots of grape (*Vitis*). Adults active in late spring and summer, feed on grape leaves; also at light. Massachusetts and New York to Florida, west to Ontario, North Dakota, Colorado, Kansas, and Texas. *Fidia longipes* (Melsheimer) (4.5–5.5 mm) is smaller, usually blackish, with femoral bases or tibia lighter. (3)

Glyptoscelis pubescens **(Fabricius)** (7.0–11.0 mm) is elongate, oblong, stout and robust, dark brown or blackish with a bronze or pinkish-bronze luster and lightly and evenly clothed in mixture of brown and white reclining pubescence. Pronotum widest at middle. Elytra with distinct depression around scutellum. Appendages dark reddish brown. Claws incised at tips. Adults active late spring and summer, found on various tree, shrubs, and vines, especially pine (*Pinus*); also attracted to light. Québec and Ontario to Florida, west to Manitoba, Minnesota, Iowa, and Texas. (3)

Graphops pubescens **(Melsheimer)** (3.2–4.4 mm) is oblong-oval, sparsely setose, with shiny metallic bronze or coppery sheen. Pronotum wider than long. Elytra more than twice as long as pronotum, with prominent humeri and fine, inconspicuous setae, and rows of fine punctures. Abdomen with pygidium lacking conspicuous groove down middle. Legs with apices of middle and hind tibiae distinctly notched, front femora each with small tooth, and claws with long inner tooth. Adults active spring and early summer, found on evening primrose (*Oenothera*). Widespread in eastern North America. (8)

Xanthonia decemnotata **(Say)** (3.0–3.5 mm) is small, reddish brown, coarsely punctate dorsally, and clothed in fine, pale setae. Eyes prominent. Pronotum broader than long, with side margins rounded, narrower than base of elytra. Elytra with 8–10 distinct or indistinct variable spots that may or may not coalesce, punctures scattered on surface, in rows only along suture and margins. Abdomen with lateral margins smooth and continuous. Adults active in summer, found on various deciduous trees, including oak (*Quercus*), beech (*Fagus*), and elm (*Ulmus*). Nova Scotia and New Brunswick to Georgia, west to Saskatchewan, Montana, Nebraska, Oklahoma, and Texas. (7)

Dogbane Beetle *Chrysochus auratus* **(Fabricius)** (8.0–13.0 mm) is one of the most spectacular leaf beetles in eastern North America. Relatively large, oval, shiny; brilliantly iridescent green, coppery green, golden green or bluish green body is distinctive. Head retracted into pronotum and last five antennomers slightly enlarged. Adults and larvae associated exclusively with spreading dogbane (*Apocynum androsaemifolium*); diurnal adults found on leaves. Across most of southern Canada and all but California and Florida in continental United States. (1)

Grape Colaspis *Colaspis brunnea* **(Fabricius)** (3.9–5.1 mm) is yellowish brown above, darker below. Last antennomere, sometimes tip of previous, dark. Pronotum coarsely punctate. Prothoracic and elytral margins narrowly metallic and abdomen dark (northern populations), or not (southern populations). Each elytron with eight ridges, two near suture widest. Male with small tubercle on fifth abdominal ventrite. Legs yellowish brown. Adults active late spring through early fall, found on various plants, especially tick trefoil (*Desmodium*), lespedeza (*Lespedeza*), also fruits and vegetables; attracted to light. Québec and Ontario to Georgia, west to Minnesota, South Dakota, and Texas. (14)

Rhabdopterus **species** (4.0–6.0 mm) are somewhat compact, cylindrical, and dark reddish brown to blackish with a metallic luster. Head fully exposed, not withdrawn into prothorax. Pronotum smooth, shiny, with very fine punctures. Abdomen with pygidium grooved down middle. Adults found in various habitats in late spring and summer and feed on various plants; attracted to light. Examination of male genitalia needed for identification, females indistinguishable without associated males. (6)

455

Tymnes tricolor **(Fabricius)** (6.0–7.5 mm) is elongate, somewhat parallel-sided, dark metallic green, blue, bronze, or brown, with appendages usually pale. Head recessed in pronotum. Elytra with faint ridges and coarsely punctate to apex. Sides of metathorax finely punctate. Hind tibiae unmodified. Adults found on various trees and shrubs, including hickory (*Carya*), walnut (*Juglans*), tulip tree (*Liriodendron*), oak (*Quercus*), blackberry (*Rubus*), and grape (*Vitis*) from late spring through midsummer; also attracted to light. New Hampshire to Florida, west to Ohio, Tennessee, Arkansas, and Texas. (4)

Metachroma pellucidum **Crotch** (3.4-3.8 mm) is shiny yellowish brown, usually with head and pronotum darker, reddish brown. Head with punctures very fine to absent. Head not inserted into prothorax. Pronotum wider than long, finely but not densely punctate, with distinct keel on sides. Elytra wider than pronotum, with only traces of grooves, punctures not deep, especially at sides and apices. Legs with femora not toothed, claws with basal tooth long. Adults active in summer, feed on bayberry (*Morella*), oak (*Quercus*); attracted to light. New York to Florida, west to Indiana and Texas. (23)

456

Strawberry Rootworm *Paria fragariae* **Wilcox** (2.5–3.5 mm) is somewhat robust, convex, without setae or scales, color confusingly variable, ranging from uniformly reddish brown to black. Head with distinct suture between frons and clypeus. Head deeply set in prothorax. Pronotum very finely wrinkled, usually pale with basal black spot, occasionally entirely black. Elytra with sides somewhat parallel, sometimes with four relatively dull spots not in contact with each other, or spotless. Legs reddish brown, front femora each with small tooth. Adults active spring and summer, on plants in rose family (Rosaceae); also attracted to light, in Malaise traps. Widespread in eastern North America. (18)

Paria quadrinotata **(Say)** (3.4–4.0 mm) is somewhat elongate, with spots. Head with clypeus finely wrinkled, punctate, inserted into prothorax. Pronotum black, with punctures not merging together. Elytra pale with spots, pale with dark side margins and without spots, or dark, seam along sides complete to apex. Underside with metasternum and abdomen black. Legs with middle and hind tibiae notched near apices, front and hind femora each with a tooth. Adults and larvae feed on walnut (*Juglans*). Adults active late spring and summer, found on various trees and shrubs; also attracted to light. Québec and Ontario to Florida, west to South Dakota, Kansas, and Texas. (18)

Syneta ferruginea (Germar) (5.0–7.0 mm) is uniformly reddish yellow, coarsely punctate, lacks setae. Pronotum slightly longer than wide, with rounded sides each bearing three sharp teeth, front and rear angles also distinct. Elytra wider at base than pronotum, somewhat lighter overall with suture darker, each elytron with four ridges separated by three rows of punctures. Pygidium grooved down middle. Middle and hind tibiae lack notch just before apices. Adults active spring through early summer, found on various trees and shrubs. Atlantic Canada and New England to Georgia, west to Manitoba, Wisconsin, Iowa, Missouri, and Tennessee. (2)

PINE FLOWER SNOUT BEETLES, FAMILY NEMONYCHIDAE
(NE-MO-*NICK*-IH-DEE)

The Nemonychidae consists of five genera in North America, of which only *Cimberis* occurs in the east. Adults are active in late winter and spring and feed on pine (*Pinus*) pollen released by male cones (megasporangiate strobili). The larvae also eat pollen and drop to the ground to pupate in the soil.

FAMILY DIAGNOSIS Adult nemonychids have straight, not elbowed antennae, an elongate rostrum with a distinct labrum and two distinct grooves on underside, maxillary palps with four flexible palpomeres, elytra without grooves or rows of punctures, and apical spurs on all tibiae. Rostrum becoming wider and antennae attached at tip. Pygidium hidden by elytra. Tarsi appear 4-4-4, actually 5-5-5, tarsomere 3 deeply lobed, 4 small.

SIMILAR FAMILIES
- *Mycterus* (Mycteridae) – rostrum broad; antennae not clubbed; tarsi 5-5-4 (p.369)
- *Rhinosimus* (Salpingidae) – rostrum broad; antennae with loose club, tarsi 5-5-4 (p.376)

- fungus weevils (Anthribidae) – antennae long; tibiae with spurs; pygidium exposed (p.458)
- cycad weevils (Belidae) – femora enlarged (p.462)
- leaf-rolling, tooth-nose, and thief weevils (Attelabidae) – antennae attached at base of rostrum (p.462)
- straight-snouted, pear-shaped weevils (Brentidae) – body long and straight-sided, or pear-shaped (p.466)
- weevils (Curculionidae) – antennae elbowed (p.469)

COLLECTING NOTES *Cimberis* is seldom collected because of its specialized habits and limited seasonal activity. Look for adults early in the year on male pine cones. Also occasionally found in Malaise traps.

457

FAUNA 15 SPECIES IN FIVE GENERA (NA); TWO SPECIES IN ONE GENUS (ENA)

Cimberis pilosa (LeConte) (2.0–3.8 mm) is reddish brown to black without brassy luster and clothed in conspicuous and nearly erect, fine white setae; rostrum, prothorax, appendages, and underside often darker. Antennae not elbowed, antennomere 5 about as long as 3 or 4. Slender rostrum extended forward, flat and wide at tip. Eyes small and circular. Pronotum convex, punctures elongate and dense, surface coarse. Elytra without striae. Adults and larvae feed on pollen of pines (*Pinus*). New Brunswick and Maine to Florida, west to Manitoba and Texas. *Cimberis elongata* (LeConte) (2.9–5.1 mm) is more elongate, has a brassy tinge and flat or slightly concave pronotum. (2)

FUNGUS WEEVILS, FAMILY ANTHRIBIDAE
(AN-*THRIB*-IH-DEE)

Anthribids are uncommonly collected and their biology and natural histories are poorly known. The larvae eat vegetable materials and feed inside twigs and branches, in hard or polypore fungi, or under the bark of dead and dying trees. Adults of stem-feeding larvae generally eat pollen of the same plant. In fungus feeders, the larvae bore inside, while the adults graze on the surface. Adults of wood-boring larvae are often found on dead and dying branches and might eat bark. A predatory European species, *Anthribus nebulosus* Foster, is now established in northeastern United States, where it was introduced to control scale insects.

FAMILY DIAGNOSIS Adult anthribids have a broad, flat rostrum with grooves underneath, clubbed antennae that are straight and not elbowed, pronotum with sharp margin across base, pygidium not covered by elytra, and tarsomere 3 with spongy pubescent pad underneath. Abdomen underneath with ventrites 1–4 fused. Tarsi appear 4-4-4, actually 5-5-5.

SIMILAR FAMILIES
- *Mycterus* (Mycteridae) – rostrum broad; antennae not clubbed; tarsi 5-5-4 (p.369)
- *Rhinosimus* (Salpingidae) – rostrum broad; antennae with loose club, tarsi 5-5-4 (p.376)
- pine flower snout weevils (Nemonychidae) – pygidium covered by elytra (p.457)
- cycad weevils (Belidae) – femora enlarged (p.462)
- leaf-rolling, tooth-nose, and thief weevils (Attelabidae) – antennae attached at base of rostrum (p.462)
- straight-snouted, pear-shaped weevils (Brentidae) – body long and straight-sided, or pear-shaped (p.466)
- weevils (Curculionidae) – antennae elbowed (p.469)

COLLECTING NOTES The most effective method for collecting anthribids is to beat dead or diseased branches (especially if fungi are evident), clumps of dead twigs or leaves, or tangles of dead vines. Inspect the sheet right away since anthribids are relatively fast and take wing quickly. Other species are found on fungi growing on tree trunks. Sweeping weedy fields with fungal-infected and smutty grasses may also be productive. Species in several genera are collected in Malaise traps.

FAUNA 88 SPECIES IN 30 GENERA (NA); 48 SPECIES IN 23 GENERA (ENA)

Marbled Fungus Weevil *Euparius marmoreus* **(Olivier)** (4.5–8.8 mm) is distinctively marked with mixed yellow and/or gray, black, and white pubescence. Middle tibiae with a single pale band at middle. Adults found under bark in winter and usually associated with polypore fungi *Megasporoporia*, *Panis*, *Pereniporia*, *Phlebia*, *Trametes*, and *Trichaptum* in spring and summer; sometimes attracted to lights. Nova Scotia to Florida, west to Manitoba, Montana, Nebraska, and Texas. (3)

Euparius paganus Gyllenhal (3.3–5.8 mm) is elongate, robust, and clothed in brown mixed with yellowish and grayish pubescence. Head covered with dense, white pubescence, rostrum flat and as long as head, and mandibles tipped with three teeth. Antennae attached to sides of head right in front of prominent eyes, reaching base of elytra. Pronotum with basal ridge just in front of margin. Elytra with pale gray or whitish scales behind basal bump, often followed by black mark. Middle tibiae with two distinct pale rings. Adults and larvae feed on polypore fungi, including *Irpex lacteus*. Québec to Florida, west to Manitoba, Montana, Nebraska, and Texas. (3)

Ischnocerus infuscatus Fåhraeus (7.0–10.0 mm) is oblong and brown or black, with intermixed yellowish-brown and pale gray pubescence. Rostrum broad, longer than head, wider at tip, with fine and shiny ridge on top. Eyes long and elliptical, coarsely faceted, and not notched in front. Antennae long and slender, attached to rostrum on sides closer to mandibles than to eyes, club with three antennomeres. Pronotum longer than wide, front margin with small toothlike angles behind eyes. Elytra each with swellings at base and rows of deep punctures. Claws toothed. Larvae develop in dead branches. Maryland to Florida, west to Texas. (1)

Piesocorynus moestus (LeConte) (2.8–6.0 mm) is oblong, cylindrical, and blackish with white spots on pronotum sometimes indistinct or absent. Eyes oval, coarsely faceted, and not notched. Antennomere 3 longer than 2 or 4. Scutellum white. Pronotum with callus on top, spot on front margin, two on base. Elytra lobed at base and extending over base of pronotum, with rows of moderate, deep punctures, spaces between punctures with rows of black and gray squares. Legs ringed with gray. New Jersey to Florida, west to Ohio and Texas. (3)

Goniocloeus bimaculatus (Olivier) (4.5–6.0 mm) is slender, oblong, black, with numerous scattered tufts of black setae. Head not white in front, finely faceted eyes distinctly bulging, not distinctly notched in front. Rostrum flat, short, wider than long and not longer than head. Antennae short, slender, attached to side of head, club with 4 antennomeres, not reaching base of prothorax. Prothorax cone-shaped, widest at base. Elytra with rows of coarse, deep punctures, grayish-white angles and band behind middle. Adults found under bark; at light. Massachusetts to Georgia, west to Wisconsin and Texas. (1)

Toxonotus cornutus **(Say)** (3.5–5.8 mm) is elongate, somewhat cylindrical, and brown with conspicuous tufts of dark setae on pronotum and elytra; antennae and legs ringed with pale setae. Pronotum densely punctate, narrowed before middle and parallel behind, front margin with two tufts. Elytra each with white spot before middle, faint light and dark markings down sides of suture. Legs with tarsomere 1 lacking apical spine on top. Adults active spring and summer, found in Malaise trap; attracted to light. New Jersey to Florida, west to Indiana and Texas. (2)

Trigonorhinus sticticus **(Boheman)** (2.5–3.0 mm) is oblong, robust, brown, and clothed in dark brown and grayish-yellow setae. Rostrum narrowed from base to tip, longer at middle than sides. Eyes notched at bases of antennae. Pronotum convex, brown to blackish, widest in front of or at basal ridge. Scutellum U-shaped. Elytra each with central brown spot and other variable markings. Legs reddish brown, femora with dark at middle, tibiae without rings or spots, tarsomere 3 on all feet distinctly lobed. Adults associated with yellow nutsedge (*Cypereus esculentus*) and corn smut (*Utilago maydis*). In east from New Brunswick and Québec to Florida, west to Indiana and Texas. (3)

460

Eurymycter tricarinatus Pierce (6.2–8.5 mm) has a broad patch of white pubescence on rostrum and behind middle of elytra. Rostrum with three ridges, outer ridges long, parallel, and distinct; middle ridge less distinct. Pronotum wider than long with surface uneven, narrowly grooved down middle. Abdomen brown in middle and white or gray at sides. Hind tibiae with setae forming one pale band at middle. Adults found on dead twigs and on fungus growing on beech (*Fagus*), sycamore (*Platanus*), and other hardwoods in late spring and summer; also attracted to lights. Larvae develop in fungi, including *Daldinia* and *Hypoxylon*, associated with woody plants. Québec to North Carolina, west to Illinois and Arkansas. (3)

Gonotropis gibbosus LeConte (4.5–6.0 mm) is convex, somewhat ovate, and dull black. Sides of head with dense fine white pubescence. Pronotum with broad triangular impression bordered by triangular patch of light brown pubescence. Elytra wider than prothorax, with two prominent tubercles at base, front half with large saddle-shaped patch of pale pubescence, with rows of deep punctures, spaces between raised. Abdomen underneath with tip rounded in both sexes. Adults collected on dead hemlock (*Tsuga*). Alaska and Canada south to Pennsylvania and Colorado. (1)

Eusphyrus walshi (**LeConte**) (2.3–3.0 mm) is elongate, oval, robust, and clothed in brownish or grayish pubescence mottled with irregular patches of yellowish-white setae. Pronotum with sharp ridge just in front of base that comes in contact with elytral base. Elytra with rows of deep irregular punctures. Appendages reddish brown, sometimes with antennal club and femora darker. Adults active in late spring and summer, found on dead branches or under bark of deciduous trees and shrubs, including oak (*Quercus*), elm (*Ulmus*); also in Lindgren funnel and Malaise traps, and at light. Québec to Florida, west to Michigan and Texas. (3)

Ormiscus saltator LeConte (1.5–2.0 mm) is brownish black or black with spots or bands of grayish-white pubescence forming distinct elytral band before middle and expanded toward scutellum. Head with eyes notched and rostrum squarish, antennal club with antennomeres fused, with uniformly gray (male) or mottled (female) pubescence. Pronotum squarish, at sides densely covered with pale setae. Elytra with rows of large, deep punctures, spots at humeri and behind middle less conspicuous than elytral band, parallel-sided. Hind tibiae of male with barely visible hook. Adults capable of jumping; no firm association with fungi. Ontario to Florida, west to Michigan, Illinois, Kansas, and Texas. (14NA)

Choragus sayi LeConte (2.1–2.5 mm) is small, elongate-oval, somewhat cylindrical and pubescent, and dark brown. Head not capable of being withdrawn into prothorax, eyes elongate-oval, not very convex and closer on top of head than bottom, antennae attached on top of rostrum, club with three antennomeres. Rostrum short, flat, directed down. Pronotum minutely and densely punctured with single ridge on each side, with basal margin double-arched. Elytra with rows of deep punctures, spaces between them somewhat convex. Larvae develop in hard, dry, velvety brown or black and charcoal-like pyrenomycete fungi. Adults found on dead twigs of beech (*Fagus*) and other hardwoods with fungi; also Lindgren funnel traps. Maritime Provinces to Georgia, west to Québec, Indiana and Texas. (6)

CYCAD WEEVILS, FAMILY BELIDAE
(*BEL*-IH-DEE)

Belids are small, odd weevils represented in North America in south Florida by a single genus, *Rhopalotria*, where both species are associated with native and adventive *Zamia* cycads. Adults gather on the male cones, or strobili, to feed, mate, and lay eggs. They inadvertently carry pollen to the female cones as they move about and may be obligate pollinators of cycads.

FAMILY DIAGNOSIS Adult belids have clubbed antennae with 11 antennomeres, 9–11 forming loose club, pronotum with entire sides sharply margined or keeled, elytra short and exposing pygidium, legs short with greatly expanded front femora in males. Tarsi appearing 4-4-4, actually 5-5-5, tarsomeres 2–3 broadly lobed, claws simple. Abdomen with five distinct ventrites.

SIMILAR FAMILIES The above diagnosis and the exclusive association of these beetles with cycads are definitive.

COLLECTING NOTES Look for *Rhopalotria* on the reproductive structures of cycads.

FAUNA TWO SPECIES IN ONE GENUS (NA, ENA)

Rhopalotria slossonae **(Schaeffer)** (3.5–4.2 mm) is oblong, somewhat flattened, reddish yellow, elytra black with long reddish-yellow spots on humeri. Head with clubbed antennae straight, with rostrum slender, slightly curved, punctate (male) or smooth (female). Pronotum subequal in width to base of elytra, with front margin broadly rounded. Elytra slightly diverging toward broadly and individually rounded tips, slightly shorter than abdomen, one tergite exposed. Legs with all femora enlarged, especially in male. Larvae feed, develop, and pupate in male cones of cycads, including the native coontie, *Zamia pumila*. Adults feed, mate, and lay eggs in male cones. Florida. *Rhopalotria mollis* (Sharp) is adventive; uniformly reddish yellow. (2)

LEAF-ROLLING AND THIEF WEEVILS, AND TOOTH-NOSE SNOUT BEETLES, FAMILY ATTELABIDAE
(AT-TEH-*LAB*-IH-DEE)

Attelabids are either leafrollers, leaf miners, or live on other plant tissues, especially reproductive structures. Female leaf-rolling weevils (*Homoeolabus*, *Synolabus*) lay one or more eggs on a leaf, then use their mandibles to chew and cut the base of the leaf and roll it around the eggs with their front legs. The rolled-up barrel-like leaf serves as both food and shelter for the developing larva(e). Species in the genus *Pterocolus* are called thief weevils because the females take over the rolled leaf nurseries of other attelabids by destroying their eggs and replacing them with their own. Tooth-nose snout beetles have mandibles toothed on the inner and outer margins. Their larvae are leaf miners (*Eugnamptus*) or develop in flower heads (*Auletobius*, *Haplorhynchites*, *Involvulus*, *Temnocerus*). Most species are of no economic importance, but *Merhynchites*, which develops in buds and shoots, sometimes damages cultivated blackberries, raspberries, and roses.

FAMILY DIAGNOSIS Adult leaf-rolling weevils are more or less stout, broad across elytral bases, without setae; tooth-nose snout beetles are elongate (*Eugnamptus*) or very small and oval; *Pterocolus* is very small and broadly oval. Attelabids have clubbed antennae with 11 antennomeres, straight, not elbowed, 9–11 forming loose club. Rostrum long and slender (*Eugnamptus*) or short and broad, mandibles toothed only on inner margin (*Himatolabus, Homoeolabus, Synolabus*) or on the inner and outer margins. Pronotum distinctly narrower than base of elytra. Elytra cover the entire abdomen. Tarsi appearing 4-4-4, but are 5-5-5; tarsomere 4 small, partially hidden within lobes of heart-shaped tarsomere 3, claws equal in size and toothed. Abdomen with five ventrites becoming progressively shorter toward the rear, 1–2 fused.

SIMILAR FAMILIES

■ pine flower snout beetles (Nemonychidae) – associated with male pine cones; rostrum with distinct labrum (p.457)

■ fungus weevils (Anthribidae) – rostrum broad; antennae long; pygidium exposed (p.458)

■ straight-snouted weevils (Brentidae) –body pear-shaped or long, straight; long, cylindrical trochanter with femur attached at tip is unique (p.466)

■ weevils (Curculionidae) – antennae elbowed; compact club comprising one to three antennomeres (p.469)

COLLECTING METHODS Beating shrubs, trees, and vines, and sweeping flowers are the most productive methods for collecting attelabids in the field. Some attelabids are abundant in spring and early summer on oak (*Quercus*), while those species that develop in plants in the rose family (Rosaceae) are likely to be found in spring and fall.

FAUNA 51 SPECIES IN 11 GENERA (NA); 15 SPECIES IN 9 GENERA (ENA)

Himatolabus pubescens **(Say)** (4.0–7.2 mm) is pear-shaped, robust, uniformly dull reddish brown or darker and irregularly clothed in short, yellowish pubescence. Rostrum short, coarsely punctate in front of antennal bases. Pronotum smooth, coarsely punctate with narrow groove down middle, without lobes in front covering eyes. Elytra without bumps at base, with close-set rows of coarse punctures, spaces between finely punctate. Adults are active mostly in summer, found on hazelnut (*Corylus*), alder (*Alnus*), oak (*Quercus*), and rosemallow (*Hibsicus*). Maritime Provinces and Québec to Virginia, west to Manitoba, North Dakota, Colorado, New Mexico, and Alabama; Mexico. (1)

Homoeolabus analis **(Illiger)** (5.0–6.0 mm) lacks setae and is short, wide, and mostly bright red with base of head, appendages, and pterothorax black. Front legs of both sexes unarmed, front tibiae of female strongly curved. Male with two rows of sharp tubercles on abdomen. Adults active during spring and summer and are found on oak (*Quercus*); female lays eggs in freshly rolled leaves where larvae develop. Ontario to Florida, west to Manitoba, Kansas, and Texas. (1)

Synolabus bipustulatus **(Fabricius)** (3.0–4.0 mm) lacks setae and is black tinged with blue with an oblong red spot on humerus of each elytron. Adults found on oak (*Quercus*), hickory (*Carya*), and walnut (*Juglans*) and at light in late spring and summer. Larva develops individually in a single leaf rolled up by female beetle. Nova Scotia to Florida, west to Ontario, Wisconsin, and Texas. (2)

Synolabus nigripes **(LeConte)** (3.5–4.5 mm) lacks setae and is usually bright red with rostrum and appendages black without bluish tinge. Front femora with either one blunt spine (female) or two (male). Adults active spring and summer and found on sumac (*Rhus*) or at light. Rhode Island and New York to Florida, west to Minnesota, Colorado, Kansas, and Arizona. (2)

Auletobius cassandrae **(LeConte)** (1.8–2.2 mm) is oblong-oval, brownish yellow to reddish brown or blackish, and sparsely clothed in patches of long, white pubescence; pubescence denser on head, front and down middle of pronotum, and in two irregular bands across elytra. Antennae inserted at basal third of rostrum. Pronotum wider than long, sides weakly arched and not keeled. Scutellum with short, adjacent grooves absent. Elytra with punctate grooves irregular, spaces between indistinct, all punctures similar in size. Pygidium exposed. *Auletobius ater* (LeConte) (3.3–3.8 mm) blackish, sparsely, uniformly clothed in fine setae, with antennae inserted near middle of rostrum. Eastern North America. (2)

Eugnamptus angustatus **(Herbst)** (3.5–5.1 mm) is elongate with head and pronotum nearly equal in length, variably colored. Head, elytra, and underside of abdomen usually black, reddish black, or blue-black. Pronotum, legs, and portions of pterothorax yellowish orange, reddish, or black. Head with eyes bulging, less so in female. Pronotum as wide as long. Elytra widest at apical third, ventrites 1 and 2 fused, surface with rows of punctures. Larvae mine leaves of various deciduous trees and shrubs. Adults active in spring and summer. Vermont and Ontario to Florida, west to Nebraska and Texas. (2)

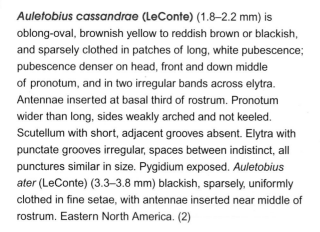

Sunflower Headclipping Weevil *Haplorhynchites aeneus* **(Boheman)** (3.9–6.6 mm) is coarsely punctate, wholly black with slight bronze luster , or with dull reddish-brown elytra, and clothed in long, bristly setae. Rostrum slender, longer than head and prothorax, antennae attached just behind middle. Pronotum as long as wide, widest at base, but decidedly narrower than elytra. Elytra with shallow grooves with fine punctures, spaces between with irregular rows of smaller punctures. Larva develops in flower head of composites (Asteraceae). Adults active in summer, found on larval hosts. Widespread in North America; throughout eastern United States. (1)

Rose Curculio *Merhynchites bicolor* **(Fabricius)** (5.0–6.5 mm) is bicolored red and black and clothed in erect yellowish pubescence; appendages black. Rostrum grooved, black, long as head and pronotum combined. Head black, sometimes reddish behind eyes. Pronotum red, nearly wide as long, narrower than elytra. Elytra red with distinct rows of punctures. Underside of pterothorax and abdomen black. Larvae develop in buds and hips of rose (*Rosa*), and blackberries and raspberries (*Rubus*). Widespread; in east from Ontario to South Carolina, west to Dakotas and Kansas. (1)

465

Pterocolus ovatus **(Fabricius)** (2.0–3.7 mm) is strongly ovate, broad, convex, and uniformly deep metallic blue or greenish black. Rostrum straight and shorter than head. Pronotum with distinct side margins and deep, long punctures. Elytra grooved with deep, close-set punctures and round tips exposing part of abdomen. Females take over the rolled leaves of other attelabids. Adults active in late spring and summer, found on many trees and shrubs. New England and Ontario to Florida, west to Wisconsin, Iowa, and Arizona. (1)

Eastern Rose Curculio *Temnocerus aeratus* **(Say)** (2.1–2.8 mm) is oblong-convex, black with upper surface usually coppery or with bluish or purplish luster. Head with rostrum more or less staight-sided and narrowest between antennae and tip; male rostrum shorter than prothorax, female's one-fourth longer. Prothorax somewhat cylindrical, slightly longer than wide. Elytra half again as wide as pronotum, grooves with large punctures, spaces between narrow. Adults found on vegetation, including willow (*Salix*); also attracted to light. Ontario and Maine to Florida, west to Minnesota, Colorado, and Arizona. (4)

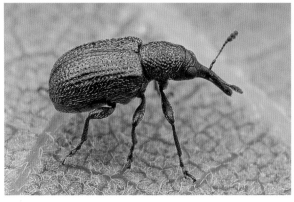

STRAIGHT-SNOUTED AND PEAR-SHAPED WEEVILS, FAMILY BRENTIDAE
(BRENT-IH-DEE)

Brentids are composed of primarily tropical beetles and most are very small and difficult to identify. The larvae of some species tunnel in living and dying hardwoods, degrading the value of standing timber and recently logged trees felled and harvested for wood products. Other brentid larvae attack developing fruits, or mine stems and leaves and may cause the development of galls. The larva of the adventive sweet potato weevil, *Cylas formicarius* (Fabricius), attacks sweet potato vine and tubers, as well as other morning glories (Convolvulaceae). Larvae of *Trichapion* and its relatives are associated with numerous flowering plants, especially in the legume (Fabaceae) and sunflower (Asteraceae) families. They mine stems, developing fruits, and seeds. A few seed-feeding species were purposely imported into North America as biological control agents of invasive shrubs and weeds, including purple loosestrife (*Lythrum salicaria*).

FAMILY DIAGNOSIS Adult brentids are difficult to characterize as a family. They are long, slender, and parallel-sided (*Arrenodes*, *Brentus*, *Paratrachelizus*, *Stereodermus*), stout and pear-shaped (*Trichapion* and relatives), antlike (*Cylas*), or large and robust with a short, broad rostrum (*Ithycerus*). Head with rostrum somewhat to very long, slender, and cylindrical; males (*Arrenodes*, *Brentus*, *Paratrachelizus*, *Stereodermus*) tend to have broader or longer rostra. Body lacks setae or scales, or with distinct, short pubescence (*Ithycerus*). Antennae usually straight, occasionally elbowed or geniculate (*Nanodactylus*, *Nanophyes*, *Pseudotychius*), and attached to sides at middle of rostrum. Legs with tarsal formula 5-5-5. Abdomen with first two ventrites fused and longer than ventrites 3 and 4; these first two ventrites are on a different plane (examine from side) from ventrites 3–5.

SIMILAR FAMILIES

- pine flower snout beetles (Nemonychidae) – antennae attached near tip of rostrum; tibiae with spurs, labrum visible and free (p.457)
- fungus weevils (Anthribidae) – labrum visible, antennae attached at base of rostrum, tibiae without spurs, labrum visible and free (p.458)
- cycad weevils (Belidae) – short legs with femora swollen (esp. male), elytral apices truncate (on cycads; Florida only) (p.462)
- leaf-rolling weevils (Attelabidae) – labrum not free (p.462)
- weevils (Curculionidae) – antennae elbowed (geniculate) with distinct club (p.469)

COLLECTING NOTES Look for brentids under bark or on trunks of dead or dying trees at night, or locate them by beating or sweeping flowers and vegetation, especially on composites (Asteraceae) and legumes (Fabaceae). Many species are attracted to lights.

FAUNA 151 SPECIES IN 30 GENERA (NA); ~30 SPECIES IN 22 GENERA (ENA)

Oak Timberworm *Arrenodes minutus* (Drury) (6.0–17.0 mm) is long, slender, nearly cylindrical, shiny dark reddish brown to blackish with narrow yellowish spots often joined to form bars on elytra. Head with rostrum broad in male, slender in female. Prothorax longer than wide. Adults found on bark of dead or dying trees and at light at night in late spring and early summer; sometimes cluster under loose bark. Larva takes two to three years to develop, pupation occurs in gallery near exit. Ontario and Québec to Florida, west to Wisconsin, Nebraska, and Texas. (1)

Sweet Potato Weevil *Cylas formicarius* **(Fabricius)**
(5.0–6.0 mm) is small, slender, antlike, smooth, shiny, and
brightly colored. Antennomere 11 long and cylindrical
(male) or shorter and oval (female). Prothorax, legs, and
antennae reddish, head bluish black, rostrum black, elytra
and abdomen blue. Pronotum markedly constricted before
base, surface without punctures. Elytra convex, humeri
not sharp, and with narrow, finely punctate grooves.
Adults active year-round, found on sweet potato (*Ipomoea*)
and wild relatives. Virginia to Florida, west to New Mexico,
south to South America. (1)

Perapion curtirostre **(Germar)** (1.7–2.6 mm) is black
with somewhat metallic luster, and fine, pale, inconspicuous
vestiture. Rostrum short, thick. Pronotum nearly cyclindrical.
Elytra with spaces between grooves with one or two rows
of fine setae. Bases of middle legs touching, not separated
by thoracic process, first hind tarsomere longer than wide,
that of male with spine underneath, and claws of both
sexes not toothed. Adults found on dock (*Rumex*). Europe;
established from Maritime Provinces and Maine to New
York. (1)

Neapion herculanum **(Smith)** (2.0–3.5 mm) is pear-
shaped, convex, reddish brown to blackish brown with pale
pubescence. Rostrum curved, as long as prothorax, of
equal width throughout. Prothorax as long as broad, widest
at base, with sides sinuate, fine punctures, and short,
narrow groove down middle. Elytra distinctly grooved with
deep punctures, spaces between broader and flat, and
broad band without setae across middle fringed in front
and rear with dense pubescence. New England to North
Carolina, west to Wisconsin, Illinois, and Tennessee. (1)

Hollyhock Weevil *Rhopalapion longirostre* **(Olivier)**
(2.6–3.2 mm) is pear-shaped, black with reddish-brown
legs, clothed in grayish pubescence. Rostrum of female
thicker and very long, twice that of male's. Antennae
straight, first antennomere (scape) shorter than next three
antennomeres of funicle, funicle with seven antennomeres,
club with sutures distinct. Pronotum with vestiture directed
toward midline. Pygidium of male without deep groove
across tip. Legs with front femora lacking polished area
underneath, bases of middle legs separated by thoracic
sternal processes, and all claws toothed at base. Adults
found on hollyhock (*Alcea rosea*) and cotton (*Gossypium*).
Eurasia; widely established in North America. (1)

Betulapion simile (Kirby) (1.7–2.2 mm) is elongate, somewhat slender, black, and clothed in conspicuous and sparse whitish to yellowish-white long, fine scales. Head with eyes moderately prominent, rostrum slightly curved, slightly longer (male) or 1.5–2.0 times longer (female) than pronotum. Pronotum barely wider than long at base. Elytra with deep grooves and fine scales, with spaces between usually with one row of fine scales. Tips of middle and hind legs with spinelike processes equal in size. Adults and larvae on paper birch (*Betula papyrifera*). Eurasia; established from Newfoundland and North Carolina, west to Pacific Northwest and Utah. (1)

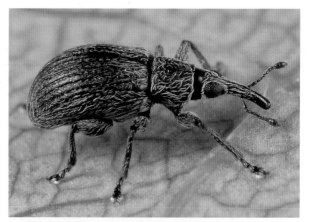

White Clover Weevil *Ischnopterapion virens* (Herbst) (1.8–2.6 mm) is oblong, convex, and black with metallic reflections. Head with eyes prominent, rostrum not distinctly expanded at point of antennal insertion. Pronotum wider than long, broadest at base, with side margins parallel in basal half. Elytra oblong to elongate with sides round, uniformly shining metallic green or greenish blue, grooves with moderately deep punctures. Legs black with metallic greenish or bluish femora. Larvae and adults feed on clover (*Trifolium*); larvae mine petioles, stem, and roots, adults eat foliage. Europe; established from Connecticut and New York to Virginia. (1)

Trichapion rostrum (Say) (3.0–3.5 mm) is robust, black, and sparsely clothed in fine, white scales, more so on sides of pterothorax. Head with eyes prominent, rostrum slightly curved, slightly longer (male) or 1.5–2.0 times longer (female) than pronotum. Pronotum with moderately deep punctures, widest at base, rounded to slightly constricted toward front. Elytra with deep grooves, spaces between usually convex, sometimes flat, with two rows of fine punctures bearing fine scales. Middle and hind tibiae of male with equal-sized spines. Larvae develop in seedpods of indigo (*Baptisia*). Adults on foliage of larval host, especially on seedpods. New York to West Virginia, west to Wisconsin and Iowa. (45 NA)

Coelocephalapion perminutum (Smith) (1.2–1.5 mm) is small, robust, pear-shaped, blackish, with inconspicuous pubescence; rostrum and appendages contrastingly pale yellowish or reddish. Rostrum slender, shorter than head and prothorax, with antennae attached near barely expanded base. Prothorax wider than long, widest behind middle. Elytra widest at middle with rows of deep and widely spaced punctures, spaces between rows slightly convex. Adults associated with low-growing herbage; larvae develop in seeds of hempvine (*Mikania*). Massachusetts and New York to Florida, west to Texas. (22 NA)

New York Weevil *Ithycerus noveboracensis* (Forster)
(12.0–18.0 mm) is brown or black, broad-shouldered, with
pronotum and elytra covered with light and dark scales
forming a distinctive pattern. Larvae feed inside roots
on outer vascular tissues. Adults rarely encountered;
feed on the shoots, leaf petioles, leaf buds, and other
vegetative structures of various deciduous hardwoods,
especially beech (*Fagus*), hickory (*Carya*), oak (*Quercus*),
crabapple (*Malus sylvestris*), and peach and plum (*Prunus*).
Widespread in eastern United States, north to Ontario and
Québec. (1)

WEEVILS, AND SNOUT, BARK AND AMBROSIA BEETLES, FAMILY CURCULIONIDAE
(CUR-CUE-LEE-ON-IH-DEE)

The Curculionidae is the largest family of beetles and includes many important pantry, garden, agricultural, and forest pests. A great number of weevil pests were introduced into North America from Europe in ornamental plants and stored products. Others were purposely introduced as biocontrol agents of numerous invasive plants, including purple loosestrife (*Lythrum salicaria*) and thistle (*Cirsium*). As a group, adult and larval weevils feed as generalists or specialists on every kind of living aquatic or terrestrial plant and are associated with all their vegetative and reproductive structures. Most species are associated with flowering plants, but some are adapted to conifers, especially pines. Larvae that are generalist feeders burrow through the soil and feed externally on the roots of many kinds of plants and sometimes produce characteristically shaped galls. Specialists often feed internally in the stems, roots, leaves, or reproductive structures of one or more closely related species of plants. A few species feed on leaves, living or dead, mining inner tissues or grazing on their outer surfaces. Most adults eat leaves, pollen, flowers, and fungi, but others attack fruits and nuts, or burrow into wood. A few species are capable of reproducing without mating, a cloning process called parthenogenesis. Among parthenogenetic weevils, males are rare or entirely unknown. Bark and ambrosia beetles live mostly in injured, weakened, or dying trees, shrubs, and woody vines. Bark beetles feed on the phloem of the inner bark and leave characteristic galleries and tunnels behind. Ambrosia beetles cultivate and feed on symbiotic ambrosia fungi in the xylem of the host plant. Some bark and ambrosia beetles are well-known vectors of tree diseases and degrade or kill vast expanses of forests annually.

FAMILY DIAGNOSIS Adult curculionids are incredibly diverse and are broadly oval, long, and cylindrical to strongly humpbacked beetles. Rostrum is long and slender, short and broad, greatly reduced, or entirely absent. Surface sometimes scaled, with varied patterns of black, brown, or gray, sometimes with weak to decidedly metallic reflections. Eyes present, reduced, or very rarely absent. Clubbed and elbowed antennae have 11 antennomeres, 9–11 forming a compact club. Pronotum long or short, slightly wider than the head, without sharp margins or keels on sides. Scutellum small or hidden. Elytra rounded or parallel-sided, almost or completely concealing abdomen.

Tarsal formula appearing 4-4-4, usually 5-5-5, tarsomere 4 very small and hidden within lobes of heart-shaped 3, claws mostly equal in size and simple. Abdomen with five ventrites, first two usually fused.

SIMILAR FAMILIES
- *Rhinosimus* (Salpingidae) – rare, associated with dead wood; antennae straight, body with a distinct green metallic sheen (p.376)
- pine flower snout beetles (Nemonychidae) – rare, on male pine strobili; antennae straight, club with three antennomeres; labrum distinct (p.457)

469

- fungus weevils (Anthribidae) – beak broad; antennae not elbowed, club faint or absent in species with long antennae; pygidium exposed (p.458)
- some leaf-rolling weevils (Attelabidae) – antennae straight, club loose with three antennomeres; elytra nearly as wide as long, covering the abdomen; body never covered with scales; claws lobed or toothed at base (p.462)
- straight-snouted weevils (Brentidae)– antennae straight, club with three antennomeres; long, cylindrical trochanter with femur attached at tip (p.466)

COLLECTING METHODS Look for weevils on developing foliage, especially plants in bloom or bearing fruit. Beating and sweeping these and a wide variety of plants during the day and after dark will increase the diversity of your catch. A few species come to lights. When disturbed, many species play dead and resemble seeds, buds, and other plant structures. Ambrosia and bark beetles are best captured with a net, by hand, or at lights. Look for piles of fine sawdust in bark crevices or on the ground under a dead or dying tree and peel back the bark to search for adults. Rearing ambrosia and bark beetles from infested wood is the most productive method of collection, especially for species that develop in cones, twigs, and branches. Freshly killed trees are more attractive to beetles than those that have been dead for a long time.

FAUNA 2,919 SPECIES IN 501 GENERA (NA)

Dryophthorus americanus Bedel (2.5–2.8 mm) is elongate, dull grayish brown with appendages paler. Eyes on head, not rostrum. Antennae with four antennomeres between elbow and club. Rostrum more than half as long as pronotum. Pronotum longer than wide, distinctly constricted just behind front, and sculpted with broad, shallow punctures. Elytra with distinct rows of punctures, spaces between narrow and convex. Larvae develop in decaying pine (*Pinus*). Adults active in spring and summer, found in leaf litter and under pine bark; attracted to light. Nova Scotia, New Brunswick to Florida, west to Manitoba, Kansas, and Arkansas. (1)

Mexican Bromeliad Weevil *Metamasius callizona* (Chevrolat) (11.0–16.0 mm) is black with a single yellow or orange bar across each elytron just before middle. Abdomen with first two ventrites indented, sometimes brownish (male) or flat, black (female). Adults active year-round; a serious threat to native bromeliads (*Tillandsia*) in natural areas and parks, also pest of horticultural plants in nurseries and greenhouses. Mexico to Panama; established in southern Florida. (3)

470

Silky Cane Weevil *Metamasius hemipterus sericeus* **(Olivier)** (9.0–14.0 mm) is large, shiny red to yellow and with variable black markings, not spots. Pronotum and underside black to red and black. Legs red to yellow, femora with black tips, bands or clouds. Elytra with basal third to half red or yellow, rest mostly black. Larva pest of sugarcane, palms, bananas, and other tropical plants by boring through stems. Long-lived adults active year-round, usually associated with injured larval host plants. Central Mexico and Caribbean to northern Argentina and Bolivia; established in Florida. (3)

Cocklebur Weevil *Rhodobaenus quinquepunctatus* **(Say)** (5.0–7.5 mm) has a black elytral suture and apex, while those of *R. tredecimpunctatus* are red. Unlike *R. tredecimpunctatus*, some *R. quinquepunctatus* have almost entirely black elytra. Black elytral suture and apices is most common color pattern. Host plants include several genera of composites, including ragweed (*Ambrosia*), thistle (*Carduum*), ironweed (*Vernonia*), joe pye weed (*Eutrochium*), sunflower (*Helianthus*), marsh elder (*Iva*), and rosin-weed (*Silphium*). Québec to Florida, west to South Dakota and Texas. (2)

471

Rhodobaenus tredecimpunctatus **(Illiger)** (6.0–10.0 mm) has a black head, rostrum, underside, and appendages. Elytra mostly red with distinct black spots. Pronotum with round black spots; median spot similar in size to other spots. Basal dilation of rostrum deeply grooved. Adults found on stems of sunflower (*Helianthus*) and other composites during the summer. Larvae develop inside the stems of composite flowers. Southern Ontario and New York to Florida, west to Washington and California; Mexico. (2)

Palmetto Weevil *Rhynchophorus cruentatus* **(Fabricius)** (19.0–30.0 mm) is large, elongate-oval, shiny black to almost completely red with variable black pattern; largest weevil in North America and palm pest. Rostrum rough (male) or smooth (female). Elytra deeply grooved. Larvae develop in wounded cabbage palmetto (*Sabal palmetto*), saw palmetto (*Serenoa repens*), and many ornamental palms. Adults active spring and summer, found on larval hosts. South Carolina to Florida, west to southern Texas. (1)

Sisal Weevil *Scyphophorus acupunctatus*
Gyllenhal (8.0–24.0 mm) is black or reddish black with rostrum nearly straight. Head with eyes nearly touching underneath. Antennae with six antennomeres before club; tip of club obliquely truncate, spongy, and contained within penultimate antennomere. Elytra with basal margin broadly concave, tips straight, appearing cut off (truncate). Legs with third tarsomere with only a fringe of dense, stiff setae along apical border. Adults found on *Agave* and *Yucca* in summer. South Carolina to Florida, west to California, also Mexico; introduced into Hawaii and Africa. (1)

Rice Weevil *Sitophilus oryzae* **(Linnaeus)** (2.1–2.8 mm) is not coated, somewhat dull reddish brown to black, upper and lower surfaces densely and coarsely punctured, long rostrum three-fourths length of pronotum, and with elytra of most individuals bearing four reddish spots. Sides of pronotum mostly rounded before head. Elytra have closely set double rows of punctures. A serious pest of stored grains; larvae develop and feed inside individual grains and hollow them out. Cosmopolitan; widely distributed across southern Canada and United States. (5)

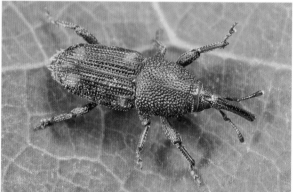

472

Claycolored Billbug *Sphenophorus aequalis* Gyllenhal (9.0–21.0 mm) is black with grayish or ivory-colored enamel-like coating; coating darkens and wears off with age. Pronotum with three slightly raised areas with fine punctures separated by broad paler stripes with large punctures. Elytra with rows of large round punctures separated by rows of very fine punctures. Tibiae each tipped with sharp tooth, tarsi black with tarsomere 3 of front and middle legs broad. Larvae feed on the roots of bulrush (*Schoenoplectus*) and corn (*Zea mays*). Adults active spring and summer. Eastern North America. (42)

Hunting Billbug *Sphenophorus venatus vestitus*
Chittenden (8.0–11.0 mm) is black or reddish, with or without enamel-like coating. Pronotum coarsely punctate with three bare stripes, middle stripe Y-shaped and enclosing a faint or distinct depression just behind head. Elytra variable with punctures in grooves larger than those between; third and fifth intervals somewhat raised. Adults found in turf and in various traps; also attracted to light. District of Columbia to Florida, west to Kansas and eastern Texas; *S. v. venatus* (Say) occurs from New England to New Jersey, west to Ohio. (42)

Rice Water Weevil *Lissorhoptrus oryzophilus* **Kuschel**
(2.6–3.8 mm) is dark with dense coating of flat tan and
brown scales. Antennae with base of club large, shiny.
Pronotum wider than long, somewhat convex and slightly
constricted near base. Middle tibia distinctly curved with
long slender setae, hind tibia with finely notched tooth on
tip (male) or with simple tooth and smaller tooth above
(female). Larva develops in cultivated rice (*Oryza sativa*).
Adults active spring through summer, found on vegetation
surrounding wetlands; attracted to light. Widely distributed
in eastern United States. (5)

Anthonomus haematopus **Boheman** (2.5–3.0 mm) is
broadly oblong-oval, dull blackish, elytra and abdomen
reddish, with sparse pubescence. Rostrum curved, densely
punctate and fine ridge on top, as long as head and thorax
combined. Antennae yellowish brown. Pronotum usually
reddish along front margin. Elytra one-third wider at base
than pronotum, with rows of shallow, close-set punctures,
space between nearly flat and finely wrinkled. Abdomen with
ventrites 2–5 each decreasing in length toward rear. Legs
bright reddish brown or blackish, front femora with single
tooth. Larva develops in stem galls of willow (*Salix*). Adults
active in late spring and summer, found on laurel (*Kalmia*).
In east from Maritime Provinces and New England to North
Carolina, west to Ontario, Kansas, and Louisiana. (41)

473

Apple Curculio *Anthonomus quadrigibbus* **Say**
(2.3–4.5 mm) is dark red, rostrum and appendages paler,
head and apical two-thirds with sparse red and gray setae,
and pronotum and basal third of elytra moderately clothed
in gray setae. Pronotum cone-shaped with three pale stripes.
Elytra broadly impressed across base with very distinct
convex tubercles on apical third. Front femora with two teeth,
middle and hind femora usually with one tooth each. Larval
hosts include hawthorn (*Crataegus*), apple (*Malus*), and pear
(*Pyrus*). Adults found in spring on flowers of serviceberry
(*Amelanchier*), hazelnut (*Corylus*), hawthorn, and cherry
(*Prunus*). Throughout eastern North America. (41)

Strawberry Bud Weevil *Anthonomus signatus* **Say** (2.0–
3.0 mm) is pear-shaped with elytra widely rounded, pale
yellowish brown to blackish, thinly clothed in whitish hairlike
setae that become dense on midline of pronotum and
scutellum. Rostrum longer than head and pronotum. Elytra
reddish with dark suture and side patches sometimes faint
and white setae around side patches sometimes rubbed off.
All femora with a small tooth. Adults found on strawberry
(*Fragaria*) and blackberry (*Rubus*) in spring and summer.
Québec to Florida, west to North Dakota and Texas. (41)

Currant Fruit Weevil *Pseudanthonomus validus* Dietz
(1.7–2.7 mm) is oval, convex, pale reddish brown and
sparsely clothed with fine pale whitish or yellowish setae;
pronotal and elytral scales pointed. Head with rostrum
uniformly curved, antennal funicle with six antennomeres.
Pronotum half as long as wide, with dense setae forming
median stripe on basal half. Elytra more or less smooth,
extreme bases of third interval prominently elevated, intervals
uniform in width. Abdomen with ventrites 4 and 5 equal in
width. Seed-feeding larvae develop in fruits of currant (*Ribes*)
and blueberry (*Vaccinium*). Adults also on *Amelanchier* and
Prunus in summer. Eastern North America. (7)

Yellow Poplar Weevil *Odontopus calceatus* (Say) (3.0–
4.0 mm) is broadly oval and shiny black, with antennae and
tarsi reddish brown. Rostrum long as head and pronotum
combined. Pronotum wider than long, narrowed toward
front, coarsely and deeply punctured. Elytra squarish, with
rows of deep, coarse punctures, spaces between flat and
rough with punctures and small granules. Front femur with
very large serrated tooth on inner margins. Larvae mine
leaves of tulip tree (*Liriodendron tulipifera*) and sassafras
(*Sassafras*). Adults active in spring and summer, found on
dogwood (*Cornus*), magnolia and sweetbay (*Magnolia*), and
tulip tree; capable of defoliating trees. Connecticut and New
York to Florida, west to Michigan, Indiana, and Missouri. (1)

Figwort Weevil *Cionus scrophulariae* (Linnaeus) (4.5–
5.0 mm) is grayish or blackish with yellowish and brown
markings; antennae and tarsi brown. Head and pronotum
yellowish. Elytra completely cover abdomen, with two bold
black spots along suture and distinct black and white ridges.
Larva constructs a cocoon on host plant resembling small,
shiny round fruit. Attacks figwort (*Scrophularia*) and mullein
(*Verbascum*), also plum (*Prunus*). Europe; eastern records
include Québec, Indiana, Louisiana, Massachusetts, New
York, and Vermont. (1)

Acorn weevils *Curculio* **species** (4.3–9.5 mm) are more
or less diamond-shaped in outline, widest at the humeri and
tapered at both ends. Head with rostrum short and curved to
very long and straight, shorter or longer than body, longer in
females; mandibles move vertically, not horizontally; antennae
set midway on rostrum. Prothorax with bases of front legs
in contact with each other and set far back. North American
species with all femora armed with a tooth. Females chew
holes in acorns, hickory nuts, beechnuts, hazelnuts, and
pecans in which to lay their eggs. Larvae develop in nut, nut
falls, mature larvae leave nut and pupate in soil. Sometimes
pests in nut crops. Eastern North America. (17)

Dorytomus laticollis **LeConte** (4.5–5.0 mm) is oblong, somewhat cylindrical, yellowish to black with scattered brown and white spots and stripes; antennae and tarsi reddish brown. Rostrum moderately slender and curved. Pronotum one-third wider than long, with brown setose stripe down middle sparsely flanked by coarse white setae. Femora each with small, sharp tooth. Adults found on aspen, poplar, cottonwood (*Populus*). Across Alaska and Canada, south to Florida, Wisconsin, and Iowa. (14)

Myrmex myrmex **(Herbst)** (3.8–4.5 mm) is narrow-waisted, shiny black with long erect setae; setae darker above, white underneath and on scutellum. Rostrum short with two parallel grooves on top. Pronotum convex, longer than wide. Elytra oblong, widest behind middle, sides straight, with rows of deep, coarse, close-set punctures and spaces between with minute, long punctures. Underside with conspicuous band of white setae just below elytra. Front tibiae stout, sinuate, widest at tip; femora swollen, club-shaped, each with large, triangular tooth. Adults active spring and summer on various plants and shrubs; related species associated with galls on oak (*Quercus*). Connecticut and Québec to Florida, west to Iowa and Mississippi. (4)

Piazorhinus pictus **LeConte** (2.0–2.5 mm) is broadly ovate, reddish brown, and clothed in narrow scales. Head with eyes almost meeting on top, antennae not elbowed. Rostrum short and broad, shorter than pronotum, becoming wider toward tip, and finely punctate. Pronotum wider than long, coarsely and sparsely punctate, with distinctive scale pattern directed to short, narrow ridge down middle. Elytra deeply grooved with fine close-set punctures, spaces between flat and coarsely punctate, and yellowish with irregular brownish bands. Legs with femora toothed. Adults active mostly spring and summer, found on oak (*Quercus*) and hickory (*Carya*). Nova Scotia and New England to Florida, west to Ontario, Michigan, Illinois, and Mississippi. (4)

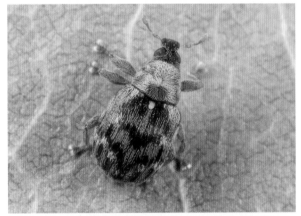

Piazorhinus scutellaris **Say** (2.0–2.5 mm) is broadly ovate, somewhat shiny black, clothed in narrow scales; antennae and tarsi pale brownish yellow. Eyes almost meeting on top, antennae not elbowed. Rostrum short and broad, shorter than pronotum, becoming wider toward tip, and coarsely punctate. Pronotum wider than long, coarsely and sparsely punctate, with distinctive scale pattern directed to short, narrow ridge down middle. Elytra deeply grooved with fine close-set punctures, spaces between flat and coarsely punctate. Femora toothed. Adults active mostly spring and summer, found on oak (*Quercus*). Maritime Provinces to Georgia, west to Ontario, Minnesota, Nebraska, and Arizona. (4)

***Isochnus sequensi* (Stierlin) (formerly *I. populicola* (Silfverberg))** (2.0–2.5 mm) is shiny black with somewhat short, curved rostrum, and pale brown appendages. Pronotum shiny, coarsely punctate, narrower than base of elytra, base with narrow band of pale setae. Elytra punctostriate, punctures large and deep. Larvae mine leaves of willow (*Salix*) and poplar (*Populus*); pupation takes place in mine. Adults found on larval host plants. Europe; now established from Maritime Provinces to New Jersey, west to Indiana. Best separated from *Isochnus rufipes* (LeConte) by examination of male genitalia, basal margin of pronotum sometimes, at most, with narrow band of white scales. (2)

***Tachyerges ephippiatus* (Say)** (2.0–2.9 mm) is broadly oval, clothed in dark and light setae, mostly black, elytra reddish orange or yellowish brown underneath; antennae, part of legs reddish. Eyes nearly touching, seven antennomeres between elbow and club. Pronotum widest before base. Scutellum white. Elytra with broad triangular patch across base and narrow irregular band just before tips sometimes narrowly connected along suture. Legs with hind femora enlarged. Adults active spring and summer, found on willow (*Salix*), aspen and poplar (*Populus*). Across Canada; in east from Maritime Provinces and New England to South Carolina, west to Ontario and Kansas. (3)

***Lignyodes fraxini* (LeConte)** (3.1–4.0 mm) is elongate-oblong, reddish brown, and thickly clothed in reddish-yellow hairlike scales. Head with large eyes nearly meeting on top. Rostrum stout (male) or slender (female), with elongate pit on sides parallel. Prothorax wider than long, narrowed in front. Elytra with crossbar often faint. Front tibiae of male expanded at apical three-fourths and concave beneath, edges of concavity with curved and narrowed bristles. Larvae develop in ash (*Fraxinus*) seeds. Adults active spring and early summer, found on ash. New England and Québec to District of Columbia, west to Saskatchewan, Michigan, Illinois, and Kansas. (5)

Ligustrum Weevil *Ochyromera ligustri* Warner (3.0–4.7 mm) is broadly oval, yellowish brown and black, and clothed in erect, orange-yellow setae. Rostrum curved, longer than prontum. Femora enlarged, each with large, triangular tooth. Elytral suture and apices often darker, with prominent tubercles near apex. Adults eat leaves of privet (*Ligustrum*), lilac (*Syringa*), and grape (*Vitis*) in late spring and summer; also at light. Larvae develop inside fruits and eat seeds of adult host plants. Sometimes a horticultural pest of, or biocontrol for, Chinese privet (*L. sinense*). Asia; established from Virginia to Florida. (1)

Bagous planatus LeConte (2.7–3.0 mm) is densely clothed in dark ashy gray or brown scales; antennae and tarsi brownish yellow. Rostrum stout, punctate, curved, almost as long as prothorax. Eyes partly covered by prothoracic lobes. Pronotum with three whitish stripes, longer than wide, sides parallel, abruptly converging toward head, surface coarsely granulate; underneath with channel for rostrum. Elytra wider than prothorax, humeri prominent, white spots (not bumps) flanking suture behind middle, with rows of fine punctures, spaces between flat, each tip with pair of cone-shaped bumps. Third tarsomere broad, notched. Adults found on streamside and floating vegetation. New Brunswick to Virginia, west to North Dakota and Nebraska. (34)

Dirabius rectirostris (LeConte) (3.2–6.0 mm) is elongate, oval, finely wrinkled, somewhat shiny black with inconspicuous scales; antennae and tarsi dark reddish brown. Rostrum nearly straight, long as pronotum, sculptured and stout (male) or longer, slender, and smooth (female). First two antennomeres of stem long, club slender. Pronotum about as long as wide, sides straight to apical third. Elytra twice as long as pronotum, with rows of fine, deep punctures, spaces between rough with fine punctures. Adults active in spring and early summer, found on stems of sedge (*Carex*). Maritime Provinces to South Carolina, west to Minnesota and Missouri. (8)

Geraeus picumnus (Herbst) (1.9–2.9 mm) is oval, robust, dark chestnut brown to black, and densely clothed in narrow yellowish or white scales. Rostrum long and slender, half as long as body, with finely punctate grooves (male) or coarsely punctate at base and polished beyond (female). Antennomere 2 three times longer than wide. Pronotum cone-shaped, half again as wide as long, densely punctate with scales arranged obliquely, underneath with scales directed backward and a pair of long sharp spines in male. Elytra completely covering abdomen, setae uniformly colored. Adults found on flowers, especially sunflowers (Asteraceae). Connecticut to Florida, west to Nebraska, to Arizona. (4)

Linogeraeus neglectus (LeConte) (2.9–4.5 mm) is densely clothed in yellowish and some scattered dark scales. Rostrum with distinctly triangular mandibles with smooth inner margins not overlapping, parallel-sided (female). Pronotum with sides convergent at base, underneath without short triangular spines (male), scales radiating out from central pit behind head. Elytra completely cover abdomen, with narrow grooves, broader spaces between. Claws separate at base. Virginia to Florida, west to Iowa, Nebraska, and Texas; Mexico and Central America. (7)

Odontocorynus umbellae (**Fabricius**) (3.0–4.7 mm) is oblong-oval, robust, black or reddish brown and clothed in white scales. Antennae with scape gradually becoming wider from middle, base of male club notched with cone-shaped process. Rostrum coarsely sculptured, longer than head and pronotum, strongly curved in male, with antennae attached at about basal quarter. Pronotum coarsely sculptured without sharp tubercles on sides near front. Scutellum more densely clothed in scales. Elytra with rows of scales roughly equal in width, grooves with fine setae. Adults active late spring and summer, found on various flowering plants, especially in the sunflower family (Asteraceae). New Hampshire to Florida, west to Minnesota, Missouri, and Texas. (6)

Oligolochus ornatus (**Casey**) (2.6–2.8 mm) is broadly oval, moderately convex, black with reddish legs and yellowish setae; setae dense on sides and basal lobe of pronotum, and base of elytra. Rostrum slender, evenly curved, and long as pronotum (male) or head and pronotum (female). Pronotum wider than long with sides round, with small punctures and smooth line down middle of basal half. Elytra longer than pronotum, with humeri bulging, deeply grooved with area between with single row of punctures. Adults active in late spring and summer. Carolinas west to Indiana, Missouri, Arkansas, and Alabama. (6)

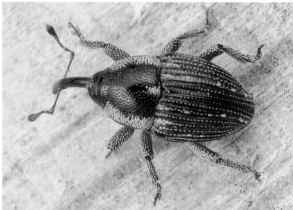

Sibariops confusa (**Boheman**) (2.7–3.5 mm) is elongate, oval, sparsely clothed in hairlike scales, and black with paler antennae. Rostrum shorter than pronotum with small and dense punctures. Pronotum slightly wider than long, punctures separated and dense, with smooth line down middle; males with slender spines below. Elytra with grooves deep, narrow, spaces between with two irregular rows of coarse punctures. Adults found on flatsedge (*Cyperus*) and rice (*Oryza*). New England to Florida, west to Indiana, Nebraska, and Mississippi. Genus needs revision.

Cosmobaris scolopacea (**Germar**) (3.0–3.3 mm) is oblong-oval, convex, and black with patches of brownish, whitish, and yellowish scales on sides of pronotum and elytra. Rostrum long as head and pronotum combined, conspicuously sculptured. Pronotum slightly wider than long with large, dense punctures. Elytra two-fifths (male) or half (female) as long as wide. Underside with band of white scales next to base of elytra. Adults active spring and summer, found on ragweed (*Ambrosia*) and goosefoot (*Chenopodium*). Europe; established from New Brunswick and New England to South Carolina, west to Ontario, Minnesota, Kansas, and Texas. (1)

Potato Stalk Borer *Trichobaris trinotata* **(Say)** (3.0–5.0 mm) is narrowly oblong, somewhat flat, black, and densely clothed in white slender scales. Rostrum slender, nearly long as pronotum (male) or longer (female). Black spots conspicuous on humeri, under sides of pronotum, and on scutellum. Pronotum slightly longer than wide, coarsely and densely punctate. Most spaces between rows of punctures on elytra with three rows of scales. Abdominal sternum 5 with narrow, deep impression in male. Adults active late spring and summer, found on jimsonweed (*Datura*), ground-cherry (*Physalis*), and nightshade (*Solanum*). New York and Ontario to Florida, west to Michigan, Kansas, and Texas. (3)

Glyptobaris lecontei **Champion** (3.6–4.6 mm) is oblong-oval, convex, shiny dark reddish brown with bands of long yellowish scales at base and behind middle often connected by a similar broad patch of scales along suture. Elytra at base slightly wider than pronotum and narrowed toward tips, with deep, notched grooves, spaces between flat with distinct rows of large, widely spaced punctures. Adults active from spring through summer and found on various plants; also Malaise traps. Pennsylvania to South Carolina, west to Nebraska, Oklahoma, and Mississippi; Mexico. (1)

Madarellus undulatus **(Say)** (2.6–4.7 mm) is obovate, shiny black or with red head and pronotum, without scales or setae. Rostrum slender, one-fourth body length. Pronotum twice as wide as long with sides broadly rounded, then abruptly constricted just behind head. Elytra narrower than pronotum, with narrow rows of deep punctures, spaces between on middle flat, smooth, and finely punctate, distinctly rougher at sides. Adults active spring and summer; found on creeper (*Parthenocissus*), grape (*Vitis*), eastern poison ivy (*Toxicodendron radicans*), and milkweed flowers (*Asclepias*). Nova Scotia to Florida, west to Ontario, South Dakota, Kansas, and Texas. (1)

Stethobaris ovata **(LeConte)** (2.5–3.0 mm) is somewhat oval, robust, convex, and shining black, with appendages and tip of rostrum reddish brown. Rostrum curved, tapered to tip. Prothorax wider than long, widest at base, narrowed toward front, front margin rounded, surface coarsely but not densely punctured, with feeble ridge down middle, and channeled between legs to receive rostrum. Elytra with rows of small, deep punctures, spaces between wider. Adults associated with orchids. Massachusetts to Maryland, west to Indiana. (7)

Ceutorhynchus americanus **Buchanan** (2.1–3.0 mm) is oval, blackish with brassy reflections, and metallic blue or green elytra. Head with rostrum slender, curved, more than half again as long as pronotum, seven antennomeres between elbow and club. Pronotum narrowed toward head and constricted just before front margin, underneath with short distinct channel between forelegs. Elytra with patch of small white scales behind scutellum. Middle and hind femora each with a tooth, tarsomere 5 shorter than combined lengths of 2 and 3. Adults active spring and summer, found on mustard (*Brassica*). In east from Atlantic Canada to South Carolina, west to Dakotas and Texas. (31)

Dietzella zimmermanni (**Gyllenhal**) (2.4–3.2 mm) is broad, oval, convex, densely clothed in black and white scales, with a distinctly bicolored pronotum. Head sometimes withdrawn into prothorax, and six antennomeres between elbow and club. Rostrum short, three times longer than wide. Prothorax barely wider than long with sharp tubercles on sides, front margin with pair of small teeth. Elytra with crosslike markings. Femora unarmed, claws each with a long, slender tooth. Adults found on beggar's-ticks (*Bidens*) and willowherb (*Epilobium*). Newfoundland to Georgia, west to Wisconsin, Arkansas, and Louisiana; British Columbia. (1)

480

Perigaster obscura (**LeConte**) (2.4–3.1 mm) is broadly oval, reddish brown, and thinly clothed in brown, coppery, and whitish scales. Rostrum small, stout, shorter than pronotum and expanded at tip. Eyes prominent, clearly visible, with margins raised above surface. Pronotal surface uneven with distinct swelling at middle, sides whitish. Elytra with pair of small white spots at basal fourth, surfaces between grooves finely roughened. Legs with claws simple. Adults active spring and summer, found on primrose-willow (*Ludwigia*); also attracted to light. New York to Florida, west to Arkansas and Louisiana. (4)

Iris Weevil *Mononychus vulpeculus* (**Fabricius**) (4.5–5.0 mm) is broadly ovate, shiny black with dorsal surface nearly devoid of scales. Rostrum straight, nearly cylindrical, and received into distinct groove between bases of front and middle legs. Eyes partially hidden by lobes on prothorax. Pronotum narrowed toward head, sides yellow. Elytra with rows of rectangular punctures, suture with broad yellowish scales, spaces between broad and rough. Legs each with a single claw. Pygidium with sharp bumps (male) or concave (female). Underside clothed in broad yellowish scales. Adults found in seedpods and flowers of wild iris (*Iris*). Maine and Québec to Georgia, west to Minnesota and Iowa. (1)

Rhinoncus castor (Fabricius) (2.1–3.2 mm) is somewhat oval, robust, convex, clothed in narrow white and brown scales and setae. Pronotum with front margin sometimes reddish. Antennae with seven antennomeres between elbow and club, eyes without ridges above. Scutellum hidden. Elytral grooves with sparse setae, spaces between rough with large, widely spaced, raised dots. Adults active spring and summer, found on alfalfa (*Medicago*), dock (*Rumex*), and waterdropwort (*Oenanthe*). Europe; established from Maritime Provinces and New England to Georgia, west to Wisconsin, Missouri, and Tennessee; Pacific Northwest. (6)

Rhinoncus longulus LeConte (2.3–3.0 mm) is oblong, oval, thinly clothed in short setae and long white scales, and reddish to black with appendages paler. Sides of head clothed in white scales. Eyes without distinct ridge above. Seven antennomeres between elbow and club. Prothorax wide as long, coarsely punctate with concentrations of white scales on sides and channel before scutellum. Elytra with short, conspicuous white stripe behind scutellum. Underside with scattered white scales. Elytra with rows of deep punctures, spaces between rough. Adults found spring and summer on knotweed (*Polygonum*). In east from Connecticut, New York, and southern Ontario to Florida, west to Wisconsin, Kansas, and Texas. (6)

Acallodes ventricosus LeConte (2.8–4.0 mm) is ovate, convex, and blackish with fine pubescence and white oval scales; appendages reddish. Rostrum long as pronotum, broader at tip. Pronotum barely wider than long, about equal in width to elytra, with faint white stripes. Scutellum white. Elytra widest at or behind middle, suture white at base, with irregular bands across middle and tip. Legs with femora becoming wider toward tips and armed with small tooth. Adults active late spring and early summer, found on apple (*Malus*). Ontario to Virginia, west to Manitoba, North Dakota, and Missouri. (3)

Acoptus suturalis LeConte (3.2–4.5 mm) is elongate, somewhat cylindrical, and black with dense gray and blackish-brown scales. Rostrum long as pronotum. Antennal clubs large. Pronotum slightly wider than long, with a ridge down middle not reaching front or rear margins. Elytra wider than pronotum with broad impression at basal third, remaining surface convex. Larvae develop in dead wood of deciduous trees such as hopornbeam (*Ostrya*), beech (*Fagus*), and butternut (*Juglans*). Adults active late spring and summer, found on hickory (*Carya*) and larval hosts. Maritime Provinces to Georgia, west to Michigan and Illinois. (1)

Lechriops oculatus (Say) (2.3–3.2 mm) is short, mostly black, oval in outline, and densely covered with black, rusty brown, turquoise, and white scales. Rostrum longer than head and antennae inserted near middle. Antennae and tarsi pale reddish brown. Elytra somewhat flattened, one-third wider than prothorax, and with conspicuous spot of white scales at middle. Adults commonly found by beating and sweeping vegetation, especially oak (*Quercus*), hickory (*Carya*), sassafras (*Sassafras albidum*), ash (*Fraxinus*), viburnum (*Viburnum*), and hawthorn (*Crataegus*) in spring and summer. Québec and Ontario to Florida, west to Manitoba, Iowa, and Texas. (1)

Tachygonus lecontei Gyllenhal (2.0–2.5 mm) is broadly oval, narrowed in front, rounded in back, somewhat flat, variably dark reddish brown to black, and densely clothed in white and tan comblike scales, black and white bristles, and tufts of black or white setae. Rostrum short, broad. Antennae not elbowed, antennomere 1 very short. Pronotum bell-shaped, rounded on sides and narrowed toward head. Elytra nearly twice width of pronotum, widest behind base, with rows of coarse punctures. Hind legs long, femora enlarged (not for jumping). Adults active in spring, found on oak (*Quercus*); larva mines oak leaves. New York to Florida, west to Texas: Mexico, Guatemala. (5)

Cylindrocopturus quercus (Say) (2.5–3.0 mm) is elongate, stout, and black with dorsal surface clearly visible between distinct patches of black and white scales. Rostrum slender, about as long as prothorax. Pronotum with sides and middle across base white. Elytra flat, only slightly wider at base than pronotum, with suture and two interrupted bands white. Femora without spines. Abdomen with last three ventrites abruptly sloped to rear when viewed from side. Connecticut to Georgia, west to Michigan, Iowa, Arkansas, and Alabama. (5)

Cossonus impressifrons Boheman (3.5–5.5 mm) is elongate, somewhat cylindrical, slightly flattened, black or blackish with short, broad rostrum distinctly widened at tip. Eyes at junction of head and rostrum. When viewed from above, tip of rostrum abruptly widened, wider than long, with sides of base straight and diverging away from head. Seven antennomeres between scape and club. Pronotum slightly longer than wide, wider or narrower than elytra at base. Adults active spring through summer, found under bark of dead deciduous hardwoods, including oak (*Quercus*), sycamore (*Platanus*), and elm (*Ulmus*). Québec and Ontario to Florida, west to Wisconsin, Kansas, and Texas. (4)

482

Himatium errans LeConte (2.0–2.2 mm) is elongate, slender, straight-sided, coarsely sculptured, dull reddish brown, and densely clothed in curved yellowish setae. Rostrum weakly curved, slightly shorter than pronotum. Pronotum somewhat cylindrical, half again as long as wide. Scutellum very small, but distinct. Elytra with sides parallel to apical third, one-fourth wider than pronotum; striae with deep and square punctures narrowly separated from one another. Adults found under bark and in galleries of *Ips* bark beetles on pine (*Pinus*); also reared from dead maple branches (*Acer*), extracted from leaf litter; at light. Nova Scotia and New England to Florida, west to Québec and Ohio. (2)

Hexarthrum ulkei Horn (2.5–3.2 mm) is almost cylindrical and moderately shiny blackish or dark reddish brown, and without vestiture. Rostrum slightly longer than head, densely punctured. Antennae short and thick, with six antennomeres before club. Pronotum wide as long, slightly narrowed in front, and coarsely punctate. Elytra slightly wider than pronotum, shallowly grooved with coarse round to somewhat squarish punctures. Bases of front legs (coxae) closed, not touching, and last tarsomere long. Adults are associated with conifers. Québec and Ontario to Florida, west to Indiana. (1)

Stenoscelis brevis (Boheman) (2.7–3.8 mm) is oblong, robust, nearly cylindrical, coarsely punctured, and black, with brownish or blackish appendages; antennae and tarsi paler. Rostrum half length of head. Head with short antennal grooves in front of eyes, antennae not elbowed. Pronotum half as long as wide, coarsely and densely punctate. Elytra swollen and rough at base, followed by rows of coarse, deep punctures, spaces between somewhat convex with fine punctures, and tips without setae. Legs with tibiae smooth, without teeth, and all tarsi with tarsomere 5 long and curved. Nova Scotia and New England to Florida, west to Ontario, Minnesota, Kansas, and Louisiana. (2)

Poplar and Willow Borer *Cryptorhynchus lapathi* (Linnaeus) (7.5–10.0 mm) is elongate, oval, robust, and dull black with dense sooty black and pale scales mixed with tufts of black setae. Antennae attached at middle of rostrum. Eyes partly covered. Pronotum with deep channel to receive rostrum. Larvae bore into bark of ornamental trees and shrubs. Adults active in spring and summer, found on bark, dead twigs of willow (*Salix*), poplar (*Populus*), and birch (*Betula*). Europe; southern Canada and adjacent United States; in east from Ontario to Georgia, west to Minnesota and Illinois. (7)

Eubulus bisignatus (**Say**) (2.8–4.9 mm) is oval, robust, densely covered in mostly brown, some black scales. Head without pit, eyes separated by about two-thirds width of rostrum. Pronotum of freshly emerged individuals with tuft of broad scales on middle. Elytra with alternate intervals ridged, with pair of short oblique white bands at middle. All femora with two very small teeth on inner margin. Abdomen underneath with scales on ventrites 3–5 lighter, 1 concave in male. Adults on oak (*Quercus*), beech (*Fagus*), birch (*Betula*), hickory (*Carya*), and maple (*Acer*); in Malaise traps, attracted to light. New Hampshire and Québec to Florida, west to Ontario, Nebraska, and Texas. (3)

Gerstaeckeria hubbardi (**LeConte**) (7.5–9.5 mm) is black and clothed in black, white, and brown scales, with white patch behind elytral angles. Rostrum with ridges, but with shiny line at base. Head with elongate, deep pit between eyes. Pronotum coarsely sculptured with distinct ridge down middle, narrower than elytra at base. Elytra globose, humeri not prominent, grooves with punctures deep and not all equally spaced, spaces between becoming more convex away from suture, with white or brown band behind middle. Larvae mine pads of cactus (*Opuntia*) and hollow out smaller cacti (*Coryphantha*, *Mammillaria*). Flightless and nocturnal adults found year-round on cactus. Georgia and Florida to Alabama. (1)

Tyloderma aereum (**Say**) (2.1–3.1 mm) is somewhat oval, and brassy brown with antennae brownish red. Rostrum with ridge near middle. Head with short shallow groove down front, punctures dense near eyes. Pronotum longer than wide, finely and evenly punctured, surface finely wrinkled and appearing dull, underneath with lobes extending toward eyes. Elytra widest behind middle, with rows of large punctures becoming faint just behind middle, spaces between wide and smooth. Adults active in late spring and summer; attracted to light. Québec and Ontario to Florida, west to Minnesota, Iowa, Kansas, and Texas. (24)

Tyloderma foveolatum (**Say**) (3.1–5.7 mm) is elongate, oval, dull black with patches of whitish or yellowish scales, and coarsely punctured. Rostrum short with deep grooves and punctures. Eyes almost completely covered by prothoracic lobes. Pronotum with deep, large punctures becoming larger on sides. Elytra with rows of punctures, about same size as those on pronotum. Adults active in summer, found on primrose-willow (*Ludwigia*), meadowbeauty (*Rhexia*), and beaksedge (*Rhynchospora*) growing along margins of wetlands. New York and Ontario to Florida, west to Dakotas, Nebraska, and Texas. (24)

Cophes obtentus **(Herbst)** (4.7–6.8 mm) is elongate-oval, sooty black, densely clothed in small flat scales and bristles. Rostrum coarsely, densely punctate; antennae with funicular antennomeres 3–7 gradually decreasing in length. Pronotum wider than long, sides nearly parallel at basal third, with long white spot down middle. Scutellum white or yellow. Elytra each with two ridges, and shared large yellow spot behind middle. Underside with metasternum long, bases of middle legs widely separated, hind tibiae with apical comb with double row of setae, claws not toothed. Adults found on dead twigs, branches; also at light. New York to Florida, west to Illinois and Texas. (3)

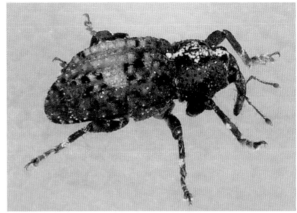

Vegetable Weevil *Listroderes costirostris* **Schoenherr** (6.4–8.7 mm) has a rostrum half as long as pronotum. Pronotum widest behind front margin, with sides straight, diverging from base to widest point; light stripe down middle. Dark reddish brown with rows of mixed light and dark scales and setae. Elytra with dark scales forming oblique bands and cone-shaped tubercle near tips. Femora with scales and setae. Feeds on many kinds of wild and ornamental plants, as well as many vegetable crops. Adults damage or kill young agricultural, ornamental, and native plants by damaging or girdling stems. Larvae burrow through fleshy roots, stems, and leaves. South America; established across southern third of United States. (2)

485

Listronotus appendiculatus **(Boheman)** (4.2–6.5 mm) is elongate, slender, black with dense yellow scales. Rostrum nearly as long as pronotum with ridge along top. Mandibles notched at tip, with two teeth. Eyes partly covered by prothoracic lobes. Head largely covered by round scales. First antennomere past elbow shorter than second. Pronotum longer than wide, with sides rounded and surface coarsely and densely punctate. Elytra with rows of fine punctures, spaces between with short, curved setae. Adults active in summer, found on sedge (*Carex*) and arrowhead (*Sagittaria*). Widespread in eastern North America. (51)

Listronotus sparsus **(Say)** (4.0–5.0 mm) is elongate-oblong, densely clothed in grayish or brownish scales, dark reddish brown to blackish; appendages reddish brown. Pronotum cylindrical, slightly wider than long, sometimes with pale scales on sides, and with indistinct impression on top. Elytra wider than pronotum, humeri distinct, fine grooves with large punctures, every other space between convex with rows of setae, with common dark stripe down suture from base to apical third. Adults active in summer on plants in or near water; seldom attracted to light. Québec and Ontario to Florida, west to Dakotas, Kansas, and Texas. (51)

Agraphus bellicus (**Say**) (6.5–8.5 mm) is densely covered with grayish, sometimes dusky scales; scales worn off in older specimens reveal dark, shiny brown elytra. Antennal scape longer than remaining antennomeres, including club. Pronotum wider than long, elytra strongly convex, grooves indicated by large, shallow depressions. Flightless adults found in sandy coastal habitats and inland in Florida. Atlantic Coast, from New York south to Florida. (1)

Imported Longhorned Weevil *Calomycterus setarius* **Roelofs** (3.0–3.5 mm) is oval, robust, dark reddish brown to black, and densely clothed in small, whitish scales and erect bristles. Head and rostrum longer than prothorax. Rostrum with two grooves and V-shaped ridge on expanded tip. Pronotum with side slightly rounded, widest along front, and front margin with lobes behind eyes. Scutellum not visible. Elytra at base barely wider than pronotum, egg-shaped, convex, humeri not evident, grooves with fine punctures, spaces between slightly convex with a row of bristles; flightless. Only females known, found on various plants, pest on soybeans (*Glycine*). Asia; established eastern Ontario and southern Québec, eastern United States to Iowa and Kansas. (1)

Asiatic Oak Weevil *Cyrtepistomus castaneus* (**Roelofs**) (4.1–5.8 mm) has a long antennal scape extending well beyond anterior margin of pronotum. Elytra distinctly grooved. Inside margin of hind tibiae with spur. Fresh specimens have metallic greenish scales along sides of dark body. Adults are minor defoliators of foliage of various hardwoods, especially oaks (*Quercus*) and red maple (*Acer rubrum*); also attracted to lights in spring and summer. Reproduce parthenogenetically and lay eggs in soil. Larvae feed on roots and develop at bases of oak seedlings. Connecticut to Florida, west to Ohio and Texas. (1)

Peach Root Weevil *Oedophrys hilleri* (**Faust**) (3.3–4.0 mm) is oval, dark, and densely covered with tan, gray, white, and dark brown scales. Eyes small, separated from prothorax by three or more scales. Pronotum brown and elytra mottled. Elytra one-third wider than pronotum at base with humeral angles distinct and intervals flat. Femora each with a small tooth. Adults active in summer and feed on foliage of various plants in the rose family (Rosaceae), including peach (*Prunus persicae*) and pear (*Pyrus communis*). Larvae develop on the roots of adult host plants. Asia; established from Connecticut and Pennsylvania south to South Carolina. (1)

Sesbania Clown Weevil *Eudiagogus pulcher* **Fåhraeus** (5.0–8.0 mm) is oblong-oval, and densely clothed in brownish black, tan, copper, and greenish metallic scales. Head, except for dark spot at base of rostrum, covered with tan and coppery scales. Pronotum with coppery scales forming crossbars. Elytra with narrow greenish suture flanked by broad black stripes, narrow stripes along sides broken at middle. Larva feeds on roots of riverhemp (*Sesbania*). Adults active mostly late spring and summer on riverhemp. North Carolina to Florida, west to California. *Eudiagogus maryae* Warner with elytral stripes along sides unbroken. (3)

Eudiagogus rosenschoeldi **Fåhraeus** (4.1–7.1 mm) is oblong-oval, and densely clothed in brownish black, tan, copper, and greenish metallic scales. Head, except for dark spot at base of rostrum, covered with tan and coppery scales. Pronotum with two broad dark stripes. Elytra with narrow greenish suture flanked by broad black irregular stripes with variable markings along sides. Larva feeds on roots of riverhemp (*Sesbania*). Adults active mostly late spring and summer on riverhemp. South Carolina to Florida, west to Texas. (3)

487

Brachystylus sayi **Alonso-Zarazaga** (7.5–9.0 mm) is oblong, somewhat slender, and brownish gray with dense tan and brown scales. First antennomere (scape) short. Tips of rostrum and mandibles with long setae. Pronotum somewhat conical, narrowed to straight front margin, base slightly sinuate. Elytra wider at base than pronotum, with oblique pale or dark brown band behind white band at middle, and somewhat pointed tips. Abdomen with ventrite 5 rounded (male) or sharply triangular (female). Adults active spring and summer, found on persimmon (*Diospyros*). New York to Florida, west to Illinois, Missouri, and Texas. (1)

Epicaerus imbricatus **(Say)** (7.5–11.5 mm) is ovate, somewhat pear-shaped, densely clothed in brownish and pale gray scales. Top of rostrum continuous with head, distinctly impressed on sides. Pronotum cone-shaped, sides nearly parallel at base, narrowed toward head, with three irregular stripes. Elytra broadly oval, slightly wider at base than pronotum, with humeri not distinct, rows of coarse deep punctures, spaces between narrow, with surface slope at tips almost vertical when viewed from side. Adults active spring and summer, found on lespedeza (*Lespedeza*), onion (*Allium*), cabbage (*Brassica*), potato (*Solanum*), clover (*Trifolium*), and other vegetation. New York to Georgia, west to South Dakota and Texas; Mexico. (2)

Hormorus undulatus (Uhler) (7.5 mm) is elongate-oval, robust, dark brown, and sparsely clothed in white scales and scalelike hairs. Rostrum longer and narrower than head, widened at tip. Antennae with 7 antennomeres between elbow and club. Pronotum slightly longer than wide. Elytra slightly wider at base than pronotum, grooves with deep, closely spaced punctures, spaces between narrower and covered with small granules. Abdomen with ventrites 1–2 broadly impressed in male. Larvae feed externally on tubers of false lily of the valley (*Maianthemum racemosa*) and Solomon's seal (*Polygonatum*). Adults active spring and summer, found on leaves of larval host plants. Québec to Maryland, west to Minnesota and Iowa. (1)

Fuller Rose Weevil *Naupactus cervinus* Boheman (6.0–8.5 mm) is oblong-oval, dark brown, and uniformly clothed in small gray, brown, and pinkish scales, with characterisitic, sometimes faint oblique whitish bar behind middle on sides of elytra. Rostrum very short and broad. Sides of body with or without paler scales, never with distinct stripe fringed with darker scales. Pronotum with front and side margins rounded. Elytra with humeri lacking, not wider than base of pronotum. Flightless adults active year-round, found on many plants; parthenogenetic. South America; widespread in North America. (3)

Whitefringed Weevil *Naupactus leucoloma* Boheman (8.0–12.0 mm) is oblong, oval, black, and densely clothed in brownish or gray scales. Rostrum short, broad, with distinct ridge on sides. Eyes convex. Prothorax and elytra flanked by a broad, pale stripe bordered in black. Pronotum somewhat rough, widest at base, with setae across base directed toward head. Elytra wider at base than pronotum, with humeri distinct and round-oval scales. Only females known in United States, active mainly in spring and summer, feed on many horticultural plants and vegetables. South America; established from Virginia to Florida, west to Illinois, Missouri, and Louisiana. (3)

Naupactus peregrinus (Buchanan) (6.0–9.5 mm) is oblong-oval, brown to black, and covered with small brownish, pinkish, or greenish scales. Pronotum and elytra with broad pale stripe on sides bordered with black. Pronotum with setae on front half directed forward and backward on back half. An immigrant species known only from parthenogenetic females. Adults feed on a variety of plants and can become a garden crop pest. South America; established from Virginia to Florida, west to Arkansas and Texas. (3)

Strawberry Root Weevil *Otiorhynchus ovatus*
(Linnaeus) (5.0–6.0 mm) is almost antlike, coarsely
sculptured, and shiny black with prothorax and elytra
each distinctly rounded. Rostrum flat, coarsely and
roughly punctate. Front of head with long pit between eyes.
Pronotum with frontal and basal margins straight, top with
curved rows of setose bumps separated by deep grooves.
Elytra wider than pronotum with rows of deep, setose
punctures more distinct along sides. Legs with femora
toothed, front femur with tooth notched, others usually
simple. Europe; widespread in North America. (3)

Rough Strawberry Root Weevil *Otiorhynchus*
rugosostriatus **(Goeze)** (6.5–8.0 mm) is oblong-oval, rough,
dark brown to black, somewhat antlike, and rough with curled
reddish setae; appendages reddish brown. Rostrum short,
broad, with wide, shallow depression flanked by ridges,
tip with Y-shaped ridge. Pronotum round, wider than long,
with raised setal bumps. Elytra oval, nearly twice as wide as
pronotum; surfaces between rows of punctures with two rows
of small setal bumps. Front femora not toothed. Flightless
adults parthenogenetic, found on many plants, sometimes
pest on strawberry (*Fragaria*). Europe; established in
southeastern Canada to Georgia; also in West. (3)

489

Black Vine Weevil *Otiorhynchus sulcatus* **(Fabricius)**
(8.3–9.2 mm) is dull brownish black with reddish to blackish
antennae. Rostrum short, broad, with shallow depression,
a pair of ridges, and Y-shaped ridge at tip. Pronotum
oval with sides rounded, longer than wide, and coarsely
granulate. Elytra round, twice as wide as pronotum,
coarsely punctate and granulate with patches of yellowish
setae, with tips each distinctly rounded. Adults known
only from parthenogenetic females and feed on a variety
of plants; sometimes pests in greenouses and nurseries.
Europe; established from Newfoundland to South Carolina,
west to Wisconsin and Missouri. (3)

Aphrastus taeniatus **Say** (4.7–5.8 mm) is light to dark
red and densely clothed in light and dark brown scales.
Rostrum short with broad, bare area without scales
contained within a V-shaped ridge. Elytra with tenth row
of punctures ending at base of hind legs. Larvae develop
on grass roots. Diurnal adults are found on various
composites, including ragweed (*Ambrosia*), pokeweed
(*Phytolacca*), ironweed (*Vernonia*), and various deciduous
shrubs in late spring and summer. Ontario and Québec
south to Florida and Mississippi. (2)

European Snout Beetle *Phyllobius oblongus* (Linnaeus) (4.0–7.0 mm) is elongate, oblong, black, clothed in long, pale setae; elytra and legs yellowish to reddish brown. Pronotum widest at middle, coarsely and unevenly punctate. Rows of elytral punctures separated by flat intervals with small bumps bearing setae. Diurnal adults defoliate hardwoods, especially maple (*Acer*), elm (*Ulmus*), birch (*Betula*), and serviceberry (*Amelanchier*); leaf damage consists of a series of semicircular scallops along margins. Larvae eat tree roots and overwinter in soil. Europe; established from New Brunswick to Virginia, west to Ohio. (3)

Polydrusus sericeus (Schaller) (5.1–7.0 mm) is elongate, oblong, robust, light reddish brown to black, and densely clothed in oval bright green scales; appendages yellowish brown. Rostrum short, narrow, not constricted behind eyes, with tip wider than base. Antennae long, scape just reaching rear margin of eye. Elytra without distinct rows of setae in spaces between grooves. Adults eat leaves of hardwoods, especially seedlings of birch (*Betula*), basswood (*Tilia*), ironwood (*Ostrya*), and maple (*Acer*). Larvae burrow in soil, eat roots of adult host plants. Eurasia; established from Prince Edward Island to Connecticut, west to Wisconsin and Illinois. (4)

490

Barypeithes pellucidus (Boheman) (2.9–4.0 mm) is oval, light to dark reddish brown or blackish with pale appendages and sparsely clothed in erect setae. Rostrum very short, broad. Pronotum round, convex, coarsely punctate. Elytra shining, wider than pronotum, with distinct rows of large, deep, close-set, and setose punctures, spaces between flat with rows of long, inclined setae. Adults active late spring and summer, found on lichen-encrusted rocks, oak (*Quercus*), elm (*Ulmus*), cherry (*Prunus*), hawthorn (*Crataegus*), blackberry (*Rubus*), and strawberry (*Fragaria*). Europe; established from Maritime Provinces and New England to North Carolina, west to Manitoba, Wisconsin, and Illinois; British Columbia. (1)

Blue-green Citrus Root Weevil *Pachnaeus litus* (Germar) (9.0–10.5 mm) is oblong-oval, black, and densely clothed in bright blue-green to aqua scales. Pronotum with sides, middle, and base paler. Elytra each with base and angle projecting forward and 10 rows of pits. Femora toothed. Larvae are root feeders. Adults active in summer, eat many species of plants by feeding on edges of young leaves, including ornamentals and commercially grown citrus (*Citrus*) in various lowland habitats. Southern Florida; West Indies and Mexico. *Pachnaeus opalus* (Olivier) with pronotum pale on sides and base, elytral bases and angles not projecting or produced; New Jersey to northern Florida, west to Mississippi. (2)

Pandeleteius hilaris (Herbst) (3.2–5.6 mm) has moderately enlarged forelegs and variably distinct patterns of dense, small grayish and brownish scales. Head with eyes small, rounded, hemispherical; tip of rostrum with small triangular projection over mandibles. Pronotum longer than wide, long dark spot on middle flanked by light and dark indistinct stripes. Elytra faintly constricted behind humeri, grooves shallowly to deeply punctate, sometimes with black scales outlining white markings. Front tibiae curved at tip with straight inner edge bearing 7–14 teeth of equal size, sometimes with smaller teeth between. Adults found in spring and early summer on shrubs, especially oak (*Quercus*), also ceanothus (*Ceanothus*) and beech (*Fagus*). New Hampshire to Florida, west to Iowa and Texas. (2)

Cercopeus komareki O'Brien (2.8–3.1 mm) is oblong-oval, shining dark reddish brown, and densely clothed in dark brown, pale whitish brown, and few black round to broadly oval scales with somewhat sparse, erect, coarse setae; most of antennae and tarsi reddish brown. Eyes round, surrounded by groove. Short, broad rostrum weakly curved about as long as head, with pits on sides short and deep. Antennae with seven antennomeres between elbow and compact; oval club. Elytra oval, humeri not evident. Flightless males and females found year-round in pine-hardwood litter; extracted from litter using Berlese funnel. Southern Georgia and northern Florida. (10)

Two-banded Japanese Weevil *Pseudocneorhinus bifasciatus* (Roelofs) (4.0–5.5 mm) is pear-shaped and dark brown with short, blunt snout. Elytra wider than pronotum with two bands formed by brown and gray scales. Adults and larvae feed on more than 100 species of landscape plants. Wingless adults are mostly parthenogenetic females and active from spring through fall. Adults eat leaves, while larvae feed on roots. Eggs folded into leaves. Asia; established from New England to Florida, west to Illinois and Alabama. (1)

Clover Leaf Weevil *Brachypera zoilus* (Scopoli) (formerly *Hypera punctata* Fabricius) (5.0–8.5 mm) is oval, robust, black, and densely clothed in slender gray, brown, yellowish-brown, and blackish-brown scales notched on tips and suberect bristles. Rostrum stout, two-thirds shorter than length of pronotum. Pronotum wider than long, sides parallel, then abruptly narrowed in front. Adults active year-round. Adults and larvae pests on alfalfa (*Medicago*), clover (*Trifolium*), and other legumes (Fabaceae); larvae pupate in loose cocoons attached to leaves. Europe, widespread in eastern United States to Ontario. (1)

Lesser Clover Leaf Weevil *Hypera nigrirostris* **(Fabricius)** (3.5–4.5 mm) is elongate oval, reddish brown to black, and densely clothed in greenish hairlike scales, scales on sides notched on tip; appendages reddish brown. Head black, rostrum of male long as pronotum, antennomere 1 (scape) reaching front margin of more or less elongate-oval eye. Pronotum longer than wide, often with pale line down middle, sides rounded behind middle, with base narrower than elytra. Elytra with fine, punctate grooves, spaces between with short, thick, reclining setae, humeri rounded, and side parallel. Tibiae without sharp hooks at tips, claws separate, simple. Adults active spring and summer, found on alfalfa (*Medicago*), clover (*Trifolium*), and grasses. Europe; established in east from Maritime Provinces and New England to South Carolina, west to Wisconsin and Alabama. (7)

Canada Thistle Bud Weevil *Larinus planus* **(Fabricius)** (7.0–8.0 mm) is broadly oval, dark brown or black with patches of grayish hairlike scales and fine setae; freshly emerged individuals coated with yellow wax. Rostrum of female long, curved. Scutellum short, wide. Released for biocontrol of Canada thistle (*Cirsium arvense*); also attacks native thistles. Larvae develop in flower heads, destroying developing seeds. Europe; in east established in Manitoba, Maryland, Ohio, New York, and Nova Scotia. (3)

Rhubarb Curculio *Lixus concavus* **Say** (10.0–13.5 mm) is elongate, cylindrical, robust, and black with short grayish setae; freshly emerged individuals with yellowish or rusty bloom; appendages reddish brown. Rostrum long and not expanded at tip. Pronotum narrowed in front, with large and pronounced oval depression from front to base and carrying over to elytra, base sinuate and sides continuous with those of elytra. Elytra long, with rows of small and distant punctures, spaces between finely and densely punctate. Larvae develop in stems of dock (*Rumex*). Adults active spring and summer, found on larval host plants and other herbaceous growth. New York to Florida, west to Montana, Kansas, and Texas. (19)

Lixus scrobicollis **Boheman** (5.5–10.0 mm) is slender, black, and sparsely clothed in grayish setae. Rostrum short, stout or slender. Pronotum slightly longer than wide, parallel-sided with a distinct pubescent stripe down each side. Elytra with basal impression wide and shallow and rows of large punctures. Larvae develop in ragweed (*Ambrosia*) and other Asteraceae. Adults active spring and summer, found on larval host plants. New Jersey to Florida, west to Michigan, South Dakota, Colorado, and Arizona. (19)

Laemosaccus nephele **(Herbst)** (3.2–4.5 mm) is dull black, coarsely punctured on head and pronotum, with common red spot on elytra sometimes covering nearly entire surface. Rostrum flattened, grooved, and coarsely punctured on top, and much shorter than prothorax. Prothorax bell-shaped with sides broadly rounded. Elytra at middle narrower than prothorax, apices separately rounded, rows of weakly punctured grooves; intervals convex with small bumps; two to four intervals form lobes reaching across base of pronotum. Front and middle femora with a sharp tooth. Adults on oak (*Quercus*), hickory (*Carya*), and at light in late spring and summer. Complex of several undescribed species. Eastern North America. (1)

Magdalis austera **Fall** (3.0–4.5 mm) is elongate-oblong and dull black, elytra sometimes with bluish tinge. Rostrum slightly curved, longer than pronotum. Antennal scape short. Pronotum wider than long, distinctly constricted at bisinuate base. Elytra shiny, bases overlapping pronotum, rows of large, round punctures, spaces between crossed with fine wrinkles, with sides parallel (male), or slightly widened behind middle (female). Tarsomere 3 broadly bilobed. Larvae develop in bark of dead or dying trees. New Hampshire to South Carolina, west to Ontario, Michigan, and Indiana. Shiny blue form often found from New England and Québec to New York. (14)

493

Magdalis perforata **Horn** (3.5–5.5 mm) is elongate, somewhat wedge-shaped, shiny black, and coarsely, deeply punctate; appendages blackish. Rostrum nearly as long as head and pronotum combined. Antennal club normal in both sexes. Pronotum longer than wide, with sides straight at basal half, base distinctly sinuate. Elytra gradually becoming wider toward rear, grooves with deep, close, rectangular punctures, intervals narrower, base partly overlaps base of pronotum. Femora not toothed. Adults active spring and summer, found on pine (*Pinus*); attracted to light. Nova Scotia and Maine to Florida, west to Minnesota and Iowa. (14)

Rhyssomatus lineaticollis **(Say)** (5.5–6.5 mm) is robust, oval, convex, almost devoid of setae or scales, and black with reddish antennae and tarsi. Rostrum shorter than head and prothorax combined. Pronotum wider than long, side margins strongly arched, surface with deep grooves nearly parallel to midline. Elytra one-fifth wider than pronotum, spaces between grooves distinctly ridged. Adults and larvae associated with milkweed (*Asclepias*); adults found in summer on leaves, stems, and pods; larvae develop in seedpods. Connecticut to Florida, west to North Dakota, Utah, Missouri, and Texas. (4)

Conotrachelus anaglypticus (Say) (2.9–4.7 mm) is blackish or dark reddish brown with two short, thin lines of yellowish setae on each side of pronotum. Elytra twice as wide as pronotum, with whitish or yellowish setae in broad oblique bands behind humeri and middle. Larvae develop in bark wounds of different trees. Adults resemble dried plant buds when legs are retracted. Attracted to lights in spring and summer; also found in leaf litter. A pest on peach (*Prunus persica*) and other fruit and shade trees; also attacks cotton bolls (*Gossypium hirsutum*). Massachusetts to Florida, west to Montana, Nebraska, and Texas to South America. (38)

Conotrachelus elegans (Say) (3.8–5.1 mm) is reddish and black with thinly scattered reddish-yellow to whitish setae. Rostrum longer than pronotum, with three fine grooves on sides and ridge on top. Pronotum densely, coarsely punctate without furrow down middle, and whitish lines not meeting behind head. Elytra with broad, pale band behind middle, low ridges nearest suture twice interrupted. Femora each with two teeth, claws divergent and toothed; male with apical projection (uncus) on hind tibia toothed, female unci not toothed. Underside of abdomen coarsely punctured. Breeds in *Phylloxera* galls on hickory (*Carya*). Adults found on hickory; also at light. Québec and Ontario to Florida, west to Michigan, Illinois, and Texas. (38)

Butternut Curculio *Conotrachelus juglandis* LeConte (5.9–7.1 mm) is reddish to black with sparse and slender brownish-yellow and white setae. Rostrum ridged and grooved, longer than pronotum. Pronotum with sinuate line on each side not reaching front. Elytra with rows of coarse punctures, especially along basal half, pale band behind middle, each with a pair of pale patches of setae at base and a short ridge down middle. Abdomen with first ventrite finely punctate. Adults active in late spring and summer, found on walnut (*Juglans*); attracted to light. New York and Québec to Georgia, west to Wisconsin, Iowa, and Texas. (38)

Plum Curculio *Conotrachelus nenuphar* (Herbst) (3.6–5.6 mm) is variably dark brown and black with brownish-yellow pubescence and four elytral bumps. Rostrum curved, as long as pronotum. Scutellum depressed and sloped toward front. Elytra with ridges interrupted resulting in four distinct and narrow bumps near base and at middle, surface between black and shiny, and a band of reddish-yellow or reddish-yellow and white setae behind middle. Ventrites coarsely, densely punctate. Adults found on trees and shrubs, especially *Prunus*; larvae attack fruit and berries. Maritime Provinces to Florida, west to Manitoba, Colorado, Kansas, and Texas. (38)

Conotrachelus posticatus Boheman (3.7–5.0 mm)
is dark reddish brown with irregular black spots. Rostrum
longer than pronotum, with distinct ridges and three grooves
in both sexes. Pronotum densely punctured with fine ridge
down middle. Elytra each with white spot at base, rows
of large punctures, spaces between finely ridged with a
conspicuous row of nearly erect setae, and a light band
before tip. Hind femora with distinct tooth, males with long,
sharp process on tip of front tibiae. Larvae breed in acorns.
Adults found in spring and summer on oak (*Quercus*) and
other hardwood trees. Widely distributed in eastern North
America; Mexico and Central America. (38)

Avocado Weevil *Heilipus apiatus* **(Olivier)**
(14.0–16.0 mm) is oblong and shiny black, with a broad,
white, and highly irregular stripe along the sides of pronotum
and elytra. Adults are found year-round, but reach peak
activity in summer, found on sassafras (*Sassafras*) and
under pine (*Pinus*) bark. Adults and larvae are serious
pests of avocados (*Persea*); adults eat young fruits, while
larvae bore and develop in base of trunk. Virginia to Florida,
west to Tennessee. (1)

Pales Weevil *Hylobius pales* **(Herbst)** (5.8–11.4 mm) is
oblong, robust, dark reddish brown with small scattered
patches of pale yellowish scales on pronotum and elytra.
Rostrum about same length as pronotum, distinctly wider
past antennal insertions in female. Pronotum shorter than
wide, densely punctate and wrinkled with short, sharp
ridge down middle. Tips of hind tibia not widened, male
with broad, rounded spine (uncus). Ventrites 1–2 broadly
depressed across middle in male, 1 flat and 2 slighty
convex in female. Adults found year-round feeding on pine
(*Pinus*); also attracted to light. Adults and larvae are pests
in pine plantations. Québec and Ontario to Florida, west to
Minnesota to Texas. (2)

Pitch-eating Weevil *Pachylobius picivorus* **(Germar)**
(7.0–13.0 mm) is dark brown or black with sparse clumps
of short white, yellowish, or reddish-brown setae. Rostrum
long as pronotum. Pronotum longer than wide, coarsely
punctate, with narrow smooth line down middle. Elytra
slightly wider than pronotum, shallowly grooved with oblong
punctures, sides somewhat parallel at basal third. Tip of
hind tibia broad, wide as femora, with flat, rounded plate.
Feeds on pine, especially shortleaf (*Pinus echinata*),
loblolly (*P. taeda*), and slash (*P. elliottii*). Adults eat inner
bark of small twigs and seedlings; larvae bore into roots
of recently cut or killed trees. Throughout eastern North
America, especially the Southeast. (1)

495

Lepyrus palustris (Scopoli) (9.0–10.0 mm) is elongate-oval, black, and sparsely clothed in gray and yellowish hairlike scales. Rostrum more than twice length of head. Prothorax cone-shaped with pale stripe down each side. Elytra with equally spaced rows of punctures, each with small pale spot at middle; flight wings developed. Femora each with a small tooth and ringed with white. Adults active in summer, found on willow (*Salix*) and aspen (*Populus*). In northeast from Labrador to New York, west to Ontario, Wisconsin, and Illinois. (6)

Hormops abducens LeConte (3.7–4.0 mm) is elongate-oval and reddish brown with nearly circular pronotum. Head with long eyes barely visible above and nearly touching underneath; antennae arise from deep pit just in front of eyes; rostrum very short, broad. Pronotum wider than long, base and sides broadly rounded, and distinctly punctate without fine, raised ridge down middle. Elytra somewhat flattened, wider than pronotum, with rows of punctures separated by flat, punctate spaces. Adults live in cut branches used by squirrels to build their arboreal nests; also in leaf litter, attracted to light. Maryland to Florida, west to Kansas and Texas. (1)

496

White Pine Weevil *Pissodes strobi* (Peck) (4.0–6.0 mm) is also known as the Englemann or sitka spruce weevil. Elytra with patches of white and brown scales near tips; white patch reaches elytral suture. Adults feed and breed on many species of native pines and spruces, especially eastern white pine (*Pinus strobus*) and Norway spruce (*Picea abies*). Adults emerge in spring to feed on shoots and lay eggs in small holes chewed in bark. Larvae kill terminal growth of trees. Repeated larval infestations stunt crown growth and render commercially grown trees unusable. Occurs throughout eastern North America. (8)

Cowpea Curculio *Chalcodermus aeneus* Boheman (4.8–5.5 mm) is oval, convex, and black with surface very finely wrinkled and often with bronze luster. Rostrum nearly straight, longer than pronotum, and slightly ridged. Pronotum wider than long, coarsely punctate, not wrinkled. Elytra oval, convex, sides somewhat parallel along basal half, with rows of deep, widely spaced punctures, spaces between very finely wrinkled, each with a row of fine punctures. Adults active year-round, found on cudweed (*Gnaphalium*), evening primrose (*Oenothera*), dock (*Rumex*), senna (*Senna*), fuzzybean (*Strophostyles*), verbena (*Verbena*), vetch (*Vicia*), and cowpea (*Vigna*); attracted to light. Maryland to Florida, west to Indiana, Kansas, and Texas. (3)

Black Turpentine Beetle *Dendroctonus terebrans*
(Olivier) (5.0–10.0 mm) is elongate, stout, cylindrical, and
reddish brown to black. Head densely granulate and roughly
punctate, convex in front, and visible from above. Antennae
with five short antennomeres before short club with suture
just before tip. Pronotum and elytra coarsely and shallowly
punctate. Adults and larvae attack pine (*Pinus*), especially
loblolly (*P. taeda*) and slash pine (*P. elliotti*); infested trees
with reddish to white pitch tubes that turn gray. Adults
found under bark; attracted to baited Lindgren funnel traps.
Virginia to Florida, west to Arkansas and eastern Texas. (5)

Red Turpentine Beetle *Dendroctonus valens* LeConte
(5.3–9.0 mm) is large, stout, cylindrical, and uniformly
reddish to reddish brown. Antennal club semicircular,
flattened, and crossed by three curved grooves. Pronotum
with dense, shallow punctures, underneath with sides
granulate with punctures faint or absent. Elytra with
punctures small and deep, numerous setae at base, tips
evenly convex. Larvae develop primarily in pine (*Pinus*),
occasionally in other conifers. Adults attracted to freshly
cut stumps and injured, weakened, or dying trees, usually
near ground. In North America across Canada, western and
northeastern United States, to Guatemala. (5)

497

Eastern Ash Bark Beetle *Hylesinus aculeatus* Say
(2.0–3.4 mm) is elongate, cylindrical, and dark brown with
variable light and dark patterns. Front of head flat (male)
or convex (female). Pronotum with whitish-gray scales
outlining a diamond-shaped patch of dark reddish scales,
sides with tiny spikelike projections. Elytra slightly wider
than pronotum, serrate along basal margin, brown and gray
scales forming herringbone pattern; tips convex, gradually
sloped. Fifth ventrite with hairlike setae. Breeds in large
branches, limbs, and trunks of injured, dying, or felled ash
(*Fraxinus*). Adults emerge in spring from round exit holes.
Nova Scotia to Georgia, west to Manitoba, South Dakota,
and Oklahoma. (4)

Hylurgops pinifex (Fitch) (3.4–5.0 mm) is reddish brown to
black above, black underneath, and clothed in rows of setae
and narrowly to broadly flattened scales. Pronotum narrowed
in front of middle, with equal numbers of intermixed large and
small punctures. Elytra with spaces between grooves convex
with irregular, fine notches and long, erect, hairlike setae, and
granulate on convex elytral tips. Third tarsomere broad and
bilobed. Larvae work mostly old, dead logs, stumps, and
lower parts of standing pine (*Pinus*) and spruce (*Picea*), do
not form distinct galleries. Nova Scotia to Rhode Island,
west to Alberta. (1)

Four-eyed Spruce Bark Beetle *Polygraphus rufipennis*
(Kirby) (1.8–3.7 mm) is elongate, cylindrical, very dark
brown to black, and densely clothed in whitish or yellowish
scales. Head with eyes completely divided and antennal
club unsegmented, front shallowly concave below small
bumps (male) or flat to concave with long pubescence
(female). Elytra with punctures scattered with elytral tips
evenly convex. Breeds in broken, cut, or fallen conifers,
especially spruce (*Picea*) and pine (*Pinus*); occasionally
attacks standing trees weakened by other bark beetles; one
to three broods. Across Canada, in east from Newfoundland
to North Carolina, west to New Mexico. (1)

Hickory Bark Beetle *Scolytus quadrispinosus* **Say**
(4.0–5.0 mm) is shining black to reddish brown. Head with
front and between eyes broadly impressed and strongly
pubescent (male) or convex and sparsely pubescent
(female). Elytra shining, not abruptly cut off behind, with
rows of deep punctures, intervals with single row of shallow
punctures. Abdomen abruptly ascending from thorax,
with (male) or without (female) sharp tubercles. Front
tibiae broad, flat, without spines. Serious pest of hickories
and pecans (*Carya*), and butternut (*Juglans cinerea*).
Southern Ontario and Québec to northern Florida, west to
southeastern Nebraska and eastern Texas. (5)

498

Six-spined Ips *Ips calligraphus* **(Germar)** (3.5–6.5 mm)
is elongate, cylindrical, and shiny dark reddish brown. Head
convex, granulate, setose, small bump on middle, flat and
oval antennal club with sinuate sutures. Elytra with spaces
between grooves punctate, tips concave, outer margins with
six teeth, third tooth from top largest and hooked (male) or
pointed (female). Adults and larvae found in stumps, trunks,
and larger limbs of recently logged pine trees (*Pinus*); also
colonizes and kills healthy trees. Eastern North America. (7)

Pine Engraver *Ips pini* **(Say)** (3.3–4.3 mm) is dark
reddish brown to blackish. Head coarsely punctured above,
granulate below. Elytra with surface lacking punctures
or setae between grooves; tips strongly sloping down,
shining, broadly scooped out, with four teeth along each
side. Typically attacks thin-barked portions of pine (*Pinus*)
slash, and dead or dying trees, seldom attacks healthy
trees; rarely breeds in spruce (*Picea*) or larch (*Larix*); brood
gallery distinctive. Across Canada and eastern United
States to North Carolina and Tennessee; also in West. (7)

Pityokteines sparsus (LeConte) (2.1–2.5 mm) is somewhat stout with long, erect, dense setae on front of flattened head and across anterior of pronotum (female); male head convex with ridges. Antennal club without sutures and obliquely truncate. Elytra with punctate grooves mostly not impressed, all surface punctures similar in size, and tips possessing distinct teeth, male's larger than female. Starshaped brood galleries form in phloem of limbs and boles of living, weakened, or dead balsam fir (*Abies balsamea*), also attacks other conifers. Newfoundland to Alberta, northeastern United States. (1)

Columbian Timber Beetle *Corthylus columbianus* Hopkins (3.5–4.0 mm) is stout, with one antennomere between elbow and club without any sutures. Head concave and pubescent (female) or convex and without setae (male). Elytra with tips convex with small but distinct tubercles. Middle and hind tibiae with four teeth near tips. Larvae develop in short chambers off main brood gallery deep in sapwood of hardwoods where they feed on ambrosial fungus that stains wood black and ruins its value as lumber. Ontario and Québec to Florida, west to Michigan and Arkansas. (3)

499

Yellow-banded Timber Beetle *Monarthrum fasciatum* (Say) (2.3–3.0 mm) is small, elongate, cylindrical. Antennal stalk with two antennomeres. Pronotum long, rough in front, smooth behind. Elytra entirely dark, or half to entirely pale yellow, suture and tips sometimes dark; tips appear cut off, clothed in long yellow setae with two close-set tubercles. Appendages yellowish. Usually breeds in dead or dying deciduous hardwoods, including oak (*Quercus*), maple (*Acer*), birch (*Betula*), poplar (*Populus*); sometimes attacks pine (*Pinus*) and fruit trees (*Prunus*). Females with mycangia carry spores of wood-staining ambrosia fungi. Adults active in spring and summer. Québec and Ontario to Florida, west to Wisconsin and Texas. (2)

Camphor Shot Borer *Cnestus mutilatus* (Blandford) (2.6–3.9 mm) is short, robust, cyclindrical, black, and clothed in short, erect setae. Pronotum wider than long, with front rough. Elytra short, only slightly longer than pronotum, abruptly sloping down at base third with tips lacking spines. Front legs widely separated at base. Larvae attack mostly deciduous trees, shrubs, and woody vines, including maple (*Acer*), hickory (*Carya*), dogwood (*Cornus*), beech (*Fagus*), oak (*Quercus*), cherry (*Prunus*), elm (*Ulmus*), and grape (*Vitis*); also pine (*Pinus*), plastic gas containers. Adults active in summer, attracted to Lindgren funnels baited with ethanol. Southeast Asia, established from Georgia and Florida, west to Arkansas and Texas. (1)

Xyleborus affinis **Eichhoff** (2.0–2.8 mm) is somewhat elongate, brownish yellow, with long gray pubescence. Antennae with five antennomeres between elbow and obliquely truncate club. Pronotum longer than wide, surface rough, anterior margin nearly horned at middle (male) or entire (female); surface concave (male) or convex (female), base shining. Scutellum flat. Elytra with grooves not deeply impressed, with tips convex, dull, broadly sloping with tubercles on interstriae 1 and 3 small but conspicuous, and of equal size. Larvae develop in various species of deciduous trees. Males haploid, flightless, and remain in tunnels. Ontario and Québec, eastern United States; also in Neotropics. (17)

Euplatypus compositus **(Say)** (4.0–5.0 mm) is elongate, straight-sided, cylindrical, and light to medium reddish brown. Head lacks rostrum, antennal club without sutures. Prothorax longer than wide, nearly half as long as elytra. Tips of elytra each with blunt process ending in three spines (male) or without any projection (female). Underside of abdomen of both sexes without spines. Leg with first tarsomere equal in length to rest of tarsus. Adults active spring through early winter, found in bark of maple (*Acer*), magnolia (*Magnolia*), pine (*Pinus*), and oak (*Quercus*). Widespread in eastern North America. (2)

500

Myoplatypus flavicornis **(Fabricius)** (4.0–5.7 mm) is elongate, slender, cylindrical, and light to dark reddish brown with yellowish appendages. Pronotum punctate with fine groove down middle at basal third. Eytra tipped with large, triangular process pointed at tip and serrate along sides (male) or with smaller triangular process rounded at tip (female). Abdominal ventrite 4 with (male) or without (female) pair of broad teeth. Adults found year-round; attracted to light. New Jersey to Florida, west to Louisiana. (1)

Oxoplatypus quadridentatus **(Olivier)** (4.0–4.5 mm) is long, narrow, cylindrical, and uniformly reddish brown. Antennal club lacks sutures. Pronotum with pair of large, conspicuous fungus-storing (mycangia) pores at basal third near midline present (female) or absent (male). Elytra of male with rounded processes at tip, female without processes. First tarsomere as long as tarsomeres 2–5 combined. Ventrite 4 with (male) or without (female) a pair of large hooked spines. Larva develops mostly in oaks (*Quercus*). Adults found in spring and late summer under bark; attracted to light, also Malaise and Lindgren funnel traps. Maryland to Florida, west to West Virginia to Texas. (1)

Appendix

CLASSIFICATION OF THE BEETLES COVERED IN THIS BOOK

The classification used for the species included in this book is based primarily on Beutel and Leschen (2005), Bouchard et al. (2011), and Leschen et al. (2010) (see Selected References and Resources for complete bibliographic information on these references).

ORDER COLEOPTERA

Suborder Archostemata
    Family Cupedidae
        Subfamily Cupedinae
            Cupes capitatus Fabricius
            Tenomerga cinereus (Say)
        Family Micromalthidae
            Micromalthus debilis LeConte
Suborder Myxophaga
    Superfamily Sphaeriusoidea
        Family Sphaeriusidae
            Sphaerius species
Suborder Adephaga
    Family Carabidae
        Subfamily Nebriinae
          Tribe Nebriini
            Nebria lacustris Casey
          Tribe Notiophilini
            Notiophilus aeneus (Herbst)
            Notiophilus novemstriatus LeConte
        Subfamily Carabinae
          Tribe Carabini
            Calosoma calidum (Fabricius)
            Calosoma frigidum Kirby
            Calosoma sayi Dejean
            Calosoma scrutator (Fabricius)
            Calosoma sycophanta (Linnaeus)
            Calosoma wilcoxi LeConte
            Carabus auratus Linnaeus

            Carabus maender Waldheim
            Carabus nemoralis Müller
            Carabus serratus Say
            Carabus sylvosus Say
            Carabus vinctus (Weber)
          Tribe Cychrini
            Scaphinotus andrewsii (Harris)
            Sphaeroderus stenostomus lecontei Dejean
        Subfamily Cicindelinae
          Tribe Megacephalini
            Tetracha carolina (Linnaeus)
            Tetracha virginica (Linnaeus)
          Tribe Cicindelini
            Cicindela duodecimguttata Dejean
            Cicindela hirticollis hirticollis Say
            Cicindela limbalis Klug
            Cicindela patruela Dejean
            Cicindela repanda repanda Dejean
            Cicindela scutellaris rugifrons Dejean
            Cicindela sexguttata Fabricius
            Cicindela splendida Hentz
            Cicindela tranquebarica Hentz
            Cicindelidia abdominalis (Fabricius)
            Cicindelidia punctulata (Olivier)
            Cicindelidia rufiventris rufiventris (Dejean)
            Cylindera unipunctata (Fabricius)
            Ellipsoptera hirtilabris (LeConte)
            Ellipsoptera lepida (Dejean)
            Ellipsoptera marginata (Fabricius)
            Habroscelimorpha dorsalis dorsalis (Say)

Subfamily Elaphrinae
  Tribe Elaphrini
    Elaphrus californicus Mannerheim
Subfamily Omophroninae
  Tribe Omophrini
    Omophron americanum Dejean
    Omophron labiatum (Fabricius)
    Omophron tessellatum Say
Subfamily Scaritinae
  Tribe Cliviniini
    Clivina fossor (Linnaeus)
    Clivina pallida Say
    Dyschirius sphaericollis (Say)
    Paraclivina bipustulata (Fabricius)
    Semiardistomis viridis (Say)
  Tribe Pasimachini
    Pasimachus marginatus (Fabricius)
    Pasimachus subsulcatus Say
  Tribe Scaritini
    Scarites subterraneus Fabricius
  Tribe Rhysodini
    Clinidium sculptile (Newman)
    Omoglymmius americanus (Laporte)
Subfamily Trechinae
  Tribe Trechini
    Trechus apicalis Motschulsky
  Tribe Bembidiini
    Bembidion castor Lindroth
    Bembidion rapidum (LeConte)
    Mioptachys flavicauda (Say)
    Paratachys rhodeanus (Casey)
    Tachyta kirbyi Casey
Subfamily Patrobinae
  Tribe Patrobini
    Patrobus longicornis (Say)
Subfamily Brachininae
  Tribe Brachinini
    Brachinus tenuicollis LeConte
Subfamily Harpalinae
  Tribe Pterostichini
    Cyclotrachelus sigillatus (Say)
    Myas cyanescens Dejean
    Poecilus chalcites (Say)
    Poecilus lucublandus (Say)
    Pterostichus adoxus (Say)
  Tribe Zabrini
    Amara pallipes Kirby
  Tribe Harpalini
    Acupalpus testaceus Dejean
    Amphasia interstitialis (Say)
    Anisodactylus rusticus (Say)
    Anisodactylus sanctaecrucis (Fabricius)

    Cratacanthus dubius (Palisot de Beauvois)
    Euryderus grossus (Say)
    Geopinus incrassatus (Dejean)
    Harpalus caliginosus (Fabricius)
    Harpalus erythropus Dejean
    Harpalus faunus Say
    Notiobia terminata (Say)
    Selenophorus opalinus (LeConte)
    Stenolophus comma (Fabricius)
    Stenolophus lecontei (Chaudoir)
    Stenolophus lineola (Fabricius)
    Stenolophus ochropezus (Say)
    Trichotichnus dichrous (Dejean)
  Tribe Licinini
    Badister neopulchellus Lindroth
    Dicaelus elongatus Bonelli
    Dicaelus purpuratus Bonelli
    Dicaelus sculptilis Say
    Diplocheila striatopunctata (LeConte)
  Tribe Panagaeini
    Panagaeus fasciatus Say
  Tribe Chlaeniini
    Chlaenius aestivus Say
    Chlaenius niger Randall
    Chlaenius sericeus (Forster)
    Chlaenius tomentosus (Say)
    Chlaenius tricolor Dejean
  Tribe Oodini
    Oodes fluvialis (LeConte)
  Tribe Ctenodactylini
    Leptotrachelus dorsalis (Fabricius)
  Tribe Platynini
    Agonum extensicolle (Say)
    Agonum octopunctatum (Fabricius)
    Calathus opaculus LeConte
    Platynus cincticollis (Say)
    Platynus tenuicollis (LeConte)
    Synuchus impunctatus (Say)
  Tribe Lachnophorini
    Ega sallei (Chevrolat)
  Tribe Odacanthini
    Cosnania pensylvanica (Linnaeus)
  Tribe Cyclosomini
    Tetragonoderus latipennis (LeConte)
  Tribe Lebiini
    Apenes sinuata (Say)
    Calleida punctata LeConte
    Coptodera aerata Dejean
    Cymindis limbata (Dejean)
    Lebia analis Dejean
    Lebia fuscata Dejean
    Lebia grandis Hentz

Lebia ornata Say
Lebia pectita Horn
Lebia solea Hentz
Lebia tricolor Say
Lebia viridis Say
Lebia vittata Fabricius
Phloeoxena signata (Dejean)
Plochionus timidus Haldeman
Tribe Zuphiini
Pseudaptinus pygmaeus (Dejean)
Zuphium americanum Dejean
Tribe Galeritini
Galerita bicolor (Drury)
Tribe Helluonini
Helluomorphoides praestus bicolor Harris
Family Gyrinidae
Subfamily Gyrininae
Tribe Enhydrini
Dineutus emarginatus (Say)
Tribe Gyrinini
Gyrinus species
Tribe Orectochilini
Gyretes iricolor Young
Family Haliplidae
Brychius hungerfordi Spangler
Haliplus pantherinus Aubé
Peltodytes muticus (LeConte)
Family Noteridae
Subfamily Noterinae
Hydrocanthus iricolor Say
Suphis inflatus (LeConte)
Family Dytiscidae
Subfamily Copelatinae
Copelatus glyphicus (Say)
Subfamily Laccophilinae
Tribe Agabetini
Agabetes acuductus (Harris)
Tribe Laccophilini
Laccophilus maculosus Say
Laccophilus undatus Aubé
Tribe Methlini
Celina hubbelli Young
Tribe Hydroporini
Hydroporus tristis (Paykull)
Hygrotus sayi Balfour-Browne
Neoporus undulatus (Say)
Subfamily Coptotominae
Coptotomus longulus lenticus Hilsenhoff
Subfamily Matinae
Matus bicarinatus (Say)
Subfamily Agabinae
Agabus species

Subfamily Colymbetinae
Tribe Colymbetini
Colymbetes paykulli Erichson
Ilybius biguttulus (Germar)
Rhantus wallisi Hatch
Subfamily Dytiscinae
Tribe Dytiscini
Dytiscus carolinus Aubé
Tribe Hydaticini
Hydaticus piceus LeConte
Tribe Aciliini
Acilius mediatus (Say)
Acilius semisulcatus Aubé
Graphoderus liberus (Say)
Thermonectus basillaris (Harris)
Tribe Cybisterini
Cybister fimbriolatus (Say)
Suborder Polyphaga
Series Staphyliniformia
Superfamily Hydrophiloidea
Family Hydrophilidae
Subfamily Helophorinae
Helophorus grandis Illiger
Subfamily Hydrochinae
Hydrochus squamifer LeConte
Subfamily Hydrophilinae
Tribe Sperchopsini
Sperchopsis tessellata (Ziegler)
Tribe Berosini
Berosus ordinatus LeConte
Tribe Acidocerini
Enochrus cinctus (Say)
Enochrus ochraceus (Melsheimer)
Helobata larvalis (Horn)
Helocombus bifidus (LeConte)
Tribe Hydrobiusini
Hydrobius fuscipes (Linnaeus)
Tribe Hydrophilini
Hydrochara soror Smetana
Hydrophilus ovatus Gemminger & Harold
Hydrophilus triangularis Say
Tropisternus blatchleyi D'Orchymont
Tropisternus collaris (Fabricius)
Tropisternus lateralis nimbatus (Say)
Subfamily Sphaeridiinae
Tribe Megasternini
Cercyon praetextatus (Say)
Tribe Sphaeridiini
Sphaeridium scarabaeoides (Linnaeus)
Family Histeridae
Subfamily Abraeinae
Tribe Abraeini
Plegaderus tranversus (Say)

503

Tribe Acritini
Aeletes politus (LeConte)
Subfamily Saprininae
Euspilotus assimilis (Paykull)
Hypocaccus dimidiatipennis (LeConte)
Hypocaccus fraternus (Say)
Saprinus pensylvanicus (Paykull)
Subfamily Dendrophilinae
Tribe Paromalini
Paromalus bistriatus Erichson
Platylomalus aequalis (Say)
Subfamily Histerinae
Tribe Platysomatini
Platysoma coarctatum LeConte
Platysoma leconti Marseul
Tribe Hololeptini
Hololepta aequalis Say
Tribe Histerini
Hister furtivus LeConte
Family Hydraenidae
Subfamily Hydraeninae
Tribe Hydraenini
Hydraena pensylvanica Kiesenwetter
Subfamily Ochthebiinae
Tribe Ochthebiini
Enicocerus benefossus (LeConte)
Family Ptiliidae
Subfamily Ptiliinae
Tribe Ptenidiini
Ptenidium pusillum (Gyllenhal)
Tribe Nanosellini
Nanosella atrocephala Dury
Family Agyrtidae
Subfamily Necrophilinae
Necrophilus pettiti Horn
Family Leiodidae
Subfamily Leiodinae
Tribe Leiodini
Leiodes species
Tribe Agathidiini
Agathidium species
Subfamily Cholevinae
Tribe Cholevini
Catops basilaris Say
Prionochaeta opaca (Say)
Tribe Ptomaphagini
Ptomaphagus brevior Jeannel
Subfamily Platypsyllinae
Leptinus orientamericanus Peck
Platypsyllus castoris Ritsema

Family Silphidae
Subfamily Silphinae
Necrodes surinamensis (Fabricius)
Necrophila americana (Linnaeus)
Oiceoptoma inequale (Fabricius)
Oiceoptoma noveboracense (Forster)
Thanatophilus lapponicus (Herbst)
Subfamily Nicrophorinae
Nicrophorus americanus Olivier
Nicrophorus defodiens Mannerheim
Nicrophorus orbicollis Say
Nicrophorus pustulatus Herschel
Nicrophorus sayi Laporte
Nicrophorus tomentosus Weber
Family Staphylinidae
Subfamily Omaliinae
Tribe Anthophagini
Arpedium schwarzi Fauvel
Olophrum obtectum Erichson
Trigonodemus striatus LeConte
Subfamily Pselaphinae
Tribe Batrisini
Batrisodes lineaticollis (Aubé)
Tribe Brachyglutini
Brachygluta abdominalis (Aubé)
Decarthron velutinum (LeConte)
Reichenbachia facilis (Casey)
Tribe Clavigerini
Adranes coecus LeConte
Tribe Tyrini
Cedius spinosus LeConte
Ceophyllus monilis LeConte
Tyrus semiruber Casey
Subfamily Phloeocharinae
Charhyphus picipennis (LeConte)
Subfamily Olisthaerinae
Olisthaerus substriatus Paykull
Subfamily Tachyporinae
Tribe Mycetoporini
Lordithon cinctus (Gravenhorst)
Lordithon facilis (Casey)
Lordithon fungicola Campbell
Lordithon kelleyi (Malkin)
Tribe Tachyporini
Coproporus ventriculus (Say)
Sepedophilus species
Tachinus fimbriatus Gravenhorst
Tachyporus elegans Horn
Subfamily Aleocharinae
Tribe Aleocharini
Aleochara littoralis (Mäklin)
Tribe Athetini
Meronera venustula (Erichson)

504

Tribe Falagriini
  Falagria dissecta Erichson
Tribe Gymnusini
  Gymnusa atra Casey
Tribe Homalotini
  Gyrophaena species
Tribe Hoplandriini
  Hoplandria lateralis (Melsheimer)
Tribe Lomechusini
  Drusilla canaliculata (Fabricius)
Tribe Philotermitini
  Philotermes cubitopilus Seever
Subfamily Scaphidiinae
  Tribe Scaphidiini
    Scaphidium quadriguttatum Say
  Tribe Scaphisomatini
    Baeocera species
    Scaphisoma rubens Casey
Subfamily Piestinae
  Siagonium americanum (Melsheimer)
Subfamily Osoriinae
  Tribe Thoracophorini
    Thoracophorus costalis (Erichson)
Subfamily Oxytelinae
  Tribe Blediini
    Bledius mandibularis Erichson
  Tribe Oxytelini
    Anotylus rugosus (Fabricius)
Subfamily Oxyporinae
  Oxyporus quinquemaculatus LeConte
  Oxyporus rufipennis LeConte
  Oxyporus vittatus Gravenhorst
Subfamily Scydmaeninae
  Tribe Cyrtoscydmini
    Euconnus salinator (LeConte)
Subfamily Steninae
  Stenus colon Say
Subfamily Pseudopsinae
  Pseudopsis subulata Herman
Subfamily Paederinae
  Tribe Paederini
    Astenus brevipennis (Austin)
    Homaeotarsus bicolor (Gravenhorst)
    Lathrobium convolutum Watrous
    Lobrathium collare (Erichson)
    Paederus littorarius Gravenhorst
    Sunius confluentus (Say)
  Tribe Pinophilini
    Palaminus testaceus Erichson
    Pinophilus latipes Gravenhorst

Subfamily Staphylininae
  Tribe Diochini
    Diochus schaumii Kraatz
  Tribe Othiini
    Atrecus americanus (Casey)
  Tribe Staphylinini
    Acylophorus species
    Belonuchus rufipennis (Fabricius)
    Bisnius blandus (Gravenhorst)
    Creophilus maxillosus villosus (Gravenhorst)
    Erichsonius patella (Horn)
    Hesperus baltimorensis (Gravenhorst)
    Heterothops fumigatus LeConte
    Laetulonthus laetulus (Say)
    Ocypus nitens (Schrank)
    Ontholestes cingulatus (Gravenhorst)
    Philonthus caeruleipennis (Mannerheim)
    Philonthus flumineus Casey
    Platydracus fossator (Gravenhorst)
    Platydracus maculosus (Gravenhorst)
    Quedius capucinus (Gravenhorst)
    Quedius peregrinus (Gravenhorst)
  Tribe Xantholinini
    Gyrohypnus fracticornis (Müller)
Series Scarabaeiformia
Superfamily Scarabaeoidea
  Family Lucanidae
    Subfamily Aesalinae
      Tribe Nicagini
        Nicagus obscurus (LeConte)
    Subfamily Syndesinae
      Tribe Ceruchini
        Ceruchus piceus (Weber)
    Subfamily Lucaninae
      Tribe Lucanini
        Dorcus parallelus (Say)
        Lucanus capreolus (Linnaeus)
        Lucanus elaphus Fabricius
      Tribe Platycerini
        Platycerus virescens (Fabricius)
  Family Passalidae
    Subfamily Passalinae
      Tribe Proculini
        Odontotaenius disjunctus (Illiger)
  Family Glaresidae
    Glaresis inducta Horn
  Family Trogidae
    Omorgus monachus (Herbst)
    Omorgus suberosus (Fabricius)
    Trox capillaris Say
    Trox scaber (Linnaeus)
    Trox tuberculatus (De Geer)
    Trox unistriatus Palisot de Beauvois

Family Geotrupidae
    Subfamily Bolboceratinae
        Tribe Bolboceratini
            Bolbocerosoma farctum (Fabricius)
            Bradycinetulus ferrugineus (Palisot de Beauvois)
            Eucanthus lazarus (Fabricius)
            Odonteus darlingtoni Wallis
    Subfamily Geotrupinae
        Tribe Geotrupini
            Geotrupes blackburnii blackburnii (Fabricius)
            Geotrupes splendidus (Fabricius)
            Mycotrupes cartwrighti Olson & Hubbell
            Mycotrupes retusus (LeConte)
            Peltotrupes profundus Howden
Family Ochodaeidae
    Subfamily Ochodaeinae
        Tribe Ochodaeini
            Xenochodaeus musculus (Say)
Family Hybosoridae
    Subfamily Hybosorinae
        Hybosorus roei Westwood
    Subfamily Ceratocanthinae
        Tribe Ceratocanthini
            Ceratocanthus aeneus (MacLeay)
            Germarostes aphodioides (Illiger)
Family Glaphyridae
    Subfamily Glaphyrinae
        Lichnanthe vulpina (Hentz)
Family Scarabaeidae
    Subfamily Aphodiinae
        Tribe Aphodiini
            Aphodius fimetarius (Linnaeus)
            Blackburneus stercorosus (Melsheimer)
            Calamosternus granarius (Linnaeus)
            Dialytes striatulus (Say)
            Flaviellus phalerioides (Horn)
            Labarrus pseudolividus (Balthasar)
            Pseudagolius bicolor (Say)
        Tribe Eupariini
            Ataenius imbricatus (Melsheimer)
            Ataenius spretulus (Haldeman)
    Subfamily Scarabaeinae
        Tribe Deltochilini
            Canthon pilularius (Linnaeus)
            Canthon viridis (Palisot de Beauvois)
            Deltochilum gibbosum (Fabricius)
            Melanocanthon bispinatus (Robinson)
        Tribe Coprini
            Copris fricator (Fabricius)
            Copris minutus (Drury)
        Tribe Ateuchini
            Ateuchus histeroides Weber

            Dichotomius carolinus (Linnaeus)
        Tribe Phanaeini
            Phanaeus vindex MacLeay
        Tribe Oniticellini
            Euoniticellus intermedius (Reiche)
        Tribe Onthophagini
            Digitonthophagus gazella (Fabricius)
            Onthophagus depressus Harold
            Onthophagus hecate (Panzer)
            Onthophagus nuchicornis (Linnaeus)
            Onthophagus taurus (Schreber)
    Subfamily Melolonthinae
        Tribe Sericini
            Maladera castanea (Arrow)
            Nipponoserica peregrina (Chapin)
            Serica atracapilla (Kirby)
        Tribe Melolonthini
            Amphimallon majale (Razoumowsky)
            Hypotrichia spissipes LeConte
            Phyllophaga crenulata (Froelich)
            Phyllophaga micans (Knoch)
            Polyphylla comes Casey
            Polyphylla occidentalis (Linnaeus)
            Polyphylla variolosa (Hentz)
        Tribe Diplotaxini
            Diplotaxis liberta (Germar)
            Diplotaxis sordida (Say)
        Tribe Hopliini
            Hoplia trivialis Harold
        Tribe Dichelonychini
            Dichelonyx albicollis (Burmeister)
            Dichelonyx linearis (Gyllenhal)
        Tribe Macrodactylini
            Macrodactylus angustatus (Palisot de Beauvois)
            Plectris aliena Chapin
    Subfamily Rutelinae
        Tribe Anomalini
            Anomala lucicola (Fabricius)
            Anomala undulata Melsheimer
            Callistethus marginatus (Fabricius)
            Exomala orientalis (Waterhouse)
            Popillia japonica Newman
            Strigoderma arbicola (Fabricius)
            Strigoderma pygmaea (Fabricius)
        Tribe Rutelini
            Cotalpa lanigera (Linnaeus)
            Pelidnota punctata (Linnaeus)
    Subfamily Dynastinae
        Tribe Cyclocephalini
            Cyclocephala borealis Arrow
            Dyscinetus morator (Fabricius)

Tribe Pentodontini
 Aphonus castaneus (Melshiemer)
 Eutheola humilis (Burmeister)
 Parastasia brevipes (LeConte)
 Tomarus gibbosus (De Geer)
Tribe Oryctini
 Strategus aloeus (Linnaeus)
 Strategus antaeus (Drury)
 Strategus splendens (Palisot de Beauvois)
 Xyloryctes jamaicensis (Drury)
Tribe Phileurini
 Phileurus truncatus (Palisot de Beauvois)
 Phileurus valgus (Olivier)
Tribe Dynastini
 Dynastes tityus (Linnaeus)
Subfamily Cetoniinae
Tribe Gymnetini
 Cotinis nitida (Linnaeus)
Tribe Cetoniini
 Euphoria areata (Fabricius)
 Euphoria fulgida (Fabricius)
 Euphoria herbacea (Olivier)
 Euphoria inda (Linnaeus)
 Euphoria sepulcralis (Fabricius)
Tribe Cremastocheilini
 Cremastocheilus harrisii Kirby
Tribe Trichiini
 Gnorimella maculosa (Knoch)
 Osmoderma eremicola (Knoch)
 Osmoderma scabra (Palisot de Beauvois)
 Trichiotinus affinis (Gory & Percheron)
 Trichiotinus bibens (Fabricius)
 Trichiotinus lunulatus (Fabricius)
 Trichiotinus piger (Fabricius)
 Trigonopeltastes delta (Forster)
Tribe Valgini
 Valgus canaliculatus (Fabricius)
 Valgus seticollis (Palisot de Beauvois)
Series Elateriformia
Superfamily Scirtoidea
Family Eucinetidae
 Eucinetus morio LeConte
 Nycteus oviformis LeConte
Family Clambidae
Subfamily Clambinae
 Clambus species
Family Scirtidae
Subfamily Scirtinae
 Cyphon collaris (Guérin-Ménèville)
 Cyphon padi (Linnaeus)
 Cyphon ruficollis (Say)
 Elodes maculicollis Horn

 Ora troberti (Guérin-Ménèville)
 Prionocyphon limbatus (LeConte)
 Sacodes pulchella (Guérin-Ménèville)
 Sacodes thoracica (Guérin-Ménèville)
 Sarabandus robustus (LeConte)
 Scirtes orbiculatus (Fabricius)
 Scirtes ovalis Blatchley
Superfamily Dascilloidea
Family Rhipiceridae
 Sandalus niger Knoch
 Sandalus pterophya Knoch
Superfamily Buprestoidea
Family Buprestidae
Subfamily Polycestinae
Tribe Acmaeoderini
 Acmaeodera ornata (Fabricius)
 Acmaeodera pulchella (Herbst)
 Acmaeodera tubulus (Fabricius)
Tribe Haplostethini
 Mastogenius crenulatus Knull
 Mastogenius subcyaneus (LeConte)
Tribe Ptosomini
 Ptosima gibbicollis (Say)
Subfamily Chrysochroinae
Tribe Chrysochroini
 Chalcophora liberta (Germar)
 Chalcophora virginiensis (Drury)
 Texania campestris (Say)
Tribe Dicercini
 Dicerca divaricata (Say)
 Dicerca lurida (Fabricius)
 Dicerca obscura (Fabricius)
Tribe Poecilonotini
 Poecilonota cyanipes (Say)
Subfamily Buprestinae
Tribe Actenodini
 Actenodes acornis (Say)
Tribe Anthaxiini
 Agrilaxia flavimana (Gory)
 Anthaxia quercata (Fabricius)
Tribe Buprestini
 Buprestis lineata (Fabricius)
 Buprestis rufipes (Olivier)
 Buprestis salisburyensis (Herbst)
 Buprestis striata (Fabricius)
Tribe Chrysobothrini
 Chrysobothris azurea LeConte
 Chrysobothris chrysoela (Illiger)
 Chrysobothris femorata (Olivier)
Tribe Melanophilini
 Melanophila acuminata (De Geer)
 Phaenops fulvoguttata (Harris)

507

Tribe Stigmoderini
    Spectralia gracilipes (Melsheimer)
Tribe Xenorhipidini
    Xenorhipis brendeli LeConte
Subfamily Agrilinae
    Tribe Agrilini
        Agrilus bilineatus (Weber)
        Agrilus cyanescens Ratzeburg
        Agrilus obsoletoguttatus Gory
        Agrilus ruficollis (Fabricius)
    Tribe Coraebini
        Eupristocerus cogitans (Weber)
    Tribe Tracheini
        Brachys aerosus Melsheimer
        Brachys floricolus Kerremans
        Brachys ovatus (Weber)
        Pachyschelus purpureus (Say)
        Taphrocerus nicolayi Obenberger
Superfamily Byrrhoidea
  Family Byrrhidae
    Subfamily Byrrhinae
      Tribe Byrrhini
        Byrrhus americanus LeConte
        Cytilus alternatus (Say)
    Subfamily Syncalyptinae
      Tribe Syncalyptini
        Chaetophora spinosa (Rossi)
  Family Elmidae
    Subfamily Elminae
      Tribe Ancyronychini
        Ancyronyx variegata (Germar)
      Tribe Elmini
        Dubiraphia vittata (Melsheimer)
        Optioservus trivittatus (Brown)
        Stenelmis mera Sanderson
      Tribe Macronychini
        Macronychus glabratus Say
  Family Dryopidae
    Helichus lithophilus (Germar)
    Pelonomus obscurus LeConte
  Family Lutrochidae
    Lutrochus laticeps Casey
  Family Limnichidae
    Subfamily Limnichinae
      Tribe Limnichini
        Limnichites punctatus (LeConte)
  Family Heteroceridae
    Subfamily Heterocerinae
      Tribe Heterocerini
        Heterocerus fenestratus (Thunberg)
        Heterocerus mollinus Kiesenwetter
      Tribe Tropicini
        Tropicus pusillus (Say)

Family Psephenidae
  Subfamily Eubriinae
    Ectopria leechi Brigham
  Subfamily Psepheninae
    Psephenus herricki (DeKay)
Family Ptilodactylidae
  Subfamily Cladotominae
    Paralichus trivittus (Germar)
  Subfamily Ptilodactylinae
    Ptilodactyla species
Family Chelonariidae
    Chelonarium lecontei Thomson
Family Callirhipidae
    Zenoa picea (Palisot de Beauvois)
Superfamily Elateroidea
  Family Artematopodidae
    Subfamily Artematopodinae
      Tribe Macropogonini
        Eurypogon niger (Melsheimer)
  Family Cerophytidae
    Cerophytum pulsator (Haldeman)
  Family Eucnemidae
    Subfamily Melasinae
      Tribe Melasini
        Isorhipis obliqua (Say)
    Subfamily Macraulacinae
      Tribe Macraulacini
        Deltometopus amoenicornis (Say)
        Onichodon orchesides Newman
  Family Throscidae
    Aulonothroscus constrictor (Say)
    Trixagus carinicollis (Schaeffer)
  Family Elateridae
    Subfamily Cebrioninae
      Tribe Cebrionini
        Selonodon medialis Galley
    Subfamily Agrypninae
      Tribe Agrypnini
        Danosoma brevicornis (LeConte)
        Lacon discoideus (Weber)
        Lacon marmoratus (Fabricius)
      Tribe Hemirhipini
        Alaus myops (Fabricius)
        Alaus oculatus (Linnaeus)
        Chalcolepidius viridipilis (Say)
        Pherhimius fascicularis (Fabricius)
      Tribe Oophorini
        Aeolus mellilus (Say)
        Conoderus bellus (Say)
        Conoderus lividus (De Geer)
        Conoderus scissus (Schaeffer)
        Conoderus suturalis (LeConte)
        Conoderus vespertinus (Fabricius)

Heteroderes amplicollis (Gyllenhal)
Heteroderes falli (Lane)
Tribe Pseudomelanactini
Lanelater sallei (LeConte)
Tribe Pyrophorini
Deilelater physoderus (Germar)
Subfamily Lissominae
Tribe Oestodini
Oestodes tenuicollis (Randall)
Subfamily Pityobiinae
Tribe Pityobiini
Pityobius anguinus LeConte
Subfamily Oxynopterinae
Melanactes morio (Fabricius)
Melanactes piceus (De Geer)
Subfamily Dendrometrinae
Tribe Dendrometrini
Athous acanthus (Say)
Athous cucullatus (Say)
Athous neacanthus Becker
Denticollis denticornis (Kirby)
Hemicrepidius nemnonius (Herbst)
Limonius basilaris (Say)
Limonius griseus (Palisot de Beauvois)
Limonius quercinus (Say)
Limonius stigma (Herbst)
Tribe Prosternini
Actenicerus cuprascens (LeConte)
Anostirus vernalis (Hentz)
"*Ctenicera*" *pyrrhos* (Herbst)
Eanus estriatus (LeConte)
Hadromorphus inflatus (Say)
Hypoganus sulcicollis (Say)
Pseudanostirus hamatus (Say)
Pseudanostirus hieroglyphicus (Say)
Pseudanostirus triundulatus (Randall)
Selatosomus pulcher (LeConte)
Subfamily Negastriinae
Tribe Negastriini
Paradonus pectoralis (Say)
Subfamily Elaterinae
Tribe Agriotini
Agriotes collaris (LeConte)
Agriotes lineatus (Linnaeus)
Idolus bigeminata (Randall)
Tribe Ampedini
Ampedus areolatus (Say)
Ampedus collaris (Say)
Ampedus linteus (Say)
Ampedus nigricollis (Herbst)
Ampedus rubricollis (Herbst)
Ampedus rubricus (Say)

Ampedus xanthomus (Germar)
Anchastus binus (Say)
Tribe Dicrepidiini
Dicrepidius palmatus Candéze
Tribe Elaterini
Elater abruptus Say
Orthostethus infuscatus (Germar)
Tribe Megapenthini
Megapenthes limbalis (Herbst)
Tribe Melanotini
Melanotus species
Subfamily Cardiphorinae
Cardiophorus cardisce (Say)
Cardiorphorus convexus (Say)
Horistonotus curiatus (Say)
Family Lycidae
Subfamily Dictyopterinae
Tribe Dictyopterini
Dictyoptera aurora (Herbst)
Dictyoptera munda (Say)
Subfamily Lycinae
Tribe Calopterini
Caenia dimidiata (Fabricius)
Calopteron discrepans (Newman)
Calopteron reticulatum (Fabricius)
Calopteron terminale (Say)
Leptoceletes basalis (LeConte)
Tribe Calochromini
Calochromus perfacetus (Say)
Tribe Erotini
Eropterus trilineatus (Melsheimer)
Eros humeralis (Fabricius)
Erotides sculptilis (Say)
Lopheros fraternus (Randall)
Tribe Lycini
Lyconotus lateralis (Melsheimer)
Tribe Platoderini
Plateros species
Family Phengodidae
Subfamily Phengodinae
Phengodes laticollis LeConte
Family Lampyridae
Subfamily Lampyrinae
Tribe Cratomorphini
Pyractomena dispersa Green
Tribe Lucidotini
Ellychnia corrusca (Linnaeus)
Lucidota atra (Olivier)
Photinus pyralis (Linnaeus)
Pyropyga nigricans (Say)
Subfamily Photurinae
Photuris pennsylvanica (De Geer)

Family Omethidae
  Subfamily Omethinae
    Omethes marginatus LeConte
Family Cantharidae
  Subfamily Cantharinae
    Tribe Cantharini
      Atalantycha bilineata (Say)
      Atalantycha dentigera (LeConte)
      Atalantycha neglecta (Fall)
      Pacificanthia rotundicollis (Say)
    Tribe Podabrini
      Podabrus brevicollis Fall
      Podabrus brimleyi (Green)
      Podabrus rugosulus LeConte
      Rhagonycha longula (LeConte)
      Rhagonycha mollis (Fall)
      Rhaxonycha carolina (Fabricius)
  Subfamily Silinae
    Tribe Silini
      Polemius laticornis (Say)
      Silis bidentata (Say)
    Tribe Tytthonyxini
      Tytthonyx erythrocephala (Fabricius)
  Subfamily Malthininae
    Tribe Malthinini
      Malthinus occipitalis LeConte
    Tribe Malthodini
      Malthodes fuliginosus LeConte
  Subfamily Chauliongnathinae
    Tribe Chauliognathini
      Chauliognathus marginatus (Fabricius)
      Chauliognathus pensylvanicus (De Geer)
    Tribe Ichthyurini
      Trypherus latipennis (Germar)
Series Derodontiformia
  Superfamily Derodontoidea
    Family Derodontidae
      Subfamily Derodontinae
        Derodontus esotericus Lawrence & Hlavac
      Subfamily Laricobiinae
        Laricobius rubidus LeConte
    Family Nosodendridae
      Nosodendron unicolor Say
    Family Jacobsoniidae
      Derolathrus cavernicolus Peck
Series Bostrichiformia
  Superfamily Bostrichoidea
    Family Dermestidae
      Subfamily Dermestinae
        Tribe Dermestini
          Dermestes caninus Germar
          Dermestes lardarius Linnaeus

      Subfamily Orphilinae
        Orphilus ater Erichson
      Subfamily Trinodinae
        Tribe Thylodriini
          Thylodrias contractus Motschulsky
      Subfamily Megatominae
        Tribe Anthrenini
          Anthrenus pimpinellae Fabricius
          Anthrenus verbasci (Linnaeus)
          Cryptorhopalum species
          Trogoderma glabrum (Herbst)
          Trogoderma ornatum (Say)
    Family Endecatomidae
      Endecatomus rugosus (Randall)
    Family Bostrichidae
      Subfamily Bostrichinae
        Tribe Bostrichini
          Amphicerus bicaudatus (Say)
          Lichenophanes bicornis (Weber)
        Tribe Xyloperthini
          Prostephanus punctatus (Say)
          Rhyzopertha dominica (Fabricius)
          Xylobiops basilaris (Say)
      Subfamily Lyctinae
        Tribe Lyctini
          Lyctus planicollis LeConte
        Tribe Trogoxylonini
          Trogoxylon parallelopipedum (Melsheimer)
    Family Ptinidae
      Subfamily Ptininae
        Tribe Gibbiini
          Gibbium aequinoctiale Boieldieu
        Tribe Meziini
          Mezium affine Boieldieu
        Tribe Ptinini
          Ptinus fur Linnaeus
          Ptinus quadrimaculatus (Melsheimer)
      Subfamily Eucradinae
        Eucrada humeralis (Melsheimer)
      Subfamily Ernobiinae
        Ernobius granulatus LeConte
      Subfamily Anobiinae
        Anobium punctatum (De Geer)
        Hadrobregmus notatus (Say)
        Hemicoelus carinatus (Say)
        Stegobium paniceum (Linnaeus)
        Trichodesma gibbosa (Say)
      Subfamily Ptilininae
        Ptilinus ruficornis Say
      Subfamily Xyletinae
        Tribe Xyletini
          Euvrilletta harrisii Fall

Tribe Lasiodermini
 Lasioderma serricorne (Fabricius)
Subfamily Dorcatominae
 Byrrhodes incomptus LeConte
 Caenocara oculata (Say)
 Dorcatoma pallicornis LeConte
 Protheca hispida LeConte
Subfamily Mesocoelopodinae
 Tribe Tricorynini
 Priobium sericeum (Say)
 Tricorynus species
Series Cucujiformia
Superfamily Lymexyloidea
 Family Lymexylidae
 Subfamily Hylecoetinae
 Elateroides lugubris (Say)
 Subfamily Melittommatinae
 Melittomma sericeum (Harris)
Superfamily Cleroidea
 Family Trogossitidae
 Subfamily Peltinae
 Tribe Lophocaterini
 Grynocharis quadrilineata (Melsheimer)
 Lycoptis americana (Motschulsky)
 Tribe Peltini
 Peltis septentrionalis (Randall)
 Tribe Thymalini
 Thymalus marginicollis Chevrolat
 Subfamily Trogossitinae
 Tribe Calityini
 Calitys scabra (Thunberg)
 Tribe Trogossitini
 Airora cylindrica (Audinet-Serville)
 Corticotomus parallelus (Melsheimer)
 Temnoscheila virescens (Fabricius)
 Tenebroides collaris (Sturm)
 Tenebroides laticollis (Horn)
 Family Cleridae
 Subfamily Thaneroclerinae
 Tribe Zenodosini
 Zenodosus sanguineus (Say)
 Subfamily Tillinae
 Cymatodera bicolor (Say)
 Cymatodera inornata (Say)
 Cymatodera undulata (Say)
 Lecontella brunnea (Melsheimer)
 Monophylla terminata (Say)
 Subfamily Hydnocerinae
 Tribe Hydnocerini
 Isohydnocera curtipennis (Newman)
 Phyllobaenus humeralis (Say)
 Phyllobaenus pallipennis (Say)
 Phyllobaenus unifasciatus (Say)

 Wolcottia pedalis (LeConte)
Subfamily Clerinae
 Enoclerus ichneumoneus (Fabricius)
 Enoclerus nigripes (Say)
 Enoclerus quadrisignatus (Say)
 Enoclerus rosmarus (Say)
 Placopterus thoracicus (Olivier)
 Priocera castanea (Newman)
 Thanasimus dubius (Fabricius)
 Trichodes apivorus Germar
 Trichodes nuttalli (Kirby)
Subfamily Korynetinae
 Chariessa pilosa (Forster)
 Cregya oculata (Say)
 Madoniella dislocata (Say)
 Necrobia ruficollis (Fabricius)
 Necrobia rufipes De Geer
 Necrobia violacea (Linnaeus)
 Neorthopleura thoracica (Say)
 Pelonides quadripunctatus (Say)
 Pelonium leucophaeum (Klug)
Family Melyridae
 Subfamily Melyrinae
 Tribe Melyrini
 Melyrodes basalis (LeConte)
 Subfamily Malachiinae
 Tribe Malachiini
 Anthocomus equestris (Fabricius)
 Attalus circumscriptus (Say)
 Attalus scincetus (Say)
 Collops quadrimaculatus (Fabricius)
 Hypebaeus apicalis (Say)
 Malachius aeneus (Linnaeus)
 Temnopsophus bimaculatus Horn
Superfamily Cucujoidea
 Family Byturidae
 Subfamily Byturinae
 Byturus unicolor (Say)
 Family Sphindidae
 Subfamily Sphindinae
 Sphindus americanus LeConte
 Family Biphyllidae
 Diplocoelus rudis (LeConte)
 Family Erotylidae
 Subfamily Languriinae
 Tribe Languriini
 Acropteroxys gracilis (Newman)
 Languria mozardi Latreille
 Languria taedata LeConte
 Subfamily Cryptophilinae
 Tribe Toramini
 Toramus pulchellus (LeConte)

511

Subfamily Erotylinae
  Tribe Dacnini
    Dacne quadrimaculata (Say)
  Tribe Megalodacnini
    Megalodacne fasciata (Fabricius)
    Megalodacne heros (Say)
  Tribe Tritomini
    Ischyrus quadripunctatus (Olivier)
    Triplax frontalis Horn
    Triplax thoracica (Say)
    Tritoma biguttata biguttata (Say)
    Tritoma mimetica (Crotch)
Family Monotomidae
  Subfamily Rhizopghaginae
    Rhizophagus cylindricus LeConte
    Rhizophagus remotus LeConte
  Subfamily Monotominae
    Tribe Monotomini
      Monotoma bicolor Villa & Villa
      Monotoma producta LeConte
    Tribe Europini
      Bactridium species
      Europs pallipennis (LeConte)
Family Cryptophagidae
  Subfamily Cryptophaginae
    Tribe Caenoscelini
      Caenoscelis basalis Casey
    Tribe Cryptophagini
      Antherophagus ochraceus Melsheimer
      Cryptophagus species
      Henotiderus obesulus (Casey)
      Telmatophilus americanus LeConte
Family Silvanidae
  Subfamily Brontinae
    Tribe Brontini
      Dendrophagus cygnaei Mannerheim
      Uleiota debilis (LeConte)
      Uleiota dubius (Fabricius)
    Tribe Telephanini
      Telephanus atricapillus Erichson
  Subfamily Silvaninae
    Ahasverus rectus (LeConte)
    Cathartosilvanus imbellis (LeConte)
    Nausibius major Zimmerman
    Oryzaephilus mercator (Fauvel)
    Oryzaephilus surinamensis (Linnaeus)
Family Cucujidae
  Cucujus clavipes clavipes Fabricius
  Pediacus subglaber LeConte
Family Passandridae
  Catogenus rufus (Fabricius)
  Taphroscelidia linearis (LeConte)

Family Phalacridae
  Olibrus species
  Stilbus apicalis (Melsheimer)
Family Laemophloeidae
  Charaphloeus convexulus LeConte
  Cryptolestes ferrugineus (Stephens)
  Laemophloeus biguttatus (Say)
  Laemophloeus fasciatus Melsheimer
  Placonotus modestus (Say)
Family Kateretidae
  Brachypterolus pulicarius (Linnaeus)
  Brachypterus urticae (Fabricius)
  Heterhelus abdominalis (Erichson)
Family Nitidulidae
  Subfamily Epuraeinae
    Epuraea aestiva (Linnaeus)
    Epuraea flavomaculata Mäklin
  Subfamily Carpophilinae
    Carpophilus discoideus LeConte
    Carpophilus hemipterus (Linnaeus)
    Carpophilus melanopterus Erichson
    Carpophilus sayi Parsons
  Subfamily Amphicrossinae
    Amphicrossus ciliatus (Olivier)
  Subfamily Meligethinae
    Fabogethes nigrescens (Stephens)
  Subfamily Nitidulinae
    Aethina tumida Murray
    Amphotis schwarzi Ulke
    Cychramus adustus Erichson
    Lobiopa insularis Laporte
    Lobiopa undulata (Say)
    Nitidula bipunctata (Linnaeus)
    Nitidula carnaria (Schaller)
    Omosita colon Linnaeus
    Pallodes pallidus (Palisot de Beauvois)
    Phenolia grossa (Fabricius)
    Prometopia sexmaculata (Say)
    Stelidota geminata (Say)
    Stelidota octomaculata (Say)
    Thalycra carolina Wickham
  Subfamily Cillaeinae
    Brachypeplus glaber LeConte
    Colopterus truncatus (Randall)
    Conotelus obscurus Erichson
  Subfamily Cryptarchinae
    Cryptarcha ampla Erichson
    Cryptarcha strigatula Parsons
    Glischrochilus fasciatus (Olivier)
    Glischrochilus obtusus (Say)
    Glischrochilus quadrisignatus (Say)
    Glischrochilus sanguinolentus (Olivier)
    Glischrochilus vittatus (Say)

Family Cybocephalidae
    Cybocephalus nipponicus Endrody-Younga
Family Smicripidae
    Smicrips palmicola LeConte
Family Bothrideridae
  Subfamily Bothriderinae
    Tribe Bothriderini
      Bothrideres geminatus (Say)
    Tribe Sosylini
      Sosylus costatus LeConte
Family Cerylonidae
  Subfamily Euxestinae
    Hypodacne punctata LeConte
  Subfamily Murmidiinae
    Murmidius ovalis (Beck)
  Subfamily Ceryloninae
    Cerylon unicolor (Ziegler)
    Philothermus glabriculus LeConte
Family Endomychidae
  Subfamily Merophysiinae
    Phymaphora pulchella Newman
    Rhanidea unicolor (Ziegler)
  Subfamily Endomychinae
    Endomychus biguttatus Say
  Subfamily Stenotarsinae
    Danae testacea (Ziegler)
    Stenotarsus hispidus (Herbst)
  Subfamily Lycoperdininae
    Aphorista vittata (*Fabricius*)
    Lycoperdina ferruginea LeConte
    Mycetina perpulchra (Newman)
Family Coccinellidae
  Subfamily Microweiseinae
    Tribe Microweiseini
      Microweisea misella (LeConte)
  Subfamily Coccinellinae
    Tribe Brachicanthini
      Brachiacantha quadripunctata (Melsheimer)
    Tribe Chilocorini
      Chilocorus stigma (Say)
      Exochomus marginipennis (LeConte)
    Tribe Coccidulini
      Coccidula lepida LeConte
    Tribe Coccinellini
      Adalia bipunctata (Linnaeus)
      Anatis labiculata (Say)
      Anisosticta bitriangularis (Say)
      Calvia quatuordecimguttata (Linnaeus)
      Coccinella septempunctata (Linnaeus)
      Coccinella trifasciata perplexa Mulsant
      Coleomegilla maculata lengi Timberlake
      Cycloneda munda (Say)

      Harmonia axyridis (Pallas)
      Hippodamia convergens Guerin
      Hippodamia parenthesis (Say)
      Hippodamia variegata (Goeze)
      Mulsantina hudsonica (Casey)
      Mulsantina picta (Randall)
      Myzia pullata (Say)
      Naemia seriata (Melsheimer)
      Neoharmonia venusta (Melsheimer)
      Olla v-nigrum (Mulsant)
      Propylea quatuordecimpunctata (Linnaeus)
      Psyllobora vigintimaculata (Say)
    Tribe Epilachnini
      Epilachna varivestis Mulsant
      Subcoccinella vigintiquatuorpunctata (L.)
    Tribe Hyperaspidini
      Hyperaspis octavia Casey
      Hyperaspis proba (Say)
    Tribe Scymnini
      Cryptolaemus montrouzieri Mulsant
      Diomus terminatus (Say)
      Scymnus species
Family Corylophidae
  Subfamily Corylophinae
    Tribe Orthoperini
      Orthoperus species
    Tribe Parmulini
      Arthrolips misellus (LeConte)
      Clypastraea lunata (LeConte)
    Tribe Peltinodini
      Holopsis marginicollis (LeConte)
    Tribe Rypobiini
      Rypobius marinus LeConte
    Tribe Sericoderini
      Sericoderus lateralis (Gyllenhal)
Family Latridiidae
  Subfamily Latridiinae
    Corticaria serrata (Paykull)
    Dienerella filum (Aubé)
    Enicmus aterrimus (Motschulsky)
    Melanophthalma picta LeConte
Superfamily Tenebrionoidea
  Family Mycetophagidae
    Subfamily Mycetophaginae
      Tribe Mycetophagini
        Litargus tetraspilotus LeConte
        Mycetophagus flexuosus Say
        Mycetophagus melsheimeri LeConte
        Mycetophagus obsoletus (Melsheimer)
        Mycetophagus punctatus Say
      Tribe Typhaeini
        Typhaea stercorea (Linnaeus)

Family Archeocrypticidae
    Enneboeus caseyi Kaszab
Family Ciidae
    Subfamily Ciinae
        Tribe Orophiini
            Octotemnus species
            Strigocis opacicollis Dury
Family Tetratomidae
    Subfamily Tetratominae
        Tetratoma truncorum LeConte
    Subfamily Penthinae
        Penthe obliquata (Fabricius)
        Penthe pimelia (Fabricius)
    Subfamily Hallomeninae
        Hallomenus scapularis Melsheimer
    Subfamily Eustrophinae
        Tribe Eustrophini
            Eustrophopsis bicolor (Fabricius)
        Tribe Holostrophini
            Holostrophus bifasciatus (Say)
Family Melandryidae
    Subfamily Melandryinae
        Tribe Orchesiini
            Orchesia castanea (Melsheimer)
        Tribe Dircaeini
            Dircaea liturata (LeConte)
        Tribe Serropalpini
            Amblyctis praeses LeConte
            Enchodes sericea (Haldeman)
            Rushia longula (LeConte)
            Spilotus quadripustulatus (Melsheimer)
        Tribe Hypulini
            Hypulus simulator Newman
            Microtonus sericans (LeConte)
            Symphora flavicollis (Haldeman)
        Tribe Melandryini
            Emmesa connectens Newman
            Melandrya striata Say
            Prothalpia undata (LeConte)
    Subfamily Osphyinae
        Osphya varians (LeConte)
Family Mordellidae
    Subfamily Mordellinae
        Tribe Mordellini
           Glipa hilaris (Say)
           Glipa oculata (Say)
           Hoshihananomia octopunctata (Fabricius)
           Mordella marginata Melsheimer
           Mordellaria serval (Say)
           Tolidomordella discoidea (Melsheimer)
           Tomoxia lineella (LeConte)

          Yakuhananomia bidentata (Say)
        Tribe Mordellistenini
          Falsomordellistena bihamata (Melsheimer)
          Falsomordellistena pubescens (Fabricius)
          Mordellina pustulata (Melsheimer)
          Mordellistena andreae LeConte
          Mordellistena cervicalis LeConte
          Mordellistena convicta LeConte
          Mordellistena fuscipennis (Melsheimer)
          Mordellistena liturata (Melsheimer)
          Mordellochroa scapularis (Say)
Family Ripiphoridae
    Subfamily Pelecotominae
        Pelecotoma flavipes Melsheimer
    Subfamily Ripiphorinae
        Tribe Macrosiagonini
            Macrosiagon cruentum (Germar)
            Macrosiagon dimidiatum (Fabricius)
            Macrosiagon flavipenne LeConte
            Macrosiagon limbatum (Fabricius)
            Macrosiagon pectinatum (Fabricius)
        Tribe Ripiphorini
            Ripiphorus species
Family Zopheridae
    Subfamily Colydiinae
        Tribe Colydiini
            Colydium lineola Say
            Colydium nigripenne LeConte
        Tribe Synchitini
            Aulonium parallelopipedum (Say)
            Bitoma crenata (Fabricius)
            Bitoma quadriguttata (Say)
            Endeitoma granulata (Say)
            Namunaria guttulata (LeConte)
            Paha laticollis (LeConte)
    Subfamily Zopherinae
        Tribe Monommatini
            Hyporhagus punctulatus Thomson
        Tribe Phellopsini
            Phellopsis obcordata (Kirby)
        Tribe Pycnomerini
            Pycnomerus sulcicollis LeConte
Family Tenebrionidae
    Subfamily Lagriinae
        Tribe Goniaderini
            Anaedus brunneus (Ziegler)
            Paratenetus punctatus Spinola
        Tribe Lagriini
            Arthromacra aenea (Say)
            Statira gagatina Melsheimer
    Subfamily Pimeliinae

Tribe Epitragini
  Bothrotes canaliculatus canaliculatus (Say)
  Epitragodes tomentosus LeConte
  Schoenicus puberulus LeConte
Subfamily Tenebrioninae
  Tribe Alphitobiini
    Alphitobius diaperinus (Panzer)
    Cynaeus angustus LeConte
  Tribe Amarygmini
    Meracantha contracta (Palisot de Beauvois)
  Tribe Blaptini
    Blapstinus metallicus (Fabricius)
  Tribe Bolitophagini
    Bolitophagus corticola Say
    Bolitotherus cornutus Panzer
    Eleates depressus (Randall)
    Rhipidandrus paradoxus (Palisot de
      Beauvois)
  Tribe Centronopini
    Centronopus calcaratus (Fabricius)
  Tribe Helopini
    Helops aereus Germar
    Tarpela micans (Fabricius)
    Tarpela venusta Say
  Tribe Opatrini
    Ammodonus fossor (LeConte)
  Tribe Pedinini
    Alaetrinus minimus (Palisot de Beauvois)
  Tribe Tenebrionini
    Idiobates castaneus Knoch
    Neatus tenebroides (Palisot de Beauvois)
    Tenebrio molitor Linnaeus
  Tribe Triboliini
    Tribolium castaneum (Herbst)
  Tribe Ulomini
    Uloma impressa Melsheimer
Subfamily Alleculinae
  Tribe Alleculini
    Andrimus murrayi (LeConte)
    Androchirus erythropus (Kirby)
    Androchirus femoralis (Olivier)
    Capnochroa fuliginosa (Melsheimer)
    Hymenorus obesus Casey
    Isomira pulla (Melsheimer)
    Isomira sericea (Say)
    Lobopoda punctulata (Melsheimer)
    Mycetochara haldemani (LeConte)
    Pseudocistela marginata (Ziegler)
Subfamily Diaperinae
  Tribe Crypticini
    Gondwanocrypticus platensis (Fairmaire)
    Poecilocrypticus formicophilus Gebien

Tribe Diaperini
  Adelina pallida (Say)
  Diaperis maculata Olivier
  Neomida bicornis (Fabricius)
  Platydema ellipticum (Fabricius)
  Platydema flavipes (Fabricius)
  Platydema ruficorne (Sturm)
Tribe Phaleriini
  Phaleria picipes Say
  Phaleria testacea Say
Subfamily Stenochiinae
  Tribe Cnodalonini
    Alobates morio (Fabricius)
    Alobates pennsylvanica (De Geer)
    Glyptotus cribratus (LeConte)
    Iphthiminus opacus (LeConte)
    Merinus laevis (Olivier)
    Polopinus youngi Kritsky
    Polypleurus perforatus Germar
    Upis ceramboides (Linnaeus)
    Xylopinus saperdioides (Olivier)
  Tribe Stenochiini
    Strongylium crenatum Mäklin
    Strongylium tenuicolle (Say)
Family Synchroidae
  Synchroa punctata Newman
Family Stenotrachelidae
  Subfamily Stenotrachelinae
    Stenotrachelus aeneus (Fabricius)
  Subfamily Cephaloinae
    Cephaloon lepturides Newman
    Cephaloon ungulare LeConte
Family Oedemeridae
  Subfamily Calopodinae
    Calopus angustus (LeConte)
  Subfamily Oedemerinae
    Tribe Nacerdini
      Nacerdes melanura (Linnaeus)
      Xanthochroa lateralis (Melsheimer)
    Tribe Ditylini
      Ditylus caeruleus (Randall)
    Tribe Asclerini
      Asclera puncticollis (Say)
      Asclera ruficollis (Say)
      Hypasclera dorsalis (Melsheimer)
      Oxacis taeniata (LeConte)
      Oxycopis mimetica (Horn)
      Oxycopis thoracica (Fabricius)
Family Meloidae
  Subfamily Meloinae
    Tribe Pyrotini
      Pyrota germari (Haldeman)

Tribe Epicautini
  Epicauta atrata (Fabricius)
  Epicauta funebris Horn
  Epicauta pensylvanica (De Geer)
  Epicauta vittata (Fabricius)
Tribe Lyttini
  Lytta aenea Say
  Lytta polita Say
  Lytta sayi LeConte
Tribe Meloini
  Meloe impressus Kirby
Subfamily Nemognathinae
  Tribe Nemognathini
    Nemognatha nemorensis Hentz
    Nemognatha piazata (Fabricius)
    Pseudozonitis longicornis (Horn)
    Tricrania sanguinipennis (Say)
    Zonitis vittigera (LeConte)
Family Mycteridae
  Subfamily Mycterinae
    Mycterus scaber (Haldeman)
  Subfamily Eurypinae
    Lacconotus punctatus LeConte
  Subfamily Hemipeplinae
    Hemipeplus marginipennis (LeConte)
Family Boridae
  Subfamily Borinae
    Boros unicolor Say
    Lecontia discicollis (LeConte)
Family Pythidae
  Pytho americanus Kirby
  Pytho niger Kirby
  Priognathus monilicornis (Randall)
Family Pyrochroidae
  Subfamily Pedilinae
    Pedilus lugubris (Say)
    Pedilus terminalis (Say)
  Subfamily Pyrochroinae
    Dendroides canadensis Latreille
    Dendroides concolor (Newman)
    Neopyrochroa femoralis (LeConte)
    Neopyrochroa flabellata (Fabricius)
    Schizotus cervicalis Newman
Family Salpingidae
  Subfamily Inopeplinae
    Inopeplus immunda (Reitter)
  Subfamily Salpinginae
    Rhinosimus viridaenus Randall
Family Anthicidae
  Subfamily Eurygeniinae
    Tribe Eurygeniini
      Retocomus murinus (Haldeman)

Stereopalpus mellyi LaFerté-Sénectère
Subfamily Macratriinae
  Tribe Macratriini
    Macratria confusa (Fabricius)
Subfamily Anthicinae
  Tribe Anthicini
    Acanthinus argentinus (Pic)
    Amblyderus pallens LeConte
    Anthicus cervinus LaFerté-Sénectère
    Ischyropalpus nitidulus (LeConte)
    Malporus formicarius (LaFerté-Sénectère)
    Omonadus formicarius (Goeze)
    Sapintus species
    Stricticollis tobias (Marseul)
    Vacusus vicinus (LaFerté-Sénectère)
Subfamily Notoxinae
  Notoxus desertus Casey
  Notoxus monodon (Fabricius)
  Notoxus murinipennis (LeConte)
Subfamily Tomoderinae
  Tomoderus species
Family Ischaliidae
  Ischalia costata (LeConte)
Family Aderidae
  Subfamily Aderinae
    Tribe Euglenesini
      Zonantes fasciatus (Melsheimer)
      Zonantes subfasciatus (LeConte)
    Tribe Emelinini
      Emelinus melsheimeri (LeConte)
    Tribe Aderini
      Elonus basalis (LeConte)
      Vanonus piceus (LeConte)
Family Scraptiidae
  Subfamily Scraptiinae
    Tribe Allopodini
      Allopoda lutea (Haldeman)
    Tribe Scraptiini
      Canifa pallipes (Melsheimer)
      Scraptia sericea (Melsheimer)
  Subfamily Anaspidinae
    Tribe Anaspidini
      Anaspis flavipennis Haldeman
      Anaspis nigrina (Csiki)
      Anaspis rufa Say
    Tribe Pentariini
      Pentaria trifasciata (Melsheimer)
Superfamily Chrysomeloidea
  Family Disteniidae
    Subfamily Disteniinae
      Tribe Disteniini
        Elytrimitatrix undata (Fabricius)

Family Cerambycidae
  Subfamily Parandrinae
    Tribe Parandrini
      Neandra brunnea (Fabricius)
      Parandra polita Say
  Subfamily Prioninae
    Tribe Macrotomini
      Archodontes melanoplus (Linnaeus)
    Tribe Mallodini
      Mallodon dasytomus (Say)
    Tribe Meroscelisini
      Tragosoma harrisii (LeConte)
    Tribe Prionini
      Derobrachus thomasi Santos-Silva
      Orthosoma brunneum (Forster)
      Prionus imbricornis (Linnaeus)
      Prionus laticollis (Drury)
    Tribe Solenopterini
      Sphenostethus taslei (Buquet)
  Subfamily Lepturinae
    Tribe Desmocerini
      Desmocerus palliatus (Forster)
    Tribe Encyclopini
      Encyclops caerulea (Say)
    Tribe Lepturini
      Analeptura lineola (Say)
      Anastrangalia sanguinea (LeConte)
      Anthophylax attenuatus (Haldeman)
      Anthophylax cyaneaus (Haldeman)
      Bellamira scalaris (Say)
      Brachyleptura champlaini Casey
      Brachyleptura vagans (Olivier)
      Brachysomida bivittata (Say)
      Grammoptera subargentata (Kirby)
      Evodinus monticola (Randall)
      Gaurotes cyanipennis (Say)
      Grammoptera haematites (Newman)
      Idiopidonia pedalis (LeConte)
      Judolia cordifera (Olivier)
      Judolia montivagans (Couper)
      Leptorhabdium pictum (Haldeman)
      Lepturobosca chrysocoma (Kirby)
      Lepturopsis biforis (Newman)
      Metacmaeops vittata (Swederus)
      Pidonia ruficollis (Say)
      Pseudostrangalia cruentata (Haldeman)
      Stenelytrana emarginata (Fabricius)
      Stenocorus cinnamopterus (Randall)
      Stenocorus schaumii (LeConte)
      Stictoleptura canadensis (Olivier)
      Strangalepta abbreviata (Germar)
      Strangalia acuminata (Olivier)

      Strangalia bicolor (Swederus)
      Strangalia famelica Newman
      Strangalia luteicornis (Fabricius)
      Strangalia sexnotata Haldeman
      Strophiona nitens (Forster)
      Trachysida mutabilis (Newman)
      Trigonarthris minnesotana (Casey)
      Typocerus acuticauda acuticauda Casey
      Typocerus velutinus (Olivier)
      Typocerus zebra (Olivier)
      Xestoleptura octonotata (Say)
    Tribe Rhagiini
      Rhagium inquisitor (Linnaeus)
  Subfamily Spondylidinae
    Tribe Asemini
      Arhopalus foveicollis (Haldeman)
      Asemum striatum (Linnaeus)
    Tribe Atimiini
      Atimia confusa (Say)
    Tribe Spondylidini
      Neospondylis upiformis (Mannerheim)
      Scaphinus muticus (Fabricius)
  Subfamily Necydalinae
    Necydalis mellita (Say)
  Subfamily Cerambycinae
    Tribe Achrysonini
      Achryson surinamum (Linnaeus)
    Tribe Agallissini
      Osmopleura chamaeropis (Horn)
    Tribe Anaglyptini
      Cyrtophorus verrucosus (Olivier)
      Tilloclytus geminatus (Haldeman)
    Tribe Callichromatini
      Plinthocoelium s. suaveolens (Linnaeus)
    Tribe Callidiini
      Meriellum proteus (Kirby)
      Phymatodes ameonus (Say)
      Phymatodes testaceus (Linnaeus)
      Pronocera collaris (Kirby)
      Ropalopus sanguinicollis (Horn)
    Tribe Clytini
      Calloides nobilis (Harris)
      Clytus marginicollis Laporte & Gory
      Clytus ruricola (Olivier)
      Glycobius speciosus (Say)
      Megacyllene decora (Olivier)
      Megacyllene robiniae (Forster)
      Neoclytus mucronatus (Fabricius)
      Sarosesthes fulminans (Fabricius)
      Xylotrechus aceris Fisher
      Xylotrechus colonus (Fabricius)
      Xylotrechus sagittatus (Germar)

Tribe Dryobiini
　　Dryobius sexnotatus Linsley
Tribe Eburiini
　　Eburia quadrigeminata (Say)
Tribe Elaphidiini
　　Anelaphus parallelus (Newman)
　　Anelaphus villosus (Fabricius)
　　Elaphidion mucronatum (Say)
　　Enaphalodes rufulus (Haldeman)
　　Parelaphidion aspersum (Haldeman)
　　Psyrassa unicolor (Randall)
　　Romulus globosus Knull
　　Stenosphenus notatus (Olivier)
Tribe Hesperophanini
　　Hesperophanes pubescens (Haldeman)
　　Tylonotus bimaculatus Haldeman
Tribe Ibidionini
　　Heterachthes quadrimaculatus Haldeman
Tribe Methiini
　　Methia necydalea (Fabricius)
Tribe Molorchini
　　Molorchus bimaculatus bimaculatus Say
　　Molorchus bimaculatus celti Knull
Tribe Obriini
　　Obrium maculatum (Olivier)
Tribe Oemini
　　Oeme rigida (Say)
Tribe Psebiini
　　Callimoxys sanguinicollis (Olivier)
Tribe Rhopalophorini
　　Rhopalophora longipes (Say)
Tribe Smodicini
　　Smodicum cucujiforme (Say)
Tribe Tillomorphini
　　Euderces picipes (Fabricius)
　　Euderces pini (Olivier)
Tribe Torneutini
　　Knulliana cincta cincta (Drury)
Tribe Trachyderini
　　Ancylocera bicolor (Olivier)
　　Batyle suturalis (Say)
　　Elytroleptus floridanus (LeConte)
　　Purpuricenus axillaris Haldeman
　　Trachyderes mandibularis (Dupont)
Subfamily Lamiinae
Tribe Acanthocinini
　　Acanthocinus nodosus (Fabricius)
　　Acanthocinus obsoletus (Olivier)
　　Astyleiopus variegatus (Haldeman)
　　Astylidius parvus (LeConte)
　　Astylopsis sexguttata (Say)
　　Dectes texanus LeConte

518

　　Eutrichillus biguttatus (LeConte)
　　Graphisurus fasciatus (De Geer)
　　Graphisurus triangulifer (Haldeman)
　　Hyperplatys aspersa (Say)
　　Hyperplatys maculata Haldeman
　　Leptostylopsis planidorsus (LeConte)
　　Leptostylus asperatus (Haldeman)
　　Leptostylus transversus (Gyllenhal)
　　Lepturges pictus (LeConte)
　　Sternidius mimeticus (Casey)
　　Styloleptus biustus (LeConte)
　　Urgleptes signatus (LeConte)
Tribe Acanthoderini
　　Acanthoderes quadrigibba (Say)
　　Aegomorphus modestus (Gyllenhal)
Tribe Agapanthiini
　　Hippopsis lemniscata (Fabricius)
Tribe Cyrtinini
　　Cyrtinus pygmaeus (Haldeman)
Tribe Desmiphorini
　　Eupogonius tomentosus (Haldeman)
　　Psenocerus supernotatus (Say)
Tribe Dorcaschematini
　　Dorcaschema cinereum (Olivier)
Tribe Hemilophini
　　Hemierana marginata ardens (LeConte)
Tribe Lamiini
　　Goes pulcher (Haldeman)
　　Goes tigrinus (De Geer)
　　Microgoes oculatus (LeConte)
　　Monochamus carolinensis (Olivier)
　　Monochamus notatus (Drury)
　　Monochamus scutellatus (Say)
　　Monochamus titillator (Fabricius)
　　Neoptychodes trilineatus (Linnaeus)
　　Plectrodera scalator (Fabricius)
Tribe Onciderini
　　Oncideres cingulata (Say)
Tribe Phytoeciini
　　Mecas cineracea Casey
　　Oberea gracilis (Fabricius)
　　Oberea tripunctata (Swederus)
Tribe Pogonocherini
　　Ecyrus dasycerus (Say)
Tribe Pteropliini
　　Ataxia crypta (Say)
Tribe Saperdini
　　Saperda calcarata (Say)
　　Saperda candida Fabricius
　　Saperda discoidea Fabricius
　　Saperda obliqua Say
　　Saperda puncticollis Say

Saperda tridentata Olivier
Tribe Tetraopini
 Tetraopes melanurus Schönherr
 Tetraopes tetraophthalmus (Forster)
Family Megalopodidae
 Subfamily Zeugophorinae
  Zeugophora scutellaris Suffrian
Family Orsodacnidae
 Subfamily Orsodacninae
  Orsodacne atra (Ahrens)
Family Chrysomelidae
 Subfamily Bruchinae
  Tribe Amblycerini
   Amblycerus robiniae (Fabricius)
  Tribe Bruchini
   Acanthoscelides alboscutellatus (Horn)
   Bruchidius villosus (Fabricius)
   Bruchus brachialis Fåhraeus
   Gibbobruchus mimus (Say)
   Megacerus cubiculus (Casey)
   Megacerus discoidus (Say)
   Meibomeus musculus (Say)
   Sennius abbreviatus (Say)
 Subfamily Donaciinae
  Tribe Donaciini
   Donacia species
  Tribe Plateumarini
   Plateumaris species
 Subfamily Criocerinae
  Tribe Criocerini
   Crioceris asparagi (Linnaeus)
   Lilioceris lilii (Scopoli)
  Tribe Lemini
   Lema daturaphila Kogan & Goeden
   Lema solani Fabricius
   Neolema sexpunctata (Olivier)
   Oulema melanopus (Linnaeus)
 Subfamily Cassidinae
  Tribe Cassidini
   Agroiconota bivittata (Say)
   Cassida rubiginosa Müller
   Charidotella purpurata (Boheman)
   Charidotella sexpunctata bicolor (Fabricius)
   Deloyala guttata (Olivier)
   Gratiana pallidula (Boheman)
   Plagiometriona clavata (Fabricius)
  Tribe Cephaloleiini
   Stenispa metallica (Fabricius)
  Tribe Chalepini
   Baliosus nervosus (Panzer)
   Chalepus bicolor (Olivier)
   Microrhopala floridana Schwarz
   Microrhopala vittata (Fabricius)

   Microrhopala xerene (Newman)
   Octotoma plicatula (Fabricius)
   Odontota dorsalis (Thunberg)
   Odontota scapularis (Olivier)
   Sumitrosis inaequalis (Weber)
  Tribe Hemisphaerotini
   Hemisphaerota cyanea (Say)
  Tribe Ischyrosonychini
   Physonota helianthi (Randall)
  Tribe Mesomphaliini
   Chelymorpha cassidea (Fabricius)
 Subfamily Chrysomelinae
  Tribe Chrysomelini
   Calligrapha alni Schaeffer
   Calligrapha philadelphica (Linnaeus)
   Calligrapha rowena Knab
   Chrysomela interrupta Fabricius
   Chrysomela mainensis Bechyné
   Chrysomela scripta Fabricius
   Gastrophysa cyanea Melsheimer
   Gonioctena americana (Schaeffer)
   Labidomera clivicollis (Kirby)
   Leptinotarsa decemlineata (Say)
   Leptinotarsa juncta (Germar)
   Microtheca ochroloma Stål
   Plagiodera versicolora (Laicharting)
   Zygogramma suturalis (Fabricius)
 Subfamily Galerucinae
  Tribe Alticini
   Agasicles hygrophila Selman & Vogt
   Altica chalybea (Illiger)
   Blepharida rhois (Forster)
   Capraita sexmaculata (Illiger)
   Capraita subvittata (Horn)
   Disonycha caroliniana (Fabricius)
   Disonycha discoidea (Fabricius)
   Disonycha pensylvanica (Illiger)
   Disonycha xanthomelas (Dahlman)
   Epitrix fasciata Blatchley
   Epitrix fuscula Crotch
   Kuschelina gibbitarsa (Say)
   Pseudolampsis guttata (LeConte)
   Systena elongata (Fabricius)
   Systena marginalis (Illiger)
   Trichaltica scabricula (Crotch)
  Tribe Galerucini
   Galerucella nymphaeae (Linnaeus)
   Monocesta coryli (Say)
   Neogalerucella calmariensis (Linnaeus)
   Ophraella conferta (LeConte)
   Pyrrhalta viburni (Paykull)
   Tricholochmaea cavicollis (LeConte)
   Trirhabda bacharidis (Weber)

Tribe Luperini
Acalymma vittatum (Fabricius)
Cerotoma trifurcata (Forster)
Diabrotica barberi Smith & Lawrence
Diabrotica cristata (Harris)
Diabrotica undecimpunctata howardi Barber
Subfamily Cryptocephalinae
Tribe Clytrini
Anomoea laticlavia laticlavia (Forster)
Babia quadriguttata (Olivier)
Coleothorpa dominica franciscana (LeConte)
Saxinis omogera (Lacordaire)
Tribe Cryptocephalini
Bassareus detritus (Olivier)
Bassareus mammifer (Newman)
Cryptocephalus guttulatus Olivier
Cryptocephalus leucomelas Suffrian
Cryptocephalus quadruplex Newman
Griburius scutellaris (Fabricius)
Pachybrachis bivittatus (Say)
Pachybrachis subfasciatus (LeConte)
Tribe Fulcidacini
Neochlamisus bebbianae (Brown)
Subfamily Eumolpinae
Tribe Bromiini
Bromius obscurus (Linnaeus)
Demotina modesta Baly
Fidia viticida Walsh
Glyptoscelis pubescens (Fabricius)
Graphops pubescens (Melsheimer)
Xanthonia decemnotata (Say)
Tribe Eumolpini
Chrysochus auratus (Fabricius)
Colaspis brunnea (Fabricius)
Rhabdopterus species
Tymnes tricolor (Fabricius)
Subfamily Synetinae
Metachroma pellucidum Crotch
Paria fragariae Wilcox
Paria quadrinotata (Say)
Syneta ferruginea (Germar)
Superfamily Cuculionoidea
Family Nemonychidae
Subfamily Cimberidinae
Tribe Cimberidini
Cimberis pilosa (LeConte)
Family Anthribidae
Subfamily Anthribinae
Tribe Cratoparini
Euparius marmoreus (Olivier)
Euparius paganus Gyllenhal

Tribe Ischnocerini
Ischnocerus infuscatus Fåhraeus
Tribe Piesocorynini
Piesocorynus moestus (LeConte)
Tribe Platyrhinini
Goniocloeus bimaculatus (Olivier)
Tribe Platystomini
Toxonotus cornutus (Say)
Tribe Trigonorhinini
Trigonorhinus sticticus (Boheman)
Tribe Tropiderini
Eurymycter tricarinatus Pierce
Gonotropis gibbosus LeConte
Tribe Zygaenodini
Eusphyrus walshi (LeConte)
Ormiscus saltator LeConte
Subfamily Choraginae
Tribe Choragini
Choragus sayi LeConte
Family Belidae
Subfamily Oxycoryninae
Tribe Oxycorynini
Rhopalotria slossonae (Schaeffer)
Family Attelabidae
Subfamily Attelabinae
Tribe Attelabini
Himatolabus pubescens (Say)
Homoeolabus analis (Illiger)
Synolabus bipustulatus (Fabricius)
Synolabus nigripes (LeConte)
Subfamily Rhynchitinae
Tribe Auletini
Auletobius cassandrae (LeConte)
Tribe Rhynchitini
Eugnamptus angustatus (Herbst)
Haplorhynchites aeneus (Boheman)
Merhynchites bicolor (Fabricius)
Pterocolus ovatus (Fabricius)
Temnocerus aeratus (Say)
Family Brentidae
Subfamily Brentinae
Tribe Arrhenodiini
Arrenodes minutus (Drury)
Subfamily Cycladinae
Cylas formicarius (Fabricius)
Subfamily Apioninae
Tribe Apelmonini
Perapion curtirostre (Germar)
Tribe Ixapiini
Neapion herculanum (Smith)
Tribe Malvapiini
Rhopalapion longirostre (Olivier)

Tribe Oxystomatini
  Betulapion simile (Kirby)
  Ischnopterapion virens (Herbst)
  Trichapion rostrum (Say)
  Incertae sedis
  Coelocephalapion perminutum (Smith)
Subfamily Ithycerinae
  Ithycerus noveboracensis (Forster)
Family Curculionidae
Subfamily Dryophthorinae
  Tribe Dryophthorini
    Dryophthorus americanus Bedel
  Tribe Rhynchophorini
    Metamasius callizona (Chevrolat)
    Metamasius hemipterus sericeus (Olivier)
    Rhodobaenus quinquepunctatus (Say)
    Rhodobaenus tredecimpunctatus (Illiger)
    Rhynchophorus cruentatus (Fabricius)
    Scyphophorus acupunctatus Gyllenhal
    Sitophilus oryzae (Linnaeus)
    Sphenophorus aequalis Gyllenhal
    Sphenophorus venatus vestitus Chittenden
Subfamily Erirhininae
  Tribe Stenopelmini
    Lissorhoptrus oryzophilus Kuschel
Subfamily Curculioninae
  Tribe Anthonomini
    Anthonomus haematopus Boheman
    Anthonomus quadrigibbus Say
    Anthonomus signatus Say
  Tribe Camarotini
    Odontopus calceatus (Say)
  Tribe Cionini
    Cionus scrophulariae (Linnaeus)
  Tribe Curculionini
    Curculio species
  Tribe Ellescini
    Dorytomus laticollis LeConte
  Tribe Otidocephalini
    Myrmex myrmex (Herbst)
  Tribe Piazorhinini
    Piazorhinus pictus LeConte
    Piazorhinus scutellaris Say
  Tribe Rhamphini
    Isochnus sequensi (Stierlin)
    Tachyerges ephippiatus (Say)
  Tribe Tychiini
    Lignyodes fraxini (LeConte)
    Ochyromera ligustri Warner
Subfamily Bagoinae
  Bagous planatus LeConte

Subfamily Baridinae
  Tribe Apostasimerini
    Dirabius rectirostris (LeConte)
    Geraeus picumnus (Herbst)
    Linogeraeus neglectus (LeConte)
    Odontocorynus umbellae (Fabricius)
    Oligolochus ornatus (Casey)
    Sibariops confusa (Boheman)
  Tribe Baridini
    Cosmobaris scolopacea (Germar)
    Trichobaris trinotata (Say)
  Tribe Madarini
    Glyptobaris lecontei Champion
    Madarellus undulatus (Say)
  Tribe Madopterini
    Stethobaris ovata (LeConte)
Subfamily Ceutorhynchinae
  Tribe Ceutorhynchini
    Ceutorhynchus americanus Buchanan
    Dietzella zimmermani (Gyllenhal)
    Perigaster obscura (LeConte)
    Tribe Mononychini
    Mononychus vulpeculus (Fabricius)
  Tribe Phytobiini
    Rhinoncus castor (Fabricius)
    Rhinoncus longulus LeConte
  Tribe Scleropterini
    Acallodes ventricosus LeConte
Subfamily Conoderinae
  Tribe Lechriopini
    Acoptus suturalis LeConte
    Lechriops oculatus (Say)
  Tribe Tachygonini
    Tachygonus lecontei Gyllenhal
  Tribe Zygopini
    Cylindrocopturus quercus (Say)
Subfamily Cossoninae
  Tribe Cossonini
    Cossonus impressifrons Boheman
    Himatium errans LeConte
  Tribe Onycholipini
    Hexarthrum ulkei Horn
    Stenoscelis brevis (Boheman)
Subfamily Cryptorhychinae
  Tribe Cryptorhynchini
    Cryptorhynchus lapathi (Linnaeus)
    Eubulus bisignatus (Say)
    Gerstaeckeria hubbardi (LeConte)
    Tyloderma aereum (Say)
    Tyloderma foveolatum (Say)
  Tribe Gasterocercini
    Cophes obtentus (Herbst)

Subfamily Cyclominae
  Listroderes costirostris Schoenherr
  Listronotus appendiculatus (Boheman)
  Listronotus sparsus (Say)
Subfamily Entiminae
  Tribe Agraphini
    Agraphus bellicus (Say)
  Tribe Cyphicerini
    Calomycterus setarius Roelofs
    Cyrtepistomus castaneus (Roelofs)
    Oedophrys hilleri (Faust)
  Tribe Eudiagogini
    Eudiagogus pulcher Fåhraeus
    Eudiagogus rosenschoeldi Fåhraeus
  Tribe Eustylini
    Brachystylus sayi Alonso-Zarazaga
  Tribe Geonemini
    Epicaerus imbricatus (Say)
  Tribe Homorini
    Hormorus undulatus (Uhler)
  Tribe Naupactini
    Naupactus cervinus Boheman
    Naupactus leucoloma Boheman
    Naupactus peregrinus (Buchanan)
  Tribe Otiorhynchini
    Otiorhynchus ovatus (Linnaeus)
    Otiorhynchus rugosostriatus (Goeze)
    Otiorhynchus sulcatus (Fabricius)
  Tribe Phyllobiini
    Aphrastus taeniatus Say
    Phyllobius oblongus (Linnaeus)
  Tribe Polydrusini
    Polydrusus sericeus (Schaller)
  Tribe Sciaphilini
    Barypeithes pellucidus (Boheman)
  Tribe Tanymecini
    Pachnaeus litus (Germar)
    Pandeleteius hilaris (Herbst)
  Tribe Trachyphloeini
    Cercopeus komareki O'Brien
    Pseudocneorhinus bifasciatus (Roelofs)
Subfamily Hyperinae
  Tribe Hyperini
    Brachypera zoilus (Scopoli)
    Hypera nigrirostris (Fabricius)
Subfamily Lixinae
  Tribe Lixini
    Larinus planus (Fabricius)
    Lixus concavus Say
    Lixus scrobicollis Boheman

Subfamily Mesoptilinae
  Tribe Laemosaccini
    Laemosaccus nephele (Herbst)
  Tribe Magdalidini
    Magdalis austera Fall
    Magdalis perforata Horn
Subfamily Molytinae
  Tribe Cleogonini
    Rhyssomatus lineaticollis (Say)
  Tribe Conotrachelini
    Conotrachelus anaglypticus (Say)
    Conotrachelus elegans (Say)
    Conotrachelus juglandis LeConte
    Conotrachelus nenuphar (Herbst)
    Conotrachelus posticatus Boheman
  Tribe Hylobiini
    Heilipus apiatus (Olivier)
    Hylobius pales (Herbst)
    Pachylobius picivorus (Germar)
  Tribe Lepyrini
    Lepyrus palustris (Scopoli)
  Tribe Petalochilini
    Hormops abducens LeConte
  Tribe Pissodini
    Pissodes strobi (Peck)
  Tribe Sternechini
    Chalcodermus aeneus Boheman
Subfamily Scolytinae
  Tribe Hylesinini
    Dendroctonus terebrans (Olivier)
    Dendroctonus valens LeConte
    Hylesinus aculeatus Say
    Hylurgops pinifex (Fitch)
    Polygraphus rufipennis (Kirby)
  Tribe Scolytini
    Scolytus quadrispinosus Say
  Tribe Ipini
    Ips calligraphus (Germar)
    Ips pini (Say)
    Pityokeines sparsus (LeConte)
  Tribe Corthylini
    Corthylus columbianus Hopkins
    Monarthrum fasciatum (Say)
  Tribe Xyleborini
    Cnestus mutilatus (Blandford)
    Xyleborus affinis Eichhoff
Subfamily Platypodinae
  Tribe Platypodini
    Euplatypus compositus (Say)
    Myoplatypus flavicornis (Fabricius)
    Oxoplatypus quadridentatus (Olivier)

GLOSSARY

abdomen: last major region of the beetle body, usually partly or entirely covered by the elytra

adecticous pupa: a pupa without functioning mouthparts

alutaceous: dulled by a minute network of fine cracks resembling those of human skin

ambrosia: mutualistic fungus grown in tunnels by some bark and ambrosia beetles (Curculionidae) as food

angulate: edge of structure forming an angle

antenna (pl. antennae): pair of jointed sensory appendages on head attached above mouth

antennomere: article of antenna, including scape, pedicel, and flagellum

anterior: in front

apical: at the tip of a structure

aposematic: possessing distinctive, often contrasting color patterns that serve a defensive purpose by warning predators of unpalatability

appendages: the mouthparts, antennae, and legs of a beetle

appendiculate claw: claw bearing a broad flange at base

apterous: without flight wings

band: a marking across the body, from one side to the other

basal: near the base of a structure

bilobed: divided into two lobes

bioluminescence: production of light involving oxidation of luciferin through the action of luciferase in Lampyridae, Phengodidae, and Elateridae

bipectinate antennae: or comblike, with short antennomeres bearing two prolonged extensions

brachypterous: flight wings present, but reduced; flightless

campodeiform larva: slender, leggy, active beetle larva

canthus: exoskeletal process that partly or completely divides compound eye

capitate antennae: with outermost antennomeres abruptly enlarged to form a round or oval symmetrical club

carina (pl. carinae): a raised narrow ridge or keel along or across a structure

carrion: decomposing dead animal

cercus (pl. cerci): a paired appendage on tip of some beetle abdomens

clavate antennae: antennomeres gradually becoming broader toward apex

claw: typically paired, sharp, hooked structures at apex of tarsus

cleft claw: claw that is split or forked at tip

club: expanded terminal antennomere(s)

clypeus: sclerite typically covering mouthparts of beetles

coccoon: a silken case within which larvae pupate in a few beetle species

Coleoptera: beetles; order of insects that typically have chewing mouthparts and leathery or sheathlike forewings, and develop by holometaboly (i.e., egg, larva, pupa, adult)

commensalism: symbiosis in which one organism benefits and the other derives no benefit, nor is harmed

compound eye: primary organ of sight consisting of multiple facets or lenses

concave: hollowed out, like interior of sphere

confused punctures: punctures not arranged in rows

connate ventrites: visible adominal sternites not freely movable or fused, sutures between sometimes faint or absent

contractile: ability to withdraw appendages tightly against body

convex: rounded, like exterior of sphere

coxa (pl. coxae): basal segment of leg

crepuscular: active at dusk or dawn

cylindrical: having the shape of a cylinder; usually applied to elongate, parallel-sided species with convex dorsal and ventral surfaces and suggests that they would appear almost circular in cross section

dehiscent: separated toward the tip

detritus: accumulation of mostly decomposed plant material

diurnal: active during the day

dorsal: above or on top

eclosion: in beetles, to emerge from the pupa

ectoparasitoid: an external parasite that typically kills its host

elateriform larva: a slender larvae with tough exoskeleton, short legs, and very few setae

elongate: long or lengthened

elytron (pl. elytra): leathery or shell-like forewing of beetles

elytral suture: seam down back of beetle where elytra meet

emarginate: notched, sometimes broadly so, along margin

endosymbiotic microorganism: an organism that lives inside another

epipleuron (pl. epipleura): turned-under fold along lateral edge of elytra

erect: upright

eruciform larva: legged beetle larva that is caterpillar-like in form

exarate pupa: pupa with legs and wings free from body and a movable abdomen

exoskeleton: the protective outer covering of beetles that functions as both skeleton and skin; serves internally as a foundation for powerful muscles and organ systems, while externally providing a platform for sensory and morphological structures

family: taxonomic subdivision ending in -idae

feces: waste or excrement expelled from anus

femur (pl. femora): third leg segment from body between trochanter and tibia

filiform antennae: or threadlike, with segments uniformly cylindrical, or nearly so

flabellate antennae: or fanlike, with segments each bearing a long extension that fit together like a fan

flagellomere: an article of the flagellum

flagellum: antennal articles after the scape and pedicel that lack their own musculature and are not true segments

frass: plant fragments, especially wood, mixed with feces

frontoclypeal suture: transverse suture between frons and clypeus

frons: upper portion of head between eyes and vertex

geniculate antennae: abruptly bent or elbowed

gin-trap: defensive pinching device on opposable abdominal tergites of some beetle pupae

glabrous: surface smooth, devoid of setae or sculpturing

glaucous: grayish or bluish, usually with a coating of waterproof wax secreted by epidermal glands underlying the exoskeleton; easily rubbed off or dissolved in chemical preservatives

granulate: surface rough with small grains or granules

gula: a plate at the back of the underside of head in prognathous beetles

head: first body region, bearing mouthparts, antennae, and eyes

hemispherical: highly convex dorsally, flat or concave ventrally

hemolymph: beetle blood

herbaceous: small, soft plants without woody tissues

holometaboly: development with four distinct stages (egg, larva, pupa, adult); also called complete metamorphosis

humerus (pl. humeri): outer shoulder-like angles at base of elytra

hydrofuge: dense, water-repellent setae

hypermetamorphosis: type of holometaboly where larvae develop through very different forms, usually found in parasitic beetles (Meloidae, Rhipiceridae, Ripiphoridae)

hypognathous: mandibles directed downward

immature: egg, larval, and pupal stages of beetles

impunctate: without punctures

incised claw: claw that is split, or cleft, at tip

instar: stage between larval molts

interval: space between striae on elytra

iridescent: shimmering metallic colors that change with angle of light

labium: the "lower lip" beneath the maxilla

labrum: the "upper lip" over the mandibles that is under or extends beyond clypeus

lamellate antennae: with outermost segments short, flat, and forming a distinctly lopsided club

lanceolate: oblong and tapering at one end or spear- or lance-shaped, often in reference to shape of scales

larva (pl. larvae): second stage of holometabolous development; sometimes called grub in beetles

larviform: an adult female beetle that resemble a larva

lateral: on the side or sides

mandibles: first of two pairs of jaws in beetles, used for chewing

maxilla: second of two pairs of jaws in beetles, used for manipulating food

mentum: ventral head sclerite between mouth and gulum

mesepimeron: rear plate of pleuron of mesothorax

mesepipleuron: pleuron of mesothorax

mesoternum: ventral or sternal portion of mesothorax

mesothorax: middle segment of thorax bearing second pair of legs and elytra

metasternum: ventral or sternal portion of metathorax

metathorax: third thoracic segment bearing the third pair of legs and flight wings (if present)

molt: the action each time a larva sheds its exoskeleton in order to grow

moniliform antennae: or beadlike, with round antennomeres of uniform size

mutualism: when two symbiotic organisms both benefit from the relationship

mycangium (pl. mycangia): an exoskeletal pocket-shaped receptacle used to carry symbiotic fungi in bark beetles (Curculionidae)

mycetome: a structure housing intracellular symbiotic bacteria, yeasts, and fungi, often found in gut lining of wood-boring beetle larvae

mycophagous: feeds on fungus

myrmecophile: lives with ants

nocturnal: active at night

notopleural suture: ventral suture separating pronotum from proepisternum in beetles of suborder Archostemata, Myxophaga, and Adephaga

obovate: egg-shaped or ovate, with narrow end directed downward

obtect pupa: legs and wings tightly appressed to body of pupa, abdomen immobile

ocellus: simple eye in some adult beetles (see stemmata)

oval: elliptical, with end equally rounded

oviposition: act of laying eggs

ovipositor: abdominal structure in female beetles that facilitates oviposition

paedogenesis: production of eggs or larvae by a larva

palpomere: article of palp

palp (pl. palpi, palps): fingerlike appendage of mouth associated with maxillae and labia

parasite: dependent on another host organism for its existence; usually does not kill host

parasitoid: a parasite that typically kills its host

parthenogenesis: development from unfertilized eggs

pectinate antennae: or comblike, with short antennomeres each bearing a prolonged extension

pectinate claw: claw with comblike teeth

pedicel: second antennal segment, located between scape and flagellum

penultimate: next to last

pheromones: chemicals produced by special glands and released into environment to communicate with other members of same species

phoresy: a symbiotic relationship in which a smaller organism is carried by a larger organism strictly for the purpose of transportation

plastron: a thin layer of air trapped in a velvety mesh of dense setae that surrounds the body of some aquatic beetles

plastron breathing: a method of respiration used by some aquatic beetles in which a plastron is used to obtain dissolved oxygen from surrounding water and expel carbon dioxide

pleuron (pl. pleura): lateral sclerites of thoracic segments

plumose antennae: or featherlike, with antennomeres bearing long, slender, and flexible extensions

posterior: behind

predaceous: an animal that hunts and feeds on other animals

prepupa: last larval instar

pretarsus: last segment of the leg bearing claws and associated structures

procoxa (pl. procoxae): basal segment of front leg

procoxal cavity: prothoracic housing for procoxae

prognathous: head and mandibles directed straight forward, or nearly so

pronotum: dorsal sclerite of prothorax

propleuron: lateral sclerite of prothorax

propygidium: abdominal tergite before pygidium in beetles

prosternal process: posterior projection of prosternum that may partly overlap mesosternum

prosternum: underside of prothorax, mostly between procoxae

prothorax: first thoracic segment that bears first pair of legs; midsection of beetle body

proximal: toward base of structure

pruinose: having a waxy light blue, gray, white, or yellowish bloom on some freshly emerged adult beetles

psammophilic: sand-inhabiting

pterothorax: fused wing-bearing meso- and metathorax covered by elytra

punctostriate: rows of elytral punctures that may or may not occur within striae

punctures: small and/or coarse surface pits. Punctures range from very small (*finely punctate*) to large (*coarsely punctate*) and may be shallow or deep

pupa: stage of holometabolous development between larva and adult

pygidium: last dorsal abdominal tergite in beetles

raptorial: adapted for seizing prey, such as forelegs of Gyrinidae

recumbent: lying down or reclining

reflex bleeding: a defensive release of blood through intersegmental membranes between leg joints and body segments

reticulate: raised network of ridges, as in elytral sculpturing of Lycidae

riparian: narrow band of woodland growing along streams and rivers

rostrum: snoutlike projection of mouthparts (some Lycidae, Mycteridae, and Curculionidae)

rugopunctate: surfaces have punctures so tightly spaced that the surface appears rough

rugose: wrinkled

saproxylic: feeding on decayed wood

scale: flattened seta

scape: first of two true antennal segments, followed by pedicel

scarabaeiform larvae: C-shaped grub with well-developed head and legs

scavenger: feeds on decaying plant and fungal tissues and carrion

sclerite: small exoskeletal plate surrounded by sutures or membranes

scutellum: small, often triangular sclerite at base of and between elytra

segment: subdivision of body or appendage distinguished by joints, articulations, or sutures

serrate antennae: or saw-toothed, with flattened, triangular antennomeres

serrate claw: claw with jagged, saw-toothed edge

seta (pl. setae): Setae are fine or bristly, stand straight up (*erect*), or lie nearly flat on the surface (*recumbent*). Flattened setae, or *scales*, range in outline from nearly round, to oval (egg-shaped), obovate (pear-shaped), lanceolate (spear-shaped), or linear (long and slender). Densely setose or scaled surfaces may be partially or completely obscured from view, while the complete absence of setae or scales altogether is referred to as *glabrous*.

simple claw: claw without teeth or other modifications

species: basic biological unit of classification; a group of sexually reproducing beetles that can potentially reproduce with one another and is reproductively isolated from other species

spermatheca: a female organ that stores and nourishes sperm until fertilization and oviposition

spur: movable or socketed spine located at tip of leg segment

stemmata: simple eyes in larval beetles

sternite: a subdivision of the sternum

sternum (pl. sterna): underside of a thoracic or abdominal segment

stria (pl. striae): an impressed groove along length of pronotum or elytron, with or without punctures

stridulation: act of sound production by rubbing one body surface against another, usually filelike spines or tubercles across a carina or series of carinae

stripe: a marking that runs along the long axis of body

subapical: just before apex of structure

subelytral cavity: a space beneath elytra used by aquatic beetles to store air and bring it in contact with thoracic and abdominal spiracles; also serves in thermoregulation in terrestrial species living in dry habitats

surface sculpture: raised or impressed markings on surface of exoskeleton

sutures: membranes of pure chitin joining segments, seen as narrow furrows separating them

symbiotic: an organism living in association with another, does not imply nature of relationship (see commensalism, mutualism, parasite, phoresy)

tarsal formula: shorthand for number of tarsomeres (including pretarsus) on front, middle, and hind legs, respectively; 5-5-5, 5-5-4, 4-4-4, etc.

tarsomere: an article of the foot that does not bear claws

tarsus (pl. tarsi): foot, including both tarsomere(s) and pretarsus

teneral: freshly eclosed pale and soft-bodied adult

tergum (pl. terga): dorsal sclerite of beetle abdomen

tergite: a plate or portion of tergum

termitophile: lives with termites

thanatosis: act of playing dead as a defensive tactic so that predators lose interest

thorax: middle body region, bearing legs and wings, subdivided into pro-, meso-, and metathorax

tibia (pl. tibiae): fourth segment of leg from base, located between femur and tarsus

toothed claw: claw with one or more teeth

triungulin: small campodeiform larva that develops by hypermetamorphosis

trochanter: second leg segment from body, located between coxa and femur

truncate: appearing cut- or squared-off

tubercle: small raised bump or knob

urogomphus (pl. urogomphi): a fixed and paired, sometime articulated process on tip of larval abdomen in some species

ventral: below or underside

ventrite: visible abdominal sternite; in beetles, first ventrite is usually second abdominal sternite

vermiform larva: legless, almost wormlike beetle larva

vertex: top of head

SELECTED REFERENCES AND RESOURCES

GENERAL INFORMATION ON NATURAL HISTORY AND BEHAVIOR

Crowson, R.A. 1980. *The Biology of the Coleoptera*. London: Academic. 802 pp. (out of print).

Evans, A.V., and C.L. Bellamy. 2000. *An Inordinate Fondness for Beetles*. Berkeley: University of California Press. 208 pp.

Evans, A.V., and J.N. Hogue. 2004. *An Introduction to California beetles*. Berkeley: University of California Press. 299 pp.

Klausnitzer, B. 1981. *Beetles*. New York: Exeter. 213 pp. (out of print).

Stehr, F.W. (ed.). 1991. *Immature Insects*. Vol. 2. Dubuque, IA: Kendall/Hunt. 973 pp.

HIGHER CLASSIFICATION OF BEETLES

Beutel, R.G., and R.A.B. Leschen (eds.). 2005. *Handbook of Zoology. Arthropoda: Insecta. Coleoptera, Beetles. Vol. 1: Morphology and Systematics (Archostemata, Adephaga, Myxophaga, Polyphaga partim)*. Berlin: Walter de Gruyer. 567 pp.

Bouchard, P., Y. Bousquet, A.E. Davies, M.A. Alonso Zarazaga, J.F. Lawrence, C.H.C. Lyal, A.F. Newton, C.A.M. Reid, M. Schmitt, S.A. Slipinski, and A.B.T. Smith. 2011. Family-group names in Coleoptera (Insecta). *ZooKeys* 88: 1–972.

Leschen, R.A.B., R.G. Beutel, and J.F. Lawrence (eds.). 2010. *Handbook of Zoology. Arthropoda: Insecta. Coleoptera, Beetles. Vol. 2: Morphology and Systematics (Elateroidea, Bostrichiformia, Cucujiformia partim)*. Berlin: Walter de Gruyer. 786 pp.

NORTH AMERICAN GUIDES AND REFERENCES

Arnett, R.H., Jr., N.M. Downie, and H.E. Jacques. 1980. How to know the beetles. *The Pictured Key Nature Series*. Dubuque, IA: William C. Brown. 416 pp.

Arnett, R.H., Jr. and M.C. Thomas (eds.). 2000. *American Beetles. Vol. 1: Archostemata: Myxophaga, Adephaga, Polyphaga: Staphyliniformia*. Boca Raton, FL: CRC Press. 443 pp.

Arnett, R.H., Jr., M.C. Thomas, P.E. Skelley, and J.H. Frank (eds.). 2002. *American Beetles. Vol. 2: Polyphaga: Scarabaeoidea through Curculionidae*. Boca Raton, FL: CRC Press. 861 pp.

Bousquet, Y. 1990. *Beetles Associated with Stored Products in Canada: An Identification Guide*. Publ. 1837. Research Branch, Agriculture Canada. 214 pp.

Bousquet, Y., P. Bouchard, A.E. Davies, and D.S. Sikes. 2013. *Checklist of Beetles of Canada and Alaska*. Second edition. Pensoft Series Faunistica 109. Sofia, Bulgaria: Pensoft. 402 pp.

Brown, H.P. 1972. Aquatic dryopoid beetles (Coleoptera) of the United States. *Biota of Freshwater Ecosystems Identification Manual No. 6*. Water Pollution Control Research Series. Cincinnati, OH: US Environmental Protection Agency. 82 pp. (reprinted in 1976).

Erwin, T.L. 2007. *A Treatise on the Western Hemisphere Caraboidea (Coleoptera). Their Classification, Distributions, and Ways of Life. Vol. 1 (Trachypachidae, Carabidae-Nebriiformes)*. Sofia, Bulgaria: Pensoft. 365 pp.

Erwin, T.L. 2011. *A Treatise on the Western Hemisphere Caraboidea (Coleoptera). Their Classification, Distributions, and Ways of Life. Vol. 3 (Carabidae-Loxomeriformes, Melaeniformes)*. Sofia, Bulgaria: Pensoft. 412 pp.

Erwin T.L., and D.L. Pearson. 2008. *A Treatise on the Western Hemisphere Caraboidea (Coleoptera). Their Classification, Distributions, and Way of Life. Vol. 2 (Carabidae – Nebriiformes 2 – Cicindelitae)*. Sofia, Bulgaria: Pensoft. 365 + [1] pp. + 33 plates.

Pearson, D.L., C.B. Knisley, and C.J. Zakilek. 2006. *A Field Guide to the Tiger Beetles of the United States and Canada. Identification, Natural History, and Distribution of the Cicindelidae*. Oxford: Oxford University Press. 227 pp.

White, R.E. 1983. *A Field Guide to the Beetles of North America*. Boston: Houghton Mifflin. 368 pp.

EASTERN REGIONAL BOOKS

Blatchley, W.S. 1910. *An Illustrated Descriptive Catalogue of the Coleoptera or Beetles (Exclusive of the Rhynchophora) Known to Occur in Indiana with Bibliography and Descriptions of New Species*. Indianapolis. 1386 pp. (out of print).

Blatchley, W.S., and C.W. Leng. 1916. *Rhynchophora or Weevils of North Eastern America.* Indianapolis: The Nature Publishing Company. 682 pp. (out of print).

Bousquet, Y. 2010. *Illustrated Identification Guide to Adults and Larvae of Northeastern North American Ground Beetles (Coleoptera: Carabidae).* Sofia, Bulgaria: Pensoft. 562 pp.

Choate, P.M. 2003. Tiger Beetles. *A Field Guide and Identification Manual for Florida and Eastern U.S.* Gainesville, FL: University Press of Florida. 197 pp.

Ciegler, J.C. 2003. Water beetles of South Carolina (Coleoptera: Gyrinidae, Haliplidae, Noteridae, Dytiscidae, Hydrophilidae, Hydraenidae, Scirtidae, Elmidae, Dryopidae, Limnichidae, Heteroceridae, Psephenidae, Ptilodactylidae, and Chelonariidae). *Biota of South Carolina, Vol. 3.* Clemson, SC: Clemson University. 207 pp.

Ciegler, J.C. 2007. Leaf and seed beetles of South Carolina (Coleoptera: Chrysomelidae and Orsodacnidae). *Biota of South Carolina, Vol. 4.* Clemson, SC: Clemson University. 246 pp.

Ciegler, J.C. 2010. Weevils of South Carolina (Coleoptera: Nemonychidae, Attelabidae, Brentidae, Ithyceridae, Curculionidae). *Biota of South Carolina, Vol. 6.* Clemson, SC: Clemson University. 276 pp.

Ciegler, J.C. 2013. Tenebrionoidea of South Carolina (Coleoptera: Mycetophagidae, Archeocrypticidae, Tetratomidae, Melandryidae, Mordellidae, Ripiphoridae, Zopheridae, Tenebrionidae, Synchroidae, Oedemeridae, Stenotrachelidae, Meloidae, Mycteridae, Boridae, Pythidae, Pyrochroidae, Salpingidae, Anthicidae, Ischaliidae, and Aderidae). *Biota of South Carolina, Vol. 8.* Clemson, SC: Clemson University (in press).

Dillon, E.S., and L.S. Dillon. 1961. *A Manual of Common Beetles of Eastern North America.* Evanston, IL: Row, Peterson. 884 pp. (Reprinted in 1972 by Dover, New York, as two volumes) (out of print).

Downie, N.M., and R.H. Arnett, Jr. 1996. *The Beetles of Northeastern North America. Vols. 1 and 2.* Gainesville, FL: Sandhill Crane Press. 1721 pp. (out of print).

Epler, J.H. 2010. *The Water Beetles of Florida. An Identification Manual for the Families Chrysomelidae, Curculionidae, Dryopidae, Dytiscidae, Elmidae, Gyrinidae, Haliplidae, Helophoridae, Hydraenidae, Hydrochidae, Hydrophilidae, Noteridae, Psephenidae, Ptilodactylidae and Scirtidae.* Final report for FDEP Contract Number WM940. Tallahassee: State of Florida, Department of Environmental Protection, Division of Environmental Assessment and Restoration. 414 pp.

Harpootlian, P.J. 2001. Scarab beetles (Coleoptera: Scarabaeidae) of South Carolina. *Biota of South Carolina, Vol. 2.* Clemson, SC: Clemson University. 157 pp.

Harpootlian, P.J., and C.L. Bellamy. 2013. Jewel beetles (Coleoptera: Buprestidae) of South Carolina. *Biota of South Carolina, Vol. 7.* Clemson, SC: Clemson University. 127 pp.

Knisley, C.B., and T.D. Schultz. 1997. *The Biology of Tiger Beetles and a Guide to the Species of the South Atlantic States.* Special Publication 5. Virginia Museum of Natural History. 210 pp.

Larson, D.J., Y. Alarie, and R.E. Roughley. 2000. *Predaceous Diving Beetles (Coleoptera: Dytiscidae) of the Nearctic Region, with Emphasis on the Fauna of Canada and Alaska.* Ottawa: National Research Council of Canada Research Press. 982 pp.

Lingafelter, S.W. 2008. *Illustrated Key to the Longhorned Woodboring Beetles of the Eastern United States.* North Potomac, MD: Coleopterists Society. 206 pp.

Marshall, S.A. 2006. Insects. *Their Natural History and Diversity. With a Photographic Guide to Insects of Eastern North America.* Buffalo, NY: Firefly Books. 732 pp. (includes more than 1,000 images of beetles).

Paiero, S.M., M.D. Jackson, A. Jewiss-Gains, B.D. Gill, and S.A. Marshall. 2012. *Field Guide to the Jewel Beetles (Coleoptera: Buprestidae) of Northeastern North America.* Ottawa: Canadian Food Inspection Agency. 411 pp. (also available in French).

Yanega, D. 1996. *Field Guide to Northeastern Longhorned Beetles (Coleoptera: Cerambycidae).* Manual 6. Champagne: Illinois Natural History Survey. 174 pp.

COLLECTING, PRESERVING, AND REARING TECHNIQUES

Martin, J.E.H. 1977. *The Insects and Arachnids of Canada. Part 1. Collecting, Preparing, and Preserving Insects, Mites, and Spiders.* Ottawa: Biosystematics Research Institute, Ottawa, Ontario. 182 pp. (also available in French).

McMonigle, O. 2012. *The Ultimate Guide to Breeding Beetles. Coleoptera Laboratory Culture Methods.* Landisville, PA: Coachwhip. 206 pp.

Schauff, M. (ed.). 1986. *Collecting and preserving insects and mites. Techniques and tools.* www.ars.usda.gov/SP2UserFiles/ad_hoc/12754100CollectingandPreservingInsectsandMites/collpres.pdf (accessed 1 January 2014).

INFORMATION ON RARE AND ENDANGERED SPECIES

Natureserv Explorer. An authoritative source for information on more than 70,000 plants, animals, and ecosystems of the United States and Canada that includes in-depth coverage of rare and endangered species. www.natureserve.org/explorer/ (accessed 1 January 2014).

United States Fish and Wildlife Service Endangered Species. Includes an interactive map with endangered species information by state. www.fws.gov/endangered/ (accessed 1 January 2014).

BEETLE SOCIETIES

The Coleopterists Society: An international organization devoted to the study of all aspects of systematics and biology of beetles of the world; publishes the quarterly Coleopterists Bulletin; archive for various beetle newsletters. http://coleopsoc.org (accessed 25 January 2014).

BEETLE LISTSERVS

CARABID: This LISTSERV is for people interested the Carabidae. To subscribe, visit www.mail-archive.com/carabid@lists.berkeley.edu/ (accessed 1 January 2014).

CERAMBYX: A LISTSERV based at the University of Montana for those interested in longhorn beetles (Cerambycidae) and their relatives. All are invited to contribute. To subscribe, send an e-mail message with subscribe cerambyx [your name] to listserv@listserv.montana.edu.

SCARABS-L: This list is for professionals, amateurs, and students interested in scarab beetle taxonomy. It is used for posting questions, information, and new discoveries regarding scarab systematics, biology, and nomenclature. Subscribe at http://listserv.unl.edu/cgi-bin/wa?SUBED1=SCARABS-L&A=1 (accessed 6 September 2013).

STAPHLIST: This LISTSERVE is for people interested in Staphylinidae and related groups. To subscribe, visit: https://sympa.uio.no/nhm.uio.no/info/staphlist (accessed 1 January 2014).

TENEB-L: This LISTSERV is for those interested in any family within the superfamily Tenebrionoidea and is based at Arizona State University. To subscribe, visit https://lists.asu.edu/cgi-bin/wa?SUBED1=TENEB-L&A= (accessed 1 January 2014).

BEETLES OF EASTERN NORTH AMERICA ON THE WEB

Atlantic Canada Coleoptera: This site highlights the beetle fauna of Nova Scotia, New Brunswick, Prince Edward Island, and Newfoundland. www.chebucto.ns.ca/environment/NHR/atlantic_coleoptera.html (accessed 1 January 2014).

BugGuide.net: An outstanding resource for identified beetle images, taxonomic information, and other online resources. www.buguguide.net (accessed 1 January 2014).

Canadian Journal of Arthropod Identification: A product of the Biological Survey of Canada, this web-based journal is devoted to documenting Canada's arthropods and includes guides to Lampyridae and Staphylinidae. www.biology.ualberta.ca/bsc/ejournal/ejournal.html (accessed 1 January 2014).

Cerambycoid. Primary types of the Smithsonian Institution: An online searchable database for primary type specimens of longhorned woodboring beetles that includes types of Casey and others. http://elaphidion.com (accessed 1 January 2014).

The Ground Beetles of Canada: Images and catalogue of Canadian species. http://www.cbif.gc.ca/spp_pages/carabids/phps/index_e.php (accessed 1 January 2014).

Introduction to the darkling beetles of eastern North America: Images, distributions, and natural history notes on many species of Tenebrionidae. http://entnemdept.ufl.edu/teneb/intro.htm (accessed 1 January 2014).

MCZ type database @ Harvard Entomology: This online database contains records and images of the primary types housed in one of the largest entomology collections in North America, the Museum of Comparative Zoology (MCZ). The beetle types of LeConte, Horn, Fall, and others are housed here. http://insects.oeb.harvard.edu/MCZ/index.php (accessed 1 January 2014).

BEETLE BOOKS, COLLECTING EQUIPMENT, AND SUPPLIES

Atelier Jean Paquet Matériel Entomologique, 4656, route Fossamault, Sainte-Catherine-de-la-Jacques-Cartier, Québec G3N 1S8 CANADA; phone 418-875-2276; fax 418-873-1866; www.atelierjeanpaquet.com (accessed 1 January 2014).

BioQuip Products, Inc., 2321 Glawick Street, Rancho Dominguez, CA 90220; phone 310-667-8800; fax 310-667-8808; www.bioquip.com (accessed 1 January 2014).

PHOTO AND ILLUSTRATION CREDITS

All illustrations in this book (Figures 2a–n, 9a–b, family key) are original and were rendered by Jennifer Read. Figures 2a–m are based on images taken by Nicolas Gompel, while Figure 2n is a reworking of an image taken by John Ott.

The photo credits are given below. All photographs are by the author with the exception of the following:

KEN ALLEN
Andrimus murrayi (p.351); *Megacerus cubiculus* (p.431); *Plectris aliena* (p.167); *Pseudolampsis guttata* (p.446).

DAVID ALMQUIST
Fig. 24; *Cercopeus komareki* (p.491); *Cnestus mutilatus* (p.499); *Dendroctonus terebrans* (p.497); *Ellipsoptera hirtilabris* (p.72); *Geotrupes blackburnii blackburnii* (p.151); *Gerstaeckeria hubbardi* (p.484); *Hypotrichia spissipes* male, female (p.164); *Mycotrupes cartwrighti* (p.151); *Onthophagus depressus* (p.162); *Pachnaeus litus* (p.490); *Pasimachus subsulcatus* (p.75); *Polopinus youngi* (p.358); *Pseudagolius bicolor* (p.158); *Rhynchophorus cruentatus* (p.471); *Strigoderma pygmaea* (p.169); *Thalycra carolina* (p.301).

JERRY ARMSTRONG
Necrophilus pettiti (p.117).

LYN ATHERTON
Ischnocerus infuscatus (p.459).

TROY BARTLETT
Babia quadriguttata (p.450).

CHRISTY BEAL
Chalcodermus aeneus (p.496); *Strategus splendens* (p.171).

PAUL BEDELL
Knulliana cincta cincta (p.414).

CHRISTOPH BENISCH
Rhyzopertha dominica (p.251); *Anobium punctatum* (p.254); *Stegobium paniceum* (p.255).

THOMAS BENTLEY
Agrilaxia flavimana (p.189); *Agrilus cyanescens* (p.192); *Anastrangalia sanguinea* (p.392); *Atalantycha neglecta* (p.239); *Batyle suturalis* (p.414); *Brachypera zoilus* (p.491); *Brachys aerosus* (p.193); *Brachys ovatus* (p.194); *Chlaenius sericeus* (p.86); *Chrysobothris azurea* (p.190); *Coleothorpa dominica franciscana* (p.451); *Cryptocephalus guttulatus* (p.452); *Cychramus adustus* (p.298); *Diabrotica cristata* (p.450); *Disonycha pensylvanica* (p.445); *Dorcaschema cinereum* (p.422); *Haplorhynchites aeneus* (p.465); *Hormorus undulatus* (p.488); *Ithycerus noveboracensis* (p.469); *Listronotus sparsus* (p.485); *Lytta aenea* (p.367); *Mecas cineracea* (p.425); *Omophron tessellatum* (p.73); *Pachyschelus purpureus* (p.194); *Pidonia ruficollis* (p.396); *Plagiometriona clavata* (p.436); *Podabrus brevicollis* (p.240); *Rhagonycha mollis* (p.241); *Rhaxonycha carolina* (p.241); *Sphenophorus aequalis* (p.472); *Systena elongata* (p.446); *Trichaltica scabricula* (p.447); *Trichodes apivorus* (p.268); *Trichodes nuttalli* (p.268); *Yakuhananomia bidentata* (p.335); *Zonitis vittigera* (p.369); *Zygogramma suturalis* (p.443).

ASHLEY M. BRADFORD
Figs 12a, b; *Calomycterus setarius* (p.486); *Cryptocephalus leucomelas* (p.452); *Heterachthes quadrimaculatus* (p.411); *Hormops abducens* (p.496); *Linogeraeus neglectus* (p.477); *Melittomma sericeum* (p.259); *Parelaphidion aspersum* (p.410); *Perigaster obscura* (p.480); *Styloleptus biustus* (p.420).

DONNA BRUNET
Necydalis melitta (p.403).

VALERIE BUGH
Elytroleptus floridanus (p.415); *Epicaerus imbricatus* (p.487); *Neoharmonia venusta* (p.318); *Oeme rigida* (p.412); *Trachyderes mandibularis* (p.415).

ROBERT CARLSON
Lepturopsis biforis (p.396).

CHRISTOPHER CARLTON, LOUISIANA STATE ARTHROPOD MUSEUM
Nosodendron unicolor (p.245).

CARMEN CHAMPAGNE
Sperchopsis tessellata (p.106).

JANET C. CIEGLER
Mycterus scaber (p.370).

PATRICK COIN
Anomala undulata (p.167); *Anomoea laticlavia laticlavia* (p.450); *Bothrotes caniculatus caniculatus* (p.346); *Calosoma sayi* (p.65); *Carabus vinctus* (p.67); *Colydium lineola* (p.341); *Cybister fimbriolatus* (p.104); *Hemierana marginata ardens* (p.422); *Hydrophilus ovatus* (p.108); *Hypocaccus fraternus*

(p.112); *Lebia vittata* (p.92); *Melanactes piceus* (p.219); *Oncideres cingulata* (p.424); *Plateros* sp. (p.233); *Ptilodactyla* (p.205); *Scarites subterraneus* (p.75); *Sphenostethus taslei* (p.391); *Strangalia bicolor* (p.398); *Strangalia sexnotata* (p.399); *Tetraopes melanurus* (p.427).

ALAN CRESSLER
Figs 18, 35; *Desmocerus palliatus* (p.391).

STEPHEN CRESSWELL
Ataenius imbricatus (p.158); *Belonuchus rufipennis* (p.138); *Byturus unicolor* (p.274); *Charhyphus picipennis* (p.127); *Cylindrocopturus quercus* (p.482); *Dialytes striatulus* (p.157); *Eupristocerus cogitans* (p.193); *Hypulus simulator* (p.331); *Osmoderma eremicola* (p.175); *Palaminus testaceus* (p.137); *Pyrota germari* (p.366); *Ripiphorus* (p.340); *Scaphinotus andrewsii* (p.67); *Stenocorus schaumii* (p.397).

ROB CURTIS
Agrilus obsoletoguttatus (p.193); *Archodontes melanoplus* (p.389); *Calathus opaculus* (p.87); *Chalcolepidius viridipilus* (p.215); *Cotalpa lanigera* (p.169); *Deilelater physoderus* (p.218); *Enchodes sericea* (p.330); *Helobata larvalis* (p.107); *Iphthiminus opacus* (p.357); *Leptotrachelus dorsalis* (p.87); *Megacyllene decora* (p.406); *Meracantha contracta* (p.347); *Metamasius hemipterus sericeus* (p.471); *Mycetochara haldemani* (p.353); *Poecilus chalcites* (p.79); *Sennius abbreviatus* (p.432); *Subcoccinella vigintiquatuorpunctata* (p.319).

DENIS DOUCET
Anostirus vernalis (p.222).

JOSEPH DVORAK
Zeugophora scutellaris (p.428).

CHARLEY EISEMAN
Fig. 38; *Ampedus rubricus* (p.226); *Caenia dimidiata* (p.230); *Canthon viridis* (p.159); *Capraita subvittata* (p.444); *Dietzella zimmermanni* (p.480); *Erotides sculptilis* (p.232); *Fabogethes nigrescens* (p.297); *Leptoceletes basalis* (p.231); *Oxyporus quinquemaculatus* (p.133); *Pseudanthonomus validus* (p.474); *Pyrrhalta viburni* (p.448); *Rhinoncus longulus* (p.481); *Selenophorus opalinus* (p.82); *Stenolophus comma* (p.83).

MARDON ERBLAND
Agriotes lineatus (p.224).

JOHN FRISCH
Tetracha virginica (p.68).

DAVID FUNK
Paralichus trivittus (p.205).

STAN GILLIAM
Cophes obtentus (p.485).

NICHOLAS GOMPEL
Adranes coecus (p.126).

HENRI GOULET
Agonum extensicolle (p.87); *Amphasia interstitialis* (p.80); *Anisodactylus rusticus* (p.80); *Bembidion castor* (p.76); *Bembidion rapidum* (p.77); *Calosoma calidum* (p.65); *Calosoma frigidum* (p.65); *Calosoma sycophanta* (p.66); *Carabus nemoralis* (p.66); *Carabus serratus* (p.67); *Chlaenius niger* (p.86); *Chlaenius tomentosus* (p.86); *Cicindela duodecimguttata* (p.68); *Clivina fossor* (p.74); *Diplocheila striatopunctata* (p.85); *Dyschirius sphaericollis* (p.74); *Euryderus grossus* (p.81); *Harpalus erythropus* (p.82); *Myas cyanescens* (p.78); *Nebria lacustris* (p.64); *Oodes fluvialis* (p.86); *Patrobus longicornis* (p.78); *Platynus tenuicollis* (p.88); *Poecilus lucublandus* (p.79); *Pterostichus adoxus* (p.79); *Sphaeroderus stenostomus lecontei* (p.68); *Synuchus impunctatus* (p.88); *Tachyta kirbyi* (p.77); *Tenebrio molitor* (p.351); *Trechus apicalis* (p.76).

BOB GRESS
Nicrophorus americanus (p.122).

JOYCE GROSS
Figs 8h, 15h; *Anaedus brunneus* (p.345); *Bruchus brachialis* (p.431); *Carpophilus hemipterus* (p.296); *Celina hubbelli* (p.100); *Cosnania pensylvanica* (p.89); *Conotrachelus nenuphar* (p.494); *Cryptolaemus montrouzieri* (p.312); *Dubiraphia vittata* (p.197); *Emmesa connectens* (p.332); *Eurymycter tricarinatus* (p.460); *Gastrophysa cyanea* (p.441); *Glischrochilus quadrisignatus* (p.303); *Hadrobregmus notatus* (p.255); *Hallomenus scapularis* (p.328); *Holostrophus bifasciatus* (p.329); *Laccophilus maculosus* (p.100); *Lema daturaphila* (p.433); *Lycoperdina ferruginea* (p.310); *Lyctus planicollis* (p.252); *Mordellaria serval* (p.334); *Mycetina perpulchra* (p.310); *Necrobia ruficollis* (p.269); *Necrobia rufipes* (p.270); *Nicrophorus pustulatus* (p.123); *Nicrophorus tomentosus* (p.123); *Olibrus* (p.291); *Optioservus trivittatus* (p.197); *Oryzaephilus mercator* (p.287); *Platypsyllus castoris* (p.120); *Prionocyphon limbatus* (p.182); *Psephenus herricki* (p.204); *Ptilinus ruficornis* male (p.256); *Rhopalapion longirostre* (p.467); *Scaphidium quadriguttatum* (p.132); *Sumitrosis inaequalis* (p.438); *Telephanus atricapillus* (p.286); *Thanatophilus lapponicus* (p.122); *Thylodrias contractus* (p.247); *Thymalus marginicollis* (p.261); *Triplax thoracica* (p.280); *Tritoma mimetica* (p.280).

JEFF GRUBER
Hypodacne punctata (p.307); *Lutrochus laticeps* (p.200).

GUY HANLEY
Adalia bipunctata (p.314); *Ancylocera bicolor* (p.414); *Arhopalus foveicollis* (p.401); *Astylidius parvus* (p.416); *Calopus angustus* (p.362); *Calvia quatuordecimguttata* (p.315); *Coccidula lepida* (p.314); *Dendroctonus valens* (p.497); *Elater abruptus* (p.227); *Eucanthus lazarus* (p.150); *Geopinus incrassatus* (p.81); *Glaresis inducta* (p.146); *Hesperophanes pubescens* (p.411); *Hister furtivus* (p.114);

531

Meriellum proteus (p.404); *Plectrodera scalator* (p.424); *Ropalopus sanguinicollis* (p.405).

RANDY HARDY
Achryson surinamum (p.403).

PHILLIP J. HARPOOTLIAN
Bradycinetulus ferrugineus (p.150); *Euphoria areata* (p.173); *Mycotrupes retusus* (p.151); *Odonteus darlingtoni* (p.150); *Strategus antaeus* (p.171).

JEFF HOLLENBECK
Osmopleura chamaeropsis (p.403).

SCOTT JUSTIS
Allopoda lutea (p.385); *Altica chalybea* (p.443); *Anthonomus haematopus* (p.473); *Aphorista vittata* (p.310); *Astenus brevipennis* (p.135); *Aulonium parallelopipedum* (p.342); *Bitoma quadriguttata* (p.342); *Brachys floricolus* (p.194); *Carpophilus discoideus* (p.296); *Cerotoma trifurcata* (p.449); *Coelocephalapion perminutum* (p.468); *Diplocoelus rudis* (p.276); *Eleates depressus* (p.348); *Gondwanocrypticus platensis* (p.354); *Isohydnocera curtipennis* (p.265); *Lobiopa insularis* (p.298); *Megalodacne fasciata* (p.279); *Microrhopala vitatta* (p.437); *Namunaria guttulata* (p.343); *Neolema sexpunctata* (p.434); *Neorthopleura thoracica* (p.270); *Octotemnus* (p.326); *Oligolochus ornatus* (p.478); *Olla v-nigrum* dark form (p.318); *Osphya varians* (p.332); *Phyllobaenus unifasciatus* (p.266); *Scirtes orbiculatus* (p.183); *Sepedophilus* (p.129); *Sitophilus oryzae* (p.472); *Stenoscelis brevis* (p.483); *Tachygonus lecontei* (p.482).

JAMES A. KALISCH
Dectes texanus (p.417).

WONGUN KIM
Acanthoscelides alboscutellatus (p.431); *Calochromus perfacetus* (p.231); *Corticocomus parallelus* (p.261); *Griburius scutellaris* (p.452); *Oxoplatypus quadridentatus* (p.500); *Protheca hispida* (p.257); *Saxinis omogera* (p.451); *Semiardistomis viridis* (p.75); *Tomoderus* (p.381); *Wolcottia pedalis* (p.266).

THOR KRISTIANSEN
Stenotrachelus aeneus (p.361).

JERRI LARSSON, BIOQUIP PRODUCTS, INC.
Fig. 43.

JESSICA LAWRENCE
Trichiotinus lunulatus (p.175).

RENÉ LIMOGE
Amphimallon majale (p.163).

ILONA LOSER
Lacconotus punctatus (p.370); *Temnopsophus bimaculatus* (p.273).

STEPHEN LUK
Figs 15g, 39; *Ceophyllus monillus* (p.127); *Cimberis pilosa* (p.457); *Cymatodera inornata* (p.264); *Deltometopus amoenicornis* (p.211); *Dicerca obscura* (p.188); *Elateroides lugubris* female (p.259); *Helophorus grandis* (p.106); *Lopheros fraternus* (p.232); *Melanophila acuminata* (p.191); *Mezium affine* (p.253); *Omosita colon* (p.299); *Onichodon orchesides* (p.211); *Ormiscus saltator* (p.461); *Oxyporus rufipennis* (p.134); *Pelecotoma flavipes* (p.338); *Phaenops fulvoguttata* (p.191); *Phenolia grossa* (p.300); *Phymatodes testaceus* (p.405); *Ptinus fur* (p.253).

TED MACRAE
Cicindela limbalis (p.68); *Elytrimitatrix undata* (p.387); *Plinthocoelium suaveolens* (p.404).

CRYSTAL MAIER, LOUISIANA STATE ARTHROPOD MUSEUM
Ancyronyx variegata (p.197).

DANIEL MARLOS, WHAT'S THAT BUG?
Cylas formicarius (p.467).

STEPHEN A. MARSHALL
Amblyctis praeses (p.330).

OLE MARTIN
Alphitobius diaperinus (p.347).

CHARLES MATSON
Nacerdes melanura (p.363).

JOHN MAXWELL
Conoderus vespertinus (p.217); *Metachroma pellucidum* (p.456); *Polyphylla variolosa* (p.165).

SEAN MCCANN
Lyconotus lateralis (p.233); *Metamasius callizona* (p.470); *Phanaeus vindex* (p.161).

RICHARD MIGNEAULT
Fig, 21; *Anthophylax cyaneus* (p.392); *Bassareus mammifer* (p.451); *Bromius obscurus* (p.453); *Calligrapha rowena* (p.440); *Pacificanthia rotundicollis* (p.239); *Chrysomela mainensis* (p.441); *Dendrophagus cygnaei* (p.285); *Glischrochilus sanguinolentus* (p.303); *Lepturobosca chrysocoma* (p.396); *Lepyrus palustris* (p.496); *Malachius aeneus* (p.273); *Monochamus notatus* (p.423); *Podabrus rugosulus* (p.240); *Poecilonota cyanipes* (p.188); *Polydrusus sericeus* (p.490); *Pyropyga nigricans* (p.236); *Saperda calcarata* (p.426); *Saperda obliqua* (p.427); *Syneta ferruginea* (p.457); *Upis ceramboides* (p.358).

GRAHAM MONTGOMERY
Acylophorus (p.138); *Acanthoderes quadrigibba* (p.420); *Agasicles hygrophila* (p.443); *Bactridium* (p.282); *Bothrideres geminatus* (p.306); *Collops quadrimaculatus* (p.272);

Conotrachelus posticatus (p.495); *Danae testacea* (p.309); *Digitonthophagus gazella* (p.161); *Eudiagogus pulcher* (p.487); *Eudiagogus rosenschoeldi* (p.487); *Gibbium aequinoctiale* (p.253); *Heteroderes amplicollis* (p.217); *Hippopsis lemniscata* (p.421); *Hoplandria lateralis* (p.131); *Laemophloeus biguttatus* (p.292); *Laemophloeus fasciatus* (p.293); *Lissorhoptrus oryzophilus* (p.473); *Mastogenius crenulatus* (p.186); *Ophraella conferta* (p.448); *Oryzaephilus surinamensis* (p.287); *Otiorhynchus sulcatus* (p.489); *Poecilocrypticus formicophilus* (p.354); *Trichobaris trinotata* (p.479); *Trogoxylon parallelopipedum* (p.252).

ROY F. MORRIS II
Romulus globosus (p.410).

TIM MOYER
Thermonectus basillaris (p.104).

TOM MURRAY
Acallodes ventricosus (p.481); *Acanthocinus obsoletus* (p.416); *Acilius mediatus* (p.103); *Acilius semisulcatus* (p.104); *Acoptus suturalis* (p.481); *Actenicerus cuprascens* (p.221); *Aeletes politus* (p.111); *Agabetes inductus* (p.100); *Agabus* (p.102); *Agonum octopunctatum* (p.87); *Agriotes collaris* (p.224); *Agroiconota bivittata* (p.434); *Aleochara littoralis* (p.130); *Ampedus areolatus* (p.225); *Anaspis flavipennis* (p.385); *Anaspis rufa* (p.386); *Anisodactylus sanctaecrucis* (p.80); *Anisosticta bitriangularis* (p.314); *Anotylus rugosus* (p.133); *Antherophagus ochraceus* (p.283); *Anthonomus quadrigibbus* (p.473); *Anthophylax attenuatus* (p.392); *Aphonus castaneus* (p.170); *Athous acanthus* (p.219); *Athous cucullatus* (p.219); *Athous neacanthus* (p.219); *Atomaria distincta* (p.285); *Atrecus americanus* (p.137); *Auletobius cassandrae* (p.464); *Aulonothroscus constrictor* (p.212); *Badister neopulchellus* (p.84); *Baeocera* (p.132); *Bagous planatus* (p.477); *Barypeithes pellucidus* (p.490); *Batrisodes lineaticollis* (p.125); *Betulapion simile* (p.468); *Bisnius blandus* (p.138); *Bitoma crenata* (p.342); *Blepharida rhois* (p.444); *Boros unicolor* (p.371); *Brachygluta abdominalis* (p.125); *Brachypterolus pulicarius* (p.294); *Brachypterus urticae* (p.294); *Brachysomida bivittata* (p.393); *Byrrhodes incomptus* (p.257); *Byrrhus americanus* (p.195); *Caenoscelis basalis* (p.284); *Calleida punctata* (p.89); *Calligrapha alni* (p.440); *Callimoxys sanguinicollis* (p.413); *Cardiophorus convexus* (p.228); *Carpophilus sayi* (p.297); *Cephaloon ungulare* (p.361); *Cerylon unicolor* (p.308); *Ceutorhynchus americanus* (p.480); *Chaetophora spinosa* (p.196); *Chalcophora liberta* (p.187); *Chalepus bicolor* (p.437); *Charaphloeus convexulus* (p.292); *Cionus scrophulariae* (p.474); *Clambus* (p.179); *Clypastraea lunata* (p.321); *Coccinella trifasciata perplexa* (p.315); *Colaspis brunnea* (p.455); *Colopterus truncatus* (p.301); *Colymbetes paykulli* (p.102); *Conoderus bellus* (p.216); *Conotrachelus elegans* (p.494); *Conotrachelus juglandis* (p.494); *Coptotomus longulus lenticus* (p.101); *Corticaria serrata* (p.322); *Corthylus columbianus* (p.499); *Cosmobaris scolopacea* (p.478); *Crioceris asparagi* (p.433); *Cryptarcha strigulata* (p.302); *Cryptophagus* (p.284); *Cryptorhynchus lapathi* (p.483); *Cymindis limbatus*

(p.90); *Cyphon collaris* (p.180); *Cyphon padi* (p.181); *Cyphon ruficollis* (p.181); *Cytilus alternatus* (p.196); *Danosoma brevicorne* (p.214); *Decarthron velutinum* (p.126); *Dendroides canadensis* (p.374); *Dendroides concolor* (p.374); *Dermestes lardarius* (p.247); *Diabrotica barberi* (p.449); *Dienerella filum* (p.322); *Diochus schaumi* (p.137); *Diplotaxis liberta* (p.165); *Dirabius rectirostris* (p.477); *Ditylus caeruleus* (p.363); *Dorcatoma pallicornis* (p.257); *Dorytomus laticollis* (p.475); *Drusilla canaliculata* (p.131); *Dytiscus carolinus* (p.103); *Eanus estriatus* (p.222); *Elodes maculicollis* (p.181); *Enicmus aterrimus* (p.323); *Epilachna varivestis* (p.319); *Epuraea aestiva* (p.296); *Epuraea flavomaculata* (p.296); *Erichsonius patella* (p.139); *Eubulus bisignatus* (p.484); *Eucinetus morio* (p.178); *Euconnus salinator* (p.134); *Eucrada humeralis* (p.254); *Eugnamptus angustatus* (p.464); *Euparius paganus* (p.459); *Eurypogon niger* (p.208); *Euspilotus assimilis* (p.111); *Euvrilletta harrisii* (p.256); *Evodinus monticola* (p.394); *Exochomus marginipennis* (p.313); *Falagria dissecta* (p.130); *Galerucella nymphaeae* (p.447); *Geraeus picumnus* (p.476); *Glischrochilus vittatus* (p.303); *Glycobius speciosus* (p.406); *Glyptoscelis pubescens* (p.454); *Goniocloeus bimaculatus* (p.459); *Gonioctena americana* (p.441); *Grammoptera haematites* (p.394); *Grammoptera subargentata* (p.394); *Graphoderus liberus* (p.104); *Gymnusa atra* (p.130); *Gyrohypnus fracticornis* (p.142); *Gyrophaena* (p.131); *Harmonia axyridis* (p.316); *Harpalus faunus* (p.82); *Helluomorphoides praestus bicolor* (p.94); *Hemicoelus carinatus* (p.255); *Hemicrepidius nemnonius* (p.220); *Henotiderus obesulus* (p.284); *Hesperus baltimorensis* (p.139); *Heterhelus abdominalis* (p.294); *Heterocerus fenestratus* (p.202); *Heterothops fumigatus* (p.139); *Himatolabus pubescens* (p.463); *Hippodamia convergens* (p.316); *Hippodamia parenthesis* (p.316); *Hippodamia variegata* (p.317); *Homaeotarsus bicolor* (p.135); *Hydaticus piceus* (p.103); *Hydraena pensylvanica* (p.115); *Hydrocanthus oblongus* (p.98); *Hydrochara soror* (p.108); *Hydrochus squamifer* (p.106); *Hydroporus tristis* (p.101); *Hygrotus sayi* (p.101); *Hylurgops pinifex* (p.497); *Hyperaspis octavia* (p.312); *Hyperplatys aspersa* (p.418); *Hyperplatys maculata* (p.418); *Hypoganus sulcicollis* (p.223); *Idiopidonia pedalis* (p.395); *Idolus bigeminata* (p.225); *Ilybius biguttulus* (p.102); *Ischnopterapion virens* (p.468); *Ischyropalpus nitidulus* (p.379); *Isochnus sequensi* (p.476); *Judolia montivagans* (p.395); *Laccophilus undatus* (p.100); *Laetulonthus laetulus* (p.139); *Lathrobium convolutum* (p.136); *Lebia fuscata* (p.90); *Lebia ornata* (p.91); *Lebia pectita* (p.91); *Lebia solea* (p.91); *Lebia tricolor* (p.92); *Lebia viridis* (p.92); *Leiodes* (p.118); *Lichnanthe vulpina* (p.155); *Lignyodes fraxini* (p.476); *Lilioceris lillii* (p.433); *Limnichites punctatus* (p.201); *Limonius basilaris* (p.221); *Limonius quercinus* (p.222); *Limonius stigma* (p.222); *Listronotus appendiculatus* (p.485); *Lobiopa undulata* (p.299); *Lobrathium collare* (p.136); *Lordithon cinctus* (p.128); *Lordithon facilis* (p.128); *Lordithon fungicola* (p.128); *Lordithon kelleyi* (p.128); *Macratria confusa* (p.378); *Madarellus undulatus* (p.479); *Madoniella dislocata* (p.269); *Magdalis austera* (p.493); *Malporus formicarius* (p.379); *Malthodes fuliginosus* (p.242); *Matus bicarinatus* (p.102); *Melanophthalma picta* (p.323);

Merhynchites bicolor (p.465); *Meronera venustula* (p.130); *Microtonus sericans* (p.331); *Microweisea misella* (p.311); *Mononychus vulpeculus* (p.480); *Monophylla terminata* (p.265); *Monotoma bicolor* (p.282); *Monotoma producta* (p.282); *Mordella marginata* (p.334); *Mordellina pustulata* (p.336); *Mordellistena andreae* (p.336); *Mordellistena cervicalis* (p.336); *Mordellistena convicta* (p.337); *Mulsantina hudsonica* (p.317); *Mulsantina picta* (p.317); *Naemia seriata* (p.318); *Neapion herculanum* (p.467); *Necrobia violacea* (p.270); *Nemognatha nemorensis* (p.368); *Neogalerucella calamariensis* (p.448); *Nitidula bipunctata* (p.299); *Nitidula carnaria* (p.299); *Notiobia terminata* (p.82); *Notiophilus aeneus* (p.64); *Notoxus desertus* (p.380); *Nycteus oviformis* (p.178); *Oestodes tenuicollis* (p.218); *Oiceoptoma inequale* (p.121); *Olisthaerus substriatus* (p.127); *Omonadus formicarius* (p.379); *Orchesia castanea* (p.329); *Otiorhynchus ovatus* (p.489); *Ocypus nitens* (p.140); *Oxyporus vittatus* (p.134); *Pachybrachis bivittatus* (p.453); *Pachybrachis subfasciatus* (p.453); *Paederus littorarius* (p.136); *Pallodes pallidus* (p.300); *Paradonus pectoralis* (p.224); *Paria quadrinotata* (p.456); *Peltis septentrionalis* (p.260); *Perapion curtirostre* (p.417); *Philonthus flumineus* (p.140); *Philothermus glabriculus* (p.308); *Phymaphora pulchella* (p.309); *Phymatodes amoenus* (p.404); *Physonota helianthi* mottled form (p.439); *Piazorhinus pictus* (p.475); *Piazorhinus scutellaris* (p.475); *Pityokteines sparsus* (p.499); *Plagiodera versicolora* (p.443); *Platysoma coarctatum* (p.113); *Plegaderus transversus* (p.111); *Polygraphus rufipennis* (p.498); *Priobium sericeum* (p.258); *Priognathus monilicornis* (p.373); *Pronocera collaris* (p.405); *Propylea quatuordecimpuncta* (p.319); *Prostephanus punctatus* (p.251); *Pseudanostirus hamatus* (p.223); *Pseudanostirus triundulatus* (p.223); *Pseudopsis subulata* (p.135); *Psyrassa unicolor* (p.410); *Ptomaphagus brevior* (p.119); *Pytho niger* (p.372); *Quedius capucinus* (p.141); *Quedius peregrinus* (p.141); *Reichenbachia facilis* (p.126); *Rhabdopterus* (p.455); *Rhanidea unicolor* (p.309); *Rhantus wallisi* (p.103); *Rhinoncus castor* (p.481); *Rhinosimus viridiaeneus* (p.376); *Rhizophagus cylindricus* (p.281); *Rhizophagus remotus* (p.281); *Rypobius marinus* (p.321); *Sacodes pulchella* (p.182); *Saperda candida* (p.426); *Sapintus* (p.380); *Sarabandus robustus* (p.182); *Scaphisoma rubens* (p.132); *Schizotus cervicalis* (p.375); *Selatosomus pulcher* (p.224); *Sericoderus lateralis* (p.321); *Sibariops confusa* (p.478); *Sphindus americanus* (p.275); *Spilotus quadripustulatus* (p.331); *Stelidota geminata* (p.300); *Stelidota octomaculata* (p.301); *Stenispa metallica* (p.436); *Stenolophus lecontei* (p.83); *Stethobaris ovata* (p.479); *Stictoleptura canadensis* (p.398); *Stricticomus tobias* (p.380); *Strigocis opacicollis* (p.327); *Tachinus fimbriatus* (p.129); *Tachyerges ephippiatus* (p.476); *Tachyporus elegans* (p.129); *Taphrocerus nicolayi* (p.194); *Telmatophilus americanus* (p.284); *Toramus pulchellus* (p.278); *Trichapion rostrum* (p.468); *Trichotichnus dichrous* (p.84); *Tricorynus* (p.258); *Trigonodemus striatus* (p.125); *Trigonorhinus sticticus* (p.460); *Tritoma biguttata biguttata* (p.280); *Trixagus carinicollis* (p.212); *Tropisternus blatchleyi* (p.109); *Tyloderma aereum* (p.484); *Tyloderma foveolatum* (p.484); *Tylonotus bimaculatus* (p.411); *Typhaea stercorea* (p.325); *Tyrus semiruber* (p.127); *Uleiota debilis* (p.286); *Vanonus piceus* (p.384); *Xanthonia decemnotata* (p.455); *Xestoleptura octonotata* (p.401); *Xyleborus affinis* (p.500); *Zonantes fasciatus* (p.383); *Zonantes subfasciatus* (p.383).

STEVE NANZ

Actenodes acornis (p.189); *Arthromacra aenea* dark bronze form (p.345); *Cynaeus angustus* (p.347); *Dichelonyx albicollis* (p.166); *Hydrobius fuscipes* (p.108); *Pentaria trifasciata* (p.386); *Polemius laticornis* (p.241); *Toxonotus cornutus* (p.460); *Tropisternus lateralis nimbatus* (p.109).

SCOTT NELSON

Derobrachus thomasi (p.390); *Euoniticellus intermedius* (p.161); *Pelonomus obscurus* (p.199).

PENNSYLVANIA DEPT. OF CONSERVATION AND NATURAL RESOURCES/BUGWOOD

Ips pini (p.498).

MARK O'BRIEN

Fig. 8f.

JENNIFER FORMAN ORTH

Leptorhabdium pictum (p.395); *Prothalpia undata* (p.332).

JOHN OTT

Figs 2n, 8k; *Acanthinus argentinus* (p.378); *Adelina pallida* (p.354); *Ahasverus rectus* (p.286); *Amphotis schwarzi* (p.298); *Anchastus binus* (p.227); *Arpedium schwarzi* (p.124); *Ataenius spretulus* (p.159); *Conoderus scissus* (p.216); *Conoderus suturalis* (p.217); *Cryptolestes ferrugineus* (p.292); *Cyclotrachelus sigillatus* (p.78); *Cymatodera undulata* (p.264); *Ega sallei* (p.88); *Endeitoma granulata* (p.342); *Europs pallipennis* (p.282) *Glipa hilaris* (p.333); *Heteroderes falli* (p.217); *Hyporhagus punctulatus* (p.343); *Languria taedata* (p.278); *Lecontella brunnea* (p.265); *Myoplatypus flavicornis* (p.500); *Octotoma plicatula* (p.438); *Otiorhynchus rugostriatus* (p.489); *Paha laticollis* (p.343); *Phloeoxena signata* (p.92); *Piesocorynus moestus* (p.459); *Pityobius anguinus* (p.218); *Polypleurus perforatus* (p.358); *Priocera castanea* (p.268); *Pseudaptinus pygmaeus* (p.93); *Pseudostrangalia cruentata* (p.397); *Rhipidandrus paradoxus* (p.348); *Selonodon medialis* (p.214); *Stenotarsus hispidus* (p.310); *Tenebroides collaris* (p.262); *Thanasimus dubius* (p.268); *Zuphium americanum* (p.93).

NIKOLA RAHMÉ

Gonotropis gibbosus (p.460).

JON RAPP

Lepturges pictus (p.419); *Tricrania sanguinipennis* (p.369).

JENNIFER READ

Figs 1a–b, 3a–b, 7, 9a–b, 10, 11a–f; *Brychius hungerfordi* (p.96); *Enicocerus benefossus* (p.115); *Laricobius rubidus* (p.244); *Lasioderma serricorne* (p.256); *Orthosoma brunneum* (p.390); *Prionochaeta opaca* (p.119); *Ptenidium pusillum* (p.116).

DAVID REED
Hylesinus aculeatus (p.497).

LAWRENCE R. REEVES
Fig. 27; *Purpuricenus axillaris* (p.415).

CHARLES ROBERTSON
Stenelytrana emarginata (p.397).

MATT ROTH
Goes pulcher (p.422).

KURT SCHAEFER
Megacerus discoidus (p.431).

LYNNETTE SCHIMMING
Hypera nigrirostris (p.492); *Neospondylis upiformis* (p.402); *Onthophagus nuchicornis* (p.162).

KEN R. SCHNEIDER
Amblyderus pallens (p.378).

KYLE SCHNEPP
Ateuchus histeroides (p.160); *Copris fricator* (p.160); *Derodontus esotericus* (p.244); *Gyretes iricolor* (p.95); *Leptinus orientamericanus* (p.120); *Omethes marginatus* (p.237); *Peltotrupes profundus* (p.152); *Tetratoma truncorum* (p.327); *Xenorhipis brendeli* (p.192).

TOM D. SCHULTZ
Dryobius sexfasciatus (p.408).

ROY SEWALL
Fig. 42.

JAMES SHERWOOD
Calloides nobilis (p.405).

MARVIN SMITH
Atimia confusa (p.402); *Microgoes oculatus* (p.423).

SOEBE/WIKIMEDIA
Carabus auratus (p.66).

GAYLE AND JEANELL STRICKLAND
Ataxia crypta (p.426); *Berosus inordinatus* (p.106); *Brachystylus sayi* (p.487); *Chrysobothris chrysoela* (p.191); *Clytus marginicollis* (p.406); *Dicrepidius palmatus* (p.227); *Ecyrus dasycerus* (p.425); *Gratiana pallidula* (p.436); *Parandra polita* (p.389); *Ips calligraphus* (p.498); *Leptostylus asperatus* (p.419); *Methia necydalea* (p.411); *Nemognatha piazata* (p.368); *Neoptychodes trilineatus* (p.424); *Odontopus calceatus* (p.474); *Pachylobius picivorus* (p.495); *Pelonides quadripunctatus* (p.270); *Prionus imbricornis* (p.390); *Saperda tridentata* (p.427); *Spectralia gracilipes* (p.192); *Strongylium tenuicolle* (p.359); *Tetragonoderus latipennis* (p.89); *Trirhabda bacharidis* (p.449); *Xanthochroa lateralis* (p.363).

TRACY SUNVOLD
Physonota helianthi green form (p.439).

MICHAEL C. THOMAS
Brachypeplus glaber (p.301); *Ceratocanthus aeneus* (p.154); *Cybocephalus nipponicus* (p.304); *Derolathrus cavernicolus* (p.245); *Enneboeus caseyi* (p.326); *Hemipeplus marginipennis* (p.370); *Lecontia discicollis* (p.371); *Lycoptis americana* (p.260); *Murmidius ovalis* (p.307); *Nausibius major* (p.287); *Pediacus subglaber* (p.288); *Rhopalotria slossonae* (p.462); *Schoenicus puberulus* (p.346); *Smicrips palmicola* (p.305); *Sphaerius* (p.62); *Suphis inflatus* (p.98); *Taphroscelidius linearis* (p.289).

ALEXEY TISHECHKIN
Paromalus bistriatus (p.112).

EDWARD TRAMMEL
Dicaelus sculptilis (p.85).

DONNA WATKINS
Texania campestris (p.187).

ALEX WILD
Fig. 15d; *Olla v-nigrum* pale form (p.318); *Aethina tumida* (p.298); *Micromalthus debilis* (p.61); *Sandalus niger* (p.184); *Tribolium castaneum* (p.351).

CHRISTOPHER C. WIRTH
Figs 6, 8a, 8c, 8e, 14, 15a, 16a, 17, 19, 20, 23, 25, 26; *Acalymma vittatum* (p.449); *Acmaeodera ornata* (p.185); *Acmaeodera tubulus* (p.186); *Acropteroxys gracilis* (p.278); *Acupalpus testaceus* (p.80); *Aeolus mellilus* (p.216); *Agrilus ruficollis* (p.193); *Alaetrinus minimus* (p.350); *Ampedus nigricollis* (p.226); *Amphicerus bicaudatus* (p.250); *Amphicrossus ciliatus* (p.297); *Analeptura lineola* (p.392); *Anaspis nigrina* (p.386); *Anomala lucicola* (p.167); *Anthicus cervinus* (p.379); *Anthrenus pimpinellae* (p.247); *Anthrenus verbasci* (p.248); *Apenes sinuata* (p.89); *Arthrolips misellus* (p.320); *Arthromacra aenea* purplish-green form (p.345); *Asclera puncticollis* (p.363); *Attalus scincetus* (p.272); *us nervosus* (p.436); *Blackburneus stercorosus* (p.157); *Brachiacantha quadripunctata* (p.313); *Brachyleptura champlaini* (p.393); *Brachyleptura vagans* (p.393); *Bruchidius villosus* (p.430); *Buprestis salisburyensis* (p.190); *Caenocara oculata* (p.257); *Calamosternus granarius* (p.157); *Calligrapha phildelphica* (p.440); *Canifa pallipes* (p.385); *Cathartosilvanus imbellis* (p.287); *Catops basiliaris* (p.119); *Cedius spinosus* (p.126); *Chilocorus stigma* (p.313); *Choragus sayi* (p.461); *Chrysomela scripta* (p.441); *Cicindela patruela* (p.69); *Cicindelidia abdominalis* (p.71); *Cicindelidia punctulata* (p.71); *Cicindelidia rufiventris rufiventris* (p.71); *Coccinella septempunctata* (p.315); *Conotelus obscurus* (p.302); *Copelatus glyphicus* (p.99); *Coproporus ventriculus* (p.129); *Cryptocephalus quadruplex* (p.452); *Cryptorhopalum* (p.248); *Curculio* (p.474); *Cycloneda munda* (p.316); *Cyrtophorus verrucosus* (p.403); *Dacne quadrimaculata* (p.279); *Deloyala guttata* (p.435); *Denticollis denticornis* (p.220); *Diabrotica*

INDEX

541

555

557